MAGIC DAYS

MAGIC DAYS

Your Daily Astrology, Numerology and Tarot Guide

NADINE JANE

◻ SQUARE PEG

1 3 5 7 9 10 8 6 4 2

Square Peg, an imprint of Vintage, is part of the Penguin Random House group of companies whose addresses can be found at global.penguinrandomhouse.com

Penguin
Random House
UK

First published by Square Peg in 2022

Penguin.co.uk/vintage

A CIP catalogue record for this book is available from the British Library

ISBN 9781529902594

Typeset in Adobe Caslon Pro
Designed by Cassandra Garruzzo Mueller

Printed and bound in Great Britain by Clays Ltd, Elcograf S.p.A.

The authorised representative in the EEA is Penguin Random House Ireland, Morrison Chambers, 32 Nassau Street, Dublin D02 YH68

Penguin Random House is committed to a sustainable future for our business, our readers and our planet. This book is made from Forest Stewardship Council® certified paper.

Dedicated to anyone who has ever
lost touch with Magic.

ACKNOWLEDGMENTS

Books are never created by one person, so I would first like to acknowledge the two most important Megs in my life: Meg Leder, my editor and the editorial director at Penguin Life, who invited me to dream big and never compromise while helping me to perfect every word of this book, and Meg Thompson, my agent and the founder of Thompson Literary Agency, who put the crazy idea in my head that I could write a book in the first place.

I would also like to acknowledge the rest of the team at Penguin, without whose skills and expertise this book would not exist: Brian Tart (publisher of Penguin Life), Amy Sun (editor), Annika Karody (editorial assistant), Matt Giarratano (executive managing editor), Norina Frabotta (senior director, Production Editorial), Megan Gerrity (assistant director, Production Editorial), Marlene De Jesus (director, Production), Sabrina Bowers (associate director, Art/Design), Elizabeth Yaffe (senior designer), Molly Fessenden (assistant director, Marketing), Kristina Fazzalaro (manager, Publicity), and everyone from the Penguin sales team.

And last but certainly not least, I would like to acknowledge my close friends, my family, my parents, my dear sister, and my beloved partner, Nick, for offering me support in times of fear, encouragement in times of insecurity, and the laughs I needed to enjoy the wild journey of writing this book.

CONTENTS

Dear Reader,

If you don't know me already, hi! I'm Nadine. I'm an astrologer, an Aquarius-sun-and-moon-Virgo-rising, a graphic designer, the daughter of academics, and a yet-to-be-fully-functioning person. I cannot tell you how excited I am to share *Magic Days* with you. But to tell you about everything that this book is, I must first and foremost tell you about my relationship with my dear friend *Magic*. . . .

My earliest memory of *Magic* was in first grade, when I would wake up each morning with a tingling feeling in my belly. It felt so special, like a present that was gifted just for me, and despite growing up without religion, I couldn't help but wonder if it was the thing the other kids at school called God. I would swing wildly from great heights on the playground, scaring my parents half to death, but I knew for certain that *Magic* had my back. When my friend Holly and I dug into the ground during recess in third grade and found rainbow claylike mud, like a treasure we had resurrected from a lost dimension, I knew *Magic* had left it there especially for us to find.

As I grew, I began to build a deeper relationship with *Magic* through art. I started doodling faces from my imagination, faces I had never seen before that I believed were spirits who just wanted to come say hi and have their portrait drawn. When I was thirteen, I began obsessively drawing planets and stars all over my notebooks and binders and even my white pair of Vans, perfecting the ring of Saturn more times than I can count. I didn't know much about astrology or astronomy, but I knew that the shapes felt familiar, like a town I had never visited and yet desperately wanted to go back to.

But then puberty set in. Insecurities. Fears. Gender and sexual binaries. Gossip. Trauma. Grades. Social pressure. Applying to college. Teachers, my parents, and even peers began asking me big questions I had no easy answers to. Do you like boys or girls? What do you want to study in college? Why do you dress like that? Have you lost your virginity yet? Do you think art will land you a financially stable job?

Gradually, my relationship with *Magic* became a luxury—or even worse, a liability. I no longer felt applauded for asking the big questions but instead felt like a complete failure for not coming up with any answers. So I turned my back on *Magic* and went searching. I felt certain that there was some otherworldly thing that would one day reveal itself to me and give me the answers to all of life's most troublesome questions. I just needed to find it. And there my journey began.

First, I thought that beauty and fashion had all the answers. The models, celebrities, stylists, and editors in their black sunglasses looked as if they had it all figured out. If

I only could dress and present myself the right way, if I only could get my weight down to a number that my body never intended to be, I would figure it out, too. Next, I thought that thing could be men. Then I thought that thing was New York City. Then I thought that thing could be success.

But at twenty-one years old, I was shown my astrological birth chart for the first time. My Venus in Pisces told me of my love of music and animals, while calling me out on my romanticizing of the hero-savior complex that often plagued my love life. My Plutonian Moon told me of my mother's great influence in my life and the ancestral rage we both carried. My Mercury-ruled ascendant and midheaven told me I was a writer before I had any notion that this one day would come true. I couldn't understand how this spiritual practice knew such precise details about me, but I knew at that moment that I had made contact with this thing I had been searching for, the thing with all the answers, and it was speaking directly to me as an adult for the first time.

Fast-forward to 2015. I was a digital designer and the "in-house astrologer" at a very popular beauty startup in Soho. I was completely obsessed with reading birth charts, so I took it upon myself to take every new and willing employee out to lunch and read their chart. As the company grew from thirty to one hundred people during my three years there, I learned a fair bit about the personal and outer planets, aspects, and houses.

And just like any millennial who thinks they know something, on September 1, 2017, I started an Instagram account called @nadinejane_astrology. I took my amateur mental encyclopedia of astrology, my well-trained design eye, and my love for one-liners, and poured it all into twelve posts, one for each sign. It felt as if all the searching I had done over the years finally came together in harmony, like a symphony from a song that I knew by heart but had not written myself. The account became a special portal that I could visit, a place where I knew I again could make conscious contact with that thing with all the answers, whenever I wanted. Or so I thought.

By March 2018, I had quit my job to pursue astrology full time, privileged enough to turn my passion into a job. I suddenly felt as though I was no longer able to just ask questions, but instead, once again I felt an immense amount of pressure to have the answers. So I approached it like any well-trained daughter of an academic would: I studied my ass off. I read as much as I could retain, taught myself how to interpret transits and write horoscopes, and eventually enrolled in an online school. My readings got more precise, my horoscopes more involved, and the opportunities even larger. But somewhere in this whirlwind of spiritual content creation, in my desire to predict the future, I lost sight of what made me fall in love with astrology in the first place: *Magic*.

And then came this book. I thought it was going to be a simple and straightforward book about what astrology, numerology, and tarot say about each day and birthday of the year. I thought that I would churn through all 365 days of the year in a logical and organized fashion, interpreting these ancient spiritual practices with as much precision as I could humanly muster. I thought, foolishly, that I had all the answers.

But this book revealed itself to be mysterious and wild, bucking me off its back enough times for me to know for certain that it could not and would not be tamed. It prodded at my imposter syndrome, asked me to break rules that I barely felt that I understood, leaving me both terrified and excited that there was no perfect answer. It wanted me to ask questions instead of knowing the answers, and it preferred me when I was curious rather than smart. It forced me into an even deeper state of humility and guided me through a quest of the unknown, where the only way to write was from complete surrender. This book didn't need me to be an expert; it didn't need me to arrive; it wasn't linear. Instead, it needed me to be as curious as I was when I was a child.

So I went back to the beginning, to a time before I knew anything about being a "professional" astrologer. I woke up every morning, still and quiet enough to feel the tingling in my belly. I let myself rediscover what it felt like to sit under a full moon with no clue as to what sign it was in but with the openness to experience exactly how it felt. I started shuffling my tarot deck every single morning—pulling The Fool more times than I would like to admit—and slowly developing a more personal relationship with these otherworldly guides. I let myself believe as I did as a child, without an ounce of judgment, that the numbers *123* were the universe's way of nodding at me because I was born on January 23. I committed deeply to the belief that everything has meaning and yet nothing is certain.

It was then that I realized that the thing I had been searching for all along, and the very thing that I had lost in my quest to contain it, was my old friend *Magic*. I couldn't help but wonder, what if astrologers, scientists, and adults, just like children, aren't here to have all the answers, but instead to ask the big questions? What if we are all just searching for the same thing? What if we are all just reaching for, longing for, yearning for *Magic*?

And therein lies my greatest hope for this book.

My hope is that this book enables you to connect, or reconnect, with the *Magic* of your journey. I hope it inspires you to bear witness to the inexplicable wonder that exists in every moment of every single day of the year. I hope it invites you to find meaning in the seemingly mundane miracles that alter the course of your day, like noticing the clock at 11:11 or catching a glimpse of a butterfly on your walk to work. I hope it gives you permission to have a childlike relationship with the spiritual world, without having to explain to yourself or others why something resonates with you, like relishing a magic trick without having to look up how it was performed. I hope it encourages you to stare up at the big blue sky, chasing infinite wonder instead of finite answers. And I hope it reminds you that your life is an ever-unfolding journey—a spiritual, mythical journey—in which you can only hope never to arrive, never to understand this world, so as not to miss the *Magic*.

I'd like you to know a few things before diving into *Magic Days*.

This is a book about journeys. *Magic Days* isn't about how you started or how you will someday end, but instead devotes itself to your mystical, magical in-between. No matter who you are and no matter where you are, this book believes that your journey, not your successes nor your failures, is the tale worth telling.

As you engage with *Magic Days*, I invite you to view yourself as the hero and the book as the guide to the unique spiritual journey you are invited on every day of the year and throughout your lifetime.

This isn't a book about astrology. It does use astrology, tarot, and numerology as guides to help illuminate the hero's journey. I've used astrology to describe the day's energy and to tell the story of you, the hero; I've included the numerology of the day to explore the spiritual path you are invited to walk; and I've listed the tarot cards of the day to illuminate the boundless lessons you can uncover along the way. I have given each of your guides a name to help personify these esoteric practices, allowing you to engage with them as you would a trusted friend. In a world that demands clear formulas for how to succeed, *Magic Days* utilizes astrology, numerology, and tarot as an open invitation to engage with the spiritual world, rather than as a definitive prediction of how your day will go.

On the next few pages, you can find more information about what these spiritual practices are and how they are used within the context of this book. Then I begin the days with March 21, the first day of Aries season, rather than the Western calendar's January 1, because the former marks the start of the astrological new year.

On each day's spread, you'll find information for that day, along with special information if it's your birthday. The left-hand page tells you about the journey that particular day will take you on, including a high-level overview of the day's journey, mantras, and journal prompts to get you inspired, as well as a few notable people born on that day. You can use this as a guide for how to approach your day, inspiration for self-development, or a simple affirmation that you are on the right track.

If you want to flip directly to your birthday, the right-hand page of each day's spread tells you about the journey your soul will go on in this lifetime. It includes an overview of your journey, your journey's purpose, and relationship dynamics to aid you along your quest.

This is a book for anyone, every day. It is for the excitable novice looking for their first introduction to spiritual practices. It is for the lost soul who could use some direction in life. It is for the jaded expert looking for a new point of view on the topics they know far too well. It is for the empathic people-reader who loves to understand others. And it is for the complete skeptic who considers this "spiritual nonsense" while secretly delighting in the inexplicable accuracy of it all.

I hope *Magic Days* will live and breathe alongside you in your daily struggles, walk in step with you as you climb your soul's highest mountain, and swim fearlessly alongside you as you navigate the deepest tidal waters.

Happy *Magic Days*!

Love,
Nadine

THE SPIRITUAL PRACTICES
USED IN *MAGIC DAYS*

ASTROLOGY

THE PERSONALITY OF
THE DAY AND BIRTHDAY

What is used: **The transits of the sun**

Example: **January 23 = 1st Decan of Aquarius Season**

Astrology is an ancient form of divination that studies the qualities and movements of the planets in the sky and interprets how they influence the human experience. Astrology can be used for a wide variety of practices; by following the transits of the sun, *Magic Days* uses astrology to define the energy of the day you are embarking on as well as the general personality archetype of the individual born on that day.

NUMEROLOGY

THE PATH OF
THE DAY AND BIRTHDAY

What is used: **The month + the day = up to 9**

Example: **January 23 = 1 + 23 = 24; 2 + 4 = 6**

Numerology is an ancient belief system in which numbers are thought to have both predictive and spiritual meaning. It can be used in a number of different ways (see what I did there?), and *Magic Days* uses numerology to define the path you are invited on for each day of the year as well as the general path you are invited to take in this lifetime based on your birthday. The most traditional way to define the number of a given day is to separate all the numbers and add them (e.g., January 23 = 1 + 2 + 3), but in this book, the whole number of the month and the whole number of the day are added to get a single digit between 1 and 9 (e.g., January 23 = 1 + 23 = 24; 2 + 4 = 6).

TAROT MINOR ARCANA

THE LESSON OF THE DAY AND BIRTHDAY

What is used: **The month + the day + the element of the zodiac sign**

Example: **January 23 = 1 + 23 = 24; 2 + 4 = 6; 6 + air = 6 of Swords**

The tarot is a deck of cards that dates to the mid-fifteenth century and began to be used for divination in the late eighteenth century. The deck is composed of seventy-eight cards, which include forty Minor Arcana cards, organized into four suits, one for each element, with ten cards each. The Minor Arcana can be used and interpreted in a wide variety of ways, and *Magic Days* uses these cards to define the lesson or obstacles you will encounter on a daily basis as well as in this lifetime.

TAROT MAJOR ARCANA

THE HIGHEST CALLING OF THE DAY AND BIRTHDAY

What is used: **The month + the day = up to 21**

Example: **January 23 = 1 + 23 = 24; 2 + 4 = 6 = The Lovers**

The tarot includes 21 Major Arcana cards. The Major Arcana can be used in a wide variety of ways, and *Magic Days* uses these cards to represent the highest karmic purpose of the day and for the individual born on that day.

ASTROLOGY:

The Personality of the Day and Birthday

By following the decanates, or divisions, of the sun, *Magic Days* uses astrology to define the energy of the day you are embarking on as well as the personality archetype of the individual born on that day.

ARIES

The 1st Decanate of Aries | Ruler: Mars, Subruler: Mars | March 21–31

Day: The energy of the day is ambitious and inspired yet incredibly impulsive.

Birthday: You are an Aries with extra fire and impact. Some may find you domineering, knowing that by sheer force of will you usually win any argument or competition.

The 2nd Decanate of Aries | Ruler: Mars, Subruler: The Sun | April 1–10

Day: The energy is bold and inspiring, but be wary of the ego taking over.

Birthday: You are easily excitable, enabling you to approach life with a sunnier disposition than most Aries. You are a natural leader, preferring to inspire confidence in others rather than maintaining control and authority.

The 3rd Decanate of Aries | Ruler: Mars, Subruler: Jupiter | April 11–19

Day: The energy is expansive and driven, yet it may be hard to focus on just one goal.

Birthday: You are an Aries who needs to run free. Winging life is a natural talent of yours, so no need to overplan—just follow the beat of your intuitive drum.

TAURUS

The 1st Decanate of Taurus | Ruler: Venus, Subruler: Venus | April 20–30

Day: The energy is earthly and materially driven, but be wary of excess and overspending.

Birthday: You are a Taurus with grace and elegance. You know how to make the world a more beautiful place; just make sure not to fixate on appearances.

The 2nd Decanate of Taurus | Ruler: Venus, Subruler: Mercury | May 1–10

Day: The energy is grounded yet communicative, but watch out for stubbornness.

Birthday: You are a lifelong student of the arts. A grounded communicator at heart, you shed light on the topics and crafts that bring us all closer to the physical world.

The 3rd Decanate of Taurus | Ruler: Venus, Subruler: Saturn | May 11–20

Day: The energy is responsible and loyal yet can make it hard to go with the flow.

Birthday: You have a sturdy determination that is powerful. You do not rely on the whims of inspiration nor are you swayed by popular opinion—you only care about building something real.

GEMINI

The 1st Decanate of Gemini | Ruler: Mercury, Subruler: Mercury | May 21–31

Day: The energy is curious and intellectual yet can overstimulate the mind.

Birthday: You are a Gemini who thinks a million miles a minute. Your mental agility is hard to beat, giving you the next best answer to any riddle life throws your way.

The 2nd Decanate of Gemini | Ruler: Mercury, Subruler: Venus | June 1–10

Day: The energy is highly social, but try not to chameleon yourself to please others.

Birthday: You are a Gemini who can connect with just about anyone on a social level. Although your ability to engage others is a highly coveted skill, you have to practice true vulnerability to experience true intimacy.

The 3rd Decanate of Gemini | Ruler: Mercury, Subruler: Uranus | June 11–20

Day: The energy is mentally stimulating yet erratic, so be careful not to say something impulsive.

Birthday: You are an unconventional Gemini. Know that not everyone can match your speed of thought, but you inspire others to think for themselves and explore uncharted mental territory.

CANCER

The 1st Decanate of Cancer | Ruler: The Moon, Subruler: The Moon | June 21–30

Day: The energy is nurturing and gentle but makes it difficult to get out of the coziness of bed.

Birthday: You are as Cancerian as they come. Your emotions ride with the waves of the moon, allowing you to experience and emphasize with every up and down of the human experience.

The 2nd Decanate of Cancer | Ruler: The Moon, Subruler: Pluto | July 1–11

Day: The energy is highly emotional, so give yourself extra space as you engage with others.

Birthday: You are sensitive and hyperaware, enabling you to see others for who they truly are. The trick is learning how not to let your powerful emotions turn into self-destruction.

The 3rd Decanate of Cancer | Ruler: The Moon, Subruler: Neptune | July 12–22

Day: The energy is nostalgic and dreamy yet can make it easy to project your feelings onto others.

Birthday: You are a very romantic and dreamy Cancer—and highly creative! But spending time alone can help you get in touch with your intuition as well as your creative vitality.

LEO

The 1st Decanate of Leo | Ruler: The Sun, Subruler: The Sun | July 23–August 1

Day: The energy is bright and bold yet can make you more self-conscious than usual.

Birthday: You shine bright like a diamond, at every angle, on any given day. You do not shy away from the spotlight and can easily lead a group with your innate and generous sense of authority.

The 2nd Decanate of Leo | Ruler: The Sun, Subruler: Jupiter | August 2–12

Day: The energy is expansive and optimistic yet overly idealistic in extremes.

Birthday: You are willing to step up to the plate when others cower in fear because you know how to laugh at your mistakes. As you accept your shortcomings, others will learn to accept theirs, too.

The 3rd Decanate of Leo | Ruler: The Sun, Subruler: Mars | August 13–22

Day: The energy is confident and assertive but can easily lead to conflicts of the ego.

Birthday: You are like an uncontrollable hot flame. You have intense periods of inspiration followed by the occasional energy crash, but it's all in the name of fun! You want to feel alive.

VIRGO

The 1st Decanate of Virgo | Ruler: Mercury, Subruler: Mercury | August 23–September 1

Day: The energy is highly intellectual and pragmatic but easily can lead to anxiety.

Birthday: You are incredibly rational and intelligent, finding yourself thriving on details, deadlines, and the like. You often place your high standards on others, so you know that you must live by example.

The 2nd Decanate of Virgo | Ruler: Mercury, Subruler: Saturn | September 2–12

Day: The energy is hardworking and humble but can lead to burnout when taken to extremes.

Birthday: You don't crumble; you thrive under pressure, finding intense satisfaction from a hard day's work. Diligence and humility are hallmarks of your character, allowing others to trust you implicitly.

The 3rd Decanate of Virgo | Ruler: Mercury, Subruler: Venus | September 13–22

Day: The energy is giving and compassionate yet can cause people-pleasing.

Birthday: Your humble nature combined with the calming energy of Venus makes you virtually impossible to dislike or distrust! You can be friendly yet unsure of your power, causing you to look for validation in public approval.

LIBRA

The 1st Decanate of Libra | Ruler: Venus, Subruler: Venus | September 23–October 2

Day: The energy is highly romantic, but be wary of codependency and idealizing others.

Birthday: You are talented at making the world a more beautiful and tranquil place, whether that be from your style, art, or love for humanity. You may put too much weight on what others think, but you are undeniably charming.

The 2nd Decanate of Libra | Ruler: Venus, Subruler: Uranus | October 3–13

Day: The energy is socially exciting yet unexpected, so watch out for strange interactions with others.

Birthday: Your combination of innovation and social grace can give you a highly original artistic style and role in society. You are independent in your thinking yet thrive in collaboration and partnership.

The 3rd Decanate of Libra | Ruler: Venus, Subruler: Mercury | October 14–22

Day: The energy is creative and compassionate—just be careful not to overpromise.

Birthday: You have a quick mind that you choose to use fairly and diplomatically. You enjoy digging through information and coming out with a balanced view, shying away from polarizing opinions and dogmatic thinking.

SCORPIO

The 1st Decanate of Scorpio | Ruler: Pluto, Subruler: Pluto | October 23–November 1

Day: The energy is psychologically aware and probing, but be wary of morbid reflection.

Birthday: You are a sincere Scorpio. You may love the mysterious and unknown darkness of life, contemplating taboo topics like it's a hobby. Not all who know you understand you, but that is part of your magic.

The 2nd Decanate of Scorpio | Ruler: Pluto, Subruler: Neptune | November 2–11

Day: The energy is deeply spiritual and healing, yet it can be difficult to harness all the emotion.

Birthday: You have significant psychological and spiritual gifts for healing. You are a romantic at heart, believing that real intimacy comes from seeing all the good, bad, and ugly in someone and accepting them completely.

The 3rd Decanate of Scorpio | Ruler: Pluto, Subruler: The Moon | November 12–21

Day: The energy is emotionally sincere and pensive but can be intensely introverted.

Birthday: You are as deep as they come, with intuition guiding you to each new milestone. Your emotions run like a wild river, and it can feel challenging to contain them, even with yourself.

SAGITTARIUS

The 1st Decanate of Sagittarius | Ruler: Jupiter, Subruler: Jupiter | November 22–December 1

Day: The energy is expansive and worldly but can be excessively idealistic.

Birthday: You are an eternal student of human nature. You believe strongly in personal freedom and make sure to share this expansive optimism with others as often as you can.

The 2nd Decanate of Sagittarius | Ruler: Jupiter, Subruler: Mars | December 2–11

Day: The energy is highly optimistic but can make it difficult to sit still.

Birthday: You are a natural optimist while maintaining the level of concentration required to achieve what you set out to do. If you can continue growing in your ambitions, life is yours for the taking.

The 3rd Decanate of Sagittarius | Ruler: Jupiter, Subruler: The Sun | December 12–21

Day: The energy is joyful and wonder-filled, yet it is not suited for the mundanity of daily work.

Birthday: You are here to experience the very best joy life has to offer. You are a gifted crowd-pleaser, with a natural optimism that is contagious to everyone who surrounds you.

CAPRICORN

The 1st Decanate of Capricorn | Ruler: Saturn, Subruler: Saturn | December 22–December 31

Day: The energy is serious and responsible but can feel quite burdensome at times.

Birthday: You can self-manage and manage others in a way that is highly effective and sustainable. If you are given a task, you always complete it, from start to finish, even at the expense of fun.

The 2nd Decanate of Capricorn | Ruler: Saturn, Subruler: Venus | January 1–10

Day: The energy is interpersonal and devotional, but try not to make promises you can't keep.

Birthday: You are a very devoted lover and friend and take relationships seriously. Despite your unbreakable loyalty, you still keep others at an emotional distance that allows you to maintain control.

The 3rd Decanate of Capricorn | Ruler: Saturn, Subruler: Mercury | January 11–19

Day: The energy is intellectually grounded and mature yet makes it hard to think creatively.

Birthday: You are disciplined yet malleable, enabling you to adapt quickly to any situation and "flex" yourself to fit others' needs. Your brain is your secret power, pushing you to new heights of leadership.

AQUARIUS

The 1st Decanate of Aquarius | Ruler: Uranus, Subruler: Uranus | January 20–29

Day: The energy is visionary yet erratic, leading to new ideas that may not always work in reality.

Birthday: You think one hundred years ahead of the rest of the world, so you may find you have an excellent skill for invention. The trick is learning how to accept human emotion, rather than rationalizing your way out of it.

The 2nd Decanate of Aquarius | Ruler: Uranus, Subruler: Mercury | January 30–February 8

Day: The energy is mentally inspired and future-oriented but can make it hard to stay grounded.

Birthday: You know how to speak the truth of the future. Not all people understand your way of thinking, but with time, the world will remember you fondly for your radically new perspective.

The 3rd Decanate of Aquarius | Ruler: Uranus, Subruler: Venus | February 9–18

Day: The energy is socially minded and compassionate yet can be blocked from true emotion.

Birthday: You are a radical individual with a flair for the creative. Your progressive lens may bring new ideas to the beauty and art space, allowing you to transport others to new worlds through creativity.

PISCES

The 1st Decanate of Pisces | Ruler: Neptune, Subruler: Neptune | February 19–29

Day: The energy is dreamy and creative yet can leave your head and heart in the clouds.

Birthday: You are a Pisces with enough imagination to rebuild the world. You are empathic, even to a fault, bending and twisting as you go about life, healing those who feel profoundly misunderstood through your creativity.

The 2nd Decanate of Pisces | Ruler: Neptune, Subruler: The Moon | March 1–10

Day: The energy is empathic and reflective but can leave you stuck rehashing old feelings.

Birthday: You are a Pisces who can pick up on anyone's emotions, which can be exhausting at times. You are sensitive and treat others with care, although you should aspire to have the same devotion reciprocated from your loved ones.

The 3rd Decanate of Pisces | Ruler: Neptune, Subruler: Pluto | March 11–20

Day: The energy is deeply emotional and sensitive, leading to unexplained subconscious reactions.

Birthday: You are highly reflective, needing periods of solace to reconnect with your inner power. Your love is based on total acceptance of self and others, allowing you to break down walls and heal old wounds.

NUMEROLOGY:

The Path of the Day and Birthday

Magic Days uses the 9 numbers in numerology to define the path you are invited on for each day of the year as well as the general path you are invited to take in this lifetime based on your birthday. To find the number of the day, add the whole month and the whole date up to 9. The most traditional way to define the number of a given day is to separate all the numbers and add them (e.g., January 23 = 1 + 2 + 3), but in this book, the whole number of the month and the whole number of the day are added (e.g., January 23 = 1 + 23 = 24; 2 + 4 = 6).

(Month) + (Date) = Numerology Path

E.g., January 23 = (1) + (23) = 24; 2 + 4 = 6

E.g., December 5 = (12) + (5) = 17; 1 + 7 = 8

ONE: *Autonomy*

This path inspires self-belief through the art of self-reliance, encouraging you to choose your own way even if no one has walked it before. To master this path, make your intuition your copilot.

TWO: *Balance*

This path encourages you to find grace in even the most excruciating of circumstances and to seek peace even with the most difficult of people. To master this path, always aim toward the middle road.

THREE: *Flexibility*

This is a path of connection and change, encouraging you to have your voice heard as well as remain curious about the opinions of others. To master this path, don't give in to stubbornness.

FOUR: *Discipline*

This is a path that asks for action rather than words, inviting you to make integrity the foundation of your purpose rather than focusing on the end goal. To master this path, worship humility rather than success.

FIVE: *Courage*

This is not a path that asks you to walk with your back straight in a perfect line, but rather inspires you to dance your way through its zigzagging maze of wonder. To master this path, move from your heart, not your head.

SIX: *Devotion*

This path encourages you to show your love and your profound gifts through humble service to those around you. To master this path, look for how collective healing is the ultimate self-gratification.

SEVEN: *Commitment*

This path requires personal discernment as you commit to the people, ideas, and goals that mean the most to you. To master this path, prioritize quality over quantity.

EIGHT: *Power*

This path encourages you to go after what you want by being entirely yourself and doing the internal inventory required to stay honest. To master this path, realize that abundance isn't a number but a state of mind.

NINE: *Experience*

This path allows you to be a wise teacher through the complete admission that you yourself are an eternal student of life. To master this path, learn by doing.

TAROT MINOR ARCANA:

The Lesson of the Day and Birthday

Magic Days uses the Minor Arcana cards of the tarot to define the hurdles and obstacles you encounter on a daily basis as well as in this lifetime. There are forty Minor Arcana cards in the tarot, organized into four suits. Each element in astrology (fire, earth, air, and water) has an equivalent Minor Arcana suit (Wands, Pentacles, Swords, and Cups). So to find the Minor Arcana card for each day, pair the numerology and zodiac season of the day with the corresponding tarot suit.

(Month) + (Date) + (Zodiac element) = (Number up to 9) + (Minor Arcana suit)

Fire sign = *Wands suit,* earth sign = *Pentacles suit*, air sign = *Swords suit*, water sign = *Cups suit*

E.g., January 23 = (1) + (23) = 24; 2 + 4 = 6 + (air sign) = Six of Swords

E.g., December 5 = (12) + (5) = 17; 1 + 7 = 8 + (fire sign) = Eight of Wands

WANDS | *Fire Sign*

ACE OF WANDS:

Potential

Potential is a fiery invitation to believe in your soul's calling. It doesn't require any planning but rather a profound "yes" to your next best idea.

TWO OF WANDS:

Preparation

Preparation is a contrary invitation to slow down and cover your bases. Your inspiration may be at an all-time high, but first ground yourself in a practical plan of action.

THREE OF WANDS:

Expansion

Expansion is a sparkling invitation to be both the apprentice and the master. While carrying the knowledge you possess, try something new, divine, and inspiring.

FOUR OF WANDS:

Celebration

Celebration is a warm invitation to enjoy what you have accomplished. Rather than seeking external approval or success, find fulfillment within your friends and chosen family.

FIVE OF WANDS:

Conflict

Conflict is a playful invitation to take competition, opposition, and your ego less seriously. Find the freedom in competing without any armor, until you realize that no one drew their weapon in the first place.

SIX OF WANDS:

Confidence

Confidence is a loud invitation to take humble pride in your accomplishments. You have earned the right to celebrate the work you have done, so don't skip the recognition you deserve.

SEVEN OF WANDS:

Perseverance

Perseverance is a fierce invitation to believe in your cause. No matter what forces attempt to block you, tap into the power of self-belief and power through adversity.

EIGHT OF WANDS:

Momentum

Momentum is an exciting invitation to align your actions with your intuition. By trusting your gut instinct and following through with confidence, you can make great strides in your goals.

NINE OF WANDS:

Persistence

Persistence is a fearless invitation to push through no matter how difficult the opposition may seem. By leaning on those who are in your corner, you can discover the divine satisfaction in sticking things out.

PENTACLES | *Earth Sign*

ACE OF PENTACLES:

Manifestation

Manifestation is a grounded invitation to believe in your powers of abundance. Rather than focusing on what you may lack, take the next step toward financial and material growth.

TWO OF PENTACLES:

Prioritization

Prioritization is a much-needed invitation to balance how, when, and where you spend your energy. You cannot be in two places at once, so plan and delegate where necessary.

THREE OF PENTACLES:

Collaboration

Collaboration is a rooted invitation to share and receive from others. While remaining confident in your abilities and abundance, you can participate in the natural exchange of skills and resources.

FOUR OF PENTACLES:
Conservation

Conservation is an earthly invitation to reground yourself. By pausing your hustle, you can find the security that lives within your relationship with your body and the earth itself.

FIVE OF PENTACLES:
Scarcity

Scarcity is a strict invitation to take inventory of your needs. Whether you are overspending, overworking, underearning, or underappreciating your value, try to prioritize your foundational well-being.

SIX OF PENTACLES:
Reciprocity

Reciprocity is an abundant invitation to share what you have with those who need it most. Even when your cup seems to be running low, it is benevolence rather than scarcity that will refill it.

SEVEN OF PENTACLES:
Sustainability

Sustainability is a serious invitation to invest in your future. By keeping your relationship with the spiritual world in harmony with the physical, you can save and spend where it counts.

EIGHT OF PENTACLES:
Repetition

Repetition is a masterful invitation to never outgrow the tasks that keep you sharp in your talents. With this energy, it is the daily, seemingly small pieces of work that amount to the wholeness of your craft.

NINE OF PENTACLES:
Self-sufficiency

Self-sufficiency is a luxurious invitation to appreciate what you have earned. By taking note of the hard work that got you to your current position of abundance, you can bask in the glory of self-earned plenty.

SWORDS | *Air Sign*

ACE OF SWORDS:
Clarity

Clarity is a mischievous invitation to believe in your intellectual genius. No need for credentials or secondary education here; instead, believe in the innate resources within your mind.

TWO OF SWORDS:
Doubt

Doubt is a rational invitation to make a decision even if you aren't entirely sure of the outcome. By staying calm and collected, you can take a look before you leap, without overthinking it.

THREE OF SWORDS:
Trigger

Trigger is a tough invitation to listen to both your collaborators and naysayers. It's okay to be perfectly wrong so that you can one day discover the right answer.

FOUR OF SWORDS:
Restoration

Restoration is a solitary invitation to take deep, mental rest, giving your brain and body a much-needed break. By taking the space you need, you can separate the ego from inspiration as you plan your next greatest idea.

FIVE OF SWORDS:
Maturity

Maturity is a cutting invitation to think before you speak. Rather than intellectually overpowering others, lay down your mental weapons and surrender to the humility of understanding.

SIX OF SWORDS:
Transition

Transition is a deep invitation to let go of old and outdated patterns of thinking. No longer do you need to torment yourself with the past. Instead, by releasing what was, you can finally embrace what is to come.

SEVEN OF SWORDS:
Hypervigilance

Hypervigilance is a spiritual invitation to stay in the present moment, rather than strategizing or manipulating your current situation. By surrendering to what is, rather than what could be, you can find internal peace.

EIGHT OF SWORDS:
Negativity

Negativity is a humbling invitation to release yourself from your mental cages. Rather than staying stuck in self-pity or victimhood, you can make a choice to take total responsibility for your well-being.

NINE OF SWORDS:
Anxiety

Anxiety is a rational invitation not to believe all the mean voices that keep you up at night. By choosing to see the possibilities rather than the potential failures, you can release yourself from the chains of fear.

CUPS | *Water Sign*

ACE OF CUPS:
Vulnerability

Vulnerability is an intuitive invitation to believe in your heart. You don't need to justify or intellectualize your actions—only to follow your gut no matter what.

TWO OF CUPS:
Worthiness

Worthiness is a mature invitation to dip your toes before you plunge into new emotional waters. Taking one rational step at a time, approach your relationships with loving caution and self-worth.

THREE OF CUPS:
Belonging

Belonging is a sweet invitation to dive into the intimacy of friendship. Witness and be witnessed by your chosen family, emotional scars and all.

FOUR OF CUPS:
Reflection

Reflection is a personal invitation to create intimacy within yourself. By putting your needs first, you emotionally fill your cup so you can overflow into the cups of the ones you love.

FIVE OF CUPS:
Grief

Grief is an incisive invitation to reconsider whom and what you give your heart to. If your devotion is not being reciprocated or valued, be willing to take responsibility for your part and walk away.

SIX OF CUPS:

Nostalgia

Nostalgia is a heartfelt invitation to revisit your childlike self. By remembering what you used to love and cherish growing up, you can reconnect with the joyful innocence that lives within you.

SEVEN OF CUPS:

Illusion

Illusion is a meaningful invitation to stay out of fantasy and exist deeply in reality. By making a choice, rather than staying stuck in what could be, you can discover the grounded potential of what your heart desires.

EIGHT OF CUPS:

Disappointment

Disappointment is an introspective invitation to let go of the attachments that no longer fit your growth. By making space for the grief within change, you can honor the place they once occupied in your heart.

NINE OF CUPS:

Gratitude

Gratitude is a sincere invitation to appreciate the things in your life that are filling your cup. Although contentment is never permanent, seek to find happiness in any moment.

TAROT MAJOR ARCANA:
The Highest Calling of the Day and Birthday

Magic Days uses the Major Arcana cards of the tarot to represent the highest karmic purpose of the day and for the individual born on that day. There are twenty-two of these cards, numbered 0 to 21, so to find the Major Arcana card for each day, add the numerology of the day up to 21.

(Month) + (Date) = Major Arcana cards up to 21

E.g., January 23 = (1) + (23) = 24; 2 + 4 = 6 = The Lovers

E.g., December 5 = (12) + (5) = 17 = The Star

0. THE FOOL: *Faith*

While none of the guides in *Magic Days* can add up to its attributed number of 0, *Faith* is an inherent part of the start of every journey. *Faith* invites you to dive into new, uncharted territory with blind faith, humble confidence, and the gift of beginner's luck. Ready, set, leap!

1. THE MAGICIAN: *Magic*

Magic is a high calling to believe in the inexplicable moments of wonder that happen within and outside yourself. You may notice that no day of the year can add up to the number 1, which is no accident, as *Magic Days* is guided entirely by this card.

2. THE HIGH PRIESTESS: *Intuition*

Intuition is an invitation to turn inward in this lifetime, trusting your powerful unseen truths over the opinions of others. By trusting the ebb and flow of your emotions, you can work in spiritual partnership with your inner knowing.

3. THE EMPRESS: *Abundance*

Abundance is a higher calling to choose to embrace the receptive, creative, and "yin" energy that lives within. By opening yourself to receive the goodness that life has to offer, you will learn to fill your spiritual cup.

4. THE EMPEROR: *Self-mastery*

Self-mastery is an invitation to go after what you want and learn how to unapologetically take up space in the world. By trusting yourself to lead, you will create order in the world around you.

5. THE HIEROPHANT: *Wisdom*

Wisdom is a higher calling to find your grounded place as both the teacher and the student. By remaining both discerning and open-minded, you will discover that knowledge can't be possessed; it can only be shared.

6. THE LOVERS: *Choice*

Choice is a higher calling to prioritize love above all other worldly desires. By constantly striving toward a lifetime of emotional maturity, you'll find that happiness and connection are born from a place of self-love.

7. THE CHARIOT: *Evolution*

Evolution is a higher calling to crawl out of your shell and choose movement over safety. By taking a chance on yourself, you can come to realize that you are always capable of building new muscles.

8. STRENGTH: *Resilience*

Resilience is a higher calling to avoid the whims of passion or emotion. Instead, by recognizing that your strengths are yours to harness, you can create self-esteem through estimable actions.

9. THE HERMIT: *Instinct*

Instinct is a higher calling to question your purpose and travel fearlessly through the darkness of uncertainty. By listening to nothing but the voice of your intuition, you can reach a place of profound meaning.

10. WHEEL OF FORTUNE: *Impermanence*

Impermanence invites you to embrace the mysterious intelligence of the universe. By trusting the highs and lows that life throws at you, you can learn to enjoy the ride of a lifetime.

11. JUSTICE: *Truth*

Truth is a higher calling toward radical accountability. By believing deeply in the spiritual consequences of behavior, you can act in accordance with the laws of karma.

12. THE HANGED MAN: *Surrender*

Surrender is a higher calling to choose spiritual growth over having your way. By surrendering to a power greater than yourself, you can view life from an entirely new perspective.

13. DEATH: *Transformation*

Transformation is a higher calling to surrender to the cyclical and impermanent nature of life. By discovering the renewal within loss, you can turn even the deepest of grief into radical metamorphosis.

14. TEMPERANCE: *Serenity*

Serenity is a higher calling to choose reason over drama, patience over passion. By finding the balance within, you can access internal peace no matter what life throws your way.

15. THE DEVIL: *Shadow*

Shadow is a higher calling to release the patterns of shame that keep you from blossoming. By realizing that there is no bypassing healing, you can stay present to the entirety of the human experience.

16. THE TOWER: *Upheaval*

Upheaval is a higher calling to release your grip on life and take a trust fall. By accepting that the universe will do for you what you cannot do for yourself, you can learn to respect the unplanned nature of change.

17. THE STAR: *Hope*

Hope is a higher calling to dip into your inner resources of optimism. By believing deeply in your inner magic and the gifts that are uniquely yours, you can show the rest of us that anything is possible.

18. THE MOON: *Memory*

Memory is a higher calling to confront the past so you can see the world around you with renewed clarity. By clearing away the wreckage of your past, you can learn to trust your intuition at last.

19. THE SUN: *Vitality*

Vitality is a higher calling to shine with the light of authentic power. By birthing your subconscious truths into creative reality, you give the rest of us permission to express ourselves.

20. JUDGMENT: *Awakening*

Awakening is a higher calling to accept and integrate the harsh but honest realities. By bravely acknowledging the larger patterns at play in the world around you, you can make more clear and conscious decisions.

21. THE WORLD: *Perspective*

Perspective is a higher calling to zoom out and witness the grand adventure of life. By finding gratitude and understanding for each peak and valley along your journey, you can appreciate the human experience.

On each of the following day spreads, you'll find information for that particular day of the year, along with special information if it's your birthday. The left-hand page of each spread, "The Journey of . . . ," tells you about the journey that day will take you on, including a high-level overview of the day's mantras, rituals, and journal prompts to get you inspired. You can use this as a guide for how to approach your day, as inspiration for self-development, or as a simple affirmation that you are on the right track.

If you want to flip directly to your birthday, the right-hand page of each day's spread, "The Journey of Those Born on . . . ," tells you about the journey your soul will go on in this lifetime. It includes a key to your guides, an overview of your journey, your journey's purpose, and relationship dynamics to aid you along your quest, as well as a few notable people born on that day.

WELCOME TO

ARIES
SEASON

The Journey of
MARCH 21

Welcome to March 21, a heartfelt journey toward unconditional love.

Marking the first day of the fiery Aries season, *Devotion* (The Number Six) invites you to cool your passions and act from a place of complete sincerity. Whatever you do today, help others, and do it from the heart. What is your soul calling you to be of service to? Big or small, put compassion on the top of your to-do list as you work to make the world a better place.

And make sure to pat yourself on the back throughout the day. *Confidence* (Six of Wands) invites you to feel good about the work you are doing and the person you are becoming. If public or interpersonal recognition comes your way in the form of a compliment or accolade, accept the honor with humble pride and know that you deserve it.

Besides, there is no better time to fall in love with yourself. *Choice* (The Lovers) asks you to accept the adoration and connection from those around you by first and foremost internalizing how worthy you are of receiving it. Treat yourself today, and every day, as you would someone you love, knowing that the most important relationship you have is the one you have with yourself.

———————————————————◇———————————————————

JUST FOR TODAY

TODAY'S MANTRA

I am worthy of receiving the kind of love I give to others.

TODAY'S JOURNAL PROMPT

What is one thing, big or small, about myself that I find loveable?

TODAY'S RITUAL

Use the power of turquoise to help you channel your confidence. If you have a piece of turquoise jewelry or a piece of clothing that is the color turquoise, adorn yourself with it as you go about today.

———————————————————◇———————————————————

BORN ON THIS DAY

HENRY OSSIAN FLIPPER, American soldier, former enslaved person, and first Black cadet to graduate from the US Military Academy at West Point

ALBERT KAHN, American architect known as the "Architect of Detroit"

"We are hungry for tenderness, in a world where everything abounds, we are poor of this feeling which is like a caress for our heart, we need these small gestures that make us feel good. Tenderness is a disinterested and generous love, that does not ask anything else to be understood and appreciated."—**ALDA MERINI**, Italian writer and poet

The Journey of Those Born on
MARCH 21

Y ou were born of transcendent imagination and worldliness that can block you from doing the inner healing work you need most. You will have to turn inward to experience the love you want, as your journey is one of goodwill, praise, and self-acceptance.

Early on in your journey, you will meet your trustworthy guide, *Devotion* (The Number Six). *Devotion* steers you away from a life of fair-weather plans and toward a path of sincere action. You will meet *Devotion* in your soul's deepest callings that gently guide you to where you can be of service to the people around you. If you can choose honor over temporary fun, you'll pursue a life of meaning.

And if you choose this noble path, *Confidence* (Six of Wands) invites you to recognize your accomplishments. It is easy to mistake low self-worth for humility, but it's important to have a positive image of yourself. You will meet *Confidence* in moments of joyous self-recognition, when the world is cheering you on, but you already have all the applause you'll ever need from within.

YOUR GUIDES

Astrology: Your Energy
Aries (Mars)

Numerology: Your Path
Devotion (The Number Six)

Minor Arcana: Your Lesson
Confidence (Six of Wands)

Major Arcana: Your Highest Calling
Choice (The Lovers)

By answering these calls of the heart, you will uncover the genius of *Choice* (The Lovers). *Choice* empowers you to make a decision, every single day, to love yourself. You will meet *Choice* in moments of interpersonal self-worth, when you are able to discern who truly knows your value. By filling your own cup and never accepting anything less than you deserve, you'll discover the emotional abundance that can only come from self-love.

———————————————○———————————————

ARIES
RULER: MARS

PURPOSE
*To love yourself unconditionally
in order to love others generously.*

RELATIONSHIPS

You are ambitious and worldly, yet your relationships should be a place of humble service and sweet sincerity. By seeking out partners who love you unconditionally while honoring their own sense of worthiness, you will discover that true love is the ultimate potential of openhearted intimacy.

The Journey of
MARCH 22

Welcome to March 22, a laser-focused journey toward self-progress.

Commitment (The Number Seven) asks you to get clear on what you are fighting for today. Whether it be a relationship or a deep ambition you've had for quite some time, aim directly for what you desire most. Actions speak louder than words right now, so make your intentions known.

But don't give up, no matter what. As you navigate your way through the intensity of Aries season, *Perseverance* (Seven of Wands) asks you to welcome any challenge or opposition that comes your way today, proving to the universe itself just how devoted you are to your cause. If someone disagrees with your point of view or tries to dismantle your progress, channel any anger or frustration toward your irrefutable success.

And if you stay true to your goals, *Evolution* (The Chariot) ensures that you won't end today where you began. Limitless growth possibilities exist today, as long as you do the legwork to get there, so let the world see your grit. If you can work passionately guided by the power of self-belief, you will make radical advancement.

JUST FOR TODAY

TODAY'S MANTRA
Today is mine for the taking, as long as I am willing to fight for it.

TODAY'S RITUAL
Wear something that makes you feel strong. Whether it be a protective armor of leather or a favorite childhood sweater, dress yourself as if you are going into battle.

TODAY'S JOURNAL PROMPT
What do I want to fight for today?

BORN ON THIS DAY

CONSTANCE WU, American actor

MARCEL MARCEAU, French actor and mime artist

"Doing begets more doing. It sounds simple, but I'm a firm believer that action can solve so many worries, and just powering through, no matter what, can give you the confidence you need when you feel like you've got nothing to offer."—REESE WITHERSPOON, American actor

The Journey of Those Born on
MARCH 22

You were born of undeniable self-power and stubbornness that can block your true potential. You will have to fight for the person you hope to become, as your journey is one of focus, tenacity, and radical progress.

Early on in your journey, you will meet your determined guide, *Commitment* (The Number Seven). *Commitment* calls you away from a life of playing it safe and toward a path of consequential purpose. You will meet *Commitment* in each of your most desired targets, when you are so sure of what you want that you stop at nothing to achieve it. If you can aim the entirety of your being directly at the heart of the matter, you will never miss.

But if you choose this weighty path, *Perseverance* (Seven of Wands) will challenge you to fight for what you believe in, despite any obstacles. You will meet *Perseverance* in the face of your detractors, when you have no choice but to look within yourself for the strength of conviction to defeat any opposition.

YOUR GUIDES

Astrology: Your Energy
Aries (Mars)

Numerology: Your Path
Commitment (The Number Seven)

Minor Arcana: Your Lesson
Perseverance (The Seven of Wands)

Major Arcana: Your Highest Calling
Evolution (The Chariot)

By answering these calls for action, you will get swept away by the winds of *Evolution* (The Chariot). As long as you do your part to suit up and show up, *Evolution* reveals that there are no limits to your potential as you soar to new heights of self-progress. You will meet *Evolution* in the momentum of self-advancement, when your mind can't quite catch up with how far your soul has come. If you can keep on keeping on, you'll grow with the divine speed of spiritual progress.

ARIES
RULER: MARS

PURPOSE
*To commit to and fight for
your highest potential.*

RELATIONSHIPS

You are seriously independent by nature, but your relationships should be a place of reciprocity and equality. By seeking out partners who respect your ambitions and goals while offering you the encouragement you desire, you will discover that true love supports you no matter what.

The Journey of
MARCH 23

W elcome to March 23, a journey that uncovers the strength that lies within.
Aries season is not known for its introspective qualities, but *Power* (The Number Eight) calls you away from unconscious reaction and into deep self-reflection. Today is a wonderful time to do any therapeutic work, whether that be with a trained counselor, recovery partner, friend, or your journal. Strip back the mask and get honest about who you are and what you are going through.

And listen to the inner callings. *Momentum* (Eight of Wands) doesn't need you to do today perfectly; it just needs you to show up as authentically as you can. So be brave. Be bold. Be direct. If your gut is calling you to act, don't miss out on this momentum because you never know when this level of internal alignment will happen again.

There's no worst-case scenario because you can handle anything. *Resilience* (Strength) empowers you to use your emotional muscles, relying on them in moments of discomfort or fear. Rather than getting lost in self-destructive behaviors or fits of volatile feeling, reach down into the recesses of your soul and find fortitude in the part of you that has overcome so much.

JUST FOR TODAY

TODAY'S MANTRA

I will feel the fear but do it anyway.

TODAY'S RITUAL

Light a match—in a safe and contained space, of course. When it's ignited, say, "Bring me movement," and then blow it out. Repeat this for a total of eight times.

TODAY'S JOURNAL PROMPT

If fear couldn't stop me, what truth would I like to accept within myself?

BORN ON THIS DAY

DANE RUDHYAR, French-born American author, modernist composer, and pioneer of modern astrology

CHAKA KHAN, American singer-songwriter and musician

"To be an artist means to search, to find and look at these realities. To be an artist means never to look away."—AKIRA KUROSAWA, Japanese director and screenwriter

The Journey of Those Born on
MARCH 23

Y ou were born of intuitive confidence and a pridefulness that can stop you from healing repressed shame and trauma. You will have to go inward to the places that scare you, as your
journey is one of introspection, momentum, and emotional fortitude.

Early on in your journey, you will meet your intuitive guide, *Power* (The Number Eight). *Power* calls you
away from the distractions of drama and toward a path
of deep reflection. By shedding light on even the darkest corners of your soul, you'll learn that the truth is
only as scary as it is denied. If you can integrate the
parts of you that you once hid in the closet, and share
them with the people you trust, you'll discover the gift
of authentic connection.

And if you choose this honest path, *Momentum*
(Eight of Wands) teaches you how to act upon your
truth. Although you're never fully prepared for vulnerability, take this leap of faith anyhow. You will meet
Momentum in moments of intuitive action, when you
forgo perfection and strike while the iron's hot.

By answering these brave calls, you will tap into *Re-*
silience (Strength). *Resilience* is your enduring emotional underbelly, built by the muscles that
have held you through even the worst of times. You will meet *Resilience* in moments of personal
fortitude, when you thought the worst had happened and yet you find yourself only growing in
self-trust. If you can lean on this invisible power, you'll receive the keys to infinite strength.

> ## YOUR GUIDES
>
> *Astrology: Your Energy*
> Aries (Mars)
>
> *Numerology: Your Path*
> Power (The Number Eight)
>
> *Minor Arcana: Your Lesson*
> Momentum (The Eight of Wands)
>
> *Major Arcana: Your Highest Calling*
> Resilience (Strength)

ARIES
RULER: MARS

PURPOSE
*To realize that limitless power comes
from self-acceptance.*

RELATIONSHIPS

You are courageous and magnificent, and your relationships should be a place of emotional transparency and honesty. By seeking out partners who unconditionally accept all the layers of your
dynamic soul, you will discover that true love doesn't require you to hide.

The Journey of
MARCH 24

W elcome to March 24, a high-minded journey that gets you in touch with your purpose. *Experience* (The Number Nine) invites you to be fearless in your quest for insight today. Track down that worldly adviser and pick their brain, throw yourself into that new project at work, or make an impulse decision to start an entirely foreign field of study. Make big moves to expand your perspective today.

But amidst the ambition of Aries season, make sure you don't burn out too quickly. *Persistence* (Nine of Wands) encourages you to take a small rest when possible throughout today, recharging your battery without giving up entirely on the tasks that lie ahead. Create necessary boundaries for yourself when appropriate, never biting off more than you can chew.

The good news is that your gut will tell you everything you need to know. As you explore new and uncharted territory, *Instinct* (The Hermit) calls you to trust the intuitive voice that lives within to guide you along the winding roads of today. You don't have to plan ahead or map your day in advance; simply drop into your soul's center and listen for divine direction.

JUST FOR TODAY

TODAY'S MANTRA

I don't have to have the answers. I just have to be brave enough to explore.

TODAY'S JOURNAL PROMPT

What tools, elements, and practices help me get in touch with my intuition?

TODAY'S RITUAL

Go outside and collect nine sticks or twigs—ideally small enough to keep in your desk drawer. Tie them together with a black band or ribbon and hold them in your hands whenever you are in need of power today. Repeat the spell, "Nine of Wands, please bring to me the persistence I need."

BORN ON THIS DAY

DOROTHY HEIGHT, American civil rights and women's rights activist

STEVE MCQUEEN, American actor called the "King of Cool"

"My Brain is the key that sets me free."—**HARRY HOUDINI**, Hungarian-born American magician and escape artist

The Journey of Those Born on
MARCH 24

You were born of fierce compassion and a belief in others that you don't as easily extend toward yourself. You will have to grow to trust yourself, as your journey is one of searching, endurance, and intuitive knowledge.

Early on in your journey, you will meet your high-minded guide, *Experience* (The Number Nine). *Experience* calls you away from a life of mundanity and toward a path of fearless searching. You will meet *Experience* in the excitement of the unknown, when you have found your next great question and yet you have no idea how to find the answer. If you consistently can push your boundaries of understanding, you'll discover the limitless gift of curiosity.

But if you choose this demanding path, *Persistence* (Nine of Wands) will ask you to finish your goals to completion. It is easy to have enthusiasm at the beginning of an endeavor, but *Persistence* asks you to sustain your energy so that you can see your ambitions through. You will meet *Persistence* in moments of strategic boundaries, when you keep your spark alive through pragmatic self-care.

By answering these calls for growth, you will have to lean on *Instinct* (The Hermit). *Instinct* asks you to listen to the intuitive navigator who lives within, guiding you through even the murkiest of roads with no clear destination in sight. You will meet *Instinct* in total darkness, when there is no plan and no leader to follow except yourself. If you can realize that the only searching you need to do is within, *Instinct* illuminates the internal hallways of truth.

ARIES
RULER: MARS

PURPOSE
To instinctually and strategically explore new heights of understanding.

RELATIONSHIPS

You are fearlessly devoted, and your relationships should be a place of expansion and wanderlust. By seeking out partners who are as endlessly fascinating as they are adventurous, you will discover that true love takes you to jaw-dropping heights of personal growth.

The Journey of
MARCH 25

W elcome to March 25, an ambitious journey with no guarantees.
   Autonomy (The Number One) invites you to pursue today on your own terms, entirely on your own and with no precedent. Set a high-reaching goal and hurl your entire will in that direction. There's no need to overthink, overprepare, or seek outside counsel; just reach for radical bravery over careful planning.

To coincide with the independent nature of Aries season, *Potential* (Ace of Wands) invites you to pursue your passions. Believe in your next best idea, turning inspiration into forceful action. Take a step, any step, in the direction of your dreams, and follow through with grit and tenacity. Shut yourself off from the naysayers—today is about a resounding "yes."

But completely surrender the outcome. *Impermanence* (Wheel of Fortune) invites you to witness life's wild ride today, taking neither the highs nor the lows too seriously. Luck, whether good or bad, is fleeting, so roll with the punches and keep your perspective on the big picture. Are you still reaching for your dreams? If you can tend to this flame that lives within, regardless of your present circumstances, you'll discover the gift of faith.

JUST FOR TODAY

TODAY'S MANTRA
The potential of my ambition is more important than the outcome.

TODAY'S JOURNAL PROMPT
What are my beliefs around fate and karma?

TODAY'S RITUAL
On a piece of paper, write down what the numbers 1 through 9 represent to you (e.g., 1 = independence, 8 = truth). Every hour on the hour, roll a dice and see what the universe wants you to channel.

BORN ON THIS DAY

ARETHA FRANKLIN, American singer-songwriter known as the "Queen of Soul" and first female performer inducted into the Rock and Roll Hall of Fame in 1987

BÉLA BARTÓK, Hungarian pianist and composer of *Concerto for Orchestra*

"Without leaps of imagination, or dreaming, we lose the excitement of possibilities. Dreaming, after all, is a form of planning."—GLORIA STEINEM, American journalist, feminist, and publisher

The Journey of Those Born on
MARCH 25

Y ou were born of fierce ambition and laser focus that makes it hard to accept failure. You will have to let go of expectation, as your journey is one of independence, fearlessness, and destiny.

Early on in your journey, you will meet your formidable guide, *Autonomy* (The Number One). *Autonomy* calls you away from a life of excess responsibility and toward a path of personal freedom. You will meet *Autonomy* in the bold aloneness that comes from creating a blueprint for living that has never been done before. If you can trust your intuition over external opinion, you'll be able to draw upon the power of self-reliance.

And if you accept this daring path, you will meet your bright coconspirator, *Potential* (Ace of Wands). The most coveted currency in life is ambition, and *Potential* asks you to follow through on the lightbulb ideas you carry within. You will meet *Potential* in the very beginning stages of a new endeavor, when you brave your first step toward the life of your dreams.

YOUR GUIDES
Astrology: Your Energy Aries (Mars)
Numerology: Your Path Autonomy (The Number One)
Minor Arcana: Your Lesson Potential (The Ace of Wands)
Major Arcana: Your Highest Calling Impermanence (The Wheel of Fortune)

By answering these calls for bravery, you will come to respect the laws of *Impermanence* (Wheel of Fortune). *Impermanence* reminds you that the quickest way to make the universe laugh is to tell it your plans, so relinquish control and believe in destiny. You will meet *Impermanence* in the ups and downs, the ebbs and flows, forever reminding you that the only constant on this roller coaster is change. If you can throw your hands up in playful surrender, you'll enjoy the ride.

ARIES
RULER: MARS

PURPOSE
To utilize the power of will while believing in fate.

RELATIONSHIPS

You are serious in your responsibilities, yet your relationships should be a place of freedom and independence. By seeking out partners who know how to fill their life with meaning on their own accord, you will discover that true love comes without expectation.

The Journey of
MARCH 26

Welcome to March 26, a patient journey toward justice.

Balance (The Number Two) encourages you to relax and let it flow today. There's no need for frantic or impulsive action, but instead, do the things that feel easy and organic. And bring a partner or friend with you throughout your day, leaning on them in moments that feel overwhelming.

If you don't get anything concrete done, don't worry because *Preparation* (Two of Wands) wants you to lay the necessary groundwork before making your next big move. To counteract the urgency of Aries season, align your short- and long-term goals, planning for what's to come while getting clear on your intentions. If you can draw up a course of action today, you can hit the ground running tomorrow.

And what is it that you're preparing for exactly? *Truth* (Justice) empowers you to consider how your goals are impacting the world around you. Use this time to consider the cause and effect of your ambitions, helping you narrow your aim toward a higher purpose. Balance logic with intuition as you fuse your actions with your moral values.

———————————o———————————

JUST FOR TODAY

TODAY'S MANTRA
I will prepare internally for the fair and just future I want to build.

TODAY'S JOURNAL PROMPT
Do my moral and social values align with my current professional ambitions?

TODAY'S RITUAL
Drink honeysuckle tea. Fairly easy to find at your local health food store, honeysuckle helps you channel the calmness of today. As you sip your tea, close your eyes and repeat the words, "Balance. Preparation. Truth."

———————————o———————————

BORN ON THIS DAY

ROBERT FROST, American poet

KATE RICHARDS O'HARE, American Socialist Party activist, editor, and orator

"We don't accomplish anything in this world alone . . . and whatever happens is the result of the whole tapestry of one's life and all the weavings of individual threads form one to another that creates something."—**SANDRA DAY O'CONNOR**, first American woman to serve as a US Supreme Court Justice

The Journey of Those Born on
MARCH 26

You were born of pure passion and a depth of power that can be intimidating to many. You will have to learn to catch more flies with honey, as your journey is one of harmony, patience, and intention.

Early on in your journey, you will meet your steady guide, *Balance* (The Number Two). *Balance* calls you away from the unpredictability of passion and toward a path of harmonious partnership. You will meet *Balance* in moments of trust, when you recognize that when you ask for help, life isn't so hard after all. If you can reach for tranquility over prideful autonomy, you'll develop a sense of internal peace.

And if you choose this gentle path, you will have to contend with *Preparation* (Two of Wands). Although you have a penchant for impulsivity, *Preparation* asks you to think things through anyhow. You will meet *Preparation* in times of careful planning, when your head wants things to be done in an instant, but your soul knows that the goal is too important to rush through. If you can take the time to aim your arrows directly at your target, you can never miss.

By answering these calls to slow down, you will be able to hear *Truth* (Justice). *Truth* lives within the irrefutable laws of karma, reminding you time and again that your actions, and ambitions, have consequences. *Truth* invites you to align your values with your goals so that you can create the change you hope to see in the world. If you can fight for justice over self, you'll tap into the power of spiritual accountability.

ARIES
RULER: MARS

PURPOSE
To slow down enough to realize what is worth fighting for.

RELATIONSHIPS

You are autonomous and powerful, yet your relationships should be a place of healthy dependency and trust. By seeking out partners who aim to make your life just a little bit easier and never shame you for asking for help, you will discover that true love creates peace from mutual partnership.

The Journey of
MARCH 27

Welcome to March 27, a beautiful but winding journey of open-mindedness.

Aries season can make you believe you need all the right answers, but *Flexibility* (The Number Three) invites you to forgo your pride and ask the right questions. Seek out any and every opportunity to learn and grow today, and don't be afraid to look silly in the process. Don't take yourself too seriously but do pursue your curiosity in earnest.

Expansion (Three of Wands) asks you to double down on these efforts by trying your hand at something new. Test out that dance class you thought you'd be terrible at, ask out that person who you believe to be out of your league, or start studying that new language you've been dying to try.

If you put yourself out there, you can begin to receive. *Abundance* (The Empress) offers you gifts of the unknown today, encouraging you to enjoy the beauty, connection, and wonder that these new experiences bring. If you receive a compliment or a token of appreciation from someone, stay present with this joy, and know that you are worthy.

―――――○―――――

JUST FOR TODAY

TODAY'S MANTRA
There is an abundance of life to live if I'm willing to be a beginner.

TODAY'S JOURNAL PROMPT
What are my fears around starting something new and not being in control or an expert?

TODAY'S RITUAL
Spend time watching an animal today. It could be a dog, cat, bird, or field mouse—it doesn't matter! Watch them playfully and intuitively go about their day as a reminder not to take everything so seriously.

―――――○―――――

BORN ON THIS DAY

ANNA MAE AQUASH, First Nations activist and Mi'kmaq tribal member

MARIAH CAREY, American singer

"Don't write what you think people want to read. Find your voice and write about what's in your heart."―QUENTIN TARANTINO, American director and screenwriter

The Journey of Those Born on
MARCH 27

You were born of intellectual independence and limitless intuition that place you in a permanent state of authority. You will have to open yourself to being a beginner, as your journey is one of curiosity, exploration, and abundance.

Early on in your journey, you will meet your inquisitive guide, *Flexibility* (The Number Three). *Flexibility* calls you away from a life of isolating contemplation and toward a path of perspective-building connection. You will meet *Flexibility* in the fear of not having the answers, when humility leaves you completely open-minded to the opinions and experiences of others. If you can choose connection over pride, you'll discover the benefits of adaptability.

If you take this winding path, you will open yourself to *Expansion* (Three of Wands). Channel your expert knowledge into a new passion that requires you to be a student. You will meet *Expansion* in the thrill of uncharted territory, when beginner's luck allows you to grow in ways you never thought possible.

> ### YOUR GUIDES
>
> *Astrology: Your Energy*
> Aries (Mars)
>
> *Numerology: Your Path*
> Flexibility (The Number Three)
>
> *Minor Arcana: Your Lesson*
> Expansion (The Three of Wands)
>
> *Major Arcana: Your Highest Calling*
> Abundance (The Empress)

By answering these mind-altering calls, you will tap into *Abundance* (The Empress). Abundance asks you to not play it safe by keeping your life small, but instead, invites you to say "yes" to receiving all the richness that life has to offer. You will meet *Abundance* in moments of plenty, when your cup is so full you can't help but share this joy with others. If you can remember you are worthy of these blessings, you'll discover the gift of spiritual prosperity.

ARIES
RULER: MARS

PURPOSE
To be open enough to receive all the knowledge, connection, and abundance life has to offer.

RELATIONSHIPS

You are assertive and intuitive, yet your relationships should be a place of letting go and having fun. By seeking out partners who never take themselves too seriously, you will discover that true love is a lighthearted adventure of its own.

The Journey of
MARCH 28

Welcome to March 28, a hardworking journey toward self-leadership.

Discipline (The Number Four) invites you to put your head down and do the work required today. There's no need for excuses or postponement, so do the mundane and seemingly insignificant tasks that you would otherwise leave for tomorrow. To counteract the unpredictability of Aries season, control what you can through personal integrity.

When you're done with your responsibilities, leave some time for *Celebration* (Four of Wands). Work as hard as you play by spending fun time with the people you love. Whether you throw a party or go out for a night of comedy, reward yourself for a job well done.

This reasonable approach is needed, as *Self-mastery* (The Emperor) knows a compassionate leader would never let their team work themselves to the bone. Step into a place of authority in your life, and be discerning about when to rest, when to work, and when to simply let loose and have a good time. It is a worthwhile tightrope you must walk today, but if you lose your balance, tap into the divine wisdom that lives within.

○

JUST FOR TODAY

TODAY'S MANTRA

There is a time to work and a time to enjoy, and my gut knows the difference.

TODAY'S RITUAL

Get out of your head and have fun—it's that simple. Dance like no one's watching, turn your kitchen upside down baking something delicious, or paint an imperfect masterpiece.

TODAY'S JOURNAL PROMPT

Am I more prone to overworking or overplaying, and what is the reason behind that?

○

BORN ON THIS DAY

ARISTIDE BRIAND, French politician, eleven-time prime minister of France, and Nobel Peace Prize winner

LADY GAGA, American singer-songwriter and actor

"Prayer is an act of love. Words are not needed."—**SAINT TERESA OF ÁVILA**, Spanish noblewoman, Carmelite nun, prominent Spanish mystic, religious reformer, author, and theologian

The Journey of Those Born on
MARCH 28

You were born of fierce ambition and an impulsiveness that can get you in trouble. You will have to learn to harness your passions, as your journey is one of restraint, self-improvement, and a bit of fun.

Early on in your journey, you will meet your stern guide, *Discipline* (The Number Four). *Discipline* calls you away from a life built on self-propulsion and toward a path of integrity and hard work. You will meet *Discipline* in the grittiest of hours, when your head wants to give up, but your soul carries you forward anyhow. If you can mean what you do and do what you say, you'll build a foundation that can stand for a lifetime.

But if you choose this demanding path, *Celebration* (Four of Wands) will ask you to let down your hair from time to time. Your ambitions may be fierce, but *Celebration* asks you to pursue a well-rounded life. You will meet *Celebration* in the joy of being with your chosen family, when you forget about what must be done and exist in the moment with the people you call home.

YOUR GUIDES

Astrology: Your Energy
Aries (Mars)

Numerology: Your Path
Discipline (The Number Four)

Minor Arcana: Your Lesson
Celebration (The Four of Wands)

Major Arcana: Your Highest Calling
Self-mastery (The Emperor)

By answering these calls for maturity, you will reach new heights of *Self-mastery* (The Emperor). Rather than getting caught up in the dramas of emotion, *Self-mastery* asks you to react to life from a place of objective wisdom. You will meet *Self-mastery* in moments of spiritual growth, when you become a respected leader by being a leader toward yourself. If you can choose reason over passion, you'll tap into the power of integrity.

○

ARIES
RULER: MARS

PURPOSE
To be a thoughtful and balanced leader toward yourself.

RELATIONSHIPS

You are independent, even to a fault, yet your relationships should be a place of deep emotional grounding. By seeking out partners who feel like home as they help you rest and take the stress off the day, you will discover that true love brings a profound sense of emotional safety.

The Journey of
MARCH 29

Welcome to March 29, a fearsome journey toward self-knowledge.

Courage (The Number Five) asks you to throw caution to the wind and act from a place of bold authenticity today. Say "yes" to any invitations for vulnerability, whether it be an unexpected leadership position at work or a spotlight on social media. To channel the passion of Aries season, tell the world exactly who you are and what you believe in most.

And don't run away from *Conflict* (Five of Wands). Remain open to feedback and come to terms with the inevitability of such opposition when you are finding your voice. Try your best to objectively sort through any contradictory opinions that come your way, neither taking them as fact nor denying their potential value.

Besides, *Wisdom* (The Hierophant) knows that truth is subjective. Whether you are processing a comment from a friend or listening to a respected leader, step into a place of personal authority as you separate the true from the false. Be a discerning student today as you wade through the endless piles of opinions, knowing that the only answers and approval you need lie within.

JUST FOR TODAY

TODAY'S MANTRA
No one's truth is more important than mine.

TODAY'S JOURNAL PROMPT
When did I learn to silence my opinion due to fear of authority?

TODAY'S RITUAL
Seek out the wisdom of the owl. Whether it be a figurine, an image, a painting, or an actual owl (!) hold it in your gaze as you repeat the chant, "Owl wisdom please help me see, the intuitive teacher that lives within me."

BORN ON THIS DAY

PEARL BAILEY, American actor and singer

MICHAEL LEONARD BRECKER, American jazz saxophonist and composer who earned fifteen Grammy Awards as a performer and composer

"The star player must slay his ego and learn teamwork and communication skills before he can achieve the ultimate in sport."—WALT "CLYDE" FRAZIER JR., American NBA basketball player

The Journey of Those Born on
MARCH 29

You were born of intuitive balance and a need for acceptance that can block from you finding your true voice. You will have to listen deeply to the truth that lives within, as your journey is one of bravery, diversity, and self-knowledge.

Early on in your journey, you will meet your bold guide, *Courage* (The Number Five). *Courage* calls you away from making yourself small to please others and toward a path of unapologetic self-expression. You will meet *Courage* in moments of vulnerability, when you risk your reputation in favor of being entirely and completely yourself. If you can prioritize authenticity over appeasement, *Courage* offers you the gift of personal freedom.

But if you choose this daring path, you will have to contend with *Conflict* (Five of Wands). You will meet *Conflict* in the face of your adversaries and contrarians, when you are forced to get clear on what feedback is useful or plain hurtful. Rather than reacting, reflect upon where you have room to learn while appreciating all the courage it took you to get here.

By answering these calls for bravery, you will tap into *Wisdom* (The Hierophant). Your truth can, and will be, different from others', so *Wisdom* encourages you to trust your gut while remaining open to the perspectives of others. You will meet *Wisdom* in the messiness of subjectivity when you realize that no one and nothing has a monopoly on knowledge. If you can hold on to your intuitive power, you'll learn to trust that the answers to your deepest questions must come from within.

ARIES
RULER: MARS

PURPOSE
To courageously trust yourself while remaining teachable.

RELATIONSHIPS

You are passionate about equality and peace, yet your relationships should be a place of healthy conflict and understanding. By seeking out partners who share their truth as strongly as they listen to yours, you will discover that true love inspires courage.

The Journey of
MARCH 30

Welcome to March 30, a sincere journey toward emotional contentment.

Aries season is not known for its sentimentality, but *Devotion* (The Number Six) invites you to give generously from the heart today anyway. Offer your talents and abundance of energy everywhere you go. Whether it be paying a stranger a compliment or going out of your way to help a neighbor with a tough project, ensure that your actions align with a higher purpose.

And don't be shy to accept any praise that comes your way. *Confidence* (Six of Wands) encourages you to acknowledge the progress you make today, reveling in the good feelings that come from personal integrity. Give yourself a metaphorical or physical pat on the back and use this positivity to move forward with pride.

And how can you make the most of this day, exactly? *Choice* (The Lovers) champions emotional reciprocity, inspiring you to deepen your connections with the people who always aim to meet you halfway. Spend time with a loved one who's actions always make you feel truly seen and heard, and hold compassionate space for them in return. There's so much love in the air, so make sure you receive as much as you give.

JUST FOR TODAY

TODAY'S MANTRA

Love can only be shared if it is received.

TODAY'S JOURNAL PROMPT

Do I give more than I receive from others? If so, what blockages do I have around receiving?

TODAY'S RITUAL

Give yourself a hug—you might be surprised by how good this feels! Wrap your arms as tightly around yourself as you can, inhale the sweet aroma of your skin, and repeat the phrase, "I will love myself unconditionally."

BORN ON THIS DAY

INGVAR KAMPRAD, Swedish businessman and founder of IKEA

CÉLINE DION, Canadian singer

"Be clearly aware of the stars and infinity on high. Then life seems almost enchanted after all."—VINCENT VAN GOGH, Dutch artist, painter, and pioneer of Expressionism

The Journey of Those Born on
MARCH 30

You were born of social ambition and a generousness that you rarely extend to yourself as easily as you do to others. You will have to get to know the beauty of your heart, as your journey is one of sincerity, progress, and true love.

Early on in your journey, you will meet your sweet guide, *Devotion* (The Number Six). *Devotion* calls you away from a life of social domination and toward a path of meaningful service. You will meet *Devotion* in the causes that mean the most to you when you are willing to put social pressure aside in favor of a higher purpose.

But if you choose this noble path, you will have to make room for *Confidence* (Six of Wands). *Confidence* asks you to enjoy your reputation and embrace the applause and accolades you earn along the way. Be careful not to mistake self-denial for humility by acknowledging your hard-earned success.

By answering these calls for sincerity, you will tap into a new sense of self-respect. *Choice* (The Lovers) reminds you that the only way to share your cup is to keep it full, inspiring you to make yourself available to receiving love. You will meet *Choice* in moments of compassionate care, when you decide to prioritize the people, projects, and ideas that love you. If you can treat yourself as you would like to treat others, you'll discover the gift of eternal self-love.

YOUR GUIDES

Astrology: Your Energy
Aries (Mars)

Numerology: Your Path
Devotion (The Number Six)

Minor Arcana: Your Lesson
Confidence (The Six of Wands)

Major Arcana: Your Highest Calling
Choice (The Lovers)

ARIES
RULER: MARS

PURPOSE
To give from the heart to others and, most importantly, to yourself.

RELATIONSHIPS

You are excitable and forever searching for more, yet your relationships should be a place of emotional contentment and nourishment. By seeking out partners who love as openly and generously as you do, you will discover that true love gives you the everlasting energy of loyal support.

The Journey of
MARCH 31

W elcome to March 31, an intentional journey of self-progress.

Commitment (The Number Seven) asks you to focus your attention on your deepest ambitions today. It's a wonderful time to make a vision board so you can align your actions with your long-term goals. Show up to the responsibilities that coincide with your dreams and approach your obligations with courageous conviction.

And don't let anything stop you. *Perseverance* (Seven of Wands) isn't afraid to make you sweat to see just how loyal you are to your cause. Aries season has a penchant for hotheadedness, so greet any opposition with fierce determination and clarity of purpose. If criticism or fear of failure get the best of you at any point today, get centered and remember what it is you are fighting for.

It'll be worth the battle, as *Evolution* (The Chariot) wants you to go far today. Whether you accomplish a big milestone or embrace a huge internal breakthrough, you'll experience the gift of momentum in exchange for hard work and dedication. Keep your eye on the prize, and you will be amazed by the progress you can make in a single day.

JUST FOR TODAY

TODAY'S MANTRA

My purpose is stronger than my fear of defeat.

TODAY'S JOURNAL PROMPT

Where do I hope to evolve toward today?

TODAY'S RITUAL

Write down on paper the name of your greatest threat. It can be a person, a system, or a part of you. Roll the paper very tightly and light it on fire somewhere safe and contained. Stomp out the flame as you chant the words, "Evolution, I am ready for you."

BORN ON THIS DAY

RENÉ DESCARTES, French philosopher

ALEXANDRA KOLLONTAI, Russian revolutionary, politician, diplomat, and Marxist feminist

"To make a great dream come true, the first requirement is a great capacity to dream; the second is persistence."—CESAR CHAVEZ, American labor leader and cofounder of the United Farm Workers

The Journey of Those Born on
MARCH 31

You were born of controlled passion and a restraint that can hold you back from your ultimate potential. You will have to throw yourself fearlessly toward your purpose, as your journey is one of certainty, challenge, and limitless potential.

Early on in your journey, you will meet your thoughtful guide, *Commitment* (The Number Seven). *Commitment* calls you away from a life of meaningless work and toward a path of deliberate action. You will encounter *Commitment* in the spiritual contracts that you sign when you choose to devote yourself entirely to a cause. If you can narrow your focus to your soul's deepest callings, you'll learn how to stick to your word.

But if you choose this discerning path, you will have to contend with *Perseverance* (Seven of Wands). *Perseverance* won't let you back down without a fight, encouraging you to stand up for what you believe in no matter what opposes you. You will meet *Perseverance* in moments of conviction, when you believe so earnestly in your cause that nothing and no one can slow you down.

By answering these calls for integrity, you will grow with the power of *Evolution* (The Chariot). *Evolution* asks you to show your devotion through consistent and hard work in exchange for the divine momentum of self-progress. You will meet *Evolution* in radical breakthroughs, when you somehow manage to smash the ceiling of success you never thought could budge. If you can fight for the highest potential for the future, *Evolution* ensures you will get there.

———————————————————————○———————————————————————

ARIES
RULERS: MARS, THE SUN

PURPOSE
To hurl yourself toward your highest potential.

RELATIONSHIPS

You are hardworking and self-reliant, and your relationships should be a place of hard work and mutual integrity. By seeking out partners who want to share the small and large burdens in life with you, you will discover that true love is a shared responsibility.

The Journey of
APRIL 1

Welcome to April 1, a radical journey toward self-knowledge.

Take center stage in your life today. Whether it be on social media, in the classroom, or at the office, Courage (The Number Five) asks you to grab the microphone and tell the world exactly who you are and what you stand for. To coincide with the fiery qualities of Aries season, throw caution to the wind and act from a place of passion rather than logic.

However, know that with self-expression comes inevitable feedback. *Conflict* (Five of Wands) warns against defensiveness of any kind, encouraging you to receive criticism as a growth opportunity rather than a lethal threat. If you can set aside your ego and search for the ounce of truth in what your perceived enemies say, you'll see eye to eye with people who are your unlikely teachers.

But don't give away your power entirely. Just because you are open to the opinions of others doesn't mean you have to disregard your own. *Wisdom* (The Hierophant) empowers you to trust your gut throughout this day, deciding on your own definition of true and false as you remain teachable to the knowledge that comes your way.

───────────○───────────

JUST FOR TODAY

TODAY'S MANTRA

I can learn from others while I decipher what is true for me.

TODAY'S JOURNAL PROMPT

How do I typically respond to criticism? Is there a way I can remain more open to it today?

TODAY'S RITUAL

Surrender your defenses. Lie facedown on your bed or somewhere comfortable (even a field of grass could be nice!) and spread your arms and legs in a starfish position. Breathe in deeply, and as you exhale, imagine dropping your shield of armor, knowing that the universe has your back.

───────────○───────────

BORN ON THIS DAY

SOPHIE GERMAIN, French mathematician

TOSHIRO MIFUNE, Japanese actor

"Human rights are not things that are put on the table for people to enjoy. These are things you fight for and then you protect."—WANGARI MUTA MAATHAI, Kenyan environmentalist, political activist, and founder of the Green Belt Movement

The Journey of Those Born on
APRIL 1

You were born of unfiltered intuition and a fearlessness that can appear reckless at times. You will have to channel your bravery into higher knowledge, as your journey is one of self-expression, contention, and revelation.

Early on in your journey, you will meet your bold guide, *Courage* (The Number Five). *Courage* asks you to transform passion into vulnerability as you follow a path of self-expression. You will meet *Courage* in the uncertainty of authenticity, when you put yourself out there without any guarantee of a positive outcome. If you can enjoy the wild ride of being unapologetically yourself, you'll open yourself to the gift of being real.

But if you choose this daring path, you will have to contend with *Conflict* (Five of Wands). Rather than getting lost in blind rage or indigent pride, listen to the critics you come up against in order to grow. You will meet *Conflict* in the ounce of truth that lives within negative feedback when you drop your defenses and surrender to the growing pains of being human.

YOUR GUIDES

Astrology: Your Energy
Aries (Mars, The Sun)

Numerology: Your Path
Courage (The Number Five)

Minor Arcana: Your Lesson
Conflict (The Five of Wands)

Major Arcana: Your Highest Calling
Wisdom (The Hierophant)

By embracing these calls for honesty, you will step into the realm of *Wisdom* (The Hierophant). *Wisdom* asks you to listen to the internal knowing that lives within, helping you differentiate your truth from the false prophets and gurus who attempt to tell you how you should think. You will encounter *Wisdom* in moments of spiritual discernment, when you are teachable while remaining loyal to yourself as you wade through the endless unknown.

───────────────○───────────────

ARIES
RULERS: MARS, THE SUN

PURPOSE
To walk the divine tightrope of being fearlessly teachable and intuitively discerning.

RELATIONSHIPS

You are uncompromisingly independent, yet your relationships should be a place of heartfelt vulnerability and passion. By seeking out partners who rock your world and open your heart to possibility, you will discover that true love is the giver of life.

The Journey of
APRIL 2

Welcome to April 2, a sincere journey toward true love. Despite the self-oriented nature of Aries season, look out for how you can be of service to others today. Whether it be complimenting a stranger on the street or helping a coworker, do these acts of kindness behind the scenes and do not expect anything in return. *Devotion* (The Number Six) reminds you that true character is what you do when no one is watching.

But you might just be rewarded after all. *Confidence* (Six of Wands) encourages you to accept praise when it is given today. If you have been working tirelessly on a project that is finally reaching a meaningful milestone, take a moment to truly pat yourself on the back for everything you have done to make this happen. And if you are offered this recognition on a more public level, embrace it with humility.

At the end of the day, emotional fulfillment is a *Choice* (The Lovers). Prioritize your happiness through intentional action, seeking out the partners and projects that give back in return for your efforts. If something is feeling one-sided or draining, don't be afraid to cut ties so you can focus on the life-giving responsibilities that fill your cup.

JUST FOR TODAY

TODAY'S MANTRA
I will give and receive the love that I know I deserve through action.

TODAY'S JOURNAL PROMPT
What is something I am proud of right now?

TODAY'S RITUAL
Give yourself a compliment. I know, this can be hard for some of us. But tell yourself one nice thing you could say about a personal quality you possess. If you are truly stumped, call a loving person and ask them to help you come up with something true.

BORN ON THIS DAY

ANNALENA TONELLI, Italian lawyer and social activist

RODNEY KING, American victim of Los Angeles Police Department violence

"To be of use to the world is the only way to be happy."—HANS CHRISTIAN ANDERSEN, Danish author best known for his collection of fairy tales

The Journey of Those Born on
APRIL 2

You were born of fierce helpfulness and a fearlessness that you use to save others rather than saving yourself. You will have to learn to receive the love you so easily give, as your journey is one of purpose, praise, and self-worth.

Early on in your journey, you will meet your sincere guide, *Devotion* (The Number Six). Despite any predispositions toward lethargy or procrastination, *Devotion* calls you toward a path of generous service. You will meet *Devotion* in the sweat that pours from you in the midst of a meaningful project, when your body feels tired but your heart begs you to do just a bit more.

If you choose this path of purpose, be sure to take in the applause along the way. *Confidence* (Six of Wands) knows that esteem built through estimable action never amounts to arrogance, so don't feel guilty over hard-earned praise. You will meet *Confidence* in moments of humble success, when the universe rewards the invisible work that amounts to sincere progress.

By answering these meaningful calls, *Choice* (The Lovers) will have a simple decision for you to make: to drain your emotional cup through extreme self-sacrifice or to fill up your cup and let it overflow through complete self-love. The answer is only easy in theory, but *Choice* asks you to take active steps to prioritize reciprocal relationships and ambitions that nourish your holistic well-being and happiness. If you can treat yourself as gently as you would another person, you'll discover the gift of emotional contentment.

> ## YOUR GUIDES
>
> *Astrology: Your Energy*
> Aries (Mars, The Sun)
>
> *Numerology: Your Path*
> Devotion (The Number Six)
>
> *Minor Arcana: Your Lesson*
> Confidence (The Six of Wands)
>
> *Major Arcana: Your Highest Calling*
> Choice (The Lovers)

ARIES
RULERS: MARS, THE SUN

PURPOSE
To give and receive unconditional love through meaningful action.

RELATIONSHIPS

You are relationship-driven by nature, and your relationships should be a place of unconditional love. By seeking out partners who aim to lighten your load rather than burden you with responsibilities that are not yours, you will discover that true love doesn't have to feel so heavy after all.

The Journey of
APRIL 3

Welcome to April 3, an ambitious journey toward self-actualization.

What do you care about most today? *Commitment* (The Number Seven) encourages you to narrow your focus and show loyalty to your goals and relationships through action. It's easy to get distracted by shiny-new-toy syndrome, but now is the time to bring complete intention to everything you are devoted to.

And be sure you are willing to fight for them. Amidst the fiery passion of Aries season, *Perseverance* (Seven of Wands) empowers you to stand up for what you love in the face of any opposition. Whether it be a troll discrediting your name online or a frenemy undercutting your actions through false words, use the unstoppable force of self-belief to combat these lower beings. Rise high rather than stooping to their level.

Besides, you are moving on up. *Evolution* (The Chariot) pushes you to be ambitious and hungry for progress today. Harness your willpower as you blaze through the competition and toward your highest self. Even if fear or imposter syndrome creep in, just keep moving, just keep working. Fortune favors the bold today, so dazzle the rest of us with your audacious bravery.

JUST FOR TODAY

TODAY'S MANTRA
I won't let my dreams go down without a fight.

TODAY'S JOURNAL PROMPT
How do I normally react to opposition or threat? How can I learn to persevere?

TODAY'S RITUAL
Exert some high energy for seven minutes straight without stopping. Go for a run, a brisk walk, or something physically strenuous that you are capable of handling for this length of time.

BORN ON THIS DAY

EDDIE MURPHY, American actor and comedian

EARL LLOYD, first Black American basketball player in the NBA

"What you do makes a difference, and you have to decide what kind of difference you want to make."—JANE GOODALL, English primatologist and anthropologist

The Journey of Those Born on
APRIL 3

You were born of fierce curiosity and a restlessness that can make it hard to remain loyal to just one thing. You will have to set your sights on a life of purpose, as your journey is one of intention, grit, and self-progress.

Early on in your journey, you will meet your stately guide, *Commitment* (The Number Seven). *Commitment* knows of your penchant for unpredictability but pushes you toward a path of thoughtful action instead. You will meet *Commitment* in necessary sacrifice, when you realize the limits of your time and energy and make an intentional choice to focus solely on the things that matter. If you can remain faithful to the callings of the heart, you'll reap the fruits of loyalty.

But if you take this thoughtful path, you will have to fight for what you care about most. *Perseverance* (Seven of Wands) knows that nothing real can be threatened, empowering you to champion the things that you love in the face of opposition. You will meet *Perseverance* in moments of conviction, when there is no one and nothing that can pull you down from the height of authentic intention.

By answering these calls to action, *Evolution* (The Chariot) will propel you forward. *Evolution* amplifies your hard work and dedication with radical progress, pushing you through unimaginable levels of success and satisfaction. You will meet *Evolution* in upward momentum, when your determination aligns with your faith and you find yourself breaking through the next highest ceiling. If you can work hard, very hard, *Evolution* ensures your efforts will pay off.

ARIES
RULERS: MARS, THE SUN

PURPOSE
To focus on and fight for the inspired callings of the heart.

RELATIONSHIPS

You are larger than life and generous to a fault, and your relationships should be a place of divine equality. By seeking out partners who give as much as they take and who support you in your ambitions, you will discover that true love is a mutual commitment.

The Journey of
APRIL 4

Welcome to April 4, an honest journey toward internal strength.

Aries season encourages action over reflection, but *Power* (The Number Eight) invites you inward to accept the best and the seemingly worst of yourself today. Get vulnerable with yourself or a trusted person as you express the feelings that you would normally bury due to their messy nature. There's no need to be perfect as you reveal your humanity.

And from there, make some necessary changes. *Momentum* (Eight of Wands) invites you to act upon any emotional revelations you may have today. Whether it be shedding any superficial layers of yourself or confronting some interpersonal issues, now is the time to be as honest in your actions as you are in your thoughts.

And know that you can handle your truth. *Resilience* (Strength) reminds you of how much you have endured and the spiritual strength that carried you through. If the day feels overwhelming at any point, tap into the emotional fortitude that lives within as you strengthen the muscles required to live a life of radical honesty.

JUST FOR TODAY

TODAY'S MANTRA
I will get to know the depth of who I am.

TODAY'S JOURNAL PROMPT
When was the last time I had to rely on my emotional resilience?

TODAY'S RITUAL
Write down eight truths about yourself and be sure to include the ones that are hard to swallow. Fold the piece of paper and place it somewhere healing (with a piece of lavender for good measure!) for the day and pray for acceptance. Return to it at night and reread the truths, seeing which ones feel easier to digest.

BORN ON THIS DAY

DOROTHEA DIX, American pioneering nurse and social activist who created the first American mental hospital

ROBERT DOWNEY JR., American actor

"You may shoot me with your words, you may cut me with your eyes, you may kill me with your hatefulness, but still, like air, I'll rise!"—MAYA ANGELOU, American poet and author

The Journey of Those Born on
APRIL 4

You were born of fierce discipline and a need for perfection that can block you from experiencing your full magic. You will have to uncover and discover who you truly are, as your journey is one of honesty, alignment, and internal strength.

Early on in your journey, you will meet your probing guide, *Power* (The Number Eight). *Power* calls you away from a life of mundane work and toward a path of deep introspection and intimacy. You will meet *Power* in the complex layers of your emotions, when you peel back one truth only to discover the richness of humanity that lies underneath. If you can choose honesty over shame, you'll connect meaningfully with others.

But if you take this path, *Momentum* (Eight of Wands) will demand that you act upon these revelations. The more you know, the better you can do, so hurl yourself fearlessly toward a life of astounding truth. You will meet *Momentum* in moments of irrefutable clarity, when you know exactly what the universe wants you to do next and the only thing left is to act.

By answering these deep calls, you will discover your capacity for *Resilience* (Strength). *Resilience* introduces you to the impenetrable spiritual strength that lives inside of you that you have unconsciously relied on in the most devastating of times. By becoming aware of these divine emotional muscles within, *Resilience* shows you that you no longer have to fear the worst-case scenarios in life, but instead, you can trust that your limitless power can handle anything.

YOUR GUIDES

Astrology: Your Energy
Aries (Mars, The Sun)

Numerology: Your Path
Power (The Number Eight)

Minor Arcana: Your Lesson
Momentum (The Eight of Wands)

Major Arcana: Your Highest Calling
Resilience (Strength)

ARIES
RULERS: MARS, THE SUN

PURPOSE
To fear nothing of truth that lies within.

RELATIONSHIPS

You are serious and at times emotionally stoic, yet your relationships should be a place of deep intimacy. By seeking out partners who unconditionally accept you for your worst while inspiring you to be your best, you will discover that true love can only come from radical honesty.

The Journey of
APRIL 5

Welcome to April 5, a divine adventure that requires soul-searching.

Forget about what you know to be true as *Experience* (The Number Nine) invites you on a quest of the unknown. Begin studying something new, explore a different part of town, or pick the brain of someone with a different life experience than you. If it makes you a bit uncomfortable due to your sheer lack of familiarity, know that you are on the right track.

And see the adventure through to completion. Despite the impulsivity of Aries season, *Persistence* (Nine of Wands) asks you to preserve your energy throughout the day so you don't lose enthusiasm for your goals. As you climb today's mountain of wisdom, accept every small opportunity to rest and reset before you continue trudging onward.

If you feel lost at any point, *Instinct* (The Hermit) calls you inward to a place of intuitive intelligence. Where is your gut telling you to go next? Rather than seeking outside counsel or consulting the internet, listen deeply to the voice that beckons you toward a higher purpose. If you can work to trust yourself, you'll be open to the gift of introspection.

○

JUST FOR TODAY

TODAY'S MANTRA
I will seek higher knowledge while listening deeply to my intuition.

TODAY'S JOURNAL PROMPT
What are small but effective ways I can preserve my energy throughout today?

TODAY'S RITUAL
Let your instinct pick a spot to explore on a map, whether it be a physical globe or a map on your computer. Close your eyes and intuitively point to a place. After you've chosen, spend nine minutes researching a bit about this foreign land.

○

BORN ON THIS DAY

PHARRELL WILLIAMS, American musician and music producer

BAHAREH HEDAYAT, Iranian student activist and campaigner for women's rights

"I have learned that success is to be measured not so much by the position that one has reached in life as by the obstacles which he has had to overcome while trying to succeed."—BOOKER T. WASHINGTON, American education pioneer and first Black American on a US postage stamp

The Journey of Those Born on
APRIL 5

You were born of fierce confidence and a pridefulness that can be mistaken for arrogance. You will have to find growth in humility, as your journey is one of seeking, endurance, and radical self-trust.

Early on in your journey, you will meet your wise guide, *Experience* (The Number Nine). Despite your innate intelligence, *Experience* calls you away from closed-mindedness and toward a quest of wild searching. You will meet *Experience* in the complete unknown, when you break out of your comfort zone and discover the wisdom that lies in foreign experiences.

But if you choose this winding path, you must preserve your energy for the long haul. *Persistence* (Nine of Wands) knows how unbridled passion can lead to burnout, so take small but crucial pauses to restore your energy along your journey. You will meet *Persistence* in the final push, when you have one crucial hurdle to get over before completing your next milestone.

YOUR GUIDES

Astrology: Your Energy
Aries (Mars, The Sun)

Numerology: Your Path
Experience (The Number Nine)

Minor Arcana: Your Lesson
Persistence (The Nine of Wands)

Major Arcana: Your Highest Calling
Instinct (The Hermit)

By answering these daring calls to explore, you will have to rely on *Instinct* (The Hermit). You will meet *Instinct* in the wilderness of the unfamiliar, when you are forced to tap into the divine intelligence that lives within. Rather than using logic or precedent, *Instinct* empowers you to feel rather than think your way through the world. If you can use your gut to light your way through even the darkest of moments, you'll discover the wisdom of intuition.

ARIES
RULERS: MARS, THE SUN

PURPOSE
To travel fearlessly through the unknown guided by nothing but intuition.

RELATIONSHIPS

You are captivating and endlessly fascinating, and your relationships should be a place of divine awakening. By seeking out partners who help you question the status quo and encourage you to grow toward self-trust, you will discover that true love is a faithful teacher.

The Journey of
APRIL 6

Welcome to April 6, a daring adventure that requires total faith.

To coincide with the independence of Aries season, *Autonomy* (The Number One) invites you to strike out on your own today. No need to consult friends or society as you set about your day's aspirations—you only need to rely on your intuition. What goal does your gut tell you to pursue?

The good news is, *Potential* (Ace of Wands) encourages you to take risks. Forget about being an expert and having a set plan. Instead, hurl yourself toward a high-reaching ambition, and don't be afraid to look foolish in the process. You have the gift of beginner's luck on your side today, so remember that you have nothing to lose.

But don't get too fixated on any one outcome. *Impermanence* (Wheel of Fortune) asks you to ride the roller coaster of today with total faith in the universe's greater vision for you. If you are feeling down on your luck at any point, stay open to the idea that this is simply your perception. Perhaps the worst-case scenario of today is an absolute miracle in disguise, only to be revealed tomorrow.

JUST FOR TODAY

TODAY'S MANTRA
I will take a leap of faith and leave the outcome up to the universe.

TODAY'S JOURNAL PROMPT
What would I pursue today if I wasn't afraid of looking dumb?

TODAY'S RITUAL
Do a small act intentionally wrong, like cracking an egg too quickly and getting shells everywhere or wearing your shirt inside-out. Lean in to the feeling of imperfection, and try to laugh in the process.

BORN ON THIS DAY

ROSE SCHNEIDERMAN, Polish-born American socialist, feminist, and labor union leader

PAUL RUDD, American actor

"Knowing 'why' (an idea) is more important than learning 'what' (the fact)."—JAMES WATSON, American molecular biologist, geneticist, and zoologist

The Journey of Those Born on
APRIL 6

You were born of fierce generosity and a selflessness that can distract you from true personal fulfillment. You will have to take a leap of faith on yourself, as your journey is one of self-reliance, confidence, and karmic fate.

Early on in your journey, you will meet your formidable guide, *Autonomy* (The Number One). *Autonomy* calls you away from a life of selfless devotion and toward a path of independence. You will meet *Autonomy* as you carve out an entirely unique path for yourself, never minding the opinions or recommendations of others. If you can progress to the beat of your intuition, *Autonomy* offers you a life of self-made satisfaction.

And if you brave this noble path, you will meet your co-conspirator *Potential* (Ace of Wands). Potential asks you to take a chance on your best ideas, inspiring you to put yourself out there for new and far-reaching opportunities. You will meet *Potential* in the thrill of being a complete beginner, when all you have to rely on is your enthusiasm for progress.

By answering these brave calls, you will have to throw expectations out the window. *Impermanence* (Wheel of Fortune) invites you to trust the cyclical nature of the human experience rather than clinging to imagined certainty. You will meet *Impermanence* in the highs as well as the lows in life, when you have no choice but to surrender to the divine powers at be. If you can believe in fate instead of a false sense of control, you'll embrace your highest potential.

───────────────○───────────────

ARIES
RULERS: MARS, THE SUN

PURPOSE
To take the risk so you don't lose the chance.

RELATIONSHIPS

You are a tender-hearted leader, yet your relationships should be a place of radical independence. By seeking out partners who champion your individuality while maintaining their own set of aspirations, you will discover that true love never limits personal possibility.

The Journey of
APRIL 7

Welcome to April 7, a patient journey toward the truth.

To counteract the impulsivity of Aries season, *Balance* (The Number Two) asks you to take the middle road today. Rather than getting lost in impulsive ambition, aim for sustainable goals and rely on partnership to help you get there. Remember that Rome wasn't built in a day, and it definitely wasn't built without the help of others.

So if you don't accomplish anything concrete, know that today was still a success. *Preparation* (Two of Wands) calls for deliberate planning over forcefulness, so slow down and get clear on what it will take to meet your next goal. Keep longevity at the forefront of your mind, neither overpromising nor overcommitting to tasks that will only burn you out in the long run.

And while you plan, consider the greater ramifications of your ambitions. *Truth* (Justice) reminds you of the profound cause and effect of your actions, so consider whether your goals will lead to the advancement or disillusionment of the world around you. If you can think before you speak and prepare before you act, you can align your larger plans with your moral values.

JUST FOR TODAY

TODAY'S MANTRA
Patient planning yields more meaningful results.

TODAY'S JOURNAL PROMPT
What am I rushing through in my life right now, and what steps can I take to slow down?

TODAY'S RITUAL
Sit down—on the grass, on the floor of your apartment, or anywhere that feels rooted to you—and get grounded. Breathe in as you repeat the word "no" and breathe out as you repeat the word "rush." Do this as many times as it takes to feel that there truly is no rush.

BORN ON THIS DAY

RAVI SHANKAR, Bengali Brahmin sitar master and Indian classical music composer

FRANCIS FORD COPPOLA, American director

"If you copy, it means you're working without any real feeling. No two people on earth are alike, and it's got to be that way in music or it isn't music."—BILLIE HOLIDAY, American jazz singer

The Journey of Those Born on
APRIL 7

Y ou were born of irrefutable power and an ambition that can have you wasting time on fruit-less efforts. You will have to learn to harmonize rather than fight through life, as your jour-ney is one of peace, planning, and justice.

Early on in your journey, you will meet your calm guide, *Balance* (The Number Two). *Balance* calls you away from unsustainable passion and toward a path of patience and partnership. You will meet *Balance* in moments of ease when you uncomplicate your goals through delegation and healthy moderation. If you can choose tranquility over power, you'll discover success doesn't have to be so hard.

And if you choose this stable path, you will meet your great teacher, *Preparation* (Two of Wands). You're deeply ambitious, but the most important plans in life must be well thought out. You will meet *Preparation* in the humble groundwork when you find yourself laying the foundation of respect for your wildest of dreams.

By answering these calls for reason, you will step into the wisdom of *Truth* (Justice). Your actions have consequences, and *Truth* asks you to deeply consider how your ambitions feed into the betterment or destruction of the world around you. You will meet *Truth* in moments of divine alignment, when your moral values, rather than your ego, are propelling your vision forward. If you can aim fearlessly at the heart of justice, *Truth* of-fers you eternal peace of mind.

> ## YOUR GUIDES
>
> *Astrology: Your Energy*
> Aries (Mars, The Sun)
>
> *Numerology: Your Path*
> Balance (The Number Two)
>
> *Minor Arcana: Your Lesson*
> Preparation (The Two of Wands)
>
> *Major Arcana: Your Highest Calling*
> Truth (Justice)

ARIES
RULERS: MARS, THE SUN

PURPOSE
To take the middle road
toward divine purpose.

RELATIONSHIPS

You are fearlessly ambitious and at times dramatic, yet your relationships should be a place of peace and tranquility. By seeking out partners who help you slow down and smell the roses, you will discover that true love is the deep rest you always needed.

The Journey of
APRIL 8

Welcome to April 8, an adventurous journey toward spiritual surrender.

Let go of your plans. Completely. It may feel strange during the ambitiousness of Aries season, but *Flexibility* (The Number Three) asks you to free yourself from any preconceived notions of how your day should go so you can be open to new ideas and relationships. Know that these possibilities are endless.

So say "yes" to anything that lies outside your comfort zone. *Expansion* (Three of Wands) encourages you to pursue something foreign today, whether it be an intimidating field of study or an uncharacteristic friendship. As long as you open your mind and grow expertise, you'll benefit from the gift of growth.

But growth isn't always comfortable. Sacrifice your rigid ways of being today as *Surrender* (The Hanged Man) invites you to see life through an entirely new perspective. Embrace the experiences and relationships that force you to rethink everything you once thought to be true, and watch as they rocket you into the next dimension of existence. If you can remain willing to be wrong as you step out on the ledge of uncertainty, you'll have the spiritual breakthrough you needed most.

───────────────○───────────────

JUST FOR TODAY

TODAY'S MANTRA
To yield all expectations and plans in the pursuit of a spiritual experience.

TODAY'S JOURNAL PROMPT
What beliefs or ambitions am I afraid to surrender, and why?

TODAY'S RITUAL
Take a chance on the road less traveled, whether it be a small change in your walk to work or taking the long drive home. See how exciting it can be to try something different.

───────────────○───────────────

BORN ON THIS DAY

BETTY FORD, American feminist, thirty-eighth first lady of the United States, and founder of the Betty Ford Center clinic

HELEN BEATRICE JOSEPH, South African anti-apartheid activist

"The future belongs to you, but it can only belong to you if you participate and take charge."
—KOFI ANNAN, Ghanaian diplomat and seventh secretary-general of the United Nations

The Journey of Those Born on
APRIL 8

Y ou were born of fearless strength and a powerful sense of self that makes it difficult to try new things. You will have to learn to adapt to uncertainty, as your journey is one of open-mindedness, exploration, and perspective-building.

Early on in your journey, you will meet your enthusiastic guide, *Flexibility* (The Number Three). *Flexibility* calls you away from a life of morbid self-reflection and toward a path of curiosity. Rather than worrying about having any of the answers, ask the right questions as you open your mind to the diverse perspectives of others. If you can reach for understanding over pride, you'll discover a wealth of knowledge.

And if you choose this winding path, *Expansion* (Three of Wands) will invite you to grow into uncharted territory. You're a talented leader, but *Expansion* asks you to be a student so that you can continue to grow in your humility and effectiveness. You will meet *Expansion* in the foreign subjects, people, or lands that offer you the ah-ha moment you needed to pursue your next greatest idea.

By answering these calls for open-mindedness, you will have to let go of the outcome completely. *Surrender* (The Hanged Man) requires you to release control and embrace unexpected pauses and disruptions to your ambitious plans. You will meet *Surrender* when your hands are metaphorically tied behind your back, and you have no choice but to reflect and reevaluate your goals. If you can remain forever willing to go back to the drawing board, you might just get the breakthrough you never knew you needed.

―――――――――――――――――○――――――――――――――――

ARIES
RULERS: MARS, THE SUN

PURPOSE
*To be adventurous enough to
let go of expectation.*

RELATIONSHIPS

You are seriously serious about most things in life, yet your relationships should be a place of expansion and flexibility. By seeking out partners who are constantly working to grow and change and inspire you to do the same, you will discover that true love never stops evolving.

The Journey of
APRIL 9

W elcome to April 9, a deliberate journey toward personal metamorphosis.
Despite the unpredictable nature of Aries season, *Discipline* (The Number Four) encourages you to devote yourself to the tasks you have on deck today. Big or small, gratifying or mundane, put your most humble foot forward as you work your way through the things you would normally put off until tomorrow.

But be sure to leave some room for fun. *Celebration* (Four of Wands) wants you to reward yourself for a job well done today, so look for any opportunity to let loose on life's metaphorical dance floor. What does carefree fun look like to you? Whether it be late-night karaoke or a wild bake-off in the kitchen, make time for joy today.

Besides, *Transformation* (Death) knows that you must always balance seriousness with unapologetic levity. Try to let go of some version of yourself today, whether it be a long-term ambition that never came to pass or an identity that is no longer serving you, and leave room for the grief as well as the optimism in this transition. If you feel scared or uncertain at any point today, remember that stars shine the brightest in the dark.

JUST
FOR
TODAY

TODAY'S MANTRA
I will balance sincerity with levity as I move closer to the truth of who I am.

TODAY'S JOURNAL PROMPT
What part of me am I ready to outgrow to grow deeper into authenticity?

TODAY'S RITUAL
Celebrate who you once were through meditation. Take a comfortable seated position and close your eyes. Visualize the version of yourself that you are ready to let go of, and adorn that person with celebratory flowers, awards, or anything you see fit. Thank them for what they have done for you as you say your goodbyes.

BORN ON THIS DAY

EMILY HOBHOUSE, English welfare campaigner, anti-war activist, and pacifist

CYNTHIA NIXON, American actor and activist

"Live your life to its fullest potential and don't really care too much about what other people think of you."—LIL NAS X, American singer-songwriter and rapper

The Journey of Those Born on
APRIL 9

You were born of intuitive knowledge and a wanderlust that can make you unreliable at times. You will have to grow into a deeper sense of responsibility, as your journey is one of development, triumph, and personal metamorphosis.

Early on in your journey, you will meet your deliberate guide, *Discipline* (The Number Four). *Discipline* calls you away from a life of endless searching and toward a focused path of hard work. You will meet *Discipline* in the tirelessly long hours when you steadily build the muscles required to master your craft. If you can choose integrity over pretension, you'll grow in your self-respect.

But if you choose this demanding path, you better have some fun along the way. *Celebration* (Four of Wands) wants you to smile and laugh, so enjoy the present moment as the people you love honor everything you have accomplished. You will meet *Celebration* in the glitz and confetti when you find yourself basking in the light of hard-earned merriment.

By answering these divine calls to action, you will learn to the importance of *Transformation* (Death). The hardest yet most rewarding work in life is to live in authenticity, and *Transformation* asks you to shed the layers of superficiality that once protected you from harm. You will meet *Transformation* in moments of transition when you are ready to let go of who you once were but are not quite sure who you are becoming. If you can find joy in each rebirth, *Transformation* offers you the keys to infinite growth.

ARIES
RULERS: MARS, THE SUN

PURPOSE
To shed the superficial layers that hide the truth that is worth celebrating.

RELATIONSHIPS

You are driven and independent to a fault, yet your relationships should be a place of grounding and respect. By seeking out partners whose actions match their words and make you feel safe, you will discover that true love is an act of mutual integrity.

The Journey of
APRIL 10

Welcome to April 10, a heroic journey toward spiritual moderation.

Courage (The Number Five) invites you to take center stage of your life today. Although it's always easier to hide in the confines of the mind, express yourself wildly and unapologetically to the world around you. Take to social media or stand on your favorite street corner and tell us what you believe in most.

And don't be afraid of a little feedback. To counterbalance the fiery reign of Aries season, *Conflict* (Five of Wands) asks you to remain open to the opinions of others as you grow in your understanding and effectiveness. Reach for humility over pride as you look for the intention and purpose behind what others say. Perhaps even the worst of trolls is a teacher in a disguise.

But don't get caught up in the drama of it all. *Serenity* (Temperance) inspires emotional restraint today, reminding you that internal peace is always accessible if you try. If you get overwhelmed or flustered at any point, take a comfortable seated position and breathe slowly and intentionally. Everything is okay in the present moment, as long as you come back to your center.

───────────────○───────────────

JUST FOR TODAY

TODAY'S MANTRA
I can balance external courage with internal peace today.

TODAY'S RITUAL
Make the most of lavender's calming properties. Carry a fresh stem or oil with you throughout the day. If you are feeling overwhelmed at any point, stop and deeply inhale the healing aroma.

TODAY'S JOURNAL PROMPT
What actions help me calm down and come back to my center?

───────────────○───────────────

BORN ON THIS DAY

JOSEPH PULITZER, American politician and newspaper publisher

SAMUEL HAHNEMANN, German physician best known as the founder of homeopathy

"It's only when we're relaxed that the thing way down deep in all of us—call it the subconscious mind, the spirit, what you will—has a chance to well up and tell us how we shall go."—FRANCES PERKINS, American labor rights advocate, US secretary of labor, and first woman and first LGBTQ+ person to serve in the US Cabinet

The Journey of Those Born on
APRIL 10

You were born of fierce independence and an extreme nature that can make it difficult to find internal peace. You will have to find the courage to live in the gray, as your journey is one of passion, surrender, and spiritual growth.

Early on in your journey, you will meet your audacious guide, *Courage* (The Number Five). Rather than getting lost in isolation, explore a path of radical self-expression. You will meet *Courage* in moments of visibility, when you throw shame out the window and step bravely into the limelight of your authentic spirit. If you can choose to be real rather than perfect, you'll be true to yourself.

But if you choose this path of raw vulnerability, never take the words of others too personally because *Conflict* (Five of Wands) requires you to drop your armor and surrender to the wisdom that lives within each critique. Although no one's opinion is all-powerful or factual, look for the ounce of truth that you can use to your advantage, turning negativity into powerful opportunities for growth.

By answering these calls for vulnerability, you will come to understand the vital need for *Serenity* (Temperance). Nothing extreme leads to emotional contentment, so consider the middle road when it comes to your thoughts and especially your actions. You will meet *Serenity* in moments of self-restraint, when you choose to tap into your intuition rather than giving in to the heat of passion. If you can choose peace over drama, *Serenity* offers you a life of eternal tranquility.

ARIES
RULERS: MARS, JUPITER

PURPOSE
To access the courage to reach for peace in any hardship.

RELATIONSHIPS

You are independent and ever-evolving, yet your relationships should be a place of peaceful honesty. By seeking out partners who can handle the truth in a calm and collected manner, you will discover that true love doesn't have to require any drama.

The Journey of
APRIL 11

Welcome to April 11, a loving journey toward internal healing.

To harness the limitless enthusiasm of Aries season, *Devotion* (The Number Six) encourages you to show your heart through action. Without missing a beat, show up for the people and projects that your soul calls you toward. Initiate a project that benefits others, lend a helping hand to someone in need, or send sincere words of encouragement to someone who is down on their luck.

And know that it is okay to feel good about yourself! *Confidence* (Six of Wands) invites you to step into the sunlight of your benevolent spirit, soaking in the kind feedback you are receiving from others or giving yourself a gentle pat on the back for a job well done. Know that you deserve generosity in return.

If this joy comes with a surprising amount of psychological discomfort, find compassion for the self-destructive coping mechanisms that may emerge today. *Shadow* (The Devil) asks you to look through an empathetic lens at these behaviors and try to reflect on when and why you learned that it was unsafe to feel good being yourself. Don't turn your back on this internal work because it offers you the gift of healing.

JUST FOR TODAY

TODAY'S MANTRA

I will bring compassion to everyone and everything I pursue today, especially myself.

TODAY'S JOURNAL PROMPT

What are some healthy coping mechanisms I can use to stay present with emotional discomfort today?

TODAY'S RITUAL

Spend fifteen minutes in privacy, and let your inner shadow talk, the part of you that acts out compulsively whenever life becomes too much for you to handle. Don't overthink what this part of you wants to say, and reach for compassion as you listen to this part of yourself.

BORN ON THIS DAY

PERCY LAVON JULIAN, American chemist

MARY WHITE OVINGTON, American suffragist, journalist, and cofounder of the NAACP

"For anyone to achieve something, he will have to show a little courage. You're only on this earth once. You must give it all you've got."—ETHEL KENNEDY, American human rights advocate

The Journey of Those Born on
APRIL 11

You were born of fierce diplomacy and an intense sense of right and wrong that can lead you to extremes. You will have to soften to your heart, as your journey is of one of sincerity, earned praise, and emotional mending.

Early on in your journey, you will meet your earnest guide, *Devotion* (The Number Six). *Devotion* calls you away from a life of black-and-white thinking and toward a path of loving-kindness. You will meet *Devotion* in the callings of the heart, when you selflessly give to the people and projects that make the world a sweeter place. If you can reach for purpose over prestige, you'll discover a soulful life of meaning.

And if you choose this noble path, make way for *Confidence* (Six of Wands). Hard-earned success deserves endless praise, so don't shy away from the adoration and applause that is yours to enjoy. Appreciate all the radical progress you have made and remember you how good it feels to be seen.

By answering these calls for emotional contentment, you will have to heal any deep-seated fear with *Shadow* (The Devil). You will meet *Shadow* in the compulsive behaviors that take you out of the present moment, when you are forced to consider why it is so hard to be in the here and now. *Shadow* invites you to do the unseen healing work, looking inward to find the psychological wounds that disguise themselves as coping mechanisms. If you can find compassion for the behaviors that have helped you survive great pains in the past, you'll be able to move toward a new place of spiritual freedom.

> ### YOUR GUIDES
>
> *Astrology: Your Energy*
> Aries (Mars, Jupiter)
>
> *Numerology: Your Path*
> Devotion (The Number Six)
>
> *Minor Arcana: Your Lesson*
> Confidence (The Six of Wands)
>
> *Major Arcana: Your Highest Calling*
> Shadow (The Devil)

ARIES
RULERS: MARS, JUPITER

PURPOSE
To do the healing work required to be emotionally present to life's great joys.

RELATIONSHIPS

You are intuitive in all matters of partnership, and your relationships should be a place of unconditional love and deep healing. By seeking out partners who admire you for your light as much as your shadow, you will discover how *acceptance* is just another word for "true love."

The Journey of
APRIL 12

Welcome to April 12, an intentional journey with no certain outcome.

Aim your focus on the things that matter most to you today. Despite the unpredictable energy of Aries season, *Commitment* (The Number Seven) urges you away from distractions and toward a path of thoughtful action. Give your all to the projects and people you are responsible for by showing up with no excuses and a positive attitude.

And if you are met with any opposition, don't back down without a fight. In the face of any covert naysayers or downright competitors, *Perseverance* (Seven of Wands) empowers you to draw upon your sharp weapon of conviction. Believe in the goals and ambitions you have set out to accomplish today, and don't let anything or anyone get in your way.

But don't get too carried away with expectations. Today is filled with unexpected change, as *Upheaval* (The Tower) may put into motion the scary changes you may not be ready to make yourself. If an unanticipated circumstance requires you to adjust, look for the revelation that lies within the perceived turmoil. Perhaps what looks like a mistake is really the miracle of awakening in chaotic disguise.

JUST FOR TODAY

TODAY'S MANTRA

I will commit to my goals while trusting in the unexpected nature of life.

TODAY'S JOURNAL PROMPT

When was the last time unexpected change ended up being a surprising miracle to me?

TODAY'S RITUAL

Try to balance on one foot for up to seven minutes—it's harder than you might think! Notice how strenuous it is to withstand such a precarious position, and as you try to balance, say the mantra, "Tower, if I fall, help me fall with grace."

BORN ON THIS DAY

YAYORI MATSUI, Japanese journalist and women's rights activist

SAOIRSE RONAN, American Irish actor

"I have found that the only thing that does bring you happiness is doing something good for somebody who is incapable of doing it for themselves."—DAVID LETTERMAN, American comedian and talk show host

The Journey of Those Born on
APRIL 12

You were born of fearless curiosity and a flexibility that can err on the side of unreliability. You will have to get serious about self-trust, as your journey is one of intention, challenge, and unexpected change.

Early on in your journey, you will meet your deliberate guide, *Commitment* (The Number Seven). Despite your restless nature, *Commitment* calls you away from a life of unpredictability and toward a path of sincere action. You will meet *Commitment* when you prioritize the things that matter over frivolous fun. By doing what you say and meaning what you do, you'll live in integrity.

But if you walk this intentional path, you will have to protect what is rightfully yours. *Perseverance* (Seven of Wands) emboldens you to fight your way through the toughest of competition using self-belief as your only weapon. You will meet *Perseverance* in the face of the opposition who unexpectedly threatens your stance, forcing you to dig your heels in deeper as you find a stronger sense of conviction.

YOUR GUIDES

Astrology: Your Energy
Aries (Mars, Jupiter)

Numerology: Your Path
Commitment (The Number Seven)

Minor Arcana: Your Lesson
Perseverance (The Seven of Wands)

Major Arcana: Your Highest Calling
Upheaval (The Tower)

By answering these brave calls, you will meet the divine in the unexpected. While you aim your focus at the heart of your purpose, *Upheaval* (The Tower) thrusts you out of the old and into new and uncharted revelations. You will meet *Upheaval* in times of sudden change, when the tectonic plates shift beneath you and you are forced to have total faith in the universe's chaotic plans. If you can remember that the change you didn't ask for is the very change you need most, you'll awaken to the potential of your future.

ARIES
RULERS: MARS, JUPITER

PURPOSE
To fight for what you believe in while surrendering to the larger forces of fate at play.

RELATIONSHIPS

You are charismatic and larger than life, and your relationships should be a place of complete respect and commitment. By seeking out partners who are willing to work together through even the most difficult of times, you will discover that true love is made of a strong foundation of trust.

The Journey of
APRIL 13

Welcome to April 13, a revealing journey of divine optimism.

Get vulnerable with yourself and others today. *Power* (The Number Eight) detests insincerity and superficial masks and encourages you to peel back the layers that block your authentic spirit. There may be some murky subconscious fears to work through as you do, so talk to a trusted friend or therapist, or write in your journal, as you pursue a day of complete self-honesty.

To complement the forward-moving energy of Aries season, *Momentum* (Eight of Wands) encourages you to act upon this awareness and go after the goals that feel deeply authentic to you. What would you work toward today if you were acting in alignment with your truth? Even if it doesn't fit the status quo, attack these ambitions with wild abandon.

And if you feel fearful or insecure at any point, rely upon *Hope* (The Star). Reach down into the depths of your soul and look for the impenetrable optimism that lives within you, using divine faith to decipher the next best action for your day. It is through internal enthusiasm, rather than unnecessary doubt, that you can renew your excitement for the future.

JUST FOR TODAY

TODAY'S MANTRA
I will heal the shame that buries my hope for the future.

TODAY'S JOURNAL PROMPT
What am I secretly optimistic I could accomplish today?

TODAY'S RITUAL
Wish upon a star—literally. Step outside at night, and even if you can't see them, tell the stars exactly what you hope, and what you secretly believe, could come true for you.

BORN ON THIS DAY

VIDA GOLDSTEIN, Australian suffragist and social reformer

AL GREEN, American singer-songwriter and record producer

"Hope is not optimism, which expects things to turn out well, but something rooted in the conviction that there is good worth working for."—SEAMUS HEANEY, Irish poet and playwright

The Journey of Those Born on
APRIL 13

Y ou were born of fierce discipline and a radical emotional awareness that can make it hard to focus on the positive. You will have to go inward to a place of hopeful truth, as your journey is one of healing, alignment, and internal optimism.

Early on in your journey, you will meet your probing guide, *Power* (The Number Eight). *Power* calls you away from a life of relentless work and toward a path of compassionate self-honesty. To enhance your introspective nature, *Power* invites you to make peace with who you are rather than denying your enigmatic nature. You will meet *Power* in moments of self-acceptance, when you begin to integrate the uncomfortable truths you once thought would get the best of you.

YOUR GUIDES

Astrology: Your Energy
Aries (Mars, Jupiter)

Numerology: Your Path
Power (The Number Eight)

Minor Arcana: Your Lesson
Momentum (The Eight of Wands)

Major Arcana: Your Highest Calling
Hope (The Star)

But if you accept this awakening path, *Momentum* (Eight of Wands) requires you to act upon these revelations. You will meet *Momentum* when the metaphysical meets the physical world and you find your daily life evolving at the same rate as your internal healing. If you can push forward to the places that scare you most, you'll discover the gift of authentic movement.

By answering these introspective calls, you will have no choice but to reach for *Hope* (The Star). *Hope* reveals the sparkling light of optimism that lives within you, helping you realize your divine calling as you courageously retire old and outdated ways of being. If you can worship at the altar of possibility rather than fear, *Hope* invites you to take a divine chance on yourself.

ARIES
RULERS: MARS, JUPITER

PURPOSE
To peel back the layers of fear and shame that block divine hope.

RELATIONSHIPS

You are ambitious and hardworking, and your relationships should be a place of radical authenticity and encouragement. By seeking out partners who cheer you on as you reveal the many layers that make you uniquely you, you will discover that true love never requires you to dim your shine.

The Journey of
APRIL 14

Welcome to April 14, an expansive journey that can take you to new heights of internal healing.

Pursue the unknown with wild abandon today. *Experience* (The Number Nine) encourages you to pursue uncharted territory, so now is the time to sign up for a course or pursue that ambition that is just far enough outside your comfort zone to make you deeply uncomfortable. To make the most of the ambition of Aries season, move toward the goals that scare you.

But be sure to preserve your energy throughout the day. *Persistence* (Nine of Wands) requires you to see things through, reminding you that a car simply cannot make it to a destination on an empty tank of gas. So fill your metaphorical tank with the self-care of your choosing—hopefully, one that includes some time to rest.

And as you step into the unknown, don't be surprised if some old fear comes up. *Memory* (The Moon) encourages you to reflect on the unaddressed trauma from your past that projects itself onto your daily life. Bring great compassion to these unhealed stories that live within you as you work to integrate them into your consciousness.

JUST FOR TODAY

TODAY'S MANTRA

I will pursue the unknowns of my future as well as my past.

TODAY'S RITUAL

Sit underneath the moon tonight and tell it a story from your history that has been hard for you to heal. Then repeat the prayer, "Moon magic, please help me be the intuitive healer that inspires safety within me."

TODAY'S JOURNAL PROMPT

What experiences from my past still haunt me to this day, and what steps can I take to integrate them?

BORN ON THIS DAY

LORETTA LYNN, American country singer-songwriter

JESSIE AITKEN, New Zealand community worker and political activist

"Indifferentism is the worst kind of disease that can affect people."—B. R. AMBEDKAR, Indian politician, jurist, and social reformer

The Journey of Those Born on
APRIL 14

You were born of fierce confidence and a worldly ambition that can distract you from internal growth. You will have to go to the places that scare you, as your journey is one of searching, self-care, and subconscious healing.

Early on in your journey, you will meet your sage guide, *Experience* (The Number Nine). Instead of trying to be an expert, pursue a path of understanding. You will meet *Experience* in the questions that you seek, when you find yourself in uncharted lands that push you out of your comfort zone and teach you everything you need to know. By choosing perspective-building over pride, *Experience* offers the road to enlightenment.

If you choose this daring path, *Persistence* (Nine of Wands) requires you to complete your ambitions to the finish line, despite any hurdles. You will meet *Persistence* in the final uphill battle when your enthusiasm is depleted and you must slow down to preserve your energy. Pause to rest whenever you can as you learn how to see things through.

By answering these calls to new heights of self-realizations, *Memory* (The Moon) invites you to heal your wounds on your way back down. You will meet *Memory* when you project your past onto the present, clouding your reality with the haze of unaddressed fear and trauma. If you can integrate these historical experiences into your conscious mind, *Memory* helps you separate hypervigilance from sacred intuition.

ARIES
RULERS: MARS, JUPITER

PURPOSE
To climb great personal milestones without leaving the past behind.

RELATIONSHIPS

You are expansive enough on your own, so your relationships should be a place of exploration and understanding. By seeking out partners who inspire you to explore not only the external world, but your internal world as well, you will discover that true love knows no bounds.

The Journey of
APRIL 15

Welcome to April 15, a fearless journey toward authenticity.

While Aries season always encourages independence, *Autonomy* (The Number One) asks you to take it up a notch. Use your intuition and skills to navigate today completely on your own, relying on nothing but the beat of your ambition. It's a wonderful time to begin a new project or goal, one that does not require you to be dependent on anyone or anything.

Besides, *Potential* (Ace of Wands) knows that anything is possible if you are willing to be a beginner. Don't be afraid to be bad at things today because it is the perfect time to throw paint against the wall and see what sticks. If you find yourself excited and inspired about something, hurl your entire focus toward it and forget about the outcome. Success looks like trying today.

And if you take a chance on yourself, *Vitality* (The Sun) invites you to shine as bright as you can. Something special happens when a person steps into their authentic nature, and today invites you to do precisely this. Who would you be if you weren't afraid of what people thought? Be big. Be bold. Be brave. Be unapologetically you!

JUST FOR TODAY

TODAY'S MANTRA
I will be vulnerable enough to try something new today.

TODAY'S JOURNAL PROMPT
If I am willing to make mistakes and be a beginner, what project or goal am I excited to begin today?

TODAY'S RITUAL
Shed some light on yourself. Go outside and bask underneath the sun or stand in front of warm light in your home as you chant, "Shine your light on my authentic spirit so I can shine it back on others."

BORN ON THIS DAY

LEONARDO DA VINCI, Italian painter, sculptor, scientist, and visionary

VIMALA THAKAR, Indian social activist and spiritual teacher

"Don't feel stupid if you don't like what everyone else pretends to love."—**EMMA WATSON**, English actor and activist

The Journey of Those Born on
APRIL 15

You were born of fierce empathy and a buried sense of shame that requires great healing. You will have to step into the light of your authentic spirit, as your journey is one of independence, potential, and exuberance.

Early on in your journey, you will meet your fiery guide, *Autonomy* (The Number One). *Autonomy* champions your ambitious nature while calling you away from the intoxicating drama of self-destruction. You will meet *Autonomy* as you walk a path that has never been traveled before. If you can trust your instinct and innate skills, you'll move toward a life that is custom-made for you.

But if you choose this independent path, *Potential* (Ace of Wands) requires you to be an endless beginner. Throw yourself into the goals that feel beyond your reach, faking it until you make it to the big leagues. You will meet *Potential* in the thrill of what could be when your hunger for radical growth far outweighs any imposter syndrome. If you can remain forever willing to try, you'll never fail.

By answering these passionate calls to action, you will bask in the light of *Vitality* (The Sun). It feels good to express who you are, no matter what the circumstance. You will meet *Vitality* in moments of authentic alignment, when the person you are exposing to the world is in perfect congruence with who you are behind closed doors. If you can accept all the qualities that make you uniquely you, *Vitality* shows you that these are the very things that make you shine.

ARIES
RULERS: MARS, JUPITER

PURPOSE
*To be fearlessly yourself and inspire
others to do the same.*

RELATIONSHIPS

You are deeply complex yet compassionate, and your relationships should be a place of total freedom and acceptance. By seeking out partners who are secure enough in themselves to let you shine in your authentic spirit, you will discover that true love never requires you to play it small.

The Journey of
APRIL 16

Welcome to April 16, a patient journey toward radical awareness.

Despite the passionate demands for autonomy of Aries season, *Balance* (The Number Two) invites you to find ease as you share your day with the people you trust. How can today go more smoothly if spent in partnership? Lean on these coconspirators as you steadily work toward a common goal.

But know that much of this work must be spent in *Preparation* (Two of Wands). Prioritize careful planning over hasty progress and try not to fit a square peg in a round hole just to call your projects complete. Rather than acting in the now, plan for the future by creating a detailed outline of what must happen between point A and point Z.

Besides, not much can get done until you get clear on your intentions. *Awakening* (Judgment) emboldens you to surrender to and integrate the toughest of truths so you can align your actions with the highest of good. Whether it be accepting the imperfections of a relationship or bringing awareness to an inconvenient societal reality, seek clarity over comfort. The truth is only as scary as it is denied, so reach for acceptance instead.

JUST FOR TODAY

TODAY'S MANTRA

I cannot rush. I can only surrender to the epiphanies that are available to me today.

TODAY'S JOURNAL PROMPT

What tough truths and realities have I been denying for quite some time now?

TODAY'S RITUAL

Ask for the awakening rather than avoiding it. Sit in front of a mirror with your hands on your knees and your palms face up. To your reflection, repeat the question, "If the truth is only as scary as it is denied, what would you have me accept?" Continue with your day and see what new awareness comes up.

BORN ON THIS DAY

SUCHENG CHAN, Chinese American author, historian, scholar, and professor

CHANCE THE RAPPER, American rapper and record producer

"You'll never find a rainbow if you're looking down."—CHARLIE CHAPLIN, English actor and comedian

The Journey of Those Born on
APRIL 16

Y ou were born of fierce conviction and a penchant for disruption that can distract you from
the truth. You will have to come to terms with even the most inconvenient aspects of reality, as your journey is one of harmony, planning, and awareness.

Early on in your journey, you will meet your calming guide, *Balance* (The Number Two). Despite your independent nature, *Balance* calls you away from a life of unreliability and toward a path of grounded peace and partnership. You will meet *Balance* in the ease that comes from interpersonal trust, when you share the burdens of your ambitions and find yourself accomplishing more than you could have ever done on your own.

But if you choose this shared path, *Preparation* (Two of Wands) requires you to think before you act. While inspiration and passion have their uses, temper your impatience to create a sustainable plan. You will meet *Preparation* in the outlines of your visions when you have laid a thoughtful foundation upon which you can achieve your deepest desires.

By answering these calls to take your time, you will begin to see things as they really are. *Awakening* (Judgment) invites you to level up your consciousness by recognizing and integrating the hard truths in life. The more you know, the better you can do, so work to accept the realities that are initially tough to swallow because they will inspire work that serves the highest good. If you can find divinity in even the scariest of revelations, you'll discover the gift of radical awareness.

YOUR GUIDES

Astrology: Your Energy
Aries (Mars, Jupiter)

Numerology: Your Path
Balance (The Number Two)

Minor Arcana: Your Lesson
Preparation (The Two of Wands)

Major Arcana: Your Highest Calling
Awakening (Judgment)

ARIES
RULERS: MARS, JUPITER

PURPOSE
To slowly but surely awaken to the call to actions of truth.

RELATIONSHIPS

You are ambitious and unrelenting, yet your relationships should be a place of deep calm. By seeking out partners who feel like a sigh of relief amidst a chaotic world, you will discover that true love is the place you go to take the day off.

The Journey of
APRIL 17

Welcome to April 17, a curious adventure that builds perspective.

There's no need to overplan or overthink today. *Flexibility* (The Number Three) asks you to keep an open mind as you say "yes" to the unexpected invitations that come your way. Whether it be working on a spontaneous team project or attending an unanticipated event, now is the time to forgo expectations.

And perhaps you'll learn something new along the way. To complement the bravery of Aries season, *Expansion* (Three of Wands) brings you the gift of beginner's luck today, encouraging you to step outside your comfort zone as you pursue a new skill or ambition. The more foreign the better, so forget about being an expert.

As you climb new heights of consciousness, be sure to pause and take in the view. *Perspective* (The World) inspires gratitude by helping you zoom out, so take note of the small and large miracles that encourage you along this winding path toward the unknown. Get out your journal or call a dear friend at the end of today and tell the wild tale that came from the invitation that spontaneity dropped on your doorstep this morning.

○

JUST FOR TODAY

TODAY'S MANTRA
I will hurl myself into the unknown and find my footing with gratitude.

TODAY'S RITUAL
Go for a climb, whether it be to the peak of a nearby mountain or the top of the Empire State Building. Soak in the view as you forget about the minutiae of your life down below.

TODAY'S JOURNAL PROMPT
What am I not very good at that I'd like to be brave enough to learn today?

○

BORN ON THIS DAY

SIRIMAVO BANDARANAIKE, Sri Lankan prime minister and first female head of state

MARGUERITE BOURGEOYS, French nun and founder of the Congregation of Notre Dame of Montreal

"I was never a natural. I got there in the end because I did believe that if you work hard enough, then you can achieve a lot."—VICTORIA BECKHAM, English singer

The Journey of Those Born on

APRIL 17

You were born of unbridled enthusiasm and an introversion that can keep you from experiencing the fruits of connection. You will have to remain forever open to the unknown of others, as your journey is one of curiosity, growth, and perspective-building.

Early on in your journey, you will meet your spontaneous guide, *Flexibility* (The Number Three). Despite your love for being alone, *Flexibility* calls you away from isolation and toward a social path of learning. You will meet *Flexibility* in the philosophies of others, when your hunger for new wisdom allows you to listen with an open heart and mind.

And if you embrace this meandering path, *Expansion* (Three of Wands) will ask you not just to learn but to experience. While you are a natural leader, dare to be a complete beginner, pursuing far-reaching ambitions with a willingness to make mistakes along the way. You will meet *Expansion* when you step out onto the ledge of a foreign goal, relying on nothing but your excitement for growth.

By answering these wild calls, you will eventually meet your great teacher, *Perspective* (The World). *Perspective* invites you to stop when you reach your next highest mountain and take in the view, soaking in gratitude for the people and experiences that brought you to this point. *Perspective* lives within the big picture, when you can zoom out and forget about the minutiae of your daily life. If you can appreciate the beauty of the peaks as well as the valleys, *Perspective* offers you an adventure of a lifetime.

YOUR GUIDES

Astrology: Your Energy
Aries (Mars, Jupiter)

Numerology: Your Path
Flexibility (The Number Three)

Minor Arcana: Your Lesson
Expansion (The Three of Wands)

Major Arcana: Your Highest Calling
Perspective (The World)

ARIES
RULERS: MARS, JUPITER

PURPOSE

To find gratitude for the experience rather than the destination.

RELATIONSHIPS

You are powerfully intuitive and brave, and your relationships should be a place of curiosity and expansion. By seeking out partners who push your limits and teach you something new every single day, you will discover that love never has to be boring.

The Journey of
APRIL 18

Welcome to April 18, a grounded journey that builds self-respect.

Despite the impulsivity of Aries season, take a methodical approach to today. *Discipline* (The Number Four) asks you to complete the tasks you normally would sweep under the rug and address all your responsibilities rather than just the ones that are most convenient. Bring personal integrity to everything that you touch, and know that you are building a strong foundation for tomorrow.

And if you're feeling worn out at any point today, make time for *Celebration* (Four of Wands). Whether you spend a night out on the town or perform the world's greatest bake-off in the comfort of your kitchen, it's time to have some fun. If you can prioritize play with the people you call family, today offers you the gift of the present moment.

Because at the heart of things, *Self-mastery* (The Emperor) wants you to be a thoughtful leader when it comes to managing your life. Zoom out and make objective decisions today, considering both your present needs and the goals you have for your future. How can you prioritize a healthy balance today? By taking a logical and strategic approach to everything you do, you can have your cake and eat it, too.

JUST FOR TODAY

TODAY'S MANTRA

I am the authority in my life, and I will make balanced choices that prioritize both work and play.

TODAY'S JOURNAL PROMPT

What are some healthy, joyful ways for me to blow off steam today?

TODAY'S RITUAL

Celebrate with four candles at the end of today, whether it be four birthday candles placed on a cupcake or four scented candles that hold meaning for you. Light them, and as you blow them out, make the wish, "The magic four, please help me enjoy the fruits of my labor."

BORN ON THIS DAY

JESSIE STREET, Australian suffragist, Indigenous rights activist, and Australia's first female delegate to the United Nations

TADEUSZ MAZOWIECKI, Polish author, journalist, philanthropist, and prime minister

"I have always felt that doubt was the beginning of wisdom."—CLARENCE DARROW, American lawyer

The Journey of Those Born on
APRIL 18

You were born of intuitive power and a vivid emotional memory that can make it hard to stay in the present. You will have to keep your feet firmly planted on the ground, as your journey is one of hard work, self-restraint, and a healthy dose of fun.

Early on in your journey, you will meet your discerning guide, *Discipline* (The Number Four). While you are passionate and unpredictable, *Discipline* calls you away from a life of endless searching and toward a path of meaningful work. You will meet *Discipline* within humility, when you place one foot in front of the other as you build an unshakable foundation of integrity.

But if you choose this humble path, be sure to enjoy the fruits of your labor. *Celebration* (Four of Wands) invites you to rejoice in completed milestones with the company of those you love most. You will meet *Celebration* in moments of splendor, when you forget about the many miles ahead and enjoy the present moment. If you can balance work and play, *Celebration* refills your energetic cup.

> ## YOUR GUIDES
>
> *Astrology: Your Energy*
> Aries (Mars, Jupiter)
>
> *Numerology: Your Path*
> Discipline (The Number Four)
>
> *Minor Arcana: Your Lesson*
> Celebration (The Four of Wands)
>
> *Major Arcana: Your Highest Calling*
> Self-mastery (The Emperor)

By answering these calls for maturity, you will come to respect the power of *Self-mastery* (The Emperor). *Self-mastery* inspires you to access the grounded authority that lives within, ushering you toward wise decisions that nurture a deep sense of self-respect. You will meet *Self-mastery* in moments of spiritual restraint, when you choose long-term gain over instant gratification. By being a humble leader to yourself, you'll be empowered to be a leader to many others.

ARIES
RULERS: MARS, JUPITER

PURPOSE
To celebrate self-respect rather than instant gratification.

RELATIONSHIPS

You are highly attuned to the feelings of others, yet your relationships should be a place of emotional safety and grounding. By seeking out partners who are straightforward and loyal to their word, you will discover that true love doesn't need hypervigilance.

The Journey of
APRIL 19

Welcome to April 19, a fearless journey that inspires radical self-trust.

Express yourself with wild abandon today. Whether you call that lover and tell them how you feel or pursue that public stage you always felt was out of your reach, choose bravery over complacency. *Courage* (The Number Five) invites you to grab the metaphorical microphone.

In the final hours of Aries season, prepare for *Conflict* (Five of Wands). Embrace the opposition that comes your way today, in the form of criticism or competition, and look for the silver lining that lies within this battle. Perhaps there is a pearl of truth within the pushback you are receiving, helping you grow in your understanding and effectiveness.

But don't give away your power entirely. *Wisdom* (The Hierophant) asks you to find the balance between personal authority and open-mindedness, humbling yourself to absorb new information while using your gut to discern what is true for you. Don't take any opinions or supposed facts at face value, but instead sit with them in meditation, asking yourself what they uniquely mean to you.

JUST FOR TODAY

TODAY'S MANTRA
I can share and receive information while trusting the wisdom within.

TODAY'S RITUAL
Drop your defenses. Lie down on your back somewhere comfortable and close your eyes. Do a full-body scan, making your way from the top of your head to the bottom of your feet. Notice where you're holding tension in your body, and as you work your way down, release it.

TODAY'S JOURNAL PROMPT
What actions can I take to get closer in touch with my truth today?

BORN ON THIS DAY

ALICE SALOMON, German social reformer and pioneer of social work as an academic discipline

PALOMA PICASSO, French Spanish fashion designer and businesswoman, daughter of Pablo Picasso

"The irony is that when we take care of ourselves first, we are in a much stronger place to take care of those we love."—KATE HUDSON, American actor and entrepreneur

The Journey of Those Born on
APRIL 19*

Y ou were born of fearless vitality and a self-reliance that can keep you stuck in isolation. You will have to the art of vulnerability, as your journey is one of self-expression, necessary strife, and higher knowledge.

Early on in your journey you will meet your bold guide, *Courage* (The Number Five). To complement your outgoing nature, *Courage* calls you away from a life of isolation and toward a path of authentic expression. You will meet *Courage* when you step into the spotlight and shine your truth for the rest of the world to see. If you can choose creativity over perfection, *Courage* makes your life a work of art.

But if you choose this exposing path, you will have to contend with *Conflict* (Five of Wands). As you draw upon your fiery passion, *Conflict* requires you to stand strong in the face of opposition while surrendering to the wisdom that lies in this battle. If you can absorb the inevitable feedback and criticism that comes with a life of radical authenticity, you'll grow while remaining true to yourself.

> ### YOUR GUIDES
>
> *Astrology: Your Energy*
> Aries (Mars, Jupiter)
>
> *Numerology: Your Path*
> Courage (The Number Five)
>
> *Minor Arcana: Your Lesson*
> Conflict (The Five of Wands)
>
> *Major Arcana: Your Highest Calling*
> Wisdom (The Hierophant)

By answering these calls for self-awareness, *Wisdom* (The Hierophant) invites you to be both the teacher and the student. Neither believing you have all the answers nor giving away your power to the authorities, *Wisdom* encourages humility as you think for yourself and separate the true from the false. If you can filter external knowledge through your internal intelligence, you'll open yourself to the gift of higher consciousness.

ARIES
RULERS: MARS, JUPITER

PURPOSE
To balance courage with humility while growing toward higher consciousness.

RELATIONSHIPS

You are larger than life, with energy to spend, and your relationships should be a place of healthy conflict and growth. By seeking out partners who expand your perspective while respecting your unique point of view, you will discover that true love is a radical vehicle to understanding.

*Are you a Taurus born on this day? Head to page 759 to find your additional birthday guide!

WELCOME TO

TAURUS
SEASON

The Journey of
APRIL 20

Welcome to April 20, a heartfelt journey toward personal abundance.

Marking the first day of the earnest Taurus season, give from a place of sincerity today. Whether it be offering time, resources, or words of kindness, *Devotion* (The Number Six) asks you to get off the couch and make the world a better place. By giving without expectation of return on your investments, you'll discover the gift of purpose.

But only give what you have. *Reciprocity* (Six of Pentacles) wants you to check your emotional and physical tanks to see how full or how drained you are. If you are running on empty, use today to receive, filling yourself with the warm hug of a loved one or a delicious meal. If you are overflowing with abundance, use this day to give to those who need it most.

Because at the end of the day, love is a *Choice* (The Lovers). If you feel someone or something is getting the best of you, make an active decision to move away from them or it so you can move closer to the life-giving exchanges you have with others. Remain loyal to yourself as you share your heart with others, participating in the equal exchange of healthy boundaries and unconditional love.

JUST FOR TODAY

TODAY'S MANTRA

I can give and receive in a way that feels balanced today.

TODAY'S JOURNAL PROMPT

Does my cup tend to run on empty, or do I take active steps to ensure it is overflowing?

TODAY'S RITUAL

Get in touch with your heart's center. Take a seated position, and place your left hand over your heart and your right hand over your lower stomach. Repeat the mantra, "Help me give what I can and receive what I need."

BORN ON THIS DAY

JESSICA LANGE, American actor

SEYRAN ATEŞ, German lawyer, feminist, and civil rights activist

"It's very unlikely that people are going to cause you an issue just because you are being yourself. And if they're concerned, that's on them. You're happy."—TAN FRANCE, English American fashion designer, television personality, and author

The Journey of Those Born on
APRIL 20

Y ou were born of intuitive balance and a need for stability that can keep you taking emotional chances. You will have to live completely from the heart, as your journey is one of service, altruism, and unconditional love.

Early on in your journey, you will meet your caring guide, *Devotion* (The Number Six). *Devotion* thrusts you out of a life of complacent comfort and toward a path of meaningful action. By listening to your heart's calls to action, you'll be able to mean what you say and do what you mean. If you can choose purpose over sloth, you'll open yourself to the divine gift of usefulness.

And if you walk this path of sincerity, *Reciprocity* (Six of Pentacles) will ask you to check in on your physical reserves. Is your energetic cup empty? If so, receive the gifts that are available to you, like a warm bath or a hug from a dear friend. Is your energetic cup overflowing? If so, share your wealth widely, spilling your plenty into the cups of those who need it most.

By answering these benevolent calls, you will discover that personal plenty is a *Choice* (Lovers). By prioritizing the relationships and contracts that fill your heart and doing away with the ones that drain you of your resources, you take the driver's seat on the road to happiness. You will meet *Choice* in the discernment that self-advocacy requires, when you make an active decision to love yourself so you can love others with the wholeness of your heart.

TAURUS
RULER: VENUS

PURPOSE
To be generous with yourself in order to be generous with others.

RELATIONSHIPS

You are partnership-driven by nature, and your relationships should be a place of complete devotion and romance. By seeking out partners who make your heart overflow with love and adoration, you will discover that true love isn't a fairy tale, but it is pretty damn close.

The Journey of
APRIL 21

Welcome to April 21, a discerning journey of grounded progress.

Show up for the things you care about most today. *Commitment* (The Number Seven) favors focus over fleeting entertainment, so keep your feet moving in the direction of the people, projects, and plans that hold deep meaning. If you said you would do something today, show up with no excuses and stick to your word.

But don't expect results from your actions to come to fruition today, and perhaps not even tomorrow. Coinciding with the perseverance of Taurus season, *Sustainability* (Seven of Pentacles) encourages you to work toward long-term rather than short-term gratification. Plant the seeds of integrity that you hope to come to harvest when the time is right and find joy in the simple labor.

And if you act with this level of humility, *Evolution* (The Chariot) reminds you that progress isn't always on the surface, so look for it within. By laying the groundwork for an abundant future today, you can reach new heights of conviction for the goals you hold most dear. Celebrate this forward momentum, recognizing how much faith and hard work it took you to get here.

―――――○―――――

JUST FOR TODAY

TODAY'S MANTRA

I can work patiently toward my future, with integrity being my greatest reward.

TODAY'S JOURNAL PROMPT

Do I tend to rush through my goals or procrastinate, and why?

TODAY'S RITUAL

Write down seven small, tangible actions you can take today, and as you set about the day's work, say the affirmation, "I am committed to my realistic growth." Work to complete these simple tasks by the end of today.

―――――○―――――

BORN ON THIS DAY

JOHN MUIR, Scottish American naturalist

NARGES MOHAMMADI, Iranian human rights activist

"What you want to ignite in others must first burn inside yourself."—CHARLOTTE BRONTË, English novelist

The Journey of Those Born on
APRIL 21

Y ou were born of grounded curiosity and a calmness that can err on the side of laziness when taken too far. You will have to work hard for the progress you desire, as your journey is one of intention, longevity, and determination.

Early on in your journey, you will meet your forthright guide, *Commitment* (The Number Seven). Despite your desire for comfort, *Commitment* calls you away from a life that lacks focus and toward a path of purposeful action. You will meet *Commitment* in the most meaningful obligations you have to others and yourself, when you choose to attend to these duties rather than get lost in self-centered procrastination.

And if you follow this path of integrity, you will have to practice patience when it comes to the fruits of your labor. *Sustainability* (Seven of Pentacles) asks you to favor long-term gain versus short-term gratification, inspiring you to never cut corners just to call a job complete. You will meet *Sustainability* in the small wins along the way, when you get a wink from the universe to remind you that diligence is always worth your while.

> ### YOUR GUIDES
>
> *Astrology: Your Energy*
> Taurus (Venus)
>
> *Numerology: Your Path*
> Commitment (The Number Seven)
>
> *Minor Arcana: Your Lesson*
> Sustainability (The Seven of Pentacles)
>
> *Major Arcana: Your Highest Calling*
> Evolution (The Chariot)

By answering these calls for accountability, you will find yourself working with the divine momentum of *Evolution* (The Chariot). *Evolution* creates the unseen wind beneath your sails that propels you forward whenever you show up, do the work, and believe in your cause. You will meet *Evolution* in purposeful movement, when your footwork is in complete alignment with the direction that your intuition tells you to go.

───────────────○───────────────

TAURUS
RULER: VENUS

PURPOSE
To slowly but surely move in the direction that the universe inspires.

RELATIONSHIPS

You are sociable and worldly, yet your relationships should be a place of intentionality and responsibility. By seeking out partners who inspire you to keep your word as they do theirs, you will discover that true love is the safe foundation from which you can fly.

The Journey of
APRIL 22

Welcome to April 22, an introspective journey toward self-respect.

Despite the material focus of Taurus season, *Power* (The Number Eight) asks you to go deeper today. Take a look at the parts of yourself that you normally hide due to shame and offer yourself complete self-compassion as you bring them to the surface. Call a close friend or trusted therapist as you wade through these healing but murky waters.

When you need a break from introspection, get your hands dirty with some diligent work. *Repetition* (Eight of Pentacles) reminds you that no one gets it right on their first try, so put in the time and effort to improve upon the skills you want to have today. Whether it be repeating chords on your new guitar or writing the worst of first drafts, don't be afraid to start from square one.

Today isn't a walk in the park, but you may discover your *Resilience* (Strength) in the process. If you are feeling overwhelmed at any point today, take a second to appreciate how much you have been through and what you have overcome. From there, tap into the never-ending resource of emotional fortitude that lives within as you pursue a day of authentic integrity.

JUST FOR TODAY

TODAY'S MANTRA
I can do the hard work of being myself while leaning on my emotional resilience.

TODAY'S JOURNAL PROMPT
What are times in my life when I accomplished a seemingly impossible goal? What steps did I take to get there?

TODAY'S RITUAL
Bring an infinity symbol with you today, whether it be a drawing that you make, an image that you print, a symbol from your home, or an object that you purchase. Gaze at this symbol whenever you are feeling low on energy today, remembering that anything in life is possible if you believe in yourself.

BORN ON THIS DAY

MARÍA ZAMBRANO, Spanish essayist and philosopher

CHARLES MINGUS, American jazz musician, composer, and bandleader

"Rules for Happiness: something to do, someone to love, something to hope for."—IMMANUEL KANT, German philosopher

The Journey of Those Born on
APRIL 22

You were born of earthly discipline and a focus on material security that block you from true emotional freedom. You will have to discover the abundance that lies within, as your journey is one of authenticity, mastery, and internal strength.

Early on in your journey, you will meet your empathic guide, *Power* (The Number Eight). Despite your focus on the material world, *Power* calls you away from the hamster wheel of financial gain and toward a path of internal abundance. By doing the introspective work and psychological healing required, *Power* invites you to get to know who you are underneath the superficial ties that bind you.

But if you choose this path of authenticity, you will have to earn the right to be an ace of your chosen craft. *Repetition* (Eight of Pentacles) requires you to put in hours of mundane study and humble yourself enough to learn from those who came before you. You will meet *Repetition* in the spirituality of monotony, when the seemingly ceaseless repetition teaches you everything you need to know about being a master.

By answering these introspective calls, you will access *Resilience* (Strength). *Resilience* asks you to look within to find the foundation of strength that lives inside you, encompassing the muscles you have developed throughout your hardest struggles. You will meet *Resilience* in emotional fortitude, when what you thought would end you instead introduces you to your limitless power. If you can sit back and witness how much you have endured, you'll remember you can handle anything.

TAURUS
RULER: VENUS

PURPOSE
To chip away at the layers of superficiality to find limitless internal strength.

RELATIONSHIPS

You are a grounded leader in most areas of your life, and your relationships should be a place of deep sharing and vulnerability. By seeking out partners who let you be imperfect while challenging you to grow to new heights of authenticity, you will discover that true love never judges and only inspires.

The Journey of
APRIL 23

Welcome to April 23, an educational journey toward internal awareness.

Pursue foreign territory today. Whether you try to garden and develop a green thumb or try your hand at a new project at work, *Experience* (The Number Nine) inspires you to get your hands dirty in the process of learning something new. There's no time for comfort zones, so break free of your limiting beliefs as you pursue the unknowns that today offers.

But it is Taurus season, after all, so be sure to enjoy the material world along the way. *Self-sufficiency* (Nine of Pentacles) encourages you to spoil yourself in some way, shape, or form today. Take yourself out to a gorgeous dinner, luxuriate in your nightly skin-care routine, or treat yourself to a walk in nature. Whatever it is, be sure you are in charge of your form of self-care.

And as you go about this fruitful day, listen to the voice of *Instinct* (The Hermit). Quiet the noise of the outside world as you go inward to the place of intrinsic intelligence that directs you to the next right action. If you find it hard to quiet your mind, spend a few minutes in silent meditation. It is through soul-searching that you will find divine direction today.

JUST FOR TODAY

TODAY'S MANTRA

Growth can be enjoyable and even luxurious if I'm willing to listen to my inner voice.

TODAY'S JOURNAL PROMPT

When do I feel most at home in my physical body?

TODAY'S RITUAL

Do nine small acts of self-care throughout today. Nine, I know! It sounds like a lot but let yourself thoroughly enjoy this abundance. Get creative; self-care is completely subjective.

BORN ON THIS DAY

SHIRLEY TEMPLE BLACK, American actor, singer, dancer, and diplomat

MICHAEL MOORE, American filmmaker and activist

"Have more than you show, Speak less than you know."—WILLIAM SHAKESPEARE, English poet and playwright

The Journey of Those Born on
APRIL 23

Y ou were born of grounded confidence and an innate wisdom that can be mistaken for arrogance. You will have to grow further in your understanding, as your journey is one of education, personal abundance, and intuitive knowledge.

Early on in your journey, you will meet your philosophical guide, *Experience* (The Number Nine). Rather than resting on your intellectual laurels, *Experience* calls you away from a life of educating others and toward a path of the unknown. By seeking out the answers to the questions you don't know, and never taking the words of others at face value, *Experience* inspires you to be fearless and discerning in your quest for information.

And if you choose this winding path, you will find yourself wrapped in the arms of *Self-sufficiency* (Nine of Pentacles). *Self-sufficiency* inspires you to enjoy the fruits of your labor, relishing the hard-earned comforts that you and you alone earned. You will meet *Self-sufficiency* in moments of plenty, when you look around the castle of spiritual wealth you have built and pat yourself on the back for a job well done.

> ## YOUR GUIDES
>
> *Astrology: Your Energy*
> Taurus (Venus)
>
> *Numerology: Your Path*
> Experience (The Number Nine)
>
> *Minor Arcana: Your Lesson*
> Self-sufficiency (The Nine of Pentacles)
>
> *Major Arcana: Your Highest Calling*
> Instinct (The Hermit)

By answering these calls for growth, you will have to get in touch with *Instinct* (The Hermit). *Instinct* asks you to listen to quiet voice of intelligence within to light your way through the murkiest of situations. You will meet *Instinct* when you are profoundly lost and are forced to rely on your intuitive powers to navigate your way toward your divine purpose. If you can silence the voices of the outside world, *Instinct* teaches you how to listen deeply to yourself.

TAURUS
RULER: VENUS

PURPOSE
To pursue the unknown by relying on the voice that lives within.

RELATIONSHIPS

You are courageous and at times stubborn, but your relationships should be a place of freedom and expansion. By seeking out partners who think for themselves as you both fearlessly conquer uncharted territory, you will discover that true love knows no limits.

The Journey of
APRIL 24

Welcome to April 24, an ambitious journey that can't fight fate.

Go after what you want today. *Autonomy* (The Number One) invites you to trailblaze your way to material success, never letting anything or anyone get in your way. Don't wait for permission or rely on others to help you meet your goals because today favors independence over collaboration.

But to live in harmony with the grounded earth of Taurus season, *Manifestation* (Ace of Pentacles) reminds you that a dream is best backed up with a realistic vision. Take a pragmatic lens to your plans today and see which of them needs a healthy dose of realism to come true. Anything is possible, as long as you are willing to work within reality.

And leave the outcome up to the divine powers that be. *Impermanence* (Wheel of Fortune) reminds you that luck is fleeting, but hard work and a positive attitude are forever available. No matter if your prospects are up or down, trust that fate is unfolding as it should. Turn it over to the universe once, twice, or as many times as you need to let go of expectation.

—◯—

JUST FOR TODAY

TODAY'S MANTRA

There are no limits to what I can dream, but I surrender my fate to the universe today.

TODAY'S JOURNAL PROMPT

Do I trust that the universe has my back on a practical and material level, and why?

TODAY'S RITUAL

Get your hands on some basil (if you can't, find an image of the plant online) and repeat the mantra, "With positive thinking, I can manifest the physical abundance I desire most."

—◯—

BORN ON THIS DAY

SACHIN TENDULKAR, Indian cricket batsman and national team captain

KAMLA BHASIN, Indian feminist activist, poet, author, and social scientist

"Art does not exist only to entertain, but also to challenge one to think, to provoke, even to disturb, in a constant search for truth."—BARBRA STREISAND, American singer and actor

The Journey of Those Born on
APRIL 24

You were born of earthly generosity and a patience that can err on the side of passivity. You will have to learn to seize the moment, as your journey is of one of independence, manifestation, and turns of fate.

Early on in your journey, you will meet your powerful guide, *Autonomy* (The Number One). Although you naturally would like to keep the peace, *Autonomy* calls you away from a life of staying small and toward a path of intuitive ambition. By carving out a path that has never been walked before, *Autonomy* empowers you to trust your gut and rely on your survival skills as you pursue the callings of your soul.

And if you choose this daring path, you will have to grow in your powers of *Manifestation* (Ace of Pentacles). Your internal dreams have the potential to turn into physical reality as long as you are willing to pragmatically work toward your far-reaching ideals. If you can keep one foot firmly on the ground while the other aims toward the stars, *Manifestation* offers you an abundance of realistic self-belief.

YOUR GUIDES

Astrology: Your Energy
Taurus (Venus)

Numerology: Your Path
Autonomy (The Number One)

Minor Arcana: Your Lesson
Manifestation (The Ace of Pentacles)

Major Arcana: Your Highest Calling
Impermanence (The Wheel of Fortune)

By answering these ambitious calls, you will have to surrender the outcome to fate. *Impermanence* (Wheel of Fortune) asks you to balance ambition with spiritual trust, forever reminding yourself that although you are capable of much, the universe knows best. You will meet *Impermanence* in the peaks and valleys in life, when you discover that thing you can rely on in life is a positive mindset.

TAURUS
RULER: VENUS

PURPOSE
To balance ambition with pragmatism while surrendering the outcome.

RELATIONSHIPS

You are as sweet and loyal as they come, but your relationships should be a place of independence and self-trust. By seeking out partners who have a strong sense of self and inspire you to have the same, you will discover that true love must come from within.

The Journey of
APRIL 25

Welcome to April 25, a balanced journey toward justice.

To complement the peacefulness of Taurus season, *Balance* (The Number Two) asks you to breathe in and take it easy today. There's no rush, so slow down your racing mind with a calming cup of chamomile tea or the voice of a soothing partner. You can accomplish much today, as long as you don't struggle.

But before you get going with any plans, *Prioritization* (Two of Pentacles) asks you to take on only what you can handle. How can you delegate some of your responsibilities today? Even if it's asking for more time with the obligations you have toward others, reach for self-compassion as you surrender some of the burdens in your day.

Besides, you'll need space as you work in harmony with the *Truth* (Justice). Put equality at the top of your to-do list today, looking for the ways in which you need to give or receive to reach balance with the world around you. If you feel that your cup is full, stand up for others. But if you are running on empty, be sure to stand up for your needs in a thoughtful but powerful manner.

JUST FOR TODAY

TODAY'S MANTRA

By reaching internal balance, I can easefully work toward a sense of justice.

TODAY'S RITUAL

Carry two coins with you today. When you are feeling low on energy and stretched thin, rub your thumb over one of the coins and repeat the mantra, "I am worthy of receiving." When you are feeling abundant, rub your thumb over the other coin and repeat the mantra, "I will give what I can toward justice."

TODAY'S JOURNAL PROMPT

What obligations, responsibilities, or burdens can I share with those I trust today?

BORN ON THIS DAY

HIND AL-HUSSEINI, Palestinian social worker and educator, notable for rescuing fifty-five survivors of the Deir Yassin massacre

AL PACINO, American actor

"It isn't where you came from, it's where you're going that counts."—ELLA FITZGERALD, American jazz singer

The Journey of Those Born on
APRIL 25

You were born of grounded ambition and diligent focus that can lead to burnout. You will have to devote yourself to a life of peace, as your journey is one of partnership, balance, and intuitive justice.

Early on in your journey, you will meet your tranquil guide, *Balance* (The Number Two). Rather than doing everything on your own, *Balance* calls you away from a life of exhaustion and toward a path of easeful patience. By relying on the people you trust and never rushing to meet unrealistic goals, *Balance* helps you build a life of serenity.

But if you choose this earthly path, you will have to contend with *Prioritization* (Two of Pentacles). *Prioritization* reminds you that if you put your hand in too many honey pots, you'll never have the time or focus to enjoy the sweetness. You will meet *Prioritization* in divine delegation, when you surrender some of your worldly desires in exchange for the gratification that comes from pure intention.

Astrology: Your Energy
Taurus (Venus)

Numerology: Your Path
Balance (The Number Two)

Minor Arcana: Your Lesson
Prioritization (The Two of Pentacles)

Major Arcana: Your Highest Calling
Truth (Justice)

By answering these calls for patience, you will discover that integrity is the deepest form of satisfaction. *Truth* (Justice) inspires you to get in touch with your moral compass so your life can align with your personal values. You will meet *Truth* in the consequences of your actions, when you realize that what you give out is what you receive in return. If you can stand for what you believe in most, *Truth* offers you complete clarity of mind and heart.

TAURUS
RULER: VENUS

PURPOSE
To find internal peace through thoughtful action.

RELATIONSHIPS

You are daring and forceful, yet your relationships should be a place of equality and interdependence. By seeking out partners who give as much as they take and encourage you to do the same, you will discover that true love flourishes in fairness.

The Journey of
APRIL 26

Welcome to April 26, a sociable journey toward personal expansion.

Go with the flow today. Rather than having a set plan, stay open to the invitations that come your way. Whether you start a new project at work or go on a last-minute date, *Flexibility* (The Number Three) favors spontaneity over comfort. Despite the mild complacency of Taurus season, say "yes" to stepping out of your comfort zone as you absorb the unexpected.

From there, be sure to prioritize *Collaboration* (Three of Pentacles). Work in harmony with others today, relying on their expertise while offering your skills to the group as well. There's no need to make yourself seem small or large; simply show up as an equal as you coconspire with a diverse team of people.

But don't forget to enjoy yourself. *Abundance* (The Empress) invites you to soak in life's pleasures as you spend time with others today. If you receive a compliment or are treated to a free cup of coffee, bring total presence of mind to these gifts as you learn to receive. Don't worry if fears of unworthiness come up—simply hold them with loving-kindness as you absorb the treasures of today.

JUST FOR TODAY

TODAY'S MANTRA
I can try new things and work with people who bring me joy.

TODAY'S JOURNAL PROMPT
Do I feel comfortable in collaboration? Why or why not?

TODAY'S RITUAL
Seek out two friends or colleagues today and think of a project or goal that the three of you could work toward. Pay special attention to their skills and perspectives as you work in harmony.

BORN ON THIS DAY

FREDERICK LAW OLMSTED, American writer and landscape architect

CAROL BURNETT, American actor, comedian, singer, and writer

"Stop worrying about missed opportunities and start looking for new ones."—I. M. PEI, Chinese American modernist architect

The Journey of Those Born on
APRIL 26

You were born of grounded awareness and a deep sense of self that can make it hard to embrace new things. You will have to grow and change through connection, as your journey is one of open-mindedness, teamwork, and receiving.

Early on in your journey, you will meet your curious guide, *Flexibility* (The Number Three). Despite your fixed ways, *Flexibility* calls you away from a life of solitude and toward a path of mental exploration. You will meet *Flexibility* in the knowledge and opinions that differ from your own, when you are forced to reconsider your point of view as you integrate new information. If you can stay open to the limitless wisdom of others, you'll learn how to grow in connection.

But if you choose this sociable path, you will have to answer the calls of *Collaboration* (Three of Pentacles). By recognizing that no one is an expert while paying deep respect to the skills of your peers, *Collaboration* invites you to work in harmony with others. There's no need to compete or manipulate in authentic teamwork—instead, put your faith in those you admire.

YOUR GUIDES
Astrology: Your Energy Taurus (Venus)
Numerology: Your Path Flexibility (The Number Three)
Minor Arcana: Your Lesson Collaboration (The Three of Pentacles)
Major Arcana: Your Highest Calling Abundance (The Empress)

By answering these calls for community, you will be asked to receive all the goodness that life has to offer. As easy as this may sound, *Abundance* (The Empress) asks you to find compassion for the deep wounds that block your capacity to receive what you need while working toward enjoying the earthly pleasures that life offers you. If you can work to heal the limiting beliefs you have around worthiness, you'll open yourself to the gift of spiritual bounty.

———————————————————O———————————————————

TAURUS
RULER: VENUS

PURPOSE
To open yourself to the spiritual bounty of friendship and collaboration.

RELATIONSHIPS

You are deeply grounded and self-aware, but your relationships should be a place of joyful expansion. By seeking out partners who playfully push you out of your comfort zone and help you enjoy more pleasure, you will discover that true love doesn't have to be so serious after all.

The Journey of
APRIL 27

Welcome to April 27, a pragmatic journey toward self-respect.

Take a grounded and methodical approach to your responsibilities today. *Discipline* (The Number Four) asks you to diligently blaze through the long list of tasks you would normally procrastinate on until tomorrow. So do what you say you're going to do, and look for the small wins that come from a job well done.

But don't tire yourself out too quickly because Taurus season never encourages burnout. If you are feeling low on energy at any point today, *Conservation* (Four of Pentacles) invites you to rest and take it easy. There's no shame in taking the time you need to recharge, so soak in every ounce of healing energy that you can find.

Because at the end of the day, you are in charge of your well-being. *Self-mastery* (The Emperor) encourages strong self-leadership, empowering you to make the objective and thoughtful decisions that will better your life in the long run. What steps can you take today to build a strong foundation for your future? Whether it be strategically planning what work to prioritize or setting healthy boundaries in your relationships, be a humble authority in your life today.

〇

JUST FOR TODAY

TODAY'S MANTRA

I will oversee my responsibilities to my well-being today.

TODAY'S RITUAL

Do four things that ground you and recharge your batteries. It could be taking a long bath, enjoying a peaceful walk with your pet, or spending some time in bed. Whatever they are, spread out these activities during the day.

TODAY'S JOURNAL PROMPT

In what ways do I overextend myself physically or emotionally on a daily basis?

〇

BORN ON THIS DAY

MARY WOLLSTONECRAFT, English writer, philosopher, and women's rights advocate

SHEILA SCOTT, English aviator and first person to fly an aircraft over the North Pole

"Hate is too great a burden to bear. It injures the hater more than it injures the hated."—CORETTA SCOTT KING, American author, activist, and civil rights leader

The Journey of Those Born on
APRIL 27

Y ou were born of intuitive power and an expansive imagination that can take you away from reality. You will have to ground yourself in the work that lies ahead, as your journey is one of tenacity, necessary rest, and personal authority.

Early on in your journey, you will meet your rigorous guide, *Discipline* (The Number Four). Despite your worldly aspirations, *Discipline* calls you away from a life of wanderlust and toward a path of hard work. You will meet *Discipline* in the humble hours that contribute to your long-term success, when you put in the time and effort undeniably worthy of respect. If you can place one brick on top of the other, you'll build an impenetrable emotional foundation to stand upon.

But if you choose this gratifying path, you will have to make time for *Conservation* (Four of Pentacles). The body and the soul can only take so much at a time, so slow down and recover between each mountain you climb. You will meet *Conservation* in the sweet surrender, when you soak in the much-needed rejuvenation you require to keep going.

> ### YOUR GUIDES
>
> *Astrology: Your Energy*
> Taurus (Venus)
>
> *Numerology: Your Path*
> Discipline (The Number Four)
>
> *Minor Arcana: Your Lesson*
> Conservation (The Four of Pentacles)
>
> *Major Arcana: Your Highest Calling*
> Self-mastery (The Emperor)

By answering these calls for humble balance, you will step into the wisdom of *Self-mastery* (The Emperor). *Self-mastery* encourages you to tap into the objective but loving authority that lives within so that you can know when to push and when to pull. Rather than giving away your energy, consider what is and is not worthy of your magic. If you can balance logic with intuition, you'll receive the gift of personal dignity.

―――――――――――○―――――――――――

TAURUS
RULER: VENUS

PURPOSE
To master the balance between hard work and self-respect.

RELATIONSHIPS

You are emotionally philosophical and deeply intelligent, and your relationships should be a place of uncomplicated and uncompromising respect. By seeking out partners who show their loyalty through reliable action and ask you to do the same, you will discover that true love is solid enough to fall back on.

The Journey of
APRIL 28

Welcome to April 28, a heroic journey that connects you to your personal power.

In spite of the slow and steady pace of Taurus season, *Courage* (The Number Five) invites you to throw caution to the wind and express yourself with wild abandon today. Say "yes" to every opportunity to have your voice heard, and don't back down due to fear or imposter syndrome. Know that you are worthy of this calling.

But you may still have to confront issues of *Scarcity* (Five of Pentacles). If you feel that there is not enough room for you to be as big and bold as you are, look inward to see where this story is coming from. When did you first learn that you couldn't get your needs met? These are old wounds that need your attention today.

And as you learn to take up space, tap into *Wisdom* (The Hierophant). Listen to the anchor of divine intelligence that lives within, helping you discern what is true for you versus other people. Rather than taking as fact feedback or insight from others today, show up as your own authority as you navigate what is useful information and what isn't.

———————————○———————————

JUST FOR TODAY

TODAY'S MANTRA
I can put myself out there while staying grounded in my self-worth.

TODAY'S RITUAL
Take note of your scarcity mentality. On a piece of paper, write down five financial, material, or emotional beliefs you have around not getting enough. Then rip up the page and repeat the mantra, "I am enough."

TODAY'S JOURNAL PROMPT
Do I feel comfortable taking up space in the world? Why or why not?

———————————○———————————

BORN ON THIS DAY

JESSICA ALBA, American actor and businesswoman

PAULINE DEMPERS, Namibian human rights activist and politician

"The one thing that doesn't abide by majority rule is a person's conscience."—HARPER LEE, American author

The Journey of Those Born on
APRIL 28

You were born of grounded potential and a self-reliance that can keep you from receiving support. You will have to learn to ask for what you need, as your journey is one of vulnerability, perceived lack, and higher knowledge.

Early on in your journey, you will meet your audacious guide, *Courage* (The Number Five). Although you are ambitious by nature, *Courage* calls you away from a life of independence and toward a path of radical vulnerability. By putting your heart on the line and revealing the entirety of who you are to the world around you, you'll move toward a life of complete authenticity.

But if you embrace this brave path, you will have to address *Scarcity* (Five of Pentacles). You will meet *Scarcity* when you feel that there are not enough pieces of the pie to go around, forcing you to either steal what isn't yours or give up on getting your needs met entirely. It is by looking inward to the wounds and beliefs that create this sense of not-enoughness that you will discover that asking for help is the greatest gift of all.

By answering these calls to acknowledge your inherent worth, you will tap into a higher state of consciousness. *Wisdom* (The Hierophant) wants you to be brave yet self-contained, never giving away your power to the authorities and remembering that you are the only knower of what is best for you. By listening to others while remaining forever loyal to your sense of personal truth, *Wisdom* offers you the gift of self-derived prosperity.

> ## YOUR GUIDES
>
> *Astrology: Your Energy*
> Taurus (Venus)
>
> *Numerology: Your Path*
> Courage (The Number Five)
>
> *Minor Arcana: Your Lesson*
> Scarcity (The Five of Pentacles)
>
> *Major Arcana: Your Highest Calling*
> Wisdom (The Hierophant)

TAURUS
RULER: VENUS

PURPOSE
To discover the abundance that comes from being loyal to yourself.

RELATIONSHIPS

You are independent and forever evolving, and your relationships should be a place of complete vulnerability and mutual respect. By seeking out partners who aim to see you for who you are rather than what they want you to be, you will discover that true love is a gateway to self-acceptance.

The Journey of
APRIL 29

W elcome to April 29, a tender journey toward life-giving love.
    Try to make yourself of service in the physical world today. While Taurus season is known for its comforts, *Devotion* (The Number Six) asks you to be of service instead. Share your energy and resources freely and watch as your day unfolds with the gifts of purpose.

    But check in on your reserves through the day. *Reciprocity* (Six of Pentacles) only wants you to give what you have, rather than draining your cup past the point of empty. If you are in need of receiving, don't be ashamed to ask for what you desire most. It is only in reaching a place of personal plenty that you can share your own authentic happiness.

    Remember, your sense of self-worth is a *Choice* (The Lovers). It can be easy to give away our power to the shiny things that we think will solve our self-esteem issues, but today encourages you to make decisions that are in your best interest. By saying a resounding "no" to the things that drain you today, you can prioritize the people and projects that feed your soul.

JUST FOR TODAY

TODAY'S MANTRA
I can give generously to the things that fill my cup in return.

TODAY'S TODAY'S JOURNAL PROMPT
What relationships or projects in my life allow for a mutual exchange of give and take?

TODAY'S RITUAL
Give away something tangible for free, whether it be a one-dollar bill, something homemade and delicious, or your jacket to a friend who is cold. Share your generosity on a physical level.

BORN ON THIS DAY

JERRY SEINFELD, American comedian and actor

RAZAN ZAITOUNEH, Syrian human rights lawyer and civil society activist

"A problem is a chance for you to do your best."—DUKE ELLINGTON, American bandleader, composer, and pianist

The Journey of Those Born on
APRIL 29

Y ou were born of earthly patience and a care for others that cause you to take less than you deserve. You will have to learn to ask for what you need, as your journey is one of sincerity, balance, and self-worth.

Early on in your journey, you will meet your sweet guide, *Devotion* (The Number Six). To enhance your caring spirit, *Devotion* calls you away from a life of comfort and toward a path of meaningful service. By aligning your thoughtful actions with the things that call to your soul, *Devotion* teaches you to choose purpose over complacency. If you can make yourself useful to everything you love, you'll build a life of value.

And if you accept this sincere path, you will have to learn to give and to take. *Reciprocity* (Six of Pentacles) means you can only be as benevolent to others as you are to yourself, so participate in life's ever-flowing exchange of resources. When you are brimming with energy, share it with those who need it most. But when you are down on your luck or feeling drained, don't be afraid to receive what you need in return.

YOUR GUIDES

Astrology: Your Energy
Taurus (Venus)

Numerology: Your Path
Devotion (The Number Six)

Minor Arcana: Your Lesson
Reciprocity (The Six of Pentacles)

Major Arcana: Your Highest Calling
Choice (The Lovers)

By answering these calls for vulnerability, you will come to understand the importance of *Choice* (The Lovers). *Choice* reminds you that love must be reciprocal, pushing you to seek out partners, community, and projects that are life-giving rather than emotionally draining. You will meet *Choice* when you act in your best interest, allowing your cup to overflow into the hearts of those around you.

TAURUS
RULER: VENUS

PURPOSE
To receive love in order to give love in a sustainable and fulfilling way.

RELATIONSHIPS

You are partnership-focused by nature, and your relationships should be a place of unconditional kindness and complete devotion. By seeking out partners who give with no expectation of return, you will discover that true love is the safest place to protect your heart.

The Journey of
APRIL 30

Welcome to April 30, a focused journey of self-progress.

Decide what you care about most today and let your actions align with this *Commitment* (The Number Seven). Rather than getting lost in fleeting entertainment, keep your focus on the tasks at hand and remember what it is you are trying to achieve. Bring intention to everything you do to let others know how much you mean what you say.

But amidst the tenacity of Taurus season, don't expect instant gratification from your earnest service. *Sustainability* (Seven of Pentacles) asks you to lay a thoughtful foundation for your aspirations, never minding the outcome and devoting yourself entirely to the process. Whether you dive into a spreadsheet to plan your finances or slowly chip away at your most important project, today is about the work, not the payoff.

If you can put your most sincere foot forward, you might make some meaningful progress anyhow. *Evolution* (The Chariot) invites you to see the small but crucial changes that occur when you act from a place of complete integrity. The universe reacts differently when it knows you're serious. By doing the legwork and turning over the results, you'll discover that the most important breakthroughs happen within.

JUST FOR TODAY

TODAY'S MANTRA
I will do what I say and mean what I do, and that is radical progress.

TODAY'S JOURNAL PROMPT
Do I tend to think short term or long term, and why?

TODAY'S RITUAL
Write down a tangible long-term goal at the top of a piece of paper. Below that, write down seven actionable steps you can take to reach that goal. Light a candle and repeat the mantra, "Slow and steady wins the race."

BORN ON THIS DAY

HELOISE BRAINERD, American activist and proponent of Latin American women's participation in the peace movement

GAL GADOT, Israeli actor

"It is not knowledge, but the act of learning, not possession but the act of getting there, which grants the greatest enjoyment."—CARL FRIEDRICH GAUSS, German mathematician

The Journey of Those Born on
APRIL 30

You were born of warm compassion and an internal abundance that can make it all too easy to rest on your laurels. You will have work for your long-term potential, as your journey is one of intentionality, endurance, and self-made progress.

Early on in your journey, you will meet your straight-forward guide, *Commitment* (The Number Seven). Despite your insatiable appetite for luxury, *Commitment* calls you away from a life of meaningless excess and toward a path of sincere focus. By discerning what matters most to you in life, *Commitment* teaches you how to stay true to the spiritual contracts you have signed with the universe itself.

But if you take this narrow path, don't lose your patience if your work doesn't come to fruition right away. *Sustainability* (Seven of Pentacles) requires you to plant the seeds of your aspirations and tend to the soil so that they can grow to their highest potential. You will meet *Sustainability* when you lay the internal groundwork for your future and experience the small miracles that come from humble perseverance.

By answering these calls for sincerity, you will find your efforts pay off with the power of *Evolution* (The Chariot). You will meet *Evolution* in the growth that happens slowly and then all of a sudden, when years of unseen effort finally amount to an opportunity of a lifetime. By keeping your head fully immersed in the work and leaving the rest up to fate, you'll open yourself to the gifts of divine timing.

YOUR GUIDES

Astrology: Your Energy
Taurus (Venus, Mercury)

Numerology: Your Path
Commitment (The Number Seven)

Minor Arcana: Your Lesson
Sustainability (The Seven of Pentacles)

Major Arcana: Your Highest Calling
Evolution (The Chariot)

TAURUS
RULERS: VENUS, MERCURY

PURPOSE
To allow personal progress to happen by earnest effort rather than happy accident.

RELATIONSHIPS

You are sociable and brimming with comforting energy to share, and your relationships should be a place of deep commitment and mutual respect. By seeking out partners who are as devoted to the work that goes into a relationship as you are, you will discover that true love is never lazy.

The Journey of
MAY 1

Welcome to May 1, a journey of giving that teaches you how to receive.
Amidst the abundance of Taurus season, act from a place of sincerity today. *Devotion* (The Number Six) encourages you to wear your heart on your sleeve as you give yourself to the people and projects you care about most. Whether you lend financial help to a person in need or surprise a friend with a token of affection, share your innermost kindness widely.

But within all this benevolence, don't forget to receive. *Reciprocity* (Six of Pentacles) goes both ways, so accept any sweetness that comes your way. If you are feeling drained at any point, let your close partners and friends know how they could best show up for you. And when you are full of happiness again, be sure to pay it forward.

Keep in mind throughout the day that self-love is a *Choice* (The Lovers). Prioritize the reciprocal relationships you have, both personally and professionally. If someone refuses to respect a boundary or condemns you for being honest, now is the time to consider who is really on your team. By accessing your sense of self-worth, you can stick up for your needs and cherish those who aim to meet them.

JUST FOR TODAY

TODAY'S MANTRA
If I am first generous toward myself, I can then be generous toward others.

TODAY'S JOURNAL PROMPT
Do I tend to feel more comfortable in the position of giving or receiving, and why?

TODAY'S RITUAL
Meditate on how best to treat yourself. Sit comfortably with your back pressed against a wall (holding an aventurine or emerald if you have one, or look at an image of one online if you don't), close your eyes, and in your head, repeat the mantra, "Pleasure is a birthright." See what ideas come to mind.

BORN ON THIS DAY

MAX ROBINSON, first Black American network television anchor

TIM MCGRAW, American country singer-songwriter and actor

"Do what you love, and you will find the way to get it out to the world."—JUDY COLLINS, American singer-songwriter, musician, and social activist

The Journey of Those Born on
MAY 1

You were born of unfailing intuition and a self-reliance that makes it impossible to ask for help when you need it most. You will have to learn to receive from the heart, as your journey is one of good faith, reciprocity, and self-worth.

Early on in your journey, you will meet your earnest guide, *Devotion* (The Number Six). Despite your fierce independence, *Devotion* calls you away from a life of isolation and toward a path of wholehearted action. By grounding yourself in the people, projects, and ideas that speak to your soul rather than your ego, you will discover that meaningful work never drains your emotional cup.

If you choose this humble path, you will be greeted by your abundant friend, *Reciprocity* (Six of Pentacles). *Reciprocity* isn't interested only in how you give, but also in your capacity to receive. You will meet *Reciprocity* in the mutual exchange of spiritual wealth, when you are able to surrender to the joys that come from others' kindness. If you can remember that benevolence is a two-way street, you'll learn you are worthy of such gifts.

> ### YOUR GUIDES
>
> *Astrology: Your Energy*
> Taurus (Venus, Mercury)
>
> *Numerology: Your Path*
> Devotion (The Number Six)
>
> *Minor Arcana: Your Lesson*
> Reciprocity (The Six of Pentacles)
>
> *Major Arcana: Your Highest Calling*
> Choice (The Lovers)

By answering these emotional calls, you will understand the genius of *Choice* (The Lovers). *Choice* reminds you that true love must first come from within. You will meet *Choice* when you prioritize the relationships and responsibilities that make your cup overflow with purpose, realizing that the emotional vampires in your life are simply not worth your time. By choosing self-love over self-destruction, you can uncover the gift of worthiness.

———————————————○———————————————

TAURUS
RULERS: VENUS, MERCURY

PURPOSE
To find self-love in the balance between giving and receiving.

RELATIONSHIPS

You are independent yet romantic, and your relationships should be a place of emotional generosity and divine affection. By seeking out partners whose benevolent actions beat any fairy tale you ever imagined, you will discover that true love is even better than the movies.

The Journey of
MAY 2

Welcome to May 2, a gritty journey toward personal progress.

Do what you say you are going to do today. *Commitment* (The Number Seven) asks you to show up, without excuse, to the responsibilities and obligations you have. Get organized as you approach your day, making sure that you are using your time and energy wisely rather than scattering it widely.

But don't wait on the results of your actions. To coincide with the slow-paced nature of Taurus season, *Sustainability* (Seven of Pentacles) invites you to take the long view today. Planting the seeds of intention will one day grow into a rich harvest. Lay the necessary groundwork for the relationships and goals you care about most, and practice patience and trust around the outcome.

If you access this level of humility, *Evolution* (The Chariot) ensures great progress today. Who do you hope to become? It's your opportunity to cosmically level up, so access your willpower and determination as you set your sights on a meaningful long-term vision. By aligning your actions with the highest good, you'll ensure your success will move at the divine speed of fate.

JUST FOR TODAY

TODAY'S MANTRA

I will show the universe my grit and determination while leaving the outcome up to fate.

TODAY'S RITUAL

Plant a seed—literally. Use anything that is available to you. (A castor bean or coleus will grow well indoors.) Tend to the soil of your seed today and repeat the mantra, "Growth takes time."

TODAY'S JOURNAL PROMPT

Who do I hope to become in the long run?

BORN ON THIS DAY

BIANCA JAGGER, Nicaraguan human rights advocate and actor

WILLEMIJN POSTHUMUS-VAN DER GOOT, Dutch feminist, radio broadcaster, and the first woman to attain a doctorate in economics in The Netherlands

"Blood, sweat, and respect. First two you give. Last one you earn."—DWAYNE "THE ROCK" JOHNSON, American professional wrestler, actor, and producer

The Journey of Those Born on
MAY 2

You were born of earthly tranquility and a need for stability that can keep you stuck in complacency. You will have to get serious about your personal progress, as your journey is one of focus, durability, and willpower.

Early on in your journey, you will meet your decisive guide, *Commitment* (The Number Seven). Despite your even-keeled nature, *Commitment* calls you away from a life of passivity and toward a path of exalted intention. By strategically pouring your energy only into the relationships and responsibilities that will mean something to you in the long run, you'll never drift away from your purpose.

But if you choose this discerning path, you will have to practice patience. Nothing worthwhile comes quickly, and *Sustainability* (Seven of Pentacles) requires you to tend to your goals devotedly, even when they are not showing the results you desire. You will meet *Sustainability* in humble endurance, when you are able to remember that life is a marathon, not a sprint.

YOUR GUIDES

Astrology: Your Energy
Taurus (Venus, Mercury)

Numerology: Your Path
Commitment (The Number Seven)

Minor Arcana: Your Lesson
Sustainability (The Seven of Pentacles)

Major Arcana: Your Highest Calling
Evolution (The Chariot)

By answering these deliberate calls to action, you will hit your stride with the momentum of *Evolution* (The Chariot). You can grow greatly if you put forth sheer determination and grit. You will meet *Evolution* in moments of success, when your resolve makes you willing to go to any lengths to conquer your goal. If you can show the universe just how serious you are, you'll discover the gift of radical advancement.

TAURUS
RULERS: VENUS, MERCURY

PURPOSE
To find true purpose in determination, allowing success to be secondary.

RELATIONSHIPS

You are easygoing and gentle with those you care about, and your relationships should be a place of responsibility and longevity. By seeking out partners who earn and give trust through action rather than words, you will discover that true love, when handled with respect, can last a lifetime.

The Journey of
MAY 3

Welcome to May 3, an exposing journey that relies on emotional durability.

Step into your *Power* (The Number Eight). Ask yourself what you want most today as you strip away the layers of people-pleasing that block you from your boldest potential. By embracing every inch of who you are and what you believe in, you can reach new heights of prestige and earthly influence.

But despite the slow pace of Taurus season, be sure to put in the hours to grow. *Repetition* (Eight of Pentacles) asks you to back up your ambitions with humility, showing the universe just how serious you are about what you desire. Whether you repeat the same chord on the guitar hundreds of times until you get it right or send endless prospecting emails to potential clients, there is no room for pridefulness today.

And if you feel tired or overwhelmed at any point, tap into your *Resilience* (Strength). Reach within during moments of strife today, accessing a place of emotional fortitude that allows you to handle all the ups and downs that come your way. If you can stay grounded amidst the ever-changing tides of fate, you'll discover the gift of internal strength.

JUST FOR TODAY

TODAY'S MANTRA
I can access personal power and mastery by relying on my emotional fortitude.

TODAY'S RITUAL
Tap to find your internal strength. Take a comfortable seated position and tap on the inner wrist of your nondominant hand as you repeat the affirmation, "My body is resilient. I can handle anything."

TODAY'S JOURNAL PROMPT
Am I comfortable asserting my personal power? Why or why not?

BORN ON THIS DAY

GOLDA MEIR, Israeli politician, teacher, and Israel's first female prime minister

BING CROSBY, American singer and actor

"I believe unconditionally in the ability of people to respond when they are told the truth. We need to be taught to study rather than believe, to inquire rather than to affirm."—SEPTIMA POINSETTE CLARK, American educator and civil rights activist

The Journey of Those Born on
MAY 3

Y ou were born of grounded curiosity and luckiness that, on your worst day, can make you prone to laziness. You will have to get in touch with the strength that lies within, as your journey is one of unveiling, skill-building, and emotional fortitude.

Early on in your journey, you will meet your illustrious guide, *Power* (The Number Eight). Despite your flexible nature, *Power* asks you to take off your mask of people-pleasing as you reveal your sincerest of ambitions. If you can continue to take an honest inventory of yourself while accumulating great honor and prestige, you'll discover that worldly success doesn't matter unless it is true.

If you choose this honest path, you will have to pay respect to your tough teacher, *Repetition* (Eight of Pentacles). *Repetition* shows you the quiet magic of practice and the undeniable skills that can only grow from time and patience. You will meet *Repetition* in the drudgery of mundane work and in the menial tasks that feel beneath you. If you can remember that in every apprentice lies a master, you'll tap into the irrefutable power of humility.

> ### YOUR GUIDES
>
> *Astrology: Your Energy*
> Taurus (Venus, Mercury)
>
> *Numerology: Your Path*
> Power (The Number Eight)
>
> *Minor Arcana: Your Lesson*
> Repetition (The Eight of Pentacles)
>
> *Major Arcana: Your Highest Calling*
> Resilience (Strength)

By answering these revealing calls, you will discover your profound spiritual fortitude. *Resilience* (Strength) reveals to you the never-ending resource that lives within, the source of strength that has held you through even the toughest of times. You will meet *Resilience* when fate whirls its unpredictable weather, and yet your internal strength will keep your feet firmly planted on the ground. If you can remember how much you have withstood in life, you'll be empowered to handle anything.

―――――――――――――――○―――――――――――――――

TAURUS
RULERS: VENUS, MERCURY

PURPOSE
To methodically build personal power through emotional strength.

RELATIONSHIPS

You are optimistic and jovial, and your relationships should be a place of deep connection and authenticity. By seeking out partners who aren't afraid to be honest while remaining loyal, you will discover that with hard work, true love can withstand any truth.

The Journey of
MAY 4

Welcome to May 4, a far-reaching journey guided by intuition.

Taurus season typically aims for comfort, but *Experience* (The Number Nine) invites you to lean in to the unfamiliar today. Seek out opportunities to expand your knowledge, and never back down from situations that lie well outside your comfort zone. Dive into a foreign study, try a cuisine you've never tasted before, or plan your next trip abroad.

And while you're exploring, make room for *Self-sufficiency* (Nine of Pentacles). More than likely you have been working quite hard at something, and today enjoy the fruits of your labor. Treat yourself to something physically fulfilling, like a deep massage or a luxurious meal. There's no need to post about it on social media; these moments are for you.

But if you are feeling overwhelmed with opportunity at any point today, get in touch with *Instinct* (The Hermit). Listen to the voice of divine intelligence that lives within you as you traverse this plentiful day. If your gut is saying "yes" to something, don't let your conscious thoughts talk you out of it due to fear. Move confidently in the direction of your soul, knowing that it is never wrong.

JUST FOR TODAY

TODAY'S MANTRA

I can fearlessly explore the bounty of today by relying on my instinctual intelligence.

TODAY'S JOURNAL PROMPT

Growing up, what was my relationship with luxury and abundance?

TODAY'S RITUAL

Make a list of nine physical things that bring you pleasure. You could include a cup of warm tea, your pet, or the grass at your neighborhood park. Carry this list with you today, and whenever you feel ungrounded, access one of them or visualize one in your mind.

BORN ON THIS DAY

AUDREY HEPBURN, English actor

RUTH FIRST, South African anti-apartheid activist

"Seek not greatness, but seek truth and you will find both."—**HORACE MANN**, American educator, author, and editor who pioneered public schools

The Journey of Those Born on
MAY 4

You were born of earthly pleasure, fiscal responsibility, and impenetrable self-discipline. You will have to expand your horizons, however, as your journey is one of personal adventure, financial abundance, and intuitive growth.

Early on in your journey, you will be asked by your guide, *Experience* (The Number Nine), to lift your head from your endless should-do list and discover the road less traveled. Fearlessly question what life tells you to do in favor of the subjects, concepts, and people that ignite your curiosity. You will meet *Experience* in moments of personal fascination, when the courage required to step outside your comfort zone has generously paid off in the form of higher consciousness.

If you choose to pursue this path of the unknown, you will find yourself in the abundant hands of *Self-sufficiency* (Nine of Pentacles). *Self-sufficiency* reminds you of your material power, teaching you the art of luxury through creative self-reliance. You will meet *Self-sufficiency* in moments of hard-earned pleasure, when you take a step back from the hustle and feast on the fruits of your labor.

By answering these calls for expansion, you will have to tap into *Instinct* (The Hermit). *Instinct* invites you to release fear-based control and rely on nothing but the intuitive voice of intelligence that lives within. You will meet *Instinct* in moments when you feel the most lost, the most alone, and the most afraid of the murkiness of the unknown. By believing in the power of your own abilities in conjunction with the kindness of the universe itself, your way will be lit with the divine brightness of self-trust.

TAURUS
RULERS: VENUS, MERCURY

PURPOSE
To explore and expand through trusting your intuitive power.

RELATIONSHIPS

You are pragmatic and thrive in the familiar, and your relationships should be a place of growth and understanding. By seeking partners whose inherent wanderlust and curiosity for the unknown rubs off on you, you will discover that true love is meant to expand your perspective.

The Journey of
MAY 5

Welcome to May 5, a self-led adventure that requires you to trust. Do what you want today without asking for permission. Despite the harmonious nature of Taurus season, *Autonomy* (The Number One) invites you to carve your own path and make things up as you go. Rely on your instinct whenever you are at a loss today and know that you can't go wrong if you are listening to yourself.

In this self-trust, you will discover the power of *Manifestation* (Ace of Pentacles). Believe in your earthly ideas by planting seeds of potential that you hope to grow into a future bounty. Apply to that job, buy the supplies needed to make that garden, or do your first push-up on the road to a stronger body. No matter what it is, now is the day to begin.

But don't take the highs and lows too personally. *Impermanence* (Wheel of Fortune) encourages you to rely on faith rather than giving away your power to your external circumstances. If things go perfectly today, so be it. If things don't go as planned, so be it. Ride the roller coaster and try your best to stay open to the fateful perspectives you'll gain along the way.

JUST FOR TODAY

TODAY'S MANTRA
I can pursue the things I want most while surrendering the outcome to fate.

TODAY'S JOURNAL PROMPT
How high or low does my confidence in myself feel today?

TODAY'S RITUAL
Start your day by watching a detailed video on how a plant grows. Pay attention to how it is planted and tended to and the metamorphosis it undergoes over time. Carry this visual throughout your day, as you decide what goal you would like to grow in your life.

BORN ON THIS DAY

ADELE, English singer-songwriter

NELLIE BLY, American journalist, industrialist, inventor, and charity worker

"Keep people from their history, and they are easily controlled."—KARL MARX, German philosopher, economist, historian, sociologist, political theorist, journalist, and socialist revolutionary

The Journey of Those Born on
MAY 5

You were born of earthly wisdom and a sense of authority that can make it scary to make mistakes. You will have to take a leap of faith into the unknown, as your journey is one of independence, potential, and karmic understanding.

Early on in your journey, you will meet your sovereign guide, *Autonomy* (The Number One). Despite your proud nature, *Autonomy* calls you away from a life of comfort and toward a path of complete innovation. By following your instinct rather than popular opinion, *Autonomy* inspires you to do what has never been done before as you carve out a one-of-a-kind road map for others to follow in wonder.

If you choose this daring path, you will have to work with *Manifestation* (Ace of Pentacles). By believing that anything is possible, you'll be inspired to plant the seeds of hope that will one day blossom into grand opportunities. You will meet *Manifestation* within pure potential, when you move so bravely toward what you want that you leave stress and fear in the dust.

> ### YOUR GUIDES
>
> *Astrology: Your Energy*
> Taurus (Venus, Mercury)
>
> *Numerology: Your Path*
> Autonomy (The Number One)
>
> *Minor Arcana: Your Lesson*
> Manifestation (The Ace of Pentacles)
>
> *Major Arcana: Your Highest Calling*
> Impermanence (The Wheel of Fortune)

By answering these calls for courage, you will have to surrender your perception of the outcome. *Impermanence* (Wheel of Fortune) knows that good luck is just as subjective as bad, so practice detachment as you ride the ever-winding roller coaster of life. By releasing control and trusting that every high and every low has its divine purpose, you'll learn that internal contentment is simply a shift in perspective.

TAURUS
RULERS: VENUS, MERCURY

PURPOSE
To try again and again without losing sleep over perceived failures.

RELATIONSHIPS

You are romantically bold and at times attracted to drama, yet your relationships should be a place of independence born out of complete trust. By seeking out partners who are so true to themselves they just let you be you, you will discover that true love wants you to be whole rather than half.

The Journey of
MAY 6

Welcome to May 6, an easeful journey toward radical accountability.

There's no need for extreme action, so take in a calming breath as you begin to plan your day. When you are centered, approach today with complete *Balance* (The Number Two). To complement the deep grounding of Taurus season, take things slow and steady, ignoring any faux emergencies that the world tries to hurl at you. Nothing important needs to be rushed.

You'll need this extra time to make thoughtful choices. *Prioritization* (Two of Pentacles) asks you to only take on what you can handle, delegating responsibilities when you can. Don't be shy admitting you're at your limit; the universe is always here to help.

Besides, you have high-level choices to consider. *Truth* (Justice) invites you to consult your moral compass as you stand up for fairness and equality throughout today. Whether you defend a close colleague or push for the promotion you know you deserve at work, now is the time to fight for what you believe to be true. Ensure you hold yourself and others accountable for the undeniable karmic law of cause and effect.

JUST FOR TODAY

TODAY'S MANTRA
Through internal balance, I can stand for much-needed justice.

TODAY'S JOURNAL PROMPT
What extra responsibilities and burdens can I delegate to others today?

TODAY'S RITUAL
Meditate to balance the responsibility you have on your plate today. Close your eyes and visualize each responsibility you have as a weight. Put the professional weights on your left shoulder and your interpersonal and personal weights on your right and take note of any stark imbalances. If so, ask yourself what you can release from the heavily weighted side.

BORN ON THIS DAY

GLORIA RICHARDSON, American civil rights activist and leader of the Cambridge Movement

ROBERT PEARY, American Arctic explorer who claimed to be the first to reach the geographic North Pole

"In the small matters trust the mind, in the large ones the heart."—SIGMUND FREUD, Austrian neurologist often called the "father of psychoanalysis"

The Journey of Those Born on
MAY 6

You were born of emotional loyalty and an extreme generosity that can take you off balance at times. You will have to aim for harmony in everything you do, as your journey is one of tranquility, priorities, and the karmic laws of cause and effect.

Early on in your journey, you will meet your peaceful guide, *Balance* (The Number Two). To enhance your gentle nature, *Balance* calls you away from a life of overwork and toward a path of easeful living. You will meet *Balance* in the slow and steady, when you take your time and rely on partnership rather than spinning yourself into exhaustion. If you can walk the middle road, you'll discover a life of serenity.

But if you choose this tranquil path, you will have to grapple with *Prioritization* (Two of Pentacles). You simply can't be in two places at once, so narrow your focus on the responsibilities that you hope to harvest in the long run. You will meet *Prioritization* in the necessary compromises required to remain loyal to the things that matter most.

By answering these calls to slow down, *Truth* (Justice) will embolden you to fight for fairness and equality. By discerning right and wrong according to your personal moral compass, you'll need to speak up and out about the injustices you see in the world around you. If you can remain accountable for your actions while holding others to the same standard, you'll tap into the gift of personal integrity.

YOUR GUIDES

Astrology: Your Energy
Taurus (Venus, Mercury)

Numerology: Your Path
Balance (The Number Two)

Minor Arcana: Your Lesson
Prioritization (The Two of Pentacles)

Major Arcana: Your Highest Calling
Truth (Justice)

TAURUS
RULERS: VENUS, MERCURY

PURPOSE
To find true purpose in the balance.

RELATIONSHIPS

You are as sweet and romantic as they come, and your relationships should be a place of peace and harmony. By seeking out partners who treat you the way they want to be treated in return, you will discover that true love always aims to be fair.

The Journey of
MAY 7

Welcome to May 7, a sociable journey that requires you to shed old ways of being. Stay open-minded today. Although Taurus season has us all feeling a bit stubborn, *Flexibility* (The Number Three) encourages you to step outside your lived experience and absorb the perspectives of others. By asking the questions rather than having the answers, you can open new doors of possibility.

This curiosity comes in handy, as *Collaboration* (Three of Pentacles) means learning to play well with others. Say "yes" to any team projects that are thrown your way, offering your unique set of skills while championing others to do the same. Many hands make light work today, so treasure the coconspirators who share your vision.

But as you integrate the brilliance of others, you may have to *Surrender* (The Hanged Man) what you once thought to be true. It's okay to grow and change, so lower your walls and let in the bounty of wisdom that surrounds you. If deep-seated emotional pain comes up today as your beliefs are tested, know that this temporary discomfort births spiritual breakthroughs. Let go of what is holding you back so you can untether your soul from the rigidity of fear.

JUST FOR TODAY

TODAY'S MANTRA

New information and collaboration leads me to the uncomfortable growth I need most.

TODAY'S JOURNAL PROMPT

What fears do I have around letting go of my rigid beliefs?

TODAY'S RITUAL

Call on the power of three. Find three meaningful physical objects in your home, take a seated position, and place the objects at your feet. Repeat the affirmation, "Two is better than one, but three can set me free."

BORN ON THIS DAY

OLYMPE DE GOUGES, French playwright, abolitionist, feminist, and social activist

PYOTR ILYICH TCHAIKOVSKY, Russian composer of the late-Romantic period

"The most important lesson that man can learn from life, is not that there is pain in this world, but that it is possible for him to transmute it into joy."—RABINDRANATH TAGORE, Indian philosopher, poet, and writer

The Journey of Those Born on
MAY 7

Y ou were born of deep loyalty and a sense of certainty that can err on the side of stubbornness. You will have to break out of your mold, as your journey is one of curiosity, teamwork, and spiritual untethering.

Early on in your journey, you will meet your mutable guide, *Flexibility* (The Number Three). Despite your narrow focus, *Flexibility* calls you away from a life of control and toward a path of open-mindedness. You will meet *Flexibility* in the endless perspectives of others, when you recognize that there is no one-size-fits-all approach to truth. If you can reach for understanding over pride, you'll discover intellectual freedom.

If you choose this path of knowledge, you will begin to understand the importance of *Collaboration* (Three of Pentacles). Although you have more than a few skills to offer, seek the magic of many as you pursue your long-term goals. By prioritizing teamwork above self-gratification, you can accomplish new heights of collective progress.

By answering these calls to broaden your potential, you will have to *Surrender* (The Hanged Man) what you once thought life should look like. You will meet *Surrender* in moments of divine shedding, when you forgo your rigid ways of being in favor of a spiritual experience. If you can embrace the uncomfortable between of growing but not quite becoming, you'll learn that discomfort is a necessary stepping-stone toward radical metamorphosis.

TAURUS
RULERS: VENUS, MERCURY

PURPOSE
To hang from the ledge of uncertainty and surrender to divine growth.

RELATIONSHIPS

You are certain of most things in life, yet your relationships should be a place of questioning and curiosity. By seeking out partners who playfully push your limiting beliefs and encourage you to try new things, you will discover that true love can widen your perspective.

The Journey of
MAY 8

Welcome to May 8, a foundational journey that prepares you for transition.
Put in the necessary groundwork today. Despite Taurus season's call for pleasure, *Discipline* (The Number Four) encourages you to do the tough and seemingly mundane tasks that you would normally postpone until next week. Find safety and grounding in the consistent effort you put in today.

But don't burn yourself out too quickly. *Conservation* (Four of Pentacles) asks you to address your physical needs, so be sure you are eating and resting in the ways that your body requires. Slow down throughout the day and center yourself within your body, thanking it for all it has done and asking it exactly what it needs to thrive.

You'll need this internal grounding because some aspect of your life is in need of *Transformation* (Death). What do you need to let go of? What do you need to mourn the loss of? Closure is never easy but use today to make peace with what is gone so you can begin to get curious and even excited about what is to come. There is divinity within loss, so lean into the grief of change and set your sights on the beauty of tomorrow.

JUST FOR TODAY

TODAY'S MANTRA
I can ground myself as I transform.

TODAY'S JOURNAL PROMPT
What are small, meaningful ways that I can practice rest throughout today?

TODAY'S RITUAL
Prepare a grief ceremony for yourself. Write down the things you are mourning and are ready to release. Repeat the mantra, "Within death, there is new life," and throw them into a safely contained bonfire. If you don't have access to safe fire practices, light a few candles and place them in a circle surrounding you, repeating the same mantra and recycling the paper when you're done.

BORN ON THIS DAY

DAVID ATTENBOROUGH, English naturalist, television producer, and host

ENRIQUE IGLESIAS, Spanish singer-songwriter

"Through thickest gloom look back, immortal shade, On that confusion which thy death has made."—**PHILLIS WHEATLEY**, first published female Black American poet

The Journey of Those Born on
MAY 8

You were born of earthly mastery and a deep knowing that can make it difficult to internalize necessary change. You will have to embrace the discomfort of growth, as your journey is one of hard work, self-moderation, and radical transformation.

Early on in your journey, you will meet your no-nonsense guide, *Discipline* (The Number Four). Despite your love for the luxuries in life, *Discipline* asks you to step away from overindulgence and toward a path of humble work. You will meet *Discipline* in moments of sweat and exhaustion, when you pour your entire being into your goal with no guarantee on return. By never letting you rest on your laurels, *Discipline* teaches you that nothing tastes as sweet as personal integrity.

If you choose this earnest path, you will have to pause for *Conservation* (Four of Pentacles). Overwork can take a toll on the body and soul, so tend to your physical and material needs. By slowing down and filling your cup, you'll gather what you need to thrive throughout your long road ahead.

By answering these grounding calls, you will have a

YOUR GUIDES

Astrology: Your Energy
Taurus (Venus, Mercury)

Numerology: Your Path
Discipline (The Number Four)

Minor Arcana: Your Lesson
Conservation (The Four of Pentacles)

Major Arcana: Your Highest Calling
Transformation (Death)

sturdy-enough foundation to embrace *Transformation* (Death). Nothing in life is meant to last forever, so practice accepting the inevitability of loss. You will meet *Transformation* in cyclical changes, when something you once relied on comes to a necessary end and you must trust that it will blossom into something even better. If you can release control and embrace the ever-changing seasons of life, you'll find the divine opportunity within loss.

―――――――――――――○―――――――――――――

TAURUS
RULERS: VENUS, MERCURY

PURPOSE
*To find spiritual grounding
in the inevitability of change.*

RELATIONSHIPS

You find deep comfort in familiarity, and your relationships should be a place of safety amidst necessary change. By seeking out partners who feel like home and encourage you to evolve to new heights of self-realization, you will discover that true love can ground you through even the scariest of transitions.

The Journey of
MAY 9

Welcome to May 9, a dramatic journey toward emotional regulation.

Put yourself out there today. *Courage* (The Number Five) invites you to throw the caution of Taurus season to the wind as you express your truth to the world around you. Don't fret over the what-ifs of vulnerability—just seize the moment and do what feels intuitive. Live from your heart rather than your head today.

But don't succumb to *Scarcity* (Five of Pentacles). If today doesn't offer you the gifts and adoration you were hoping for, try not to get lost in what you believe you are lacking. Instead, turn your attention to the abundance that is within or around you. If no one else is giving praise, give yourself the compliment you want to hear most.

And remember, life is only as hard as you make it. *Serenity* (Temperance) means that tranquility is always available if you are willing to center yourself. If and when you are feeling overwhelmed, quiet the noise and tap into a place of harmony. By surrendering any extremes of emotion, you will discover that peace is simply a state of mind.

JUST FOR TODAY

TODAY'S MANTRA
Just because I am vulnerable doesn't mean I need to lose my sense of balance today.

TODAY'S JOURNAL PROMPT
What are tangible things I can do to tap into a place of serenity?

TODAY'S RITUAL
Ward off scarcity by taking the contrary action of letting go of some physical things. Go through your home, your office, or your closet, and get rid of the old items that are no longer bringing you joy.

BORN ON THIS DAY

TEGLA LOROUPE, Kenyan long-distance runner and activist for peace, women's rights, and education

JOHN BROWN, American abolitionist and revolutionary

"Out of respect for the things that I was never destined to do, I have learned that my strengths are a result of my weaknesses, my success is due to my failures, and my style is directly related to my limitations."—BILLY JOEL, American rock musician and singer-songwriter

The Journey of Those Born on
MAY 9

You were born of earthly intelligence and a need for internal peace that can keep you at arm's length from true intimacy. You will have to find calm amidst the necessary drama of vulnerability, as your journey is one of self-expression, perceived lack, and spiritual moderation.

Early on in your journey, you will meet your fearless guide, *Courage* (The Number Five). Despite your humble resistance to the spotlight, *Courage* calls you away from a life of invulnerability and toward a path of radical visibility. You will meet *Courage* in moments of heartfelt expression, when you put yourself out there with no guarantee of how the rest of the world will react.

But if you choose this audacious path, you will have to contend with your lower companion, *Scarcity* (Five of Pentacles). You will meet *Scarcity* when you feel robbed of the things you want most and believe that the universe can never fully meet your needs. But if you instead bring awareness to the gifts that are present in your life, you'll learn abundance is a state of mind.

By answering these brave calls, you will come to understand the importance of *Serenity* (Temperance). *Serenity* invites you to tap into the tranquil center within, reminding you that things are never as bad, or dramatic, as they seem. Rather than getting lost in black-and-white thinking, practice emotional moderation amidst the chaos that life ensues. If you can reach for internal balance, you'll build a life of external peace.

———————————————————○———————————————————

TAURUS
RULERS: VENUS, MERCURY

PURPOSE
To look for the gifts that are inherent to a life of vulnerability.

RELATIONSHIPS

You are emotionally grounded and wise, and your relationships should be a place of tenderhearted expression and vulnerability. By seeking out partners who accept your emotional whims with grace and compassion, you will discover that true love encourages imperfections.

The Journey of
MAY 10

W elcome to May 10, a tenderhearted journey toward internal healing.

Act from a place of love today. Despite the fixed modality of Taurus season, *Devotion* (The Number Six) encourages fluid connection and vulnerable acts of kindness. Whether you send flowers to your partner or call your chosen family and tell them how much you care, today favors sincerity over ambition.

Embrace *Reciprocity* (Six of Pentacles) from all angles. If you feel as though you are overflowing with internal prosperity, spread it widely for all who need it most. But if you are feeling drained or down on your luck, today is the right time to accept the acts of grace that others extend to you. *Reciprocity* is best when it goes both ways.

But accepting love is easier said than done. *Shadow* (The Devil) asks you to look at the hidden fears, trauma, and shame that block you from embracing the authentic connections you have in your life. When did you learn that self-sabotage was better than the risk of getting hurt by others? Use today to do the unseen work, finding compassion for these unhealed parts of yourself while opening up to new forms of intimacy.

○

JUST FOR TODAY

TODAY'S MANTRA

I can love others while healing the parts of myself that are afraid to be loved in return.

TODAY'S RITUAL

Do six random acts of kindness today. It could be giving a compliment to a stranger, giving away a bit of spare change, or offering half of your lunch to a friend who forgot theirs.

TODAY'S JOURNAL PROMPT

What coping mechanisms have helped me suppress my feelings in the past? How can I begin to unburden and heal these self-defense strategies?

○

BORN ON THIS DAY

BONO, Irish singer-songwriter and member of U2

MIRAI SHIDA, Japanese actor

"We're really quite nice and friendly, but everyone has a beastly side to them, don't they?"—SID VICIOUS, English bassist and member of the Sex Pistols

The Journey of Those Born on
MAY 10

You were born of earthly ambition and a stoic independence that can make you invulnerable at times. You will have to soften to the heart of the matter, as your journey is one of sincerity, give and take, and internal healing.

Early on in your journey, you will meet your earnest guide, *Devotion* (The Number Six). Despite your independent streak, *Devotion* calls you away from a life of isolation and toward a path of meaningful service. It is by giving your body, mind, and soul to the things you love that you can discover your true purpose.

But if you choose this sincere path, you will have to learn when to give and when to receive. While you can do it all, *Reciprocity* (Six of Pentacles) encourages you to check in with your needs and get honest about what you can afford to share. You will meet *Reciprocity* in moments of reciprocity, when you give the best of yourself in exchange for the best in others.

By answering these tenderhearted calls, you will have to unearth the baggage that is blocking you from true contentment. *Shadow* (The Devil) asks you to look at your penchant for self-sabotage—when you harm yourself so that the outside world can't do it first. By shining light on these behaviors and mental patterns, you'll find the compassion needed to heal. If you can go to the places that scare you, you'll realize they are the birthplace of emotional freedom.

YOUR GUIDES

Astrology: Your Energy
Taurus (Venus, Saturn)

Numerology: Your Path
Devotion (The Number Six)

Minor Arcana: Your Lesson
Reciprocity (The Six of Pentacles)

Major Arcana: Your Highest Calling
Shadow (The Devil)

TAURUS
RULERS: VENUS, SATURN

PURPOSE
To learn to give and receive love from an emotionally aware place.

RELATIONSHIPS

You are sturdy and independent, yet your relationships should be a place of sweet surrender and devotional kindness. By seeking out partners who make you feel held for your worst as well as your best, you will discover that true love is a portal to healing.

The Journey of
MAY 11

Welcome to May 11, a paradoxical journey of pursuit and surrender.

Get clear on your intentions for the day. *Commitment* (The Number Seven) means your feet should be firmly planted in what matters as you prioritize your list of responsibilities. What people, projects, and plans are at the top of your list? As long as they serve an authentic purpose, throw your energy toward them with complete focus.

And be sure to think about the long haul. In congruence with the grounding nature of Taurus season, *Sustainability* (Seven of Pentacles) wants you to work steadily toward your goals rather than impatiently waiting for them to come to fruition. Spend thoughtful time with your partner, clean up that spreadsheet, or begin with a form of exercise that you can stick with. Perseverance wins over instant gratification.

You'll need a level of certainty because this day brings unexpected change. There may be some necessary shift that you have been postponing, so embrace the radical progress that is set into motion. In the form of something big and game-changing, *Upheaval* (The Tower) serves as an act of divine intervention. If at any point you feel this day is trying to break you, know that this is the day that *makes* you.

JUST FOR TODAY

TODAY'S MANTRA

I will pursue what matters so I can let go of what is no longer mine to keep.

TODAY'S JOURNAL PROMPT

When was the last time unexpected change brought me the revelation I really needed?

TODAY'S RITUAL

Go somewhere you've never been before in your local area, and say an affirmation to the planet Uranus, "I trust that you will do for me what I cannot do for myself, God of the Sky. Thank you for everything you've given me and everything you've taken away."

BORN ON THIS DAY

MARTHA GRAHAM, American modern dancer and choreographer

LANA CONDOR, Vietnamese American actor, producer, and singer

"Intelligence without ambition is a bird without wings."—SALVADOR DALI, Spanish surrealist artist

The Journey of Those Born on
MAY 11

You were born of internal harmony and a desire for comfort that can keep you stuck in complacency. You will have to make friends with change, as your journey is one of intention, perseverance, and unexpected revelation.

Early on in your journey, you will meet your sure-footed guide, *Commitment* (The Number Seven). Despite your steady and tranquil nature, *Commitment* calls you away from a life of ease and toward a path of thoughtful action. Uncertainty serves no purpose for you, but by prioritizing your efforts only around the people and projects that mean the most to you, you'll open yourself to a life of sincerity.

And if you choose this demanding path, you will have to consider *Sustainability* (Seven of Pentacles). Not all plants come to harvest in a timely manner, yet *Sustainability* asks you to devotedly tend this precious soil anyhow. You will meet *Sustainability* in your investments, when you pour your physical and emotional energy strategically and systematically toward a long-term vision. Keep your eye on the prize while practicing patience.

By answering these calls for intentionality, you will come to respect the power of *Upheaval* (The Tower). *Upheaval* asks you to embrace the uninvited change that life hurls your way, when you are forced into the unknown you were resisting and yet find yourself in a much better place than you could have ever planned. If you can trust in the powers that be as the world shakes beneath you, you'll discover the revelations you need most.

YOUR GUIDES

Astrology: Your Energy
Taurus (Venus, Saturn)

Numerology: Your Path
Commitment (The Number Seven)

Minor Arcana: Your Lesson
Sustainability (The Seven of Pentacles)

Major Arcana: Your Highest Calling
Upheaval (The Tower)

TAURUS
RULERS: VENUS, SATURN

PURPOSE
To pursue what matters while surrendering what life must take away.

RELATIONSHIPS

You are partnership-driven and a natural diplomat, and your relationships should be a place of respect and longevity. By seeking out partners who work for the long haul and show their loyalty amidst great change, you will discover that true love can withstand the chaos of life.

The Journey of
MAY 12

W elcome to May 12, an authentic journey that inspires optimism.

Be commanding with your honesty today. Taurus season thrives in emotional comfort, but *Power* (The Number Eight) asks you to reveal the imperfect but deeply authentic parts of yourself as you pursue what you desire most. You can have a tremendous influence on others as you unveil layers of superficiality and expose just how dynamic you are.

But as you pursue this day of truth-seeking, remember that true mastery takes time. *Repetition* (Eight of Pentacles) asks you to be willing to chip away at the things you desire most rather than rushing toward any finish line. Practice makes perfect, so put one foot in front of the other as you walk toward your potential.

Hope (The Star) reminds you of how much potential there is. If you are feeling uncertain at any point today, tap into how excited you are about your future. What ideas or plans fill you with so much optimism that fear can't stand a chance? Reach within and rely on that inner cheerleader who wants nothing more than for you to be radically yourself.

———————————————○———————————————

JUST FOR TODAY

TODAY'S MANTRA
I will peel back the layers that block my belief in myself.

TODAY'S JOURNAL PROMPT
What skill took me many hours to master?

TODAY'S RITUAL
Draw a large infinity symbol, horizontally, on a piece of paper. In the right-hand loop, write the wildest hopes and dreams you have for yourself. In the left-hand loop, write eight practical things you can master to achieve these grand visions.

———————————————○———————————————

BORN ON THIS DAY

KATHARINE HEPBURN, American actor

CLARIBEL ALEGRÍA, Nicaraguan Salvadoran poet, essayist, novelist, and journalist

"How very little can be done under the spirit of fear."—FLORENCE NIGHTINGALE, English nurse who revolutionized nursing during the Crimean War

The Journey of Those Born on
MAY 12

Y ou were born of grounded curiosity and a social awareness that can keep you from being fully authentic. You will have to accept every aspect of yourself to reach your true potential, as your journey is one of introspection, humble mastery, and intrinsic optimism.

Early on in your journey, you will meet your enigmatic guide, *Power* (The Number Eight). Despite your many external interests, *Power* calls you away from a life of fleeting meaning and toward a path of deep self-awareness. You will meet *Power* in the soul-bearing ambitions you pour yourself into, when you build true purpose and prestige from complete authenticity. If you can embrace this level of honesty, you'll open yourself to the spiritual wealth of vulnerability.

But if you choose this path of authenticity, you will have to work for who you want to become. While you are good at a lot, *Repetition* (Eight of Pentacles) asks you to put in the long, mundane hours required to be a master of your chosen craft. By looking for the small joys that come from humble work, *Repetition* reminds you that nothing good comes easy.

> ### YOUR GUIDES
>
> *Astrology: Your Energy*
> Taurus (Venus, Saturn)
>
> *Numerology: Your Path*
> Power (The Number Eight)
>
> *Minor Arcana: Your Lesson*
> Repetition (The Eight of Pentacles)
>
> *Major Arcana: Your Highest Calling*
> Hope (The Star)

By answering these calls for authenticity, you will have to rely on *Hope* (The Star). *Hope* reveals the thread of divine optimism that has carried you through even the most upsetting of times. You will meet *Hope* in the sparkling ideas you have for your future, when the sheer potential gets you out of bed and on your feet. If you can believe in yourself, you'll find light within the dark.

TAURUS
RULERS: VENUS, SATURN

PURPOSE
*To work to uncover the pure hope
that lives within.*

RELATIONSHIPS

You are flexible and romantic, and your relationships should be a place of total vulnerability and truth-telling. By seeking out partners who want to peel back your many layers, you will discover that true love never needs you to hide your magic.

The Journey of
MAY 13

W elcome to May 13, a far-reaching journey that inevitably brings you home to yourself.
View today as an adventure. Despite the stability of Taurus season, *Experience* (The
Number Nine) means expanding your consciousness through foreign and exciting experiences. Listen to that podcast whose political views differ from yours, open that dusty book you never thought you could handle, or suggest a date that throws you out of your norm. The scarier, the better.

And integrate *Self-sufficiency* (Nine of Pentacles) into these growth opportunities. Seize every moment to enjoy yourself today, whether you go out for your favorite meal or soak your tired feet in the tub. Tap into the physical luxuries available to you and savor every bit of them.

But don't be surprised if a few emotional ghosts pop up along the way. *Memory* (The Moon) projects the past onto the present so you can heal the experiences you normally try to deny. If an exchange or circumstance triggers an inappropriate emotional response today, go inward to meet the part of you that is frozen in time. Use your intuition as you gently uncover, discover, and discard the baggage that has been weighing you down for quite some time.

JUST FOR TODAY

TODAY'S MANTRA
I will seek new and enjoyable experiences that give me insight into the unhealed parts of my past.

TODAY'S RITUAL
Draw upon the awareness of the moon. Go out after dark tonight and sit somewhere comfortable while looking up toward the moon, even if it isn't visible from your vantage point. Repeat the phrase, "Moon wisdom, please help me free the long-buried stories that I most need to see."

TODAY'S JOURNAL PROMPT
What stories and experiences from my past still impact me to this day?

BORN ON THIS DAY

WITOLD PILECKI, Polish World War II resistance fighter

CAROLYN R. PAYTON, American psychologist and first female and first Black American director of the US Peace Corps

"Music, at its essence, is what gives us memories. And the longer a song has existed in our lives, the more memories we have of it."—STEVIE WONDER, American singer-songwriter and musician

The Journey of Those Born on
MAY 13

You were born of grounded discipline and a hidden depth that you don't easily reveal to others. You will have to integrate all the complexity that lies within, as your journey is one of seeking, indulgence, and internal healing.

Early on in your journey, you will meet your worldly guide, *Experience* (The Number Nine). Despite your fear of the unknown, *Experience* calls you away from a life of uninspired work and toward a limitless path of exploration. By asking questions whose answers only lead to more curiosity, you can access the humility that opens you to new heights of consciousness. If you walk outside your comfort zone, it'll never be crowded.

And if you traverse this winding path, you will meet your abundant friend, *Self-sufficiency* (Nine of Pentacles). Your brave searching builds incredible abundance, so pause from time to time to enjoy the fruits of your labor. Whether you take a fun-filled sabbatical before beginning a new job or treat yourself to a luxurious dinner date, remember that life is meant to be appreciated.

But the more you grow, the more important it will be to look back. *Memory* (The Moon) asks you to reflect upon the fundamental experiences that swim through your subconscious so that they don't project their unhealed stories onto your present life. You will meet *Memory* in déjà vu, when a present circumstance forces you to address the history that underpins your reaction. If you can bring the unconscious to the surface, *Memory* offers you the gift of emotional integration.

———————————————————○———————————————————

TAURUS
RULERS: VENUS, SATURN

PURPOSE
To grow far enough away from the past to get the perspective required to heal it.

RELATIONSHIPS

You are as steady and reliable as they come, yet your relationships should be a place of growth and expansion. By seeking out partners who challenge your beliefs and push you outside your comfort zone, you will discover that true love knows no physical limits.

The Journey of
MAY 14

Welcome to May 14, a self-led quest in pursuit of creative authenticity.

Follow the path of your intuition today. Despite Taurus season's desire to work in harmony with others, *Autonomy* (The Number One) encourages you to do your own thing and see what you can accomplish with self-reliance. Whether you start a new independent project at work or spend the day pursuing a personal goal, rely completely on your gut instinct.

As you do, tap into the power of *Manifestation* (Ace of Pentacles). There is much you can achieve today as long as you believe in the plausibility of your goals. A dream without a plan is simply wishful thinking, so if your plans feel too far-reaching, integrate them into reality by visualizing the steps it may require to achieve them.

From there, let your excitement for these ideas shine. *Vitality* (The Sun) asks you to step into the sunlight of your authentic spirit, uplifting others with your zest for life. Step out to the center stage of your world today and accept every invitation for creative leadership that comes your way. By living in accordance with your originality, you never know who you might inspire to do the same.

JUST FOR TODAY

TODAY'S MANTRA

I will ground myself in my intuition as I step into the light of my authentic spirit.

TODAY'S RITUAL

Soak in the energy of the sun. Go outside at some point today, and whether the sun is visible or hidden, repeat the phrase, "Life giver I hope to be, the ray of light that sets others free."

TODAY'S JOURNAL PROMPT

When, and with what company, do I tend to shine the brightest?

BORN ON THIS DAY

CATE BLANCHETT, Australian actor

JILL STEIN, American physician and former political candidate

"Soon the day will come when science will win victory over error, justice a victory over injustice, and human love a victory over human hatred and ignorance."—MAGNUS HIRSCHFELD, German physician, sexologist, and gay and trans rights activist

The Journey of Those Born on
MAY 14

You were born of serious wisdom and need for tranquility that can block you from taking risks. You will have to shine bright with the light of self-belief, as your journey is one of independence, earthly potential, and self-expression.

Early on in your journey, you will meet your fearsome guide, *Autonomy* (The Number One). Despite your harmonious nature, *Autonomy* calls you away from a life of peacekeeping and toward a path of innovation. By moving to the beat of your own drum and drowning out the opinions of others, *Autonomy* invites you to carve out a road map that is uniquely crafted to your ambitions.

And if you accept this brave path, you will have to rely on your inner resources to keep moving forward. *Manifestation* (Ace of Pentacles) asks you to believe deeply in the grounded yet inspiring ideas that lie within. If you can bring your wildest dreams into the earthly plane by realistically envisioning how they can be made into reality, you'll discover that with confidence and sensibility, anything is possible.

YOUR GUIDES

Astrology: Your Energy
Taurus (Venus, Saturn)

Numerology: Your Path
Autonomy (The Number One)

Minor Arcana: Your Lesson
Manifestation (The Ace of Pentacles)

Major Arcana: Your Highest Calling
Vitality (The Sun)

By embracing these fear-reaching calls, you will step into the light of *Vitality* (The Sun). *Vitality* knows how brightly you glow when you are creating from a place of authenticity, so express yourself from the soul. You will meet *Vitality* in moments of personal exuberance, when you can't help but leave a sparkle on everything you touch. By giving yourself permission to take up life-giving space in the world around you, you will empower others to do the same.

———————————————◯———————————————

TAURUS
RULERS: VENUS, SATURN

PURPOSE
*To manifest a self-made life of
creative authenticity.*

RELATIONSHIPS

You are more interested in harmony than drama, yet your relationships should be a place of courageous independence. By seeking out partners who are completely themselves, no matter what the context, and who inspire you to do the same, you will discover that true love is never afraid to shine brightly.

The Journey of
MAY 15

Welcome to May 15, a gradual journey toward radical consciousness.

Relax and take it easy today. To complement the peacefulness of Taurus season, *Balance* (The Number Two) invites you to take a softer approach to your goals and ambitions, never minding the hustle culture that you may live in. Meditate throughout the day to calm your racing mind and ask yourself how you can make your life simpler.

More than likely, this simplicity comes through *Prioritization* (Two of Pentacles). You can't be in two places at once today, so delegate or postpone the tasks that keep you away from the present moment. Give your full attention to the activities that bring meaning to you, and don't apologize for the decisions you must make to do so.

You'll need this extra space and time as you integrate new, and potentially uncomfortable, truths. It is easy to sleep-walk through life but *Awakening* (Judgment) encourages you to open your eyes to the larger patterns at play that may require great change. Whether you come to terms with the fading of a relationship or surrender to the inconvenient reality of your current career, favor acceptance over denial.

JUST FOR TODAY

TODAY'S MANTRA
I will pare down my day so I can slowly but surely awaken to the truth.

TODAY'S JOURNAL PROMPT
What are some responsibilities I can let go of today? Who can I recruit to help me?

TODAY'S RITUAL
Write down two uncomfortable truths about yourself or the world around you—truths that you are not quite ready to digest. Go outside to a place that feels comforting and balancing to you, and let the sunlight hit the paper as you internally repeat, "I can balance the truth with internal peace."

BORN ON THIS DAY

MU SOCHUA, Cambodian politician and human rights activist

BIRDY, English singer-songwriter and musician

"No equality without peace, no peace without equality."—ICHIKAWA FUSAE, Japanese feminist, politician, and a leader of the Japanese women's suffrage movement

The Journey of Those Born on
MAY 15

You were born of tenderheartedness and a buried self-hatred that can lead to subconscious self-destruction. You will have to slowly and steadily awaken to your authentic power, as your journey is one of harmony, choice, and spiritual awareness.

Early on in your journey, you will meet your gentle guide, *Balance* (The Number Two). Although you have endless love to give, *Balance* calls you away from a life of overextension and toward a path of tranquility. By never biting off more than you can chew, *Balance* encourages you to slow down and remember that nothing important needs to be rushed.

If you choose this harmonic path, you will meet your sage teacher, *Prioritization* (Two of Pentacles). Despite your capacity to juggle many projects, *Prioritization* asks you to make thoughtful choices about where and how you spend your energy. By allowing your mind and body to focus on the present task rather than scattering your attention, you'll harness the gift of intentionality.

By answering these calls to slow down and pay attention, you will make yourself available to *Awakening*

YOUR GUIDES

Astrology: Your Energy
Taurus (Venus, Saturn)

Numerology: Your Path
Balance (The Number Two)

Minor Arcana: Your Lesson
Prioritization (The Two of Pentacles)

Major Arcana: Your Highest Calling
Awakening (Judgment)

(Judgment). *Awakening* invites you to pay attention to the larger patterns that are unfolding in and around you, imperceptible to the naked eye yet deeply crucial to self-development. By bringing consciousness to the pieces that make up your individual puzzle—your past triumphs, lessons learned, heartbreaks, pains, joys, and traumas—you can wake up to the necessary changes that lead you to new heights of self-actualization.

TAURUS
RULERS: VENUS, SATURN

PURPOSE
To gently awaken to life-changing spiritual truths.

RELATIONSHIPS

You are sweet yet emotionally guarded, so your relationships should be a place of trust built from equality and mutual respect. By seeking out partners who aim to live in harmony with you by honoring your needs and boundaries, you will discover that true love can be tranquil rather than painful.

The Journey of
MAY 16

Welcome to May 16, a synergistic journey that inspires gratitude.

Step outside your lived experience today. Despite the fixed modality of Taurus season, *Flexibility* (The Number Three) encourages you to ask the right questions rather than offering what you believe to be the right answers. Pick the brains of your colleagues, friends, and family, and welcome every opportunity to shift your perspective.

This open-mindedness will help as *Collaboration* (Three of Pentacles) requires you to grow in harmony with others today. What work do you have to do that would be best served with a team of coconspirators? Usher in the genius that comes from collective thinking as you pursue new heights of shared progress.

And be sure to high-five each other along the way. *Perspective* (The World) inspires you to take a bird's-eye view on your team's growth so you can appreciate the divine momentum that is occurring. Pause throughout the day to witness the amazing breakthroughs that only could have come from trusting others with your grand plans. And if you feel compelled to, openly share your gratitude for the things you have learned from others.

○

JUST FOR TODAY

TODAY'S MANTRA
I can climb to greater heights of consciousness if I trust in the knowledge and experience of others.

TODAY'S RITUAL
Borrow three physical items from three different people today. The items could be as simple as a pencil or a warm jacket. Before you ask, repeat the affirmation, "I can ask for help today."

TODAY'S JOURNAL PROMPT
What role do I tend to perform best in when I am collaborating?

○

BORN ON THIS DAY

OLGA KORBUT, Soviet gymnast and six-time Olympic medalist

ANNE O'HARE MCCORMICK, English American journalist and first woman to receive a Pulitzer Prize in a major journalism category

"The things that happen in your life are either your choices or opportunities and lessons the universe has put before you. Life on earth is like college and we're all just trying to pass the courses."—MEGAN FOX, American actor

The Journey of Those Born on
MAY 16

You were born of emotional loyalty and a subconscious desire for instability that can lead you away from the contentment you seek. You will have to find grounding in teamwork and gratitude, as your journey is one of curiosity, trust, and worldly perspective.

Early on in your journey, you will meet your excitable guide, *Flexibility* (The Number Three). Despite your desire for certainty, *Flexibility* calls you away from a life of fearful stubbornness and toward a path of free-thinking. By embracing the many perspectives of others and integrating new information over time, *Flexibility* reminds you that it is always okay to change your mind. If you can favor freedom over dogmatism, you'll open yourself to a life of limitless growth.

And if you accept this fruitful path, you will discover the joys of *Collaboration* (Three of Pentacles). You don't need to do everything on your own. Instead, by offering your unique skills while trusting in the varying expertise of others, you can reach previously unimaginable realms of progress. Plus, by embracing this new sense of teamwork, you'll learn that work can be fun after all.

YOUR GUIDES

Astrology: Your Energy
Taurus (Venus, Saturn)

Numerology: Your Path
Flexibility (The Number Three)

Minor Arcana: Your Lesson
Collaboration (The Three of Pentacles)

Major Arcana: Your Highest Calling
Perspective (The World)

By answering these awareness-raising calls, you will begin to build *Perspective* (The World). By walking up the mountain of consciousness in step with the coconspirators you now call friends, *Perspective* invites you to stop at the peak, take in the view, and recognize how much you have learned along the way. If you can always keep a gracious eye on your growth, you'll open yourself to the gift of appreciation.

〇

TAURUS
RULERS: VENUS, SATURN

PURPOSE

To traverse new heights of consciousness through collaboration while taking time to appreciate the view.

RELATIONSHIPS

You are fiercely devoted to the people you care about most, and your relationships should be a place of spontaneity and travel. By seeking out partners who have an insatiable hunger for adventure, you will discover that true love purposefully breaks through comfort zones.

The Journey of
MAY 17

Welcome to May 17, a grounded journey toward personal authority.

Put your head down and do the work today. Despite the indulgent nature of Taurus season, *Discipline* (The Number Four) asks you to spend the hours and energy required to meet your long-term goals. There's no time like the present to make concrete progress on your plans, so why not get moving.

But be sure you have what you need to last the whole day. *Conservation* (Four of Pentacles) encourages you to create boundaries around your resources, neither overspending nor overprotecting what you have. Whether you take inventory of your finances or your physical energy levels, this is the time to get clear on where you need to extend or pull back.

To help you traverse this deliberate day, tap into the objective authority that lives within. *Self-mastery* (The Emperor) reminds you that you are the only leader you need, so make the difficult yet crucial decisions that will catapult you into a higher realm. Act in your own best interest, but don't rely on emotion. Instead, balance intuition with logic as you rule over your day with a lovingly discerning eye.

JUST FOR TODAY

TODAY'S MANTRA

I can be a loving yet discerning leader toward myself as I make decisions for the long term.

TODAY'S JOURNAL PROMPT

How can I remain objective in my decision-making when difficult emotions are at play?

TODAY'S RITUAL

Check in to see where you need to practice physical boundaries. Lie on your back, close your eyes, and mentally scan up and down your body. Where does it hurt? Where is it tired? Next, visualize a protective shield surrounding those parts of your body. Carry this image with you throughout the day.

BORN ON THIS DAY

EDWARD JENNER, English physician who pioneered the use of vaccinations and created the smallpox vaccine

COOL PAPA BELL, American Baseball Hall of Fame center fielder in Negro Leagues baseball

"Fame and success are very different things."—ENYA, Irish singer-songwriter

The Journey of Those Born on
MAY 17

Y ou were born of impenetrable power and an optimism that can make your goals unrealistic at times. You will have to find strength in restraint, as your journey is one of hard work, rest, and emotional fortitude.

Early on in your journey, you will meet your resolute guide, *Discipline* (The Number Four). Despite your abundant desires, *Discipline* calls you away from a life of excess and toward a path of sincere effort. You will meet *Discipline* in the long and arduous hours that will one day amount to a life beyond your wildest dreams. If you can place one foot in front of the other, you'll discover the gratification that comes from humility.

But if you choose this conscientious path, you will have to listen to the warnings of *Conservation* (Four of Pentacles). *Conservation* urges you not to drain your internal and external resources too quickly, preserving what will sustain you for the long haul. You will meet *Conservation* when you take inventory of what you need to carry you through, rationing out what you require while letting go of the scarcity that is holding you down.

By answering these grounded calls, you will step into the power of *Self-mastery* (The Emperor). *Self-mastery* asks you to be a judicial yet loving internal authority, inviting you to listen to the intrinsic voice that pushes you to make rational and careful decisions for your future. Rather than getting swept away by the unpredictability of emotion, *Self-mastery* encourages you to operate from a place of personal discernment. If you can choose long-term stability over short-term pleasure, you'll open yourself to eternal respect.

———————————————○———————————————

TAURUS
RULERS: VENUS, SATURN

PURPOSE
To humbly step into a position of self-leadership.

RELATIONSHIPS

You are expansive and bright, and your relationships should be a place of healthy boundaries and emotional safety. By seeking out partners who mean what they do and do what they mean, you will discover that the foundation of true love is mutual respect.

The Journey of
MAY 18

Welcome to May 18, a bold yet destabilizing journey that requires internal trust.
Reveal yourself to the world around you today. Whether you channel your truth into art, movement, or business, *Courage* (The Number Five) means stepping out on the ledge of vulnerability. Despite the humble nature of Taurus season, take center stage in your life and shine bright with the belief in yourself.

As you put yourself out there, watch out for *Scarcity* (Five of Pentacles). Don't get stuck in a lack mindset; be aware of when you are only seeing the worst in your situation. If you feel your needs are not being met on a physical or financial level, consciously look for the help that is available to you.

But don't give away your power too easily. *Wisdom* (The Hierophant) empowers you to think for yourself as you open to new information. If you meet a new teacher or study a new practice, humble yourself at the feet of this knowledge while tapping into the divine intelligence that lives within. Through internal trust, you can access the truth of today.

JUST FOR TODAY

TODAY'S MANTRA
I can balance humility with courage and knowledge with intuition.

TODAY'S RITUAL
To combat feelings of scarcity, give away something physical that you no longer need. Whether you donate old clothes or pass along your leftovers to someone in need, create abundance through action.

TODAY'S JOURNAL PROMPT
Do I consider myself an introvert or extrovert, and why?

BORN ON THIS DAY

REGGIE JACKSON, American Baseball Hall of Fame baseball player

MADELEINE PELLETIER, French psychiatrist, feminist, and activist who died in an asylum where she was sentenced for giving abortions to poor women

"Only by letting go can we truly possess what is real."—CHOW YUN-FAT, Hong Kong actor

The Journey of Those Born on
MAY 18

Y ou were born of earthly wisdom and sharp memory that can keep you stuck on the past. You will have to make friends with the unknown, as your journey is one of self-expression, perceived lack, and higher knowledge.

Early on in your journey, you will meet your wild guide, *Courage* (The Number Five). In spite of your humble nature, *Courage* calls you away from a life of guarded privacy and toward a path of creative brilliance. By bringing who you are and what you stand for into the physical world, you can inspire others to do the same. If you can choose tangible vulnerability over safety, *Courage* makes your life a work of art.

But if you choose this daring path, you will have to contend with your lower companion, *Scarcity* (Five of Pentacles). *Scarcity* highlight the voice of lack that lives within that believes you cannot have the life that you want without a cost. You will meet *Scarcity* in moments of spiritual shortage, when fear blinds you from the help that is available to you. If you can open your eyes to the abundance that surrounds you, *Scarcity* offers you an opportunity to heal.

By answering these brave calls, you will tap into *Wisdom* (The Hierophant). *Wisdom* invites you to rely on the anchor of intelligence that lives within, teaching you how to listen to others while discerning what is true for you versus true for them. You will meet *Wisdom* when you balance being the teacher and the student, trusting your intellectual authority above the critiques and beliefs of others. If you can listen deeply to yourself, *Wisdom* introduces you to the truth.

TAURUS
RULERS: VENUS, SATURN

PURPOSE
To courageously listen to the
abundant knowledge that lives within.

RELATIONSHIPS

You are intuitive and knowledgeable, and your relationships should be a place of fearless vulnerability and growth. By seeking out partners who push you to share your truth while asking to be heard in return, you will discover that true love is inherently courageous.

The Journey of
MAY 19

Welcome to May 19, an earnest journey that teaches you how to share and receive.
To lean in to the abundance of Taurus season, give from the heart today. Whether you lend a bit of money to a stranger in need or prepare a delicious meal for your overworked partner, *Devotion* (The Number Six) inspires meaningful action born from true compassion. There's no need for self-protection if your intentions are sincere, so put your soul on the line as you make the world a sweeter place.

And make special room for the people and projects that reciprocate your *Reciprocity* (Six of Pentacles). If you receive a wonderful gift from a friend or an unexpected raise at work, step into this well-deserved state of abundance. Once you are brimming with gratitude, be sure to pay your enthusiasm forward.

Because at the end of this day, love is a *Choice* (The Lovers). By carving out thoughtful time and effort for the life-giving connections you have, you'll remember that your happiness is contingent on the decisions you make. Be the loving partner, friend, colleague, and person you wish to be in the world, and watch as your cup overflows with emotional peace.

JUST FOR TODAY

TODAY'S MANTRA
If I want the universe to be generous with me, I must be generous in return.

TODAY'S JOURNAL PROMPT
When was the last time someone was truly generous with me?

TODAY'S RITUAL
Sit in a comfortable position and mentally scan your body, noticing the strength of your arms and the integrity of your back. Repeat aloud the question, "Body, how would you have me use your strength today?"

BORN ON THIS DAY

LORRAINE HANSBERRY, American playwright and first Black female author to have a play performed on Broadway

NANCY ASTOR, American-born English politician and first female MP in the British House of Commons

"We need more light about each other. Light creates understanding, understanding creates love, love creates patience, and patience creates unity."—**MALCOLM X**, American human rights activist and Muslim minister

The Journey of Those Born on
MAY 20*

You were born of intuitive balance and a deep awareness that can err on the side of judgmental. You will have to keep your focus on your side of the street, as your journey is one of intentionality, persistence, and determination.

Early on in your journey, you will meet your conscientious guide, *Commitment* (The Number Seven). Despite your seemingly easygoing personality, *Commitment* calls you away from complacency and toward a path of pure focus. By aligning your heart, mind, and body toward your meaningful responsibilities and commitments, your actions will always match your intentions.

But if you choose this formidable path, you will have to find patience. *Sustainability* (Seven of Pentacles) reminds you that anything too fast, too big, or too expensive is never reliable for the long haul, so it is best to invest in the daily humble work instead. You will meet *Sustainability* when you work diligently toward your long-term success, thoughtfully tending to your goals without rushing them to come to harvest.

By answering these calls for accountability, you will hit your stride with the power of *Evolution* (The Chariot). Evolution simply wants to see that you care, inspiring you to persevere through even the grittiest of circumstances and rewarding you with self-made progress. You will meet *Evolution* in moments of gradual self-realization, when the seemingly thankless hours you never thought could pay off suddenly blossom into tangible success. If you can work without expectation of return, you'll always move forward.

TAURUS
RULERS: VENUS, SATURN

PURPOSE
To humbly persevere while letting success unfold naturally with time.

RELATIONSHIPS

You are even-keeled and self-aware, and your relationships should be a place of hard work and commitment. By seeking out partners who are willing to grow together to sustain the long haul, you will discover that true love lasts if you are both willing to persevere.

Are you a Gemini born on this day? Head to page 759 to find your additional birthday guide!

WELCOME TO

The Journey of
MAY 21

Welcome to May 21, an introspective journey that introduces you to your intrinsic strength. To start Gemini season with a bang, step into your *Power* (The Number Eight) today. Access a place of deep authenticity as you pursue your ambitions with personal confidence and uncompromising truth. You will discover the influence that you can wield if you are brave enough to take up honest space in the world.

But as you expand, don't be surprised if *Negativity* (Eight of Swords) rears its fearful head. Rather than surrendering to the self-deprecating voices that lie within, combat them with a positive sense of courage. The only thing that can restrict you today is your mind, so let it be a tool for empowerment rather than limitation.

And know there is nothing you can't handle, as *Resilience* (Strength) reminds you of your emotional fortitude. If you feel overwhelmed or unsure of yourself at any point, slow down and look within to find the spiritual strength you need to persevere. You have been through a lot, so rather than getting swept away by the unpredictability of feeling, tap into the solid foundation of emotional toughness you have built over time.

JUST FOR TODAY

TODAY'S MANTRA
Through personal strength and positive thinking, I can handle anything.

TODAY'S JOURNAL PROMPT
What mean and limiting negative thoughts tend to dominate my head?

TODAY'S RITUAL
Lie facedown on your bed. Visualize the negative thoughts you have in your head as daggers in your back. Imagine your higher self gently pulling them out of you one by one. When you are finished, turn onto your back. Take in a deep breath, and exhale with relief.

BORN ON THIS DAY

ANDREI SAKHAROV, Russian nuclear physicist and activist

THE NOTORIOUS B.I.G., aka Biggie Smalls, American rapper and songwriter

"Do not fear truth, let it be ever so contrary to inclination and feeling. Never give up the search after it; and let me take courage, and try from the bottom of my heart to do that which I believe truth dictates."—ELIZABETH FRY, English prison and social reformer and Quaker minister

The Journey of Those Born on
MAY 21

You were born of sharp wit and a wanderlust that can make it hard to look inward. You will have to heal in order to access your intrinsic strength, as your journey is one of self-acceptance, restriction, and emotional fortitude.

Early on in your journey, you will meet your enigmatic guide, *Power* (The Number Eight). Despite your flexible mind, *Power* calls you away from a life of uncertainty and toward a path of authentic force. By doing the inventory required to remain deeply self-aware, you can pursue the worldly ambitions you desire most without getting swept away by ego.

But if you choose this introspective path, you will have to confront your lower companion, *Negativity* (Eight of Swords). You will meet *Negativity* in moments of self-imposed restriction, when your poor self-image keeps you from pursuing the things you desire most. If you can bring these voices into the light of day, you'll discover these harmful beliefs are old protective coping mechanisms that you can now let go.

YOUR GUIDES

Astrology: Your Energy
Gemini (Mercury)

Numerology: Your Path
Power (The Number Eight)

Minor Arcana: Your Lesson
Negativity (The Eight of Swords)

Major Arcana: Your Highest Calling
Resilience (Strength)

By answering these calls for self-awareness, you will come to understand the importance of *Resilience* (Strength). *Resilience* holds up a mirror to the spiritual grit that underpins your personal strength, gracefully carrying you through even the worst of circumstances. You will meet *Resilience* in moments of staying power, when you preserve rather than letting your feelings get the best of you. If you can remember how strong you are, *Resilience* offers you the gift of emotional stamina.

GEMINI
RULER: MERCURY

PURPOSE
To realize that authentic power comes from internal strength.

RELATIONSHIPS

You are curious and excitable, and your relationships should be a place of emotional honesty and authenticity. By seeking partners who accept you for your worst and your best, you will discover that true love is strong enough to withstand the truth.

The Journey of
MAY 22

Welcome to May 22, an adventurous journey that requires self-trust.
Explore the unknown today. Despite the mercurial nature of Gemini season, *Experience* (The Number Nine) asks you to get out of your head and into the present moment, hurling yourself into new and uncomfortable situations that can help widen your perspective. If you get invited to study a new subject or meet a new person, say an enthusiastic "yes."

But as you try new things, watch out for *Anxiety* (Nine of Swords). The brain is a tricky thing that can either be used as a helpful tool or a fearsome weapon, so be mindful of the latter. What fearful visions of the future are blocking you from freely exploring? Bring this angst into the light by calling a friend or writing it down on paper.

And after you are able to clear away those fears, tap into *Instinct* (The Hermit). If you are feeling lost or uncertain at any point, spend some time on your own so you can tap into the divine wisdom that lives within. More than likely, all the answers you need are right in front of you, as long as you trust yourself.

JUST FOR TODAY

TODAY'S MANTRA
I won't let fear block me from instinctually exploring new things.

TODAY'S JOURNAL PROMPT
What area of my life holds the most anxiety for me at the moment, and why?

TODAY'S RITUAL
Surrender your negativity. Take a seated position, and with your index and middle finger, tap the palm of your nondominant hand as you repeat the mantra, "Just because I have negative thoughts, does not mean I have to believe them."

BORN ON THIS DAY

BETTY WILLIAMS, Irish peace activist

HERGÉ, Belgian cartoonist and comic book creator

"Hope will never be silent."—HARVEY MILK, American politician and gay activist

The Journey of Those Born on
MAY 22

Y ou were born of mental strength and a need for control that can keep you from growing. You will have to continue in your search for understanding, as your journey is one of seeking, fear, and internal knowledge.

Early on in your journey, you will meet your daring guide, *Experience* (The Number Nine). Despite your innate intelligence, *Experience* calls you away from a life of expertise and toward a path of deep questioning. You will meet *Experience* in the great unknown, when you leave your comfort zone in search of a wider perspective. If you can choose possibility over limitation, you'll open yourself to the wisdom of adventure.

But if you choose this uncharted path, you will have to contend with *Anxiety* (Nine of Swords). *Anxiety* highlights the voice of fear that lives within, telling you unfounded stories of what might happen in the future. If you can remember that these terrifying dreams are simply a figment of your imagination, you'll begin to address the unhealed dread that is buried within your subconscious.

> ## YOUR GUIDES
>
> *Astrology: Your Energy*
> Gemini (Mercury)
>
> *Numerology: Your Path*
> Experience (The Number Nine)
>
> *Minor Arcana: Your Lesson*
> Anxiety (The Nine of Swords)
>
> *Major Arcana: Your Highest Calling*
> Instinct (The Hermit)

By answering these brave calls, you will access the power of *Instinct* (The Hermit). You will meet *Instinct* when you are seemingly lost and forced to soul-search in order to make the next right step into the unknown. It is through self-trust, rather than logic, that you can guide yourself through the murkiest of transitions. If you can listen deeply to yourself when you are the most alone, you'll open yourself to self-discovery.

GEMINI
RULER: MERCURY

PURPOSE
To explore the unknown, guided by divine intuition rather than fear.

RELATIONSHIPS

You are knowledgeable and wise, and your relationships should be a place of searching and understanding. By seeking out partners who push you out of your comfort zone and into the unknown, you will discover that true love always asks you to grow.

The Journey of
MAY 23

Welcome to May 23, an independent mental journey that is anything but predictable. Carve out your own path today. *Autonomy* (The Number One) encourages you to think for yourself as you pursue the untapped potential of your intellect. There's no need to tell others what you are up to because they may not understand, so rely on your own wit and sensibility as you explore new realms of innovation.

The good news is, *Clarity* (Ace of Swords) has you brimming with new and exciting ideas. To coincide with the mental sharpness of Gemini season, let your mind wander as it cooks up your next brilliant plan. Get out a notepad or open a document on your computer and be sure to get down all these thoughts for future use.

But don't get too fixated on outcomes today. *Impermanence* (Wheel of Fortune) reminds you that life is in a constant state of change, so adapt to whatever circumstances are thrown your way. If you are on a mental high, ride the wave as far as it'll take you. But if you hit a low at any point, make peace with what you can't control while remaining optimistic about what is to come.

―――――――――○―――――――――

JUST FOR TODAY

TODAY'S MANTRA
I will run with my ideas as far as they'll take me.

TODAY'S JOURNAL PROMPT
What does my relationship with my imagination look like?

TODAY'S RITUAL
Clear your mind with peppermint. Pour yourself a piping hot cup of peppermint tea, or dab peppermint oil on your hand, and deeply inhale the aroma as you repeat the prayer, "Peppermint, please clear from me the mental fog that blocks ideas coming through me."

―――――――――○―――――――――

BORN ON THIS DAY

AILEEN HERNANDEZ, American union organizer, civil rights activist, and women's rights activist

CAROL LINNAEUS, Swedish botanist and explorer known as the "father of modern taxonomy"

"Love bravely, live bravely, be courageous; there's really nothing to lose."—JEWEL, American Grammy Award–winning singer-songwriter

The Journey of Those Born on
MAY 23

You were born of fierce intelligence and a relentless need to be taken seriously. You will have to be willing to risk failure, as your journey is one of innovation, purity, and the turning tides of fate.

Early on in your journey, you will meet your formidable guide, *Autonomy* (The Number One). Rather than caring what others may think of you, move toward a path of intuitive vision. You will meet *Autonomy* as you fearlessly traverse uncharted territory, carving out new roads to travel with no one to thank but yourself. If you can follow the beat of your own drum, you'll stay on the cutting edge.

And if you choose this daring path, you will meet your incisive friend *Clarity* (Ace of Swords). *Clarity* comes to you in the sparkling purity of new ideas, when the sheer potential of what you envision is enough to get you started. By listening to these acts of divine mental intervention, you can discover new heights of mercurial progress.

> ### YOUR GUIDES
>
> *Astrology: Your Energy*
> Gemini (Mercury)
>
> *Numerology: Your Path*
> Autonomy (The Number One)
>
> *Minor Arcana: Your Lesson*
> Clarity (The Ace of Swords)
>
> *Major Arcana: Your Highest Calling*
> Impermanence (The Wheel of Fortune)

By answering these bold calls, you will have to learn to roll with the tides. *Impermanence* (Wheel of Fortune) reminds you that the highs are just as fleeting as the lows, so you might as well make the most of your present circumstances. You will meet *Impermanence* when you surrender to destiny, trusting that the roller coaster of life is guiding you to where you are meant to go. If you can lean in, you'll learn how to enjoy the ride.

GEMINI
RULER: MERCURY

PURPOSE
To embrace the mental roller coaster of innovation.

RELATIONSHIPS

You are brave and wholehearted, and your relationships should be a place of independence and mental breakthroughs. By seeking out partners who think for themselves and ignite new ideas within you, you will discover that true love is always stimulating.

The Journey of
MAY 24

Welcome to May 24, a middle road toward personal clarity.

Despite the mental stimulation of Gemini season, *Balance* (The Number Two) asks you to live in the gray area today. Instead of jumping to conclusions or taking things to extremes, aim for compromise with the people and ideas you come up against. Take the easier, softer way.

But don't get stuck in *Doubt* (Two of Swords). Be mindful of the impassivity that can come from internal confusion and try not to let your thoughts get the best of you. If there seems like no perfect solution to a problem, look for a simple answer. More than likely, it's right in front of you.

And if you can reach a place of internal peace, you can access the *Truth* (Justice). There are no clear-cut answers to life's greatest dilemmas, so reach inside yourself as you decipher your moral compass today. By clarifying what is fair and reasonable to you, you can act in alignment with this belief system and stand up for what you care about most without being dogmatic. Justice hangs in the balance today, so get comfortable in this state of flexibility.

JUST FOR TODAY

TODAY'S MANTRA
I will reach for inner peace so I can fight fairly for justice.

TODAY'S JOURNAL PROMPT
How do I tend to address important decision-making?

TODAY'S RITUAL
Build inner trust by making a small but intentional decision to start your day, whether it be choosing what you are having for breakfast or intuitively choosing your route to work. Trust your gut, and don't overthink it.

BORN ON THIS DAY

DANIEL GABRIEL FAHRENHEIT, Polish Dutch physicist, inventor, and scientific instrument maker, who invented the thermometer and Fahrenheit scale

MARIE GOEGG-POUCHOULIN, Swiss pioneer in the women's rights and women's peace movements

"May you always know the truth and see the lights surrounding you."—**BOB DYLAN**, American singer-songwriter

The Journey of Those Born on
MAY 24

You were born of humble intelligence and a need for acceptance that can quiet your truth. You will have to find your voice within justice, as your journey is one of partnership, uncertainty, and equality.

Early on in your journey, you will meet your tranquil guide, *Balance* (The Number Two). Despite your active mind, avoid overthinking and move toward a path of harmonic coexistence with your partners, friends, and colleagues. You will meet *Balance* in moments of intellectual understanding, when you meet others halfway and grow to a place of mutual understanding.

But if you walk this gentle path, you will have to contend with *Doubt* (Two of Swords). You will meet *Doubt* in the crippling voice of uncertainty that lives within, making it difficult to come to any decision. By realizing that the simplest answer is always the best answer, *Doubt* asks you to act from a place of internal peace.

By answering these calls for the middle road, you will step into the light of *Truth* (Justice). *Truth* asks you to tap into the moral compass that lives inside, helping you balance what you believe to be right and wrong in the world around you. You will meet *Truth* in moments of the clarity of your convictions, when you align your actions with your belief system and fight for fairness and equality. If you can practice what you preach, you'll be empowered to pursue justice.

GEMINI
RULER: MERCURY

PURPOSE
To fight for justice from a state of internal harmony and mental balance.

RELATIONSHIPS

You are generous and affectionate with your words, and your relationships should be a place of equality and reciprocity. By seeking out partners who are good listeners and aim to understand and be understood, you will discover that true love always tries to be fair.

The Journey of
MAY 25

Welcome to May 25, an abundant journey that requires an open mind.

Stay available to the opinions and perspectives of others. To complement the mercurial nature of Gemini season, *Flexibility* (The Number Three) invites you to take in new information and be a humble student rather than an expert. Who can you learn from today? Listen and receive, and see where the day takes you.

But watch out for misinterpreting the words of others. *Trigger* (Three of Swords) warns against taking things too personally, so bring self-awareness to the emotional reactions that might come up today. While others are responsible for their actions, you are accountable to your emotions, so go inward to heal these ancient wounds rather than lashing out.

If you can clear your side of the street, you will make room for *Abundance* (The Empress). Many gifts are around you, if only you can take notice of the joys and connections that are filling your cup. By expressing gratitude and appreciation for the wonders of the natural world as well as your community, you can leave today with a profound sense of spiritual contentment.

JUST FOR TODAY

TODAY'S MANTRA

I will keep an open mind and make room for personal abundance.

TODAY'S RITUAL

Meditate on the topic of belonging. Close your eyes and think about your earliest memories of trying to fit in. How did you feel in your skin when you were learning to engage socially? Send love to your inner child as you go about your day.

TODAY'S JOURNAL PROMPT

What are three things that are filling my emotional cup right now?

BORN ON THIS DAY

ALICE HERZ, German peace activist and the first person in the US known to have immolated herself in protest of the Vietnam War

RALPH WALDO EMERSON, American essayist and philosopher

"Be transparent as wind . . . be what moves things forward without needing to leave a mark, be part of this collection of molecules that begins somewhere unknown and can't help but keep rising."—v, aka Eve Ensler, American playwright, performer, feminist, and activist

The Journey of Those Born on
MAY 25

You were born of mental conviction and a desire for certainty that can block you from absorbing new information. You will have to remain open to the abundance around you, as your journey is one of curiosity, temporary pain, and spiritual bounty.

Early on in your journey, you will meet your inquisitive guide, *Flexibility* (The Number Three). Although you are certain about many things, you don't need to be an expert, so move toward a path of humble questioning instead. You will meet *Flexibility* in the opinions and perspective of others when you remain open-minded enough to take in new and diverse information.

But if you choose this social path, you will have to contend with *Trigger* (Three of Swords). You will meet *Trigger* in the words that sting, when a flippant comment goes straight into an unhealed wound. If you can look within and realize that your reaction is born from historical pain rather than present harm, you'll open yourself to greater emotional maturity.

By answering these calls for connection, you will step into the light of *Abundance* (The Empress). Enjoy the present moment with the people you love rather than getting lost in your overactive imagination. You will meet *Abundance* in the spiritual beauty in life, when your breath is taken away by the joy of a friendly smile or a blossoming flower. If you can look for the good, you'll tap into a greater sense of spiritual wealth.

YOUR GUIDES

Astrology: Your Energy
Gemini (Mercury)

Numerology: Your Path
Flexibility (The Number Three)

Minor Arcana: Your Lesson
Trigger (The Three of Swords)

Major Arcana: Your Highest Calling
Abundance (The Empress)

GEMINI
RULER: MERCURY

PURPOSE
To stay open to the mental healing and abundance that comes from connection.

RELATIONSHIPS

You are serious about most things in life, yet your relationships should be a place of playful wonder and joy. By seeking out partners who make you laugh and keep your world forever interesting, you will discover that true love exists in the present moment.

The Journey of
MAY 26

Welcome to May 26, a journey of mental fortitude that doesn't care for excuses.

Follow through on your intellectual responsibilities for the day. Despite the mutable nature of Gemini season, *Discipline* (The Number Four) calls you back down to earth and places your feet firmly in the work at hand. If you have been procrastinating on some tasks, now is the time to execute.

But if you feel depleted at any point, don't run on empty. *Restoration* (Four of Swords) encourages you to pause between efforts, checking in to make sure your brain is being used wisely. Take a break by meditating or going for a walk, giving your mind the space it needs to reset. If there are strategic ways you can streamline your day, seize the opportunity to narrow your focus.

As you follow through on your ambitions, remember that you are in charge of yourself. Even when fleeting emotions arise, *Self-mastery* (The Emperor) empowers you to remain objective and act from a place of logic rather than feeling. Step into a place of leadership as you make thoughtful decisions that take into consideration your long-term mental health and well-being.

―――――――――――――○―――――――――――――

JUST FOR TODAY

TODAY'S MANTRA

I will keep an objective eye on the mental work I have at hand today.

TODAY'S JOURNAL PROMPT

What are four tangible ways I can take a break today?

TODAY'S RITUAL

Create a homelike environment in your mind. Visualize the most comforting, safe space for your mind to go to when the day feels overwhelming. Are there cushions, pillows, animals, or rainbows? Dream up a place of serenity and go there whenever you need rest today.

―――――――――――――○―――――――――――――

BORN ON THIS DAY

MILES DAVIS, American jazz musician, trumpeter, and composer

SALLY RIDE, American astronaut and first American woman to go to space

"I always wanted to be a motivator of positive change."—LAURYN HILL, American singer-songwriter, rapper, record producer, and actor

The Journey of Those Born on
MAY 26

You were born of vast intelligence and a depth that can keep you trapped in morbid reflection. You will have to use your brain wisely, as your journey is one of hard work, necessary pause, and self-restraint.

Early on in your journey, you will meet your demanding guide, *Discipline* (The Number Four). Despite your powerful disposition, *Discipline* calls you away from overconfidence and toward a path of sincere effort. You will meet *Discipline* in the long hours of arduous mental work that will one day amount to unparalleled success. If you can choose diligence over cockiness, you'll experience the satisfaction of self-respect.

But if you embrace this humble path, you will have to pause for *Restoration* (Four of Swords). Before finding your next intellectual mountain to climb, you must stop and recharge, reflecting on the previous work you have done. You will meet *Restoration* amidst much-needed time off, when you give your mind the room and space to take a bird's-eye view as you prepare for your next challenge.

By answering these earnest calls, you will harness the power of *Self-mastery* (The Emperor). *Self-mastery* introduces you to the calm, pragmatic authority within that allows you to make thoughtful decisions that benefit you and others in the long run. Rather than getting lost in paranoia or overthinking, *Self-mastery* encourages you to remain objective in your thinking as you act from a place of integrity. If you can aim for reason over emotion, you'll become a thought leader for others.

———————————○———————————

GEMINI
RULER: MERCURY

PURPOSE
*To harness the power of
mental fortitude.*

RELATIONSHIPS

Your emotional resilience knows no limits, yet your relationships should be a place of grounding and rest. By seeking out partners you can lean on and who encourage you to take care of yourself amidst your ambitions, you will discover that true love always considers the long run.

The Journey of
MAY 27

Welcome to May 27, an intellectually stimulating journey that requires authenticity.
Speak your mind today. To harness the mental powers of Gemini season, *Courage* (The Number Five) invites you to share your knowledge and perspective with the world around you. Whether you take to social media or speak up at work, now is the time to find your voice. Say it loud and say it proud.

But prepare for the inevitable opposition that comes from sharing your truth. *Maturity* (Five of Swords) warns against internal defensiveness, instead encouraging you to accept others' opinions without having to be right. Aim for mutual understanding by looking for the ounce of truth that may live in these opposing perspectives and embrace the growth that comes from challenging your own point of view.

Besides, no one has a monopoly on truth. *Wisdom* (The Hierophant) asks you to walk the fine line between teacher and student today, neither shoving your ideas down people's throats nor surrendering your power to popular opinion. By listening to your gut as you separate the true from the false, you'll find a place of intellectual confidence that no one can penetrate.

○

JUST FOR TODAY

TODAY'S MANTRA
I will confidently share my truth while allowing others to have their own perspective, too.

TODAY'S JOURNAL PROMPT
How do I typically react to criticism or opposing opinions?

TODAY'S RITUAL
If you find yourself getting worked up or defensive, spend five minutes sipping chamomile tea and focusing on calming your mind. Repeat the mantra, "I will practice restraint of pen and tongue."

○

BORN ON THIS DAY

AMELIA BLOOMER, American women's rights and temperance advocate

IBN KHALDŪN, North African Islamic scholar, philosopher, and historian

"Knowing what I do, there would be no future peace for me if I kept silent."—RACHEL CARSON, American marine biologist, conservationist, and writer

The Journey of Those Born on
MAY 27

You were born of worldly intellect and a deep humility that can keep you from speaking your mind. You will have to find your voice, as your journey is one of self-expression, understanding, and higher consciousness.

Early on in your journey, you will meet your daring guide, *Courage* (The Number Five). Despite your humble wisdom, *Courage* calls you away from a life of isolation and toward a path of mental confidence. By grabbing life's metaphorical microphone and saying what you think, *Courage* pushes you to be part of the larger social conversation.

But if you choose this public path, you will have to answer the calls of *Maturity* (Five of Swords). You will meet *Maturity* in the face of verbal opposition, when your words are twisted and contorted to fit the views of the contradicting side. Instead of giving in to these petty acts of aggression, take the high road by believing in yourself. If you can make peace with your naysayers without overexplaining your side, you'll find mental freedom.

By embracing these calls for vulnerability, you will access *Wisdom* (The Hierophant). The truth can be subjective, so think for yourself and remain available to the perspectives and knowledge that live outside you. You will meet *Wisdom* when you practice mental discernment and step into a place of intellectual authority. If you can listen to your gut while remaining teachable, you'll discover the most important answers lie within.

GEMINI
RULER: MERCURY

PURPOSE
To find intellectual bravery born from
a place of internal wisdom.

RELATIONSHIPS

You thrive in mental isolation, yet your relationships should be a place of honest expression and vulnerability. By seeking out partners who aren't afraid to speak their truth and encourage you to do the same, you will discover that true love never asks you to hide.

The Journey of
MAY 28

W elcome to May 28, a compassionate journey toward true intimacy.
Use your words for good today. While Gemini season has your mind moving a million miles per minute, *Devotion* (The Number Six) invites you to aim your mental power toward matters of the heart. Send words of appreciation to someone you love, making their day just a little bit sweeter.

But be willing to receive support in return. You may be letting go of an old mental pattern today, and *Transition* (Six of Swords) encourages you to lean on the friends and partners who get how your brain works the best. It is scary to surrender the cages of the mind that used to make you feel safe, so offer compassion toward yourself because you'll need extra reassurance and encouragement today.

At the end of the day, disconnection and connection are both a *Choice* (The Lovers). Make a special effort to prioritize the relationships that feed your soul by participating in the natural exchange of support that intimacy requires. There is no room for pride, so surrender your fears of rejection as you open your heart and mind to the generosity of those you care about most.

JUST FOR TODAY

TODAY'S MANTRA
I will share and receive the words of affirmation I need most.

TODAY'S JOURNAL PROMPT
What mental patterns or ways of thinking am I ready to surrender today? Who can I call upon for support in this?

TODAY'S RITUAL
Confide in someone you love today. Call or invite this person of trust to lunch and ask them to simply hold space as you share your truth about a transition you are going through, whether it be personal, mental, or professional.

BORN ON THIS DAY

T-BONE WALKER, American blues guitarist

KYLIE MINOGUE, Australian pop singer-songwriter

"I wish you power that equals your intelligence and your strength. I wish you success that equals your talent and determination. And I wish you faith."—**BETTY SHABAZZ**, American educator and civil rights activist

The Journey of Those Born on
MAY 28

You were born of intuitive confidence and an impulsive mind that can get you into trouble. You will have to align your head with your heart, as your journey is one of thoughtful service, letting go, and emotional surrender.

Early on in your journey, you will meet your tender guide, *Devotion* (The Number Six). Despite your detached and independent nature, move away from self-serving tendencies, and instead head toward a path of meaningful expression. You will meet *Devotion* when you communicate your innermost generosity to the people and projects you love, earnestly sharing words of affection to make the world just a bit sweeter.

But if you choose this openhearted path, you will have to call upon support during times of *Transition* (Six of Swords). You will meet *Transition* in moments of letting go, when you are ready to release a destructive and outdated mental pattern but are fearful of what life would feel like without it. By reaching out for a helping hand from those you care about most, you'll reach your destination with gentle compassion.

By answering these meaningful calls, you will discover that connection is a *Choice* (The Lovers). By playing an active part in creating and building the emotional relationships you desire most, you can be vulnerable as you fall into the arms of true intimacy. If you can let the words of truth flow from your heart to the hearts of others, you'll tap into the gifts of shared empathy.

GEMINI
RULER: MERCURY

PURPOSE
To use the power of the mind for love, release, and understanding.

RELATIONSHIPS

You are independent even to a fault, yet your relationships should be a place of sweet devotion and compassionate communication. By seeking out partners who are as earnest with their words as they are with their actions, you will discover that true love is a safe place to surrender your heart.

The Journey of
MAY 29

Welcome to May 29, a mentally progressive journey that requires focus.

Pour your attention into the intellectual and interpersonal responsibilities that matter most to you today. Despite the scatterbrained nature of Gemini season, *Commitment* (The Number Seven) asks you to remain focused as you show your loyalty and devotion through action. Keep to your word and make a difference by showing up with complete presence of mind.

But watch out for paranoia. *Hypervigilance* (Seven of Swords) warns against unnecessary self-protective measures, so try to remain aware of how fear is blocking you from trusting others. If you find yourself plotting to attack your perceived enemies to avoid getting hurt first, slow down and surrender to the peace that exists in the present moment. More than likely, your mind is getting the best of you.

Letting go of this emotional defensiveness will allow you to make much faster progress anyhow. *Evolution* (The Chariot) ensures you can grow to new heights of consciousness, as long as you put your sincerest of mental efforts forward. If a grand yet intimidating invitation to learn comes your way, rise to this occasion, leaning on your power of mental fortitude to soar.

———————————————◯———————————————

JUST FOR TODAY

TODAY'S MANTRA
I will commit to my mental progress without getting sidetracked by paranoia and fear.

TODAY'S JOURNAL PROMPT
Do I often distrust the intentions of others when they try to support me? If so, why?

TODAY'S RITUAL
Let down your physical guard. Throughout the day, try to notice whenever you feel your shoulders getting tense, your hands bunching into fists, or your jaw clenching. Take a deep breath as you consciously release this tension from your body.

———————————————◯———————————————

BORN ON THIS DAY

TENZING NORGAY, Tibetan mountaineer and one of the first climbers to reach the summit of Mount Everest

JOHN F. KENNEDY, senator and thirty-fifth president of the United States

"I believe if we have something that we love to do, that can save our lives. That can get us through."—LAVERNE COX, American actor and LGBTQ+ advocate

The Journey of Those Born on
MAY 29

You were born of internal balance and a diplomacy that can make it difficult to know where you stand on any one issue. You will have to learn to fight for what you believe in most, as your journey is one of sincerity, surrender, and divine progress.

Early on in your journey, you will meet your serious guide, *Commitment* (The Number Seven). Despite your even-keeled nature, *Commitment* calls you away from a life of ambiguity and toward a path of clear direction. By harnessing your mental energy toward the people and projects that call your soul, rather than scattering your focus, you'll discover the gifts of intentionality.

But if you take this discerning path, you will have to contend with *Hypervigilance* (Seven of Swords). You will meet *Hypervigilance* in situations that cause the hair on the back of your neck to stand up, when you feel your safety is being threatened, placing you into a state of intense self-protection. If you can recognize this reaction as an outdated coping mechanism from a time in your life when you had no choice but to be on guard, you'll discover a greater mental peace.

> ## YOUR GUIDES
>
> *Astrology: Your Energy*
> Gemini (Mercury)
>
> *Numerology: Your Path*
> Commitment (The Number Seven)
>
> *Minor Arcana: Your Lesson*
> Hypervigilance (The Seven of Swords)
>
> *Major Arcana: Your Highest Calling*
> Evolution (The Chariot)

By answering these calls for strength, *Evolution* (The Chariot) ensures you will make mental leaps and bounds. You will meet *Evolution* in the momentum of internal progress, when you are willing to leave old beliefs in the dust as you blaze toward higher realms of consciousness. If you can keep your mind moving forward into expansion no matter what, you'll experience radical advancement.

GEMINI
RULER: MERCURY

PURPOSE
*To focus on purpose
rather than fear.*

RELATIONSHIPS

You are a naturally harmonious partner, and your relationships should be a place of straightforwardness and progress. By seeking out partners who aim for growth over complacency, you will discover that true love has limitless potential.

The Journey of
MAY 30

Welcome to May 30, a mentally testing day that introduces you to your strength.
Step into your intellectual *Power* (The Number Eight). Rather than making your ideas smaller to avoid intimidating others, speak from a place of humble truth as you learn to take up space in the world around you. As long as your words are real, you can expand into great success today.

But be prepared for some internal backlash as you grow into this abundance. Gemini season speeds up the mind, but *Negativity* (Eight of Swords) asks you to be mindful of the cruel voices in your head that keep you in a state of victimhood. Spend some time today tending to these self-protective coping mechanisms, bringing compassion to them while acknowledging how harmful they are to your growth.

And if you feel overwhelmed, remember how much you have been through. *Resilience* (Strength) asks you to rely on your mental fortitude rather than giving into the whims of feeling. By employing these emotional muscles to carry you through the highs as well as the lows, you can channel your fear, grief, or frustration into your future progress. You can handle anything, so keep your eye on the prize.

JUST FOR TODAY

TODAY'S MANTRA
By releasing old fear and shame, I can grow into my authentic power.

TODAY'S JOURNAL PROMPT
What in my life am I most afraid of growing toward right now?

TODAY'S RITUAL
Expel all the negative thoughts in your head by writing them down on a piece of paper. Read them back to yourself out loud, crossing out the ones that feel less true as you bring them into the daylight. If any remain, repeat the mantra, "Let me see the positive in this negative."

BORN ON THIS DAY

YOONA, South Korean singer and actor

BRIAN KOBILKA, American Nobel Prize–winning chemistry professor

"You can't get it all right all the time, but you can try your best. If you've done that, all that's left is to accept your shortcomings and have the courage to try to overcome them."—IDINA MENZEL, American actor and singer

The Journey of Those Born on
MAY 30

You were born of mental flexibility and an expansive intelligence that makes it easier to analyze your emotions rather than to feel them. You will have to get to know all the complexity of your internal world, as your journey is one of authenticity, perspective-shifting, and emotional fortitude.

Early on in your journey, you will meet your mysterious guide, *Power* (The Number Eight). Despite your humble curiosity, *Power* calls you away from uncertainty and toward a path of sincere self-confidence. By remaining authentic and self-aware no matter how much you succeed in your worldly desires, *Power* reminds you that as long as it's true, expansion is yours for the taking.

But if you choose this abundant path, you will have to contend with *Negativity* (Eight of Swords). You will meet *Negativity* in mental self-harm, when you speak to yourself in a manner that you would never dream of speaking to another. When did you learn to protect yourself from expansion? If you can heal the wounds that block you from enjoying your growth, you'll discover a crucial shift in perspective.

> ## YOUR GUIDES
>
> *Astrology: Your Energy*
> Gemini (Mercury)
>
> *Numerology: Your Path*
> Power (The Number Eight)
>
> *Minor Arcana: Your Lesson*
> Negativity (The Eight of Swords)
>
> *Major Arcana: Your Highest Calling*
> Resilience (Strength)

And if you answer these deep calls, you will come to understand your *Resilience* (Strength). *Resilience* lies in the emotional muscles that you have strengthened during times of great strife and hardship. You will meet *Resilience* in moments of perseverance, when you harness tough emotions and channel them into your next greatest triumphant victory. If you can reach within, you can handle anything.

GEMINI
RULER: MERCURY

PURPOSE
To quiet the negative voices within in order to hear your true authentic power.

RELATIONSHIPS

You are flexible and inquisitive, and your relationships should be a place of vulnerability that brings real intimacy. By seeking out partners who champion your authentic power, you will discover that true love is born of truth.

The Journey of
MAY 31

Welcome to May 31, an intellectually expansive journey that requires intuition.

Go to the places that scare you today. *Experience* (The Number Nine) invites you to make friends with the unknown, so embrace every opportunity to step outside your comfort zone. Whether you explore a foreign subject or try your hand at an intimidating project, now is the time to learn by doing.

But don't be surprised if some fear pops up along the way. Gemini season always gets the mind racing, but *Anxiety* (Nine of Swords) warns against unnecessary future-tripping. If you find yourself fixating on the worst-case scenario at some point today, take a deep breath and try to find peace in the present moment. More than likely, these frightening visions are simply a self-protective coping mechanism rather than a potential reality.

Within that space of clarity, you can tap into *Instinct* (The Hermit). Trust your gut throughout today, balancing your mental awareness with internal wisdom. Where is your intuition telling you to go? Only you know what the next right action is, so consult your divine compass of intelligence as you move in the direction of instinctual purpose.

JUST FOR TODAY

TODAY'S MANTRA

I can explore new heights of consciousness by following my intuitive compass.

TODAY'S JOURNAL PROMPT

What does my relationship with fear look like historically and presently?

TODAY'S RITUAL

Create a space that calms your anxiety. Put on some meditative music, shut off all your distracting electronic devices, and turn off all artificial lights. Lie in this space with your hand over your heart for as long as you need to feel more relaxed.

BORN ON THIS DAY

IRMA SCHWAGER, Austrian anti-fascist resistance fighter and politician

BROOKE SHIELDS, American model and actor

"Re-examine all that you have been told . . . dismiss that which insults your soul."—WALT WHITMAN, American poet and volunteer nurse during the Civil War

The Journey of Those Born on
MAY 31

You were born of grounded intellect and a mental restraint that can make it hard to get to know your intuition. You will have to explore deeper realms of consciousness, as your journey is one of knowledge, psychological clearing, and divine intuition.

Early on in your journey, you will meet your sage guide, *Experience* (The Number Nine). Although we all desire control, *Experience* calls you away from a life of rigidity and toward a path of wild searching. You will meet *Experience* in the foreign, when you leap out of your comfort zone in pursuit of mental expansion. If you can aim for growth over certainty, you'll have the intellectual ride of a lifetime.

But if you choose this brave path, you will have to contend with *Anxiety* (Nine of Swords). Exploring uncharted territory can be destabilizing, but look at the subconscious fear that blocks you from true expansion. By going inward to unburden the parts of you that are terrified of the unknown, you can free yourself from old mental cages.

By answering these fear-reaching calls, you will have to rely on *Instinct* (The Hermit). *Instinct* invites you to listen to the voice of intuitive intelligence that lives within, guiding you through the passages in life that feel the most uncertain. You will meet *Instinct* in uncharted territory, when you have no map to reference and are forced to rely on your gut. If you can trust your divine internal genius, you'll discover your highest purpose.

YOUR GUIDES

Astrology: Your Energy
Gemini (Mercury, Venus)

Numerology: Your Path
Experience (The Number Nine)

Minor Arcana: Your Lesson
Anxiety (The Nine of Swords)

Major Arcana: Your Highest Calling
Instinct (The Hermit)

―――――――――――○―――――――――――

GEMINI
RULERS: MERCURY, VENUS

PURPOSE
*To find self-trust and release old fear
by exploring the unknown.*

RELATIONSHIPS

You are confident and a natural authority, and your relationships should be a place of mental expansion. By seeking out partners whose diverse life experience forces you out of your comfort zone, you will discover that true love always asks you to grow.

The Journey of
JUNE 1

Welcome to June 1, a progressive journey that requires mental discernment.

Stick to your word. Despite the airiness of Gemini season, *Commitment* (The Number Seven) encourages you to show your loyalty through action. Whether you show up for professional or personal responsibilities, narrow your focus so you can bring your complete attention to the tasks at hand.

But as you put your best foot forward, watch out for *Hypervigilance* (Seven of Swords). Be mindful of the ways in which you distrust others and try to preemptively protect yourself against betrayal. If you find your mind racing away with imagined thoughts of getting hurt, call a logical friend who can help you get regrounded into the present moment.

The good news is, *Evolution* (The Chariot) asks you to look toward the future rather than over your shoulder. Get serious about where you are going, setting your sights on meaningful goals that align with your most treasured obligations. Put one mental foot in front of the other as you take the necessary steps required to grow into your highest potential. By working hard, you'll go farther than you could have imagined.

──────────○──────────

JUST FOR TODAY

TODAY'S MANTRA
I am committed to my responsibilities, healing, and growth.

TODAY'S JOURNAL PROMPT
What commitments do I have today? Which ones matter to me, and which ones could I let go of?

TODAY'S RITUAL
Draw seven lines (they don't have to be perfect or straight) on a piece of paper. Beneath each line write a person, circumstance, or project you fear will end in betrayal. Stare at the paper as you repeat the affirmation, "I can't control others, but I trust that the universe has my back." Rip up the paper and recycle it immediately.

──────────○──────────

BORN ON THIS DAY

ISABEL FRANCES LONGWORTH, Australian dentist and peace activist

ALANIS MORISSETTE, Canadian American musician and singer-songwriter

"Challenge yourself; it's the only path which leads to growth."—**MORGAN FREEMAN**, American Academy Award–winning actor

The Journey of Those Born on
JUNE 1

You were born of dynamic intellect and a blind ambition that can steer you away from meaningful growth. You will have to redefine your direction for growth, as your journey is one of discernment, awareness, and thoughtful progress.

Early on in your journey, you will meet your faithful guide, *Commitment* (The Number Seven). Despite your playful desire to explore the next best thing, *Commitment* calls you away from being a fair-weather friend and toward a path of intentionality. By deciding what you care about most in life, you can surrender the distractions that pull you away from your responsibilities. If you can keep your powerful mind centered, you'll discover less is more.

But if you choose this deliberate path, you will have to contend with *Hypervigilance* (Seven of Swords). You will meet *Hypervigilance* in moments of distrust in others, when you find yourself preparing for a betrayal that, so far, only exists in your mind. By letting down your guard and acknowledging that you cannot predict or control the actions of others, you'll find peace of mind.

YOUR GUIDES

Astrology: Your Energy
Gemini (Mercury, Venus)

Numerology: Your Path
Commitment (The Number Seven)

Minor Arcana: Your Lesson
Hypervigilance (The Seven of Swords)

Major Arcana: Your Highest Calling
Evolution (The Chariot)

And if you answer these calls for mental strength, you will climb to new heights of *Evolution* (The Chariot). *Evolution* shows you the undeniable progress that comes from sincere and devotional effort. You will meet *Evolution* when you are crossing the finish line of a hard-earned goal and are already setting your sights on somewhere greater. If you can show the universe just how serious you are about what matters, your dreams will become even larger.

―――――――――――――――――○―――――――――――――――――

GEMINI
RULERS: MERCURY, VENUS

PURPOSE
To focus diligently on what matters in order to widen the scope of possibilities.

RELATIONSHIPS

You are independent and easily bored, and your relationships should be a place of sincere commitment and progress. By seeking out partners who show their loyalty through action and inspire you to grow, you will discover that true love is forever evolving.

The Journey of
JUNE 2

Welcome to June 2, a courageous journey that introduces you to your authentic strength. Step into your *Power* (The Number Eight) today. Go inward, get clear on who you are and what you stand for, and hold your head high as you pursue your worldly ambitions. Don't make yourself small to make others comfortable, but instead, act from a place of confidence as you experience the full breadth of your individuality.

As you pursue your truth, watch out for *Negativity* (Eight of Swords). Gemini season has a tendency to make the mind wander, so if you begin to feel trapped by critical and limiting self-beliefs, try to redirect the channel of your brain somewhere more positive. Whether you call a dear friend or put on a soothing video, now is the time to free yourself from harmful thoughts.

Besides, you are brave and powerful, thanks in large part to your *Resilience* (Strength). As you navigate such a vulnerable day, look inward and acknowledge the place of internal strength that has carried you through the many highs and lows life has thrown your way. You have a set of emotional muscles that are always available to you, so reach for them throughout today.

JUST FOR TODAY

TODAY'S MANTRA
My emotional strength is the foundation of my authentic power.

TODAY'S RITUAL
Change the channel in your mind. Throughout the day, notice the many thoughts that come into your mind. Whenever you witness a negative thought, repeat the affirmation in your mind, "Positivity will always triumph over negativity."

TODAY'S JOURNAL PROMPT
Is there a person in my life who easily inspires positivity within me?

BORN ON THIS DAY

MARQUIS DE SADE, French philosopher and writer

CHARLIE SIFFORD, first Black American golfer to join the PGA Tour

"Strength is a full gamut. You've got to be strong from top to bottom, but you also have to raise your hand and say, 'I'm feeling weak right now. I need some help.' There is true strength in being able to ask for help."—ABBY WAMBACH, American soccer player

The Journey of Those Born on
JUNE 2

You were born of intellectual harmony and a diplomacy that, when taken too far, can extend into people-pleasing. You will have to discover your strength of conviction, as your journey is one of authenticity, release, and internal fortitude.

Early on in your journey, you will meet your intimidating guide, *Power* (The Number Eight). Despite your ability to be a social chameleon, *Power* calls you away from niceties and toward a path of brave vulnerability. By discovering and owning exactly who you are on a psychological and spiritual level without apology, you can achieve great honor and prestige in the physical world.

But if you choose this authentic path, you will have to heal with your lower companion, *Negativity* (Eight of Swords). You will meet *Negativity* in the limiting beliefs that you have about yourself when you obsess over feeling trapped and victimized by your present circumstances. Rather than giving in to these destructive thought patterns, you'll discover that internal empowerment is simply a state of mind.

YOUR GUIDES

Astrology: Your Energy
Gemini (Mercury, Venus)

Numerology: Your Path
Power (The Number Eight)

Minor Arcana: Your Lesson
Negativity (The Eight of Swords)

Major Arcana: Your Highest Calling
Resilience (Strength)

By answering these courageous calls, you will come to recognize *Resilience* (Strength). *Resilience* reveals the spiritual backbone within that has supported you, in even the most excruciating of circumstances, building its strength as you persevere through the unthinkable. You will meet *Resilience* in moments of self-empowerment when you rise to the occasion rather than falling into the depths of despair. If you can grow toward the places that scare you, you'll learn that pain teaches you what to fight for.

GEMINI
RULERS: MERCURY, VENUS

PURPOSE
To fight through the fear of being authentically powerful.

RELATIONSHIPS

You are relationship-driven by nature, and your relationships should be a place of deep connection and shared vulnerability. By seeking out partners who know how to communicate their affection as well as their uncomfortable truths, and empower you to do the same, you will discover that true love never hides from the truth.

The Journey of
JUNE 3

Welcome to June 3, an expansive journey that requires personal faith.

Explore what you don't know today. Gemini season thrives on intellectual expertise, but *Experience* (The Number Nine) encourages you to seek answers to the unknowns in your day. What subject, project, or person feels foreign but exciting to you? Step out onto the ledge of uncertainty as you expand your perspective.

But bring compassion to yourself if you bump into *Anxiety* (Nine of Swords) along the way. It is natural to experience fear when wading through uncharted territory, so if you find yourself paralyzed with worry at any point, call up a dear friend and share what your worst-case scenario is. More than likely, they can offer you a different point of view, allowing you to recenter and get back to the present moment.

After you've calmed your mind, tap into *Instinct* (The Hermit). When it comes to how and where you should explore, your intuition is the most powerful force at play. Seek out a few moments of solace during your day, meditating on what your gut is trying to direct you toward. By trusting yourself, you'll discover your divine internal compass.

JUST FOR TODAY

TODAY'S MANTRA
If I can quiet my fear, my instinct directs me through the unknown.

TODAY'S RITUAL
Find a calming place in your house and take a seated position. Close your eyes and put your hand over your lower belly. Draw in your breath to the count of nine and, as you exhale, repeat the phrase, "My gut will guide me through." Repeat this exercise at least nine times.

TODAY'S JOURNAL PROMPT
Who is a calming person who always helps relieve my anxiety?

BORN ON THIS DAY

JOSEPHINE BAKER, American-born French song-and-dance revue artist, actor, and civil rights activist

RAFAEL NADAL, Spanish tennis player

"To gain your own voice, forget about having it heard. Become a saint of your own province and your own consciousness."—ALLEN GINSBERG, American beat poet and counterculture icon

The Journey of Those Born on
JUNE 3

Y ou were born of mental flexibility and social ambition that can get you caught up in the minutiae of gossip. You will have to get out of your head and into the present moment, as your
journey is one of seeking, psychological healing, and divine knowledge.

Early on in your journey, you will meet your sage
guide, *Experience* (The Number Nine). Although you
would rather stick within your intellectual comfort
zone, *Experience* calls you away from being an expert
and toward a path of the unknown. By getting curious
about the foreign, you'll expand your perspective and
reach higher consciousness.

But if you choose this mentally expansive path, you
will have to address *Anxiety* (Nine of Swords). *Anxiety*
is the voice of angst that lives inside you, weaving its in-
tricate tales of worst-case scenarios throughout your
subconscious. You will meet *Anxiety* in the fear that
keeps you up at night, when you feel suffocated by the
weight of what you can't control. If you can look within
and discover where these distressed parts of you come
from, you'll begin to break the cycle of dread.

> ### YOUR GUIDES
>
> *Astrology: Your Energy*
> Gemini (Mercury, Venus)
>
> *Numerology: Your Path*
> Experience (The Number Nine)
>
> *Minor Arcana: Your Lesson*
> Anxiety (The Nine of Swords)
>
> *Major Arcana: Your Highest Calling*
> Instinct (The Hermit)

By answering these brave calls, you will come to rely on the power of *Instinct* (The Hermit).
You will meet *Instinct* in moments of mental bewilderment, when your mind has no idea where
to go next and yet your intrinsic intelligence moves you closer to your destined purpose. As you
explore uncharted territory and release yourself from the mental cages of fear, *Instinct* teaches
you how to light your way through the unknown with the brilliance of your intuition.

○

GEMINI
RULERS: MERCURY, VENUS

PURPOSE
*To rely on your gut, rather than fear,
to explore the world of knowledge.*

RELATIONSHIPS

You are as intelligent and self-aware as they come, and your relationships should be a place of
growth and expansion. By seeking out partners who push you out of your comfort zone and into
the unknown, you will discover that true love knows no bounds.

The Journey of
JUNE 4

Welcome to June 4, a fateful journey of mental independence.

Think for yourself today. Although Gemini season encourages open-mindedness, *Autonomy* (The Number One) asks you to go inward for the answers. What ideas do you believe in most? Rely on your intellectual and spiritual powers as you trailblaze through new paths of self-realization.

And look for *Clarity* (Ace of Swords). If a magical spark of inspiration hits you today, follow it with wild abandon. It's not a time to fret about the journey nor the outcome, but rather, a perfect moment to get excited about the potential of it all. Chase the vision, and you can worry about the rest tomorrow.

But prepare for anything that comes your way today. *Impermanence* (Wheel of Fortune) invites you to see the good in any circumstance, trusting that the universe has your best interests at heart. If you feel down on your luck, surrender to what is while trying to find the silver lining in the discomfort. If you are feeling high on success, pay it forward to someone who is hurting. And remember above all else, everything in life, the good and the bad, is temporary.

JUST FOR TODAY

TODAY'S MANTRA
I will chase my mental enthusiasm today and not worry about the outcome.

TODAY'S JOURNAL PROMPT
Do I feel comfortable thinking for myself? Why or why not?

TODAY'S RITUAL
Manifest clarity with peppermint. Bring this oil, tea, or leaf with you throughout the day, and inhale its invigorating aroma as you repeat the affirmation, "My clearest ideas come from within."

BORN ON THIS DAY

RUSSELL BRAND, English comedian and television personality

ALEXEI NAVALNY, Russian political activist and leader of opposition party Russia of the Future

"You'd think, 'What if I make a mistake today, I'll regret it.' I don't believe in regret, I feel everything leads us to where we are and we have to just jump forward, mean well, commit and just see what happens."—ANGELINA JOLIE, American actor and humanitarian

The Journey of Those Born on
JUNE 4

You were born of mental discipline and pragmatism that can stop you from taking healthy risks. You will have to take a chance on fate, as your journey is one of independence, certainty, and divine timing.

Early on in your journey, you will meet your sovereign guide, *Autonomy* (The Number One). Although you like to keep your ideas grounded, *Autonomy* asks you not to play it safe as you move toward an unfounded path of self-reliance. You will meet *Autonomy* when you are in the heat of intuitive action, carving out a blueprint for success that others will follow for years to come.

And if you traverse this self-guided path, you will have to count on *Clarity* (Ace of Swords). *Clarity* is the spark of an idea, made of pure potential that hasn't quite formed into a concrete plan yet. You will meet *Clarity* when your mind is hit with an electrifying breakthrough and you know exactly where your efforts must move toward next.

> ## YOUR GUIDES
>
> *Astrology: Your Energy*
> Gemini (Mercury, Venus)
>
> *Numerology: Your Path*
> Autonomy (The Number One)
>
> *Minor Arcana: Your Lesson*
> Clarity (The Ace of Swords)
>
> *Major Arcana: Your Highest Calling*
> Impermanence (The Wheel of Fortune)

By answering these calls for independence, you will have to leave your destiny up to fate. *Impermanence* (Wheel of Fortune) knows of your all-too-human desire for certainty and yet asks you to throw expectation to the wind as you ride the fateful cycles of life. You will meet *Impermanence* in the highs as well as the lows, when you are forced to surrender to your present circumstances and make the most of the journey. If you can trust that everything is temporary, you'll better enjoy the ride.

———————————————○———————————————

GEMINI
RULERS: MERCURY, VENUS

PURPOSE
To mentally place one independent foot in front of the other and not worry about the destination.

RELATIONSHIPS

You are grounded and loyal, and your relationships should be a place of independence and mental inspiration. By seeking out partners who light your imagination on fire while encouraging you to recognize your own power, you will discover that true love allows you to grow into yourself.

The Journey of
JUNE 5

Welcome to June 5, a gentle journey toward personal conviction.

Aim for *Balance* (The Number Two) today. Don't get too hung up on personal opinions, but instead, look for understanding and compromise as you work in peaceful coexistence with others. By sharing ideas, you can reach new heights of shared understanding.

But because Gemini season puts the mind in overdrive, don't waste any time on *Doubt* (Two of Swords). If you find yourself overthinking and getting paralyzed with uncertainty, take a few calming breaths to get back to your emotional center. Action is better than indecision. The right choice may not be crystal clear, but as long as your intentions are good, you can't make a mistake.

As you trek along this middle road, aim for *Truth* (Justice). A calm and centered moral compass lives within you, allowing you to stand for your convictions while remaining open to the varying perspectives of others. When you are in alignment with your values, what change do you hope to see in the world? Take a balanced and fair approach as you stand up for the things you care about most.

JUST FOR TODAY

TODAY'S MANTRA
I can work in harmony with others as I make fair decisions based on justice.

TODAY'S JOURNAL PROMPT
Who is a trustworthy partner I can reach out to if I'm stuck in indecision?

TODAY'S RITUAL
If at some point today you find that you can't make a decision, flip a coin. Witness your gut reaction to the visible side, and if you get a resounding "yes" or "no," go with your intuition.

BORN ON THIS DAY

ELENA CORNARO PISCOPIA, Italian mathematician and one of the first women to receive an academic degree from a university

BREONNA TAYLOR, American medical technician who was shot and killed by police officers in her own home

"The bottom line is, if you stay home, your message stays home with you. If you stand for justice and equality, you have an obligation to find the biggest possible megaphone to let your feelings be known. Don't let your message be buried and don't bury yourself."—**JOHN CARLOS**, American sprinter and civil rights activist

The Journey of Those Born on
JUNE 5

Y ou were born of fierce intellect and an intensity of opinion that can make you difficult to argue with. You will have to walk the middle road toward justice, as your journey is one of harmony, decision-making, and integrity.

Early on in your journey, you will meet your calming guide, *Balance* (The Number Two). You have much knowledge to share, but *Balance* calls you away from a life of intellectual debate and toward a path of peaceful coexistence. By thinking and collaborating in harmony with personal and professional partners, you'll keep an open mind. If you can choose tranquility over righteousness, you'll tap into the gift of unity.

But if you choose this amicable path, try not to get lost in *Doubt* (Two of Swords). You will meet *Doubt* in the mental gymnastics of uncertainty, when you can't quite make up your mind due to paralyzing fear that you will make the wrong decision. By recognizing that by trying your best there is no such thing as a mistake, you'll be empowered to move bravely through ambiguity.

Besides, the *Truth* (Justice) lies in your intuition. Although there are no individual authorities on justice, *Truth* invites you to build a divine and personal relationship with the concepts of fairness and equality. You will meet *Truth* in your individual moral compass, when you search within to decide what you believe in and are willing to stand for. If you can align your values with your actions, you'll learn to hold fairness and personal conviction with equal weight.

YOUR GUIDES

Astrology: Your Energy
Gemini (Mercury, Venus)

Numerology: Your Path
Balance (The Number Two)

Minor Arcana: Your Lesson
Doubt (The Two of Swords)

Major Arcana: Your Highest Calling
Truth (Justice)

GEMINI
RULERS: MERCURY, VENUS

PURPOSE
To find personal conviction in the balance of justice.

RELATIONSHIPS

You are bold and openhearted, and your relationships should be a place of equality and balance. By seeking out partners who aim to grow in peaceful harmony with you, you will discover that true love is always fair.

The Journey of
JUNE 6

Welcome to June 6, a perspective-shifting journey that requires an open mind. To coincide with the inquisitive nature of Gemini season, *Flexibility* (The Number Three) wants you to be the student rather than the teacher today. Get curious about the experiences of others as you ask the questions that can lead to unexpected mind-bending epiphanies. It's mentally invigorating not to have all the answers.

But watch out for any sensitivity today. *Trigger* (Three of Swords) reminds you that if your response to another's words is hysterical, the issue is probably historical, so take the necessary inventory required to own and understand your reaction. Ask yourself what past unhealed wound their words uncovered and find compassion for the person you thought was trying to harm you.

Besides, putting yourself in someone else's shoes is the fastest shortcut to a personal awakening. *Surrender* (The Hanged Man) encourages you to sacrifice your rigid ways of thinking today, so step out of your comfort zone and try to see things from a new angle. More than likely, by embracing the discomfort that comes from changing your point of view, you can discover new heights of spiritual consciousness.

JUST FOR TODAY

TODAY'S MANTRA

The mental breakthroughs I want most are just a simple shift in perspective.

TODAY'S JOURNAL PROMPT

How do I typically respond when my point of view is questioned or threatened?

TODAY'S RITUAL

Read the news from three drastically different outlets today with an open mind. After you take in the information, sit in a meditative position and close your eyes. Repeat the affirmation, "I can stay true to my values while remaining open to different perspectives."

BORN ON THIS DAY

SUKARNO, first president of Indonesia

HYUNA, South Korean singer-songwriter, rapper, and model

"If you don't like the way the world is, you change it. You have an obligation to change it. You just do it one step at a time."—MARIAN WRIGHT EDELMAN, American children's rights activist

The Journey of Those Born on
JUNE 6

You were born of social compassion and tenderheartedness that can make it difficult to try new things. You will have to become willing to surrender to the unknown, as your journey is one of curiosity, emotional pain, and spiritual sacrifice.

Early on in your journey, you will meet your open-minded guide, *Flexibility* (The Number Three). To coincide with your great capacity for understanding, *Flexibility* calls you away from a life of certainty and toward a path of perspective-building. By being humble enough to not have the answers and learning from others, you'll access the gift of interpersonal connection.

But if you choose this sociable path, you will have to contend with your lower companion, *Trigger* (Three of Swords). You will meet *Trigger* in moments of hurt feelings, when the words of another slash through an unhealed wound from your past. If you can look inward rather than blaming others for your pain, you can uncover new depths of self-compassion and learn to take full emotional responsibility for yourself.

YOUR GUIDES

Astrology: Your Energy
Gemini (Mercury, Venus)

Numerology: Your Path
Flexibility (The Number Three)

Minor Arcana: Your Lesson
Trigger (The Three of Swords)

Major Arcana: Your Highest Calling
Surrender (The Hanged Man)

By answering these calls for growth, you will begin to see things from an entirely new perspective. *Surrender* (The Hanged Man) asks you to shed protective layers of the ego and open yourself to radical states of awareness. You will meet *Surrender* in moments of conscious sacrifice, when you willingly give up something you once relied upon in order to hang freely from new heights of universal understanding. If you can let go of your old ideas completely, *Surrender* offers you the keys to a spiritual awakening.

GEMINI
RULERS: MERCURY, VENUS

PURPOSE
To give up old ways of thinking to find new freedom.

RELATIONSHIPS

You are generous and at times sentimental, and your relationships should be a place of understanding and perspective shifting. By seeking out partners who challenge your rigid ways of thinking and honor your capacity for growth, you will discover that true love inspires great change.

The Journey of
JUNE 7

Welcome to June 7, a transformational journey that requires personal integrity. While Gemini season is not known for its reliability, do what you say you are going to do today. *Discipline* (The Number Four) asks you to put your head down and do the work you are responsible for, making no excuses for outside distractions. If it is an issue of mind over matter, focus your brain on the tasks at hand.

But be sure to take a mental pause before any drastic action. *Restoration* (Four of Swords) encourages you to align your mind with a higher purpose by taking the necessary time required to get clear on your purpose. Don't be afraid to spend some time in isolation until you reach a place of internal clarity.

All this work should amount to great growth, as long as you are willing to shed old emotional skin from the past. *Transformation* (Death) empowers you to let go of what is no longer true for you today, surrendering any attachments you have to outdated identities or coping mechanisms. Who are you in the process of becoming? Take a moment to grieve who you were as you get excited about a more authentic tomorrow.

JUST FOR TODAY

TODAY'S MANTRA
I will work hard and take my time at becoming a more authentic version of myself.

TODAY'S RITUAL
Write down four practical things you can focus your mind on today. They can be personal or professional, and they should be easily achievable. As you complete them today, say the affirmation, "I can work hard at what I can and surrender the rest."

TODAY'S JOURNAL PROMPT
What version of my identity am I ready to let go of?

BORN ON THIS DAY

SUSAN BLOW, American educator who pioneered kindergarten education

DEAN MARTIN, American singer, comedian, and actor

"There's always a rainbow at the end of every rain."—PRINCE, American funk, rock, and R&B singer-songwriter and musician

The Journey of Those Born on
JUNE 7

You were born of mental conviction and desire for certainty that can block you from the growth you need most. You will have to work through the many ego deaths within life, as your journey is one of preparation, pause, and rebirth.

Early on in your journey, you will meet your formidable guide, *Discipline* (The Number Four). Despite your strong will, *Discipline* calls you away from prideful ignorance and toward a path of humble action. By trudging through the long hours required to master your intellectual goals, *Discipline* helps you build a strong foundation of integrity upon which you can grow. If you can choose honor over power, you'll discover the gift of stability.

But if you choose this serious path, you will have to quiet your mind for *Restoration* (Four of Swords). Although you are ambitious beyond belief, *Restoration* asks you to take a thoughtful pause between completed milestones so you can don't waste time on fruitless efforts. You will meet *Restoration* in the necessary breaks in life, when you wait for the spiritual direction to guide your next right action.

By answering these discerning calls, you will have to contend with *Transformation* (Death). *Transformation* invites you to embrace the natural changes that happens over time, when you let go of who you once were to embrace the potential of who you are becoming. By surrendering the conscious attachments you have to your identity and believing in the power of metamorphosis, you'll slowly but surely unveil your true authentic nature.

YOUR GUIDES

Astrology: Your Energy
Gemini (Mercury, Venus)

Numerology: Your Path
Discipline (The Number Four)

Minor Arcana: Your Lesson
Restoration (The Four of Swords)

Major Arcana: Your Highest Calling
Transformation (Death)

GEMINI
RULERS: MERCURY, VENUS

PURPOSE
To build a strong mental foundation upon which to emotionally transform.

RELATIONSHIPS

You are loyal by nature, and your relationships should be a place of safety and growth. By seeking out partners you can lean on during times of great change and transformation, you'll discover that true love always has your back.

The Journey of
JUNE 8

W elcome to June 8, a journey of vulnerability that requires personal moderation.
Put your ideas out there today. *Courage* (The Number Five) favors audacity over cowardness, so grab the metaphorical microphone and say what you are thinking. Whether you take to social media or engage publicly in your work, now is the time to have your voice heard.

But be sure to practice *Maturity* (Five of Swords). Gemini season encourages healthy communication of any kind, but not all words are useful or productive, so watch out for combativeness if you come up against any criticism or conflict. It is easy to get lost in the heat of battle, so surrender your verbal weapons and don't be afraid to apologize for any harm done.

If you find yourself in a place of urgency today, more than likely you are acting out of fear or scarcity rather than *Serenity* (Temperance). Remember, a bit of restraint never hurt anyone. There's no need to respond to that email or text message until you reach a place of internal peace that will allow you to engage in a healing manner. You can access this centeredness in patience today, so calm your mind and wait until your mind, body, and spirit are aligned.

JUST FOR TODAY

TODAY'S MANTRA

Emotional centeredness allows me to act from a place of authenticity rather than react from a place of fear.

TODAY'S JOURNAL PROMPT

What are practical ways for me to calm my mind and reach a place of serenity?

TODAY'S RITUAL

Make amends for any past harm done. Make a list of any people you have harmed with your words and write a short but concise letter to them owning your mistakes. If you feel compelled and if it is appropriate, reach out to one of them today and ask if you can make this apology to them directly.

BORN ON THIS DAY

ANNIE ROBINSON, Scottish suffragist and pacifist

KANYE WEST, American rapper, songwriter, and record producer

"Less is only more where more is no good."—**FRANK LLOYD WRIGHT**, American architect recognized as the "greatest American architect of all time"

The Journey of Those Born on
JUNE 8

Y ou were born of intellectual power and a depth of intelligence that can lead you down rabbit holes of morbid reflection. You will have to balance bravery with moderation, as your journey is one of self-expression, conflict, and divine restraint.

Early on in your journey, you will meet your bold guide, *Courage* (The Number Five). To channel your influential mind, *Courage* calls you away from a life of materialism and toward a path of radical vulnerability. By telling the world exactly who you are and what you believe in most, you'll build a creative platform made of honesty.

But if you choose this visible path, you will have to wrestle with *Maturity* (Five of Swords). Just because you can speak your mind doesn't mean it's always in your best interest. You will meet *Maturity* in moments of bad blood, when an opponent or naysayer threatens your stance and you are forced to decide whether or not you are going to react. By choosing your battles wisely and learning to apologize when it is warranted, you'll gain greater emotional wisdom.

> ### YOUR GUIDES
>
> *Astrology: Your Energy*
> Gemini (Mercury, Venus)
>
> *Numerology: Your Path*
> Courage (The Number Five)
>
> *Minor Arcana: Your Lesson*
> Maturity (The Five of Swords)
>
> *Major Arcana: Your Highest Calling*
> Serenity (Temperance)

By answering these daring calls, you will discover the importance of *Serenity* (Temperance). *Serenity* asks you to tap into the tranquility that comes from self-moderation, when you don't allow yourself to be pulled to extremes and instead walk the middle road of spiritual restraint. By living in flow with the universe itself, *Serenity* shows you that it is safe to lay down your mental weapons and surrender to the here and now. If you can reach for patience over drama, you'll discover greater peace.

GEMINI
RULERS: MERCURY, VENUS

PURPOSE
To find internal peace through balancing radical vulnerability with spiritual moderation.

RELATIONSHIPS

You are powerful and mentally persuasive, and your relationships should be a place to grow in conflict and compromise. By seeking out partners who are not afraid of honesty and yet aim for understanding, you will discover that true love can bring peaceful coexistence.

The Journey of
JUNE 9

W elcome to June 9, a transformative journey that inspires deep healing.
Live from a place of sincerity today. To channel the romantic end of Gemini season, wear your heart on your sleeve as you express your affection and *Devotion* (The Number Six) through words and actions. Extend a generous compliment to someone who seems down on their confidence, or tell a loved one just how much they mean to you.

You will have to lean on these special people in return, as *Transition* (Six of Swords) asks you to let go of some subconscious ways of operating. If there is a mental pattern that you are aware you need to let go of, now is the time. This can bring up huge discomfort and fear, however, so call up a dear friend and ask for them to hold healing space during this transition.

As you do this internal shedding, *Shadow* (The Devil) encourages you to look at the self-destructive behaviors that block you from true happiness and presence. What historical coping mechanisms do you lean on when life feels overwhelming? Take the day to find compassion for these acts of survival, and aim to surrender them as you embrace true vulnerability.

JUST FOR TODAY

TODAY'S MANTRA
I am willing to surrender the subconscious blocks I have around accepting love and happiness.

TODAY'S JOURNAL PROMPT
What mental patterns are currently harming me? Am I ready to let them go?

TODAY'S RITUAL
Consider one emotional survival mechanism you had to utilize when growing up. Think back to when you had to begin using this skill. Visualize the age you were and make up a name for the inner child who had to take on this burden. Then, put your hand over your heart and repeat the affirmation to this inner child, "You do not need to carry this any longer. I am here to protect you."

BORN ON THIS DAY

NATALIE PORTMAN, Israeli American actor

BERTHA VON SUTTNER, Austrian Bohemian pacifist and novelist

"The more I expect, the more unhappy I am going to be. The more I accept, the more serene I am."—MICHAEL J. FOX, Canadian actor, author, comedian, and activist

The Journey of Those Born on
JUNE 9

You were born of intuitive intellect and a deep introversion that closes you off to true connection. You will have to surrender to the power of love, as your journey is one of sincerity, healing, and internal mending.

Early on in your journey, you will meet your soulful guide, *Devotion* (The Number Six). Despite your desire to escape discomfort through exploration, *Devotion* calls you away from wanderlust and toward a path of meaningful work and intimacy. By generously giving your mind, body, and heart to the people and projects that mean the most to you, you'll discover the gifts of sincere connection.

If you choose this heartfelt path, *Transition* (Six of Swords) will ask you to unburden outdated mental patterns along the way. You will meet *Transition* when you know that you must change, yet are terrified of what will happen if you do. By leaning on your chosen people through these destabilizing times, you can thank the past for what it taught you while growing toward higher levels of personal truth.

> ## YOUR GUIDES
>
> *Astrology: Your Energy*
> Gemini (Mercury, Venus)
>
> *Numerology: Your Path*
> Devotion (The Number Six)
>
> *Minor Arcana: Your Lesson*
> Transition (The Six of Swords)
>
> *Major Arcana: Your Highest Calling*
> Shadow (The Devil)

By embracing these calls for love, you will have to heal with the power of *Shadow* (The Devil). You will meet *Shadow* when things are going well in life and yet you can't manage to enjoy them. *Shadow* reveals the unconscious block you have around emotional freedom, manifesting in the self-destructive behaviors that numb you from the necessary lows as well as the gorgeous highs of the human experience. If you can surrender these coping mechanisms while honoring how they have helped you survive, you'll gain the chance to thrive.

─────────────────○─────────────────

GEMINI
RULERS: MERCURY, VENUS

PURPOSE
To understand and release the mental barriers that block the heart.

RELATIONSHIPS

You are intellectually and spiritually larger than life, and your relationships should be a place of heartfelt surrender. By seeking out partners who make you feel emotionally safe through their actions, you will discover that true love doesn't require any walls.

The Journey of
JUNE 10

Welcome to June 10, a fateful journey that requires complete surrender.

Show up to your responsibilities today. Despite the airy quality of Gemini season, *Commitment* (The Number Seven) asks you to say what you mean and do what you say. There's no room for fair-weather plans or half-hearted attempts, so meet your obligations with complete attention and focus. The world wants to see how serious you are.

And be mindful of who you trust. *Hypervigilance* (Seven of Swords) warns against unnecessary paranoia and self-defensiveness yet encourages you to take careful inventory of who you are letting into your inner circle. Does your gut feel uneasy when you are around a specific individual? Make the change, if necessary, so you can finally let down your guard.

But prepare for the unexpected. Welcome unanticipated change, and trust that *Upheaval* (The Tower) is an act of divine intervention rather than punishment. Perhaps there is a decision you have been delaying for quite some time now, and the universe can't wait any longer. If you can believe that fate is unfolding as it should, you'll move forward on the road to your divine destiny.

───────○───────

JUST FOR TODAY

TODAY'S MANTRA
I trust that the universe, and the people I am committed to, have my back.

TODAY'S RITUAL
Embrace change by switching up your appearance. Whether you try out an exciting, bold new shade of makeup or get a drastic haircut, lean in to the unexpected and get comfortable with discomfort.

TODAY'S JOURNAL PROMPT
Are there any relationships in my life that inspire paranoia or distrust?

───────○───────

BORN ON THIS DAY

HATTIE MCDANIEL, first Black American actor to win an Oscar

SHIVA NAZAR AHARI, Iranian human rights activist

"Unexpected intrusions of beauty. This is what life is."—**SAUL BELLOW**, Canadian-born American author

The Journey of Those Born on
JUNE 10

Y ou were born of intellectual independence and a subconscious need for change that can make you unreliable. You will have to learn to be responsible for what you can, as your journey is one of intention, surrender, and divine change.

Early on in your journey, you will meet your decisive guide, *Commitment* (The Number Seven). Despite your desire for freedom, *Commitment* calls you away from selfishness and toward a path of personal responsibility. By showing up for the obligations you have to yourself and others, you'll learn the importance of follow-through. If you can choose loyalty over the whims of passion, you'll reap the rewards of keeping to your word.

If you choose this faithful path, you will have to watch out for *Hypervigilance* (Seven of Swords). *Hypervigilance* highlights the paranoia that creeps in when you feel unsafe in relationships with others, forcing you to question what is fear versus intuition. By taking careful inventory of who you keep in your life and investing only in the partners you know have your back, you can learn to let down your guard.

By answering these calls for accountability, *Upheaval* (The Tower) will remind you that there are some things in life you simply can't plan for. *Upheaval* comes to you in unforeseen change, when fate steps in and does for you what you cannot do for yourself. Although these moments can feel destabilizing, trust that your destiny is unfolding as it should. If you can surrender your plans to the divine powers, you'll learn that when you fall, the universe will catch you.

─────────────────────○─────────────────────

GEMINI
RULERS: MERCURY, URANUS

PURPOSE
To surrender self-will in favor of divine trust in fate.

RELATIONSHIPS

You are independent even to a fault, yet your relationships should be a place of earnest commitment and reciprocal responsibility. By seeking out partners who say what they mean and do what they say, you will discover that true love is an act of integrity.

The Journey of
JUNE 11

Welcome to June 11, an empowering journey that renews your faith in the future.

Step into your strength today. Despite the breezy nature of Gemini season, *Power* (The Number Eight) asks you to take up space in the world and stand firmly in your personal authority. By being authentically yourself, you can share greater intimacy with the people you love while inspiring others to do the same.

But as you expand, watch out for the cages of the mind. *Negativity* (Eight of Swords) warns against self-destructive thinking today, so practice mindfulness and witness the restrictive stories your brain is telling you. Even if things seem impossible, more than likely, the solution is standing right in front of you.

And if you are finishing a difficult time in your life or closing out a weighty chapter, *Hope* (The Star) reminds you of how much you must look forward to. Try to wash away the leftover debris of the past so that you can bask in the bright light of optimism. You are growing and changing, so seize the opportunity to feel excited again about who you are becoming.

JUST FOR TODAY

TODAY'S MANTRA

The only thing more powerful than fear is optimism.

TODAY'S JOURNAL PROMPT

What chapter of my life is ending, and what am I looking forward to taking its place?

TODAY'S RITUAL

The head carries a lot of emotional weight, so do a deep-cleansing wash of your scalp at night. Use apple cider vinegar or your favorite shampoo, and as you cleanse your scalp, repeat the affirmation, "I am ready to wash away the mental cages of the past."

BORN ON THIS DAY

JEANNETTE RANKIN, American politician and first woman elected to the US Congress

ADDIE WAITES HUNTON, American suffragist, race and gender activist, writer, political organizer, and educator

"The sea, once it casts its spell, holds one in its net of wonder forever."—JACQUES COUSTEAU, French oceanic explorer

The Journey of Those Born on
JUNE 11

You were born of mental balance and a desire for peace that can leave you bending to the will of others. You will have to step into your innate sense of authority, as your journey is one of authenticity, positive thinking, and internal optimism.

Early on in your journey, you will meet your enigmatic guide, *Power* (The Number Eight). Despite your social diplomacy, *Power* calls you away from a life of people-pleasing and toward a path of radical personal truth. By revealing who you are and what you stand for, you'll discover the undeniable influence you can have on others and the worldly success you can gain by simply being yourself.

But if you choose this empowered path, you will have to grapple with *Negativity* (Eight of Swords). *Negativity* highlights the self-doubt and criticism that prevents you from pursuing what is best for you. You will meet *Negativity* in moments of being mentally blocked, when you are so focused on the problem that you can't see the solution. If you can slow your racing thoughts, you'll discover the answer is more simple than you think.

YOUR GUIDES

Astrology: Your Energy
Gemini (Mercury, Uranus)

Numerology: Your Path
Power (The Number Eight)

Minor Arcana: Your Lesson
Negativity (The Eight of Swords)

Major Arcana: Your Highest Calling
Hope (The Star)

By answering these weighty calls, *Hope* (The Star) will shine light on your potential. *Hope* invites you to use the divine waters of optimism to wash away the debris of the past, allowing you to move toward a brighter future. You will meet *Hope* in times of personal renewal, when you have grieved your ego and suddenly find yourself basking in the celestial glow of healing, optimism, and excitement. By shining brightly in the dark, you'll discover it's never too late to begin again.

──────────○──────────

GEMINI
RULERS: MERCURY, URANUS

PURPOSE
*To find power in simplicity
as you move toward a brighter future.*

RELATIONSHIPS

You are a natural diplomat who aims for equality, and your relationships should be a place of authenticity and renewal. By seeking out partners who empower you to be yourself while embracing the change that happens over time, you will discover that true love wants you to shine.

The Journey of
JUNE 12

W elcome to June 12, an adventure into the far-reaching walls of your subconscious mind. Get out of your comfort zone today. Rather than playing games in your head, *Experience* (The Number Nine) invites you to step into the present moment by taking on projects and relationships that push you into the unknown. If something makes you excited yet nervous, pursue it with wild abandon.

But as you explore, be sure to address *Anxiety* (Nine of Swords). Gemini season has the mind in overdrive but try not to get lost in the dread that comes from fear-based thinking. If you find yourself spiraling down the hole of worst-case scenarios, call a dear friend and ask them to calmly bring you back to reality.

If you can move fear out of the way, you can tap into *Memory* (The Moon). If a situation today triggers an emotional response from your past, place logic to the side and listen to what your emotions are trying to tell you. There can be great wisdom in these internal responses. The subconscious is far more intelligent than we give it credit for, so live in accordance with what your nervous system is telling you.

JUST FOR TODAY

TODAY'S MANTRA
I will make peace with my fear of the unknown.

TODAY'S JOURNAL PROMPT
How was I taught to deal with fear and anxiety while growing up?

TODAY'S RITUAL
On a piece of paper, write down a memory that is quite hard for you to make peace with. Leave this note, weighed down by a rock, somewhere outside overnight so it can bask underneath the moon, even if it isn't visible to the naked eye. Before you leave it, repeat the prayer, "Lunar magic, help me heal the past so I can bring the power of my subconscious into the present."

BORN ON THIS DAY

PETE FARNDON, English musician

EGON SCHIELE, Austrian Expressionist painter

"What a wonderful thought it is that some of the best days of our lives haven't even happened yet."—ANNE FRANK, German Dutch diarist and victim of the Nazi Holocaust

The Journey of Those Born on
JUNE 12

Y ou were born of sharp wit and a social flexibility that can take you far away from your truth. You will have to explore your way back to yourself, as your journey is one of seeking, psychological healing, and subconscious integration.

Early on in your journey, you will meet your adventurous guide, *Experience* (The Number Nine). Despite your innate intelligence, *Experience* calls you to get out of your head and into the present moment. You will meet *Experience* in the perspective-shifting unknown, when you jump off the ledge of certainty in the pursuit of greater knowledge. If you can engage in life rather than staying inside the confines of your mind, *Experience* offers you the gift of higher consciousness.

But if you travel this far-reaching path, you will have to address *Anxiety* (Nine of Swords). *Anxiety* highlights the internal voices of dread that keep you up at night as they paint daunting images of fear on the walls of your subconscious. Instead of believing in these panicked thoughts, look inward to heal the parts of yourself that have been afraid to let go of control.

YOUR GUIDES

Astrology: Your Energy
Gemini (Mercury, Uranus)

Numerology: Your Path
Experience (The Number Nine)

Minor Arcana: Your Lesson
Anxiety (The Nine of Swords)

Major Arcana: Your Highest Calling
Memory (The Moon)

By answering these calls for healing, you will come to understand the importance of *Memory* (The Moon). *Memory* invites you to integrate the stories of your past so that you no longer project your historical experiences onto the present moment. You will meet *Memory* in moments of déjà vu, when a nostalgic smell or sound transports you back to a crucial time, forcing you to heal something from your subconscious. If you can confront and integrate the wisdom of the past, you'll meet your divine intuition.

—————————————————◯—————————————————

GEMINI
RULERS: MERCURY, URANUS

PURPOSE
To go to the places that scare you in order to heal the buried memories of the past.

RELATIONSHIPS

You are an expert genius in your own right, and your relationships should be a place of growth and subconscious reckoning. By seeking out partners who push you out of your comfort zone and inspire you to address your deepest wounds, you will discover that true love encourages deep healing.

The Journey of
JUNE 13

W elcome to June 13, an independent journey toward mental freedom.

Do your own thing today. *Autonomy* (The Number One) asks you to follow the sound of your intuitive genius as you trailblaze new ground. There's no need to seek out insight or the opinions of others, but instead, turn inward for the answers. What is your mind the most excited to explore?

As you decide, look out for *Clarity* (Ace of Swords). Gemini season has a knack for stirring up new thoughts, so if you have in mind a clear, concise, but not fully realized idea, pursue it with wild enthusiasm. It is a time of beginnings rather than in-betweens, so don't waste time worrying about how the project or relationship will go—simply get started.

Vitality (The Sun) reminds you not to take yourself so seriously, but instead, to wear your heart on your sleeve as you explore the unknowns of today. By accessing the free-spirited side of your personality, you can break through old walls of fear and come up with more inspired ideas than ever before. You are called to be a fearless innovator today, but one who knows how to have a good time along the way.

○

JUST FOR TODAY

TODAY'S MANTRA
I can pursue new ideas with childlike enthusiasm and joy.

TODAY'S JOURNAL PROMPT
What is my inner child most excited about doing?

TODAY'S RITUAL
Pull up a picture of you as a child. Bring this image out into the sun, and smile at it, even if it feels unnatural at first. Repeat the prayer, "Sunlight, please help reveal my authentic spirit."

○

BORN ON THIS DAY

MIMI SVERDRUP LUNDEN, Norwegian educator, nonfiction writer, and women's rights advocate

MARY-KATE AND ASHLEY OLSEN, American actors, fashion designers, and twins

"You have to take ownership and leadership of tomorrow. For that to be possible, you have to strengthen your capacity and widen your vision as a global citizen."—BAN KI-MOON, South Korean politician and eighth secretary-general of the United Nations

The Journey of Those Born on
JUNE 13

Y ou were born of grounded intellect and a depth of feeling that can get you lost in dark reflection. You will have to pursue joy fearlessly, as your journey is one of independence, ideation, and authentic power.

Early on in your journey, you will meet your emboldened guide, *Autonomy* (The Number One). Despite your desire for certainty, *Autonomy* calls you away from a life of restriction and toward a path of self-trust. By moving to the beat of your own genius, *Autonomy* encourages you to innovate as you carve out a design for living that has never been done before. If you can choose sovereignty over submission, you'll begin to listen more keenly to your intuition.

And if you choose this daring path, you will learn to work with *Clarity* (Ace of Swords). *Clarity* invites you to pursue the seedling of an idea, one that is not quite fully formed and yet has endless potential. You will meet *Clarity* in the small ah-ha moments, when you get just enough vision that pure enthusiasm can carry you the rest of the way through. If you can act upon even the rawest of inspiration, you'll be reminded of what that idea can become.

> ### YOUR GUIDES
>
> *Astrology: Your Energy*
> Gemini (Mercury, Uranus)
>
> *Numerology: Your Path*
> Autonomy (The Number One)
>
> *Minor Arcana: Your Lesson*
> Clarity (The Ace of Swords)
>
> *Major Arcana: Your Highest Calling*
> Vitality (The Sun)

By embracing these calls for action, you will step into the spotlight of *Vitality* (The Sun). *Vitality* knows that an inspired leader is within you, encouraging you to own your expertise and talents as you take center stage in your life. Rather than shrinking under the pressure, *Vitality* teaches you how to rise to the occasion as you access the unfiltered child within. If you can dare to be so vulnerable, *Vitality* shows you how to shine.

───────────────○───────────────

GEMINI
RULERS: MERCURY, URANUS

PURPOSE
*To trailblaze toward the sunlight
of authenticity.*

RELATIONSHIPS

You are grounded and humble, and your relationships should be a place of encouragement and recognition. By seeking out partners who cheer you on as you climb new heights of self-realization, you will discover that true love never asks you to stay small.

The Journey of
JUNE 14

Welcome to June 14, a gentle journey that wakes you to the truth.

Try to find *Balance* (The Number Two) today. Rather than letting your mind go to extremes, aim to understand and work in harmony with the people who cross your path. Nothing has to be as difficult as it seems, so look for opportunities to thrive in partnership through peaceful coexistence.

But don't get stuck in *Doubt* (Two of Swords). Gemini season has a way of letting the mind run wild, so if you find yourself paralyzed with indecision due to the sheer number of possible outcomes, make a choice and surrender the results. More than likely, there is no perfect answer, so all you need to worry about are your intentions.

You'll need this internal ease because *Awakening* (Judgment) demands that you open your eyes to the truth. Whether you find renewed clarity around a relationship, project, or larger social issue, now is the time to run toward honesty rather than away from it. The truth is rarely comfortable or easy, but by embracing what you once denied, you can make more informed decisions that benefit you and others in the long run.

JUST FOR TODAY

TODAY'S MANTRA

I will practice mental and emotional balance as I awaken to the truth.

TODAY'S RITUAL

If you run into a tough decision today, flip a coin to come to an answer. This simple act of faith serves as a reminder that choices are not as complicated and finite as they seem.

TODAY'S JOURNAL PROMPT

What does my inner child get the most excited about doing?

BORN ON THIS DAY

HARRIET BEECHER STOWE, American author and abolitionist

STEFFI GRAF, German tennis player

"Every person has the truth in his heart. No matter how complicated his circumstances, no matter how others look at him from the outside, and no matter how deep or shallow the truth dwells in his heart, once his heart is pierced with a crystal needle, the truth will gush forth like a geyser."—**CHE GUEVARA**, Argentinean Marxist revolutionary, author, and physician

The Journey of Those Born on
JUNE 14

You were born of radical intelligence and an emotional restraint that can keep you from witnessing the full extent of the truth. You will have to gracefully balance the weight of honesty, as your journey is one of harmony, uncertainty, and radical recognition.

Early on in your journey, you will meet your fair-minded guide, *Balance* (The Number Two). Despite your sharp tongue and passionate mind, *Balance* calls you away from a life of self-serving drama and toward a path of peaceful coexistence. By always thinking of how you can reach shared understanding and cooperation with those you respect, you'll discover again that two heads are always better than one.

But if you take this amicable path, you will have to wrestle with *Doubt* (Two of Swords). *Doubt* comes to you in the form of indecision, when fear of making the wrong choice paralyzes you from moving forward at all. If there are multiple ways to solve a problem, don't let your mind fret about which one is right. *Doubt* invites you to simply make a call, recognizing that there is never a perfect solution and leaving the results up to fate.

> ### YOUR GUIDES
>
> *Astrology: Your Energy*
> Gemini (Mercury, Uranus)
>
> *Numerology: Your Path*
> Balance (The Number Two)
>
> *Minor Arcana: Your Lesson*
> Doubt (The Two of Swords)
>
> *Major Arcana: Your Highest Calling*
> Awakening (Judgment)

By answering these meaningful calls, you will begin the process of *Awakening* (Judgment). You will meet *Awakening* when your eyes are wide open to the truth, surrendering your mental comfort zone in favor of larger universal realities. It is never convenient or easy to come to terms with the harsher aspects of the human experience, but by integrating these tough-to-swallow pills of honesty, you'll become a part of something larger than yourself.

○

GEMINI
RULERS: MERCURY, URANUS

PURPOSE
To gracefully balance the inconvenient, but crucial, weight of the truth.

RELATIONSHIPS

You are a wild freethinker, yet your relationships should be a place of balance and equality. By seeking out partners who aim to grow and understand in harmony with you, you will discover that true love thrives in peaceful coexistence.

The Journey of
JUNE 15

Welcome to June 15, a mentally collaborative journey that builds perspective.
To complement the inquisitive nature of Gemini season, *Flexibility* (The Number Three) asks you to learn from others today rather than staying in your intellectual comfort zone. Actively invite your friends and coworkers to share their experience and knowledge so you can grow in your level of understanding.

But be wary of *Trigger* (Three of Swords). Today warns against taking things too personally, so try to practice self-awareness if you find yourself in pain from the words of others. Rather than reacting, get curious about where this pain originated. Did they unintentionally hit an unhealed wound? Although they are accountable for their actions, you can be responsible for your feelings.

And if you can practice this level of emotional maturity, you can take a step back and find *Perspective* (The World). Instead of getting lost in the minutiae or drama of the day, zoom out and notice how far you have come. Perhaps you have completed a major milestone and deserve to pause and appreciate the lessons you've learned along the way. It is within gratitude that you can find the emotional satisfaction you are looking for.

JUST FOR TODAY

TODAY'S MANTRA
Gratitude helps me be a better listener and friend.

TODAY'S JOURNAL PROMPT
Am I completing any major milestone in my life?

TODAY'S RITUAL
Practice mindful gratitude. Sit in a meditative position, close your eyes, and visualize yourself hovering over your life. What are three things you are grateful for? Place your hand over your heart, holding rose quartz if you have it, and say thank you to these blessings.

BORN ON THIS DAY

HELEN HUNT, American actor

LISA DEL GIOCONDO, Italian noblewoman whose name was given to the *Mona Lisa*

"I get ideas from everything. A big color, the sound of water and wind, or a flash of something cool. Playing is like life. Either you feel it or you don't."—ERROLL GARNER, American jazz pianist

The Journey of Those Born on
JUNE 15

Y ou were born of compassionate genius that you rarely extend toward yourself. You will have to find emotional healing in the bigger picture, as your journey is one of collaboration, social awareness, and gratitude.

Early on in your journey, you will meet your amicable guide, *Flexibility* (The Number Three). Although you are curious but fearful, *Flexibility* calls you away from a life of isolation and toward a path of intellectual growth. By making yourself available to the wisdom of the people and subjects you aren't familiar with, you can step outside your mental comfort zone.

But if you take this sociable path, you will have to contend with *Trigger* (Three of Swords). *Trigger* comes to you in moments of emotional pain when the words and actions of another shoot straight into an unhealed wound. While others are accountable for their actions, *Trigger* reminds you that you are responsible for your reactions. By reflecting rather than blaming, you'll have a chance to heal the hurt from your past.

YOUR GUIDES

Astrology: Your Energy
Gemini (Mercury, Uranus)

Numerology: Your Path
Flexibility (The Number Three)

Minor Arcana: Your Lesson
Trigger (The Three of Swords)

Major Arcana: Your Highest Calling
Perspective (The World)

By answering these calls for understanding, you will begin to see life through the lens of *Perspective* (The World). You will see *Perspective* when you zoom out and look at the big picture, recognizing how every twist and turn of the human experience amounts to a grand masterpiece. If you can take a meditative pause for gratitude between completed milestones throughout your journey, *Perspective* offers you the gift of spiritual contentment.

GEMINI
RULERS: MERCURY, URANUS

PURPOSE
To step far enough outside your mental comfort zone to find spiritual perspective.

RELATIONSHIPS

You are generous yet guarded, so your relationships should be a place of thoughtful communication and conscious gratitude. By seeking out partners who push you to share your innermost thoughts while keeping an eye on the big picture, you will discover that true love is about perspective.

The Journey of
JUNE 16

Welcome to June 16, a purposeful journey of divine restraint.

Get to work today. Despite the unpredictability of Gemini season, *Discipline* (The Number Four) asks you to control what you can. Create a thorough list of your responsibilities for the day ahead and execute them with focus and perseverance. You can do anything you set your mind to.

But make time for *Restoration* (Four of Swords). Rather than moving forward without a plan, pause and reconsider what efforts are worth your time. If you need a few hours of rest and relaxation to clear your mind, that's okay—you need a full tank of energy as you move toward your purpose.

Because at the end of the day, you are the only leader you need. *Self-mastery* (The Emperor) wants you to self-regulate today, checking in with your mental health while showing up to the commitments and obligations you have. If you find yourself burning the candle at both ends, know that you have the power to change the course of your day. Tap into this sense of personal authority as you decipher when to push and when to pull, balancing intuition with objective reason.

JUST FOR TODAY

TODAY'S MANTRA

I can take care of my responsibilities and my mental health.

TODAY'S RITUAL

Make room for mental clarity today. Set aside thirty minutes (or at much time as you can afford), and lie down on your back. Close your eyes, and visualize a single sword resting beneath your back, symbolizing your purpose. Ask your intuition, "What does this sword represent?"

TODAY'S JOURNAL PROMPT

How could I create some room for self-care today?

BORN ON THIS DAY

ADAM SMITH, Scottish economist and moral philosopher

TUPAC SHAKUR, American rapper and actor

"Wisdom and peace come when you start living the life the creator intended for you." —GERONIMO, Apache leader and resistance fighter

The Journey of Those Born on
JUNE 16

Y ou were born of mental conviction and chaotic genius that can lead you to dangerous extremes. You will have to find divine purpose in restraint, as your journey is one of hard work, contemplation, and personal authority.

Early on in your journey, you will meet your serious guide, *Discipline* (The Number Four). In spite of your unpredictable mind, *Discipline* calls you away from disorder and toward a path of humble perseverance. You will meet *Discipline* in the grit of a hard day's work, when your emotion tells you to give up but your fixed mindset carries you through. If you can invest diligently in your future, *Discipline* shows you the rewards of integrity.

But if you choose this demanding path, you will have to take pause for *Restoration* (Four of Swords). You will meet *Restoration* in the forced breaks between ambitions, when you want to trailblaze forward but must stop and wait for your next divine direction. If you can use this time off to take care of your tired body, mind, and soul, you'll remember that success is never worth the cost of burnout.

And if you answer these calls for regulation, you will discover the power of *Self-mastery* (The Emperor). *Self-mastery* encourages you to listen to the objective authority that lives within, helping you make thoughtful decisions for the long haul. Rather than giving in to whims of passion, remember that internal leadership is born from a place of reason. By keeping your mind firmly planted on the ground, you'll tap into the gift of personal composure.

GEMINI
RULERS: MERCURY, URANUS

PURPOSE
To find personal authority within hard work, patience, and reason.

RELATIONSHIPS

You are unpredictable and exciting, and your relationships should be a place of mutual respect and grounding. By seeking out partners who are willing to put in the work for the long run, you will discover that true love is a reliable place to call home.

The Journey of
JUNE 17

Welcome to June 17, an expressive journey toward intellectual humility.

Share what you are inspired about today. *Courage* (The Number Five) doesn't need you to hold anything back as long as you are expressing it for the sake of creativity and joy. By putting yourself out there and revealing your innermost power, you can inspire others to do the same.

But don't get caught in the crossfire of opinion. Although Gemini season encourages you to speak your mind, *Maturity* (Five of Swords) reminds you that some words cannot be taken back. If you are met with criticism or contention, look for the silver lining of truth that can help you grow rather than defending your personal stance.

Because at the end of the day, you decide what is true for you. *Wisdom* (The Hierophant) reminds you that you have power over what gets under your skin, so remain discerning as you take in the opinions and perspectives of others. Instead of putting your self-esteem in the hands of others, ask yourself how you feel about your actions. If you are aligned with your highest and best, there is nothing to fear.

JUST FOR TODAY

TODAY'S MANTRA
I can courageously listen to my internal truth while remaining open to constructive feedback.

TODAY'S JOURNAL PROMPT
How do I typically respond to criticism? What are tactful ways I can handle it today?

TODAY'S RITUAL
Write down any feelings of frustration, anger, or resentment on a piece of paper. Say anything you'd like, even the words that you wouldn't want anyone else to read. When you feel relieved, rip up the paper and repeat the affirmation, "Better out than in, but I won't use my words to hurt others."

BORN ON THIS DAY

JAMES WELDON JOHNSON, American Harlem Renaissance poet, lyricist, civil rights activist, and leader of the NAACP

IGOR STRAVINSKY, Russian composer

"I don't focus on what I'm up against. I focus on my goals and I try to ignore the rest."—VENUS WILLIAMS, American tennis star, considered one of the all-time greats of women's tennis

The Journey of Those Born on
JUNE 17

Y ou were born of powerful intellect and a jovialness that can make you avoid tough conversations. You will have to stand up for your innermost truths, as your journey is one of vulnerability, self-awareness, and higher knowledge.

Early on in your journey, you will meet your audacious guide, *Courage* (The Number Five). Despite your understated nature, *Courage* calls you away from restraint and toward a path of wild visibility. By displaying your deepest thoughts on the center of the stage called life, you can take pride in your bravery. If you can choose self-expression over fear, you'll turn your words into a work of art.

But if you choose this vulnerable path, you will have to cross swords with *Maturity* (Five of Swords). Although you have a wicked way with words, *Maturity* asks you not to give in to mental combat when you come up against criticism or competitors. By remaining teachable and open to feedback, no matter how loud the applause gets, you'll discover the value of humility.

By rising to these grand occasions, you will access *Wisdom* (The Hierophant). *Wisdom* empowers you to tap into the divine intelligence that lives within, helping you decipher what information is worthy of absorption and what opinions are a downright waste of your time. By understanding that truth is subjective, you'll begin to think for yourself rather than giving away your power to false authority. If you can continue growing while remaining loyal to yourself, you'll reach a state of higher consciousness.

YOUR GUIDES
Astrology: Your Energy Gemini (Mercury, Uranus)
Numerology: Your Path Courage (The Number Five)
Minor Arcana: Your Lesson Maturity (The Five of Swords)
Major Arcana: Your Highest Calling Wisdom (The Hierophant)

GEMINI
RULERS: MERCURY, URANUS

PURPOSE
To dance to the delicate beat of humility and intellectual power.

RELATIONSHIPS

Your emotional power runs deep, and your relationships should be a place of radical honesty and mutual growth. By seeking out partners who are willing to have tough conversations for the sake of intimacy, you will discover that true love is a victory worth fighting for.

The Journey of
JUNE 18

Welcome to June 18, a sincere journey that introduces you to your worth.
Wear your heart on your sleeve today. Although Gemini season is more intellectual than emotional, *Devotion* (The Number Six) asks you to make decisions based on your intimate desires and loyalty. Share generously, whether it be kind words to the people you love most or offering a helping hand to a project you deeply believe in.

But prepare to *Transition* (Six of Swords) what is holding you back emotionally. If a protective yet destructive coping mechanism is blocking you from the personal fulfillment you seek most, reach out to your trusted support system for help willing yourself to part ways with this defense.

It is scary to shed old survival skills, but *Choice* (The Lovers) reminds you of how much potential there is for love. Make self-affirming decisions today to prioritize the healthy and nourishing relationships and obligations that you have in your life. If something or someone is draining your emotional tank, now is the time to take personal agency over your happiness and make room for something more true. Remain loyal to yourself at all costs, and the love you seek will follow.

───────────○───────────

JUST FOR TODAY

TODAY'S MANTRA
I can love others generously while advocating for my heart and happiness.

TODAY'S RITUAL
Take a warm bath with a large scoop of Epsom salt. Soak in a meditative state for a minimum of six minutes, repeating the affirmation, "My mental patterns can change."

TODAY'S JOURNAL PROMPT
What was my earliest experience of emotional belonging?

───────────○───────────

BORN ON THIS DAY

GEORGE MALLORY, English mountaineer who took part in the first three British expeditions to Mount Everest

CARMEL BUDIARDJO, English human rights activist, lecturer, and author

"It's a little better all the time."—**PAUL McCARTNEY**, English singer-songwriter, musician, and member of the Beatles

The Journey of Those Born on
JUNE 18

You were born of intuitive brilliance and an attachment to the past that can keep you from your future. You will have to learn to let go in order to move forward, as your journey is one of dedication, transition, and self-worth.

Early on in your journey, you will meet your sincere guide, *Devotion* (The Number Six). Despite your keen intellect, *Devotion* calls you away from mental isolation and toward a path of meaningful action. By channeling your feelings into thoughtful acts of service and words of affection, you'll learn how to wear your heart on your sleeve. If you can put love before ego, *Devotion* offers you the gift of honest connection.

But if you choose this earnest path, you will have to surrender your swords to *Transition* (Six of Swords). *Transition* calls you to part ways with the mental patterns that are holding you back from true emotional freedom, encouraging you to explore uncharted waters of intimacy. By relying on the support of your loved ones as you walk through the discomfort of internal transition, you can shed old protective skin.

YOUR GUIDES

Astrology: Your Energy
Gemini (Mercury, Uranus)

Numerology: Your Path
Devotion (The Number Six)

Minor Arcana: Your Lesson
Transition (The Six of Swords)

Major Arcana: Your Highest Calling
Choice (The Lovers)

By answering these calls for vulnerability, you will understand the power of *Choice* (The Lovers). *Choice* reminds you that you are responsible for protecting your heart and happiness, encouraging you to prioritize self-love over public praise. You will meet *Choice* in moments of disillusion, when something you once thought would fill the emotional void didn't end up satisfying. If you can look within for the love you desire most, you'll discover a lasting sense of personal contentment.

─────────────────○─────────────────

GEMINI
RULERS: MERCURY, URANUS

PURPOSE
To generously share your heart by seeking love from within.

RELATIONSHIPS

You are self-protective by nature, yet your relationships should be a place of earnest vulnerability and sincere devotion. By seeking out partners who give without caution and share their heart generously, you will discover that true love is a safe space to let down your guard.

The Journey of
JUNE 19

W elcome to June 19, a progressive journey that requires your sincerest efforts.
Get serious about your day. While Gemini season has a go-with-the-flow energy to it, *Commitment* (The Number Seven) asks you to say what you mean and do what you say. What responsibilities and obligations do you have toward others? If you are stretched too thin, narrow your focus to the things that matter most.

And try to appreciate what you have rather than focusing on what you lack. *Hypervigilance* (Seven of Swords) warns against feelings of not-enoughness. If you find that even though all is well in the present moment, your eyes are still sifting through what you don't have, calm your fears through mindfulness. Take a deep breath in and surrender your self-protective fears.

It is through this level of focus and appreciation that you can make great progress. *Evolution* (The Chariot) invites you to get clear about what you are fighting for today, so channel all your energy into your higher purpose. Whether you are pursuing an idea, relationship, or project, pour your will and your skill into it entirely. Show the universe just how serious you are and watch how far you'll go.

JUST FOR TODAY

TODAY'S MANTRA

I will focus on what I care about most, rather than worrying about what I don't have.

TODAY'S RITUAL

Get your hands on some pyrite, burn a candle, or light some incense. Channel the fire within these objects, and repeat the mantra, "Fire bring me the focus I need."

TODAY'S JOURNAL PROMPT

What are my fears around not getting "enough" in life? What is my history with scarcity?

BORN ON THIS DAY

SALMAN RUSHDIE, Indian-born English American novelist

JEAN DUJARDIN, first French actor to win an Academy Award for Best Actor

"It is not a sacrifice, it's a choice. If you choose to do something, then you shouldn't say it's a sacrifice, because nobody forced you to do it."—AUNG SAN SUU KYI, Burmese politician and human rights activist

The Journey of Those Born on
JUNE 19

Y ou were born of intuitive knowledge and an expansiveness that can make it difficult to focus on just one goal. You will have to get clear on what you want to fight for, as your journey is one of focus, surrender, and mental determination.

Early on in your journey, you will meet your serious guide, *Commitment* (The Number Seven). Despite your independent nature, *Commitment* calls you away from self-seeking and toward a path of meaningful responsibility. By showing up for the people, projects, and potential that you care about most, you'll learn the importance of keeping to your word.

But if you choose this honest path, *Hypervigilance* (Seven of Swords) will ask you to question why nothing ever seems to be enough. You will meet *Hypervigilance* in moments where your soul is at peace and yet your head is constantly searching for what else can ease its discontentment. If you can make note of what you do have, trusting that you don't have to strategize and manipulate to get your needs met, you'll learn to become fulfilled in the present moment.

By answering these calls for integrity, *Evolution* (The Chariot) will take you to new realms of self-realization. *Evolution* lies in the unexpected breakthroughs, when years of loyalty, labor, and perseverance suddenly break you through a ceiling you never imagined you'd touch. Sometimes, success comes slowly and then all at once. If you can remain patient and focused on the work at hand, it'll all be worth your while.

○

GEMINI
RULERS: MERCURY, URANUS

PURPOSE
To be loyal to, and content with, the people, projects, and visions that matter most.

RELATIONSHIPS

You are brilliant and independent, yet your relationships should be a place of loyalty and integrity. By seeking partners who are committed to the growth and success of the relationship and require you to do the same, you will discover that true love always sticks to its word.

The Journey of
JUNE 20

Welcome to June 20, a self-affirming journey that requires mental fortitude.
Stay true to yourself no matter what. *Power* (The Number Eight) asks you to be honest rather than perfect, so step into the fullness of your authentic being and don't worry if it makes anyone uncomfortable. More than likely, by honoring the person you are, you can win the confidence of others and inspire them to be sincere in return.

But spend some time working on *Negativity* (Eight of Swords). Gemini season can take the mind to many places, so watch out for self-harming mental patterns that keep you stuck in the grasps of limiting beliefs. It is scary to expand into the full brilliance of your humanity, but don't let your brain steer you away from being real.

And if the fear persists, tap into *Resilience* (Strength). Remember how much you have endured and acknowledge how much your emotional muscles have strengthened over time. By reaching this place of internal power, you can handle today with personal integrity rather than getting carried away with the whims of passion, fear, and anger. You are the divine leader of how you show up emotionally today.

―――――――――――――――○―――――――――――――――

JUST FOR TODAY

TODAY'S MANTRA

When I am being real, I can access the full breadth of my emotional power.

TODAY'S JOURNAL PROMPT

When I expand into my power, what fears and negative thought patterns come up?

TODAY'S RITUAL

Look up eight positive affirmations. Even if they feel uncomfortable and untrue, say them aloud to yourself in front of the mirror. When you are finished, wrap your arms around your torso and hug yourself gently.

―――――――――――――――○―――――――――――――――

BORN ON THIS DAY

PATRISSE CULLORS, American activist, cofounder of the Black Lives Matter movement, artist, and writer

BRIAN WILSON, American singer-songwriter, musician, and member of the Beach Boys

"Greatness comes from fear. Fear can either shut us down and we go home, or we fight through it."—LIONEL RICHIE, American singer and television personality

The Journey of Those Born on
JUNE 20*

Y ou were born of intellectual diplomacy and a mental awareness that can make it difficult for
you to surrender your inhibitions. You will discover the strength in vulnerability, as your
journey is one of authenticity, perspective-shifting, and emotional tenacity.

Early on in your journey, you will meet your mysterious guide, *Power* (The Number Eight). Despite your socially harmonious personality, *Power* calls you away
from people-pleasing and toward a path of radical self-
embodiment. By stepping into the truth of who you actually are, you'll discover how influential, and successful,
you can be when you're being real.

But if you choose this empowering path, you will
have to address *Negativity* (Eight of Swords). *Negativity*
lies in the traps of the mind that hold you back through
limiting beliefs. You will meet *Negativity* in moments
of low confidence, when you question whether you are
worthy of so much prosperity. If you can find compassion for these voices that try to keep you small, you'll
also find the chance to heal.

By answering these calls for self-honesty, *Resilience*
(Strength) will remind you of how emotionally power-

YOUR GUIDES
Astrology: Your Energy
Gemini (Mercury, Uranus)
Numerology: Your Path
Power (The Number Eight)
Minor Arcana: Your Lesson
Negativity (The Eight of Swords)
Major Arcana: Your Highest Calling
Resilience (Strength)

ful you are. You will meet *Resilience* when you are forced to rely on yourself, when the worst has
happened and yet you preserve, carried by an inner knowing that everything will work out in the
long run. If you can trust in your internal strength, *Resilience* teaches you that you can handle
anything.

──────────────○──────────────

GEMINI
RULERS: MERCURY, URANUS

PURPOSE
*To be completely true to the power
that lives within.*

RELATIONSHIPS

You are diplomatic and partnership-driven by nature, so your relationships should be a place of
radical authenticity and deep honesty. By seeking out partners who want to see you for who you
are rather than who they want you to be, you will discover that true love is empowering.

Are you a Cancer born on this day? Head to page 760 to find your additional birthday guide!

WELCOME TO

CANCER
SEASON

The Journey of
JUNE 21

W elcome to June 21, an experiential journey toward internal growth.

Despite the self-protective nature of Cancer season, *Experience* (The Number Nine) asks you to step out of your emotional cocoon and into the unknown. Look for every opportunity to try something new today, even if it scares you. By keeping your mind and heart open to a diverse range of experiences, you can widen your scope of compassion.

And as you experience the foreign, make room for *Gratitude* (Nine of Cups). Between these courageous efforts, pause and zoom out so you can witness the magic that comes from the human experience. Go for a short walk or drive up to somewhere with a view and say thank you for the gifts today has brought you.

But if you ever feel lost or afraid, tap into *Instinct* (The Hermit). Instead of relying on others or the internet for direction, reach inside to access your intuitive intelligence. More than likely, this divine voice of reason knows exactly where you should be going, so put one foot in front of the other as you let your gut be your guide. By following the beat of your intuitive drum, today can help you build trust with yourself.

JUST FOR TODAY

TODAY'S MANTRA

My intuition can lead me to new heights of growth and gratitude.

TODAY'S JOURNAL PROMPT

What are nine emotional qualities that I admire in other people (e.g., kindness, loyalty, etc.)?

TODAY'S RITUAL

Go somewhere with a view. Whether you hike to the peak of a mountain or drive up to the highest spot in your town, rest at the top and enjoy the scenery. Take in nine deep breaths, and after each one repeat the affirmation, "Life is a grand adventure."

BORN ON THIS DAY

SHIRIN EBADI, Iranian lawyer, human rights activist, and first Iranian Muslim woman to receive a Nobel Peace Prize

LANA DEL REY, American singer-songwriter

"If you are lonely when you're alone, you are in bad company."—JEAN-PAUL SARTRE, French existentialist philosopher and writer

The Journey of Those Born on
JUNE 21

Y ou were born of emotional abundance and an insatiable desire for expansion. You will have to find freedom within emotional growth, as your journey is one of personal searching, gratitude, and self-trust.

Early on in your journey, you will meet your soulful guide, *Experience* (The Number Nine). *Experience* leads you away from the familiar daily hustle toward a quieter path, one that beckons you toward the truth. You will meet *Experience* when you part ways with your material ambitions and addictions so that you can run with arms wide open toward the great unknown.

If you choose this spiraling path, you will meet your great teacher, *Gratitude* (Nine of Cups). *Gratitude* asks you to rest quietly in emotional satisfaction, a task that may be harder for you than it initially appears. You are a seeker, yearning for more, but if you can bow to the gifts that the universe has given you and surrender your restless soul, you'll tap into the healing power of acknowledgment.

YOUR GUIDES

Astrology: Your Energy
Cancer (The Moon)

Numerology: Your Path
Experience (The Number Nine)

Minor Arcana: Your Lesson
Gratitude (The Nine of Cups)

Major Arcana: Your Highest Calling
Instinct (The Hermit)

By answering these calls for growth, *Instinct* (The Hermit) will remind you that you are never truly alone. *Instinct* gets you in touch with the intuitive voice within, lighting your way through the darkest night of the soul and gently guiding you toward the next right action. You will meet *Instinct* when you realize that you can't overplan or overprepare. Instead, if you can trust that you are moving toward your destiny, you'll discover the spiritual map that lies within.

CANCER
RULER: THE MOON

PURPOSE
To find emotional healing in the darkness of the unknown.

RELATIONSHIPS

You are able to hold space for even the darkest of characters, but your relationships should be a place to recharge your batteries. By attracting partners who seek to fill your cup rather than take from it, you will discover that true love doesn't always have to be painful.

The Journey of
JUNE 22

Welcome to June 22, a radical trust fall into the arms of fate.

Follow the beat of your intuition today. *Autonomy* (The Number One) encourages you to believe in your powers of perception as you carve out your unique place in society today. Don't ask for permission or wait for acceptance—just be yourself and see where the day takes you.

But don't stop there. Despite the emotionally protective nature of Cancer season, *Vulnerability* (Ace of Cups) asks you to put your heart on the line and get excited about what you care about most. Whether you are pursuing an intimate relationship or a creative endeavor, let your authentic feelings nourish the potential of these emotional connections.

And try to appreciate the ebbs and flows of the day. Even if it is scary, *Impermanence* (Wheel of Fortune) reminds you that destiny is an ever-moving target, meaning you shouldn't get too hung up on any one outcome. Perhaps your worst-case scenario is truly a blessing in disguise, so practice gratitude for each twist and turn that the day offers. Hang on to your hat and embrace the divine roller coaster of fate.

―――――――――――――――○―――――――――――――――

JUST FOR TODAY

TODAY'S MANTRA
I will put myself emotionally out there while leaving the outcome up to fate.

TODAY'S RITUAL
Hold on to a piece of celestite or go near a flowing body of water (or just run your faucet). Close your eyes and imagine the purity of your heart flowing out from you and into the world around you.

TODAY'S JOURNAL PROMPT
How do I typically react when an act of vulnerability doesn't turn out how I hoped?

―――――――――――――――○―――――――――――――――

BORN ON THIS DAY

CICELY SAUNDERS, English nurse, physician, and writer who founded the first modern hospice

VIJAY, Indian film actor, dancer, and philanthropist

"It's better to fight because if you don't fight, you can't win. Besides, even when you don't win, you can change the game."—ELIZABETH WARREN, American academic and US senator

The Journey of Those Born on
JUNE 22

You were born of emotional discipline and a sense of responsibility for the ones you love that at times can feel like a burden. You will have to learn to let go and take risks, as your journey is one of trailblazing, openheartedness, and karmic fate.

Early on in your journey, you will meet your fearless guide, *Autonomy* (The Number One). Despite your cautious tendencies, *Autonomy* calls you away from playing it safe and toward a path of intuitive progress. By listening to your gut rather than the rules of society, you can do what has never been done before. If you can move toward enthusiasm over fear, you'll learn how to seize the moment.

And if you choose this bold path, you'll need to encourage *Vulnerability* (Ace of Cups). You will meet *Vulnerability* in moments of emotional excitement, when your hopefulness about a creative or personal endeavor outweighs any insecurity or imposter syndrome. Risk putting your heart on the line in return for radical belonging.

By answering these calls for courage, don't worry about the outcome of your efforts. *Impermanence* (Wheel of Fortune) asks you to simply go along for the ride, surrendering your will so the journey can feel that much smoother. You will meet *Impermanence* in the emotional ups and well as the downs, when you have no choice but to trust that your destiny is unfolding as it should. If you can appreciate every ebb and flow of the human experience, you'll also learn how to appreciate the in-between.

CANCER
RULER: THE MOON

PURPOSE
To surrender control and make a date with destiny.

RELATIONSHIPS

You are steady and reliable, but your relationships should be a place of risk-taking and vulnerability. By putting your feelings out there with no certainty of return, you will discover that true love is a divine trust fall.

The Journey of
JUNE 23

Welcome to June 23, a partnership-driven journey that demands equality.

Aim for *Balance* (The Number Two) today. Rather than taking your emotions to extremes, try to walk the middle road as you flow in harmony with your personal and professional partners. By reaching for compassion and harmony as you coconspire with others, you may be surprised at how easy the work feels.

But listen to *Worthiness* (Two of Cups). Although Cancer season encourages us to give rather than take, make sure that your relationships are reciprocating your heartfelt efforts. Don't waste time on the obligations that drain you, but instead, give special focus to the people who are aligned with your needs. True love shouldn't have to be an uphill battle.

But *Truth* (Justice) is worth fighting for. State your perspective loud and clear to the people you trust, and be sure you are listening in return by holding yourself accountable. Equality is your north star today, so if you notice an injustice in your personal or professional setting, stop at nothing to bring this issue to light. Through calm and logical communication, you can ensure that everyone's needs are being met.

JUST FOR TODAY

TODAY'S MANTRA

Fairness, equality, and love are birthrights, so I will treat myself and others accordingly.

TODAY'S RITUAL

Find some rose quartz or rose oil and place it under your pillow when you go to sleep tonight. Just before you close your eyes to fall asleep, repeat the prayer, "Love, help me find my harmony."

TODAY'S JOURNAL PROMPT

What partnerships tend to meet me halfway, emotionally and tangibly?

BORN ON THIS DAY

JUNE CARTER CASH, American Grammy Award–winning singer-songwriter and actor

HUDA SHA'ARAWI, Egyptian feminist leader, suffragist, and nationalist

"Sometimes it is the people no one imagines anything of who do the things that no one can imagine."—ALAN TURING, English mathematician and computer scientist pioneer

The Journey of Those Born on
JUNE 23

Y ou were born of emotional passion and an unintentional penchant for emotional drama. You will have to decide what is worth fighting for, as your journey is one of harmony, reciprocation, and personal truth.

Early on in your journey, you will meet your tranquil guide, *Balance* (The Number Two). Despite your strong-willed nature, *Balance* calls you away from a life of drama and toward a path of peaceful coexistence. By staying in compassion rather than righteousness, you can build meaningful partnerships that take some of the weight off your plate. If you can aim for unity, you'll discover that two hearts are better than one.

And if you choose this partnership-driven path, you will have to embrace *Worthiness* (Two of Cups). *Worthiness* reminds you of the importance of emotional reciprocation, encouraging you to invest in the relationships that give as generously as you do. You will meet *Worthiness* in moments of interpersonal alignment when your needs and desires flow in harmony with one another.

> ## YOUR GUIDES
>
> *Astrology: Your Energy*
> Cancer (The Moon)
>
> *Numerology: Your Path*
> Balance (The Number Two)
>
> *Minor Arcana: Your Lesson*
> Worthiness (The Two of Cups)
>
> *Major Arcana: Your Highest Calling*
> Truth (Justice)

By answering these calls for intimacy, you will unlock the consciousness of *Truth* (Justice). *Truth* reminds you that equality in partnership is an ever-evolving concept that must be considered again and again over time. Rather than falling prey to the extremes of right and wrong, good and bad, *Truth* encourages you to create your own definition of fairness within your relationships. By stating your needs loud and clear and asking your loved ones to do the same, you'll discover mutuality never has to be a guessing game.

CANCER
RULER: THE MOON

PURPOSE
To actively seek justice, harmony, and emotional reciprocity within partnership.

RELATIONSHIPS

You are intuitive and wise, and your relationships should be a place of clear communication and equality. By seeking out partners who aren't afraid to state their needs while encouraging you to do the same, you will discover that true love always aims to be fair.

The Journey of
JUNE 24

Welcome to June 24, a fruitful journey of emotional connection.

Despite the sensitive and protective nature of Cancer season, *Flexibility* (The Number Three) asks you to step out of your comfort zone and learn from others. Pick the brain of a new colleague or potential friend and keep an open heart as you explore the depths of their lived experience. You never know what you can discover if you remain curious.

And embrace the power of *Belonging* (Three of Cups). Call a few old friends or reach out to a few of your trusted coworkers and share how you really feel. By putting your heart out there and earnestly looking for friendship, you can come out of today with a new sense of community.

And my, what joy this sense of belonging can bring. *Abundance* (The Empress) invites you to enjoy the day, relishing the beauty and wonder that comes from sharing. Put on a gorgeous celebration for the people you love, or go out in nature with a few of your friends and soak in every inch of pleasure that is offered to you. The more magic you give, the more you'll receive.

JUST FOR TODAY

TODAY'S MANTRA
I can give and receive good things today.

TODAY'S RITUAL
Choose three friends to extend small gifts to today. It could be a handwritten note or their favorite cup of coffee, but think carefully about what each of them would love.

TODAY'S JOURNAL PROMPT
What have been my historical experiences around friendship?

BORN ON THIS DAY

LIONEL MESSI, Argentine footballer

SOLANGE KNOWLES, American singer-songwriter, performance artist, and actor

"I have a personality defect where I refuse to see myself as an underdog."—MINDY KALING, American actor, comedian, and screenwriter

The Journey of Those Born on
JUNE 24

You were born of deep compassion and an empathy toward others that you rarely turn toward yourself. You will have to learn how to receive the support you need, as your journey is one of open-mindedness, belonging, and emotional prosperity.

Early on in your journey, you will meet your inquisitive guide, *Flexibility* (The Number Three). Despite your sentimental nature, *Flexibility* calls you away from your comfort zone and toward a path of perspective-shifting collaboration. By staying open to the wisdom and experience of new friends and colleagues, you'll discover there is much to learn if you are willing to try.

If you choose this openhearted path, you will be greeted by *Belonging* (Three of Cups). You are sensitive and empathic, but building relationships with people you grow to trust comes with huge emotional rewards. You will meet *Belonging* in times of authentic belonging, when your personal truth is accepted and nourished by a core group of supportive individuals. If you can choose vulnerability over self-protection, you'll tap into the value of community.

YOUR GUIDES

Astrology: Your Energy
Cancer (The Moon)

Numerology: Your Path
Flexibility (The Number Three)

Minor Arcana: Your Lesson
Belonging (The Three of Cups)

Major Arcana: Your Highest Calling
Abundance (The Empress)

By embracing these calls for inclusion, you will make room in your heart for *Abundance* (The Empress). *Abundance* comes when you receive the emotional support you need from others, letting your guard down and surrendering to the joy that comes from true intimacy. You will meet *Abundance* in moments of beautiful connection, when your heart overflows with happiness. If you can stay present with the excruciating vulnerability of love, your cup will always remain full.

CANCER
RULER: THE MOON

PURPOSE

To embrace the excruciating vulnerability of authentic connection and loving support.

RELATIONSHIPS

You are emotionally generous, and your relationships should be a place of mutual encouragement and positivity. By seeking out partners who champion your beauty, creativity, and magic, you will discover that true love is eternally supportive of your happiness.

The Journey of
JUNE 25

Welcome to June 25, an emotionally contained journey toward personal leadership.

Create a solid foundation of work today. Cancer season has everyone feeling extra sensitive, but *Discipline* (The Number Four) asks you to channel your heart into the tangible tasks and responsibilities you have at hand. What do you need to get done? Put one foot in front of the other, relying on integrity rather than emotion.

But if you are swimming through some murky emotional water, *Reflection* (Four of Cups) invites you to clear up some things before you look toward the future. Go inward to understand the feelings of grief, pain, sadness, or regret that you are experiencing. Have a good cry, a good scream, or a good laugh, and don't apologize for how long it takes to feel better.

Besides, *Self-mastery* (The Emperor) means you are responsible for your own well-being. Step into a place of internal authority, making concrete decisions that serve your own and others' best interests today. If you find yourself caught by a wave of erratic passion, take a slow and meditative breath as you get back to center. By balancing logic with intuition, you can be the responsible caretaker you always needed.

JUST FOR TODAY

TODAY'S MANTRA
I can balance my emotions with gentle compassion and objective reason.

TODAY'S RITUAL
Take an ice-cold bath or do a polar plunge in a cold body of water. Count backward from four and let the sobering experience clear out old emotional baggage.

TODAY'S JOURNAL PROMPT
What emotions am I experiencing that I have been denying or avoiding?

BORN ON THIS DAY

ANTONI GAUDÍ, Catalan Spanish architect

JAMES MEREDITH, American civil rights activist and first Black student admitted to the University of Mississippi

"The further a society drifts from truth the more it will hate those who speak it."—GEORGE ORWELL, English novelist, essayist, journalist, and critic

The Journey of Those Born on
JUNE 25

You were born of fearsome loyalty and an unrelenting need for control. You will have to learn to harness the power of feeling, as your journey is one of hard work, contemplation, and personal authority.

Early on in your journey, you will meet your austere guide, *Discipline* (The Number Four). Despite your sensitive and cautious nature, *Discipline* calls you away from timidity and toward a path of unstoppable dedication. By putting in long hours of consistent work, you'll learn how sustainable success is built upon a solid foundation of humility.

But if you choose this tenacious path, you will have to pause for *Reflection* (Four of Cups). Heartbreak, disappointment, and regret are all natural parts of the human experience, and *Reflection* encourages you to sit with these feelings rather than bypassing them in an attempt to not feel any pain. By listening to grief and holding yourself through discomfort, you'll discover the opportunity to heal and clear old emotions.

By answering these calls to balance perseverance with awareness, you will step into the power of *Self-mastery* (The Emperor). *Self-mastery* invites you to be an objective yet compassionate authority toward yourself. You will meet *Self-mastery* in moments of personal leadership, when you act in the best interest of yourself and others by basing your decisions on intuitive logic rather than blind passion. If you can remain patient rather than jumping to conclusions, you'll tap into the gift of empathic reason.

───────────○───────────

CANCER
RULER: THE MOON

PURPOSE
To channel even the most difficult of emotions into empathic leadership.

RELATIONSHIPS

You are compassionate and loyal, and your relationships should be a place of healthy boundaries and clear communication. By seeking out partners who bring order and structure to the boundless nature of emotion, you will discover that true love can be a safe container for your feelings.

The Journey of
JUNE 26

Welcome to June 26, an emotionally brave journey that builds personal authority.

Share honestly today. Although Cancer season encourages emotional self-protection, *Courage* (The Number Five) inspires you to push past any fears of vulnerability and take center stage in your life. Listen to your gut as you decipher when it is appropriate and important to put yourself out there and have your voice heard.

But don't overlook or attempt to bypass *Grief* (Five of Cups). If some pangs of regret come up for you, whether it be from the past or the present, hold compassionate space for yourself and others. Self-forgiveness is at the heart of progress today, so try to make peace with what was so you can open an emotional door for what is to come.

This personal healing is necessary because *Wisdom* (The Hierophant) needs you to trust yourself today. Rather than giving away your power to the powers that be, look within for the answers to your deepest questions. By listening to your divine intelligence rather than the opinions of others, you can make decisions that remind you of how powerfully intuitive you are. No one knows your truth better than you do.

───────○───────

JUST FOR TODAY

TODAY'S MANTRA
Through self-forgiveness I can bravely trust and share my truth.

TODAY'S JOURNAL PROMPT
When I put myself out there and share vulnerably, do I tend to care about others' opinions of me more than my own?

TODAY'S RITUAL
Forgive yourself. Lie on your back somewhere comfortable, close your eyes, and place your hand over your heart. Visualize an incident that you regret and ask that version of yourself why they did what they did. Repeat the affirmation, "I did the best I could at the time."

───────○───────

BORN ON THIS DAY

MARYAM AL-KHAWAJA, Bahraini human rights activist

EMMA MILLER, English Australian union organizer and suffragist

"Don't ever doubt yourselves or waste a second of your life. It's too short, and you're too special."
—ARIANA GRANDE, American singer

The Journey of Those Born on
JUNE 26

Y ou were born of intuitive power and a depth of feeling that you rarely share with others. You will have to boldly express your truth, as your journey is one of vulnerability, self-forgiveness, and personal authority.

Early on in your journey, you will meet your intense guide, *Courage* (The Number Five). Despite your introspective nature, *Courage* calls you away from morbid reflection and toward a path of emotional bravery. Rather than keeping your innermost feelings to yourself, *Courage* empowers you to find your voice and channel your emotions into works of art. If you can choose guts over safety, you'll discover a life of creative fulfillment.

But if you choose this path of visibility, you will have to contend with *Grief* (Five of Cups). You will meet *Grief* in regret, when you find yourself so consumed with despair about what didn't work out that you are unable to move forward. *Grief* asks you to forgive others, and most importantly forgive yourself, so that you can begin setting your heart onto newer and truer promises of hope. If you can hold tender space for what was, you can make emotional space for what's to come.

YOUR GUIDES

Astrology: Your Energy
Cancer (The Moon)

Numerology: Your Path
Courage (The Number Five)

Minor Arcana: Your Lesson
Grief (The Five of Cups)

Major Arcana: Your Highest Calling
Wisdom (The Hierophant)

By answering these heroic calls, you will unlock the power of *Wisdom* (The Hierophant). *Wisdom* asks you to get to know the intelligent authority that lives within, allowing you to discern what is true and false for you personally. Rather than giving away your power and expecting others to know what is best for you, *Wisdom* empowers you to be in charge of yourself. If you can remain self-assured yet teachable, you'll find the confidence you need to honor your deepest truths.

―――――――――――――――――○―――――――――――――――――

CANCER
RULER: THE MOON

PURPOSE
To forgive yourself in order to access the emotional courage of self-belief.

RELATIONSHIPS

You are deep and introspective, and your relationships should be a place of complete vulnerability and courage. By seeking out partners who don't hold back anything and empower you to do the same, you will discover that true love builds self-confidence.

The Journey of
JUNE 27

W elcome to June 27, a tenderhearted journey of courageous vulnerability.
 Act from the heart today. If you feel emotionally attached to a person, project, or idea, pour your soul into it rather than protecting your heart from such openness. *Devotion* (The Number Six) is the name of the game, so put yourself out there and discover the satisfaction that comes from sincerity.

And get in touch with your inner child. Cancer season is reflective by nature, but *Nostalgia* (Six of Cups) brings old memories to the surface so you can integrate them into the present. What personal stories is your mind drifting toward, and what might they be trying to tell you? The past is a wonderful portal into what needs to be addressed today.

Plus, this internal healing will introduce you to your worth. *Choice* (The Lovers) wants you to act in your best interests today, prioritizing the people and opportunities that fill your emotional cup in return for your generosity. If you believe that someone or something will heal you, take back your power by looking within for the validation you desire most. Nothing is more powerful than self-love.

JUST FOR TODAY

TODAY'S MANTRA

The past is a powerful portal into the self-love I need today.

TODAY'S RITUAL

Find something that transports you back to your childhood. It could be an old item of clothing or a specific ingredient or smell. As you hold this object in your hand, repeat the spell, "Memory, memory, take me back to a time that was heavenly."

TODAY'S JOURNAL PROMPT

Are there any parts of myself that I have lost since childhood? Do I want to bring them back?

BORN ON THIS DAY

PAUL LAURENCE DUNBAR, American poet

J. J. ABRAMS, American television and movie writer, producer, and director

"The best and most beautiful things in the world cannot be seen or even touched—they must be felt with the heart."—HELEN KELLER, American political activist, author, lecturer, and the first deaf and blind person to earn a bachelor's degree

The Journey of Those Born on
JUNE 27

You were born of lunar instinct and a fear of being hurt that can block you from true connection. You will have to reopen your heart to others and yourself, as your journey is one of generosity, sentimentality, and self-worth.

Early on in your journey, you will meet your tender-hearted guide, *Devotion* (The Number Six). Despite your introverted nature, *Devotion* calls you away from emotional isolation and toward a path of sincere service. By only pursuing the longings of the heart and giving your all to the people and causes that matter most, you'll build a life of compassionate purpose.

If you take this loving path, you will bump into your reflective friend, *Nostalgia* (Six of Cups). *Nostalgia* calls you back to the past, inspiring you to reintegrate your most crucial memories of happiness, belonging, sadness, grief, and fear. Not all of these stories were easy at the time, but work on healing these old wounds so you can build a strong and intimate relationship with the joyful child who lives within.

By answering these calls to peel back old emotional layers, you will come to understand the power of *Choice* (The Lovers). No one and no one thing can make you love yourself. Instead, by recognizing your worth, *Choice* empowers you to be your own best advocate as you build a profound sense of emotional self-esteem. By making decisions that fill your cup rather than drain your resources, you'll discover the love you always needed comes from within.

CANCER
RULER: THE MOON

PURPOSE
*To peel back the emotional layers
that block self-love.*

RELATIONSHIPS

You are emotionally self-sufficient, yet your relationship should be a place of tenderheartedness. By seeking out partners who are as generous with their affection as they are with their heart, you will discover that true love never holds anything back.

The Journey of
JUNE 28

W elcome to June 28, an emotionally discerning journey that leads to radical progress.
Show up to your responsibilities today. Cancer season is quite passive in nature, but *Commitment* (The Number Seven) asks you to align your actions with your loyalties. Who and what are you obligated toward? Be the reliable partner, colleague, and friend you know you are capable of becoming.

But be wary of *Illusion* (Seven of Cups). If you have been fantasizing about a dreamlike solution to your problems, today asks you to reintegrate reality into your thinking by calling an objective friend. When something seems too good to be true, more than likely there are better places you could be investing your time and energy.

And if you get serious about what matters rather than wasting time on what doesn't, *Evolution* (The Chariot) ensures you'll make great progress today. Reach inside yourself to a place of personal conviction as you narrow your focus to the relationships and projects that call your heart. Believe in your potential as you place one strategic foot in front of the other, reaching new heights of success and satisfaction. Remember, the universe always rewards sincerity.

─────────────────────○─────────────────────

JUST FOR TODAY

TODAY'S MANTRA
I will invest in the potential of the people and projects that are real.

TODAY'S JOURNAL PROMPT
Who, and what, am I emotionally responsible for today?

TODAY'S RITUAL
Get yourself a huge piece of amethyst, or if you can't access one, find an image of it online. As you stare at the amethyst, repeat the mantra, "Sobriety stone, clear my vision and guide me to the right decision."

─────────────────────○─────────────────────

BORN ON THIS DAY

ALICE MAY DOUGLAS, American newspaper editor and author of poetry, children's literature, and nonfiction

ELON MUSK, South African–born American entrepreneur and inventor

"I went from years of honing my craft to sudden recognition. It was quite a life changer."—KATHY BATES, American Academy Award–winning actor

The Journey of Those Born on
JUNE 28

You were born of intuitive ambition and an emotional unpredictability that can steer you away from your highest potential. You will have to find grounding in tangible progress, as your journey is one of decisiveness, reality, and radical progress.

Early on in your journey, you will meet your faithful guide, *Commitment* (The Number Seven). Despite your autonomous nature, *Commitment* calls you away from self-indulgence and toward a path of interpersonal responsibility. Rather than only looking out for number one, show your loyalty to others through thoughtful action.

If you invest in what matters, watch out for *Illusion* (Seven of Cups). *Illusion* warns you of the fantasy of what could be, when you believe that if you only had that one thing all your problems would be solved. However, not all dreams are what they seem, and *Illusion* calls you to break the spell by reaching out to your trustworthy and objective partners. By remaining willing to rethink your deepest desires, you'll begin to see things as they are.

YOUR GUIDES

Astrology: Your Energy
Cancer (The Moon)

Numerology: Your Path
Commitment (The Number Seven)

Minor Arcana: Your Lesson
Illusion (The Seven of Cups)

Major Arcana: Your Highest Calling
Evolution (The Chariot)

By answering these calls for personal discernment, you will move at the divine pace of *Evolution* (The Chariot). You will meet *Evolution* in the breakthrough moments of achievement. Success, however, is rarely an overnight sensation, but sheer commitment to your ambitions brings radical progress in the long run. If you can show the universe just how determined you are to meet your goals, *Evolution* will ensure you get there.

CANCER
RULER: THE MOON

PURPOSE
To pursue only what matters, prioritizing tangible progress over fantasy.

RELATIONSHIPS

You are an independent spirit, and your relationships should be a place of sincere commitment and respect. By seeking out partners who keep to their word and require you to do the same, you will discover that true love thrives when handled with integrity.

The Journey of
JUNE 29

Welcome to June 29, an empowering journey of emotional vulnerability.
Step into your *Power* (The Number Eight) today. Despite the timid and self-protective nature of Cancer season, own who you are and don't apologize for taking up space in the world. Get in honest touch with yourself as you decide what you want to pursue and how you wish to succeed.

But as you get more real, prepare for *Disappointment* (Eight of Cups). If a relationship or commitment is no longer in alignment with your future dreams, don't be afraid to part ways with it today. It's scary to move on without a clear plan but trust your intuition as you pursue greater ground.

And as you shed old layers, tap into *Resilience* (Strength). Rather than getting lost in the impermanence of feeling, channel your emotional force into a higher purpose of helping others. By being raw and vulnerable with yourself, you can spread this radical freedom to others and inspire them to live a life of truth. Invite deep conversation with your trusted partners and friends today, and remind them of just how special they are.

JUST FOR TODAY

TODAY'S MANTRA

By being radically true to myself, I can empower others to practice the same level of vulnerability.

TODAY'S JOURNAL PROMPT

Are there any emotional obligations that I am ready to walk away from?

TODAY'S RITUAL

Make an altar of your disappointments. On small scraps of paper, write down eight current regrets you are ready to move away from, and place them beside a black candle. Light the candle, and repeat the affirmation, "I am grateful for everything I have gained, everything I have lost, and everything I must let go of." In a fireproof bowl, burn these notes to ash and bury them in a nearby piece of land.

BORN ON THIS DAY

PRASANTA CHANDRA MAHALANOBIS, Indian scientist and applied statistician

CAMILA MENDES, American actor and singer

"Nobody can make you angry without your consent, nobody can disappoint you without your consent, you have to give people consent to do these things."—CHARLAMAGNE THA GOD, American radio and television personality, actor, and author

The Journey of Those Born on
JUNE 29

You were born of divine compassion and an emotional loyalty that can keep you stuck in draining relationships. You will have to move on to discover just how strong you are, as your journey is one of authenticity, discontent, and emotional fortitude.

Early on in your journey, you will meet your mystical guide, *Power* (The Number Eight). Despite your diplomatic nature, *Power* calls you away from passivity and toward a path of radical self-confidence. By stepping into the full breadth of your authentic spirit, you'll learn how to feel good in your own skin. If you can choose truth over people-pleasing, *Power* helps you change the status quo.

But if you choose this dynamic path, you will have to surrender to *Disappointment* (Eight of Cups). You will meet *Disappointment* when something you once thought would fulfill you no longer resonates deep down. It is a tough pill to swallow when you know an emotional attachment must break, but *Disappointment* reminds you that there is so much to look forward to if you are willing to be brave.

By answering these mighty calls to honesty, *Resilience* (Strength) will remind you of the enormous emotional muscles you have built over a lifetime. You will meet *Resilience* in moments of spiritual endurance, when the universe hurls the winds of fate yet you manage to keep your feelings planted firmly on the ground through integrity. If you can harness your emotions with internal strength, you'll learn just how much you can handle.

CANCER
RULER: THE MOON

PURPOSE
To step bravely away from disappointment and into the enormous power of authenticity.

RELATIONSHIPS

You are harmonious and easygoing, and your relationships should be a place of radical authenticity and self-revelation. By seeking out partners who champion you to grow into the full breadth of your power, you will discover that true love never asks you to stay small.

The Journey of
JUNE 30

Welcome to June 30, an emotional adventure that connects you to your intuition.

Go toward the feelings that are foreign to you. Despite Cancer season's desire for safety, *Experience* (The Number Nine) invites you to view today as an interpersonal adventure, so dive heart-first into the relationships and projects that push you the most. Whether you switch up your norm at home or try a new form of therapy, you'll learn by doing.

And make some space for *Gratitude* (Nine of Cups). Zoom out on your life, and express thanks to the people who have filled your cup along the way. Call an old friend or trusted adviser and let them know exactly what you gained from the relationship. By recognizing the good in your life, you can spread this abundance widely.

But as you step out on these emotional ledges, fall back on the power of *Instinct* (The Hermit). Your gut will tell you where to go today, so if you are feeling lost or confused at any point, slow down and meditate on what to do next. By trusting in the divine intelligence that lives within, you can make choices that are in alignment with your higher self.

JUST FOR TODAY

TODAY'S MANTRA
I will bravely pursue the emotional unknown, guided by my intuition.

TODAY'S JOURNAL PROMPT
What is a new and foreign way I could express my vulnerability today?

TODAY'S RITUAL
Tap into gratitude by making a list of nine things you are appreciative of. They can be people, places, or things, but make sure they are sincere choices. When you are finished, fold the paper nine times and repeat the affirmation, "Thank you for everything you have done for me."

BORN ON THIS DAY

KAHO, Japanese actor and fashion model

ASSIA DJEBAR, Algerian novelist, translator, and filmmaker

"There will be obstacles. There will be doubters. There will be mistakes. But with hard work . . . there are no limits."—MICHAEL PHELPS, American competitive swimmer and most successful and decorated Olympian of all time

The Journey of Those Born on
JUNE 30

You were born of lunar intuition and a deep desire for familiarity. You will have to grow toward the feelings that scare you, as your journey is one of adventure, recognition, and divine intelligence.

Early on in your journey, you will meet your risk-taking guide, *Experience* (The Number Nine). Despite the comfort of certainty, *Experience* calls you away from emotional complacency and toward a path of the unknown. By stepping out of your heart's comfort zone, you'll reach new heights of compassion and shared understanding.

But if you choose this wide-open path, you will have to make room in your heart for *Gratitude* (Nine of Cups). It's easy to focus on what you don't have, but *Gratitude* invites you to take a step back every time you reach a major milestone and witness all the blessings you have received along the way. By remembering there is no such thing as a final destination in life, you'll begin to view all your life's twists and turns with generous affection.

By answering these brave calls, you will come to rely on the power of *Instinct* (The Hermit). *Instinct* asks you to listen to the intuitive voice of reason that lives within, gently ushering you through uncharted territory and toward your higher purpose. You will meet *Instinct* in moments of complete uncertainty, when you have nothing and no one to guide you except your gut-level intelligence. If you can go to the places that scare you, your intuition will light your way through the dark.

―――――――――――――――○―――――――――――――――

CANCER
RULER: THE MOON

PURPOSE
To grow fearlessly toward the unknown of emotion.

RELATIONSHIPS

You are compassionate and inquisitive, and your relationships should be a place of perspective-building. By seeking out partners who push you out of your comfort zone and expand your consciousness, you will discover that true love always wants you to grow.

The Journey of
JULY 1

Welcome to July 1, an emotionally powerful day of vulnerability.

Embrace the *Power* (The Number Eight) of self-honesty today. Rather than denying your deepest feelings or silencing your truth, walk through the discomfort of vulnerability as you shed old layers of superficiality. By being entirely true to yourself, you can make more authentic internal progress than you ever thought possible.

And know that *Disappointment* (Eight of Cups) is a natural part of the healing process. You may be mourning a close relationship or dream today because it failed to bring you the sense of connection you were once hoping for. To enhance the emotional honesty of Cancer season, accept the reality of what was so you can make room in your heart for what is to come.

No matter what comes, know that you can handle it. *Resilience* (Strength) reminds you of the emotional muscles you have built over time as you endured great personal hardship. Tap into this inner strength if the day feels overwhelming at any point, knowing that sometimes the only way out of a difficult situation is the long way through. Don't bypass any feelings; simply integrate them and handle them with grace.

JUST FOR TODAY

TODAY'S MANTRA
My emotional strength allows me to handle radical honesty.

TODAY'S RITUAL
Reflect on a difficult time in your life. What did you learn about yourself in that process? When you are finished, place your hand over your heart and repeat the affirmation, "My authentic emotional strength can carry me through anything."

TODAY'S JOURNAL PROMPT
Is there a relationship, connection, or idea that I am mourning today?

BORN ON THIS DAY

AMY JOHNSON, English pilot, first female pilot to fly solo from England to Australia

MISSY ELLIOTT, American rapper, songwriter, and record producer

"I think the biggest disease the world suffers from in this day and age is the disease of people feeling unloved."—DIANA SPENCER, English humanitarian and Princess of Wales

The Journey of Those Born on
JULY 1

You were born of lunar power and an emotional independence that can keep you at arm's length from others. You will have to lead a life of vulnerable authenticity, as your journey is one of self-honesty, movement, and internal strength.

Early on in your journey, you will meet your soulful guide, *Power* (The Number Eight). Despite your sensitive nature, *Power* calls you away from personal caution and toward a path of radical truth-telling. By expanding into the full breadth of your human experience, embracing the good, the bad, and the ugly, you will discover that vulnerability is an undeniable force for change.

But if you take this revealing path, you will have to move through inevitable *Disappointment* (Eight of Cups). Not all relationships and commitments stand the test of time, and you'll need to accept these realities as you grow toward more meaningful connections. You will meet *Disappointment* in moments of grief, when you know what has ended but you are not quite sure where to go next.

By answering these calls for honesty, you will discover your capacity for *Resilience* (Strength) when times get hard. Emotions are forever changing like the tides, and *Resilience* inspires you to channel these feelings into a higher calling rather than resorting to impulsive measures. By integrating the wisdom that comes from strife and embracing your innate authority, you can discover the gift of self-trust.

CANCER
RULERS: THE MOON, PLUTO

PURPOSE
To channel emotional strife into personal power.

RELATIONSHIPS

You are as resilient as they come, and your relationships should be a place of deep honesty and vulnerability. By seeking out partners who can handle the truth and empower you to be yourself, you will discover that true love never asks you to deny your complexity.

The Journey of
JULY 2

W elcome to July 2, a daring adventure through the emotional unknown.
Rather than staying in your introverted comfort zone, aim to have an *Experience* (The Number Nine) today. Whether you explore an exciting new relationship or hurl yourself into a foreign environment at work, seize every opportunity to break out of your shell. Through this temporary discomfort you can expand your point of view.

And as you explore the unknown, be sure to reach for *Gratitude* (Nine of Cups). Count your blessings today, focusing on the joys of the journey rather than the tangible rewards of success. What twists and turns are you appreciative of? More than likely, the most unexpected peaks and valleys in life have made you into the person you are today.

But if you feel lost or uncertain of where to go today, rely on *Instinct* (The Hermit). There is an intuitive voice that leads the way to your higher purpose, so carve out some alone time to hear this divine wisdom. By sitting in a meditative state and silencing the noise of your daily hustle, you can place one crucial foot in front of the other as you move closer to your personal truth.

JUST FOR TODAY

TODAY'S MANTRA

I am grateful for what I have learned, and I am excited about what I have yet to explore.

TODAY'S JOURNAL PROMPT

How can I break out of my emotional comfort zone today?

TODAY'S RITUAL

Start your day in quiet meditation. Put on noise-canceling headphones or cover your ears as you listen to the intuitive voice within. Where is it telling you to grow today?

BORN ON THIS DAY

SYLVIA RIVERA, American gay liberation and transgender rights activist and New York community worker

ALEX MORGAN, American soccer player and cocaptain of the US women's national soccer team

"We must dissent from the indifference. We must dissent from the apathy. We must dissent from the fear, the hatred and the mistrust."—THURGOOD MARSHALL, first Black American US Supreme Court Justice

The Journey of Those Born on
JULY 2

You were born of powerful compassion and a need for partnership that can lead you to varying forms of codependency. You will have to discover the freedom that comes from relying on yourself, as your journey is one of searching, perspective, and internal trust.

Early on in your journey, you will meet your wild guide, *Experience* (The Number Nine). Despite your easygoing nature, *Experience* calls you away from a life of passivity and toward the jaw-dropping wonder of exploration. You will meet *Experience* in the foreign, when, despite fear, you hurl yourself toward an uncharted relationship or endeavor that expands your perspective.

And if you choose to this perspective-building path, you will have to pause for *Gratitude* (Nine of Cups). With every mountain you climb, you'll need to find deep emotional appreciation for the peaks and valleys it took you to get there. You will meet *Gratitude* in moments of spiritual acknowledgment, when you have to pinch yourself for how incredible the adventure has been. If you can stay present for every twist and turn, *Gratitude* teaches you how to enjoy the ride.

> ### YOUR GUIDES
>
> *Astrology: Your Energy*
> Cancer (The Moon, Pluto)
>
> *Numerology: Your Path*
> Experience (The Number Nine)
>
> *Minor Arcana: Your Lesson*
> Gratitude (The Nine of Cups)
>
> *Major Arcana: Your Highest Calling*
> Instinct (The Hermit)

By answering these calls for growth, you will come to rely on the gift of *Instinct* (The Hermit). Try to listen to the divine voice that lives within, beckoning you toward the next right action whenever you are unsure of where to go next. You will meet *Instinct* in the darkness of uncertainty, when you have nothing to rely on but your internal voice of intuition. If you can trust yourself, *Instinct* lights the path forward.

──────────────────○──────────────────

CANCER
RULERS: THE MOON, PLUTO

PURPOSE
To climb new heights of the unknown to find emotional perspective and self-trust.

RELATIONSHIPS

You are partnership-driven and a bit of a homebody, so your relationships should be a place of growth and expansion. By seeking out partners who push you out of your comfort zone and expand your perspective, you will discover that true love knows no limits.

The Journey of
JULY 3

Welcome to July 3, a fateful journey that asks you to surrender to your present circumstances.

Go your own way today. Rather than mimicking popular opinion, *Autonomy* (The Number One) encourages you to follow your intuition as you trailblaze new paths of self-realization. While it's scary to make things up as you go, trust that the answers lie inside of you. What would you do if you didn't have to ask anyone for permission?

Look within your heart rather than to your ego for the answer, because *Vulnerability* (Ace of Cups) prefers you to be soft rather than guarded. Cancer season heightens your sense of emotional awareness anyway, so act upon your innermost feelings without hesitation. Tell someone how you feel or pursue that creative project you've always wanted to express.

And above all else, take things as they come. *Impermanence* (Wheel of Fortune) reminds you that everything in life is temporary, so whether you are riding a high or enduring a low, try to make peace with your current circumstances. Oftentimes, it's easier to flow rather than to fight the winds of fate, so surrender the day's outcome to a power greater than yourself.

○

JUST FOR TODAY

TODAY'S MANTRA
I will move to the beat of my heart today while leaving the outcome up to fate.

TODAY'S JOURNAL PROMPT
If I were to listen to my innermost feelings, what would I want to pursue today?

TODAY'S RITUAL
Take a ride today in a car, on a bike, or just in your mind. As you are moving through the twists and turns of the road, repeat the affirmation, "I can't see the turns up ahead, but I trust that I am on my way to my destiny."

○

BORN ON THIS DAY

TANO JŌDAI, Japanese professor of English literature and peace activist

JULIAN ASSANGE, Australian publisher and founder of WikiLeaks

"Whatever is the scariest is almost always what I end up choosing."—AUDRA MCDONALD, American Tony, Grammy, and Emmy Award–winning actor and theatrical and operatic singer

The Journey of Those Born on
JULY 3

You were born of social compassion and a need for community that can make it hard to be alone. You will have to learn to stand on your own, as your journey is one of independence, self-trust, and divine timing.

Early on in your journey, you will meet your brave guide, *Autonomy* (The Number One). Despite your team-oriented nature, *Autonomy* calls you away from the group mentality and toward a path of radical self-trust. You will meet *Autonomy* as you carve out a unique path of your own, using your powers of perception to move through uncharted territory.

And if you choose this self-reliant path, you will have to practice *Vulnerability* (Ace of Cups). *Vulnerability* asks you to listen to your heart rather than your ego, putting yourself out there and trusting that your soul is guiding you in the right direction. Society might tell you otherwise, but you are this strong because you are willing to be so soft.

> ### YOUR GUIDES
>
> *Astrology: Your Energy*
> Cancer (The Moon, Pluto)
>
> *Numerology: Your Path*
> Autonomy (The Number One)
>
> *Minor Arcana: Your Lesson*
> Vulnerability (The Ace of Cups)
>
> *Major Arcana: Your Highest Calling*
> Impermanence
> (The Wheel of Fortune)

By answering these calls for authenticity, you will have to surrender to the inevitable ebbs and flows of life. *Impermanence* (Wheel of Fortune) invites you to swim with, rather than against, the tides of fate, trusting that each twist and turn is necessary for your evolution. You will meet *Impermanence* in the temporary, when you choose to make the most out of whatever the universe throws at you. If you can buckle up, *Impermanence* teaches you how to appreciate the ebbs and flows.

CANCER
RULERS: THE MOON, PLUTO

PURPOSE
To live in true vulnerability by swimming with, rather than against, the tides of life.

RELATIONSHIPS

You are social and compassionate, and your relationships should be a place of independence and trust. By seeking out partners who push you into a position of self-leadership rather than codependency, you will discover that true love strengthens your relationship with yourself.

The Journey of
JULY 4

Welcome to July 4, a peaceful journey that inspires higher consciousness.

Seek out *Balance* (The Number Two) today. Rather than getting burnt out emotionally and physically, look for the ways in which you can pare down your responsibilities and invite in the help you need. Whether you lean on a trusted partner or ask for more time, don't be afraid to lighten your load.

And know that you deserve to get your needs met. While Cancer season inspires compassionate caretaking, *Worthiness* (Two of Cups) encourages you to prioritize the relationships with people who meet you halfway. Who in your life goes out of their way to fill your emotional cup in return? Lean on these individuals with an open heart.

By acknowledging your own needs, you can open your eyes to the *Truth* (Justice). Equality is the name of the game today, so reach inside to access your moral compass to decide where to push and pull today. If there is a glaring injustice you witness in the world or in your personal life, now is the time to stand up for what you believe in most. Change is only possible if you are willing to fight for it.

JUST FOR TODAY

TODAY'S MANTRA

By treating myself fairly, I can fight for equality in the world around me.

TODAY'S JOURNAL PROMPT

What partners, friends, or colleagues always meet me halfway? How can I call on them for support today?

TODAY'S RITUAL

Take a piece of paper and fold it in half. On the left-hand side, write down the love languages (words of affirmation, physical touch, acts of service, gifts, and quality time) you like to give to others. On the other side, write the love languages you most like to receive. If you have a partner or friend, share this list with them and ask them to do the same in return.

BORN ON THIS DAY

RUBE GOLDBERG, American cartoonist, sculptor, author, engineer, and inventor

GINA LOLLOBRIGIDA, Italian actor and photojournalist

"You just got with the flow because life is just all about how you feel."—POST MALONE, American singer-songwriter

The Journey of Those Born on
JULY 4

Y ou were born of emotional discipline and a burdensome sense of responsibility. You will have to learn to share the weight, as your journey is one of peacefulness, reciprocation, and equality.

Early on in your journey, you will meet your tranquil guide, *Balance* (The Number Two). Despite your hardworking nature, *Balance* calls you away from rigidity and toward a path of graceful ease. If you can avoid taking on more than you can handle and ask for help from trusted partners when needed, you'll learn that life doesn't have to be so hard after all.

And if you walk this peaceful path, you will get to discover a new sense of *Worthiness* (Two of Cups). Although you are willing to give everything you have to the people you love, *Worthiness* asks you to seek emotional balance in your relationships. Are you getting your needs met in return? By prioritizing the people who want the best for you, you can always keep your cup full.

YOUR GUIDES

Astrology: Your Energy
Cancer (The Moon, Pluto)

Numerology: Your Path
Balance (The Number Two)

Minor Arcana: Your Lesson
Worthiness (The Two of Cups)

Major Arcana: Your Highest Calling
Truth (Justice)

By answering these calls for inner harmony, you will unlock the gates of *Truth* (Justice). There are no clear-cut, perfect solutions to life's greatest issues, but *Truth* invites you to follow the direction of your moral compass as you fight for justice as you see it. By holding yourself accountable for your actions, you can inspire others to do the same, making the world around you a fairer and more honest place.

CANCER
RULERS: THE MOON, PLUTO

PURPOSE
To reach the emotional balance required to fight for the truth.

RELATIONSHIPS

You are hardworking and self-contained, so your relationships should be a place of easefulness and reciprocation. By seeking out partners who aim for balance and always work to meet you halfway emotionally, you will discover that true love can be peaceful rather than painful.

The Journey of
JULY 5

Welcome to July 5, an eye-opening journey that slays the ego.

Get curious today. While Cancer season thrives in comfort, *Flexibility* (The Number Three) encourages you to step outside your lived experience and learn from the expertise of others. So dive into a group project or pick the brain of a respected colleague because now is the time to absorb the knowledge that lives beyond your mind.

And as you open yourself to others, make room for *Belonging* (Three of Cups). Whether you call some close friends and invite them to dinner or get on a group Zoom call, lean on the support of those you love most. By revealing your innermost feelings to the people you trust, you won't have to feel so alone after all.

But if these acts of vulnerability awaken new perspectives within you, don't be afraid to *Surrender* (The Hanged Man) your pride. It is never easy to rethink your position and stance on certain topics, but now is the time to awaken to the breakthroughs that come from having an open mind. Bend and twist your mind so you can understand the beliefs that challenge your own, freeing yourself to have a true spiritual experience.

○

JUST FOR TODAY

TODAY'S MANTRA

I will let go of my ego so I can learn from collaboration and connection.

TODAY'S JOURNAL PROMPT

Who would I most like to learn from today? Who would I most like to lean on today?

TODAY'S RITUAL

Get into a surrendered position by lying face-down somewhere with your arms and legs outstretched in a star-shaped position. Breathe in for a count of three, then repeat the affirmation, "I will surrender my ways so I can learn from yours."

○

BORN ON THIS DAY

A. E. DOUGLASS, American astronomer and inventor of dendrochronology

ANNA ARNOLD HEDGEMAN, American civil rights leader, politician, educator, and writer

"Things are always changing. Part of being successful here is being comfortable with not knowing what's going to happen."—SUSAN WOJCICKI, Polish American businesswoman

The Journey of Those Born on
JULY 5

You were born of lunar wisdom and a confidence that can be mistaken for pridefulness. You will have to open yourself up to a whole new perspective, as your journey is one of curiosity, connection, and ego sacrifice.

Early on in your journey, you will meet your affable guide, *Flexibility* (The Number Three). Despite your depth of knowledge, *Flexibility* calls you away from being an expert and toward a path of social understanding. By keeping an open heart and mind to the experience of every person who crosses your path, you can shift your thinking and expand your point of view.

And if you accept this dynamic path, you will step into the warmth of *Belonging* (Three of Cups). You will meet *Belonging* in deep connection, when you go out on a limb and reveal your innermost feelings and find yourself embraced through the compassion of others. By prioritizing the people who bring you this sense of emotional belonging, you can build an eternal support system that carries you through even the most difficult of times.

By answering these social calls, you will have to *Surrender* (The Hanged Man) your ways completely. *Surrender* asks you to let go of rigidity and pride so you can thoroughly welcome the mind-bending properties of a spiritual awakening. You will meet *Surrender* in moments of radical shifting, when you step outside your comfort zone and discover an entirely new way of seeing the world. If you can hang freely from the unknown, *Surrender* offers you the gift of higher consciousness.

○

CANCER
RULERS: THE MOON, PLUTO

PURPOSE
To release the blockages of the ego and awaken to the wisdom of connection.

RELATIONSHIPS

You are bold and passionate, and your relationships should be a place of laughter and shared understanding. By seeking out partners who are just as much of a friend as they are a teacher, you will discover that true love always helps you grow.

The Journey of
JULY 6

Welcome to July 6, a transformation journey that relies on emotional strength.

Practice emotional *Discipline* (The Number Four) today. Although Cancer season has us all feeling a bit more sensitive than usual, utilize logic and self-awareness as you channel these energies in a productive manner. What consistent, tangible work can you focus on? By giving yourself purpose, you can ground yourself in personal integrity and healthy boundaries.

But don't rush toward any new opportunities. *Reflection* (Four of Cups) encourages you to take personal inventory instead, making note of the relationships and connections that no longer serve you. If you are disappointed and regretful of overextending yourself in the past, now is the time to find compassion for yourself so you can make different decisions moving forward.

There is some discomfort within change, however, and *Transformation* (Death) invites you to make peace with whatever transition you are currently going through. Get honest about the layers of yourself you are currently shedding, and practice gratitude for who you were as you prepare for who you are becoming. Remember that a caterpillar doesn't become a butterfly overnight.

———○———

JUST FOR TODAY

TODAY'S MANTRA

Through personal integrity and self-honesty, I can shed old layers that block my authenticity.

TODAY'S RITUAL

Get excited about transformation by making a vision board. Whether you cut out photos from a magazine, put together an online board, or create one in your mind, bring your subconscious desires into your consciousness so you can begin manifesting your future self.

TODAY'S JOURNAL PROMPT

What version of myself, or what coping mechanism, am I currently letting go of?

———○———

BORN ON THIS DAY

TENZIN GYATSO, fourteenth Dalai Lama and Tibetan spiritual leader of the country's Lamaistic Buddhists

KEVIN HART, American comedian and actor

"At the end of the day, we can endure much more than we think we can."—FRIDA KAHLO, Mexican painter

The Journey of Those Born on
JULY 6

You were born of tenderhearted compassion and interpersonal generosity that you rarely turn inward. You will have to fall in love with your growth, as your journey is one of foundational work, awareness, and transition.

Early on in your journey, you will meet your stern guide, *Discipline* (The Number Four). Despite your emotionally driven nature, *Discipline* calls you away from the unreliability of feelings and toward a path of personal integrity. By building a strong internal foundation with bricks of consistency and accountability, you will discover that you can depend on yourself completely.

But if you choose this humble path, you will have to take pause for *Reflection* (Four of Cups). Internal awareness takes time, and *Reflection* encourages you to slow down and reevaluate where, and to whom, you are devoting your most valuable resources. If there are aspects of your life that are draining rather than life-affirming, *Reflection* asks you to grieve these losses while setting your heart on deeper and more meaningful connections.

By answering these calls for emotional fortitude, you will be ready to meet your highest calling, *Transformation* (Death). *Transformation* comes to you in moments of internal transition, when you are letting go of an old, powerful coping mechanism and preparing for what is to come. It is never easy to release the identities that make you feel safe, but *Transformation* reminds you that discomfort is a sign that you are moving closer to the truth. If you can shed these layers of superficiality, you'll discover a life of radical authenticity.

───────────────○───────────────

CANCER
RULERS: THE MOON, PLUTO

PURPOSE
To build an emotional foundation strong enough to withstand radical transformation.

RELATIONSHIPS

You are generous and heartfelt, and your relationships should be a place of awareness and integrity. By seeking out partners who work through, rather than run away from, emotional challenges, you will discover that true love means being capable of change.

The Journey of
JULY 7

Welcome to July 7, a radical journey toward divine moderation.

Put yourself out there today. Despite the introverted nature of Cancer season, *Courage* (The Number Five) asks you not to take yourself so seriously as you move to center stage in the drama of life. What truth, feeling, or creative vision do you want to express today? There's no need to hold anything back, so bring what's inside into the physical world.

But watch out for *Grief* (Five of Cups). Don't focus on the things you perceive to be a failure. It is natural to have regret when things don't go according to plan, but now is the time to acknowledge the good that is happening in your life. If you can center your emotions around what is filling your cup, you can forget about what has spilled.

Because at the end of the day, *Serenity* (Temperance) is a choice. By walking the spiritual middle path today, neither giving in to the extremes of emotion nor denying them entirely, you can find a new sense of internal peace amidst any external chaos. Take a meditative and mindful approach to your vulnerability, reaching for the limitless calm that exists in the present moment.

JUST FOR TODAY

TODAY'S MANTRA
I can balance vulnerability with internal peace.

TODAY'S RITUAL
Ward off any self-pity by making a list of five things that are filling your emotional cup these days. Once you finish the list, fold it up and hold it in the palm of your right hand as you repeat the affirmation, "I will focus on what's full rather than what's spilled."

TODAY'S JOURNAL PROMPT
What are some practical ways I can access internal peace throughout today?

BORN ON THIS DAY

RINGO STARR, English musician, singer-songwriter, and actor best known as the drummer for The Beatles

MS DHONI, Indian cricketer and captain of the Indian national team

"Let a new earth rise. Let another world be born. Let a bloody peace be written in the sky. Let a second generation full of courage issue forth; let a people loving freedom come to growth."—MARGARET WALKER, American poet and writer

The Journey of Those Born on
JULY 7

Y ou were born of intuitive direction and a loyalty that can keep you stuck in dysfunctional commitments. You will have to break free in order to find balance, as your journey is one of self-expression, maturity, and spiritual moderation.

Early on in your journey, you will meet your provocative guide, *Courage* (The Number Five). Despite your austere nature, *Courage* calls you away from taking yourself too seriously and toward a path of wild vulnerability. By putting your feelings and creativity out there for all the world to see, you can transform your experience into a work of art.

But if you take this bold path, you will have to watch out for *Grief* (Five of Cups). You will meet *Grief* in moments of obsessive regret, when you are so focused on a perceived failure that you can't make room in your heart for anything positive. While not everything in life works out the way you might have hoped, go inward and take emotional accountability for the past so you can set your sights on the future.

By answering these emotionally heroic calls, you will discover the importance of *Serenity* (Temperance). *Serenity* asks you to find the spiritual middle ground that lives within, inviting you to pull away from the extremes of emotions and center yourself in the present moment. If you can prioritize peace over drama while practicing moderation in every aspect of your life, you'll tap into the gift of divine balance.

CANCER
RULERS: THE MOON, PLUTO

PURPOSE
To handle vulnerability with spiritual moderation.

RELATIONSHIPS

You are serious about most things in life, and your relationships should be a place of heartfelt expression and peace. By seeking out partners who can handle the unfiltered truth with internal harmony, you will discover that true love lies in the balance.

The Journey of
JULY 8

Welcome to June 8, a soulful journey that asks you to heal the blocks you have around vulnerability.

Share your heart generously today. *Devotion* (The Number Six) asks you to give both your time and energy toward the people and projects that you care about most. Rather than waiting to receive or trying to look cool, find the emotional satisfaction that comes from meaningful service.

And integrate the sweetness of *Nostalgia* (Six of Cups). Cancer season always encourages reflection, so take a trip down memory lane as you reconnect with the joys of the past. What small but meaningful aspects of your childhood do you wish to reconnect with? Whether it be a favorite meal or movie, take some time to relish this wistfulness.

But as you open your heart, watch for how you psychologically contract. *Shadow* (The Devil) invites you inward to heal the wounds you have when it comes to true happiness and emotional contentment. If some self-destructive coping mechanisms come up for you today, find deep compassion for them rather than shaming yourself. It is through internal understanding, not judgment, that you can shine a light on the darkest corners of your humanity.

JUST FOR TODAY

TODAY'S MANTRA

I will release the shame that wasn't mine to bear in the first place.

TODAY'S JOURNAL PROMPT

What person or activity helps bring out my inner child?

TODAY'S RITUAL

Spend some time with your inner children through creative writing. With your dominant hand, write the question, "What is a joyful memory you'd like to share?" Respond with your nondominant hand, letting the answers flow through you. If nothing comes, practice compassion and patience for the silence.

BORN ON THIS DAY

RUBY SALES, American social justice activist, scholar, and public theologian

SON HEUNG-MIN, South Korean professional footballer

"I think the greatest thing that we can do is take care of each other."—SOPHIA BUSH, American actor, activist, director, and producer

The Journey of Those Born on
JULY 8

Y ou were born of intuitive power and emotional strength that can stop you from receiving the support you need. You will have to tend to the wounds that block you from true love, as your journey is one of sincerity, reflection, and psychological healing.

Early on in your journey, you will meet your sweet guide, *Devotion* (The Number Six). Although you are self-protective by nature, *Devotion* calls you away from fear and toward a path of heartfelt service. By giving your all to the people and projects that speak to your soul, you can build a life of meaning from vulnerability.

If you choose this gentle path, you will have to embrace *Nostalgia* (Six of Cups). *Nostalgia* asks you to reconnect with your inner children, integrating their humble levity into your conscious identity. You will meet *Nostalgia* in the sweetest of memories, when you can't help but glow as you revel in the sunlight of the past. Although no one's childhood was perfect, *Nostalgia* invites you to remember the small joys of yours.

By answering these calls for vulnerability, you will have to work with *Shadow* (The Devil). *Shadow* asks you to address the hidden fear of happiness that lives within, the part of you that subconsciously holds you back from experiencing true emotional contentment. You will meet *Shadow* in moments of profound expansion, when old destructive coping mechanisms rise to the surface to quell the discomfort of such growth. If you can find compassion for the part of you that contracts whenever life gets too big and bright, you can step out of the dark and into the light.

YOUR GUIDES

Astrology: Your Energy
Cancer (The Moon, Pluto)

Numerology: Your Path
Devotion (The Number Six)

Minor Arcana: Your Lesson
Nostalgia (The Six of Cups)

Major Arcana: Your Highest Calling
Shadow (The Devil)

CANCER
RULERS: THE MOON, PLUTO

PURPOSE
To gently peel back the layers of shame that block true connection and happiness.

RELATIONSHIPS

You are emotionally reflective but introverted, and your relationships should be a place of sweet and tenderhearted connection. By seeking out partners who make you feel safe and unconditionally supported, you will discover that true love is a soft place to land.

The Journey of
JULY 9

Welcome to July 9, an emotionally discerning test of faith.

Show up to what matters most today. While Cancer season is known for its passivity, *Commitment* (The Number Seven) asks you to pursue the responsibilities you have toward others with complete focus and intention. By sticking to your word and meeting your obligations, you can discover the power of reliability.

But watch out for *Illusion* (Seven of Cups). If a relationship or goal seems too good to be true, it probably is. Break the spell by calling up a rigorously honest friend who is willing to tell it like it is. The truth is never as pretty as fantasy, but it is much more satisfying in the long run.

No matter how much you prepare, some events you can't anticipate. *Upheaval* (The Tower) brings necessary but dramatic shifts in perspective by way of change, so embrace whatever drastic revelations come your way today. Whether something gets destabilized in your physical world or your internal one, lean in to the discomfort and trust that the universe is doing for you what you cannot do for yourself. And remember, change is just the necessary transition before a radical new beginning.

JUST FOR TODAY

TODAY'S MANTRA

I will thank the universe for every-thing it has given me and everything it has taken away.

TODAY'S JOURNAL PROMPT

Is there some aspect of my life that I am not seeing clearly? Who could help me discern between fantasy and reality?

TODAY'S RITUAL

To break the spell of illusion, get grounded in nature. Go outside and find the nearest tree, or if you don't have access, visualize it in your mind. Put both hands on the trunk as you repeat the prayer, "Sturdy tree, please help me see the beautiful reality that isn't just a dream."

BORN ON THIS DAY

TOM HANKS, American actor and filmmaker

MERCEDES SOSA, Argentine folk singer

"Maybe the purpose of being here, wherever we are, is to increase the durability and occasions of love among and between peoples."—JUNE JORDAN, American poet, essayist, teacher, and activist

The Journey of Those Born on
JULY 9

You were born of intuitive knowledge and an insatiable desire for growth. You will have to consider what it is you want to get out of this lifetime, as your journey is one of dedication, clarity, and necessary change.

Early on in your journey, you will meet your discerning guide, *Commitment* (The Number Seven). Despite your adventurous spirit, *Commitment* calls you away from wanderlust and toward a focused path of responsibility. If you can only devote your heart to the people, projects, and ideas you care about most, *Commitment* teaches you the value of intentionality.

If you take this sage path, you will have to watch out for *Illusion* (Seven of Cups). *Illusion* comes to you by way of fantasy, when you convince yourself that a shiny goal or relationship is the answer to all your problems. You will meet *Illusion* in wishful thinking, when something or someone seems too good to be true. But if you can rely on the discerning council of trusted friends, you can break the spell it holds over you.

YOUR GUIDES

Astrology: Your Energy
Cancer (The Moon, Pluto)

Numerology: Your Path
Commitment (The Number Seven)

Minor Arcana: Your Lesson
Illusion (The Seven of Cups)

Major Arcana: Your Highest Calling
Upheaval (The Tower)

By answering these discerning calls, you will come to respect the genius of *Upheaval* (The Tower). Sometimes fate steps in when you need it most, ushering in the crucial change that you were putting off. You will meet *Upheaval* in moments when the solid ground you once stood on crumbles and you have no choice but to lean in to the chaos. If you can believe that your destiny is unfolding as it should, *Upheaval* rockets you toward a brighter future.

CANCER
RULERS: THE MOON, PLUTO

PURPOSE
To commit to what matters most and to leave the rest up to destiny.

RELATIONSHIPS

You are worldly and wise, and your relationships should be a place of responsibility and commitment. By seeking out partners who hold you to your word and are discerning in nature, you will discover that true love is a divine emotional anchor.

The Journey of
JULY 10

Welcome to July 10, a hopeful journey that requires complete self-honesty.
Try to be unapologetically yourself today. Despite the emotionally protective nature of Cancer season, *Power* (The Number Eight) invites you to shed old layers of superficiality so you can experience the full breadth of your authentic spirit. Who would you be, and what would you do, if you weren't afraid of what other people thought?

But with honesty comes necessary *Disappointment* (Eight of Cups). If a relationship, commitment, or project isn't working out as you hoped it would, take some time today to make peace with this letdown so you can move forward. Whether you have the final conversation with another person or with yourself, make sure that all parties involved get the closure they need.

And from there, get excited about what's to come. *Hope* (The Star) isn't interested in the failings of the past and inspires you to set your sights on the future. Chase the ideas that keep you up at night and get you out of bed in the morning. By embracing enthusiasm rather than fear, you can wash away any bad feelings and make room for the limitless possibilities of your dreams.

JUST FOR TODAY

TODAY'S MANTRA
I can shed old layers of superficiality until I find internal optimism.

TODAY'S JOURNAL PROMPT
What ideas, personal or professional, are inspiring me right now?

TODAY'S RITUAL
Make a wish upon a star, but not just any wish. Go out at night, even if you can't see the stars, and as you look up at the sky, repeat the wish, "Star magic, I seek from thee a ray of enthusiasm to shine within me."

BORN ON THIS DAY

MARY MCLEOD BETHUNE, American educator, philanthropist, humanitarian, and civil rights activist

NIKOLA TESLA, Serbian American inventor, electrical engineer, mechanical engineer, and futurist

"I'm fearless, I don't complain. Even when horrible things happen to me, I go on."—SOFÍA VERGARA, Colombian American actor

The Journey of Those Born on
JULY 10

Y ou were born of lunar intuition and a secret penchant for emotional instability. You will have to find your grounding within optimism, as your journey is one of authenticity, dissatisfaction, and internal enthusiasm.

Early on in your journey, you will meet your enigmatic guide, *Power* (The Number Eight). Despite your independent nature, *Power* calls you away from a life of isolation and toward a path of radical self-embodiment. If you can accept every aspect of yourself—the good, the bad, and the seemingly strange—you'll discover the influence you can have on others by being real rather than perfect.

But if you choose this path of truth, you will have to build a relationship with *Disappointment* (Eight of Cups). You will meet *Disappointment* in the connections and promises that don't work out as you hoped, when you must move on and cut your losses. It is all too easy to view these experiences as failures, but *Disappointment* encourages you to view them as learning experiences as you integrate this vital information into your future choices.

> ### YOUR GUIDES
>
> *Astrology: Your Energy*
> Cancer (The Moon, Pluto)
>
> *Numerology: Your Path*
> Power (The Number Eight)
>
> *Minor Arcana: Your Lesson*
> Disappointment (The Eight of Cups)
>
> *Major Arcana: Your Highest Calling*
> Hope (The Star)

By answering these calls for emotional honesty, you will come to rely on your bright friend, *Hope* (The Star). *Hope* shines a light on the ray of enthusiasm within that inspires you to keep wishing through even the darkest of times. You will meet *Hope* in the excitement you feel when you have your next best idea. If you can trust in this divine excitement, *Hope* helps you wash away the upsets of the past.

○

CANCER
RULERS: THE MOON, PLUTO

PURPOSE
To harness the power of self-honesty and channel it into divine optimism.

RELATIONSHIPS

You are kind yet self-protective, and your relationships should be a place of radical authenticity and excitement. By seeking out partners who accept you as you are and yet inspire enthusiasm for the future, you will discover that true love always allows you to begin again.

The Journey of
JULY 11

Welcome to June 11, a comfort zone–breaking adventure that forces you to confront the past.

Get out of your cozy nest and into the wild unknown. *Experience* (The Number Nine) wants you to learn by doing as you embrace the unexpected twists and turns that saying "yes" to chance offers. Whether you take a risk by expressing your emotions or you try your hand at an intimidating new creative practice, go toward the places that scare you.

And say thank you for the growth. *Gratitude* (Nine of Cups) asks you to zoom out, recognizing the beauty that exists in the ups as well as the downs today. By acknowledging the good in everything you encounter, you will discover that emotional contentment is simply a shift in perspective.

But if this day triggers some old stories for you, know that *Memory* (The Moon) needs you to take a closer look. While Cancer season is reflective by nature, listen closely to what your intuition is telling you about where you need to heal. More than likely, some repressed feelings must come to the surface today, so be brave as you become the loving caretaker you always needed.

○

JUST FOR TODAY

TODAY'S MANTRA
I can fearlessly address the past with gratitude and compassion.

TODAY'S RITUAL
Step out under the moonlight tonight, even if it's not visible to the naked eye. As you stare up at the moon, consider nine things that you are grateful for and repeat them aloud or write them down.

TODAY'S JOURNAL PROMPT
What emotional risks am I willing to take today?

○

BORN ON THIS DAY

ADI ROCHE, Irish activist; anti-nuclear advocate; and campaigner for peace, humanitarian aid, and education

ROBERT THE BRUCE, aka Robert I, King of Scots and national hero

"Beauty comes in all forms. It's not just external; it's internal as well."—ALESSIA CARA, Canadian singer-songwriter

The Journey of Those Born on
JULY 11

Y ou were born of intuitive balance and an at times compulsive need for emotional safety. You will have to go far in order to come back home to yourself, as your journey is one of higher knowledge, perspective, and internal healing.

Early on in your journey, you will meet your sage guide, *Experience* (The Number Nine). Despite your desire for comfort, *Experience* calls you away from the safety of home and toward the fear-reaching unknown. By taking a chance on the unexpected and diving head-first in the foreign, you can see life from a new angle.

If you choose this path of understanding, make time for *Gratitude* (Nine of Cups). Although it is easy to focus on the negative, *Gratitude* encourages you to look for the silver living in each perceived setback as well as the triumphs. You will meet *Gratitude* in moments of spiritual acknowledgment, when you zoom out and notice just how miraculous the journey has been. If you can focus on what is making your glass half full, *Gratitude* teaches you how to enjoy the ride.

By answering these conscious-shifting calls, you will have to integrate the past into the present. *Memory* (The Moon) asks you to look at your personal history to see where your trauma may be projecting itself onto the opportunities that the present offers you. If you can go back to these crucial moments in time with complete self-compassion, you will understand that nothing goes away until it teaches you what you need to know. By fearlessly facing the past, you'll open yourself to the gift of emotional awareness.

CANCER
RULERS: THE MOON, NEPTUNE

PURPOSE
To integrate the emotional past into the present adventure.

RELATIONSHIPS

You are diplomatic and compassionate, and your relationships should be a place of higher education and understanding. By seeking out partners who force you out of your comfort zone and encourage you to listen to your intuition, you will discover that true love exists in the unknown.

The Journey of
JULY 12

W elcome to July 12, an emotionally brave journey that teaches you how to shine.
Do what you want today. *Autonomy* (The Number One) asks you to follow the beat of your intuition as you channel your emotions into personal fulfillment. Be a leader toward yourself in the home as well as in your intimate relationships, prioritizing your own needs rather than overly concerning yourself with the feelings of others.

And don't be afraid to practice *Vulnerability* (Ace of Cups). If your heart is guiding you somewhere, pursue that direction with complete enthusiasm instead of wasting time on the fear of rejection. By putting yourself out there and telling the universe what it is that you want, you can ensure that you will get what you deeply need.

By getting in touch with your unfiltered truth, you can glow with the power of *Vitality* (The Sun). Cancer season encourages self-protection and introversion, so let your emotions take center stage in your life today. What do you want to express to the world around you? Whether you profess your love for another or share a piece of authentic creativity, now is the time to shine a light on the authentic feelings that live within.

JUST FOR TODAY

TODAY'S MANTRA
I will glow with emotional acceptance.

TODAY'S JOURNAL PROMPT
What emotional connections or opportunities would I most like to pursue today?

TODAY'S RITUAL
Get your hands on a piece of rose quartz. Take it outside in the middle of the day and let it bask in sunlight for one hour. Bring it inside and lay it on top of your heart as you rest in silent meditation.

BORN ON THIS DAY

HENRY DAVID THOREAU, American poet, naturalist, and pacifist

PABLO NERUDA, Chilean Nobel Prize–winning poet

"When the whole world is silent, even one voice becomes powerful."—MALALA YOUSAFZAI, Pakistani activist for female education and the youngest-ever Nobel Prize recipient

The Journey of Those Born on
JULY 12

Y ou were born of deep compassion and a trust in others that can border on passivity. You will
 have to believe in yourself in order to shine, as your journey is one of independence, openheartedness, and visibility.

Early on in your journey, you will meet your daring
guide, *Autonomy* (The Number One). Despite your social nature, *Autonomy* calls you away from collaboration and toward a path of complete self-reliance. You
will meet *Autonomy* in moments of innovation, when,
by listening to the beat of your intuition, you break
new and uncharted ground.

But if you walk this ambitious path, you will have to
do so with an open heart. *Vulnerability* (Ace of Cups)
wants you to flow with your emotions, letting them or-
ganically pour out from you rather than holding them
back in fear. By exposing your innermost feelings to
the world around you, you can encourage deep connections with those who need it most.

By answering these self-revealing calls, you will step
into the light of *Vitality* (The Sun). *Vitality* invites you to tap into the brightness of embodying
your true emotional spirit. It is scary to drop the layers of protection and expose your raw authenticity, but *Vitality* empowers you to be yourself so you can inspire others to do the same. If you
can take center stage of your life, beaming with the glow of self-embodiment, you'll discover the
gift of emotional self-confidence.

CANCER
RULERS: THE MOON, NEPTUNE

PURPOSE
*To step into the limelight of
emotional authenticity.*

RELATIONSHIPS

You are a natural team player and willing to sacrifice for the good of others, yet your relationships
should be a place of independence and joy. By seeking out partners who encourage you to take up
space in the world and make you smile without even trying, you will discover that true love never
dulls your shine.

The Journey of
JULY 13

W elcome to July 13, a gentle journey that opens your eyes to reality.
Rather than going to any emotional extremes today, seek out *Balance* (The Number Two). Cancer season can heighten feelings of any kind, so try to find internal peace by lightening your to-do list and leaning on your trusted people. Call in help where you need it or ask for more time where you can get it.

Because you deserve it. *Worthiness* (Two of Cups) invites you to seek out the partners and relationships that reciprocate your generosity. Don't waste any time on the people who drain your cup; instead, get in touch with your needs and give others the opportunity to show up in the way you crave most.

And from there, try to come to terms with the inconvenient truth. *Awakening* (Judgment) wants you to open your eyes to what is actually going on in your life and the world around you. Whether it's good, bad, or downright frustrating, by accepting reality as it stands, you can make more thoughtful decisions moving forward. The only thing scarier than self-honesty is denial, so move bravely into the sunlight of radical consciousness.

JUST FOR TODAY

TODAY'S MANTRA

By relying on internal balance and trusted partnership, I can handle the truth.

TODAY'S JOURNAL PROMPT

What partners, romantic or platonic, are generous but honest with me?

TODAY'S RITUAL

Contemplate two difficult truths about yourself or the world around you. You don't have to accept them completely, but just bring them to the forefront of your mind. Light a candle and inhale deeply. As you exhale, repeat the affirmation, "The only thing scarier than self-honesty is denial."

BORN ON THIS DAY

MARY EMMA WOOLLEY, American educator, peace activist, suffragist, and first female student to attend Brown University

HARRISON FORD, American actor

"The greatest threat to freedom is the absence of criticism."—WOLE SOYINKA, Nigerian playwright and Nobel Prize–winning poet

The Journey of Those Born on
JULY 13

Y ou were born of emotional restraint and a hidden depth that you rarely bring into the light of day. You will have to slowly integrate the truth, as your journey is one of patience, reciprocation, and radical consciousness.

Early on in your journey, you will meet your temperate guide, *Balance* (The Number Two). Despite your tendency to go to extremes, *Balance* calls you away from harm and toward a path of peaceful coexistence. By taking on only what you can handle and accepting help from the people you trust most, you can begin to treat life as a marathon, not a sprint.

And if you choose this harmonious path, you will have to tap into a new sense of *Worthiness* (Two of Cups). *Worthiness* asks you to become aware of what you need in relationships with others, giving your heart in earnest while respecting your own boundaries and well-being. You will meet *Worthiness* in moments of reciprocation, when the partner you care for mirrors to you the devotion you desire most.

By answering these calls for internal peace, you will come prepared to meet *Awakening* (Judgment). *Awakening* empowers you to see life as it is rather than how you want it to be, so you can make thoughtful choices from radical awareness. *Awakening* lies in the unfiltered and unglamorous truth, the type of honesty that once noticed cannot go unseen. If you can meet reality as it stands rather than sleepwalking through life, *Awakening* hands you the keys to divine consciousness.

———————————○———————————

CANCER
RULERS: THE MOON, NEPTUNE

PURPOSE
To rely on internal and interpersonal peace while awakening to the inconvenient truth.

RELATIONSHIPS

You are emotionally controlled yet deeply complicated, and your relationships should be a place of mutual respect and peaceful harmony. By seeking out partners who aim to understand rather than contradict, you will discover that true love exists in balance.

The Journey of
JULY 14

Welcome to July 14, a winding adventure that inspires emotional wisdom. Get out of your feelings and into the experiences of others. Cancer season calls you back to your comfort zone, but *Flexibility* (The Number Three) invites you to learn something new today by breaking out of what's familiar and getting curious about what you don't know. There is so much to discover if you can keep an open heart.

So why not prioritize *Belonging* (Three of Cups)? Embrace every opportunity to connect with others today, whether it be in your work or in your personal life. Share who you actually are, and practice healthy vulnerability as you lean on the strong connections in your life. By putting yourself out there, you can create more intimacy.

And as you climb new heights of connection, look for *Perspective* (The World). Zoom out and see how every ebb and flow, twist and turn, led you to the person you are today. If you are completing a significant personal or professional milestone, spend some time reflecting on the experiences you had along the way. By taking a bird's-eye view of your life, you can access a higher state of consciousness.

○

JUST FOR TODAY

TODAY'S MANTRA

By stepping out of my emotional comfort zone, I can find new gratitude for the adventure.

TODAY'S RITUAL

Go somewhere with a view. As you soak in this new perspective, take a zoomed-out view of your life and consider what you are most grateful for. If you feel stuck or unsure, repeat the prayer, "World wisdom, please bring to me the perspective I need to appreciate what is in front of me."

TODAY'S JOURNAL PROMPT

Am I completing a significant personal or professional milestone? What did I learn along the way?

○

BORN ON THIS DAY

BEN ENWONWU, Nigerian painter and sculptor

PHOEBE WALLER-BRIDGE, English actor, writer, and director

"It's so nice to be a spoke in the wheel, one that helps to turn, not one that hinders."—GERTRUDE BELL, English archaeologist

The Journey of Those Born on
JULY 14

Y ou were born of fierce compassion and a need for emotional balance that can keep you from taking risks. You will have to learn to appreciate the unexpected nature of adventure, as your journey is one of curiosity, connection, and jaw-dropping wonder.

Early on in your journey, you will meet your excitable guide, *Flexibility* (The Number Three). Despite your flare for the dramatic, *Flexibility* calls you away from self-centeredness and toward a path of shared understanding. You will meet *Flexibility* in moments of social exchange, when you humble yourself enough to absorb the unique and diverse perspectives of others. If you can choose open-mindedness over pride, *Flexibility* reminds you there is always more to learn.

And if you choose this dynamic path, you will encounter the warm embrace of *Belonging* (Three of Cups). *Belonging* is born of true vulnerability, when you share your deepest truths with a community of trusted individuals and are rewarded with limitless compassion and support. You will meet *Belonging* in moments when, even in the hardest of emotional battles, you know that you are not alone.

By answering these calls for connection, *Perspective* (The World) will inspire you to see things through a new lens. You will meet *Perspective* at the peak of a completed milestone, when you sit back in awe at the many valleys you had to climb along the way. By reaching for deep gratitude amidst the trials and tribulations along this road called life, you can access the spiritual contentment you always desired.

CANCER
RULERS: THE MOON, NEPTUNE

PURPOSE
To climb the winding roads of connection and discover a new emotional perspective.

RELATIONSHIPS

You are seriously passionate about most things in life, so your relationships should be a place of levity and appreciation. By seeking out partners who make you laugh and remind you of the big picture, you will discover that true love never weighs you down.

The Journey of
JULY 15

W elcome to July 15, a disciplined journey of emotional discernment.
　　　　Add some much-needed structure to your day. To quell the sentimental waters of Cancer season, *Discipline* (The Number Four) invites you to focus on the seemingly mundane tasks at hand. Show up to your responsibilities with pure integrity so you can experience the emotional grounding that comes from follow-through.

But leave some time for *Reflection* (Four of Cups). Perhaps some interpersonal obligations have been draining your cup as of late. If so, take an honest inventory of where you are overextending yourself. If you are in need of rest, give your body, mind, and heart some extra space to decompress.

And remember that you are the only authority you need to listen to. *Self-mastery* (The Emperor) empowers you to make objective decisions today, so balance logic with intuition as you set healthy boundaries for yourself. It is always appropriate to say "no" to an invitation or obligation if it is not in your best interest, so stand up for your needs and don't apologize for being truthful. Be the leader you always wished for, and channel your emotions in a strategic and thoughtful manner.

JUST FOR TODAY

TODAY'S MANTRA
I can handle my emotions with self-restraint and personal integrity.

TODAY'S JOURNAL PROMPT
Are there any tough but necessary decisions or boundaries I need to make today?

TODAY'S RITUAL
Stand in front of a mirror with your legs hip-distance apart. Place your right hand over your forehead and your left over your solar plexus. While looking your reflection in the eyes, repeat the affirmation, "I am the leader I always needed."

BORN ON THIS DAY

REMBRANDT, Dutch painter, printer, and draftsman

EMMELINE PANKHURST, English suffragist who formed the Women's Social and Political Union

"I try to be like a forest: revitalizing and constantly growing.—FOREST WHITAKER, American actor, producer, director, and activist

The Journey of Those Born on
JULY 15

Y ou were born of tenderheartedness with a pinch of self-destruction. You will have to learn to harness your emotions in a productive way, as your journey is one of grounding, self-reflection, and personal integrity.

Early on in your journey, you will meet your formidable guide, *Discipline* (The Number Four). *Discipline* invites you to act from self-control rather than passing feeling, leading you through a path of undeniable hard work. You will meet *Discipline* in moments of contrary action, when your emotional nature says to quit but a deeper voice calls you to keep moving forward. If you can slowly and steadily lay one brick on top of the other, you will find yourself on a rock-solid foundation.

But if you walk this sturdy path, you will have to take a seat next to your contemplative friend, *Reflection* (Four of Cups). *Reflection* devotes itself deeply to your emotional preservation, asking you to check how empty your cup is before moving forward. You will meet *Reflection* in moments of intentional introversion, when you discover how meaningful "yes" becomes when you learn to say "no."

By answering these calls for discernment, you will be well equipped to embrace *Self-mastery* (The Emperor). It is not out of rigidity but out of deep respect that *Self-mastery* asks you to put emotions to the side to become an objective leader to yourself and others. Listen to the intelligence that lives within as you make strategic and meaningful decisions that favor your long-term well-being. If you can become the authority you always needed, you'll discover the gift of personal integrity.

———————————————————O———————————————————

CANCER
RULERS: THE MOON, NEPTUNE

PURPOSE
To harness difficult emotions through self-leadership.

RELATIONSHIPS

You are deeply emotional and introspective, and your relationships should be a place of grounding amidst the rocking tides of life. By seeking out partners who calm your fears through their deep devotion to logic and structure, you will discover that true love always has your back.

The Journey of
JULY 16

Welcome to July 16, an expressive journey that requires radical self-trust.

Although Cancer season is not known for its extroversion, *Courage* (The Number Five) invites you to put yourself out there today. Whether you express your deepest feelings online or share a body of work you have been creating for some time, choose vulnerability over self-protection. There are so many emotional riches to be gained if you are willing to be brave.

But if things don't go as you hoped, watch out for *Grief* (Five of Cups). It is far too easy to focus on the negative, but today warns against such emotional patterns and encourages you to set your sights on what is going well instead. What did you gain from the experience of self-expression? More than likely, there are more than a few silver linings to be found.

The biggest gift to look for today is self-trust. *Wisdom* (The Hierophant) invites you to listen to the beat of your intuitive genius, disregarding the unsolicited opinions of others. No one has a monopoly on the truth, so reach inside to discern what information is useful to you and what you would be better off disregarding entirely.

JUST FOR TODAY

TODAY'S MANTRA

No one's opinion of me is more important than my own.

TODAY'S JOURNAL PROMPT

If I wasn't afraid of what others thought, what emotional truths would I like to express today?

TODAY'S RITUAL

Pull up an image of an owl online and print it out if possible. As you stare into the eyes of this sage creature, repeat the prayer, "Help me be bold and brave, owl teacher, as I learn to trust internal wisdom."

BORN ON THIS DAY

KATRINA KAIF, English actor

WILL FERRELL, American actor, comedian, producer, and writer

"We had no strict laws. I know myself how irksome this strict discipline is. Good work can be done without the fear of the law."—ROALD AMUNDSEN, Norwegian polar explorer who led the first expedition to the South Pole

The Journey of Those Born on
JULY 16

You were born of emotional loyalty and an unconscious desire for chaos. You will have to learn to trust in yourself, as your journey is one of self-expression, maturity, and internal knowledge.

Early on in your journey, you will meet your inspirational guide, *Courage* (The Number Five). Despite your desire for stability, *Courage* calls you away from certainty and toward a path of radical vulnerability. You will meet *Courage* in moments of creative and emotional exposure, when you bear your soul to others and discover the satisfaction of authentic expression.

But if you choose this bold path, you will have to contend with *Grief* (Five of Cups). *Grief* asks you to acknowledge the voice of self-pity that highlights what didn't work out, pulling your focus away from all the good in your life. By recognizing and detaching from this pattern of emotion, you can begin to shift your perspective toward the possibilities of the future.

By answering these brave calls, you will meet your

trusted adviser, *Wisdom* (The Hierophant). *Wisdom* introduces you to the divine intelligence that lives within, encouraging you to remain teachable while helping you decipher your own definition of true and false. You will meet *Wisdom* in moments of discernment, when you separate what feedback is worth receiving and what isn't worth your time at all. By never giving away your power to the opinions of others, you can discover the gift of radical self-trust.

CANCER
RULERS: THE MOON, NEPTUNE

PURPOSE
To value self-opinion over the opinions of others.

RELATIONSHIPS

You are emotionally committed to the ones you love, and your relationships should be a place of radical vulnerability and higher understanding. By seeking out partners who never withhold their truth and ask you to do the same, you will discover that true love is built from honesty.

The Journey of
JULY 17

W elcome to July 17, a tenderhearted journey of self-love.
Listen to your heart today instead of your head. While it is natural to want to protect yourself from vulnerability, *Devotion* (The Number Six) asks you to invite it in with open arms as you show your loved ones just how much you care. Whether you send a thoughtful text or extend a helping hand, now is the time to give your love generously.

And while you're at it, take a gentle trip down memory lane. Cancer season always turns the mirror toward the past, but *Nostalgia* (Six of Cups) means focusing on the joy rather than the pain. What connects you with your inner child? Even if it's just a cartoon or a type of dessert, let yourself bask in the sweetness of this memory.

And as you open your heart, remember that how you treat it is a *Choice* (The Lovers). Rather than giving yourself away to the people who can never hold your feelings with care, prioritize the partners and friends who always seek to fill your emotional cup. Who makes you feel safe and understood? Go toward the people and places that soothe your soul so you can experience true internal contentment.

JUST FOR TODAY

TODAY'S MANTRA

In the right hands, I can open my heart to the people and memories that feel safe.

TODAY'S RITUAL

Hold a mirror up to your eyes. As you look at your reflection, try to imagine yourself as a child. Repeat the spell, "Child magic, please set free the sweetness of the past that lives within me."

TODAY'S JOURNAL PROMPT

What is my earliest memory of experiencing love and connection?

BORN ON THIS DAY

TONI STONE, American baseball player and one of the first women to play professional baseball full time

DAVID HASSELHOFF, American actor, singer, producer, television personality, and businessman

"When it comes to human dignity, we cannot make compromises."—ANGELA MERKEL, German politician and first female chancellor of Germany

The Journey of Those Born on
JULY 17

Y ou were born of deep compassion and an optimism that, when taken to extremes, can bypass important healing. You will have to soften to the heart of the matter, as your journey is
one of service, integration, and true love.

Early on in your journey, you will meet your tender
guide, *Devotion* (The Number Six). Despite your emotionally introverted nature, *Devotion* calls you away
from morbid reflection and toward a path of meaningful action. You will meet *Devotion* in divine acts of service, when you pour your mind, body, and soul into the
relationships and projects that mean the most to you.

And if you walk this gentle path, you will be greeted
by your reflective friend, *Nostalgia* (Six of Cups). *Nostalgia* encourages you to connect with your sweet inner
child, that voice that taps you on your shoulder from
time to time to remind you of what was. *Nostalgia*
prompts you to think back to who you were before
adulting happened, helping you remember the good so
that you can integrate the childlike innocence that lies
within.

> ## YOUR GUIDES
>
> *Astrology: Your Energy*
> Cancer (The Moon, Neptune)
>
> *Numerology: Your Path*
> Devotion (The Number Six)
>
> *Minor Arcana: Your Lesson*
> Nostalgia (The Six of Cups)
>
> *Major Arcana: Your Highest Calling*
> Choice (The Lovers)

By answering these calls for vulnerability, you will come to understand the power of *Choice*
(The Lovers). *Choice* reminds you that true emotional contentment is just one decision away, encouraging you to prioritize the relationships that fill rather than drain your cup. You will meet
Choice in moments of emotional discretion, when you walk away from an unfulfilling connection in order to run toward what your heart is truly worth. If you can receive the kind of love you
give, *Choice* ensures your heart remains full.

CANCER
RULERS: THE MOON, NEPTUNE

PURPOSE
*To soften the heart and discover true
emotional contentment.*

RELATIONSHIPS

You are emotionally powerful and brave, yet your relationships should be a place of tenderheartedness and compassion. By seeking out partners who show their devotion through kind words
and thoughtful action, you will discover that true love is as sweet as a fairy tale.

The Journey of
JULY 18

Welcome to June 18, a productive journey of interpersonal responsibility.

Keep to your word with others today. Although it is easy to get distracted by new ideas and people, *Commitment* (The Number Seven) asks you to value loyalty instead. To whom and to what are you responsible? Show up with intention and focus, letting them know just how important they are to you.

But be wary of *Illusion* (Seven of Cups). This part of Cancer season can make you see everything through rose-tinted glasses, but you'll need to practice emotional discernment if you find yourself getting lost in fantasy. If something (or particularly someone) seems too good to be true, it probably is. The easy answer to life's difficulties doesn't exist, so call a friend and get the reality check you need.

Besides, you have more important places to go. *Evolution* (The Chariot) invites personal progress today as long as you are willing to put in the work. By showing the universe just how serious you are about the people you care about most, you can make great strides in your larger ambitions. Set your sights on the future of your relationships and move toward this purpose with complete faith in yourself.

JUST FOR TODAY

TODAY'S MANTRA
I will get serious about the people who matter most and work toward our shared future.

TODAY'S JOURNAL PROMPT
To whom, and to what, am I emotionally committed? How can I prioritize them today?

TODAY'S RITUAL
Brew some tea; holy basil, peppermint, or kava will do just fine. Take a seated position as you dip your index finger in the liquid and place a drop on your forehead. Repeat the spell, "Sober tea, help me see through sober eyes."

BORN ON THIS DAY

KRISTEN BELL, American actor

PRIYANKA CHOPRA, Indian actor and singer

"I learned that courage was not the absence of fear, but the triumph over it."—NELSON MANDELA, South African anti-apartheid activist, political prisoner, and president of South Africa

The Journey of Those Born on
JULY 18

You were born of lunar intuition and an attachment to the past that can keep you from pursuing your future. You will have to channel your waves of emotion into your highest potential, as your journey is one of perseverance, sober thinking, and radical progress.

Early on in your journey, you will meet your discerning guide, *Commitment* (The Number Seven). You would rather explore the unknown, but *Commitment* calls you away from the distractions of wanderlust and toward a path of interpersonal responsibility. By keeping your word to the people, projects, and ideas that you are loyal to, you can discover the satisfaction of intentionality.

But if you choose this thoughtful path, watch out for *Illusion* (Seven of Cups). *Illusion* comes to you in fantastical thinking, when the seduction of someone or something makes you believe that your life would be better if you could only have the person or the thing. Rather than losing appreciation for the things you do have, *Illusion* invites you to break the spell with a strong dose of reality.

> ### YOUR GUIDES
>
> *Astrology: Your Energy*
> Cancer (The Moon, Neptune)
>
> *Numerology: Your Path*
> Commitment (The Number Seven)
>
> *Minor Arcana: Your Lesson*
> Illusion (The Seven of Cups)
>
> *Major Arcana: Your Highest Calling*
> Evolution (The Chariot)

By answering these calls for accountability, you will break new ground. *Evolution* (The Chariot) reminds you that success happens slowly but surely, building through a lifetime of hard work and perseverance. You will meet *Evolution* in moments of breakthrough, when all the sweat and tears you shed amount to a spectacular win. If you can place one foot in front of the other, you can go beyond what you can imagine.

———————————○———————————

CANCER
RULERS: THE MOON, NEPTUNE

PURPOSE
To commit to the people who matter most, leaving success up to timing.

RELATIONSHIPS

You are highly attuned to the feelings of others, so your relationships should be a place of responsibility and commitment. By seeking out partners who work toward, rather than against, the growth of the relationship, you will discover that true love gets better with time.

The Journey of
JULY 19

Welcome to July 19, an emotionally empowering journey toward authenticity.
Step into your *Power* (The Number Eight) today. Though it is not always easy to take up space in the world, embrace who you are rather than who you think society wants you to be so you can experience the full breadth of your honest spirit. By being unapologetically true to yourself, you can create radical intimacy and profound success.

But as you peel back the layers, don't be surprised if some *Disappointment* (Eight of Cups) comes through. Cancer season makes it difficult to let things go, but be bold and brave as you walk away from the emotional obligations that are draining your cup. By releasing what is holding you back, you can make room for better and brighter opportunities.

And if you feel overwhelmed in some way today, remember your *Resilience* (Strength). You have been through much in your life, and you have a huge emotional reservoir to tap into when you need it. Rather than letting difficult feelings get the best of you, look inward and rely on your emotional fortitude as you discover just how much you can handle.

JUST FOR TODAY

TODAY'S MANTRA
I can shed old emotional layers to reveal my authentic power.

TODAY'S RITUAL
Channel the energy of the lion. If you feel overwhelmed at any point today, close your eyes and visualize a majestic lion at the center of your heart. Repeat the affirmation, "I am the ruler of my authentic kingdom."

TODAY'S JOURNAL PROMPT
Are there any emotional obligations that I need to let go of?

BORN ON THIS DAY

HOWARD D. SCHULTZ, American businessman, and author, served as the chairman and CEO of the Starbucks Coffee Company

ANGELA TRIMBUR, American actor, writer, dancer, and choreographer

"Truth is never ugly when one can find in it what one needs."—**EDGAR DEGAS**, French impressionist painter, sculptor, and artist

The Journey of Those Born on
JULY 19

Y ou were born of lunar dreams and divine optimism that can, on its worst day, cause you to deny painful truths. You will have to make room for the healing power of darkness, as your journey is one of divine mystery, pivotal loss, and personal drive.

Early on in your journey, you will meet your enigmatic guide, *Power* (The Number Eight). *Power* asks you to drop your facades in the divine pursuit of authenticity. You will meet *Power* in moments of profound self-honesty, when the excruciating vulnerability you once thought would kill you suddenly comes to fruition in authentic success.

And if you choose this mysterious path, you will fall into the arms of your emotional teacher, *Disappointment* (Eight of Cups). *Disappointment* sheds its stark light on the aspects of your life that are no longer serving your growth. Whether it be personal, professional, or internal, *Disappointment* asks you to be willing to walk away from what no longer feels true to you. It is brave and profound to move forward in the pitch dark of the night.

> ## YOUR GUIDES
>
> *Astrology: Your Energy*
> Cancer (The Moon, Neptune)
>
> *Numerology: Your Path*
> Power (The Number Eight)
>
> *Minor Arcana: Your Lesson*
> Disappointment (The Eight of Cups)
>
> *Major Arcana: Your Highest Calling*
> Resilience (Strength)

By answering these calls for self-honesty, you will come to understand the importance of *Resilience* (Strength). *Resilience* adorns your scars with dazzling wonder, making you a beacon of spiritual optimism in a world that struggles to contend with suffering. You will meet *Resilience* in moments of self-belief, when you hold yourself through the toughest of times with emotional fortitude. If you can remember that every shade of your experience contributes to your irrefutable beauty, you will make this life an authentic masterpiece.

CANCER
RULERS: THE MOON, NEPTUNE

PURPOSE
To shine brightest in the dark.

RELATIONSHIPS

You know how to rely on your passion and talents to get by in life, yet your relationships should be a place of deep merging. By sharing your deepest thoughts, fears, and experiences with another person, you can discover that true love never hides from the truth.

The Journey of
JULY 20

Welcome to July 20, a winding adventure toward radical self-trust.

Step out into the unknown today. Despite the comfort zone–seeking nature of Cancer season, *Experience* (The Number Nine) invites you to explore new horizons with bravery and curiosity. It is more than okay to be afraid as you push your limits, but don't let these emotions block you from growth.

Somewhere amidst this exploration, take some time and access *Gratitude* (Nine of Cups). Stop and enjoy the sunset or feel the breeze on your face as you look for the grace in each peak and valley that today sends you through. By appreciating even the most uncomfortable of moments, you can have a profound shift in perspective.

But if you feel lost or overwhelmed at any point, tap into the magic of *Instinct* (The Hermit). All the direction you need today comes from within, so take a meditative moment or two to access the intuitive voice that tells you where to devote your energy next. You don't need to have the answers for tomorrow or next year; instead, align your feet with your soul as you walk through the present moment with complete personal faith.

JUST FOR TODAY

TODAY'S MANTRA

I can explore uncharted territory if I follow my intuitive voice of reason.

TODAY'S RITUAL

Get your hands on nine pieces of licorice root to use in your bath or licorice candy to eat. Before using or eating each piece of licorice, think of one thing you are grateful for today.

TODAY'S JOURNAL PROMPT

How can I step out of my emotional comfort zone today?

BORN ON THIS DAY

LYUDMILA ALEXEYEVA, Russian historian and human-rights activist

MARINA POPOVICH, Soviet Air Force colonel, engineer, and decorated test pilot

"Sometimes the future changes quickly and completely, and we're left with only the choice of what to do next. We can choose to be afraid of it. Just stand there trembling, not moving. Assuming the worst that can happen. Or we step forward into the unknown, and assume it will be brilliant."—**SANDRA OH**, Canadian American actor

The Journey of Those Born on
JULY 20

Y ou were born of intuitive balance and an intense need for emotional certainty. You will have to go to the places that scare you, as your journey is one of seeking, perspective, and internal faith.

Early on in your journey, you will meet your brave guide, *Experience* (The Number Nine). Despite your comforting disposition, *Experience* calls you away from caretaking and toward a path that helps you learn by doing. You will meet *Experience* in the vulnerability of the unknown, when you let down your guard and surrender to the divine intelligence of adventure.

And if you traverse this expansive path, you will make friends with *Gratitude* (Nine of Cups). *Gratitude* invites you to appreciate the journey, finding grace in each twist and turn that life throws at you. You will meet *Gratitude* at the height of an accomplished goal, when you take a moment to soak in the view and acknowledge how far you've come.

YOUR GUIDES

Astrology: Your Energy
Cancer (The Moon, Neptune)

Numerology: Your Path
Experience (The Number Nine)

Minor Arcana: Your Lesson
Gratitude (The Nine of Cups)

Major Arcana: Your Highest Calling
Instinct (The Hermit)

By answering these daring calls, you will have to rely on the power of *Instinct* (The Hermit). *Instinct* is the divine intelligence that lives within, directing you toward your next right action even in the murkiest of times. You will meet *Instinct* in moments of spiritual alignment, when despite the stark darkness of the incertitude, your gut knows exactly where to go on the road to your highest purpose. If you can trust in the humble genius of *Instinct*, you can discover the beauty of the unknown.

CANCER
RULERS: THE MOON, NEPTUNE

PURPOSE
To trust the intuitive intelligence within while exploring the unknown.

RELATIONSHIPS

You are generous and compassionate with everyone you encounter, and your relationships should be a place of reciprocal growth and higher understanding. By seeking out partners who expand your consciousness and push you into the unknown, you will discover that true love can be the adventure of a lifetime.

The Journey of
JULY 21

Welcome to July 21, a wild ride that requires complete openheartedness.

Trust yourself above all else. *Autonomy* (The Number One) encourages you to stand on your own two feet, guided by nothing but the voice of your intuition. Rather than seeking outside counsel if you are feeling lost today, look within and ask yourself where you'd like to go next.

But listen to your heart rather than your ego. Although Cancer season can inspire self-protection, *Vulnerability* (Ace of Cups) asks you to get excited about the possibility of connection instead. Who would you like to get to know, or what creative endeavor would you like to pursue today? If your soul is inspired, nothing can go wrong.

So let fate unfold as it should. *Impermanence* (Wheel of Fortune) asks you to leave the outcome of your actions to a power greater than yourself today, trusting that the universe has your best interests at heart. Whether you are riding a high of success or working through a temporary emotional low, try to find the good in each ebb and flow that the day offers. Nothing lasts forever, so you might as well enjoy life as it comes.

JUST FOR TODAY

TODAY'S MANTRA
I will pursue my heart's desires, while leaving the outcome up to fate.

TODAY'S JOURNAL PROMPT
If I were to trust myself, what connection or creative endeavor would I like to pursue today?

TODAY'S RITUAL
Start the day off with vulnerability. Call one beloved person in your life and ask them to hold space, without comment, as you share with them an idea or goal that you are most excited about manifesting.

BORN ON THIS DAY

ERNEST HEMINGWAY, American author

YUSUF ISLAM, aka Cat Stevens, English singer-songwriter

"I used to think that the worst thing in life was to end up alone. It's not. The worst thing in life is to end up with people who make you feel alone."—ROBIN WILLIAMS, American actor and comedian

The Journey of Those Born on
JULY 21

You were born of deep compassion and a wisdom that can make it hard to try new things. You will have to throw yourself into the unknown, as your journey is one of independence, self-revelation, and fate.

Early on in your journey, you will meet your fearless guide, *Autonomy* (The Number One). Despite your social disposition, *Autonomy* calls you away from group thinking and toward a path of radical self-trust. By carving out your own unique place in the world, you can create a life that is custom-built for your emotional contentment.

And if you walk this self-reliant path, *Vulnerability* (Ace of Cups) will ask you to lead from the heart rather than your ego. Ambition is natural, but *Vulnerability* inspires you to pursue fulfilling connections rather than fleeting goals. You will meet *Vulnerability* in the sheer possibility of connection, when your enthusiasm and hope for emotional reciprocation outweighs any fears of rejection.

YOUR GUIDES

Astrology: Your Energy
Cancer (The Moon, Neptune)

Numerology: Your Path
Autonomy (The Number One)

Minor Arcana: Your Lesson
Vulnerability (The Ace of Cups)

Major Arcana: Your Highest Calling
Impermanence (The Wheel of Fortune)

By answering these brave calls, you will have to leave the outcome of your life to destiny. *Impermanence* (Wheel of Fortune) invites you to experience the turns of fate, finding joy and meaning in even the most downtrodden of times. You will meet *Impermanence* in the peaks of your journey as well as the valleys, when you have no choice but to trust that the universe has your back. If you can believe that everything is unfolding as it should, you'll better enjoy the ride.

○

CANCER
RULERS: THE MOON, NEPTUNE

PURPOSE
To enjoy the wild roller coaster of self-trust and vulnerability.

RELATIONSHIPS

You are generous and wise, but your relationships should be a place of complete vulnerability. By seeking out partners who inspire you to put your heart and soul on the line, you will discover that true love is a radical act of bravery.

The Journey of
JULY 22

Welcome to July 22, a peaceful journey toward emotional justice.

To close out the emotional safety of Cancer season, slow down and take things easy today. *Balance* (The Number Two) encourages you to find a middle ground rather than going to extremes with your feelings, so take a deep breath if you feel overwhelmed at any point. Call a tranquil friend and ask them to help you find the serenity that comes from the present moment.

And remember that you deserve peace and happiness. *Worthiness* (Two of Cups) invites you to invest in the partnerships that reciprocate your generosity, so don't waste any time on the people who drain your emotional cup. Instead of settling for less, take note of your needs and expectations in relationships, and bring awareness to how others are treating you.

By looking inward, you can discover your own sense of *Truth* (Justice). What is your definition of right and wrong, fair and unfair, in relationships? If you notice any interpersonal injustices today, don't be afraid to stick up for what you believe in and make your voice heard. More than likely, by communicating in a calm and effective manner, you can create more equality and harmony with the people you care about most.

JUST FOR TODAY

TODAY'S MANTRA
I can communicate my needs and values in a calm and fair manner.

TODAY'S RITUAL
Bring two pieces of lavender with you throughout the day. When you are feeling emotionally imbalanced, put a stem in each hand and inhale deeply.

TODAY'S JOURNAL PROMPT
What are the values I hold when it comes to equal partnership?

BORN ON THIS DAY

EMMA LAZARUS, American author of poetry, prose, and translations and an activist for Jewish causes

SELENA GOMEZ, American singer, actor, and entrepreneur

"I try to find hope in struggle and resistance in small places as much as I can."—DANNY GLOVER, American actor, director, and civil rights activist

The Journey of Those Born on
JULY 22*

Y ou were born of emotional maturity and fierce self-discipline that can block you from seeking the help you need most. You will have to learn how to treat yourself more gently, as your journey is one of harmony, mutual partnership, and divine justice.

Early on in your journey, you will meet your gentle guide, *Balance* (The Number Two). Despite your relentlessly hardworking nature, *Balance* calls you away from burnout and toward a path of tranquil coexistence. If you can ask for help and take time off when you need it most, you'll learn to walk, rather than run, through life.

But if you choose this partnership-driven path, *Worthiness* (Two of Cups) will ask you to go inward and discover what you truly need from these relationships. Is it fun and laughter? Is it a deep sexual attraction? Is it unshakable trust? Whatever the answer may be, *Worthiness* wants you to bring awareness to your needs so that you can find yourself in a mutual and fulfilling relationship with another.

By answering these calls for emotional healing, you will come to understand the power of *Truth* (Justice). *Truth* shows you the results of your actions, positive and negative, so that you can be sure the energy you are sharing is the energy you hope to receive. You will meet *Truth* in moments of radical accountability, when you take true ownership over your life and discover the emotional freedom that comes from personal responsibility. By owning your side of the street, and nothing more, you can build a sustainably peaceful life.

YOUR GUIDES

Astrology: Your Energy
Cancer (The Moon, Neptune)

Numerology: Your Path
Balance (The Number Two)

Minor Arcana: Your Lesson
Worthiness (The Two of Cups)

Major Arcana: Your Highest Calling
Truth (Justice)

CANCER
RULERS: THE MOON, NEPTUNE

PURPOSE
To give to others as you would like to receive.

RELATIONSHIPS

You tend to love in extremes, yet your relationships should be a place of patience and equality. By getting to know yourself first and taking your time getting to know your partners, you will discover that true love can be a slow burn.

Are you a Leo born on this day? Head to page 760 to find your additional birthday guide!

WELCOME TO

The Journey of
JULY 23

Welcome to July 23, a personally fulfilling journey of expansion.

Learn from others today. Although the start of Leo season can bring a healthy boost to your self-confidence, *Flexibility* (The Number Three) asks you to remain humble as you explore the topics and modalities that don't come naturally to you. If you are willing to be a beginner, what would you like to explore today?

The good news is, *Expansion* (Three of Wands) brings you enthusiasm for your next venture. Whether you sign up for a new course or begin studying under a new mentor, now is the time to grow your skill set by trying something new. There's no need for mastery, so run toward the things that ignite your curiosity and make you feel young at heart.

And try your best to enjoy it. *Abundance* (The Empress) asks you to receive the gifts that today offers, soaking in every ounce of good fortune that comes your way. If you find yourself in the warm embrace of a friend or enjoying a delicious meal, take a moment to appreciate how good it feels to be emotionally full. Remember that you are worthy of such beauty as you go about this fruitful day.

○

JUST FOR TODAY

TODAY'S MANTRA
I can enjoy myself as I step out on a ledge and try new things.

TODAY'S JOURNAL PROMPT
If I wasn't afraid of looking inexperienced, what creative and/or professional skill would I like to try?

TODAY'S RITUAL
Take three matches. Strike them one at a time, and with each, imagine something outside your comfort zone that you would like to try before blowing the match out.

○

BORN ON THIS DAY

BARBARA DEMING, American feminist and advocate of nonviolent social change

DANIEL RADCLIFFE, English actor

"We talk a lot about our right to freedom of expression, but we need to talk more about our responsibility to freedom of expression. We all want to be heard, but let's acknowledge the difference between speaking up with intention and speaking up for attention."—MONICA LEWINSKY, American activist, television personality, fashion designer, and former White House intern

The Journey of Those Born on
JULY 23

You were born of personal authority and a confidence that can be misconstrued for arrogance. You will have to expand your consciousness through connection, as your journey is one of curiosity, progress, and spiritual abundance.

Early on in your journey, you will meet your sociable guide, *Flexibility* (The Number Three). Despite your high intelligence, *Flexibility* calls you away from having all the answers and toward an enlightening path of open-mindedness. If you're willing to be as much of a student as you are a master, you can expand your point of view by learning from the experiences of others.

And if you choose this varied path, you will meet your inspired friend, *Expansion* (Three of Wands). *Expansion* reminds you that there is always more to pursue, so consider exploring the topics and interests that are far outside your realm of understanding. You will meet *Expansion* when you set your sights on a new goal or interest, and you can't help but glow with enthusiasm for what's to come.

YOUR GUIDES

Astrology: Your Energy
Leo (The Sun)

Numerology: Your Path
Flexibility (The Number Three)

Minor Arcana: Your Lesson
Expansion (The Three of Wands)

Major Arcana: Your Highest Calling
Abundance (The Empress)

By answering these calls for open-mindedness, you will begin to see the beauty in *Abundance* (The Empress). *Abundance* invites you to enjoy life rather than just survive it, inspiring you to accept and cherish the gifts that the universe gives you. Whether you soak in a beautiful sunset or accept the offer for a dream job, *Abundance* asks you to stay present in the vulnerability of true happiness. If you can learn to receive the light you give, you'll open yourself to personal fulfillment.

———————————————————◯———————————————————

LEO
RULER: THE SUN

PURPOSE
To grow and expand while receiving the gift true happiness.

RELATIONSHIPS

You are bold and proud, yet your relationships should be a place of joyful connection and fun. By seeking out partners who keep you in the present moment through their humor and benevolence, you will discover that true love can be a lighthearted affair.

The Journey of
JULY 24

W elcome to July 24, a masterful journey that wants you to work as hard as you play.

Leo season thrives on inspiration rather than *Discipline* (The Number Four) but do what is required today. Show up for any and every responsibility you have toward yourself and others, holding yourself accountable to what you value most. Even if it takes more hours than you would like, look for the satisfaction that lies in personal integrity.

And when you're done, run straight toward *Celebration* (Four of Wands). Call up a few friends or chosen family and throw the kind of party that makes you feel rejuvenated. Whether it be a night on the dance floor or a marathon of television, let yourself enjoy the fruits of your labor. What is your definition of fun?

At the end of the day, you are your own personal authority. *Self-mastery* (The Emperor) encourages you to make discerning but loving decisions for yourself today, balancing your needs and desires in perfect harmony. There is always room for a bit of work, a bit of fun, and a bit of relaxation, so create the boundaries you need to thrive throughout this day of personal progress.

JUST FOR TODAY

TODAY'S MANTRA
There is room for work and play, as long as I set the boundaries I need to thrive.

TODAY'S JOURNAL PROMPT
What is the work I am responsible for today? What is the fun I could indulge in today?

TODAY'S RITUAL
Throw yourself a party today. It could be a simple gathering at your home or a wild night out on the town. Invite your friends and chosen family to collaborate, and be sure that instead of causing more stress, it helps you blow off steam.

BORN ON THIS DAY

AMELIA EARHART, American aviator and the first woman to fly solo across the Atlantic Ocean

JENNIFER "J.LO" LOPEZ, American actor and pop singer

"The art of victory is learned in defeat."—SIMÓN BOLÍVAR, Venezuelan military and political leader

The Journey of Those Born on
JULY 24

You were born of compassionate leadership and an extreme generosity that can distract you from your highest potential. You will have to take your future seriously, as your journey is one of hard work, homecoming, and personal authority.

Early on in your journey, you will meet your no-nonsense guide, *Discipline* (The Number Four). Despite your emotional nature, *Discipline* calls you away from the unreliability of feeling and toward a grounded path of dedication. You will meet *Discipline* in the long hours of internal endurance that will one day amount to your irrefutable success.

But don't worry; if you take this intrepid path, you will fall into the arms of *Celebration* (Four of Wands). You will meet *Celebration* when you have won the war and get to come home to your chosen family to rejuvenate your spirit. By taking some necessary time off between great personal milestones, *Celebration* teaches you how to refill your cup before going back to battle.

By answering these gratifying calls, you will tap into the realm of *Self-mastery* (The Emperor). *Self-mastery* calls you to get in touch with the objective leader who lives within, helping you separate emotion from logic as you make thoughtful decisions for yourself and others. You will meet *Self-mastery* when the cards are stacked against you and yet you somehow remain calm and collected. If you can channel your powerful feelings into rational action, *Self-mastery* shows you that you can handle anything.

LEO
RULER: THE SUN

PURPOSE
To master the art of work hard, play hard.

RELATIONSHIPS

You are tenderhearted and generous, and your relationships should be a place of emotional grounding and energetic restoration. By seeking out partners who feel like home and help you decompress between challenges, you will discover that true love always has your back.

The Journey of
JULY 25

Welcome to July 25, a courageous journey of personal authority.

Shine as bright as you can today. To complement the expressive nature of Leo season, *Courage* (The Number Five) invites you to shed any layers of shame as you step into the light of your authentic spirit. What creative talents would you like to share with the world today?

If *Conflict* (Five of Wands) comes your way in the form of criticism or competition, don't let it get you down. Instead of stooping to anyone's level or comparing yourself to others, keep your head up as you find enthusiasm for what you are expressing. No one can take away or replicate your truth or brilliance.

Because at the end of the day, you carry the *Wisdom* (The Hierophant) you need most. Look for self-confidence rather than social acceptance today, favoring your own opinion over the opinions of others. If someone claims to be an expert or professes that they have the answers, practice personal discernment as you take in their knowledge and perspective. As long as you are happy with your actions and are staying true to yourself, today is an undeniable success.

〇

JUST FOR TODAY

TODAY'S MANTRA

When it comes to expressing my vulnerability, no one's opinion is more important than my own.

TODAY'S JOURNAL PROMPT

If I were to step into the sunlight of my authentic spirit, what would I like to express today?

TODAY'S RITUAL

On a piece of paper, write down five criticisms of yourself that you would be most afraid to receive from someone else. In a fireproof bowl, light the paper on fire and let it burn to ash. As it burns, repeat the affirmation, "Courage always outshines criticism."

〇

BORN ON THIS DAY

GEOFFREY ZAKARIAN, Armenian American chef, restaurateur, television personality, and author

IMAN, Somali American fashion model, actor, and entrepreneur

"In my view, all that is necessary for faith is the belief that by doing our best we shall succeed in our aims: the improvement of mankind."—ROSALIND FRANKLIN, English chemist and co-discoverer of the structure of DNA

The Journey of Those Born on
JULY 25

You were born of strong leadership and a deep-seated need for perfection. You will have to be brave enough to step into your authenticity, as your journey is one of vulnerability, competition, and higher consciousness.

Early on in your journey, you will meet your bold guide, *Courage* (The Number Five). To enhance your passionate spirit, *Courage* calls you away from control and toward a path of radical self-expression. You will meet *Courage* in creative momentum, when you pour your heart and soul into your life.

But if you choose this public path, you will have to face *Conflict* (Five of Wands) along the way. *Conflict* comes to you by way of competitors and naysayers who make you question your worth. Rather than taking the low road and engaging in combat, *Conflict* invites you to make peace with this reality and stay in your lane. By focusing on what you are passionate about, no one can get in your way.

By answering these daring calls, you will access *Wisdom* (The Hierophant). *Wisdom* connects you to the divine intelligence that lives within, helping you decipher what information is and is not of use to you. You will meet *Wisdom* in moments of discernment, when you let another's criticism of you roll off your back as you access internal confidence. If you can care about your own opinion of yourself more than others' opinions of you, you'll tap into the power of personal authority.

LEO
RULER: THE SUN

PURPOSE
*To radically and vulnerably
listen to yourself.*

RELATIONSHIPS

You are committed by nature, and your relationships should be a place of self-expression and radical honesty. By seeking out partners who tell it like it is and empower you to be unapologetically yourself, you will discover that true love never dims your shine.

The Journey of
JULY 26

W elcome to July 26, a heartfelt journey that teaches you to receive the positivity that you send out.

Give yourself to what matters most today. *Devotion* (The Number Six) asks you to extend your energy generously toward the people and projects that speak to your soul. Rather than wasting time on superficial or unfulfilling connections, pursue what is authentic to you with wild abandon.

And accept any praise that comes your way. While Leo season always increases the spotlight, *Confidence* (Six of Wands) invites you to step into your well-earned success and embrace the applause that comes your way. Whether it be recognition from your boss or a sincere compliment from a friend, soak in this gorgeous gift and know you deserve it.

Because isn't happiness a *Choice* (The Lovers), after all? Today, make healthy decisions that prioritize your emotional and mental well-being. If an obligation or responsibility has been draining you for quite some time, don't be shy about saying "no" to it. By owning your worth and keeping your focus on the life-affirming aspects of your day, you can increase self-esteem through estimable action.

○

JUST FOR TODAY

TODAY'S MANTRA
I can give generously while remembering what I am worth in return.

TODAY'S JOURNAL PROMPT
What relationships or projects that are life-giving rather than draining could I prioritize today?

TODAY'S RITUAL
Give yourself a strong pat on the back at end of today. If you feel called, repeat out loud six things you did well throughout the day, taking a moment to bask in the warmth of self-appreciation.

○

BORN ON THIS DAY

MICK JAGGER, English rock vocalist, songwriter, and actor

JACINDA ARDERN, fortieth prime minister of New Zealand

"Do not compare, do not measure. No other way is like yours. All other ways deceive and tempt you. You must fulfill the way that is in you."—CARL JUNG, Swiss psychiatrist and psychoanalyst who founded analytical psychology

The Journey of Those Born on
JULY 26

You were born of personal nobility and an emotional strength that can block you from sharing your feelings. You will have to surrender to the power of vulnerability, as your journey is one of sincerity, recognition, and self-worth.

Early on in your journey, you will meet your sweet guide, *Devotion* (The Number Six). Despite your emotionally withdrawn nature, *Devotion* calls you away from morbid reflection and toward a path of meaningful service. By generously giving your energy to the callings of the heart, you can discover the spiritual gratification of intentionality. If you can dedicate yourself to what matters most, *Devotion* offers you a life of authentic purpose.

And if you choose this honest path, you will discover a new sense of *Confidence* (Six of Wands). *Confidence* means basking in the well-earned spotlight of your success, soaking in the praise and admiration that is extended to you. You will meet *Confidence* in moments of public recognition, when all the behind-the-scenes work you have done finally meets the surface.

By answering these calls to give as well as receive, you will come to understand the power of *Choice* (The Lovers). *Choice* reveals the special ingredient behind the love and intimacy you seek, reminding you that you can accept only the love you think you deserve. If you can work to fall in love with yourself and understand your needs, *Choice* inspires you to prioritize the relationships and commitments that fill, rather than drain, your emotional cup. By making a decision to honor yourself over others, you can put self-worth into action.

LEO
RULER: THE SUN

PURPOSE
*To learn to give and receive love with
complete openheartedness.*

RELATIONSHIPS

You are emotionally self-contained, yet your relationships should be a place of tenderheartedness and vulnerability. By seeking out partners who give their affection freely and don't hold back anything, you will discover that true love never has an ego.

The Journey of
JULY 27

W elcome to July 27, a discerning journey of personal progress.
Prioritize your loyalties today. *Commitment* (The Number Seven) asks that you stay true to your responsibilities rather than getting lost in the distractions of fleeting pleasure. To whom, and to what, are you devoted? Show your sincerity through action rather than words, proving to others and yourself just how reliable you are.

And don't back down without a fight. Because Leo season increases vitality, *Perseverance* (Seven of Wands) asks you to accept any challenges that come your way as you channel this solar energy into personal conviction. If you find yourself facing adversity or external blockages, push through these hurdles with pure passion rather than stooping low in combat.

But know that humility is the name of the game today. *Evolution* (The Chariot) reminds you that while being serious pays off big, you must keep your head down and do the work to maintain momentum. Tap into strength rather than ego as you show the universe just how committed you are to your success. By executing the necessary legwork required, you can make substantial gains.

JUST FOR TODAY

TODAY'S MANTRA

Through hard work, humility, and commitment, I can soar to new heights of progress.

TODAY'S RITUAL

On a piece of paper, write down one goal or purpose and underline it seven times. Carry the paper with you throughout your day, and if you are feeling lost, sit with your goal for seven minutes before moving into action.

TODAY'S JOURNAL PROMPT

What does my relationship to commitment look like, historically as well as today?

BORN ON THIS DAY

QUEEN MOTHER MOORE, American civil rights leader and Black nationalist

DONNIE YEN, Hong Kong Chinese actor, martial artist, director, producer, action choreographer, and multiple-time world wushu champion

"The more you do, the more you think, the better you get."—KRITI SANON, Indian actor

The Journey of Those Born on
JULY 27

You were born of bold wisdom and a self-reliance that can mask your fear of intimacy. You will have to learn to prioritize what you care about most, as your journey is one of intentionality, personal investment, and radical progress.

Early on in your journey, you will meet your serious guide, *Commitment* (The Number Seven). Despite your wanderlust, *Commitment* calls you away from unreliability and toward a path of personal discernment. By deciding to whom and to what you are loyal, you can discover the profound gift of self-accountability and interpersonal responsibility.

But if you choose this decisive path, you will have to make friends with *Perseverance* (Seven of Wands). *Perseverance* isn't interested in easy wins but instead invites you to fight for the things in life that you care about most. You will meet *Perseverance* within personal conviction, when you dig in your heels and devote yourself to the future potential of your dreams.

By answering these demanding calls, you will come to respect the power of *Evolution* (The Chariot). You will meet *Evolution* in the breakthrough moments of success, when years of strenuous hard work seem to pay off in a single second. If you can keep your head down, never minding the outcome as you continue building toward your future, *Evolution* ensures you will get further than you could have ever imagined.

YOUR GUIDES

Astrology: Your Energy
Leo (The Sun)

Numerology: Your Path
Commitment (The Number Seven)

Minor Arcana: Your Lesson
Perseverance (The Seven of Wands)

Major Arcana: Your Highest Calling
Evolution (The Chariot)

LEO
RULER: THE SUN

PURPOSE
To commit to the future, never backing down without a fight.

RELATIONSHIPS

You are forever exploring the world around you, but your relationships should be a place of personal responsibility and commitment. By seeking out partners who are loyal to their word and demand that you do the same, you will discover that true love is built from mutual respect.

The Journey of
JULY 28

Welcome to July 28, a forward-moving journey of radical self-honesty.

Step into your *Power* (The Number Eight) today. Although Leo season always helps us shine, embrace every inch of yourself, even the places you deem unlovable or unacceptable. By experiencing the full breadth of who you are, you can earn the trust of others and influence the world around you to be more true.

And take action. *Momentum* (Eight of Wands) reminds you that there is no time like the present to build the life you want most. If you were aligned with your innermost truth, what would you like to pursue today? Embrace the hustle in whatever form resonates with you, knowing that you can catch up on the rest you need tomorrow.

But if you feel overwhelmed or intimidated at any point today, tap into *Resilience* (Strength). You have a strong emotional backbone, so look within to discover your emotional fortitude. Remember how much you have been through in life as you take on the trials and tribulations of the day with grace and self-confidence. You are the hero of your story, so act in accordance with your highest and best.

○

JUST FOR TODAY

TODAY'S MANTRA

By being radically true to myself, I can pursue the life I want to live.

TODAY'S JOURNAL PROMPT

Are there any aspects of myself that I refuse to accept or acknowledge? If so, where did this self-rejection come from?

TODAY'S RITUAL

Light a candle. As you strike the match, repeat the affirmation, "My truth is powerful." When the candle is lit, count to eight and blow it out. Repeat for a total of eight times.

○

BORN ON THIS DAY

BEATRIX POTTER, English children's author and illustrator

MARCEL DUCHAMP, French sculptor and painter

"Every moment one lives is different from the other. The good, the bad, hardship, the joy, the tragedy, love, and happiness are all interwoven into one single, indescribable whole that is called life. You cannot separate the good from the bad. And perhaps there is no need to do so, either."
—JACQUELINE KENNEDY ONASSIS, American writer, editor, and thirty-fifth first lady of the United States

The Journey of Those Born on
JULY 28

Y ou were born of personal vitality and a desire for disruption that distracts you from the work you need to do most. You will have to hurl yourself toward the truth, as your journey is one of authenticity, alignment, and internal strength.

Early on in your journey, you will meet your enigmatic guide, *Power* (The Number Eight). Despite your social disposition, *Power* calls you away from people-pleasing and toward a path of radical honesty. By embracing every inconvenient truth that lives within, you can discover what you truly want out of life. If you can choose vulnerability over facades, *Power* introduces you to your true self.

If you choose this emboldened path, you will have to keep up with *Momentum* (Eight of Wands). *Momentum* asks you to act rather than react, accessing a place of internal alignment as you pursue the things you desire most in life. You will meet *Momentum* in the fast-paced nature of progress, when your mind can't quite keep up with how far you have grown.

> ### YOUR GUIDES
>
> *Astrology: Your Energy*
> Leo (The Sun)
>
> *Numerology: Your Path*
> Power (The Number Eight)
>
> *Minor Arcana: Your Lesson*
> Momentum (The Eight of Wands)
>
> *Major Arcana: Your Highest Calling*
> Resilience (Strength)

By answering these demanding calls, you will come to understand the importance of *Resilience* (Strength). *Resilience* asks you lean on the emotional backbone within that holds you steady through even the toughest of times. You will meet *Resilience* in moments of necessary discomfort, when you know that you can't stop time and have no choice but to tap into a place of emotional fortitude. If you can reach within during times of change, *Resilience* reminds you that you can handle anything.

LEO
RULER: THE SUN

PURPOSE
To step into a place of radical honesty and discover internal strength.

RELATIONSHIPS

You are confident and independent by nature, yet your relationships should be a place of deep honesty and emotional merging. By seeking out partners who never shy away from the truth and accept you for your best and worst, you will discover that true love is as real as it gets.

The Journey of
JULY 29

Welcome to July 29, a fearless journey into the unknown.

Although Leo season encourages leadership, *Experience* (The Number Nine) invites you to get out of your own experience and instead jump into the unknown today. Look for every opportunity to expand your perspective, whether you pursue a new field of study or book your next trip abroad. If it makes you excited but nervous, know that you are heading in the right direction.

But don't lose steam if things don't go smoothly right away. *Persistence* (Nine of Wands) wants to see you sweat, so show the universe just how committed you are to your personal growth. If you are met with opposition or experience exhaustion of any kind, do your best to work through it with courage and faith in yourself.

And if you feel uncertain at any point today, tap into your *Instinct* (The Hermit). You have a divine internal compass that at any time can point you to your next right action. Seek out some much-needed isolation so you can silence the outside world and get in touch with the truth of your intuition. All the answers to today's questions can be found within.

───────○───────

JUST FOR TODAY

TODAY'S MANTRA
I can grow the furthest by embracing the unknown.

TODAY'S JOURNAL PROMPT
Do I tend to listen to or ignore my intuition? How can I get in touch with this instinctual voice?

TODAY'S RITUAL
Spend some time in isolation and meditate. Close your eyes and breathe in for a count of nine and out for a count of nine. Visualize your heart as a glowing flame that can direct you through the course of your day.

───────○───────

BORN ON THIS DAY

KAWAI MICHI, Japanese educator and Christian activist

TIM GUNN, American author, actor, and television personality

"Pray that your loneliness may spur you into finding something to live for, great enough to die for."—DAG HAMMARSKJÖLD, Swedish economist, diplomat, and second secretary-general of the United Nations

The Journey of Those Born on
JULY 29

Y ou were born of diplomatic leadership and a social reliance that can block you from getting to know yourself. You will have to learn to rely on your inner resources, as your journey is one of exploration, courage, and intuition.

Early on in your journey, you will meet your adventurous guide, *Experience* (The Number Nine). You thrive in the warm embrace of partnership, but *Experience* calls you away from comfort and toward a path into the foreign. You will meet *Experience* in the complete unknown, when you break free of your lived experience in pursuit of greater truths about how the world works.

But if you choose this daring path, *Persistence* (Nine of Wands) will ask you to hold the course. You will meet *Persistence* on the edge of exhaustion, when you have endured much but need to push a bit further to meet your highest designation. If you can find the energy you need through personal conviction, you'll learn that anything is possible if you are willing to fight.

YOUR GUIDES

Astrology: Your Energy
Leo (The Sun)

Numerology: Your Path
Experience (The Number Nine)

Minor Arcana: Your Lesson
Persistence (The Nine of Wands)

Major Arcana: Your Highest Calling
Instinct (The Hermit)

By answering these calls for growth, you will come to rely on the genius of *Instinct* (The Hermit). *Instinct* is the divine voice of reason that lives within, ushering you toward a higher purpose in even the most uncertain of times. You will meet *Instinct* in the complete unknown, when there is no clear path in front of you so you must trust your gut to lead the way. If you can move toward the places that scare you, *Instinct* helps light your way through the dark.

———————————————————○———————————————————

LEO
RULER: THE SUN

PURPOSE
To persist through the unknown, guided by the light of personal intuition.

RELATIONSHIPS

You are harmonious and generous with most everyone, and your relationships should be a place of personal growth. By seeking out partners who push you out of your comfort zone and expand your perspective, you will discover that true love lies in the unknown.

The Journey of
JULY 30

W elcome to July 30, an inspired journey that introduces you to fate.
Go your own way today. *Autonomy* (The Number One) invites you to do as you please, never stopping to ask for permission or wait for the approval of others. Listen deeply to what your heart desires most and chase this enthusiasm with every ounce of energy and talent you have. What would you do today if you were to take life by the horns?

To make the most of the bravery of Leo season, believe deeply in the *Potential* (Ace of Wands) of your goals. Rather than getting hung up on a plan or preparing for the worst-case scenario, simply run with the excitement of possibility. Today is a time for beginnings, so don't lose sleep over the middles and the ends. Keep faith in your next greatest plan.

And leave the outcome up to fate. If you feel your luck is turning for the better, extend generosity toward everyone you encounter. If you feel like you are trudging through difficult terrain, try to find the silver lining. *Impermanence* (Wheel of Fortune) reminds you that life is ever-changing, so you might as well enjoy each peak and valley that the day presents you.

JUST FOR TODAY

TODAY'S MANTRA

I can run toward the things I am excited about without getting hung up on expectation.

TODAY'S JOURNAL PROMPT

Do I consider myself an independent person? Why or why not?

TODAY'S RITUAL

Get your hands on some cinnamon or ginger, and add it to your morning tea or coffee, or just pour some in the palm of your hands. As you inhale, repeat the spell, "Spice, please wake me up to the potential of the day."

BORN ON THIS DAY

ARNOLD SCHWARZENEGGER, Austrian American bodybuilder, actor, and politician

FATIMA JINNAH, Pakistani politician, dental surgeon, stateswoman, and one of the leading founders of Pakistan

"I will walk where my own nature would be leading."—EMILY BRONTË, English novelist and poet

The Journey of Those Born on
JULY 30

Y ou were born of joyous abundance and an extreme desire for connection and community. You will have to find the inspiration that can only come from within, as your journey is one of independence, possibility, and destiny.

Early on in your journey, you will meet your daring guide, *Autonomy* (The Number One). Despite your social nature, *Autonomy* calls you away from interdependence and toward a path of radical self-trust. By moving to the beat of your intuitive drum, you can carve out a life that is custom-made for your gifts and talents.

But if you accept this independent path, you will have to believe in *Potential* (Ace of Wands). *Potential* isn't concerned with outcomes but asks you to devote yourself completely to the possibility of your next greatest idea. You will meet *Potential* in the excitement of the unknown, when pure curiosity and enthusiasm for the future outweigh any fear of possible failure.

By answering these brave calls, you will come to understand the laws of *Impermanence* (Wheel of Fortune). *Impermanence* reminds you that nothing in life stays the same, inspiring you to enjoy every twist and turn that comes your way. You will meet *Impermanence* in the highs as well as in the lows along your journey, when you surrender your plans and trust that the universe has a greater vision in store for you. If you can find gratitude for even the worst of times, *Impermanence* shows you the power of staying in the present moment.

> ### YOUR GUIDES
>
> *Astrology: Your Energy*
> Leo (The Sun)
>
> *Numerology: Your Path*
> Autonomy (The Number One)
>
> *Minor Arcana: Your Lesson*
> Potential (The Ace of Wands)
>
> *Major Arcana: Your Highest Calling*
> Impermanence (The Wheel of Fortune)

LEO
RULER: THE SUN

PURPOSE
To chase enthusiasm and surrender the outcome to the power of fate.

RELATIONSHIPS

You are generous and loving by nature, yet your relationships should be a place of complete independence and mutual faith. By seeking out partners who have a rich internal life and encourage you to chase your dreams, you will discover that true love is the greatest inspiration of all.

The Journey of
JULY 31

W elcome to July 31, a slow, thoughtful journey of personal accountability.
Look for *Balance* (The Number Two) today. While Leo season is enthusiastic in nature, try not to spread your energy too thin. Instead, pare down your list of responsibilities so you can approach each task with grace and presence of mind. Call in help from the partners you trust if needed, remembering that the people you love would like to lighten your load.

And from there, spend some time in *Preparation* (Two of Wands). This is not a day for execution but rather a day for planning, so get out your pen and paper as you strategize about what is to come. What steps are needed to get you from here to your highest goals? There's no rushing this process, so practice patience as you look toward the future.

Within the spaciousness of today, tap into *Truth* (Justice). Go inward and decipher your own set of moral values so that you can act in alignment with those sets of principles. By remaining true to this internal compass, you can reassess your goals and ensure that they are in complete congruence with your personal sense of justice.

— ○ —

JUST FOR TODAY

TODAY'S MANTRA
I will pare down my duties so that I can align my goals with my moral compass.

TODAY'S JOURNAL PROMPT
How can I lighten my list of responsibilities today so that I can focus on the bigger picture?

TODAY'S RITUAL
Take a cool, calming bath. Add Epsom salt for detoxification. As you relax into this moment, repeat the prayer, "Cool waters, please help me find the truth in the balance."

— ○ —

BORN ON THIS DAY

AMELIA STONE QUINTON, American social reformer and Native American rights advocate

JUNJI ITO, Japanese horror manga artist

"The target for every great champion is to play for the team."—ANTONIO CONTE, Italian professional footballer and manager

The Journey of Those Born on
JULY 31

You were born of personal authority and a sense of responsibility that can lead to burnout. You will have to slow down to find the truth, as your journey is one of patience, planning, and intuitive justice.

Early on in your journey, you will meet your temperate guide, *Balance* (The Number Two). Despite your hardworking nature, *Balance* calls you away from overdoing it and toward a path of interpersonal harmony. By never taking on more than you can handle and prioritizing your holistic health and well-being, you can bring complete intention and focus to the responsibilities you do have.

But if you choose this tranquil path, you will have to make time for *Preparation* (Two of Wands). Rome wasn't built in a day, so slow down and get clear on your intentions before jumping into your next endeavor. Through patience and careful planning, you can use your energy more wisely.

By answering these calls for thoughtfulness, you will access your sense of *Truth* (Justice). *Truth* asks you to listen to the moral reason that comes from internal balance, helping you decipher your personal definition of justice through peace of mind. You will meet *Truth* in deep meditation, when the trappings of the mind are quiet and there is enough space to hear what feels right and what feels wrong to you. By gaining clarity around your intuitive sense of fairness, you can gracefully stand up for what you believe in most.

> ### YOUR GUIDES
>
> *Astrology: Your Energy*
> Leo (The Sun)
>
> *Numerology: Your Path*
> Balance (The Number Two)
>
> *Minor Arcana: Your Lesson*
> Preparation (The Two of Wands)
>
> *Major Arcana: Your Highest Calling*
> Truth (Justice)

LEO
RULER: THE SUN

PURPOSE
To uncomplicate your life in order to access peaceful moral reason.

RELATIONSHIPS

You are hardworking and reliable, and your relationships should be a place of emotional reciprocity and equality. By seeking out partners who harmonize your energy and always try to meet you halfway, you will discover that true love aims for peace.

The Journey of
AUGUST 1

Welcome to August 1, a reflective adventure that requires personal faith.

Embrace the unexpected today. *Experience* (The Number Nine) encourages you to break free from your comfort zone and throw yourself into the unknown. What would you want to explore if you weren't afraid? While anxiety is natural when it comes to uncharted territory, feel the fear and do it anyway.

But don't burn out too quickly. Although Leo season inspires courage, *Persistence* (Nine of Wands) emphasizes the importance of sustainable action, so take small rests throughout the day to ensure you aren't running on empty. Whether you make time for a satiating meal or a quick power nap, try to regain your enthusiasm for adventure before carrying on.

And if you feel uncertain or lost at any point today, tap into your *Instinct* (The Hermit). Rather than seeking outside opinion or following a rule book, listen to the voice inside you as you make decisions that are uniquely true for you. No one has the answers to the day's question except for your soul, so drown out the noise of society as you get to know your innate intelligence. Anything is possible if you are willing to believe in yourself.

JUST FOR TODAY

TODAY'S MANTRA

There is no road map through the unknown that is more clear than my intuition.

TODAY'S JOURNAL PROMPT

What are some efficient but effective ways I can recharge my batteries throughout today?

TODAY'S RITUAL

Set aside thirty minutes to go for a walk around a neighborhood that feels safe to you. Whenever you come to a turning point, take a brief pause and ask intuition which way it would like to turn next. Don't overthink it; just follow your gut reaction so you can learn to trust this powerful resource.

BORN ON THIS DAY

JERRY GARCIA, American guitarist and singer-songwriter

KAMALA NEHRU, Indian independence activist

"The truth is we're all searching. We're all looking for guidance, for mentors, and I'm by no means someone to follow."—JASON MOMOA, American actor, producer, and environmental activist

The Journey of Those Born on
AUGUST 1

You were born of powerful radiance and an impulsiveness that can get you in trouble from time to time. You will have to learn to trust your intuition over fleeting desire, as your journey is one of searching, resilience, and internal direction.

Early on in your journey, you will meet your adventurous guide, *Experience* (The Number Nine). Despite your ambitious nature, *Experience* calls you away from self-seeking and toward a path of higher consciousness. You will meet *Experience* in the foreign, when you step outside your comfort zone and throw yourself into uncharted territory. If you can choose courage over safety, *Experience* offers you the gift of personal growth.

If you take this daring path, you will meet your strategic coach, *Persistence* (Nine of Wands). *Persistence* asks you to see your adventures through to the end by keeping your tank full. You will meet *Persistence* in the brief breaks you take along your journey, when you recharge your soul and access the enthusiasm you need to persevere.

By answering these calls for expansion, you will come to understand the genius of *Instinct* (The Hermit). You will meet *Instinct* in the complete unknown, when you have no map to guide you except your intuition. *Instinct* asks you to silence the noise as it invites you inward to hear the voice of divine intelligence that lies deep within. By putting your faith in this innate resource, you can intuitively move toward a higher destiny.

LEO
RULER: THE SUN

PURPOSE
To light your way through the darkness of the unknown.

RELATIONSHIPS

You are independent yet magnanimous, and your relationships should be a place of expansion. By seeking out partners who force you out of your comfort zone and help you grow in your perspective, you will discover that true love is the greatest adventure of all.

The Journey of
AUGUST 2

W elcome to August 2, an inspired journey of personal faith.
Go your own way today. *Autonomy* (The Number One) invites you to make decisions from a place of intuition rather than waiting for permission or guidance from others. If your gut is telling you to move in a certain direction, don't overthink or second-guess yourself; just move toward the places that are calling your soul.

And if you're feeling uncertain at any point, chase enthusiasm. Leo season inspires passion anyhow, and *Potential* (Ace of Wands) wants you to believe in the possibility of your dreams. What idea or ambition are you the most excited about manifesting? Rather than getting lost in the anxiety of how to make it work, run toward the inspiration with the belief in its potential to bloom.

But don't fret over the outcomes of your efforts. *Impermanence* (Wheel of Fortune) reminds you that everything is temporary, so lean in to each ebb and flow that your journey brings. The only constant in this day is change, but by trusting that fate is unfolding exactly as it should, you can find the silver lining in the present moment.

JUST FOR TODAY

TODAY'S MANTRA
I will run toward my soul's callings, while leaving the outcome up to fate.

TODAY'S RITUAL
Get your hands on some fire agate, or if you can't, find an image of this gemstone. While holding the agate in your hand or looking at the image, repeat the affirmation, "By believing in my internal flame, I can light the fire I want in my life."

TODAY'S JOURNAL PROMPT
In what ways do I have an entrepreneurial spirit?

BORN ON THIS DAY

FRÉDÉRIC AUGUSTE BARTHOLDI, French sculptor who designed *Liberty Enlightening the World* (aka the Statue of Liberty)

ISABEL ALLENDE, Chilean American author

"Those who say it can't be done are usually interrupted by others doing it."—JAMES BALDWIN, American novelist and playwright

The Journey of Those Born on
AUGUST 2

You were born of social joy and limitless compassion that you rarely extend inward. You will have to learn to take a chance on yourself, as your journey is one of intuition, inspiration, and the timing of fate.

Early on in your journey, you will meet your fearless guide, *Autonomy* (The Number One). Despite your diplomatic nature, *Autonomy* calls you away from people-pleasing and toward a path of radical self-trust. By following nothing but the beat of your instinctual drum, you can blaze new ground and show the rest of us what it means to believe in oneself.

And if you choose this independent path, you will have to fight for *Potential* (Ace of Wands). You will meet *Potential* in the ray of optimism that lives within a new idea, when you have no idea how you'll make it work but you're deeply sure you're onto something good. If you can believe in limitless possibilities and chase your enthusiasm, you can discover how to turn vision into reality.

> ## YOUR GUIDES
>
> *Astrology: Your Energy*
> Leo (The Sun, Jupiter)
>
> *Numerology: Your Path*
> Autonomy (The Number One)
>
> *Minor Arcana: Your Lesson*
> Potential (The Ace of Wands)
>
> *Major Arcana: Your Highest Calling*
> Impermanence (The Wheel of Fortune)

By answering these inspired calls, you will have to surrender the outcome of your ambitions to the ever-changing tides of fate. *Impermanence* (Wheel of Fortune) invites you to have faith in the universal powers at be, trusting that each unexpected turn in your journey is a part of your larger destiny. You will meet *Impermanence* in the peaks and valleys of your success, when you are faced with a choice either to lose sleep over what you can't control or to go with the flow. If you can let go and have faith, *Impermanence* teaches you how to embrace the full breadth of the human experience.

LEO
RULERS: THE SUN, JUPITER

PURPOSE
*To take a chance on enthusiasm
rather than comfort.*

RELATIONSHIPS

You are a life-giving force of nature, but your relationships should be a place of independence and mutual trust. By seeking out partners who are content doing their own thing and championing your individuality, you will discover that true love empowers you to be free.

The Journey of
AUGUST 3

Welcome to August 3, a tranquil journey toward higher justice.

Although Leo season increases vitality, leaving you brimming with energy, *Balance* (The Number Two) asks you to take it easy and preserve your energy. Lean on your professional and personal partners as you share responsibility, reminding yourself that burdens transform into opportunities when they are thoughtfully shared with others.

And as you pare down your day, prioritize *Preparation* (Two of Wands). Rather than saying yes to every opportunity that comes your way, aim for peaceful endurance as you decipher what is and is not worth your energy today. Take a zoomed-out approach as you look at your long-term plans and goals rather than jumping straight into your next action.

As you consider your larger intentions, pay special attention to the internal voice that tells you the *Truth* (Justice). Are your ambitions aligned with your moral values? Look within and decipher your personal definition of fairness and equality. By living in accordance with the spiritual laws of karma, you can rest your head peacefully at the end of this day, knowing that you did everything you could to make the world a more just place.

———○———

JUST FOR TODAY

TODAY'S MANTRA

By slowing down and reconsidering my plans, I can ensure they align with my truest intentions.

TODAY'S JOURNAL PROMPT

What are the moral values that I hold most deeply?

TODAY'S RITUAL

Draw a bath or take a warm shower. Imagine your body as a hot flame, and as the water runs over you, imagine it calming this fire. When you are finished visualizing this calming over every part of your body, repeat the mantra, "Through patience and balance I can reignite my spark."

———○———

BORN ON THIS DAY

SARAH PLATT DOREMUS, American philanthropist

MARTHA STEWART, American business magnate and television personality

"You don't protect any of your individual liberties by lying down and going to sleep."—JOHN T. SCOPES, American educator convicted for teaching evolution

The Journey of Those Born on
AUGUST 3

You were born of social charm and a hunger for acceptance that can take you away from who you truly are. You will have to find your North Star within peace and equality, as your journey is one of tranquility, patience, and personal justice.

Early on in your journey, you will meet your peaceful guide, *Balance* (The Number Two). Despite your boundless energy, *Balance* calls you away from overdoing it and toward a path of easeful living. By never spreading yourself too thin and asking for help where you need it most, *Balance* teaches you that there is always an easier, softer way.

And if you choose this gentle path, you will have to take time for *Preparation* (Two of Wands). *Preparation* asks you what all the hurry is, encouraging you to take a thorough internal and external look before attacking your next goal. You will meet *Preparation* in thoughtful planning, when you look upon the possibilities of your future and decide exactly where and how to proceed. If you can choose patience over blind ambition, *Preparation* teaches you how to use your energy wisely.

As you slow down and get centered, you will discover your personal sense of *Truth* (Justice). *Truth* highlights your moral values, helping you get to know the internal scale that weighs what is fair and what is completely and unacceptably unjust. Listen to this internal judge as you hold yourself and others accountable to the greater karmic law of cause and effect. If you can search for *Truth* within the balance, never allowing yourself to go to extremes, you can lead a life of humble virtue.

LEO
RULERS: THE SUN, JUPITER

PURPOSE
To live for the truths that lie within patience, thoughtfulness, and internal awareness.

RELATIONSHIPS

You are as bright and generous as they come, and your relationships should be a place of harmony and equity. By seeking out partners who aim to live in peaceful coexistence and encourage the fair sharing of responsibilities, you will discover that true love thrives in balance.

The Journey of
AUGUST 4

Welcome to August 4, a perspective-shifting journey of curiosity.

Try not to be so rigid in your beliefs today. Although Leo season encourages self-confidence, *Flexibility* (The Number Three) asks you to discover the gifts of humility as you open your mind to the perspectives of others. Who or what would you like to learn from if you were willing to be wrong?

From this open space you can tap into *Expansion* (Three of Wands). Go out on a limb and attempt something new today, whether it be trying a new skill in your job or introducing yourself to a foreign language in your free time. It can be unnerving to be a beginner, but lean in to the freedom that comes from not having to be the expert.

In the big picture, *Surrender* (The Hanged Man) your ways in favor of personal growth. If you find yourself thrust into the discomfort of unfamiliarity, embrace this new perspective and see what you can discover from this alternate vantage point. By questioning everything you used to bet your life on, you will discover that there is no singular truth or authority in the spiritual world.

JUST FOR TODAY

TODAY'S MANTRA

I can discover a new perspective if I remain willing to be wrong.

TODAY'S JOURNAL PROMPT

Do I tend to dig in my heels when someone questions my perspective, or do I tend to keep an open mind? When did I learn this behavior?

TODAY'S RITUAL

Make a point to ask a question of every person you encounter today so you can discover how much there is to learn from others. You can ask a mundane question or a deep one, depending on what feels natural, but be sure you are genuinely curious about their answer.

BORN ON THIS DAY

LOUIS ARMSTRONG, American jazz trumpeter and singer

MEGHAN MARKLE, American actor and Duchess of Sussex

"Change will not come if we wait for some other person, or if we wait for some other time. We are the ones we've been waiting for. We are the change that we seek."—**BARACK OBAMA**, forty-fourth president of the United States and first Black American president

The Journey of Those Born on
AUGUST 4

You were born of personal integrity and an internalized sense of authority that can keep you stuck in an eternal position of responsibility. You will have to find the willingness to have none of the answers, as your journey is one of insatiable curiosity, grand adventure, and necessary sacrifice.

Early on in life, you will meet your energetic guide, *Flexibility* (The Number Three). *Flexibility* beckons you away from over-responsibility and toward a path of intellectual freedom and spontaneity. It's not about what you know but rather what you'd like to understand. You will meet *Flexibility* when you forego being an expert in favor of being a hungry student.

If you choose this winding path, you will meet your grand friend, *Expansion* (Three of Wands). *Expansion* invites you to broaden your horizons through new experiences and skills. You will meet *Expansion* in moments of personal growth via travel and education, when you leave behind all that is familiar in pursuit of larger truths. If you can keep a beginner's mind, *Expansion* teaches you that on the other side of humility is higher consciousness.

By embracing these fearless calls, you come to adore the power of *Surrender* (The Hanged Man). *Surrender* flips your plans, dreams, and ambitions upside down so you can take in life from an entirely new point of view. You will meet *Surrender* in moments of self-sacrifice, when you accept that what you once desired no longer fits the betterment of your personal development. If you can trust that the less you resist change the greater the reward, *Surrender* shows you that spiritual enlightenment is simply a shift in perspective.

LEO
RULERS: THE SUN, JUPITER

PURPOSE
To willingly surrender to uncertainty.

RELATIONSHIPS

You are a generous and magnetic leader, yet your relationships should be a place of humble growth. By seeking out partners that challenge and force you to grow in your understanding and effectiveness, you will discover that true love is a spiritual partnership.

The Journey of
AUGUST 5

W elcome to August 5, a grounding journey that gently inspires emotional growth.
Focus on the work you can get done today. *Discipline* (The Number Four) encourages practical action, so execute the seemingly mundane tasks that you would typically put off until tomorrow. Take a large drink of your morning coffee or splash your face with water as you prepare to get things done.

Throughout the day, make time for *Celebration* (Four of Wands). Leo season encourages fun and joy, so invite your friends and chosen family to blow off some steam. Whether it's a night out on the town or a laughter-filled lunch mid-workday, stay in the present moment as you relish the warmth of the people you love.

But give yourself some emotional space because you may be shedding old, unfulfilled dreams today. *Transformation* (Death) encourages you to mourn what you once aspired to be while beginning to set your sights on who you are becoming. What goals, ambitions, or identities are you ready to grow out of? Where do you hope to grow toward instead? These are not easy or light questions to answer, but know that discomfort is a sign you are moving closer to the truth.

———————————————————○———————————————————

JUST FOR TODAY

TODAY'S MANTRA
With support and structure, I can discover my true authentic nature.

TODAY'S JOURNAL PROMPT
Is there an outdated version of myself, a goal, or an identity that I am ready to let go of today?

TODAY'S RITUAL
Look up the life cycles of a butterfly to get inspired by the concept of metamorphosis. As you watch a video or read about it, consider where you are on your own personal journey of metamorphosis. Are you in the cocoon or are you ready to fly?

———————————————————○———————————————————

BORN ON THIS DAY

NEIL ARMSTRONG, American pilot, astronaut, and first man on the moon

HELENE FISCHER, German singer, dancer, entertainer, television presenter, and actor

"As far as expectations go, you can never work for expectations. You have to work against them."—**KAJOL**, Indian actor

The Journey of Those Born on
AUGUST 5

Y ou were born of intuitive wisdom and intellectual confidence that can err on the side of stubbornness. You will have to prioritize growth over certainty, as your journey is one of perseverance, acknowledgment, and becoming.

Early on in your journey, you will meet your practical guide, *Discipline* (The Number Four). Despite your untamable spirit, *Discipline* calls you away from over-indulgence and toward a path of self-accountability. You will meet *Discipline* in long hours of quiet work, when you put your head down and slowly but surely work your way toward a higher purpose.

But if you choose this path of integrity, you will have to make room for *Celebration* (Four of Wands). *Celebration* comes to you by way of friends and chosen family, when you kick back and allow them to shower you with the love and appreciation you need to re-charge yourself. You will meet *Celebration* in the breaks between personal milestones that inspire you to let down your guard and simply enjoy the present moment with the people you care about most.

By answering these calls to build strong internal foundations, you will come to embrace the magic of *Transformation* (Death). *Transformation* invites you to shed old versions of yourself, mourning their loss while embracing the potential of who you hope to become. Like a phoenix rising from the ashes, *Transformation* encourages you to find hope within endings, life within death. If you can bravely let go of what was, *Transformation* offers you the gift of metamorphosis.

LEO
RULERS: THE SUN, JUPITER

PURPOSE
To build the strength to withstand radical personal growth.

RELATIONSHIPS

You are confident and proud, yet your relationships should be a place of radical acceptance and personal renewal. By seeking out partners who help you recharge your batteries while encouraging you to continue to grow, you will discover that true love always has your back.

The Journey of
AUGUST 6

Welcome to August 6, an expressive journey that requires internal peace.
Channel the artistic and passionate nature of Leo season with *Courage* (The Number Five). Rather than holding back your gifts and talents, put yourself out there and take center stage of your life. What would you like to share with the world around you? Let vulnerability and authenticity be your North Star for the day.

But try not to let *Conflict* (Five of Wands) get the best of you. If you receive any criticism or come up against any competitors in your pursuit of self-expression, try to shake it off, remembering that creativity doesn't have to be taken so seriously. It is the ego, rather than the heart, that is so afraid of the opinions and acts of others.

Seek *Serenity* (Temperance) instead. Draw upon the tools of meditation and mindfulness so that you don't find yourself swept away by the chaotic waves of emotion. Reach into a place of spiritual centeredness, relying on your gifts of reason and personal moderation. Nothing needs to be done or thought of in extremes today, so find the peace that comes from the middle ground.

JUST FOR TODAY

TODAY'S MANTRA
Through self-moderation I can enjoy the rewards of vulnerability.

TODAY'S RITUAL
If there is a particular point in the day when you feel as though you are bursting with anger or passion, meditate for five minutes. Set a timer, take a seated position, and close your eyes. If you're having trouble quieting your mind, repeat the word "Temperance" over and over until time is up.

TODAY'S JOURNAL PROMPT
How do I react when I find myself in emotional extremes?

BORN ON THIS DAY

INEZ MILHOLLAND, American suffragist

ANDY WARHOL, American artist, film director, and producer who was a leading figure in the pop art movement

"Knowledge comes, but wisdom lingers."—ALFRED TENNYSON, English poet laureate

The Journey of Those Born on
AUGUST 6

You were born of emotional generosity and desire to give that can leave you feeling drained. You will have to learn to chase personal fulfillment instead, as your journey is one of vulnerability, friction, and personal moderation.

Early on in your journey, you will meet your bold guide, *Courage* (The Number Five). To complement your artistic nature, *Courage* calls you away from modesty and toward a path of inspired self-expression. You will meet *Courage* when you take center stage in your life, channeling your ingenious creativity into thought-provoking works of art.

But if you choose this audacious path, you will have to contend with *Conflict* (Five of Wands). *Conflict* comes to you by way of the critics and naysayers who attempt to poke holes in your confidence and challenge your point of view. Rather than stooping low or letting them get the best of you, *Conflict* invites you not to take yourself so seriously and let the actions of your adversaries roll off your back. By never letting others get the best of you, you can discover the power that comes from vulnerability.

By answering these daring calls, you will come to understand the importance of *Serenity* (Temperance). *Serenity* shows you the peace of mind that comes from internal balance. You will meet *Serenity* when you slow down and find your inner calm, letting spiritual centeredness guide you rather than getting swept away by the unpredictable waves of emotion. If you can reach for peace over drama, *Serenity* offers you the gift of emotional sobriety.

LEO
RULERS: THE SUN, JUPITER

PURPOSE
To balance vulnerability with emotional moderation.

RELATIONSHIPS

You are generous with your affection and energy, and your relationships should be a place of emotional honesty and peaceful coexistence. By seeking out partners who can handle the truth with a calm and rational manner, you will discover that true love is born from spiritual harmony.

The Journey of
AUGUST 7

Welcome to August 7, a vulnerable journey toward internal healing.

Show your *Devotion* (The Number Six) today. Although Leo season shines light on topics of the self, turn your focus toward the people and ideas you love through acts of service. By generously giving your time and attention, you will discover the emotional satisfaction that comes from heartfelt intention.

And as you wear your heart on your sleeve, tap into *Confidence* (Six of Wands). If you complete a milestone of some kind today, take a moment to pat yourself on the back and acknowledge how far you have come. There is a subtle difference between humility and self-denial, so step into the spotlight of your power and don't shy away from feeling good about your personal progress.

As you expand into your authentic spirit, don't be surprised if some fear comes up. *Shadow* (The Devil) reminds you of the healing work that still needs to be done, inviting you to find compassion for the parts of your subconscious that learned to fear positivity and happiness. Look within and shine compassionate light on your ancient stories that need it most.

―――――○―――――

JUST FOR TODAY

TODAY'S MANTRA

As I open my heart, I will find compassion for the parts of myself that would rather contract.

TODAY'S RITUAL

Stand naked in front of a mirror for six minutes. Bring immense compassion and patience for yourself. Scan your body from head to toe, and if you stumble upon a tender spot or a place of judgment, repeat the affirmation, "I love myself unconditionally."

TODAY'S JOURNAL PROMPT

Do I have any formative experiences that taught me to stay small and fear the breadth of my true power?

―――――○―――――

BORN ON THIS DAY

ABEBE BIKILA, Ethiopian Olympic marathon champion and Africa's first world record–breaking athlete

CHARLIZE THERON, South African actor

"To make our way, we must have firm resolve, persistence, tenacity. We can never let up."
—RALPH BUNCHE, American political scientist, diplomat, and the first Black American awarded the Nobel Peace Prize

The Journey of Those Born on
AUGUST 7

You were born of personal conviction an extreme desire for success that can block you from the emotional closure that you need most. You will have to heal the blockages around your heart, as your journey is one of sincerity, praise, and psychological breakthroughs.

Early on in your journey, you will meet your tender guide, *Devotion* (The Number Six). Although you are a serious leader, *Devotion* calls you away from blind ambition and toward a path of meaningful action. By pursuing the callings of your soul with generous effort, you can discover the emotional satisfaction of vulnerability.

And if you accept this purposeful path, you will meet your inspired friend, *Confidence* (Six of Wands). *Confidence* invites you to step into the sunlight of your spirit, basking in the warm glow of personal recognition and internal faith. While you may come upon public applause, you will meet *Confidence* in moments of self-acknowledgment, when you can't help but brim with pride for the great progress you have made.

By answering these earnest calls, you will have to respect the importance of *Shadow* (The Devil). *Shadow* invites you to look at the self-destructive behaviors that once protected you from harm but now limit you from expansion. You will meet *Shadow* in emotional contraction, when the sheer goodness of your life feels too overwhelming to bear and you find yourself shutting down. If you can take a compassionate look within, finding understanding for these wounded corners of your subconscious, you can bring what was once dark into the light of healing.

> ### YOUR GUIDES
>
> *Astrology: Your Energy*
> Leo (The Sun, Jupiter)
>
> *Numerology: Your Path*
> Devotion (The Number Six)
>
> *Minor Arcana: Your Lesson*
> Confidence (The Six of Wands)
>
> *Major Arcana: Your Highest Calling*
> Shadow (The Devil)

———————————————○———————————————

LEO
RULERS: THE SUN, JUPITER

PURPOSE
To heal the corners of the subconscious that squelch true joy and belonging.

RELATIONSHIPS

You are a confident leader by nature, yet your relationships should be a place of vulnerability and tenderhearted connection. By seeking out partners who make you feel safe and seen, you will discover that true love can break down any emotional wall.

The Journey of
AUGUST 8

Welcome to August 8, a journey of personal faith and radical fate.

Decide what you want to devote your energy to today. *Commitment* (The Number Seven) prefers you to be discerning instead of uncertain, so narrow your focus to the ideas that matter most to you. Whether it be a personal, professional, or political goal, move toward it with complete purpose.

And if you come up against any opposition by way of criticism or competitors, stand your ground. Leo season inspires strength and pride, so channel this fire into *Perseverance* (Seven of Wands), proving to yourself just how passionate you are about your long-term ambitions. You don't have to be thrown off by the doings of others—simply put your head down and do the work.

But be sure to embrace any sudden change that comes your way. Whether your plans get thrown off track or an unexpected shift in perspective dawns upon you, lean in to the possibility of what this shift could bring. *Upheaval* (The Tower) reminds you that fate steps in whenever necessary, so trust that the universe is moving you one step closer to your destiny.

—○—

JUST FOR TODAY

TODAY'S MANTRA
I won't back down in the face of my competitors, but I will surrender to fate.

TODAY'S JOURNAL PROMPT
What "failures" ended up being unexpected miracles?

TODAY'S RITUAL
Write down a long-term personal or professional goal you have. Underneath it, make a list of seven things you can commit to today to pursue this dream. After you complete each one, repeat the affirmation, "I did what I can, but I leave the results up to the universe."

—○—

BORN ON THIS DAY

ROGER FEDERER, Swiss tennis player

FAYE WONG, Hong Kong Chinese singer-songwriter and actor

"I want to die a slave to principles. Not to men."—EMILIANO ZAPATA, Mexican revolutionary

The Journey of Those Born on
AUGUST 8

Y ou were born of visionary leadership and internal strength that can be mistaken for arrogance. You will have to fight for what you believe in while remaining humble, as your journey is one of focus, integrity, and divine intervention.

Early on in your journey, you will meet your earnest guide, *Commitment* (The Number Seven). Despite your wide range of interests, *Commitment* calls you away from grandiosity and toward a path of thoughtful action. You will meet *Commitment* in the ideas you devote your life to, when you pour all your enthusiasm and skill into a higher purpose.

But if you walk this focused path, you will have to contend with *Perseverance* (Seven of Wands). You will meet *Perseverance* in the face of adversity, when others who are threatened by your power try to get the best of you by questioning your stance. By digging your heels into the ground through divine conviction, you will learn to fight like hell.

> ### YOUR GUIDES
>
> *Astrology: Your Energy*
> Leo (The Sun, Jupiter)
>
> *Numerology: Your Path*
> Commitment (The Number Seven)
>
> *Minor Arcana: Your Lesson*
> Perseverance (The Seven of Wands)
>
> *Major Arcana: Your Highest Calling*
> Upheaval (The Tower)

And if you answer these weighty calls, *Upheaval* (The Tower) ensures that any of your identities built on false ground come to a roaring, magnificent crash. You will meet *Upheaval* in moments of unanticipated change, when life abruptly thrusts you out of your comfort zone and into the next arch of your story. Whether you choose to view it as divine intervention or chaotic evil, know that fate is directing you toward a higher path of radical fulfillment. If you can trust in the divinity of disruption, you'll learn that unexpected twists of fate can be a blessing in disguise.

―――――――――○―――――――――

LEO
RULERS: THE SUN, JUPITER

PURPOSE
To fight for a singular purpose while surrendering the outcome to fate.

RELATIONSHIPS

You are mentally and emotionally strong, yet your relationships should be a place of interdependence and trust. By seeking out partners who can catch you when you fall and inspire you to get back on your feet, you will discover that true love is eternally reliable.

The Journey of
AUGUST 9

Welcome to August 9, an authentic journey of self-belief.

Step into your *Power* (The Number Eight) today. Leo season encourages vulnerability, but aim for self-acceptance rather than seeking the approval of others. By embracing each nook and cranny of your truth, you can inspire others to do the same and influence the world around you.

And don't be afraid to move forward. *Momentum* (Eight of Wands) encourages you to say "yes" to progress today, so accept every opportunity for personal or professional movement that comes your way. This day is fast-paced in nature, making it the perfect time to throw caution to the wind and act upon your deepest desires.

But if you feel insecure or unsure of yourself at any point, tap into *Hope* (The Star). Look for the light of enthusiasm within yourself or others to access the courage required to pursue your dreams. There's no need to fret about the past or waste time on regret; instead, set your sights on the potential that lives within. Through personal faith and a belief in the unknown, you can soar to heights you never thought possible today.

JUST FOR TODAY

TODAY'S MANTRA

By getting real and finding faith in myself, I can move mountains.

TODAY'S RITUAL

Get moving. Whether you go for a run, a bike ride, or a car ride, be sure you can feel the wind on your face as you speed up so you can experience the visceral feeling of momentum.

TODAY'S JOURNAL PROMPT

Is there a dream I have been sitting on for quite some time? How can I bring it to the surface today?

BORN ON THIS DAY

DANIEL LEVY, Canadian actor, writer, director, comedian, and producer

MAHESH BABU, Indian actor, producer, media personality, and philanthropist

"I decided long ago never to walk in anyone's shadow; if I fail, or if I succeed at least I'll live as I believe."—WHITNEY HOUSTON, American singer, actor, and film producer

The Journey of Those Born on
AUGUST 9

Y ou were born of sweeping intuition and a need for privacy that can keep you at arm's length from others. You will have to show the world your authentic spirit, as your journey is one of honesty, alignment, and complete faith.

Early on in your journey, you will meet your enig-matic guide, *Power* (The Number Eight). Despite your wanderlust, *Power* calls you away from outer space and toward a path of self-acceptance and worldly success. By embracing every facet of your truth, never denying yourself honesty, you can step into the full breadth of your internal force.

And if you take this genuine path, you will have to move quickly. *Momentum* (Eight of Wands) invites you to act upon your personal revelations, never waiting for permission nor postponing your fate. You will meet *Momentum* in the heat of the hustle, when your mind can't quite grasp how much progress you are making. If you can embrace this rapid pace, *Momentum* helps you make headway.

> ## YOUR GUIDES
>
> *Astrology: Your Energy*
> Leo (The Sun, Jupiter)
>
> *Numerology: Your Path*
> Power (The Number Eight)
>
> *Minor Arcana: Your Lesson*
> Momentum (The Eight of Wands)
>
> *Major Arcana: Your Highest Calling*
> Hope (The Star)

But if you answer these forceful calls, you will have to depend upon the strength of *Hope* (The Star). Hope helps you wash away the regrets of the past in favor of the possibility of the future. You will meet *Hope* in glimmering daydreams, when the pure vision of what could be completely renews your faith in your potential. If you can reach for positivity or limited thinking, *Hope* offers you the gift of self-belief.

LEO
RULERS: THE SUN, JUPITER

PURPOSE
*To find personal faith in
radical authenticity.*

RELATIONSHIPS

You are wise and experienced, yet your relationships should be a place of raw vulnerability and trust. By seeking out partners who never shy away from the truth and inspire you to own your authentic self, you will discover that true love is an act of personal faith.

The Journey of
AUGUST 10

W elcome to August 10, a healing adventure that beckons you home to yourself.
Try to *Experience* (The Number Nine) something new today. Rather than pursuing the ideas and goals that are in your wheelhouse, try to tackle ones that test your capacity for growth. In what personal or professional areas would you like to expand? There is nothing to fear but fear itself.

But don't lose steam too quickly. Leo season brings you bursts of inspiration, but *Persistence* (Nine of Wands) asks you to keep your energy sustained through conscious self-care. Take the necessary breaks throughout the day to renew your enthusiasm for your expansion, remembering that nothing good can come from personal burnout.

More than likely, the nurturing you need must come from internal healing. *Memory* (The Moon) invites you inward to reconnect with the formative experiences you buried long ago. Whether there is a moment from your past that you would like to address or a part of yourself you would like to get back in touch with, now is the time to reintegrate the things you lost along the way. If you are feeling more introverted or tender than usual, don't apologize for taking the emotional space you need.

JUST FOR TODAY

TODAY'S MANTRA
New experiences can inspire me to re-connect to the versions of myself I lost along the way.

TODAY'S JOURNAL PROMPT
What formative memory, or era of my life, could I benefit from addressing and integrating into my conscious mind?

TODAY'S RITUAL
Drive or walk somewhere at night, in an area that feels safe to you, and speak to the moon about your past. Don't worry if the moon isn't visible to the naked eye. When you are ready to go home, repeat the spell, "Moon magic, please help me free the hidden memories that chain themselves to me."

BORN ON THIS DAY

KYLIE JENNER, American media personality, socialite, model, and businesswoman

HUGO ECKENER, German inventor

"Peace produced by suppression is neither natural nor desirable."—ANNA JULIA COOPER, American author, educator, sociologist, scholar, speaker, and Black liberation activist

The Journey of Those Born on
AUGUST 10

You were born of intuitive confidence and a subconscious desire for chaos. You will have to peacefully travel back home to yourself, as your journey is one of expansion, personal faith, and internal healing.

Early on in your journey, you will meet your daring guide, *Experience* (The Number Nine). Despite your magnetic aura, *Experience* calls you away from self-absorption and toward a path of higher understanding. You will meet *Experience* in the complete unknown, when you adventure out of your comforts in pursuit of a wider perspective.

If you dare to travel this far-reaching path, *Persistence* (Nine of Wands) will ask you not to give up so easily. You will meet *Persistence* when you are close to completing, but have not quite finished, an important milestone and every inch of your body wants to give out from exhaustion. Rather than surrendering completely to this burnout, *Persistence* encourages you to take small breaks for renewal, to ensure you never completely deplete your energy.

But as you grow far and wide, *Memory* (The Moon) will call you back in. *Memory* lives in your subconscious, carrying the experiences that shaped you and ensuring that you never forget these origin stories. Through moments of hair-raising remembrance, *Memory* invites you to integrate your history into your conscious mind and heal the parts of you that you once believed were lost forever. By going back and acknowledging the past, you can clear emotional space for your intuitive truth moving forward.

―――――――――――――○―――――――――――――

LEO
RULERS: THE SUN, JUPITER

PURPOSE
To grow far and wide, only to return home to yourself with a new perspective.

RELATIONSHIPS

You are independent and infectiously self-confident, yet your relationships should be a place of subconscious healing. By seeking out partners who remind you of the person you once were and inspire you to create a home within yourself, you can discover that true love is a safe space to restore yourself.

The Journey of
AUGUST 11

W elcome to August 11, a confidence-building journey of personal faith.

Do your own thing today. *Autonomy* (The Number One) invites you to carve out a space of your own, disregarding the opinions and advice of others in favor of your intuition. Trust in your gut instinct as you ambitiously pursue the ideas that speak to your soul.

But know that you don't need to worry about the long run. *Potential* (Ace of Wands) wants you to focus on the sheer possibility of your goals, chasing your inspiration with wild abandon rather than wasting time on the details. You have the gift of beginner's luck now, so throw caution to the wind and believe that your dreams can turn into a reality.

And because Leo season inspires self-confidence, why not let yourself shine? *Vitality* (The Sun) wants you to share your enthusiasm with the world around you, wearing your heart on your sleeve and not worrying about if you will look silly in the long run. Personal belief is contagious, so step out and take center stage in your life today, knowing that it is more than okay to be the main character of today's epic tale.

○

JUST FOR TODAY

TODAY'S MANTRA
Self-confidence is contagious, so I will unapologetically embody it wherever I go today.

TODAY'S JOURNAL PROMPT
Is there a creative idea or ambition I am most enthusiastic about right now?

TODAY'S RITUAL
Visualize yourself stepping into a place of personal authority and power. What do you look like? How are you carrying yourself? What are you wearing? As you hold this clear image in your mind, strike a match and repeat the affirmation, "I am capable of anything."

○

BORN ON THIS DAY

ÚRSULA CORBERÓ DELGADO, Spanish actor and model

STEVE WOZNIAK, American pioneer of the personal computer and cofounder of Apple Computer

"There's got to be a voice deep within you that is untouched by definitions. And it is there that you become divinely who you are."—VIOLA DAVIS, American actor and producer, and the youngest actor and the first Black actor to earn an Oscar, an Emmy, and a Tony

The Journey of Those Born on
AUGUST 11

You were born of intuitive diplomacy and a desire to fit in that can stop you from actualizing your authentic potential. You will have to embrace your imperfections and inspire others to shine, as your journey is one of independence, faith, and self-expression.

Early on in your journey, you will meet your fearless guide, *Autonomy* (The Number One). Despite your innate temperance, *Autonomy* calls you away from passivity and toward a path of self-guided ambition. By pursuing a life of your own, rather than the one that makes others comfortable, you can discover the deep fulfillment that comes from personal leadership.

If you travel this daring path, you will have to believe in *Potential* (Ace of Wands). You will meet *Potential* at the beginning of each ambition, when you have no idea how you will execute these wild goals but sheer belief in yourself outweighs any fear of failure. If you can chase enthusiasm rather than safety, *Potential* shows you that anything is possible if you believe.

By answering these calls for self-trust, you will step into the light of *Vitality* (The Sun). *Vitality* shines its spotlight when you step into a place of radical authenticity, revealing to the world exactly who you are and what you stand for. You will meet *Vitality* in moments of confidence, when you accept and embrace every inch of your creative power. By dancing to the beat of your intuitive drum, you can inspire the rest of us to find our own.

> ### YOUR GUIDES
>
> *Astrology: Your Energy*
> Leo (The Sun, Jupiter)
>
> *Numerology: Your Path*
> Autonomy (The Number One)
>
> *Minor Arcana: Your Lesson*
> Potential (The Ace of Wands)
>
> *Major Arcana: Your Highest Calling*
> Vitality (The Sun)

LEO
RULERS: THE SUN, JUPITER

PURPOSE
To find authentic power through leaps of personal faith.

RELATIONSHIPS

You are a harmonious and peaceful partner by nature, but your relationships should be a place of independence and self-embodiment. By seeking out partners who are true to themselves and inspire you to be the same, you will discover that true love never needs you to dull your shine.

The Journey of
AUGUST 12

Welcome to August 12, a solemn journey that requires patience.

Seek out some *Balance* (The Number Two) in your life. The expansive nature of Leo season can have you bursting at the seams with energy, but try to pare down your day so you can work through your goals with peaceful space. Nothing good can be rushed today, so breathe in and take it easy.

Besides, now is the time for *Preparation* (Two of Wands) rather than execution. Consider your long-term ambitions, and make a thorough, strategic action plan for yourself. If you were to take a bird's-eye view of your goals, what is a sustainable vision of how you could bring them to fruition?

And as you take this step back, don't be afraid to digest some tough realities. *Awakening* (Judgment) reminds you that although self-honesty may be scary at first, it is far more productive and lucrative than self-denial. Take a look at your larger plans with a clear, sober mind, and get real about what might not make sense for you in the future. By accepting the reality of what is, you can make more conscious decisions moving forward.

○

JUST FOR TODAY

TODAY'S MANTRA

I will take a step back to see the reality of my dreams so I can make clear decisions about my future.

TODAY'S RITUAL

Drink some black tea to start your day. As you inhale this sobering aroma, repeat the spell, "Dark truths, please help me see the sobering light that sets my soul free."

TODAY'S JOURNAL PROMPT

What trusted partner, ancestor, or guide can I call upon today to help me see my goals clearly?

○

BORN ON THIS DAY

FATIMA MEER, South African writer, academic, screenwriter, and anti-apartheid activist

CANTINFLAS, Mexican comedian, actor, and filmmaker

"The energy you give off is the energy you receive."—CARA DELEVINGNE, English model, actor, and singer

The Journey of Those Born on
AUGUST 12

You were born of magnanimous social power and an insatiable desire to try new things. You will have to grow to accept life on life's terms, as your journey is one of steadiness, patience, and radical awareness.

Early on in your journey, you will meet your tranquil guide, *Balance* (The Number Two). Despite your flair for the dramatic, *Balance* calls you away from overdoing it and toward a path of steady growth. You will meet *Balance* in the middle, when instead of going to emotional extremes, you choose to seek out a more peaceful existence and take on only what you can handle.

If you walk this stable path, you will meet your cautious friend, *Preparation* (Two of Wands). *Preparation* invites you to survey the road ahead before proceeding, carefully planning where to direct your energy before wasting any time on unproductive pursuits. You will meet *Preparation* when you consider the long run and make a thoughtful action plan that can produce sustainable and meaningful results over time.

> ### YOUR GUIDES
>
> *Astrology: Your Energy*
> Leo (The Sun, Mars)
>
> *Numerology: Your Path*
> Balance (The Number Two)
>
> *Minor Arcana: Your Lesson*
> Preparation (The Two of Wands)
>
> *Major Arcana: Your Highest Calling*
> Awakening (Judgment)

By answering these calls for self-moderation, you will begin to see the bigger picture and, thus, the larger consequences of your actions. *Awakening* (Judgment) invites you to see the world through a realistic lens, never glossing over the inconvenient truths nor losing yourself within a doomsday mentality. You will meet *Awakening* in moments of conscious integration, when you look reality dead in the eye so that you can make more informed decisions moving forward. If you can choose temporary discomfort over denial, you'll inspire others not to sleepwalk through life.

LEO
RULERS: THE SUN, MARS

PURPOSE
To make thoughtful decisions based on peace, patience, and truth.

RELATIONSHIPS

You are socially dynamic and charismatic, and your relationships should be a place of longevity through consistent honesty. By seeking out partners who take their time to open up while encouraging vulnerability, you will discover that true love is a slow burn.

The Journey of
AUGUST 13

W elcome to August 13, an expansive journey that inspires gratitude.

Throw out the rulebook today. *Flexibility* (The Number Three) invites you toward the unexpected, so say "yes" to every unanticipated invitation that comes your way. Whether you go to lunch with a new friend or make a last-minute change to your plans, embrace the unknown and try your best to enjoy the ride.

As you let go of expectation, why not try your hand at something new? Although Leo season inspires leadership, *Expansion* (Three of Wands) invites you to be a student instead. What would you like to learn? While harnessing the expertise you do have, you can dive head-first into a foreign subject or project without fear of making mistakes, knowing that you have the gift of beginner's luck on your side.

Amidst this fruitful day, try to find *Perspective* (The World). Zoom out to witness the joys as well as the downfalls of your journey, searching for appreciation for each ebb and flow that comes your way. Through conscious gratitude, you can discover how each twist of fate has a divine silver lining. Gratitude is an unending resource as long as you are willing to look for it.

JUST FOR TODAY

TODAY'S MANTRA
Through interpersonal growth and expansion, I can find new perspective and appreciation for the journey.

TODAY'S JOURNAL PROMPT
Is there a new field of study, hobby, or creative pursuit I would like to try today?

TODAY'S RITUAL
Invite two companions on a hike or walk you've never been on before. They could be friends, ancestors, or guides; just be sure to invite their emotional and spiritual guidance throughout your adventure.

BORN ON THIS DAY

ALFRED HITCHCOCK, English filmmaker

SRIDEVI, Indian actor and film producer known as Indian cinema's first female superstar

"Defending peace is the duty of all."—FIDEL CASTRO, Cuban revolutionary and president and prime minister of Cuba

The Journey of Those Born on
AUGUST 13

You were born of humble leadership and a buried sense of shame that can block you from true happiness. You will have to find healing in connection and gratitude, as your journey is one of open-mindedness opportunity, and spiritual understanding.

Early on in your journey, you will meet your excitable guide, *Flexibility* (The Number Three). Despite your strong sense of personal authority, *Flexibility* calls you away from prideful ignorance and toward a path of interpersonal understanding. By remaining willing to be wrong, you can grow in your perspective as you absorb the diverse experiences and knowledge from the people around you.

If you walk this widening path, *Expansion* (Three of Wands) will ask you to go that much further. You will meet *Expansion* when you take on a new and foreign endeavor, pushing yourself outside your comfort zone in the pursuit of a higher purpose. *Expansion* invites you to enjoy the process of being a beginner, drawing upon your past experiences as you humble yourself at the feet of an uncharted goal.

YOUR GUIDES

Astrology: Your Energy
Leo (The Sun, Mars)

Numerology: Your Path
Flexibility (The Number Three)

Minor Arcana: Your Lesson
Expansion (The Three of Wands)

Major Arcana: Your Highest Calling
Perspective (The World)

By answering these calls for understanding, you will enlarge your spiritual world in the process. *Perspective* (The World) shows you just how grand the human experience is, helping you appreciate every peak and valley that leads you to each breakthrough. You will meet *Perspective* at the top of a personal milestone, when you come to realize that it was the journey, not the destination, that brought you the ah-ha moments you were searching for. If you can zoom out and acknowledge the joy of becoming, *Perspective* brings you the gift of spiritual contentment.

LEO
RULERS: THE SUN, MARS

PURPOSE
To walk a spiritual path, choosing expansive understanding over the limitations of pride.

RELATIONSHIPS

You are self-assured and wise, and your relationships should be a place of personal growth and higher consciousness. By seeking out partners who push you into the unknown and remind you how to have fun along the way, you will discover that true love knows no limits.

The Journey of
AUGUST 14

Welcome to August 14, a grounded journey toward personal authority.
As you navigate the fiery terrain of Leo season, channel your energy into *Discipline* (The Number Four). Rather than relying on the heat of passion, tap into a sense of endurance as you carry out the responsibilities you have for the day. There's no room for excuses or procrastination.

But when you feel yourself losing steam, make some time for *Celebration* (Four of Wands). Relish your hard-earned success, patting yourself on the back or allowing your chosen family or friends to help you enjoy your progress. Whether you throw an actual party or give yourself the night off to relax, be sure to refill your energetic cup.

Because at the end of the day, you are the CEO of your life, and you get to decide when to work and when to play. *Self-mastery* (The Emperor) empowers you to take charge of your destiny today, allowing you to objectively discern when to push yourself and when to let yourself relax entirely. If you were a caring authority toward yourself, how would you balance responsibility with pleasure? The answers come from within, so trust your internal voice of reason.

JUST FOR TODAY

TODAY'S MANTRA
Through self-leadership, I can strategically balance hard work and rejuvenating play.

TODAY'S RITUAL
Draw upon the leadership skills of an authority you admired when growing up. It could be a trusted adviser, parental figure, historical figure, or fictional character. How would they advise you throughout the day? Consider this as you go about your responsibilities.

TODAY'S JOURNAL PROMPT
Do I tend to overwork myself? Or do I tend to overindulge? How can I seek balance in these areas today?

BORN ON THIS DAY

STEVE MARTIN, American comedian, banjo player, author, and actor

HALLE BERRY, American actor

"Just celebrate the life you had, not the life you could've had."—EARVIN "MAGIC" JOHNSON JR., American Basketball Hall of Fame player and executive

The Journey of Those Born on
AUGUST 14

You were born of wild creativity and a need for peace that can stop you from pursuing the life you desire most. You will have to grow into the leader you always needed, as your journey is one of restraint, replenishment, and personal authority.

Early on in your journey, you will meet your stern guide, *Discipline* (The Number Four). Although you have an untamable spark, *Discipline* calls you away from unsustainable passion and toward a path of complete perseverance. You will meet *Discipline* in the long hours required to reach your lofty goals, when you put your head down and do the work, never letting up until you reach your desired destination.

But if you choose this regimented path, you will have to make time for *Celebration* (Four of Wands). *Celebration* asks you to pause between completed milestones so you can kick back and enjoy the fruits of your labor. You will meet *Celebration* in the joy of time off, when you actively seek to replenish your energy levels before setting out on your next highest climb.

YOUR GUIDES

Astrology: Your Energy
Leo (The Sun, Mars)

Numerology: Your Path
Discipline (The Number Four)

Minor Arcana: Your Lesson
Celebration (The Four of Wands)

Major Arcana: Your Highest Calling
Self-mastery (The Emperor)

By answering these calls to balance work and play, you will discover the power of *Self-mastery* (The Emperor). *Self-mastery* encourages you to make pragmatic yet compassionate choices for your future. You will meet *Self-mastery* when you harness your emotions and channel them into productive measures, ensuring that you are able to nourish your overall health and well-being for the long run. If you can act in your best interests, you'll tap into the gift of authentic self-esteem.

LEO
RULERS: THE SUN, MARS

PURPOSE
To be the objective yet compassionate authority you always needed.

RELATIONSHIPS

You are a passion-driven person by nature, yet your relationships should be a place of respect and nurturing. By seeking out partners who honor your boundaries while encouraging you to decompress at the end of a long day, you will discover that true love is a solid foundation to fall back on.

The Journey of
AUGUST 15

W elcome to August 15, a daring journey that inspires humility.
Put yourself out there today. To channel the fiery temperament of Leo season, *Courage* (The Number Five) invites you to express yourself without inhibition. What creative or personal truths would you like to share with the world? Hold nothing back as give yourself permission to shine.

But if *Conflict* (Five of Wands) comes knocking at your door, answer with internal peace. If you are met with fierce competitors or tough critics at any point today, surrender your ego so that they don't get the best of you. Nothing has to be as serious as it seems, and when you find yourself getting overwhelmed with anger or resentment, call a friend who can help you find the humor in this temporary discomfort.

Because at the end of the day, each experience is there to teach you something about yourself. *Wisdom* (The Hierophant) encourages you to remain humble today, so stay open and receptive to the new knowledge and perspectives that come your way. Find the divine balance between confidence and teachability as you grow and expand in ways you never imagined possible.

○

JUST FOR TODAY

TODAY'S MANTRA
By not taking myself too seriously, I can practice vulnerability with deep humility.

TODAY'S JOURNAL PROMPT
Who helps me find the humor in even the most difficult of circumstances?

TODAY'S RITUAL
Read through five op-ed news articles from different authors. At the end of each one, ask yourself, "What did I agree with and what did I not agree with?" Remind yourself that it is okay to not see eye to eye with everyone.

○

BORN ON THIS DAY

GERTY CORI, Austro-Hungarian American biochemist and first woman to win the Nobel Prize in Physiology or Medicine

JENNIFER LAWRENCE, American actor

"Find something you're passionate about and keep tremendously interested in it."—JULIA CHILD, American cooking teacher, author, and television personality

The Journey of Those Born on
AUGUST 15

You were born of spirited creativity and a pinch of self-destruction. You will have to decide what drama is worth fighting for, as your journey is one of self-expression, emotional maturity, and higher consciousness.

Early on in your journey, you will meet your bold guide, *Courage* (The Number Five). To enhance your innate confidence, *Courage* calls you away from undue shame and toward a path of unfiltered creative expression. You will meet *Courage* when you put your heart and soul on the line, sharing with the world exactly who you are and what you believe in.

But if you choose this audacious path, you will have to contend with *Conflict* (Five of Wands). *Conflict* comes to you by way of opposition, when your critics or competition try to get the best of you. Instead of stooping to their level or quitting entirely, *Conflict* invites you to surrender your ego and let this drama roll off your back. By never taking yourself too seriously, you can discover the resilience within humor.

By answering these calls for vulnerability, you will come to understand the true definition of *Wisdom* (The Hierophant). *Wisdom* asks you to find your place as both the teacher and the student, the expert and the novice. You will meet *Wisdom* in moments of sincere humility, when you admit what you don't know without giving away your power entirely. If you can trust your gut while remaining open to new knowledge, *Wisdom* hands you the keys to spiritual growth.

LEO
RULERS: THE SUN, MARS

PURPOSE
*To balance courage and humility,
self-trust and teachability.*

RELATIONSHIPS

You are outgoing yet private, so your relationships should be a place of radical vulnerability and healthy conflict. By seeking out partners who encourage friendly debate while creating a safe space for you to open your heart, you will discover that true love is fiercely devoted to growth.

The Journey of
AUGUST 16

W elcome to August 16, a tenderhearted journey toward authentic connection.
Stay true to your heart today. *Devotion* (The Number Six) invites you to share your love generously, letting the people and projects you cherish most know how important they are to you. Show up with complete vulnerability, knowing that sincerity is a powerful portal to personal gratification.

And let yourself feel good in the process. Leo season always inspires self-esteem, but *Confidence* (Six of Wands) wants you to acknowledge just how special you are. If you were to be your own best champion, what would you praise yourself for? If you happen to receive any external validation, accept these gifts with open arms and know that you are worthy.

Because at the end of the day, self-love is a *Choice* (The Lovers). Make an active decision to honor your value today by prioritizing the relationships and creative endeavors that fill your emotional and spiritual cup. If you have to walk away from a self-destructive behavior or connection, do so with gentle compassion and complete self-honesty. Life is too short to be spent on fruitless or unreciprocated connection, so put yourself first as you discover your intrinsic worth.

JUST FOR TODAY

TODAY'S MANTRA
I accept the love I think I deserve, and I will honor my true worth.

TODAY'S JOURNAL PROMPT
What words of affirmation do I need to hear today?

TODAY'S RITUAL
Pat yourself on your right shoulder three times, saying aloud three things you have done on an emotional level that you are proud of. Then pat yourself on your left shoulder three times, saying aloud three things you have done on a practical level that you are proud of.

BORN ON THIS DAY

STEVE CARELL, American actor, comedian, writer, producer, and director

TAMER HOSNY, Egyptian singer-songwriter, actor, composer, and director

"To be brave is to love someone unconditionally, without expecting anything in return."
—**MADONNA**, American singer-songwriter and actor

The Journey of Those Born on
AUGUST 16

You were born of fierce conviction and a subconscious penchant for chaos. You will have to soften to what your heart truly wants, as your journey is one of sincerity, acknowledgment, and divine love.

Early on in your journey, you will meet your tender guide, *Devotion* (The Number Six). Despite your tough exterior, *Devotion* calls you away from self-protection and toward a path of emotional vulnerability. By giving yourself completely to the people and ideas that matter most, you can create a life of deep and profound meaning.

And if you take this heartfelt path, you will meet your magnificent friend, *Confidence* (Six of Wands). *Confidence* invites you to bask in the sunlight of your hard-earned success, letting others shower their praise on you while you pat yourself on the back for a job well done. You will find *Confidence* in moments of personal progress, when you can't help but feel good about the breakthroughs you have made.

YOUR GUIDES

Astrology: Your Energy
Leo (The Sun, Mars)

Numerology: Your Path
Devotion (The Number Six)

Minor Arcana: Your Lesson
Confidence (The Six of Wands)

Major Arcana: Your Highest Calling
Choice (The Lovers)

By answering these meaningful calls, you will come to understand the power of *Choice* (The Lovers). *Choice* lies at the center of your soul, beckoning you toward fulfilling and reciprocal connection rather than self-destruction. You will meet *Choice* in moments of emotional discernment, when you walk away from a disappointing relationship or obligation so that you can run toward your true value. If you can listen deeply to your heart's center, *Choice* teaches you how to honor your worth.

―――――――――○―――――――――

LEO
THE SUN, MARS

PURPOSE
To run away from self-protection and toward authentic connection.

RELATIONSHIPS

You are fiercely devoted yet emotionally guarded, but your relationships should be a place of complete vulnerability and support. By seeking out partners who hold your heart with care and champion your limitless talent, you will discover that true love is a safe space to surrender.

The Journey of
AUGUST 17

Welcome to August 17, a journey that requires you to devote yourself to the present. Narrow your focus today. *Commitment* (The Number Seven) means deciding what you care about most and prioritizing the people and projects that speak to your long-term goals. Rather than getting lost in distraction, simplify your to-do list as you show your loyalty through action.

Leo season inspires passion, so channel it into *Perseverance* (Seven of Wands). If you are met with any opposition or competition, stay in your lane and keep moving forward no matter what. Rather than letting others get the best of you, control what you can by following through on your responsibilities and putting your best foot forward.

And don't fret about the long-term success of your actions. *Evolution* (The Chariot) invites you to trust that the universe will handle your future so you can keep your eyes on the tasks at hand. By devoting yourself deeply to the goals you have laid out in front of you, you can blaze new ground with grit and personal integrity. Through patience and personal faith, you may have the unexpected breakthrough you've been waiting for.

JUST FOR TODAY

TODAY'S MANTRA
I can't control my fate, but I can control my actions.

TODAY'S RITUAL
Look up a public figure you admire and do some research on how they came into their success. Take note of their personal evolution, particularly their temporary setbacks, as an inspired reminder that long-term dreams take time to become a reality.

TODAY'S JOURNAL PROMPT
How do I typically react when my goals don't come to fruition right away?

BORN ON THIS DAY

JUANITA MORROW NELSON, American activist and war tax resister

MARCUS GARVEY, Jamaican political activist, journalist, publisher, and leader of the Pan-Africanism movement

"Time goes on. So whatever you're going to do, do it. Do it now. Don't wait."—ROBERT DE NIRO, American actor, producer, and director

The Journey of Those Born on
AUGUST 17

Y ou were born of innate power and a creative magnificence that can have you resting on your laurels. You will have to get serious about your future, as your journey is one of intention, perseverance, and earth-shattering awakenings.

Early on your journey, you will meet your no-nonsense guide, *Commitment* (The Number Seven). *Commitment* asks you to chase only what you believe and avoid the compelling distractions that life throws at you. You will meet *Commitment* in moments of pivotal decision-making, when you choose to invest in less so you can devote yourself more deeply to the truth.

If you choose this serious path, your faith will be tested by your demanding teacher, *Perseverance* (Seven of Wands). *Perseverance* hurls doubt your way in the guise of authoritarian challenges, poking holes in your deepest imposter syndrome and forcing you to access an inner conviction you never knew you possessed. If you can reach for self-belief rather than self-defeat, *Perseverance* teaches you how to invest deeply in yourself.

YOUR GUIDES

Astrology: Your Energy
Leo (The Sun, Mars)

Numerology: Your Path
Commitment (The Number Seven)

Minor Arcana: Your Lesson
Perseverance (The Seven of Wands)

Major Arcana: Your Highest Calling
Evolution (The Chariot)

By answering these weighty calls, you will find yourself growing in unexpected ways. *Evolution* (The Chariot) asks you to focus solely on the work at hand by leaving the outcome of your efforts up to fate, trusting that the universe has your back. You will meet *Evolution* in radical external breakthroughs, when all your arduous internal work pays off in ecstatic success. If you can keep your focus on the daily journey, *Evolution* will take care of your future.

LEO
THE SUN, MARS

PURPOSE
To commit to the journey rather than the destination.

RELATIONSHIPS

You are forever evolving, but your relationships should be a place of interpersonal responsibility and longevity. By seeking out partners who keep to their word and build trust through action, you will discover that true love takes time.

The Journey of
AUGUST 18

W elcome to August 18, an empowering journey of self-acceptance.
Embrace every part of yourself today. *Power* (The Number Eight) reminds you of how dynamic and influential you can be when you step into the full span of your authenticity. Who would you be if you weren't trying to play it small? By taking up real space in the world around you, you can inspire others to do the same.

And be sure to follow this self-acceptance with courageous action. The end of Leo season always brings vital energy, and *Momentum* (Eight of Wands) asks you to press the gas as you move fearlessly toward your deepest ambitions. The world is yours for the taking, so don't postpone due to fear or self-denial; you are a force of nature.

Although instincts are wonderful evolutionary skills, watch out for them going too far, by way of erratic passion or uninhibited anger. Tap into your *Resilience* (Strength) as you channel this excess energy into a meaningful purpose. Whether you direct this flame toward work or your home, or by going for a last-minute sprint to calm your soul, remember that fire can be life-giving or destructive, depending how it's used.

———◯———

JUST FOR TODAY

TODAY'S MANTRA
I will light the flame of authenticity while making sure I use it wisely.

TODAY'S JOURNAL PROMPT
What are the ways in which I make myself small? How can I expand into my authentic self today?

TODAY'S RITUAL
Spend eight minutes in contemplative silence. Take a seated position, close your eyes, and visualize a flame that sits in your heart. Place your hand over your heart as you ask aloud, "Internal fire, what do you want to inspire?"

———◯———

BORN ON THIS DAY

ROBERT REDFORD, American actor, director, and activist.

G-DRAGON, South Korean rapper, singer-songwriter, and fashion designer known as the "King of K-pop"

"The more we sweat, the less we bleed."—VIJAYA LAKSHMI PANDIT, Indian diplomat, politician, and first female president of the United Nations General Assembly

The Journey of Those Born on
AUGUST 18

Y ou were born of intuitive strength and a hidden emotional sensitivity that can make you fearful of rejection. You will have to find true confidence from within, as your journey is one of authenticity, fearlessness, and self-commandment.

Early on in your journey, you will meet your enigmatic guide, *Power* (The Number Eight). To channel your creatively motivated nature, *Power* calls you away from staying small and toward a path of radical self-acceptance. You will meet *Power* when you step into the sunlight of your authentic nature, embracing every dark corner of your subconscious and inspiring others to do the same.

If you choose this self-aligned path, you will have to act fast. *Momentum* (Eight of Wands) asks you to act rather than procrastinate, seizing every opportunity for forward movement, no matter how daunting it may seem. You will meet *Momentum* in the divine hustle, when your soul aligns with your daily action as you blaze toward your chosen future.

By answering these calls for truthful action, you will come to understand the importance of *Resilience* (Strength). We each have animal instincts that can go too far when we are angry, triggered, or uninhibited. *Resilience* invites you to harness your wild soul, directing its powerful energy toward a productive and fulfilling cause. By never giving in to the unpredictable fires of passion, you can become the graceful ruler of your own kingdom.

LEO
THE SUN, MARS

PURPOSE
To access the power of authenticity and channel it into radical leadership.

RELATIONSHIPS

You are outgoing yet deeply sensitive, and your relationships should be a place of deep emotional merging. By seeking out partners who aren't afraid to love the dark as well as the light within you, you can discover that true love is unconditionally accepting.

The Journey of
AUGUST 19

Welcome to August 19, a fearless journey that requires a persistent heart.

Try to create new *Experience* (The Number Nine) today. Rather than sticking to your comfort zone, explore the ideas and ambitions that get you excited. There is nothing to be feared except fear itself, so step into the unknown and expand your consciousness.

Although Leo season brings flames of passion, try not to burn out too quickly. Instead, tap into *Persistence* (Nine of Wands) by refilling your energy throughout the day, remembering that brief pauses between efforts is a better option than quitting entirely. Whether you make sure to drink enough water or take a quick power nap, do what you need to do to keep up your enthusiasm and reach the finish line.

But if you feel overwhelmed or lost at any point, tap into *Instinct* (The Hermit). There is no road map for the course of this day, so follow your internal compass as you move intuitively through uncharted territory. It may feel like you are leading yourself through the dark, but by trusting in the divine intelligence that lives within, you can light your internal torch and make your way through with ease.

JUST FOR TODAY

TODAY'S MANTRA
While there is no clear direction through the unknown, I can take care of myself and rely on my intuition.

TODAY'S RITUAL
Come up with nine things you want to try in your lifetime. Make a calendar invite that repeats every August 19 and include this list in the invite note. Check in with yourself every year to see how you can accomplish something from this list.

TODAY'S JOURNAL PROMPT
Are there any uncharted ideas, subjects, or goals I would like to explore today?

BORN ON THIS DAY

COCO CHANEL, French fashion designer

MARGARET MORGAN LAWRENCE, American psychiatrist and psychoanalyst

"If we all worked on the assumption that what is accepted as true is really true, there would be little hope of advance."—ORVILLE WRIGHT, American aviation pioneer

The Journey of Those Born on
AUGUST 19

You were born of the vitality of the sun and a desire to be in charge that can shield you from the growth you need most. You will have to find greater wisdom in the unknown, as your journey is one of higher education, perseverance, and intuitive direction.

Early on in your journey, you will meet your brave guide, *Experience* (The Number Nine). To enhance your courageous nature, *Experience* calls you away from familiarity and toward the path of the complete unknown. You will meet *Experience* when you travel new territory, leaving behind your comfort zone in pursuit of expanded consciousness.

But if you explore this far-reaching path, you will have to absorb the lessons of *Persistence* (Nine of Wands). *Persistence* reminds you that life is a marathon, not a sprint, encouraging you to recharge your internal and external resources as you pursue your wild ambitions. You will meet *Persistence* in moments of exhaustion right before the finish line, when you take a brief pause to refill your cup before reaching your desired destination.

By answering these expansive calls, you will discover the voice of *Instinct* (The Hermit). *Instinct* gets you in touch with your internal compass so that you can navigate your way through the dark with nothing but the light of divine intelligence. You will meet *Instinct* in moments of complete isolation, when no one and nothing can lead you to your destiny and you must rely on yourself entirely. If you can trust your inherent genius, *Instinct* offers you the gift of self-guided progress.

LEO
THE SUN, MARS

PURPOSE
To discover true purpose in the wilderness of uncertainty.

RELATIONSHIPS

You are independent and self-assured, and your relationships should be a place of growth and expansion. By seeking out partners who push you into the unknown and encourage you to learn, you will discover that true love is a channel toward higher consciousness.

The Journey of
AUGUST 20

W elcome to August 20, a self-driven journey that requires radical faith.
Do your own thing today. *Autonomy* (The Number One) invites you to trust your intuition as you carve out a unique path for yourself. Disregard the suggestions and expectations of others and tap into your divine sense of courage and personal faith.

And don't hesitate—just chase your enthusiasm. Although Leo season inspires optimism, *Potential* (Ace of Wands) encourages you to believe in your next greatest idea without overthinking what you'll have to do to accomplish it. Some days are for careful planning, but today invites you to devote your energy to the power of manifestation.

But leave the outcome up to the universe. If you feel as though your luck is fading, try looking for the silver lining in the seemingly bad, knowing it will soon pass. And if you feel as though you're riding a high, pay this optimism forward with encouragement for others, knowing that it won't last forever. *Impermanence* (Wheel of Fortune) reminds you that the tides of fate are ever-changing, so make the most of your circumstances as you flow in harmony with the rhythm of the day.

―――――――――――――○―――――――――――――

JUST FOR TODAY

TODAY'S MANTRA
I will ignite my spark of enthusiasm while letting go of expectations completely.

TODAY'S RITUAL
Set an alarm for every hour of the day, from the minute you wake up to the time you go to sleep. Each time the alarm goes off, write down if you're feeling "lucky," "unlucky," or "neutral." At the end of the day, review each of these feelings, and notice how quickly your fortune can change throughout a single day.

TODAY'S JOURNAL PROMPT
What seedling of an idea am I excited about pursuing today?

―――――――――――――○―――――――――――――

BORN ON THIS DAY

ROBERT PLANT, English singer-songwriter and member of Led Zeppelin

DEMI LOVATO, American singer-songwriter and actor

"Everyone stands alone at the heart of the world, pierced by a ray of sunlight, and suddenly it's evening."—SALVATORE QUASIMODO, Italian poet, translator, and Nobel Prize winner

The Journey of Those Born on
AUGUST 20

You were born of social diplomacy and fierce self-awareness that can stop you from taking big risks. You will have to take a chance on fate, as your journey is one of independence, faith, and karmic destiny.

Early on in your journey, you will meet your daring guide, *Autonomy* (The Number One). Despite your natural people skills, *Autonomy* calls you away from codependency and toward a path of radical self-trust. By carving out your unique path, driven solely by the beat of your intuition, you can leave an unmatched legacy for others to follow.

And if you travel this brave path, you will meet your optimistic friend, *Potential* (Ace of Wands). *Potential* reminds you that the only thing better than a clear plan is an inspired idea, encouraging you to pursue the possibility of success rather than overthinking the reasons it may not work. You will meet *Potential* in the pure, unfiltered excitement of a new goal, when you are brimming with enthusiasm for what is to come.

> ### YOUR GUIDES
>
> *Astrology: Your Energy*
> Leo (The Sun, Mars)
>
> *Numerology: Your Path*
> Autonomy (The Number One)
>
> *Minor Arcana: Your Lesson*
> Potential (The Ace of Wands)
>
> *Major Arcana: Your Highest Calling*
> Impermanence (The Wheel of Fortune)

By answering these brave calls, you will have to surrender to the laws of *Impermanence* (Wheel of Fortune). *Impermanence* teaches you time and again that nothing good, and nothing bad, lasts forever, so you might as well release yourself from the grip of expectation. You will meet *Impermanence* in the ups and downs, the twists and turns, of the human experience, when you have no choice but to ride the roller coaster to your destiny. If you can believe in your plans while leaving the outcome up to chance, you'll discover how to coconspire with the universe itself.

LEO
THE SUN, MARS

PURPOSE
To fiercely pursue a life of emotional and spiritual sovereignty, no matter the outcome.

RELATIONSHIPS

You feel your best in the company of a partner, and your relationships should be a place of radical autonomy and reciprocal trust. By seeking out partners who are confident enough in themselves to support your fierce ambitions, you will discover that true love champions individual power.

The Journey of
AUGUST 21

Welcome to August 21, a thoughtful journey that invites you to consider the impact of your actions.

Seek out *Balance* (The Number Two) today. Although Leo season has a flair for the dramatic, slow down and get in touch with the peaceful center that exists within. By never going to extremes in your thinking or emotions, you can live in harmony with the world around you.

And instead of jumping into action, make time for *Preparation* (Two of Wands). Where are you heading in your creative or professional goals? What do you need to do to get there? If you can devote your day to careful planning, patiently considering every obstacle you may encounter along the way, you can hit the ground running tomorrow.

As you plan, take a step back and evaluate if your long-term ambitions are aligned with your moral values. Contemplate the cause and effect of your potential actions, making sure that fairness and equality are top of mind. While society may tell you to look out for number one, *Truth* (Justice) encourages you to pay respect to the laws of karma as you care for the betterment of your community or the world at large.

○

JUST FOR TODAY

TODAY'S MANTRA
I will take a step back from my ambitions so I can consider the greater ramifications of my actions.

TODAY'S RITUAL
Drink lots of water throughout the day to cool off the fiery flames of Leo season. If you are in need of extra calming energy, add a few slices of cucumber to your glass.

TODAY'S JOURNAL PROMPT
How can I pare down my responsibilities today so I can make some time planning for the future?

○

BORN ON THIS DAY

USAIN BOLT, Jamaican track athlete, widely considered the greatest sprinter of all time

HAFSAT ABIOLA, Nigerian human rights, civil rights, and democracy activist

"I'd rather have 100,000 people who really get what I'm doing and like it for what it is than a million who can take it or leave it."—KACEY MUSGRAVES, American country singer-songwriter

The Journey of Those Born on
AUGUST 21

You were born of internal radiance and worldly perspective that can make it hard to attend to the minutiae of interpersonal issues. You will have to slow down and pay attention to the consequences of your actions, as your journey is one of steadiness, planning, and morality.

Early on in your journey, you will meet your tranquil guide, *Balance* (The Number Two). You are passionate with your creativity, but *Balance* calls you away from extremes and toward a path of internal harmony. By never rushing to conclusions or chasing the highs and lows of drama, you can build a life of peace.

And if you walk this easeful path, you will have to make time for *Preparation* (Two of Wands). *Preparation* invites you to slow down and assess your plans before jumping into your next ambition. You will meet *Preparation* when you survey the road ahead, carefully considering where you should direct your energy. By contemplating before conquering, you can realize the power of a slow burn.

By answering these calls for patience, you will come to understand the importance of *Truth* (Justice). *Truth* asks you to consult the moral scale that lies within, helping you weigh what is fair to you, as well as what is fair to others. Consider the consequences of your actions, making sure that each strategic move aligns with your personal values. If you can act in accordance with the greater laws of karma, you'll tap into the gift of spiritual accountability.

YOUR GUIDES

Astrology: Your Energy
Leo (The Sun, Mars)

Numerology: Your Path
Balance (The Number Two)

Minor Arcana: Your Lesson
Preparation (The Two of Wands)

Major Arcana: Your Highest Calling
Truth (Justice)

LEO
THE SUN, MARS

PURPOSE
To slow down and consider the larger moral consequences of action.

RELATIONSHIPS

You are a social butterfly who can adapt to any room, but your relationships should be a place of deep equality. By seeking out partners who aim to meet you halfway—emotionally, spiritually, and intellectually—you will discover that true love always tries to be fair.

The Journey of
AUGUST 22

Welcome to August 22, an expansive journey that teaches you how to receive.
Try not to get too stuck in your ways today. Although Leo season is fierce and passionate, *Flexibility* (The Number Three) invites you to cool your flames as you remain open to the diverse perspectives of others. Ask as many questions as you can, and you'll be amazed by how much you discover along the way.

Besides, *Expansion* (Three of Wands) wants you to grow in ways you never expected. Disregard your expertise, and set your sights on a new creative, intellectual, or professional goal that requires you to start from ground zero. It is both scary and incredibly exciting to learn something from scratch, so put your ego to the side as you explore the unknown.

And try your best to enjoy it. *Abundance* (The Empress) asks you to receive all the happiness that the day has to offer, reveling in shared laughter with friends or basking in the sunlight of new experiences. It is easy to focus on what you are lacking, but now is the time to view your glass as half full by staying in the present moment.

JUST FOR TODAY

TODAY'S MANTRA
By expanding my perspective, I can discover new creative opportunities.

TODAY'S JOURNAL PROMPT
What new skill, hobby, or field of study would I like to try my hand at today?

TODAY'S RITUAL
Find a public area where many wildflowers bloom. If you can't access this easily, go to your local florist or grocery store to surround yourself with the magnificent beauty of flowers. Inhale their fresh scent if you feel inspired, appreciating the vibrant colors and natural diversity of shape.

BORN ON THIS DAY

DUA LIPA, English singer-songwriter and model

CLAUDE DEBUSSY, French composer

"It is through living that we discover ourselves, at the same time as we discover the world around us."—HENRI CARTIER-BRESSON, French photographer

The Journey of Those Born on
AUGUST 22*

Y ou were born of strong leadership and a sense of responsibility that can easily lead to over-burden. You will have to learn to enjoy life rather than control it, as your journey is one of curiosity, exploration, and beauty.

Early on in your journey, you will meet your sociable guide, *Flexibility* (The Number Three). While you are discerning in nature, *Flexibility* calls you away from rigid thinking and toward a path of mind-opening connection. By remaining receptive to and curious about the experiences and perspectives of others, you can expand your consciousness.

And if you choose this open path, you will meet your daring friend, *Expansion* (Three of Wands). *Expansion* invites you to try new things, building on your creative and professional skills through a willingness to be a beginner. No matter how far you ascend in your expertise, *Expansion* beckons you toward the great unknown, ensuring you never limit your growth.

By accepting these prolific calls, you will discover a new sense of *Abundance* (The Empress). *Abundance* encourages you to embrace the beautiful gifts that the universe gives you. You will meet *Abundance* in moments of emotional and spiritual plenty, when you find yourself basking in the beauty of a flower or receiving a warm hug from a trusted friend. If you can stay present through the excruciating vulnerability of happiness, you'll move toward spiritual fulfillment.

YOUR GUIDES

Astrology: Your Energy
Leo (The Sun, Mars)

Numerology: Your Path
Flexibility (The Number Three)

Minor Arcana: Your Lesson
Expansion (The Three of Wands)

Major Arcana: Your Highest Calling
Abundance (The Empress)

LEO
THE SUN, MARS

PURPOSE
To open to the spiritual abundance that comes from new perspectives and experiences.

RELATIONSHIPS

You are naturally authoritative, but your relationships should be a place of fun-loving freedom and expansion. By seeking out partners who make you feel like a kid again and keep you in the present moment, you will discover that true love doesn't have to be so serious after all.

*Are you a Virgo born on this day? Head to page 760 to find your additional birthday guide!

WELCOME TO

The Journey of
AUGUST 23

Welcome to August 23, a journey that demands self-accountability. To complement the humble nature of Virgo season, *Discipline* (The Number Four) asks you to stick to your word and show up to your responsibilities. Rather than putting off things until tomorrow, place one foot in front of the other as you work through your to-do list.

But be sure to leave some room for rest at the end of the day. *Conservation* (Four of Pentacles) reminds you that the body, mind, and spirit need to be recharged to thrive at full capacity. So lean in to the practices of restoration that speak to you, making no apologies for the amount of sleep or television you require to completely decompress.

And remember, you are the ultimate authority of your life. *Self-mastery* (The Emperor) encourages you to make thoughtful decisions for yourself, prioritizing your long-term well-being over instant gratification. There is a fine balance between dedication and burnout, self-care and overindulgence, so look within to find the right equilibrium for sustainable success. Through becoming an objective leader toward yourself, you can tap into a new sense of personal integrity.

JUST FOR TODAY

TODAY'S MANTRA
I will balance external work with internal nourishment.

TODAY'S JOURNAL PROMPT
Growing up, what was I taught about work-life balance?

TODAY'S RITUAL
Make a two-column list. On the left side, write the header "Responsibilities" and underneath make a list of four responsibilities you must attend to today. On the right side, write the header "Restoration" and underneath make a list of four acts of self-care that you can nourish yourself with today. For each responsibility that you accomplish today, be sure to execute an activity from your restoration list.

BORN ON THIS DAY

SAIRA BANU, Indian actor

MALVINA REYNOLDS, American folk and blues singer-songwriter and political activist

"We all have self-doubt. You don't deny it, but you also don't capitulate to it. You embrace it."—KOBE BRYANT, American basketball player

The Journey of Those Born on
AUGUST 23

Y ou were born of limitless intelligence and a fierce conviction that, when taken to extremes, can lead to conflict. You will have to lay down your weapons and learn to play the long game, as your journey is one of persistence, energy conservation, and personal restraint.

Early on in your journey, you will meet your demanding guide, *Discipline* (The Number Four). *Discipline* asks you if the drama is really worth your trouble, inviting you instead on a path toward long-term stability. You will meet *Discipline* in moments of perseverance, when you keep your head down and your feet moving forward. If you work hard, very hard, your soul will stay grounded amidst the rocking tides of life.

If you choose this hard but gratifying path, you will meet your wise friend, *Conservation* (Four of Pentacles). *Conservation* knows the limits of the body and the mind, and the serious repercussions of chronic stress, and asks you to pay respect to your well-being. If you can care for yourself as you would a loved one, you'll learn that sometimes the most productive thing is to do nothing at all.

> ### YOUR GUIDES
>
> *Astrology: Your Energy*
> Virgo (Mercury)
>
> *Numerology: Your Path*
> Discipline (The Number Four)
>
> *Minor Arcana: Your Lesson*
> Conservation (The Four of Pentacles)
>
> *Major Arcana: Your Highest Calling*
> Self-mastery (The Emperor)

And if you answer these calls for maturity, you will discover the power of *Self-mastery* (The Emperor). *Self-mastery* invites you to be an objective leader toward yourself, helping you make holistic and wise decisions for yourself in the long run. You will meet *Self-mastery* in moments of emotional restraint, when you choose to listen to your intuition and your mind instead of the unpredictable nature of feeling. By becoming the authority you always needed, you can discover the gratification of personal integrity.

VIRGO
RULER: MERCURY

PURPOSE
To choose personal integrity over interpersonal drama.

RELATIONSHIPS

You are as driven as they come, but your relationships should be a place of restoration. By seeking out partners who make you feel emotionally held and deeply cared for, you will discover that true love is a safe place to surrender.

The Journey of
AUGUST 24

Welcome to August 24, a radical journey that requires faith in vulnerability.

Live from a place of *Courage* (The Number Five) today. To channel the intellectual capacity of Virgo season, let your words flow as you tell the world exactly who you are and what you believe in. It is not a time to hold anything back, so get clear on your message and don't apologize for your perspective.

But watch out for *Scarcity* (Five of Pentacles). Today warns against self-denial, so if you are running low on any emotional, physical, or mental resources, reach out and ask for the support you need. It is undeniably uncomfortable to let people know what you need and risk rejection, but you may be pleasantly surprised by what you can gain through this act of faith.

And if you feel uncertain of yourself at any point, lean in to your innate *Wisdom* (The Hierophant). No one has the answers to today's dilemmas and opportunities except you, so reach within as you step into a place of intellectual leadership. Your mind can be used as a weapon or a treasured tool, so channel your genius into your highest and best.

JUST FOR TODAY

TODAY'S MANTRA

Through self-trust, I can say what I think, what I need, and what I believe in most today.

TODAY'S RITUAL

Call upon your ancestors to ward off any feelings of scarcity. Whether you know them by name or not, visualize the long line of people who came before you. Tell them of your fears and dreams, and repeat the mantra, "I invite all of my well-ancestors and guides to protect me today."

TODAY'S JOURNAL PROMPT

What has my relationship been with asking for help in the past? What are my greatest blockages toward this act of vulnerability?

BORN ON THIS DAY

HOWARD ZINN, American historian and activist

PAULO COELHO, Brazilian lyricist and novelist

"I may be crazy, but that don't make me wrong."—MARSHA P. JOHNSON, American gay liberation activist and self-identified drag queen

The Journey of Those Born on
AUGUST 24

You were born of humble genius and a desire to be of service that can block you from being the authority you were always meant to be. You will have to learn to fight for what you believe in, as your journey is one of self-expression, internal abundance, and divine self-trust.

Early on in your journey, you will meet your audacious guide, *Courage* (The Number Five). Despite your humble disposition, *Courage* calls you away from playing it small and toward a path of radical vulnerability. You will meet *Courage* when you share your mind with the world around you, never cowering in fear but instead rising to the occasion. If you can believe you have something to say, you'll find your voice.

But if you traverse this emboldened path, you will have to contend with *Scarcity* (Five of Pentacles). *Scarcity* comes to you in moments of emotional, spiritual, and physical lack, when your cup is so empty you can't quite see a way forward. *Scarcity* invites you to call upon the resources that are available to you, whether it be the support from your community, your ancestors, or guides. By practicing the excruciatingly vulnerable act of asking for help, you can see who has your back.

> ### YOUR GUIDES
>
> *Astrology: Your Energy*
> Virgo (Mercury)
>
> *Numerology: Your Path*
> Courage (The Number Five)
>
> *Minor Arcana: Your Lesson*
> Scarcity (The Five of Pentacles)
>
> *Major Arcana: Your Highest Calling*
> Wisdom (The Hierophant)

In answering these calls for tenacity, you will find a new kind of power within *Wisdom* (The Hierophant). *Wisdom* asks you to listen to the divine voice of reason that lives within and helps you separate the true from the false. You will meet *Wisdom* in your relationships with the powers that be, when you trust your internal compass over the commandments of those who desire control. If you can listen deeply to yourself, *Wisdom* hands you the keys to spiritual authority.

VIRGO
RULER: MERCURY

PURPOSE
To call upon the power of courage and vulnerability while fighting for the truth.

RELATIONSHIPS

You are service-oriented by nature, so your relationships should be a place of reciprocal generosity and radical devotion. By seeking out partners who have your back in even the worst of times, you will discover that true love is worth fighting for.

The Journey of
AUGUST 25

W elcome to August 25, a soul-driven journey that connects the mind with the heart.
Channel your brain into the topics, ideas, and relationships that mean the most to you. *Devotion* (The Number Six) encourages heartfelt intention, so leave your ego at the door as you show the world where your emotional loyalty lies. There is great vulnerability within sincerity, but know that you can't lose if you are being true to yourself.

If you find yourself losing steam, tap into the spiritual abundance of *Reciprocity* (Six of Pentacles). If a friend, coworker, or loved one extends a helping hand or a warm hug, embrace this gift with an open mind and heart. There is a time for giving and a time for receiving, so be sure you hold them in equal esteem throughout your day.

Because at the root of it all, self-love is a *Choice* (The Lovers). Prioritize the connections and endeavors that feed your soul, rather than draining your spiritual and mental resources on obligations that don't aim to meet your halfway. By acknowledging your self-worth, you can make pragmatic yet caring decisions for yourself and others moving forward.

JUST FOR TODAY

TODAY'S MANTRA
Through the process of self-love, I can learn to give and receive generously.

TODAY'S RITUAL
Go out into nature, find six things (rocks, seashells, twigs, leaves, or whatever strikes your fancy), and carry them with you throughout the day. If you feel inspired, give away three of them to a person who might need them, reminding yourself of how good it feels to share.

TODAY'S JOURNAL PROMPT
If I wasn't trying to look cool or protect myself, where would I want to devote my energy today?

BORN ON THIS DAY

LEONARD BERNSTEIN, American conductor, composer, pianist, music educator, author, and humanitarian

FAUSTINA KOWALSKA, Polish Roman Catholic nun and mystic

"No matter what accomplishments you make, somebody helped you."—ALTHEA GIBSON, American tennis player, golfer, and the first Black American to win a Grand Slam title

The Journey of Those Born on
AUGUST 25

Y ou were born of mental conviction and a motivation that can err on the side of blind ambition. You will have to focus on the heart of the matter, as your journey is one of sincerity,
reciprocity, and self-worth.

Early on in your journey, you will meet your sincere
guide, *Devotion* (The Number Six). Despite your incisive mind, *Devotion* calls you away from detachment
and toward a path of heartfelt action. You will meet *Devotion* in the work that means the most to you, when
you pour your focus and intention completely into a
personal calling. If you can choose connection over
power, *Devotion* helps you build a life of deep meaning.

But if you choose this vulnerable path, you will have
to learn the spiritual definition of *Reciprocity* (Six of
Pentacles). *Reciprocity* invites you to give when you are
abundant and receive when you are lacking. By never
giving in to the extremes of self-centeredness or martyrdom, *Reciprocity* teaches you that sharing is never a
one-sided exchange.

YOUR GUIDES

Astrology: Your Energy
Virgo (Mercury)

Numerology: Your Path
Devotion (The Number Six)

Minor Arcana: Your Lesson
Reciprocity (The Six of Pentacles)

Major Arcana: Your Highest Calling
Choice (The Lovers)

By answering these earnest calls, you will come to understand the importance of *Choice* (The
Lovers). *Choice* steers you away from the one-sided relationships and pushes you toward the true
emotional reciprocation. You will meet *Choice* when you own your worth, prioritizing the people
and projects that seek to fill, rather than drain, your internal reserves. If you can value your own
happiness above all else, you'll discover unconditional love.

―――――――――――――――○――――――――――――――

VIRGO
RULER: MERCURY

PURPOSE
*To channel the mind and body into a life of
heartfelt and reciprocal connection.*

RELATIONSHIPS

You are driven and pragmatic, but your relationships should be a place of tenderhearted connection. By seeking out partners who never waste time on looking cool or keeping up their guard,
you will discover that true love is a safe space to surrender.

The Journey of
AUGUST 26

Welcome to August 26, a mentally discerning journey that inspires meaningful progress. Show your *Commitment* (The Number Seven) today. Virgo season can create internal restlessness but try to channel your overactive mind into the projects and ideas that you are responsible for. Instead of getting lost in temporary distraction, find meaning in showing up for the causes that speak to your soul.

But don't exhaust yourself on fruitless investments. *Sustainability* (Seven of Pentacles) invites you to take a momentary step back from your work so you can decipher whether or not you are using your genius wisely. Are any of your current obligations turning out to be a waste of your time? Consider the long term as you make thoughtful decisions for your overall well-being.

And remember, success doesn't happen overnight. *Evolution* (The Chariot) calls you to tap into your internal determination and drive as you carry out the tasks that will one day amount to your radical progress. By believing in your cause while doing the necessary legwork required, you can move your life forward in a meaningful and consequential way. Keep your eye on the prize as you work toward your highest potential.

JUST FOR TODAY

TODAY'S MANTRA
Through deliberate and discerning action, I can move my life forward in a meaningful way.

TODAY'S JOURNAL PROMPT
Where do I envision myself growing toward in the next year?

TODAY'S RITUAL
Start the day in peaceful meditation. Take a deep breath in, close your eyes, and repeat the prayer, "Divine order, please help me discern where my mind must be used to create the progress for which I yearn."

BORN ON THIS DAY

GERALDINE FERRARO, American politician, diplomat, attorney, and the first female vice presidential nominee

THALÍA, Mexican actor and singer known as the "Queen of Latin Pop"

"Be faithful in small things because it is in them that your strength lies."—MOTHER TERESA, Albanian Indian Roman Catholic nun and missionary

The Journey of Those Born on
AUGUST 26

You were born of mental fortitude and an insatiable desire for power. You will have to narrow your focus to the ideas that speak to your soul rather than your ego, as your journey is one of intentionality, patience, and hard work.

Early on in your journey, you will meet your discerning guide, *Commitment* (The Number Seven). Despite your limitless potential, *Commitment* calls you away from insatiability and toward a path of devotional responsibility. By channeling your great mind into the topics that you are loyal to rather than spreading yourself too thin, you will discover the gratification that comes from thoughtful action.

And if you take this serious path, you will have to consider *Sustainability* (Seven of Pentacles). *Sustainability* asks you what the rush is, urging you to slow your restless spirit and take your time on these meaningful endeavors. By taking your plans day by day, balancing work and life rather than blazing toward burnout, you can invest in your long-term health and well-being.

YOUR GUIDES

Astrology: Your Energy
Virgo (Mercury)

Numerology: Your Path
Commitment (The Number Seven)

Minor Arcana: Your Lesson
Sustainability (The Seven of Pentacles)

Major Arcana: Your Highest Calling
Evolution (The Chariot)

By answering these calls for intentionality, you will begin to witness your own *Evolution* (The Chariot). *Evolution* reminds you that success builds slowly but surely over time, and even when the public calls you an overnight success, you will remember all the behind-the-scenes work that went into your progress. You will meet *Evolution* within determination, when you place one mental foot in front of the other on your magnificent climb toward self-realization.

VIRGO
RULER: MERCURY

PURPOSE
To find spiritual satisfaction in the climb rather than the destination.

RELATIONSHIPS

You are emotionally and mentally enigmatic, yet your relationships should be a place of loyalty and perseverance. By seeking out partners who consider the long-term well-being of your relationship, you will discover that true love gets even better with time.

The Journey of
AUGUST 27

Welcome to August 27, an emotionally strengthening journey that inspires authenticity. Step into your *Power* (The Number Eight) today. Rather than holding your true thoughts and feelings inside due to fear of rejection, own who you are to see just how influential you can be when you are honest. By peeling back the layers that block you from your true nature, you can tell the world what you actually mean rather than leaving yourself and others in the dark.

As you move toward greater self-honesty, be sure to put in the hours required to master your goals. To channel the humility that Virgo season requires, *Repetition* (Eight of Pentacles) asks you to attend to the mundane, foundational tasks that you would normally put off until tomorrow.

To ensure your time is used wisely, try not to get swept away by fits of passion or impulsivity. *Resilience* (Strength) invites you to channel your energy into meaningful productivity instead, so if you find yourself overcome with emotion, take some time in thoughtful meditation to calm your nervous system. The day can run much more smoothly with a sense of internal calm, so tap into your spiritual fortitude as you master the art of self-containment.

───────────────○───────────────

JUST FOR TODAY

TODAY'S MANTRA

I can step into the full breadth of my authentic power without getting swept away by ego or passion.

TODAY'S JOURNAL PROMPT

If I wasn't trying to look cool or protect myself, where would I devote my energy today?

TODAY'S RITUAL

Tap on your heart for eight minutes. Take a seated position with your legs crossed, and slowly and gently tap your heart's center, repeating the affirmation in your head, "I am the leader of my authentic self."

───────────────○───────────────

BORN ON THIS DAY

AARON PAUL, American actor and producer

YOLANDA ADAMS, American gospel singer, record producer, actor, and radio host

"I would photograph an idea rather than an object, a dream rather than an idea."—MAN RAY, American visual artist and significant contributor to the Dada and Surrealist movements

The Journey of Those Born on
AUGUST 27

Y ou were born of intuitive genius and a hidden fear of the unknown. You will have to grow into your personal strength, as your journey is one of authenticity, mastery, and internal fortitude.

Early on in your journey, you will meet your mysterious guide, *Power* (The Number Eight). Despite your introverted disposition, *Power* calls you away from hiding your genius and toward a path of radical self-revelation. You will meet *Power* when you unveil the superficial layers that block your true identity and step into the light of your authentic spirit.

But if you choose this honest path, you will have to pay respect to your diligent guide, *Repetition* (Eight of Pentacles). *Repetition* reminds you of the divine relationship between humility and mastery, encouraging you to put in the long, tedious hours of work required to meet your true potential. By never outgrowing the foundational skills that amount to your worldly success, you always can fall back on the power of comprehension.

By answering these calls for accountability, you will come to understand the importance of *Resilience* (Strength). *Resilience* introduces you to the intrinsic strength that lies within, helping you channel your impulses and instincts into a higher purpose. You will meet *Resilience* when you respond to your passions constructively rather than destructively, honoring your feelings while staying true to your beliefs. If you can tame the beast that lives within, *Resilience* shows you how influential you can be when you remain calm.

> ## YOUR GUIDES
>
> *Astrology: Your Energy*
> Virgo (Mercury)
>
> *Numerology: Your Path*
> Power (The Number Eight)
>
> *Minor Arcana: Your Lesson*
> Repetition (The Eight of Pentacles)
>
> *Major Arcana: Your Highest Calling*
> Resilience (Strength)

VIRGO
RULER: MERCURY

PURPOSE
To expand into your power through emotional fortitude and radical authenticity.

RELATIONSHIPS

You are happy and content on your own, and your relationships should be a place of emotional unveiling. By seeking out partners who accept you for who you are, without condition or reservation, you will discover that true love is a safe container for vulnerability.

The Journey of
AUGUST 28

Welcome to August 28, a self-directed adventure that inspires personal abundance.
Step out of the confines of your mind and into the foreign today. *Experience* (The Number Nine) invites you to expand your perspective by breaking out of your intellectual and spiritual comfort zones. If fear wasn't a blockage, what uncharted topics or activities would you like to explore?

And as you grow in ways you can't anticipate, be sure to take a break and treat yourself to something sweet. *Self-sufficiency* (Nine of Pentacles) encourages you to indulge in the fruits of your labor, patting yourself on the back for the hard work you've done over the past few months. Whether you indulge in a delicious meal or take a long walk in a beautiful garden, know that you are worthy of this luxury.

Virgo season is most famous for its pragmatism, but channel its more hidden powers of genius by relying on your *Instinct* (The Hermit). Let your intuition guide you throughout the day, rather than relying on the opinions and expertise of others, as you move toward a higher calling. There is no clear road map for a day like this, so tap into your voice of reason as you move confidently toward the unknown.

JUST FOR TODAY

TODAY'S MANTRA

My intuition can guide me through a day of unexpected adventure and personal indulgence.

TODAY'S RITUAL

Consider nine things you have nurtured and grown in your life. It could be plentiful friendships, financial prosperity, spiritual growth, or even a healthy house plant. When you are done, pat yourself on the back and consider how you could reward yourself for these efforts today.

TODAY'S JOURNAL PROMPT

What is a small but meaningful way I could treat myself to some indulgence today?

BORN ON THIS DAY

JACK BLACK, American actor, comedian, musician, and songwriter

EVADNE PRICE, Australian English writer, actor, and astrologer

"Life unravels the way it does, and it has an effect on you, but you have to take responsibility for dealing with it."—**SHANIA TWAIN**, Canadian singer-songwriter

The Journey of Those Born on
AUGUST 28

Y ou were born of intuitive intellect and a hidden desire for emotional chaos. You will have to learn to rely on yourself over time, as your journey is one of adventure, prosperity, and internal trust.

Early on in your journey, you will meet your fearless guide, *Experience* (The Number Nine). Despite your desire for control, *Experience* calls you out of your comfort zone and toward a path of wild unknown. You will meet *Experience* in the wisdom of the foreign, when, by breaking free of your perspective, you expand your consciousness in ways you never imagined possible.

And if you travel this far-reaching path, you will be greeted by your proud friend, *Self-sufficiency* (Nine of Pentacles). *Self-sufficiency* teaches you how to relish your hard-earned success, revealing to you the abundant potential of complete independence. You will meet *Self-sufficiency* in the fruits of your labor, when you take a moment to step back and luxuriate in the spiritual plenty you have built.

By answering these calls for expansion, you will come to rely on the power of *Instinct* (The Hermit). You will meet *Instinct* when you quiet the noise of outside opinion and come to rely deeply on your intuitive voice of reason. *Instinct* invites you to follow the direction of this divine compass, never questioning your power when you are met with contrary advice. By believing in yourself above all else, you can direct your way toward a higher calling.

—————————————————————O—————————————————————

VIRGO
RULER: MERCURY

PURPOSE
To follow the voice of intuition toward a path of spiritual and material expansion.

RELATIONSHIPS

You are independent, even to a fault, but your relationships should be a place of spiritual education and abundance. By seeking out partners who push you toward the unknown and expand your perspective, you will discover that true love is a catalyst for radical growth.

The Journey of
AUGUST 29

W elcome to August 29, an independent journey that bridges practicality with faith.
　　Do what speaks to you today rather than investing too much in the opinions of others. Amidst the mercurial air of Virgo season, *Autonomy* (The Number One) invites you to take a chance on your intuitive genius, trusting that you can carve out a better plan for yourself than anyone else. March to your own beat, knowing that you can't go wrong.

And while you're inspired, tap into the power of *Manifestation* (Ace of Pentacles). What dream would you like to bring into the fold of reality? While practicing mental and emotional discernment, seize the day by visualizing how these grand ideas could come to fruition in the physical world. There's no need for detailed planning—simply begin with the magic of self-belief.

But throw your expectations out the window. *Impermanence* (Wheel of Fortune) reminds you that the wheel of life keeps on spinning, so you might as well enjoy whatever fate brings your way. Whether you feel you are having a stroke of luck or you perceive yourself running into many obstacles, always try to find the good as you work with the tides of fate.

———————————————○———————————————

JUST FOR TODAY

TODAY'S MANTRA
I will balance rationality with intuition as I pursue my dreams while leaving the outcome up to chance.

TODAY'S JOURNAL PROMPT
What solid idea would I like to begin manifesting today?

TODAY'S RITUAL
Touch something naturally green today. It could be a tree, a leaf, or an herb. While you are making contact with it, repeat the affirmation, "With thoughtful care, my mind can manifest anything into existence."

———————————————○———————————————

BORN ON THIS DAY

CHARLIE PARKER, American jazz saxophonist, bandleader, and composer

FLEUR PELLERIN, French Korean businesswoman, civil servant, and Socialist Party politician

"You have to try it. You only have one trip, you've got to remember that."—IRIS APFEL, American businesswoman, interior designer, and fashion icon

The Journey of Those Born on
AUGUST 29

Y ou were born of mental diplomacy and a desire for internal peace that can err on the side of passivity. You will have to believe in your potential for growth, as your journey is one of independence, possibility, and unstoppable fate.

Early on in your journey, you will meet your fearless guide, *Autonomy* (The Number One). Despite your penchant for overthinking, *Autonomy* calls you away from self-doubt and toward a path of intuitive direction. By trusting in your divine genius and hurling yourself toward the ideas that spark your imagination, you can turn your dreams into a reality.

And if you choose this independent path, you will have to believe in the power of *Manifestation* (Two of Pentacles). *Manifestation* invites you to plant the seeds of your ambitions, not worrying about how they might turn out but believing deeply in their capacity to grow. You will meet *Manifestation* at the beginning of a new endeavor, when you keep your eyes on the potential, your heart in the possibility, and your feet firmly rooted in reality.

> ### YOUR GUIDES
>
> *Astrology: Your Energy*
> Virgo (Mercury)
>
> *Numerology: Your Path*
> Autonomy (The Number One)
>
> *Minor Arcana: Your Lesson*
> Manifestation (The Ace of Pentacles)
>
> *Major Arcana: Your Highest Calling*
> Impermanence (The Wheel of Fortune)

By answering these calls for radical self-trust, you will come to accept the law of *Impermanence* (Wheel of Fortune). *Impermanence* lies in the ever-changing tides of life, encouraging you to surrender control so you can rock with the ebbs and flows of fate. You will meet *Impermanence* in the ups as well as the downs, when you find grace for your circumstances while trusting that your destiny is unfolding within a larger cosmic plan. If you can detach from expectation, *Impermanence* teaches you how to enjoy the process of becoming.

VIRGO
RULER: MERCURY

PURPOSE
To thank the universe for everything that is certain and everything that is uncertain.

RELATIONSHIPS

You are more comfortable within partnership, but your relationships should be a place of independence and self-belief. By seeking out partners who encourage you to build your own spiritual and mental wealth, you will discover that true love is abundant in nature.

The Journey of
AUGUST 30

Welcome to August 30, a self-evaluating journey toward justice.

Try to find some mental *Balance* (The Number Two) today. Rather than letting your mind wander to extremes, come back to center as you easefully make your way through your plans. The simplest answer is often the best, so pare down your fantastical thinking and get grounded.

To do this successfully, you will have to let go of some of your burdens. *Prioritization* (Two of Pentacles) invites you to delegate where necessary, calling upon the resources you have or asking for more time from the people you trust. You can't be in a million places at once, so plan a realistic vision for what you can get done today and leave the rest for tomorrow.

But be sure to aim for equality in everything you do. *Truth* (Justice) asks you to zoom out and consider what is fair to you, to others, and to the world around you. Are there any imbalances in your life that need to be confronted today? Actions have consequences, so reach inside and consult your moral scale to decide where to push and where to pull.

———○———

JUST FOR TODAY

TODAY'S MANTRA
Through mental balance and thoughtful delegation, I can make fair choices for myself and others.

TODAY'S RITUAL
Brew some echinacea tea, known for its ability to ward off a cold. Inhale the aroma while meditating for two minutes. While you inhale, repeat the spell, "Healing tea, please bring to me the internal balance I need to breathe truth within me."

TODAY'S JOURNAL PROMPT
Does my to-do list feel endless these days? What tasks can I ask for help with?

———○———

BORN ON THIS DAY

MARY WOLLSTONECRAFT SHELLEY, English author

SYLVIA EARLE, American marine biologist, oceanographer, explorer, author, and lecturer

"The talk of winning our share is not the easy one of disengagement and flight, but the hard one of work, of short as well as long jumps, of disappointments, and of sweet success."—ROY WILKINS, prominent activist in the civil rights movement and leader of the NAACP

The Journey of Those Born on
AUGUST 30

Y ou were born of internal abundance and limitless intelligence, which can scatter your focus. You will have to decide where you want to devote your mental energy, as your journey is one of harmony, discernment, and higher truths.

Early on in your journey, you will meet your easeful guide, *Balance* (The Number Two). Although your brain can take you to far-reaching places, *Balance* calls you away from extremes and toward a path of tranquility. You will meet *Balance* when you walk the middle road, never taking on more than you can handle and calling upon your trusted partners when you need help.

If you choose this peaceful path, you will have to contend with your sage teacher, *Prioritization* (Two of Pentacles). *Prioritization* asks you to lay down some of your responsibilities so that you can bring your complete attention to the topics and tasks that mean the most to you. You will meet *Prioritization* in moments of strategic delegation, when you surrender your desire for control and realize that quality is better than quantity.

By answering these calls for personal equilibrium, you will quiet the noise enough to hear the voice of *Truth* (Justice). *Truth* gets you in touch with the ethical scale that lies within, helping you decipher the values upon which to base your life. You will meet *Truth* in moments of moral conviction, when you align your actions with your principles as you set out to make the world a more just place. If you can follow the intrinsic arrow that points you toward *Truth*, you will lead others by example.

───────○───────

VIRGO
RULER: MERCURY

PURPOSE
*To find the mental and emotional balance
required to stand for justice.*

RELATIONSHIPS

You are endlessly curious, and your relationships should be a place of mutual devotion and emotional contentment. By seeking out partners who bring you internal peace and inspire loyalty, you will discover that true love can be easeful.

The Journey of
AUGUST 31

W elcome to August 31, a mind-bending journey that slays the traps of the ego.
Virgo season inspires intellectual confidence, but *Flexibility* (The Number Three) invites you to forget what you know in favor of new perspectives. Pick someone's brain or open a new book, allowing yourself to be a complete beginner. The only true way to grow is to try.

And while you're at it, invite some coconspirators. *Collaboration* (Three of Pentacles) reminds you of how much more you can accomplish when you move out of isolation, so trust in the expertise of others as you create a shared vision. Call a few friends or put together a team at work, remembering that you have much to offer and so do they.

This mental expansion will come in handy because at the end of the day, *Surrender* (The Hanged Man) wants you to see things from an entirely different point of view. It is uncomfortable to consider where you may have been wrong, but today encourages complete intellectual and emotional humility. Let go of your rigid thinking or fixed beliefs by accepting that you may not have all the answers. From there, you can open yourself to a spiritual breakthrough.

○

JUST FOR TODAY

TODAY'S MANTRA
By admitting that I don't know everything, I can listen with humility.

TODAY'S JOURNAL PROMPT
When has someone taught me a profound lesson I never could have learned on my own?

TODAY'S RITUAL
Seek out a mentor who has a skill you would like to learn. The mentor could be an actual person you know, a how-to book, or an in-depth podcast. Spend at least thirty minutes listening to their expertise today, remembering how important it is to be a beginner.

○

BORN ON THIS DAY

VAN MORRISON, Irish singer-songwriter, musician, and record producer

TSAI ING-WEN, Taiwanese politician, academic, and first female president of Taiwan

"Joy, feeling one's own value, being appreciated and loved by others, feeling useful and capable of production are all factors of enormous value for the human soul."—MARIA MONTESSORI, Italian physician and educator

The Journey of Those Born on
AUGUST 31

You were born of intellectual authority and a deep-seated need for control. You will have to learn to go with the flow, as your journey is one of curiosity, teamwork, and letting go.

Early on in your journey, you will meet your excitable guide, *Flexibility* (The Number Three). Despite your fierce intelligence, *Flexibility* calls you away from closed-mindedness and toward a path of shared knowledge. You will meet *Flexibility* in the perspectives and wisdom of others, when you put your ego to the side in order to grow in your understanding and effectiveness.

And if you choose this expansive path, you will run into your social teacher, *Collaboration* (Three of Pentacles). *Collaboration* invites you to honor your skills while trusting deeply in the expertise of others, knowing that many hands make transformative work. You will meet *Collaboration* in the midst of teamwork, when a shared vision ties your brain to the genius of others, moving you to uncharted heights of communal progress.

By answering these calls for connection, you will come to understand the importance of *Surrender* (The Hanged Man). *Surrender* asks you to let go of your rigid ways of thinking so that you can open yourself to new spiritual experiences. It is through the loss of ego, rather than the fleeting power of control, that you can expand your consciousness in ways you never imagined possible. If you can choose growth over comfort, *Surrender* helps you see life from an entirely different perspective.

YOUR GUIDES

Astrology: Your Energy
Virgo (Mercury)

Numerology: Your Path
Flexibility (The Number Three)

Minor Arcana: Your Lesson
Collaboration (The Three of Pentacles)

Major Arcana: Your Highest Calling
Serenity (The Hanged Man)

VIRGO
RULER: MERCURY

PURPOSE
To discover the spiritual breakthroughs that come from keeping an open mind to the genius of others.

RELATIONSHIPS

You are as smart as they come, and your relationships should be a place of shared understanding and interpersonal growth. By seeking out partners who push you to think differently while honoring your expertise, you will discover that true love is a divine form of collaboration.

The Journey of
SEPTEMBER 1

Welcome to September 1, a self-fulfilling journey that requires complete faith.
Believe in yourself today. Although Virgo season can lead to overthinking, *Autonomy* (The Number One) invites you to forgo perfection and follow your intuitive genius. What would you do if you weren't afraid of being wrong? Rather than seeking answers from others, go inward and see where your compass points you next.

And channel the power of *Manifestation* (Ace of Pentacles). There is nothing more transformative than personal faith, so move forward with your best idea and take the necessary action to push you one step closer to tangible success. It is not a time to stay in your head, but rather a time to bring your imagination into the folds of reality.

But leave the outcome up to fate. If you find yourself with a stroke of good luck, ride this high until the wheels fall off. And if you come up against some tough odds, draw upon your internal optimism as you push through. *Impermanence* (Wheel of Fortune) reminds you that life is ever-changing, so let go of expectation and trust that your day is unfolding as it meant to.

JUST FOR TODAY

TODAY'S MANTRA

I will bring my best idea into reality, believing in myself while leaving the results up to fate.

TODAY'S RITUAL

Get in touch with your physical body in an enjoyable and intuitive way. Whether you close your eyes while dancing to some music or stretch in a way that feels nourishing, take a few minutes today to connect your mind with your body.

TODAY'S JOURNAL PROMPT

What idea have I been procrastinating on for quite some time that I would like to act upon today?

BORN ON THIS DAY

MARY GREW, American abolitionist, editor, journalist, and suffragist leader

TARSILA DO AMARAL, Brazilian painter, draftswoman, translator, and one of the leading Latin American modernist artists

"Don't try so hard to fit in, and certainly don't try so hard to be different . . . just try hard to be you."—ZENDAYA, American actor and singer

The Journey of Those Born on
SEPTEMBER 1

You were born of intuitive genius and a fierce self-reliance that at times can leave you with a sense of profound loneliness. You will have to trust in a power greater than yourself to get out of isolation, as your journey is one of independence, materialization, and unstoppable destiny.

Early on in your journey, you will meet your fearless guide, *Autonomy* (The Number One). Despite your humble disposition, *Autonomy* calls you away from doubt and toward a path of intuitive action. By listening deeply to the callings of the soul, you can carve out an unfounded legacy of genius and integrity.

If you take this path of self-trust, you will meet your coconspirator, *Manifestation* (Ace of Pentacles). *Manifestation* shows you how to turn your ideas into reality by believing deeply in their potential and seeing them through to completion. You will meet *Manifestation* when you take your first step toward fulfilling a goal, relying on nothing but the beat of your inner knowing.

But if you answer these daring calls, you will have to learn to ride with the cycles of *Impermanence* (Wheel of Fortune). *Impermanence* reminds you that nothing in life stays the same, encouraging you to have faith that when the cards seem stacked against you, everything could change for the better as soon as tomorrow. You will meet *Impermanence* in the highs as well as in the lows of your journey, and over time, you learn to detach from expectation and embrace what is. If you can believe that fate is unfolding as it should, *Impermanence* teaches you how to work with destiny.

YOUR GUIDES

Astrology: Your Energy
Virgo (Mercury)

Numerology: Your Path
Autonomy (The Number One)

Minor Arcana: Your Lesson
Manifestation (The Ace of Pentacles)

Major Arcana: Your Highest Calling
Impermanence (The Wheel of Fortune)

VIRGO
RULER: MERCURY

PURPOSE
To believe deeply in yourself, while placing destiny in the hands of fate.

RELATIONSHIPS

You are introverted by nature, but your relationships should be a place of mutual independence and unconditional support. By seeking out partners whose innate confidence allows them to champion your brilliance, you will discover that true love never asks you to hide your magic.

The Journey of
SEPTEMBER 2

Welcome to September 2, a justice-driven journey that reminds you that less is more.

Try to find *Balance* (The Number Two) in your work today. Rather than being everything for everyone, lean on your partners and coworkers, stating your limits and asking for more time when necessary. If things feel rushed or if you find yourself frazzled, slow down and ask yourself how you can simplify your day.

The best way to go about this simplification process is through *Prioritization* (Two of Pentacles). Although Virgo season rewards hard work, lean on the practices of delegation and time management to make your responsibilities more achievable. What projects, deadlines, or obligations are draining you of your resources? It is time to set the boundaries you need for moving forward.

Besides, you have more important things to focus on than overwork. *Truth* (Justice) invites you to be a champion for fairness today, fighting for a sense of equality for both yourself and for the people who surround you. If you are a witness to a grave sense of injustice, don't be afraid to be the clear voice of honesty needed to create a new sense of moral order.

JUST FOR TODAY

TODAY'S MANTRA

By paring down the obligations that drain me, I can be a voice for the moral issues that call my soul.

TODAY'S RITUAL

Call upon the calming properties of sandalwood. Whether you have some on hand, go out to buy some, or try to conjure the smell from your memory, inhale the aroma deeply while repeating the mantra, "A calm mind brings internal balance."

TODAY'S JOURNAL PROMPT

In what practical ways can I delegate some of the less important items on my list of responsibilities today?

BORN ON THIS DAY

SALMA HAYEK, Mexican American actor, film producer, philanthropist, and activist

KEANU REEVES, Canadian actor

"That knowledge and commitment to feminism were strong tools for my own empowerment at the peace table. That was also a turning point in my life."—LUZ MÉNDEZ DE LA VEGA, Guatemalan feminist writer, journalist, poet, academic, and actor

The Journey of Those Born on
SEPTEMBER 2

You were born with limitless mental energy but also a penchant for workaholism. You will have to discover how to be more effective by doing less, as your journey is one of equilibrium, delegation, and divine justice.

Early on in your journey, you will meet your grounding guide, *Balance* (The Number Two). Despite your insatiable mind, *Balance* calls you away from overstimulation and toward a path of more relaxed living. *Balance* invites you to let go of the capitalist hustle mindset and adopt a slower and more intentional way of approaching your responsibilities. By never taking on more than you can handle at any one given time, you can build a solid life upon the principles of sustainability.

If you choose this drama-free path, you will have to make tough calls with the help of *Prioritization* (Two of Pentacles). *Prioritization* asks you to consider your hierarchy of needs, never placing the expectations of others over your well-being. You will meet *Prioritization* in the boundaries you set, when you advocate for yourself while showing up for the responsibilities that matter most.

By answering these calls for intentionality, you will create enough space to hear *Truth* (Justice). Although it is noble to want to fix everyone's problems, not all issues are your battle to fight, and *Truth* empowers you to avoid the traps of overcommitting. Learn to trust the divine sense of fairness that lives within because when you are emotionally and mentally centered, it will point your moral compass toward your purpose.

YOUR GUIDES

Astrology: Your Energy
Virgo (Mercury, Saturn)

Numerology: Your Path
Balance (The Number Two)

Minor Arcana: Your Lesson
Prioritization (The Two of Pentacles)

Major Arcana: Your Highest Calling
Truth (Justice)

VIRGO
RULERS: MERCURY, SATURN

PURPOSE
To do away with the distractions of over-responsibility in order to live for the truths that matter most.

RELATIONSHIPS

You are deeply analytical, but your relationships should be a place of intuitive harmony and equality. By seeking out partners who always aim to meet you halfway and work to share responsibility, you will discover that true love thrives in emotional balance.

The Journey of
SEPTEMBER 3

Welcome to September 3, a conscious-shifting adventure of shared understanding.

While Virgo season can inspire a sense of perfectionism, try to embody the quality of *Flexibility* (The Number Three) instead. Rather than having all the right answers, seek out the varying opinions and perspectives of those around you. By letting go of the notion of certainty, you can absorb new information and learn from the unexpected.

And while you're at it, enlist the help of others through *Collaboration* (Three of Pentacles). How can your work be best served through the knowledge and expertise of your coworkers or friends? Get out of isolation, and don't be afraid to be the apprentice rather than the master. You can gain new skills as long as you are willing to drop the confines of pride.

Want to master this day? *Surrender* (The Hanged Man) your ego. By dropping the binary thinking that keeps you closed off from new experiences, you can open your mind to the spiritual breakthroughs you have been searching for all along. There is radical freedom within letting go, which inspires the mind to bend and shift and allows you to see life through an entirely new lens.

―――――――――――――――○―――――――――――――――

JUST FOR TODAY

TODAY'S MANTRA

I will sacrifice my prideful sense of certainty in favor of a spiritual breakthrough.

TODAY'S RITUAL

Try to practice mindful thinking throughout today. Notice every time your brain tells you something you "must," "should," or "have to" do, and detach yourself from these fear-based thoughts.

TODAY'S JOURNAL PROMPT

Which coworkers, friends, or historical figures could I learn something from today?

―――――――――――――――○―――――――――――――――

BORN ON THIS DAY

MADELEINE VERNET, French teacher, writer, libertarian, and pacifist

MARGUERITE HIGGINS HALL, American reporter, war correspondent, and the first woman to win a Pulitzer for Foreign Correspondence

"The key to good decision making is not knowledge. It is understanding. We are swimming in the former. We are desperately lacking in the latter."—MALCOLM GLADWELL, English-born Canadian journalist, author, and public speaker

The Journey of Those Born on
SEPTEMBER 3

You ou were born of an insatiable mind that, when used destructively, can get you in a fair bit of trouble. You will have to use humility to temper your genius, as your journey is one of curiosity, collaboration, and spiritual breakthroughs.

Early on in your journey, you will meet your inquisitive guide, *Flexibility* (The Number Three). Despite your intellectual authority, *Flexibility* calls you away from pridefulness and toward a path of shared understanding. By listening openly to others, rather than waiting to share your opinion, you can expand your consciousness in ways you never thought possible.

If you embrace this winding path, you will stumble upon your great teacher, *Collaboration* (Three of Pentacles). *Collaboration* reminds you that some projects and goals simply cannot be done in isolation, inspiring you to seek out the skills and expertise of others. You will meet *Collaboration* in the fruitfulness of teamwork, when the potential of your original idea multiplies thanks to you incorporating the perspectives of those you trust.

> ### YOUR GUIDES
>
> *Astrology: Your Energy*
> Virgo (Mercury, Saturn)
>
> *Numerology: Your Path*
> Flexibility (The Number Three)
>
> *Minor Arcana: Your Lesson*
> Collaboration (The Three of Pentacles)
>
> *Major Arcana: Your Highest Calling*
> Surrender (The Hanged Man)

By answering these calls for open-mindedness, you will come to understand the importance of *Surrender* (The Hanged Man). *Surrender* invites you to sacrifice your rigid beliefs in favor of the perspective-shifting quality of detachment. You will meet *Surrender* when you put yourself in someone else's shoes and come to realize that there is so much to be gained from dropping the confines of the ego. By letting go of the notion of certainty, you can discover that spiritual freedom comes from not having the answers.

───────────────○───────────────

VIRGO
RULERS: MERCURY, SATURN

PURPOSE
To surrender the ego in favor of the perspective-shifting promise of open-mindedness.

RELATIONSHIPS

You are highly intelligent and quick-witted, and your relationships should be a place of deep learning. By seeking out partners who ignite your curiosity and inspire you to step out of your comfort zone, you will discover that true love expands consciousness.

The Journey of
SEPTEMBER 4

Welcome to September 4, a humble journey toward personal metamorphosis.

Stick to your word today. *Discipline* (The Number Four) invites you to live in integrity by showing up to your responsibilities without any excuses. It is a wonderful time to put your head down and do the work that the day requires, rather than putting things off until tomorrow.

But be sure you sustain your energy. Virgo season can lead to overwork, so *Conservation* (Four of Pentacles) asks you to attend to your physical needs throughout the day, never letting your metaphorical gas tank run empty. What is your body telling you it needs? A nap, a workout, or a warm bath?

Besides, you may be in the process of shedding old emotional layers, so take care of yourself through this transition. If there is an identity, goal, profession, or relationship that you are mourning today, *Transformation* (Death) encourages you to face this reality head-on with complete self-compassion. It is scary and unsettling to accept what is ending, but look for the slivers of light that seep through these cracked walls of certainty. Many hidden gifts come from self-honesty.

JUST FOR TODAY

TODAY'S MANTRA

I will attend to the responsibilities I do have to myself and others while mourning the loss of what was.

TODAY'S JOURNAL PROMPT

What aspect of my life is coming to an end? How can I balance practical work with emotional healing today when processing that end?

TODAY'S RITUAL

Set four alarms: one for when you wake up, one around lunchtime, one around dinnertime, and one before bed. When each alarm rings, put your left hand on your stomach and your right hand on your heart, and ask yourself what your body needs right now.

BORN ON THIS DAY

RUTH FRY, English Quaker writer, pacifist, and peace activist

RICHARD WRIGHT, American author

"Power means happiness; power means hard work and sacrifice."—BEYONCÉ KNOWLES, American singer-songwriter, producer, and actor

The Journey of Those Born on
SEPTEMBER 4

You were born of fierce discipline and a work ethic that, when taken too far, can be used for self-destruction. You will have to devote yourself to personal metamorphosis instead, as your journey is one of integrity, restoration, and meaningful loss.

Early on in your journey, you will meet your demanding guide, *Discipline* (The Number Four). Although you are hardworking by nature, *Discipline* calls you away from distraction and toward a path of complete focus and intention. You will meet *Discipline* in the long hours of strenuous effort, when you place mind over matter and work your way toward a sense of personal fulfillment.

But if you choose this path of perseverance, you will have to make space for *Conservation* (Four of Pentacles). *Conservation* asks you what the hustle is all about, drawing your attention to your physical needs and the toll that exhaustion takes on the body and soul. You will meet *Conservation* when you consider the long haul, carefully utilizing your emotional, physical, and financial resources to last a lifetime.

> ## YOUR GUIDES
>
> *Astrology: Your Energy*
> Virgo (Mercury, Saturn)
>
> *Numerology: Your Path*
> Discipline (The Number Four)
>
> *Minor Arcana: Your Lesson*
> Conservation (The Four of Pentacles)
>
> *Major Arcana: Your Highest Calling*
> Transformation (Death)

By building the muscles of self-accountability, you will be ready to meet your highest calling, *Transformation* (Death). *Transformation* lies within great psychological and spiritual change, when you must part ways with an old identity or belief system to find a newer and truer sense of internal alignment. In moments of personal loss, *Transformation* invites you to hold grief and hope in equal esteem, allowing yourself to mourn what was while opening yourself to what's to come. By believing in the power of *Transformation*, you will discover that you can always begin again.

VIRGO
RULERS: MERCURY, SATURN

PURPOSE
To build the internal strength required to handle radical metamorphosis.

RELATIONSHIPS

You are emotionally grounded by nature, and your relationships should be a place of honesty and regeneration. By seeking out partners who honor and embrace the radical changes that happen over time, you will discover that true love is a vehicle for transformation.

The Journey of
SEPTEMBER 5

Welcome to September 5, a brave journey that requires complete self-awareness. Tap into a sense of *Courage* (The Number Five) today. To make the most of the mercurial nature of Virgo season, speak your mind while staying rooted in integrity. What truth would you like to share with the world? Whether you take to social media or speak truth to power in your work, now is the time to reveal your point of view.

Perhaps the truth you need to share is that you need support. Today warns against the pitfalls of a *Scarcity* (Five of Pentacles) mindset, so look for the abundance that comes from asking for help. If you are lacking something that you desperately need, place your pride to the side as you call upon the physical, emotional, or spiritual resources that are available to you.

And if you feel overwhelmed at any point today, reach for *Serenity* (Temperance) over emotional drama. If you find yourself overcome with fear or anger, slow down, meditate, and tap into the calm center that exists within. The best decisions come from personal moderation today, so choose the middle ground rather than taking to extremes.

JUST FOR TODAY

TODAY'S MANTRA
Through spiritual balance, I can bravely speak my truth and courageously ask for the support I need.

TODAY'S RITUAL
Find a nearby tree. Sit underneath it, resting your back against the tree if you can, for fourteen minutes as you repeat the spell, "Serenity tree, please bring to me the internal calm that breathes serenity within me."

TODAY'S JOURNAL PROMPT
What support systems am I in need of? Are there people, institutions, ancestors, or guides I could call upon?

BORN ON THIS DAY

CLAUDETTE COLVIN, American civil rights activist, nurse's aide, and first person to refuse to yield a bus seat

WILHELMINA SHERRIFF BAIN, New Zealand teacher, librarian, feminist, peace activist, and writer

"You can be anything you want to be, just turn yourself into anything you think that you could ever be."—FREDDIE MERCURY, English singer-songwriter

The Journey of Those Born on
SEPTEMBER 5

You were born of intellectual authority and a sharp tongue that can get you in trouble. You will have to balance self-confidence with self-moderation, as your journey is one of self-expression, want, and internal balance.

Early on in your journey, you will meet your audacious guide, *Courage* (The Number Five). Despite your restrictive mind, *Courage* calls you away from rigidity and toward a path of personal freedom. By speaking your truth and channeling your words into creative brilliance, you can turn your expansive mind into a work of art.

But if you brave this path, you will have to contend with *Scarcity* (Five of Pentacles). *Scarcity* comes to you in moments of perceived lack, when you are so fixated on what you don't have that you can't seem to find appreciation for what you do have. When you rewrite your definition of abundance, reaching out for help when you need it most, you'll learn that connection is the most important resource of all.

> ### YOUR GUIDES
>
> *Astrology: Your Energy*
> Virgo (Mercury, Saturn)
>
> *Numerology: Your Path*
> Courage (The Number Five)
>
> *Minor Arcana: Your Lesson*
> Scarcity (The Five of Pentacles)
>
> *Major Arcana: Your Highest Calling*
> Serenity (Temperance)

By answering these calls for vulnerability, you will come to understand the importance of *Serenity* (Temperance). *Serenity* asks you to tap into the divine balance that lives within that allows you to slow down your racing mind and find the middle ground of reason. You will meet *Serenity* when you choose not to go to emotional extremes, steering clear of drama and prioritizing your own peace of mind instead. If you can make friends with ambivalence, *Serenity* teaches you that spiritual contentment is born of personal moderation.

―――――――――――――○―――――――――――――

VIRGO
RULERS: MERCURY, SATURN

PURPOSE
To balance radical authenticity with emotional moderation.

RELATIONSHIPS

You are strong-willed and highly intelligent, and your relationships should be a place of mutual honesty and emotional balance. By seeking out partners who never shy away from conflict while always aiming for shared understanding, you will discover that true love can be peaceful rather than dramatic.

The Journey of
SEPTEMBER 6

Welcome to September 6, a heart-opening journey of emotional awareness.

To channel the service-oriented nature of Virgo season, *Devotion* (The Number Six) invites you to give yourself entirely to the projects, ideas, and relationships that call to your soul. Act from a place of complete reciprocity, expecting nothing but personal gratification in return for your sincerest of efforts.

But as you share your abundance widely, be sure to accept the love and nurturance that does come your way. *Reciprocity* (Six of Pentacles) reminds you that when your cup is running low, there is nothing wrong with getting by with a bit of help from others. Don't let pride stop you from welcoming the support you need from the people you care about most.

However, true emotional connection can be overwhelming—and in fact, downright triggering at times. *Shadow* (The Devil) asks you to find compassion for yourself if deep feelings of fear, inadequacy, or self-destruction come up as you expand into the heart of vulnerability. When has life taught you to fear, or reject, good things? Draw upon the brightness of self-compassion so that you can bring these buried fears out into the light.

―――――――――○―――――――――

JUST FOR TODAY

TODAY'S MANTRA
I will find deep compassion for myself when fear of vulnerability comes up.

TODAY'S JOURNAL PROMPT
When my life gets good, emotionally and spiritually, what fears come up for me?

TODAY'S RITUAL
Spend fifteen minutes in silent meditation. Set a timer, take a comfortable seated position, close your eyes, and visualize a shadow version of yourself standing behind you. While this can feel eerie at first, ask yourself what this unknown, shadow part of yourself might be wanting you to look at.

―――――――――○―――――――――

BORN ON THIS DAY

JANE ADDAMS, American pacifist, social activist, feminist, author, and cofounder of the ACLU

MARGARET DREIER ROBINS, American labor leader and philanthropist

"I'm an ambitious person. I never consider myself in competition with anyone, and I'm not saying that from an arrogant standpoint, it's just that my journey started so, so long ago, and I'm still on it and I won't stand still."—IDRIS ELBA, English actor, producer, director, and musician

The Journey of Those Born on
SEPTEMBER 6

You were born of humble genius and reciprocity that can turn service into martyrdom. You will have to learn to ask for what you need, as your journey is one of service, reciprocity, and psychological healing.

Early on in your journey, you will meet your tender-hearted guide, *Devotion* (The Number Six). To channel your hardworking nature, *Devotion* calls you away from unfulfilling responsibility and toward a path of meaningful action. By giving your mind and body only to the ideas and connections that speak to your soul, you can build a life based on deep personal fulfillment.

If you take this earnest path, you will have to make room for *Reciprocity* (Six of Pentacles). *Reciprocity* reminds you that there is a time to give and a time to receive, encouraging you to neither withhold your resources nor drain yourself of your energetic reserves. Instead, by paying forward abundance when you can, and asking for nourishment from others when you need it, you can take part in the mutual exchange of *Reciprocity*.

> ### YOUR GUIDES
>
> *Astrology: Your Energy*
> Virgo (Mercury, Saturn)
>
> *Numerology: Your Path*
> Devotion (The Number Six)
>
> *Minor Arcana: Your Lesson*
> Reciprocity (The Six of Pentacles)
>
> *Major Arcana: Your Highest Calling*
> Shadow (The Devil)

But as you learn to receive, you will have to heal with *Shadow* (The Devil). You will meet *Shadow* in the self-destructive tendencies that block you from accepting the love and connection you deserve. When things feel too good and bright to handle, *Shadow* invites you to look at the past experiences that taught you to put up your guard when your life began to expand. By bringing these subconscious coping mechanisms out of the dark and into the light of compassion, you can nurture yourself through the vulnerability.

VIRGO
RULERS: MERCURY, SATURN

PURPOSE
To heal the psychological blockages that impede true, reciprocal emotional connection.

RELATIONSHIPS

You are responsible and devoted to the ones you love, so your relationships should be a place of reciprocity and nurturing. By seeking out partners who aim to nourish your emotional, physical, and mental well-being, you will discover that true love is generous in nature.

The Journey of
SEPTEMBER 7

Welcome to September 7, an unexpected adventure that requires complete focus.
Stick to your word today. To channel the devotional nature of Virgo season, *Commitment* (The Number Seven) asks you to dedicate your mind and body to the projects and people you are most loyal to. Rather than spreading yourself thin or overpromising, set yourself up for success by fulfilling the obligations you have to those you care about.

And don't expect an immediate return on your efforts. *Sustainability* (Seven of Pentacles) encourages you to see your work as a long-term investment as you carefully tend to your list of responsibilities. What thoughtful, meaningful steps could you take today to build toward the future you desire?

But as you commit to your potential, embrace the unexpected chaos that may come your way. *Upheaval* (The Tower) brings the necessary yet unpredictable changes that you have been postponing due to fear. If you have been in denial or stuck in one area of your life, lean in to today's fate. More than likely, these events will be the catalyst to a change you have been desiring for quite some time.

JUST FOR TODAY

TODAY'S MANTRA
I will focus on the future while embracing change.

TODAY'S RITUAL
Find an object that represents emotional stability for you. It could be a thumb worry stone (look it up if you haven't heard of it, they're amazing!) or a sacred trinket from your childhood. Carry this object with you throughout the day, drawing upon its grounding powers if you experience any unexpected change.

TODAY'S JOURNAL PROMPT
Would I describe myself as a loyal person? Why or why not?

BORN ON THIS DAY

CHRISSIE HYNDE, American singer-songwriter and member of the Pretenders

MARÍA FERNANDA ESPINOSA, Ecuadorian politician, diplomat, poet, and essayist

"If the life approach is simple, one need not lie so frequently, nor quarrel nor steal, nor envy, anger, abuse, kill. Everyone will have enough . . . that is the beauty of simplicity."—ELA BHATT, Indian lawyer, unionist, and human rights activist

The Journey of Those Born on
SEPTEMBER 7

You were born of personal integrity and razor-sharp focus that can be confused for arrogance. You will have to work with the unexpected nature of life, as your journey is one of intention, perseverance, and necessary change.

Early on in your journey, you will meet your discerning guide, *Commitment* (The Number Seven). To channel your innate loyalty, *Commitment* calls you away from superficial connection and toward a path of mental dedication. You will meet *Commitment* in the responsibilities and obligations you have toward others, when to live in deep integrity, you must follow through on your word.

And if you choose this dedicated path, you will meet your humble friend, *Sustainability* (Seven of Pentacles). *Sustainability* asks you to forget about instant gratification and instead tend to the long-term efforts that will one day amount to meaningful success. You will meet *Sustainability* when you give your all without expectation of an immediate return.

But if you answer these devotional calls, you will have to embrace what you can't control. You will meet *Upheaval* (The Tower) in the life-altering changes that come your way. Rather than viewing these experiences as devastating, *Upheaval* encourages you to consider where there were cracks in the foundations of your plans. By doing for you what you may not yet be ready to do for yourself, *Upheaval* catapults you into the next dimension of personal growth.

VIRGO
RULERS: MERCURY, SATURN

PURPOSE
*To be deeply loyal without getting too stuck
in expectation, accepting that some
changes cannot be avoided.*

RELATIONSHIPS

You are serious and emotionally discerning, and your relationships should be a place of mutual investment and long-term commitment. By seeking out partners who put in the time and effort required to build an infallible emotional foundation, you will discover that true love can withstand the chaotic winds of change.

The Journey of
SEPTEMBER 8

Welcome to September 8, a self-affirming journey that inspires optimism.

Step into your *Power* (The Number Eight) today through complete self-acceptance. With the help of a trusted friend, ancestor, or therapist, try to make peace with the parts of yourself that you deem unacceptable. More than likely, this shame was never yours to carry in the first place, and by releasing it, you can discover how good it feels to be completely yourself.

But if you feel bogged down with how much work you have to do around the topic of self-acceptance, remember that nothing is achieved overnight. *Repetition* (Eight of Pentacles) reminds you that some days are for the tedious, mundane work we need to do in the grand pursuit of a higher vision. Put one foot in front of the other, and don't worry about the outcome quite yet.

And remember, there is always *Hope* (The Star) if you are willing to look for it. Draw upon your inner resource of optimism, or if it is nowhere to be found, seek the wisdom of a public or historical figure to renew your faith in the future. The past doesn't have to define you, so look for the shiny spark that lies within self-belief.

JUST FOR TODAY

TODAY'S MANTRA
I will do one thing today that helps me grow toward a brighter and more authentic future.

TODAY'S JOURNAL PROMPT
What hidden parts of myself do I have trouble accepting?

TODAY'S RITUAL
Tap yourself eight times on the heart while repeating the affirmation, "My past and my shame do not define my potential." Repeat this exercise as many times as you need for it to begin to feel more true.

BORN ON THIS DAY

ETHEL SNOWDEN, English socialist, human rights activist, and feminist politician

ANTONÍN DVOŘÁK, Czech composer and one of the first composers to achieve worldwide recognition

"When we stand together there is nothing, nothing, nothing we cannot accomplish."—BERNIE SANDERS, American politician and activist

The Journey of Those Born on
SEPTEMBER 8

You were born of intellectual strength and an emotional depth that can sink you into morbid reflection. You will need to brave the dark as you run toward the light of optimism, as your journey is one of authenticity, mastery, and renewal.

Early on in your journey, you will meet your soulful guide, *Power* (The Number Eight). Although you are opinionated by nature, *Power* calls you away from harsh judgment and toward a path of radical self-acceptance. By embracing every inch of yourself, the good and the seemingly bad, you can fall in love with the threads of truth that tie you to the rest of humankind.

But if you choose this self-affirming path, you will have to pay respect to *Repetition* (Eight of Pentacles). *Repetition* is not impressed by natural talent or swayed by temporary spurts of passion, but instead invites you to put in the long, arduous hours of work required to master your craft. You will meet *Repetition* in the tediousness of practice, when you have no choice but to appreciate the power of humility.

> ## YOUR GUIDES
>
> *Astrology: Your Energy*
> Virgo (Mercury, Saturn)
>
> *Numerology: Your Path*
> Power (The Number Eight)
>
> *Minor Arcana: Your Lesson*
> Repetition (The Eight of Pentacles)
>
> *Major Arcana: Your Highest Calling*
> Hope (The Star)

By answering these calls for personal integrity, you will come to rely on the limitless resource of *Hope* (The Star). *Hope* reveals the divine optimism that lives within, reminding you that even in the worst of times, there is still the potential to wash away the debris of the past while moving toward a brighter future. You will meet *Hope* in the undeniable possibility of change that carries you through even the stormiest of weather. By choosing *Hope* over despair, you can remind others that anything is possible.

VIRGO
RULERS: MERCURY, SATURN

PURPOSE
To choose empathy over judgment, humility over pride, and hope over despair.

RELATIONSHIPS

You are pragmatic in many ways, but your relationships should be a place of deep vulnerability and endless possibility. By seeking out partners who take you as you are while igniting a flame of optimism within you, you will discover that true love is spiritually abundant.

The Journey of
SEPTEMBER 9

W elcome to September 9, an introspective journey that leads to personal expansion.
Virgo season may inspire you to take pride in having all the answers, but *Experience* (The Number Nine) invites you to traverse the unknowns of the day instead. Get out of your comfort zone and try to find the freedom that comes from uncertainty.

And if you can break free from the confines of control, you may discover the abundance that comes from *Self-sufficiency* (Nine of Pentacles). You can build a sense of personal wealth through self-acknowledgment, so pat yourself on the back for all the work that has led you to this point in your life. Whether you treat yourself to a financial or emotional gift, be sure it feeds you spiritually.

But as you expand in numerous ways, *Memory* (The Moon) may call you back in time to address the things that are blocking you from moving forward. If you have a moment of déjà vu or an unexpected emotional trigger, take the time to reflect on what your subconscious is trying to tell you.

JUST FOR TODAY

TODAY'S MANTRA
I will address the subconscious blockages that keep me from expanding.

TODAY'S JOURNAL PROMPT
What memories do I have around perfection?

TODAY'S RITUAL
Go for a night walk (ensuring that it is physically safe and someone knows your whereabouts) under the moon tonight, whether the moon is visible to you or not. As you walk, repeat the affirmation, "Just like the moon, I can wax and wane, but I am always emotionally whole."

BORN ON THIS DAY

SERAFINA DÁVALOS, Paraguayan feminist and the country's first female lawyer

SARALA DEVI CHAUDHURANI, Indian educator and political activist

"In anguish of spirit I have often queried, why the lord should require me to go among a people who despise me on account of my complexion, but I have seen that it is designed to humble me, and to teach me the lesson, 'Love your enemies, and pray for them who despitefully use you.'"—SARAH MAPPS DOUGLASS, American educator, abolitionist, writer, and public lecturer

The Journey of Those Born on
SEPTEMBER 9

You were born of intuitive intelligence and a level of introspection that can unintentionally leave you feeling isolated. You will have to heal inward to grow outward, as your journey is one of discovery, abundance, and self-reflection.

Early on in your journey, you will meet your guide, *Experience* (The Number Nine). Despite your natural expertise, *Experience* calls you away from being an all-knowing authority and toward a path of experimental education. You will meet *Experience* whenever you embark on a grand and foreign adventure, throwing your comfort zone to the side in pursuit of higher understanding.

And if you traverse this winding path, you will be greeted by your dear friend, *Self-sufficiency* (Nine of Pentacles). *Self-sufficiency* shows you the rewards of independence by way of material and emotional prosperity. By leaning on nothing but your inherent talent and a belief in a benevolent universal power, you can accrue spiritual wealth over time.

By stepping out into this expansive journey, *Memory* (The Moon) will ensure that you never forget where you came from. *Memory* reminds you that when trauma goes unaddressed it dictates much of your inexplicable emotional reactions. You will meet *Memory* by way of dreams, unexpected recollections, and occasional déjà vu. *Memory* calls you inward to heal and integrate these long-buried stories so that you can make new room for intuition and internal alignment. It is scary to unpack the emotional bags of the past, but remember how light you will feel moving forward when you do.

VIRGO
RULERS: MERCURY, SATURN

PURPOSE
To grow toward the abundant unknown, slowly unpacking the subconscious baggage over time.

RELATIONSHIPS

You are pragmatic in most areas of your life, but your relationships should be a place of expansive, deep healing. By finding partners who seek to grow and understand when past wounds get triggered, rather than flee, you will discover that true love is ever-evolving rather than stagnate.

The Journey of
SEPTEMBER 10

Welcome to September 10, a confidence-boosting journey that requires you to believe in yourself.

Virgo season can make you want to double- and triple-check your work, but *Autonomy* (The Number One) invites you to throw perfection out the window and rely on your intuition instead. Do what feels right to you every step of the way today, and give yourself complete agency over your plans, knowing that you can change your mind anytime you please.

But most importantly, say "yes" to the opportunities that come your way. *Manifestation* (Ace of Pentacles) means believing deeply in the potential of your worldly desires, so don't apologize for having an appetite for success. Ask for that raise, go on that first date, or start that new class you've been curious about.

By saying "yes" to yourself, you can step into the light of your authentic spirit. *Vitality* (The Sun) invites you to shine brightly today, never dimming your power to make others comfortable. If you are feeling good about yourself, own it! Or if you find yourself in a slump, this is a good time to fake it until you make it, so dress up in a way that feels beautiful to you and remember how good it feels to be in your skin.

JUST FOR TODAY

TODAY'S MANTRA
I can turn my ideas into reality through the power of authenticity.

TODAY'S JOURNAL PROMPT
What special outfit, friend, or ritual makes me feel extra confident?

TODAY'S RITUAL
Hang out with the sun today for nineteen minutes. Whether this gorgeous ball of light is visible or not, you can sunbathe (with some SPF), make up a "sun dance" with your friends, or go for a little walk.

BORN ON THIS DAY

JACK MA, Chinese businessman, investor, and philanthropist

MEDEA BENJAMIN, American political activist and cofounder of CODEPINK

"I knew that I just didn't have it in me to give up, even if I sometimes felt like a fool for continuing to believe."—MISTY COPELAND, American ballerina and the first Black female principal dancer at American Ballet Theatre

The Journey of Those Born on
SEPTEMBER 10

Y ou were born of mental fortitude and an ambition that can keep you from enjoying the
moment. You will have to free yourself from expectation, as your journey is one of independence, opportunity, and authentic confidence.

Early on in your journey, you will meet your confident guide, *Autonomy* (The Number One). Despite
your humble nature, *Autonomy* calls you away from
playing it safe and toward a path of innovation. By listening to the voice of your intuition rather than societal pressure, you can carve out an uncharted legacy of
your own.

And if you choose this daring path, you will meet
your inspired friend, *Manifestation* (Ace of Pentacles).
Manifestation invites you to turn your thoughts into reality by way of hard work and self-belief. You will meet
Manifestation at the very beginning of a tangible goal,
when you have planted the seed of an idea with great enthusiasm and are ready to see it through to harvest.

By answering these ambitious calls, you will step
into the promise of *Vitality* (The Sun). *Vitality* reminds you of the power of vulnerability, inspiring you to hold your head high, never extinguishing your fire because someone can't handle your
flame. You will meet *Vitality* when you shine with the brightness of self-acceptance, channeling
all the internal work you have done into your work in the public. By sharing the sunlight of your
authentic spirit, you can inspire others to do the same.

> ### YOUR GUIDES
>
> *Astrology: Your Energy*
> Virgo (Mercury, Saturn)
>
> *Numerology: Your Path*
> Autonomy (The Number One)
>
> *Minor Arcana: Your Lesson*
> Manifestation (The Ace of Pentacles)
>
> *Major Arcana: Your Highest Calling*
> Vitality (The Sun)

VIRGO
RULERS: MERCURY, SATURN

PURPOSE
*To express internal confidence into
external brilliance.*

RELATIONSHIPS

You are emotionally self-contained, but your relationships should be a place of reciprocal admiration. By seeking out partners who are proud to be with you and aren't afraid to show it to the public, you will discover that true love likes to shine.

The Journey of
SEPTEMBER 11

Welcome to September 11, a consciousness-raising journey that requires some delegation. Look for *Balance* (The Number Two). There is no need to break a sweat today, so pare back your day by only paying mindful attention to the partnerships and projects that mean the most to you. If you find that some responsibilities simply must get done, call upon the support of colleagues and friends and remember that two hands are better than one.

To help you on this path, lean in to the gift of *Prioritization* (Two of Pentacles). While Virgo season can convince you that you can take on everything at once, be honest with yourself and others about what you can and cannot get done in a single day. What is highest on your list of priorities, and what could be left until tomorrow?

But be sure to put truthfulness at the top of your list. Today invites you to see the reality that is in front of you rather than wasting any time in denial. Honesty can be quite uncomfortable but *Awakening* (Judgment) reminds you that through this discomfort you can make conscious decisions that benefit you in the long run.

JUST FOR TODAY

TODAY'S MANTRA
I can make space for the uncomfortable truth by delegating and prioritizing my day wisely.

TODAY'S JOURNAL PROMPT
What tough realities, in my life or the world around me, I have been denying for quite some time?

TODAY'S RITUAL
Start the day by asking yourself two questions: What responsibilities do I need to lean away from? What responsibilities do I need to lean toward?

BORN ON THIS DAY

EUGÉNIE NIBOYET, French author, journalist, and founder of the first feminist daily newspaper in France

MINNIJEAN BROWN-TRICKEY, American civil rights activist, political figure, and member of the Little Rock Nine

"I have no sense of nationalism, only a cosmic consciousness of belonging to the human family."—ROSIKA SCHWIMMER, Hungarian pacifist, feminist, and suffragist

The Journey of Those Born on
SEPTEMBER 11

You were born of mental diplomacy and a hint of idealism that can block you from seeing the full picture of reality. You will have to prioritize truth over comfort, as your journey is one of patience, delegation, and radical consciousness.

Early on in your journey, you will meet your calming guide, *Balance* (The Number Two). Despite your hardworking nature, *Balance* calls you away from burnout and toward a path of restraint and moderation. By never taking on more than you can handle, and calling upon support when you need to, you can learn to walk, rather than sprint, through life.

By choosing this tranquil path, you will have to make friends with *Prioritization* (Two of Pentacles). *Prioritization* reminds you that you cannot be in two places at once, so delegate your responsibilities when necessary and say "no" when appropriate. You will meet *Prioritization* when you unburden yourself from draining obligations and make time for the work that matters most.

> ### YOUR GUIDES
>
> *Astrology: Your Energy*
> Virgo (Mercury, Saturn)
>
> *Numerology: Your Path*
> Balance (The Number Two)
>
> *Minor Arcana: Your Lesson*
> Prioritization (The Two of Pentacles)
>
> *Major Arcana: Your Highest Calling*
> Awakening (Judgment)

And if you answer these calls for discernment, you will slowly but surely open yourself to *Awakening* (Judgment). *Awakening* reveals the conscious-shifting quality of truth, inspiring you to make informed choices through the power of self-honesty. You will meet *Awakening* in moments of profound and uncomfortable revelation, when you take off your rose-tinted glasses and accept life on life's terms. By choosing reality over denial, you can empower others to do the same.

—————————————————○—————————————————

VIRGO
RULERS: MERCURY, SATURN

PURPOSE
To drop the distractions of overwork in order to awaken to real the purpose of life.

RELATIONSHIPS

You believe in fairness and justice above all, and your relationships should be a place of balance and radical honesty. By seeking out partners who speak their mind while always aiming to meet you emotionally halfway, you will discover that true love can handle the truth.

The Journey of
SEPTEMBER 12

Welcome to September 12, an expansive journey that builds gratitude.

Aim for *Flexibility* (The Number Three) instead of rigidity today. Virgo season can put you on a quest for answers, but try to ask the right questions instead. Pick the brain of everyone you come into contact with today, and always assume you have something to learn.

Besides, there is much to be gained from *Collaboration* (Three of Pentacles) today. Lean on the skills of others today, especially if there is a new skill or shared vision you'd like to pursue. Whether you recruit some collaborators or take on a role as an apprentice, don't stay in isolation due to fear or pride, but put yourself out there and trust in the divine expertise of others.

But if you have recently completed a huge emotional, professional, or spiritual milestone, *Perspective* (The World) asks you not to rush past this state of completion too quickly. At the end of today, take some time to pat yourself on the back for a job well done, and be sure to call the people who helped you along the way. By finding appreciation for the work you've put in to achieve this sense of wholeness, you can give meaningful thanks to others and the universe itself.

JUST FOR TODAY

TODAY'S MANTRA
I will get excited about the shared adventures to come.

TODAY'S JOURNAL PROMPT
What personal milestones have I completed and who can I thank for helping or encouraging me along the way?

TODAY'S RITUAL
Set aside twenty-one minutes (set a timer) to look through photos from the past year. As you look, ask yourself what accomplishments or experiences you are most proud of.

BORN ON THIS DAY

FLORENCE KELLEY, American social and political reformer and founder of the National Labor Committee

IRÈNE JOLIOT-CURIE, French Nobel Prize–winning chemist, physicist, and politician

"The battles that count aren't the ones for gold medals. The struggles within yourself—the invisible, inevitable battles inside all of us—that's where it's at."—**JESSE OWENS**, American track and field athlete and four-time Olympic gold medal winner

The Journey of Those Born on
SEPTEMBER 12

You were born of expansive intelligence with a surprising resistance to change. You will have to learn to appreciate the eye-opening gifts of connection, as your journey is one of understanding, collaboration, and deep gratitude.

Early on in your journey, you will meet your curious guide, *Flexibility* (The Number Three). To make the most of your expansive mind, *Flexibility* calls you away from judgment and toward a path of connective learning. By seeking to learn and listen rather than proving your point of view, you can reach new heights of consciousness through the diverse experiences of others.

And if you take this exciting path, you will come to understand the importance of *Collaboration* (Three of Pentacles). *Collaboration* invites you to work in harmony with like-minded individuals who carry their own unique set of skills and expertise. You will meet *Collaboration* when you come to realize that two or even three heads are far better, and more efficient, than one.

As you climb new heights of connection, you will find yourself with a greater sense of *Perspective* (The World). *Perspective* invites you to take in the view whenever you reach the top of a personal or professional milestone, soaking in spiritual contentment with the people who helped you along the way. You will meet *Perspective* in deep gratitude, when you zoom out and realize that each high and low amounts to the wisdom you will carry forward into the future. If you can appreciate the learning experiences as much as you do the success, you'll learn that growth is a shared journey, not an individual destination.

VIRGO
RULERS: MERCURY, VENUS

PURPOSE
To traverse the peaks and valleys of life hand in hand with others.

RELATIONSHIPS

You are self-sacrificing by nature, yet your relationships should be a place of deep belonging and shared vision. By seeking out partners who have a healthy sense of perspective and inspire you to forget petty drama, you will discover that true love helps you see the big picture.

The Journey of
SEPTEMBER 13

W elcome to September 13, a mentally grounding journey that inspires self-leadership.
Stick to *Discipline* (The Number Four) today. While Virgo season inspires hard work as it is, be sure not to get distracted by ineffective tasks but instead focus your mind on the responsibilities that matter most. Show the universe just how serious you are about your ambitions, and feel free to break a sweat along the way.

But be sure to consider the long term. *Conservation* (Four of Pentacles) reminds you not to overspend or restrict your resources, so stay away from extreme indulgence or a fierce scarcity mindset. Instead, focus on what you need to thrive in the future, whether that entails taking fiscal inventory or attending to your physical well-being.

Because at the end of the day, you are the leader you always needed. *Self-mastery* (The Emperor) empowers you to take responsibility for your success today, so make objective yet loving decisions that you know are going to benefit you over time. Instead of seeking instant gratification, step into a place of rational authority, and build the emotional and material foundations you need to last a lifetime.

JUST FOR TODAY

TODAY'S MANTRA
By discovering a sense of personal authority, I can make thoughtful and grounded decisions for the long run.

TODAY'S RITUAL
Go through your finances from the past week today. Using the software of your choosing, divide your purchases into four categories: necessity, necessary indulgence, unnecessary indulgence, and overindulgence. When you're finished, repeat the mantra, "I am in charge of my long-term safety."

TODAY'S JOURNAL PROMPT
When it comes to my physical well-being, how have I been overindulging or over-restricting?

BORN ON THIS DAY

LUTIE STEARNS, American Quaker, librarian, teacher, author, and activist

ANNIE KENNEY, English working-class suffragist and socialist feminist

"My biggest success is getting over the things that have tried to destroy and take me out of this life."—**TYLER PERRY**, American actor, director, producer, and writer

The Journey of Those Born on
SEPTEMBER 13

You were born of creative genius with a slight tendency toward morbid reflection. You will have to keep yourself grounded in personal integrity, as your journey is one of hard work, strong foundations, and necessary restraint.

Early on in your journey, you will meet your stern guide, *Discipline* (The Number Four). Despite your romantic idealism, *Discipline* calls you away from fantasy and toward a path of mental focus. *Discipline* asks you to put in the work required to be a master of your intellectual craft, rather than resting on your laurels or relying on pure talent.

But if you choose this path of integrity, you will have to contend with *Conservation* (Four of Pentacles). *Conservation* reminds you that your emotional, physical, fiscal, and spiritual resources must last you for the long haul, so take consistent inventory of where you are under- or overspending in each area of your existence. By neither giving in to complete indulgence or rigid restriction, you can win the marathon rather than the sprint.

> ### YOUR GUIDES
>
> *Astrology: Your Energy*
> Virgo (Mercury, Venus)
>
> *Numerology: Your Path*
> Discipline (The Number Four)
>
> *Minor Arcana: Your Lesson*
> Conservation (The Four of Pentacles)
>
> *Major Arcana: Your Highest Calling*
> Self-mastery (The Emperor)

By answering these calls for integrity, you will discover the importance of *Self-mastery* (The Emperor). You will meet *Self-mastery* in moments of personal leadership, when you contain your overactive mind and channel your genius into pragmatic and thoughtful decisions that will benefit you in the long run. *Self-mastery* encourages you to balance self-trust with humility, stepping into a place of authority while paying deep respect to those around you. By harnessing the power of objective reason, you can lead by example.

VIRGO
RULERS: MERCURY, VENUS

PURPOSE
To treat life as a divine marathon rather than burning out on a sprint.

RELATIONSHIPS

You are a romantic at heart, yet your relationships should be a place of emotional grounding and personal integrity. By seeking out partners who work with you to build a strong internal foundation upon which to trust one another, you will discover that true love always has your back.

The Journey of
SEPTEMBER 14

Welcome to September 14, a self-revealing journey that inspires humility.

Put yourself out there today. Although Virgo season inspires order and logic, *Courage* (The Number Five) invites you to throw the rulebook out the window and embrace the complexity of your humanity. Say what you need to say, do what you need to do, love who you need to love, and don't apologize for it along the way.

But as you practice such vulnerability, watch out for *Scarcity* (Five of Pentacles). Today warns against a lack mindset, so if you find yourself fixating on all the things you don't have on an emotional, physical, or material level, try to shift your attention to the parts of your life that are gratifying. If you find it hard to change the channel in your mind, call an optimistic friend and ask them for help remembering how much there is to be grateful for.

It is this kind of humility that inspires breakthroughs today, so remain teachable as you make yourself available to new *Wisdom* (The Hierophant). Whether you seek mentorship from a high-powered CEO or you absorb the subtle genius of a young child, open your heart and mind to the intelligence of those around you.

JUST FOR TODAY

TODAY'S MANTRA
It is an act of great courage to honor my truth while remaining teachable.

TODAY'S JOURNAL PROMPT
Who do I have something to learn from?

TODAY'S RITUAL
To ward off the traps of a scarcity mentality, make a list of five things (literal or metaphorical) that feel abundant in your life right now. If you find it hard to come up with five, call upon the wisdom of a mentor or a spiritual guide to help you answer.

BORN ON THIS DAY

MARGARET SANGER, American birth control activist, sex educator, writer, and nurse who opened the first birth control clinic in the United States

AMY WINEHOUSE, English singer-songwriter

"Lack of encouragement never deterred me. I was the kind of person who would not be put down."—CONSTANCE BAKER MOTLEY, American lawyer, state senator, civil rights movement strategist, and first Black female federal judge in the United States

The Journey of Those Born on
SEPTEMBER 14

You were born of incisive genius and a level of no-nonsense that can come across as harsh. You will have to learn to humbly and compassionately question the status quo, as your journey is one of self-expression, internal healing, and higher consciousness.

Early on in your journey, you will meet your bold guide, *Courage* (The Number Five). Despite your pragmatic approach to life, *Courage* calls you away from the confines of logic and toward a path of radical authenticity. By revealing who you are and what you stand for on an emotional and intellectual level, you can experience the full, gorgeous mess of the human experience.

But if you choose this daring path, you will have to contend with *Scarcity* (Five of Pentacle). *Scarcity* comes to you in moments of perceived lack, when you focus so much on what you don't have that you can't see what you do have. If you can take inventory of the blessings that fill your cup while calling upon the support you need in times of fear, you'll remember that abundance is a state of mind.

> ## YOUR GUIDES
>
> *Astrology: Your Energy*
> Virgo (Mercury, Venus)
>
> *Numerology: Your Path*
> Courage (The Number Five)
>
> *Minor Arcana: Your Lesson*
> Scarcity (The Five of Pentacles)
>
> *Major Arcana: Your Highest Calling*
> Wisdom (The Hierophant)

By answering these expansive calls, you will be asked to educate yourself on an intellectual, emotional, and spiritual level. *Wisdom* (The Hierophant) reminds you that truth is subjective, inviting you to question the perspectives of others without having to prove them wrong or prove yourself right. Instead, try to exist in the spiritual gray area, respecting and honoring your point of view while learning from the diverse experiences of others. By never letting your belief system go to extremes, and remaining willing to be wrong, you can experience the radical freedom that comes from true humility.

VIRGO
RULERS: MERCURY, VENUS

PURPOSE
To engage vulnerably with the messy, imperfect, gray area of the human experience.

RELATIONSHIPS

You are emotionally restrained in many ways, but your relationships should be a place of unbridled self-revealing. By seeking out partners who allow you to be completely and unapologetically vulnerable, you will discover that true love doesn't need you to be perfect.

The Journey of
SEPTEMBER 15

Welcome to September 15, a self-reflective journey of heartfelt service.

Forgo the superficial today. *Devotion* (The Number Six) invites you to draw your attention toward the relationships and ideas that speak to your soul, giving your time and energy away with generous purpose. While Virgo season can keep you in your head, try to orient your day around the matters of the heart.

And be sure you are available to give as well as receive. *Reciprocity* (Six of Pentacles) asks you to share your resources abundantly, whether you give a sincere compliment to a stranger or lend financial support to someone in need. But on the reverse end, if you are feeling drained or scarce, don't be afraid to ask for support when and where you need it most.

But beware of assuming that something outside of you will heal all your wounds. *Choice* (The Lovers) reminds you that the love you need most comes from within, so be careful not to give away your power to a shiny object that promises too much. If there is a relationship, promotion, or place that you believe could solve your issues around self-worth, look within and see how you can offer this gift to yourself.

JUST FOR TODAY

TODAY'S MANTRA

There is no gift that I can give or receive that will fill my innermost need for self-love.

TODAY'S RITUAL

Consider six traits that you would love your current or potential partner to have. When you are finished, sit in front of a mirror and repeat aloud, "I will be [insert the six traits] for myself rather than waiting for another person to be these for me."

TODAY'S JOURNAL PROMPT

What person or physical resource (e.g., money, clothing, status) do I give away my power to?

BORN ON THIS DAY

LIDIA YUSUPOVA, Russian human rights activist

ELIZABETH ODIO BENITO, Costa Rican international justice and human rights defender

"I have sometimes been wildly, despairingly, acutely miserable, racked with sorrow, but through it all I still know quite certainly that just to be alive is a grand thing."—AGATHA CHRISTIE, English crime writer

The Journey of Those Born on
SEPTEMBER 15

You were born of compassionate communication and an unconscious penchant for self-destruction. You will have to heal through the power of connection, as your journey is one of service, reciprocation, and self-acknowledgment.

Early on in your journey, you will meet your earnest guide, *Devotion* (The Number Six). To channel your generous nature, *Devotion* calls you away from superficiality and toward a path of heartfelt service. You will meet *Devotion* in the relationships and responsibilities that feed your soul, when you care so deeply for a cause that the work doesn't feel like work at all.

But if you choose this giving path, you will have to learn to receive. *Reciprocity* (Six of Pentacles) reminds you that connection is a back-and-forth sharing of unconditional support. Give what you can when you are overflowing with abundance and ask for the help and accept the gifts you need when your cup is nearing empty. If you can choose vulnerability over self-protection, *Reciprocity* offers you the support you never knew you needed.

By answering these intimate calls, you will come to understand the wisdom of *Choice* (The Lovers). You will meet *Choice* in the overwhelming desires you have, when you give away your power in the assumption that a person, identity, or place will solve all your issues of self-worth. *Choice* invites you to use this profound sense of longing as a mirror into the kind of love you must offer yourself. By reaching within rather than pulling from outside, you will discover that nothing is more powerful than belonging to oneself.

──────────○──────────

VIRGO
RULERS: MERCURY, VENUS

PURPOSE
To practice the ultimate form of intimacy, self-love.

RELATIONSHIPS

You are loving toward all yet tough on yourself, so your relationships should be a place of unconditional support and internal healing. By seeking out partners who reflect back to you just how lovable you are, you will discover that true love is a clear portal into self-acknowledgment.

The Journey of
SEPTEMBER 16

Welcome to September 16, a purposeful journey that requires your discernment. While the end of Virgo season can provoke some restless uncertainty, *Commitment* (The Number Seven) asks you to ground yourself in the relationships and responsibilities that you are loyal to. Rather than scattering your focus on meaningless desires, set your sights on the future you would like to build through and with these meaningful obligations.

And consider *Sustainability* (Seven of Pentacles). Today is the perfect day to take a step back and consider where you have been investing your energy and resources, and whether or not this is a smart use for them moving forward. Create a thoughtful and maintainable plan for your long-term goals, taking into account the reality of where your life stands today.

Amidst this humble work, look for the small signs of *Evolution* (The Chariot). Success is rarely an overnight sensation, so take a moment to acknowledge the meaningful progress you have made, while continuing to do the legwork required to move toward your desired future. By putting one humble foot in front of the other while nourishing yourself with the praise you deserve, you might be amazed by where you end up by tomorrow.

○

JUST FOR TODAY

TODAY'S MANTRA
There is no rushing meaningful progress, so I will tend to the responsibilities that are in alignment with my long-term goals.

TODAY'S JOURNAL PROMPT
Where would I like to see myself this time next year?

TODAY'S RITUAL
Take a seated position and close your eyes, visualizing yourself in a chariot on the road to your future. Ask yourself, "Where is this chariot going? Who is steering it? Who is powering it forward?"

○

BORN ON THIS DAY

SADAKO OGATA, Japanese academic, diplomat, author, administrator, and professor emeritus

AMY POEHLER, American actor, comedian, writer, producer, and director

"The beautiful thing about learning is nobody can take it away from you."—B. B. KING, American blues musician, singer-songwriter, record producer, and philanthropist

The Journey of Those Born on
SEPTEMBER 16

You were born of emotional sincerity and unexpected, and at times destabilizing, internal chaos. You will have to find your footing within thoughtful action, as your journey is one of keenness, perseverance, and divine work.

Early on in your journey, you will meet your incisive guide, *Commitment* (The Number Seven). Despite your changeable temperament, *Commitment* calls you away from unreliability and toward a path of responsible action. You will meet *Commitment* when you practice personal discernment, turning your attention away from distractions and setting your gaze fervently on the goals you are loyal to most.

But if you choose this path, you will have to contend with *Sustainability* (Seven of Pentacles). *Sustainability* asks you what your long-term plans are, pushing you to thoughtfully strategize rather than rushing forward with blind haste. You will meet *Sustainability* in humble work, when you invest in your greater ambitions rather than waste your resources on short-lived success.

> ## YOUR GUIDES
>
> *Astrology: Your Energy*
> Virgo (Mercury, Venus)
>
> *Numerology: Your Path*
> Commitment (The Number Seven)
>
> *Minor Arcana: Your Lesson*
> Sustainability (The Seven of Pentacles)
>
> *Major Arcana: Your Highest Calling*
> Evolution (The Chariot)

By answering these sage calls, you will find yourself aligned with the momentum of *Evolution* (The Chariot). *Evolution* reminds you that the breakthroughs you desire do not happen by chance, but rather are an accumulation of years of internal and external work. Do the legwork, keeping your eyes laser-focused on the responsibilities and obstacles that are right in front of you, and leave the outcome up to destiny. If you can balance humility with ambition, *Evolution* will take you further than you could have imagined.

―――――――――○―――――――――

VIRGO
RULERS: MERCURY, VENUS

PURPOSE
To find purpose in the behind-the-scenes work, leaving the external payoff up to fate.

RELATIONSHIPS

You are deeply sincere yet not always reliable, so your relationships should be a place of long-term, sustainable investment. By seeking out partners who are willing to work alongside you to build a strong foundation of trust and respect, you will discover that true love can withstand the unpredictable forces of change.

The Journey of
SEPTEMBER 17

Welcome to September 17, an emotionally fulfilling journey that requires you to dig deep. Although Virgo season inspires humility in each of us, step into your authentic *Power* (The Number Eight) and don't apologize for taking up well-deserved space. Through radical self-acceptance, you can move through the world in a more honest and meaningful way, inspiring others to do the same.

But know that this confidence may require *Repetition* (Eight of Pentacles). Authentic power is not acquired overnight, so rather than simply faking it until you make it, put in the time and effort required to reach a new level of authenticity. Whether you devote your time in therapy toward healing issues of self-esteem or practice the art of asking for what you want, know that this work will one day amount to an unshakable bedrock of self-worth.

And if you find yourself overwhelmed with emotion, tap into your *Resilience* (Strength). It is not a day to let your feelings get the best of you, but rather, a wonderful time to channel this passion into actions that build trust. By responding to your life with self-respect and sincerity, you can create self-esteem through action.

JUST FOR TODAY

TODAY'S MANTRA
There is nothing more powerful than taking accountability for my life.

TODAY'S JOURNAL PROMPT
What are some actions I can take to build self-esteem today?

TODAY'S RITUAL
Consider a list of eight qualities you have when you are living in your authentic power. Speak them aloud to your reflection in a mirror, starting each sentence with, "When I am in my authentic power I am _____."

BORN ON THIS DAY

MARII HASEGAWA, Japanese American peace activist

REINHOLD MESSNER, Italian mountaineer, explorer, author, and the first person to solo ascend Mount Everest

"All know that no permanent peace will triumph until all are ready to do justice and give justice to all."—MARY BURNETT TALBERT, American orator, activist, suffragist, and reformer

The Journey of Those Born on
SEPTEMBER 17

You were born of deep optimism that, when taken to extremes, can lift you away from reality. You will have to find anchoring within internal strength, as your journey is one of authenticity, mastery, and emotional courage.

Early on in your journey, you will meet your enigmatic guide, *Power* (The Number Eight). Despite your socially compassionate nature, *Power* calls you away from people-pleasing and toward a path of radical self-revelation. By being true to yourself in every situation, you will discover how magnetic and persuasive you can be when you aren't hiding under layers of superficiality.

But if you take this path of self-realization, you will have to pay respect to *Repetition* (Eight of Pentacles). *Repetition* reminds you that no one gets it perfect on the first try, encouraging you to never give up on your ambitions just because they require time and effort. You will meet *Repetition* in the mundanity of practice, when the slow and arduous hours of humble work one day amount to your irrefutable success.

By answering these transformative calls, you will come to rely on your intrinsic *Resilience* (Strength). *Resilience* lies within the spiritual muscles that strengthen every time you choose to practice emotional accountability. You will meet *Resilience* when you harness the extremes of passion and anger, channeling this powerful energy into the betterment of both yourself and the world around you. If you can choose internal strength over external drama, *Resilience* offers you the keys to eternal courage.

VIRGO
RULERS: MERCURY, VENUS

PURPOSE
To dig past the superficial to find innate power.

RELATIONSHIPS

You are introspective by nature, and your relationships should be a place of mutual vulnerability and true intimacy. By seeking out partners who want to know you at your worst as well as your best, you will discover that true love wants all the parts of you.

The Journey of
SEPTEMBER 18

Welcome to September 18, an intuitive journey toward personal and material growth.
Step out of your intellectual comfort zone today. Although Virgo season inspires you to be an expert, *Experience* (The Number Nine) invites you to be a student instead. If you were to place your fear of discomfort aside, what foreign field or subject would you like to learn?

As you allow your mind to grow and expand, take a few moments throughout the day to luxuriate in your hard-earned success. If you have been building toward greater financial and material safety for quite some time, *Self-sufficiency* (Nine of Pentacles) invites you to treat yourself to honor all the work you have done. So buy yourself a bouquet of flowers on the way home from work, or cook yourself a scrumptious meal.

This day is quite independent and introverted, so be sure you are listening to your *Instinct* (The Hermit) rather than the guidance of others. If you are met with a crucial crossroads at any point, consult the divine compass that lives within, knowing that your gut tells you everything you need to know to make an informed decision.

JUST FOR TODAY

TODAY'S MANTRA
By listening to my gut, I can grow in ways I never thought possible.

TODAY'S JOURNAL PROMPT
What could quality one-on-one time with myself look like today?

TODAY'S RITUAL
Channel the archetype of The Hermit today. Look up images of this tarot card online and pull up the one that speaks to you most. While looking at this card, repeat the spell, "Hermit genius, please help me feed the instinctual magic that lives within me."

BORN ON THIS DAY

JADA PINKETT SMITH, American actor, screenwriter, producer, talk show host, businesswoman, and singer

GRETA GARBO, Swedish-born American actor

"Power can never completely crush a people that cherishes its heritage—nor can power ever completely liberate a people that has abandoned its heritage."—ERICA-IRENE DAES, Greek academic, diplomat, and United Nations expert

The Journey of Those Born on
SEPTEMBER 18

Y ou were born of earthly intelligence and an empathic awareness that can lead to hypersensitivity. You will have to grow a thick skin of self-trust amidst the unpredictable adventure of life, as your journey is one of higher understanding, material success, and intuition.

Early on in your journey, you will meet your brilliant guide, *Experience* (The Number Nine). *Experience* invites you to travel a road of intellectual adventure, inspiring you to question everything that's supposed to be "true" in your path and to learn more by doing. If you can break out of your comfort zone and move toward the unknown, you'll skyrocket to new levels of spiritual consciousness.

And if you accept this path of understanding, you will be touched by the grace of *Self-sufficiency* (Nine of Pentacles). *Self-sufficiency* brings spiritual, emotional, and material gifts your way in exchange for complete self-reliance. You will meet *Self-sufficiency* in moments of personal payoff, when the fruits of your labor are ready to harvest and you have no one else to thank except your own grit and integrity.

YOUR GUIDES

Astrology: Your Energy
Virgo (Mercury, Venus)

Numerology: Your Path
Experience (The Number Nine)

Minor Arcana: Your Lesson
Self-sufficiency (The Nine of Pentacles)

Major Arcana: Your Highest Calling
Instinct (The Hermit)

By answering these calls for personal growth, you will come to rely on the power of *Instinct* (The Hermit). *Instinct* asks you to listen deeply to the internal voice of reason within so that your actions align with your higher purpose. You will meet *Instinct* in the dark nights of the soul, when the road ahead is completely stark and you have no choice but to follow the intrinsic compass that points you toward your North Star. If you can brave the uncertainty of the unknown, *Instinct* guides you toward your destiny with the divine light of self-trust.

─────────────────────────────○─────────────────────────────

VIRGO
RULERS: MERCURY, VENUS

PURPOSE
To grow and expand by following the directions of intuition.

RELATIONSHIPS

You are a student in most areas of life, and your relationships should be a place of deep understanding. By seeking out partners who have an innate willingness to grow and learn, even in the hardest of circumstances, you will discover that true love can withstand the ups and downs of the unknown.

The Journey of
SEPTEMBER 19

Welcome to September 19, an ambitious journey that requires you to trust in divine timing.

Follow your intuitive ideas today. The end of Virgo season can lead to major overthinking, but *Autonomy* (The Number One) encourages you to act on your enthusiasm and trust in your innate intelligence. There's no need to preplan or overprepare, so dive headfirst into the projects and relationships that light up your brain with wonder.

And believe in the power of *Manifestation* (Ace of Pentacles). Take the first necessary steps to turn your wildest dreams into a true reality, without worrying about what might go wrong down the line. Whether you purchase the URL or apply for that job, now is the time to put thoughts into action with a mindset of abundance.

But don't stress about the outcome today. *Impermanence* (Wheel of Fortune) invites you to ride the waves of fate, trusting that every low you encounter is about to transform into your next stroke of good fortune. There is meaning within the struggles as well as within the breakthroughs, so find faith in the greater karmic laws at play so you can bear witness to the magic unfolding of your larger destiny.

JUST FOR TODAY

TODAY'S MANTRA
While I can't control my fate, I can believe deeply in my potential.

TODAY'S RITUAL
When you first wake up, stand in front of a mirror and repeat the mantra, "I am capable of anything I set my mind to."

TODAY'S JOURNAL PROMPT
What is a tangible step I can take today to bring my inspired ideas into the fold of reality?

BORN ON THIS DAY

MABEL HYDE KITTREDGE, American home economist, social worker, and crusader for school lunches

JIMMY FALLON, American comedian, television host, and actor

"No one is born fully-formed: it is through self-experience in the world that we become what we are."—**PAULO FREIRE**, Brazilian educator, philosopher, and critical pedagogy advocate

The Journey of Those Born on
SEPTEMBER 19

You were born of mercurial charm and a pleasing temperament that can be confused for insincerity. You will have to show the world exactly who you are and what you're made of, as your journey is one of self-trust, abundance, and fateful oscillation.

Early on in your journey, you will meet your confident guide, *Autonomy* (The Number One). Despite your happy-go-lucky disposition, *Autonomy* calls you away from complacency and toward a path of intuitive action. By trusting in your gut while following the road less traveled, never minding the caution of others, you can carve out a unique legacy that others will follow in wonder and awe.

And if you choose this self-led path, you will have to rely on the power of *Manifestation* (Ace of Pentacles). *Manifestation* inspires you to turn your wildest ideas into tangible reality by doing the creative planning and humble legwork to get there. You will meet *Manifestation* at the very beginning of a long-term goal, when you aren't quite sure how you'll make it but know in your deepest of truths that it is possible.

YOUR GUIDES

Astrology: Your Energy
Virgo (Mercury, Venus)

Numerology: Your Path
Autonomy (The Number One)

Minor Arcana: Your Lesson
Manifestation (The Ace of Pentacles)

Major Arcana: Your Highest Calling
Impermanence
(The Wheel of Fortune)

By answering these calls for confidence, you will have to trust in the cycles of *Impermanence* (Wheel of Fortune). *Impermanence* reminds you that around every corner is your next stroke of good fortune, inspiring you to never quit before the miracle. You will meet *Impermanence* when you detach from expectation, trusting that your destiny is unfolding as it was always meant to. By believing deeply in the divine, cyclical nature of fate, you can gain something meaningful from each twist and turn.

VIRGO
RULERS: MERCURY, VENUS

PURPOSE
To be highly ambitious without getting too attached to the highs or the lows.

RELATIONSHIPS

You are a fine mix of romantic and independent, and your relationships should be a place of inspiration and possibility. By seeking out partners who encourage you to follow your dreams while championing their own, you will discover that true love is innately optimistic.

The Journey of
SEPTEMBER 20

Welcome to September 20, an intuitive journey toward internal justice.

Despite the hard work that Virgo season inspires, try to aim for *Balance* (The Number Two) in your day today. Look for practical ways that you can pare down your responsibilities, giving yourself the time and space you need to approach each task with peace of mind.

Get honest about what obligations you might need to forgo. *Prioritization* (Two of Pentacles) invites you to create a hierarchy of importance for your day, considering on an objective and intuitive level what must get done and what's better off left in the hands of another. You don't have to be everything for everyone, but rather enlist the support you need to show up for meaningful work with complete focus.

And if you are unsure of where to push and where to pull, reach within for the *Truth* (Justice). A moral scale lives within you, so try to weigh what feels fair to you and fair to the world around you. By accepting the reality of your circumstances, you can make rational decisions that are in accordance with your ethics and principles.

JUST FOR TODAY

TODAY'S MANTRA
With objectivity, I can create sustainable balance in my life.

TODAY'S RITUAL
Take a seated position, close your eyes, and meditate on the image of scale that lives within your lower abdomen. Visualize your list of responsibilities as bags of sand that tip the scale to the right. Then visualize the support you need as beautiful gemstones that tip the scale back to center.

TODAY'S JOURNAL PROMPT
How have I been taking on too much responsibility, or too little, as of late?

BORN ON THIS DAY

GEORGE R. R. MARTIN, American novelist, screenwriter, television producer, and short story writer

SOPHIA LOREN, Italian actor

"Reasonable ideas which find their sanction in the conscience of the righteous do not die; they are consequently realities and active forces, but they are so only to the extent that those who profess them know how to turn them to account."—**ERNESTO TEODORO MONETA**, Italian journalist, soldier, pacifist, and Nobel Peace Prize laureate

The Journey of Those Born on
SEPTEMBER 20

You were born of intellectual diplomacy and an intuitive awareness that, when taken too far, can be used as harsh judgment. You will have to find the truth that hangs in the balance, as your journey is one of ease, delegation, and personal justice.

Early on in your journey, you will meet your calming guide, *Balance* (The Number Two). Despite your restless mind, *Balance* calls you away from burnout and toward a path of tranquil living. You will meet *Balance* in a place of mental and emotional centeredness, when you take the next right action to make your days just a little smoother and more peaceful.

But if you choose this stable path, you will have to listen to *Prioritization* (Two of Pentacles). *Prioritization* reminds you that when you are juggling too many responsibilities, eventually, one of them will drop without your knowing. Instead, share your burdens with dependable partners and colleagues, trusting that you are worthy of help because you are a human being rather than a human-doing.

By answering these calls for moderation, you will

> ### YOUR GUIDES
>
> *Astrology: Your Energy*
> Virgo (Mercury, Venus)
>
> *Numerology: Your Path*
> Balance (The Number Two)
>
> *Minor Arcana: Your Lesson*
> Prioritization (The Two of Pentacles)
>
> *Major Arcana: Your Highest Calling*
> Truth (Justice)

come to appreciate the subtle genius of *Truth* (Justice). *Truth* reminds you that although life isn't always fair, you are responsible for acting in accordance with your ethical values. You will meet *Truth* in the moral scales that exist within, when you are able to balance what is happening in reality with what you have the power to change moving forward. You can be a force for progress by living in harmonic alignment with your deepest principles.

VIRGO
RULERS: MERCURY, VENUS

PURPOSE
To be a bridge between peaceful truth and radical justice.

RELATIONSHIPS

You are diplomatic yet heady, so your relationships should be a place of intuitive balance and equality. By seeking out partners who are able to communicate in a calm, peaceful manner and always aim for compromise, you will discover that true love thrives in harmony.

The Journey of
SEPTEMBER 21

Welcome to September 21, an emotionally expansive journey that requires an open mind. Aim for *Flexibility* (The Number Three) today. While the end of Virgo season always inspires curiosity, seek out new and diverse perspectives from the people around you. Whether you take a coworker out for coffee and pick their brain or say "yes" to a first date, view each interaction as a potential learning experience.

And from there, be sure to utilize the power of *Collaboration* (Three of Pentacles). If you have been sitting on a creative or intellectual goal for quite some time, try enlisting the skills and expertise of others today. If you need a mentor or could benefit from learning a new skill, don't be afraid to be the apprentice rather than the master.

Besides, there is a divine beauty in receiving the support you need most from others. *Abundance* (The Empress) reminds you that it is okay to say "yes" to the generosity that comes your way, whether it be encouraging words from a friend or a physical promotion at your work. By soaking in all the goodness of this day, you can be sure to pay it forward tomorrow.

JUST FOR TODAY

TODAY'S MANTRA

I will stay emotionally available to the acts of grace and support that come my way today.

TODAY'S RITUAL

Come up with a dream team to support you in your creative goals today. Think of three historical or current public figures you admire greatly, and as you go about your day, consider what they might say to you to encourage you along your journey.

TODAY'S JOURNAL PROMPT

When I am approaching a goal or ambition, do I tend to enlist support or work in isolation, and why?

BORN ON THIS DAY

MADEEHA GAUHAR, Pakistani actor, playwright, director, and women's rights activist

STEPHEN KING, American author of horror, supernatural fiction, suspense, science fiction, and fantasy novels

"There is a crack in everything. That's how the light gets in."—LEONARD COHEN, Canadian poet and singer-songwriter

The Journey of Those Born on
SEPTEMBER 21

Y ou were born of graceful communication and a romanticism that, when taken too far, leaves you unable to accept the mundanity of reality. You will have to find grounding within true connection, as your journey is one of understanding, collaboration, and divine receiving.

Early on in your journey, you will meet your inquisitive guide, *Flexibility* (The Number Three). To channel your social prowess, *Flexibility* calls you away from mental rigidity and toward a path of open-minded communication. You will meet *Flexibility* in the experiences and perspective of those around you, when you learn something unexpected and transformative from the brilliance of another.

If you choose this sociable path, you will have to embrace *Collaboration* (Three of Pentacles). *Collaboration* asks you to coconspire with the like-minded folks who share your passion rather than carrying it all on your shoulders. You will meet *Collaboration* in the heart of teamwork, when you come to understand that the power of a group can nourish, rather than dim, your individual creativity.

> ## YOUR GUIDES
>
> *Astrology: Your Energy*
> Virgo (Mercury, Venus)
>
> *Numerology: Your Path*
> Flexibility (The Number Three)
>
> *Minor Arcana: Your Lesson*
> Collaboration (The Three of Pentacles)
>
> *Major Arcana: Your Highest Calling*
> Abundance (The Empress)

By answering these calls for connection, you will begin to see the beauty in *Abundance* (The Empress). *Abundance* asks you to tap into the generosity that flows from you whenever you are in an openhearted state of receiving. You will meet *Abundance* in the gifts of nature and connection, when you take a second to smell a rose or look into the eyes of a cherished friend. If you can learn to receive grace rather than starving yourself with self-denial, *Abundance* hands you the keys to spiritual contentment.

—————————————————○—————————————————

VIRGO
RULERS: MERCURY, VENUS

PURPOSE
To be openhearted enough to receive the beauty, and connection, that life offers.

RELATIONSHIPS

You are idealistic in your own way, and your relationships should be a place of shared dreams and generosity. By seeking out partners who believe in your power of manifestation and nourish your deepest-held desires, you will discover that true love is abundant in nature.

The Journey of
SEPTEMBER 22

W elcome to September 22, a humble journey that builds a sense of personal integrity.
Reach for *Discipline* (The Number Four) rather than instant gratification today. Tend to your list of responsibilities, making your way through them with steady intentionality and sharp focus. By showing up without excuse for the obligations you have toward the world around you, you will discover just how reliable you are.

But while Virgo season can lead to overwork, *Conservation* (Four of Pentacles) reminds you how important it is to keep your energetic and material reserves full. Whether you make sure to meal-prep for the week ahead or pay special attention to the longevity of your finances, now is the time to consider how to sustain your needs without living through the lens of scarcity.

The good news is, *Self-mastery* (The Emperor) inspires objectivity and discernment today, helping you make thoughtful decisions for yourself and others in the long run. It is not a day to act from emotion, but rather, a time to balance logic with intuition as you step into a place of humble authority. Be the leader you always wanted by executing the tough but meaningful changes that will send you soaring to new heights of self-realization.

JUST FOR TODAY

TODAY'S MANTRA

From a place of personal objectivity, I can lead myself toward the future I always wanted.

TODAY'S RITUAL

Do four things that will assist you in your productivity this week. It could be choosing your wardrobe ahead of time, organizing your desk, or investing in a planner, but make sure that they help you streamline the work you have ahead of you.

TODAY'S JOURNAL PROMPT

What inspired examples of leadership from my life, history, or mythology can I channel today?

BORN ON THIS DAY

ANDREA BOCELLI, Italian opera tenor and multi-instrumentalist

MARTHA KARUA, Kenyan politician and social justice advocate

"Life is strong and fragile. It's a paradox. . . . It's both things, like quantum physics: It's a particle and a wave at the same time. It all exists all together."—JOAN JETT, American singer-songwriter, composer, musician, record producer, and actor

The Journey of Those Born on
SEPTEMBER 22*

You were born of creative intelligence and a fierce objectivity that, when taken to extremes, can feel uncompassionate. You will have to become a thoughtful leader toward yourself, as your journey is one of hard work, resourcefulness, and self-restraint.

Early on in your journey, you will meet your no-nonsense guide, *Discipline* (The Number Four). Despite your insatiable curiosity, *Discipline* calls you away from distractions and toward a path of humble action. You will meet *Discipline* in the long hours of work, which, over time, create a sturdy internal foundation of self-respect.

But if you choose this grounded path, you must wrestle with *Conservation* (Four of Pentacles). *Conservation* reminds you how important it is to replenish your physical and material resources, ensuring that you have enough energy, nourishment, and security to last you throughout your journey. Spend where you must, and save what you can, so you can meet your deepest needs while considering the long haul.

By answering these calls for maturity, you will begin to channel the power of *Self-mastery* (The Emperor). *Self-mastery* invites you to make tough but crucial decisions that pay equal respect to your well-being and the well-being of others. By neither taking up too much nor too little space in the world, you can discover the nuance of humble confidence and lead by example.

> ### YOUR GUIDES
>
> *Astrology: Your Energy*
> Virgo (Mercury, Venus)
>
> *Numerology: Your Path*
> Discipline (The Number Four)
>
> *Minor Arcana: Your Lesson*
> Conservation (The Four of Pentacles)
>
> *Major Arcana: Your Highest Calling*
> Self-mastery (The Emperor)

―――――――――――――――○―――――――――――――――

VIRGO
RULERS: MERCURY, VENUS

PURPOSE
To embody self-respect through emotional maturity.

RELATIONSHIPS

You are romantic yet detached, so your relationships should be a place of deep grounding and emotional rest. By seeking out partners who help carry your burdens and give you a safe space to nourish yourself at the end of the day, you will discover that true love feels like home.

*Are you a Libra born on this day? Head to page 760 to find your additional birthday guide!

WELCOME TO

LIBRA
SEASON

The Journey of
SEPTEMBER 23

Welcome to September 23, an enlightening journey that asks you to be both the teacher and the student.

Speak up and share your truth today. Whether you take to social media or tell someone how you feel, *Courage* (The Number Five) asks you to aim for honesty rather than self-denial. More than likely, by opening up and embracing exactly where you stand, you can inspire thoughtful conversation between you and the world around you.

But if conflict does come your way, lean in to *Maturity* (Five of Swords). To channel the diplomacy that Libra season inspires, try to find peaceful understanding rather than defending your perspective with harsh or unforgiving words. Today isn't about impulsive and hurtful language, so take a deep breath if you find yourself lost in the flames of anger.

The best way to find the balance between the self-expression and humility that the day requires is to tap into *Wisdom* (The Hierophant). Reach within your gut to determine where you need to learn from others and where you need to step into a place of intellectual authority. Remember that we are all both beginners and experts, so find grace for the diversity of perspectives you encounter today.

―――――――――――――――○―――――――――――――――

JUST FOR TODAY

TODAY'S MANTRA
I can honor my truth while learning from the perspectives of others.

TODAY'S RITUAL
Consider an opinion you once had that no longer rings true for you today. Do you have compassion for why you held that belief at the time? By finding understanding for how your perspective has changed over time, you can extend this same grace to the people you may disagree with today.

TODAY'S JOURNAL PROMPT
How do I typically engage with debate?

―――――――――――――――○―――――――――――――――

BORN ON THIS DAY

JOHN COLTRANE, American jazz saxophonist and composer

ANI DIFRANCO, American singer-songwriter and social and political activist

"And so, lifting as we climb, onward and upward we go, struggling and striving, and hoping that the buds and blossoms of our desires will burst into glorious fruition ere long."—MARY CHURCH TERRELL, American civil rights and suffrage activist

The Journey of Those Born on
SEPTEMBER 23

You were born of instinctual romance and a natural authority that can feel intimidating to others at times. You will have to learn through listening and grow through speaking up, as your journey is one of self-expression, growing pains, and higher consciousness.

Early on in your journey, you will meet your daring guide, *Courage* (The Number Five). Despite your harmonious nature, *Courage* calls you away from people-pleasing and toward a path of radical honesty. By speaking your truth to the powers that be, you can discover the influence that comes from unapologetic authenticity.

But if you take this audacious path, you will have to contend with *Maturity* (Five of Swords). You will meet *Maturity* in moments of interpersonal conflict, when defensiveness kicks in and you feel compelled to draw upon your verbal weapons of choice. *Maturity* reminds you, however, that just because you can say it, doesn't mean it's always in your highest and best interests. By practicing restraint of pen and tongue, you can use your words to defend your honor rather than your pride.

By answering these calls for vulnerability, you will begin to build a relationship with *Wisdom* (The Hierophant). *Wisdom* awakens the spiritual authority that lives within, helping you decipher what feedback, opinions, and information is worth learning from and what you should push back on with complete self-confidence. By remembering that you are both a student and a teacher in life, you will discover that humility is the divine balance between teachability and self-trust.

LIBRA
RULER: VENUS

PURPOSE
To speak the radical truth while remaining humble and willing to be wrong.

RELATIONSHIPS

You are as wise and generous as they come, and your relationships should be a place of complete honesty and interpersonal growth. By seeking out partners who do not shy away from healthy conflict and help you grow in your understanding and effectiveness, you will discover that true love requires humility.

The Journey of
SEPTEMBER 24

Welcome to September 24, a self-empowering day of emotional shedding.
Lead from the heart today. *Devotion* (The Number Six) means showing love through action rather than words, so let the people and projects you cherish most know where you stand. By lending a generous hand or a gesture of support, you can make the world a sweeter place.

But give yourself some emotional space if there is something you are ready to *Transition* (Six of Swords). There may be a psychological pattern that has come to your attention that you are ready to let go of, so spend the day calling upon your support system as you make your way through this temporary discomfort. Sometimes the only way out is the long way through, but with the help of others, this healing process won't seem so daunting after all.

And remember, you can make a *Choice* (The Lovers) to prioritize the love you need most. Consider your inherent value today as you set healthy boundaries that honor your truth. If there is a dysfunctional or draining relationship or identity that you give away your power to, believing that it defines your worth, make the bold and brave decision to choose yourself by walking away.

JUST FOR TODAY

TODAY'S MANTRA
Walking away can be a decision that honors my value.

TODAY'S JOURNAL PROMPT
What mental pattern, relationship, or identity am I ready to release today?

TODAY'S RITUAL
If you are grappling with fear, call upon the voice of a healthy and loving ancestor or spiritual guide. You don't have to know them by name; just consider what words of affirmation they might say to you, and when you open your eyes, write them down and carry them with you throughout your day.

BORN ON THIS DAY

ZAINAB SALBI, Iraqi American women's rights activist, writer, and public speaker

ELIZABETH MARIA MOLTENO, South African English activist for civil and women's rights in South Africa

"Society cannot trample on the weakest and feeblest of its members without receiving the curse in its own soul."—FRANCES HARPER, American abolitionist, suffragist, poet, teacher, public speaker, and writer

The Journey of Those Born on
SEPTEMBER 24

You were born of romantic idealism and emotional generosity that, when taken too far, leads to codependency. You will have to move away from the historical patterns that block you from the love you desire, as your journey is one of sincerity, transition, and self-worth.

Early on in your journey, you will meet your tender-hearted guide, *Devotion* (The Number Six). To channel your compassionate nature, *Devotion* calls you away from self-seeking and toward a path of meaningful service. By devoting your life to the betterment of the relationships and people you cherish most, you can build a sense of interpersonal purpose.

But if you choose this vulnerable path, you will have to contend with *Transition* (Six of Swords). You will meet *Transition* in times of deep psychological transition, when through self-awareness you come to accept the mental patterns you must let go of to grow. Internal change can feel scary and daunting, but know there are pieces of wisdom you will always carry from your past as you sail toward more fulfilling emotional waters.

YOUR GUIDES

Astrology: Your Energy
Libra (Venus)

Numerology: Your Path
Devotion (The Number Six)

Minor Arcana: Your Lesson
Transition (The Six of Swords)

Major Arcana: Your Highest Calling
Choice (The Lovers)

By answering these introspective calls, you will come to understand the importance of *Choice* (The Lovers). *Choice* reminds you that true love never asks you to sacrifice your authenticity, revealing to you the ways in which you make yourself small to fit the needs of partnership. Instead of basing your worth on the acceptance of others, be your own best advocate by prioritizing the relationships that nurture your power. Through honoring your inherent value, you will discover that you are the love you seek.

―――――――――――――――○―――――――――――――――

LIBRA
RULER: VENUS

PURPOSE
To do the psychological shedding required to access deeper emotional fulfillment.

RELATIONSHIPS

You are as compassionate and forgiving as they come, and your relationships should be a place of emotional safety and internal healing. By seeking out partners who inspire you to heal the wounds of your past by holding space for your truth, you will discover that true love is unconditional.

The Journey of
SEPTEMBER 25

Welcome to September 25, a progressive journey that demands your complete attention. Focus your efforts only on the people and projects that mean the most to you. Libra season inspires interpersonal *Commitment* (The Number Seven), so channel this devotional energy by making pragmatic decisions to prioritize what matters. There's no need to spread yourself too thin, but rather, utilize the power of "no" so you can give more meaning to the things you say "yes" to.

But don't waste time in comparison. *Hypervigilance* (Seven of Swords) warns against obsessing about what others have that you don't, but instead invites you to find internal peace within the present moment. What are you grateful for in your life right now? Rather than strategizing and manipulating to get what you think you need, sit with the abundance that lies within.

And from there, you might just make the progress you desire most. *Evolution* (The Chariot) asks you to do the humble legwork while the universe propels you forward to new heights of personal fulfillment. Don't let your ego worry about the outcome; just stay in integrity and let your destiny unfold as it will.

JUST FOR TODAY

TODAY'S MANTRA
By prioritizing quality over quantity, I can make meaningful progress.

TODAY'S JOURNAL PROMPT
Do I tend to compare myself to others? What are ways in which I can set internal boundaries to ensure that I remember my intrinsic value?

TODAY'S RITUAL
Get off social media and the internet entirely today to reconnect with your internal sense of contentment. When your devices are turned off or put away, repeat the mantra, "The external world does not define me."

BORN ON THIS DAY

LILIAN MASEDIBA NGOYI, South African anti-apartheid activist

DONALD GLOVER, American actor, singer, and writer

"Only if you are ready to change yourself can you be ready to change the world."—EDIT SCHLAFFER, Austrian social scientist and founder of Women Without Borders

The Journey of Those Born on
SEPTEMBER 25

Y ou were born of creative confidence and fierce loyalty that can block you from new experiences. You will have to hurl yourself toward the unknown, as your journey is one of intention, awareness, and personal progress.

Early on in your journey, you will meet your deliberate guide, *Commitment* (The Number Seven). Despite your malleable nature, *Commitment* calls you away from unreliability and toward a path of devotional action. By honoring the responsibilities and obligations that you hold closest to your heart, you can build a sense of internal purpose.

But if you choose this pointed path, you will have to wrestle with *Hypervigilance* (Seven of Swords). *Hypervigilance* comes to you when you are peeking over your shoulder at what your competitors are up to, drawing your attention away from the spiritual abundance you do have. *Hypervigilance* asks you to turn your head back around and focus your mind on what *you* are building toward.

> ### YOUR GUIDES
>
> *Astrology: Your Energy*
> Libra (Venus)
>
> *Numerology: Your Path*
> Commitment (The Number Seven)
>
> *Minor Arcana: Your Lesson*
> Hypervigilance (The Seven of Swords)
>
> *Major Arcana: Your Highest Calling*
> Evolution (The Chariot)

By answering these thoughtful calls, you will find yourself in a constant state of *Evolution* (The Chariot). *Evolution* demands that you draw upon your willpower and fight for your goals in exchange for monumental, earth-shattering progress. You will meet *Evolution* in success that builds slowly and then all of sudden, when your conscious mind can't quite keep up with how far you've come. If you can stay present with the work that lies ahead, your ambitions will only grow.

───────────○───────────

LIBRA
RULER: VENUS

PURPOSE
To focus completely on personal effort and integrity, never minding the success of others.

RELATIONSHIPS

You are partnership-driven and loyal by nature, and your relationships should be a place of soul-guided commitment to growth. By seeking out partners who don't run away when the going gets tough, but instead, choose to rise to the occasion, you will discover that true love is divine work in progress.

The Journey of
SEPTEMBER 26

Welcome to September 26, a self-empowering journey that asks you to be real.

Although Libra season can unintentionally provoke some people-pleasing, *Power* (The Number Eight) asks you to drop the facade and be radically true to yourself. Who would you be if you weren't afraid of rejection? By stepping into the full breadth of your creative, authentic spirit, you can influence the world around you through the power of self-honesty.

But be wary of the traps of *Negativity* (Eight of Swords). If you find your mind is telling you all the reasons why you can't do certain things today, take an objective look at what is fear versus reality. Whether you call a ruthlessly honest yet empowering friend or work through these mental cages on your own, begin to unravel yourself from these self-limiting beliefs.

From there, tap into the magic of *Resilience* (Strength). Although the extremes of passion, anger, and sadness are all a natural part of the human experience, do your best to balance self-compassion with rational discernment. By not letting your instincts run wild while accepting the feelings that come up today, you can channel these powerful emotions into personal strength and self-respect.

JUST FOR TODAY

TODAY'S MANTRA
Through self-empowerment, I can accept my deepest feelings without letting them overtake me.

TODAY'S RITUAL
Get out any excess physical energy. Whether you go for a quick sprint around the block or scream into a pillow, be sure you channel any erratic passion or anger into something nonharmful.

TODAY'S JOURNAL PROMPT
When in my life did I transform anger or passion into something deeply meaningful?

BORN ON THIS DAY

GERTRUD LUCKNER, English German social worker involved in the resistance to Nazism

JOEY SOLOWAY, American television creator, showrunner, director, and writer

"Being strong is never easy. Not in this world we are living in. . . . Standing up for yourself is not going to be easy, but it's always eventually respected."—SERENA WILLIAMS, American professional tennis player, widely regarded as one of the best female players of all time

The Journey of Those Born on
SEPTEMBER 26

You were born of deep compassion and internal strength that can feel overwhelming, even for you. You will have to find the true power that lives within, as your journey is one of authenticity, breakthroughs, and self-mastery.

Early on in your journey, you will meet your enigmatic guide, *Power* (The Number Eight). Despite your socially diplomatic nature, *Power* calls you away from superficiality and toward a path of radical self-embodiment. Accept every glorious and imperfect truth about yourself so that you can experience the freedom and magnetism that comes from being real.

But if you choose this self-affirming path, you will have to contend with *Negativity* (Eight of Swords). You will meet *Negativity* in the unconscious voices that keep you trapped in a state of limitation and restriction, forcing you to consider where these disempowering voices come from. By detaching from their vampiric chains, you can experience a new sense of mental freedom.

> ### YOUR GUIDES
>
> *Astrology: Your Energy*
> Libra (Venus)
>
> *Numerology: Your Path*
> Power (The Number Eight)
>
> *Minor Arcana: Your Lesson*
> Negativity (The Eight of Swords)
>
> *Major Arcana: Your Highest Calling*
> Resilience (Strength)

By accepting these calls for self-empowerment, you will discover the importance of *Resilience* (Strength). It is normal, and human, to let your animal instincts go too far, whether you get lost in passion, anger, fear, or flight. *Resilience* invites you to accept these preprogrammed parts of yourself while harnessing their energy and channeling it into a more fulfilling outlet that builds self-confidence. By making friends with the magnificent beast within, you can use its force for progress rather than self-destruction.

―――――――――○―――――――――

LIBRA
RULER: VENUS

PURPOSE
To channel unbridled passion into radical,
ceiling-breaking progress.

RELATIONSHIPS

You are romantic yet intimidating to most, so your relationships should be a place of complete self-revealing and mutual acceptance. By seeking out partners who embrace your limitless depth of character and honor your power, you will discover that true love never cowers in fear.

The Journey of
SEPTEMBER 27

Welcome to September 27, an expansive journey that requires you to go inward. Despite the comfort-driven nature of Libra season, *Experience* (The Number Nine) invites you to take the road less traveled in pursuit of higher knowledge. Rather than structuring your day in a typical fashion, seek out opportunities to explore something deeper by trying a new skill, learning a new language, or engaging in a new spiritual practice.

But be gentle if some *Anxiety* (Nine of Swords) comes up for you. If you find your mind running wild with worst-case scenarios, try to take a step back and look within. More than likely, these fears come from a historical place; so does the psychological heavy lifting to untangle and detach yourself from these stories to better approach the day with a clear vision.

And after you move some of these mental cobwebs out of the way, tap into *Instinct* (The Hermit). There is a divine compass within that can direct you through the internal work of the day, as long as you are willing to quiet the hustle and noise of the outside world. Spend some much-needed time in isolation before making any big decisions, knowing that this restorative time will connect you with your intuitive intelligence.

───────────○───────────

JUST FOR TODAY

TODAY'S MANTRA

I will adventure deep within myself to clear away the fears that block my intuition.

TODAY'S JOURNAL PROMPT

Growing up, how was I taught to manage anxiety and fear?

TODAY'S RITUAL

Go somewhere very quiet, like a public library or a secluded park, or put on noise-canceling headphones. Close your eyes, and ask yourself the question, "What would I like to explore if I wasn't afraid?"

───────────○───────────

BORN ON THIS DAY

HIRAM RHODES REVELS, American minister and first Black US senator

AVRIL LAVIGNE, Canadian singer-songwriter and actor

"We can change anything. We can make a just and peaceful world."—FAITH BANDLER, Australian civil rights activist and campaigner for the rights of Indigenous Australians and South Sea Islanders

The Journey of Those Born on
SEPTEMBER 27

You were born of creative intuition and a hidden depth of fear that can block you from your highest potential. You will have to travel fearlessly through your inner world, as your journey is one of growth, internal healing, and self-trust.

Early on in your journey, you will meet your worldly guide, *Experience* (The Number Nine). Despite your partnership-driven nature, *Experience* calls you away from codependency and toward a path of radical searching. You will meet *Experience* in the great unknown, when you push far from the shores of your comfort zone and travel the wild seas of uncertainty.

But if you choose this expansive path, you will have to contend with *Anxiety* (Nine of Swords). *Anxiety* weaves its fearful predictions through the confines of your mind, leaving you feeling virtually powerless over this sense of internal dread. Rather than dealing with these self-harming thoughts in isolation, reach out for support and shed light on the monsters that hide in your subconscious.

YOUR GUIDES

Astrology: Your Energy
Libra (Venus)

Numerology: Your Path
Experience (The Number Nine)

Minor Arcana: Your Lesson
Anxiety (The Nine of Swords)

Major Arcana: Your Highest Calling
Instinct (The Hermit)

By answering these brave calls, you will come to rely on the power of *Instinct* (The Hermit). *Instinct* empowers the divine voice of reason that lives within, helping you quiet the outside world and hear the truth of your higher purpose. You will meet *Instinct* in the peace of isolation, when you forget about societal pressure and take the time and space you need to align with your innermost intelligence. If you can choose self-trust over public approval, *Instinct* offers you the gift of internal knowing.

LIBRA
RULER: VENUS

PURPOSE
To follow the intuitive compass that points in the direction of healing.

RELATIONSHIPS

You are romantic yet private, so your relationships should be a place of gentle support and healing. By seeking out partners who never push, but rather patiently support you on your journey, you will discover that true love is a quiet act of compassion.

The Journey of
SEPTEMBER 28

Welcome to September 28, a mentally fearless adventure that asks you to let go of expectation.

Move to the beat of your intuitive drum today. Despite the partnership-driven nature of Libra season, *Autonomy* (The Number One) asks you to carve out your own path on your quest to personal fulfillment. There's no need to consult others or gain approval; simply ask yourself where you would like to grow throughout the day.

And chase the *Clarity* (Ace of Swords) of your mind. If an idea is piquing your interest, don't sweat the details; just dive right in to the possibility of this venture. What is your brain super enthusiastic about right now? If you take a leap of faith today, you can figure out a long-term plan tomorrow.

Besides, some things in life are better left up to chance. *Impermanence* (Wheel of Fortune) reminds you that your circumstances are ever-changing, so roll the dice today and surrender to whatever comes your way. By surrendering your vision and giving up control through divine trust, you can see every twist and turn as a fateful opportunity and rise to the occasion.

JUST FOR TODAY

TODAY'S MANTRA

By surrendering my expectations, I can take a leap of faith on my next best idea.

TODAY'S JOURNAL PROMPT

What is my relationship with independence? Do I feel safer in partnership, or do I thrive best on my own?

TODAY'S RITUAL

Do something on your own that normally you would do with a friend or partner. Whether you go to the movies or out to dinner alone, lean in to any temporary discomfort you may feel while trying to build a stronger relationship with yourself.

BORN ON THIS DAY

JANEANE GAROFALO, American comedian and actor

BRIGITTE BARDOT, French actor, singer, model, and animal rights activist

"Our greatest glory is not in never falling, but in rising every time we fall."—CONFUCIUS, Chinese philosopher, poet, and politician

The Journey of Those Born on
SEPTEMBER 28

You were born of the divine paradox between independence and romance, leaving even you at a loss for what you need most. You will have to take a giant bet on your potential, as your journey is one of fearlessness, possibility, and karmic destiny.

Early on in your journey, you will meet your fearless guide, *Autonomy* (The Number One). While you feel most safe within partnership, *Autonomy* calls you away from codependency and toward the road less traveled as you carve out a legacy of your own. You will meet *Autonomy* in uncharted opportunities, when you strike out in pursuit of your ambitions, leaving you with nothing and no one to rely on but your intuition.

If you choose this path of individuality, you will meet your incisive friend, *Clarity* (Ace of Swords). *Clarity* lives within mental breakthroughs, when the sheer potential of an idea is enough to send you blazing forward with complete self-confidence. If you can run toward enthusiasm without worrying about the details of your next greatest plan, you'll discover the endless capacity of the human mind.

By answering these daring calls, you will be asked to accept the laws of *Impermanence* (Wheel of Fortune). *Impermanence* lies in the ever-changing tides of fate, reminding you that no matter how much power you accrue, there are some things you simply cannot control. Surrender to the ebbs and flows of life, finding grace and opportunity within each turn in your forever-evolving story. By believing that the universe has your back, you can learn to enjoy the ride.

LIBRA
RULER: VENUS

PURPOSE
To balance fierce ambition with spiritual surrender.

RELATIONSHIPS

You are intensely self-confident, yet your relationships should be a place of mental exchange and personal evolution. By seeking out partners who speak the same intellectual language as you while pushing you to grow in even the most uncomfortable of ways, you will discover that true love inspires radical progress.

SEPTEMBER 29

Welcome to September 29, a peaceful journey toward interpersonal understanding.

Seek out *Balance* (The Number Two) within your relationships today. Libra season inspires diplomacy, so reach for harmony as you approach the interpersonal responsibilities of the day. How can the people around you support you in your efforts, and how can you have their back in return?

But don't get too stuck in indecision. Today warns against *Doubt* (Two of Swords), so if you find yourself unsure of what to do, call upon the reason and judgment of those you trust. Seek out that razor-sharp friend or incisive mentor and ask them to help you see how the best solution is often the simplest.

Amidst this people-driven day, trust in your *Truth* (Justice) rather than trying to be right. The human experience is deeply varied, so while something feels fair to you, it may feel starkly unjust to another person, and vice versa. If at any point you find yourself at odds with the opinion of another, speak up for your perspective while acknowledging and holding space for theirs. Discover the fulfillment that comes from compassionate honesty.

───────────○───────────

JUST FOR TODAY

TODAY'S MANTRA

Relationships require honesty with oneself.

TODAY'S RITUAL

Read about a current political or social issue from two vastly different news outlets. After you are finished, sit with your eyes closed for eleven minutes in silent meditation. When that time is up, open your eyes and repeat the mantra, "The truth comes from within."

TODAY'S JOURNAL PROMPT

When it comes to my opinions, am I open to changing my mind?

───────────○───────────

BORN ON THIS DAY

HALSEY, American singer-songwriter

ELIANE POTIGUARA, Brazilian author, poet, and indigenous rights leader

"Because I was the victim of hate, I have consecrated my life to converting that hate into understanding, into tolerance, and why not say it, love."—MICHELLE BACHELET, Chilean politician and the first elected female leader in South America

The Journey of Those Born on
SEPTEMBER 29

You were born of romantic idealism and an intuitive sense of right and wrong that can at times appear dogmatic. You will have to soften to the sweet center of personal virtue, as your journey is one of equilibrium, discernment, and moral consciousness.

Early on in your journey, you will meet your patient guide, *Balance* (The Number Two). Despite your emotionally generous nature, *Balance* calls you away from martyrdom and toward a path of internal tranquility. You will meet *Balance* when you walk the middle road, giving what you can while nourishing your needs for the long haul.

But if you choose this harmonic path, you will have to contend with *Doubt* (Two of Swords). *Doubt* comes to you in paralyzing indecision, when you have considered every pro and con but are left with complete uncertainty. Instead, quiet the mind and tap into your intuition, trusting that although there is never a single right answer, your gut will always lead you in a meaningful direction.

By answering these calls for tranquility, you will come to respect the nuance of *Truth* (Justice). *Truth* knows that life is subjective, messy, and excruciatingly indefinable, encouraging you to accept the gray area while discovering where your ethical boundaries lie. Act in accordance with your moral compass, speaking up when you intuitively feel called while allowing others to have their own experience and perspective. By never falling prey to the extremes of judgment, you can inspire radical justice through internal alignment.

YOUR GUIDES

Astrology: Your Energy
Libra (Venus)

Numerology: Your Path
Balance (The Number Two)

Minor Arcana: Your Lesson
Doubt (The Two of Swords)

Major Arcana: Your Highest Calling
Truth (Justice)

LIBRA
RULER: VENUS

PURPOSE
To pursue the radical truth that lies within internal peace.

RELATIONSHIPS

You are highly romantic and partnership-driven, and your relationships should be a place of intuitive equality and emotional harmony. By seeking out partners who smooth out your edges and always aim to meet you halfway, you will discover that true love hangs in the balance.

The Journey of
SEPTEMBER 30

Welcome to September 30, a mind-opening journey that inspires connection.

Because Libra season inspires understanding, try to practice mental *Flexibility* (The Number Three) in every interaction you have with others today. Rather than seeking to be right or to prove someone wrong, listen with an open mind and open heart, and be willing to question your fixed opinions.

But be wary of *Trigger* (Three of Swords). Today warns against taking the words of others too personally, so try to be self-aware and reflective if some emotions get stirred within you, rather than lashing out in anger or sadness. More than likely, these hurt feelings are a wonderful healing portal into a wound that desperately needs your care and attention.

And know that there's no rush to act on these revelations. *Surrender* (The Hanged Man) invites you to lean in to whatever holding pattern you might be in, practicing deep patience while staying open to the new information and perspectives that come your way. By dropping any set expectations of how the day should go, you can see everything from a new angle and discover the small breakthroughs that come from letting go.

JUST FOR TODAY

TODAY'S MANTRA
I can be an open-minded observer today, learning greatly from the perspectives of others.

TODAY'S JOURNAL PROMPT
Is there a person whose words have hurt me of late? Where does this hurt stem from?

TODAY'S RITUAL
Think back to an interaction between you and a friend, partner, or family member when their words negatively affected you but turned out to be a simple misunderstanding. Close your eyes and consider how you would like to approach that conversation or relationship if the same thing happened again.

BORN ON THIS DAY

MAITE NKOANA-MASHABANE, South African politician

NORA STANTON BARNEY, English-born American civil engineer, architect, and suffragist

"The opposite of love is not hate, it's indifference."—ELIE WIESEL, Romanian-born American writer, professor, political activist, Nobel Peace Prize laureate, and Holocaust survivor

The Journey of Those Born on
SEPTEMBER 30

You were born of romantic generosity and an optimism that can tend toward idealization. You will have to grow to see things from a clearer perspective, as your journey is one of curiosity, self-awareness, and spiritual awakenings.

Early on in your journey, you will meet your open-minded guide, *Flexibility* (The Number Three). To complement your diplomatic nature, *Flexibility* calls you away from rigid thinking and toward a path of shared understanding. By viewing each person you encounter as a teacher, rather than a competitor or threat, you can gain new knowledge from every relationship you have.

But if you choose this social path, you will have to contend with *Trigger* (Three of Swords). *Trigger* comes to you in moments of hurt feelings, when the words of others reignite a wound that you have been ignoring for quite some time. If you can look inward to heal, rather than lashing out in retaliation, you can build a stronger relationship with yourself through emotional accountability.

YOUR GUIDES

Astrology: Your Energy
Libra (Venus)

Numerology: Your Path
Flexibility (The Number Three)

Minor Arcana: Your Lesson
Trigger (The Three of Swords)

Major Arcana: Your Highest Calling
Surrender (The Hanged Man)

By answering these calls for understanding, you will come to understand the perspective-shifting genius of *Surrender* (The Hanged Man). You will meet *Surrender* in moments of ego sacrifice, when you are willing to be wrong and see things from someone else's point of view. Lean in to the spiritual virtue of discomfort, and approach your relationships as an educational experience rather than a struggle for power. If you can choose growth over comfort, connection over pride, *Surrender* opens your eyes to the spiritual breakthroughs that are right in front of you.

LIBRA
RULER: VENUS

PURPOSE
To sacrifice the ego to experience the transcendent power of shared understanding.

RELATIONSHIPS

You are generous with your heart, and your relationships should be a place of mutual growth and strong communication. By seeking out partners who aim to share as much as they listen, you will discover that true love is a wonderful place to learn.

The Journey of
OCTOBER 1

Welcome to October 1, a harmonious journey of interpersonal justice.
To enhance the socially diplomatic nature of Libra season, seek out *Balance* (The Number Two) in everything you do. Rather than taking on too much or too little responsibility, see how calm communication and necessary delegation can inspire a higher level of equality between you and others today.

But be conscious of the mental rabbit holes of *Doubt* (Two of Swords). While it is virtuous to try to see both sides of every situation, be careful of overthinking and indecision. If you find yourself at a crucial but overwhelming crossroads at any point today, seek out the balanced opinion of a trusted partner or meditate to get in touch with your intuition. The answer is never as complicated as it seems.

To help you navigate the gray areas of the day, rely on the guiding force of *Truth* (Justice). Reach into the moral compass that lies within, the one that instinctively knows the difference between right and wrong, fair and unjust. By seeking the wisdom of this force of reason, you can make decisions that are in alignment with your personal ethics while creating harmonious equality for everyone who crosses your path.

JUST FOR TODAY

TODAY'S MANTRA
The truth lies within.

TODAY'S RITUAL
Set an alarm for 11:11 a.m. and 11:11 p.m. When these alarms go off, spend two minutes in silent meditation to get in touch with your inner balance.

TODAY'S JOURNAL PROMPT
In what ways do I give away my power to the opinions of others?

BORN ON THIS DAY

JIMMY CARTER, American philanthropist, author, and thirty-ninth president of the United States

BRIE LARSON, American actor, singer, and director

"Better remain silent, better not even think, if you are not prepared to act."—ANNIE BESANT, English writer, social reformer, women's rights activist, and Indian independence leader

The Journey of Those Born on
OCTOBER 1

You were born of the fine line between romanticism and independence, making it hard at times to differentiate your wants versus your needs in partnership. You will have to fall in love with the gray areas in life, as your journey is one of tranquility, uncertainty, and higher truths.

Early on in your journey, you will meet your calming guide, *Balance* (The Number Two). To enhance your emotionally harmonious nature, *Balance* calls you away from over-responsibility and toward a path of peaceful living. You don't have to carry everyone's burdens, so delegate when necessary so that you can lean in to the sweet gifts of partnership and rest.

But if you choose this gentle path, you will have to contend with *Doubt* (Two of Swords). You will meet *Doubt* in moments of painstaking indecision, when, by trying to understand all sides of a situation, you lose touch with your intuitive compass altogether. *Doubt* calls you to act from a place of faithful self-reliance, trusting that while there is rarely a perfect answer to life's greatest dilemmas, your gut will always lead you to the best possible outcome.

> ### YOUR GUIDES
>
> *Astrology: Your Energy*
> Libra (Venus)
>
> *Numerology: Your Path*
> Balance (The Number Two)
>
> *Minor Arcana: Your Lesson*
> Doubt (The Two of Swords)
>
> *Major Arcana: Your Highest Calling*
> Truth (Justice)

By answering these sage calls, you will quiet the noise enough to hear *Truth* (Justice), the calm center of virtue that lies within that gently nudges you toward higher moral ground. *Truth* invites you to act in accordance with your personal code of ethics rather than falling prey to the extremes of popular opinion or social pressure. If you can meet others where they are while remaining loyal to your values, you can be a beacon of *Truth* in an unjust world.

LIBRA
RULER: VENUS

PURPOSE
To seek the emotional, mental, and spiritual balance required to make thoughtful change.

RELATIONSHIPS

You are compassionate yet self-reliant, and your relationships should be a place of physical and emotional equality. By seeking out partners who balance their intellect with intuition as they aim to meet you halfway, you will discover that true love is always fair.

The Journey of
OCTOBER 2

Welcome to October 2, a mind-altering experience of social understanding. Libra season can draw you toward a one-on-one partnership, but seek out the perspectives of many today. *Flexibility* (The Number Three) reminds you of how much you can learn when you practice curiosity. Whether you take a new coworker out to lunch or pick the brain of a blossoming friend, aim to build knowledge through community.

But be wary of *Trigger* (Three of Swords). Try not take the words of others too personally, and hold yourself accountable for the emotional reactions you have in response to your social interactions. By giving others the benefit of the doubt, inquiring why they said what they did rather than assuming or blaming, you can create a sense of shared understanding.

To continue this quest, *Surrender* (The Hanged Man) invites you to see things from a new perspective today, so let go of your rigid beliefs and fixed opinions as you open your mind to the possibility of being wrong. There is a spiritual freedom that comes from open-mindedness, so sacrifice your ego in favor of unexpected emotional enlightenment.

JUST FOR TODAY

TODAY'S MANTRA
By getting my pride out of the way, I can experience the spiritual wisdom of those around me.

TODAY'S JOURNAL PROMPT
Do I tend to be more curious or authoritative when I engage with new people?

TODAY'S RITUAL
Read a piece of literature that is outside your preferred genre today. Whether you read an article from an unlikely news outlet or pick up a book on a subject that brings up some fear, lean in to the power of intellectual and emotional discomfort.

BORN ON THIS DAY

MAHATMA GANDHI, Indian independence activist, lawyer, and spiritual leader

GROUCHO MARX, American comedian; actor; writer; and stage, film, radio, and television star

"All through my life, when faced with a difficult decision, I always ask myself—where can I learn more. Make the choice to learn." —MARIA RESSA, Filipino American journalist and author, and first Filipino Nobel Peace Prize winner

The Journey of Those Born on
OCTOBER 2

Y ou were born of romantic diplomacy that, when taken too far, can lead to people-pleasing. You will have to learn more about yourself through the art of letting go, as your journey is one of curiosity, self-awareness, and spiritual breakthroughs.

Early on in your journey, you will meet your light-hearted guide, *Flexibility* (The Number Three). Although you may feel more comfortable within partnership, *Flexibility* calls you away from codependency and toward a path of community-building and shared understanding. By keeping an open mind as you seek the wisdom of many, you can expand your consciousness by enlarging your social sphere.

But if you choose this expansive path, you will have to contend with *Trigger* (Three of Swords). You will meet *Trigger* when the words of another pierce an unhealed wound and you can't quite keep your feelings in proportion with the harm done. *Trigger* invites you to look within rather than lashing out, keeping a sense of emotional curiosity as you explore the hidden depths of your inner psyche.

> ### YOUR GUIDES
>
> *Astrology: Your Energy*
> Libra (Venus)
>
> *Numerology: Your Path*
> Flexibility (The Number Three)
>
> *Minor Arcana: Your Lesson*
> Trigger (The Three of Swords)
>
> *Major Arcana: Your Highest Calling*
> Surrender (The Hanged Man)

By answering these calls for detachment, you will come to understand the beauty in *Surrender* (The Hanged Man). You will meet *Surrender* when you let go of your ego, unshackling yourself from rigid opinions and long-held beliefs so that you can soar freely through the spiritual skies of the unknown. By sacrificing the safety of certainty, you can open yourself to wisdom that comes from being willing to be wrong.

LIBRA
RULER: VENUS

PURPOSE
To let go of certainty in order to find spiritual freedom in curiosity.

RELATIONSHIPS

You are relationship-driven and romantic, and your relationships should be a place of community-building and open communication. By seeking out partners who enlarge your social circle and inspire you to remain curious rather than guarded when you meet new people, you will discover that true love is expansive rather than isolating.

The Journey of
OCTOBER 3

Welcome to October 3, a transformative journey that builds personal strength.

Despite the airy nature of Libra season, *Discipline* (The Number Four) invites you to ground yourself in integrity and reliability. Show up for your personal and professional responsibilities with complete attention and focus.

But remember, sometimes the most productive thing to do is to do nothing at all. Before jumping into any new ambitions, take some time for *Restoration* (Four of Swords). It's a wonderful day to take a step back and nourish your mind and body so that you can get centered and decipher where your energy would be best used moving forward. Are you in need of some R&R?

You will need this self-care to carry you through because today may inspire a personal transition. *Transformation* (Death) invites you to let go of any outdated identities, relationships, or creative endeavors that you don't want to carry as you move forward. There is huge grief in this loss, but know that there is also an opportunity for renewal. By accepting the death of one part of your identity, you can create room for newer, and truer, life to grow.

JUST FOR TODAY

TODAY'S MANTRA

I will take serious care of myself as I show up for the grief and metamorphosis that today requires.

TODAY'S RITUAL

Create a four-step nighttime ritual to ensure you get adequate rest. The first step requires something with the element of earth (e.g., a nourishing, warming plant-based food). The second requires something with the element of air (e.g., stepping outside to feel the breeze on your face). The third requires something with the element of fire (e.g., lighting a candle). And the final step requires something with the element of water (e.g., a bath or drinking tea).

TODAY'S JOURNAL PROMPT

What important aspect of my life—personal, professional, or relational—am I grieving?

BORN ON THIS DAY

GEDONG BAGUS OKA, Indonesian philosopher and Hindu reformer

GWEN STEFANI, American singer-songwriter

"Mental inertia is death."—**TIMOTHY THOMAS FORTUNE**, American civil rights leader, journalist, writer, editor, and publisher

The Journey of Those Born on
OCTOBER 3

Y ou were born of creative ingenuity and an expansive nature that can take you to extremes. You will have to find the growth within restraint, as your journey is one of integrity, rest, and necessary loss.

Early on in your journey, you will meet your level-headed guide, *Discipline* (The Number Four). Despite your flair for the dramatic, *Discipline* calls you away from chaos and toward a path of humble work. You will meet *Discipline* in the long, arduous hours of repetition that will one day amount to your irrefutable sense of self-respect.

But if you choose this hardworking path, you will have to make room for *Restoration* (Four of Swords). *Restoration* reminds you to pause between goals, checking in with your mind and body long enough to restore what was lost in the heat of ambition. You will meet *Restoration* in the silence of recuperation, when you clean your energetic slate in order to find renewed clarity around where to grow next.

By answering these calls for integrity, you will build up the emotional muscles required to handle *Transformation* (Death). You will meet *Transformation* in the grief of loss, when you know that you must let go of an identity, relationship, or idea to move closer to your authentic self. *Transformation* asks you to see these emotional deaths as an opportunity to grow new life, inspiring you to keep your eyes on the future as you work through healing the past. If you can trust that when one door closes another one opens, you'll discover the art of beginning again.

LIBRA
RULERS: VENUS, URANUS

PURPOSE
To slowly but surely build the emotional foundation upon which to radically transform.

RELATIONSHIPS

You are compassionate and generous by nature, and your relationships should be a place of emotional grounding and deep rest. By seeking out partners who feel like home and remind you of the promise of tomorrow, you will discover that true love always catches you when you fall.

The Journey of
OCTOBER 4

W elcome to October 4, a nuanced journey of emotional bravery and spiritual restraint. To make the most of the creativity of Libra season, practice *Courage* (The Number Five) today. Whether you put your body of work out there for the world to see or you express your innermost feelings to an intimate partner, now is the time to be daring rather than inhibited. Be bold; be truthful; be yourself.

But don't get too carried away with your words. *Maturity* (Five of Swords) reminds you that honesty without compassion is plain cruelty, so be sure that you communicate in an effective manner if you find yourself in conflict today. While it is easy to get lost in the heat of the moment, take a second to cool off and recenter so you can approach the conversation in a balanced yet truthful manner.

To ensure that this dramatic energy doesn't get the best of you, tap into *Serenity* (Temperance). Whether you spend a better part of the day in silent meditation or take a cooling bath, reach for internal peace rather than getting carried away in external drama. By finding a place of spiritual balance, you can change the course of your day for the better.

JUST FOR TODAY

TODAY'S MANTRA

I can be peacefully brave and bravely peaceful, gently honest and honestly gentle.

TODAY'S RITUAL

If you are in the midst of an interpersonal conflict, spend fourteen minutes in silent meditation. Close your eyes and visualize this person as a young child, to the best of your imagination. As you meditate on this image, consider if it is possible to soften to this person moving forward.

TODAY'S JOURNAL PROMPT

When I am engaging in a conflict, do I tend to overcommunicate or undercommunicate?

BORN ON THIS DAY

SUSAN SARANDON, American actor and activist

C. DELORES TUCKER, American politician and civil rights activist

"Happiness lasts not forever, as despair lasts not forever."—HITONARI TSUJI, Japanese writer, composer, and film director

The Journey of Those Born on
OCTOBER 4

You were born of creative integrity and an unexpected flair for chaos. You will have to find peace amidst the drama in life, as your journey is one of self-expression, accountability, and internal harmony.

Early on in your journey, you will meet your bold guide, *Courage* (The Number Five). Despite your self-contained nature, *Courage* calls you away from emotional restriction and toward a path of radical authenticity. By expressing yourself through works of art and words of truth, you can channel the madness of emotion into creative fulfillment.

But if you choose this path, you will have to contend with *Maturity* (Five of Swords). You will meet *Maturity* in verbal conflict, when you have the perfect words to cut through your opposition but choose to live in integrity instead. *Maturity* invites you to utilize restraint of pen and tongue, drawing upon your skills of diplomacy as you balance honesty with compassion.

By answering these calls for vulnerability, you will come to understand the importance of *Serenity* (Temperance). You will meet *Serenity* in quiet meditation, when you silence the noise of the outside world and center yourself in internal tranquility. *Serenity* reminds you that nothing, and no one, is worth losing your cool over, encouraging you to take the high road through spiritual contentment. By choosing peace over drama, you can stay emotionally balanced amidst the rocking tides of reality.

> ### YOUR GUIDES
>
> *Astrology: Your Energy*
> Libra (Venus, Uranus)
>
> *Numerology: Your Path*
> Courage (The Number Five)
>
> *Minor Arcana: Your Lesson*
> Maturity (The Five of Swords)
>
> *Major Arcana: Your Highest Calling*
> Serenity (Temperance)

LIBRA
RULERS: VENUS, URANUS

PURPOSE
To be creatively wild while staying mentally, emotionally, and spiritually sober.

RELATIONSHIPS

You are loyal and reliable to the people you trust, and your relationships should be a place of careful and compassionate communication. By seeking out partners who can peacefully and transparently engage in necessary conflict, you will discover that true love can be a safe container for the truth.

The Journey of
OCTOBER 5

Welcome to October 5, an emotionally healing journey that requires internal change.

To make the most of the romantic side of Libra season, *Devotion* (The Number Six) asks you to wear your heart on your sleeve today. Discover how gratifying vulnerability can be by giving your time, energy, and words generously to the people you cherish most. What would you do and who you would be if you weren't trying to self-protect?

This emotional exposure is easier said than done, so be prepared to *Transition* (Six of Swords) the mental patterns that are getting the best of you. If there is an outdated belief system that you are ready to part ways with, hold yourself gently through this internal transition. It is courageous, yet deeply uncomfortable, to move away from what you were programmed to believe.

But as you expand into a newfound sense of emotional honesty, know that you may meet your *Shadow* (The Devil). If you have used self-destructive yet self-protective coping mechanisms to block out the emotional dangers of connection, now is the time to consider when and where you learned to fear and distrust love. By doing the internal healing required, you can experience true interpersonal belonging.

JUST FOR TODAY

TODAY'S MANTRA

I can hold my inner children with gentle compassion as I open myself to new levels of vulnerability.

TODAY'S JOURNAL PROMPT

What early experiences did I have around love and connection?

TODAY'S RITUAL

Hold yourself, as tenderly as you would a child, for a minimum of six minutes. Lie in bed or somewhere comfortable, and cradle yourself in a ball, holding your legs to your chest with your arms. If tears, discomfort, or anger arise, let the feelings be without judgment.

BORN ON THIS DAY

HERCHELLE SULLIVAN CHALLENOR, American foreign policy expert and civil rights activist

KATE WINSLET, English actor

"There are times when the greatest change needed is a change of my viewpoint."—DENIS DIDEROT, French philosopher, art critic, and writer

The Journey of Those Born on
OCTOBER 5

You were born of creative confidence and a penchant for interpersonal drama. You will have to surrender to the healing quality of change, as your journey is one of dedication, transition, and psychological shifting.

Early on in your journey, you will meet your tender-hearted guide, *Devotion* (The Number Six). Despite your bold and expressive nature, *Devotion* calls you away from self-centeredness and toward a path of meaningful action. By giving yourself generously to the people and creative endeavors that speak to your soul, you can create a life of deep meaning and consequence.

But if you choose this earnest path, you will have to come to terms with *Transition* (Six of Swords). You will meet *Transition* in times of internal change, when you know that you must part ways with a mental pattern or relationship that is no longer serving you. *Transition* reminds you that in times of uncertainty and change, it is important, and healing, to call upon the anchors of support you need through community and loved ones.

By answering these calls for intimacy, you will have to shed light on *Shadow* (The Devil). *Shadow* highlights the emotional contraction that tries to protect you from the excruciating vulnerability of happiness and authentic connection. You will meet *Shadow* when you shut down in your intimate relationships, forcing you to confront where these early coping mechanisms came from. If you can reach within to understand the parts of you that learned that love is not safe, you'll discover that compassion can shine a light on what has been kept in the dark.

LIBRA
RULERS: VENUS, URANUS

PURPOSE
To do the courageous psychological healing required to experience true emotional belonging.

RELATIONSHIPS

You are outgoing yet guarded, so your relationships should be a place of gentle understanding and deep compassion. By seeking out partners who aren't afraid of your skeletons and who hold empathetic space for your most tender secrets, you will discover that true love always supports healing.

The Journey of
OCTOBER 6

Welcome to October 6, a chaotic journey that asks for complete self-accountability.

To coincide with the devotional nature of Libra season, *Commitment* (The Number Seven) invites you to take your responsibilities and obligations seriously. Show up for the relationships you are most loyal to, whether they be personal or professional, without exception or excuse.

But be wary of *Hypervigilance* (Seven of Swords). Today warns against social paranoia of any kind, so if you find your mind obsessing over the worst possible things that others could do to you, slow that mental train to a complete stop. Whether you spend some time in peaceful meditation or call that no-nonsense friend who always brings you back to reality, remember that you can control your own behavior only.

Trust in whatever *Upheaval* (The Tower) comes your way. If a sudden and unexpected event throws you off your usual course, welcome this chaotic shift with open-mindedness and self-trust. By taking care of what you can, and approaching your actions with a sober, levelheaded mindset, you can make the most of any uncertainty that this day requires.

―――――○―――――

JUST FOR TODAY

TODAY'S MANTRA

I can't control others. I can't control fate. But I can control how I conduct myself.

TODAY'S RITUAL

Sit in quiet meditation and close your eyes. Imagine the hand of a trusted partner, friend, ancestor, or guide—someone who evokes a deep sense of safety and security—on your right shoulder. Carry this warmth with you throughout the day.

TODAY'S JOURNAL PROMPT

Am I a reliable friend, partner, or co-worker? How so and how not?

―――――○―――――

BORN ON THIS DAY

THOR HEYERDAHL, Norwegian adventurer and ethnographer

YOO AH-IN, South Korean actor

"If I fall, I'll fall five feet four inches forward in the fight for freedom. I'm not backing off."
—**FANNIE LOU HAMER**, American community organizer and women's rights and civil rights activist

The Journey of Those Born on
OCTOBER 6

Y ou were born of unconventional creativity and an openheartedness that can border on naivete. You will have to discover your innate resilience, as your journey is one of faithfulness,
trust, and radical change.

Early on in your journey, you will meet your discerning guide, *Commitment* (The Number Seven). Despite your generous spirit, *Commitment* calls you away
from spreading yourself too thin and toward a path of
complete focus. You will meet *Commitment* in tough
yet crucial decisions, when you walk away from what is
no longer serving you so you can devote yourself completely to the road ahead.

But if you choose this serious path, you will have to
contend with *Hypervigilance* (Seven of Swords). You
will meet *Hypervigilance* when you look over your
shoulder in self-protective distrust, keeping a watchful
eye on the actions of others. By remembering that you
cannot control others, nor are you responsible for their
wrongdoings, you can learn to let down your guard
and let life unfold as it must.

> ## YOUR GUIDES
>
> *Astrology: Your Energy*
> Libra (Venus, Uranus)
>
> *Numerology: Your Path*
> Commitment (The Number Seven)
>
> *Minor Arcana: Your Lesson*
> Hypervigilance (The Seven of Swords)
>
> *Major Arcana: Your Highest Calling*
> Upheaval (The Tower)

By answering these calls for maturity, you will come to understand the mad genius of *Upheaval* (The Tower). *Upheaval* lies in the winds of change that blow you out of your comfort zone
and into a higher, and more honest, dimension of existence. You will meet *Upheaval* amidst profound uncertainty, when the emotional ground beneath you is shaking and yet you hold on to the
faith that the universe has your back. If you can trust-fall into the hands of fate, you'll begin to
practice the art of starting over.

───────────────────────○───────────────────────

LIBRA
RULERS: VENUS, URANUS

PURPOSE
*To live in integrity amidst the chaotic
winds of uncertainty.*

RELATIONSHIPS

You are gentle and giving in partnership, yet your relationships should be a place of mutual respect and clear boundaries. By seeking out partners who state their needs clearly and encourage
you to do the same, you will discover that true love never keeps you guessing.

The Journey of
OCTOBER 7

Welcome to October 7, a self-revealing journey that peels back the layers that weigh you down.

Own your *Power* (The Number Eight) within your relationships today. Although Libra season always inspires a bit of people-pleasing, try to work toward being deeply honest with yourself and the ones you trust, even if it brings up some discomfort, as you can build a deeper sense of intimacy with the people around you.

But be wary of *Negativity* (Eight of Swords). If you find your mind getting wrapped around worst-case scenarios or deeply held limiting beliefs, untangle yourself from these fears as you look for the simpler solution. By moving toward emotional expansion rather than mental contraction, you can begin to see your situation as half-full rather than nearly empty.

Because at the end of the day, *Hope* (The Star) is simply a shift in perspective. Rather than fretting over the past or feeling hung up on the relationships of yesterday, try to keep your heart reaching for a new light of optimism. The future is bright and unknown.

───────────────○───────────────

JUST FOR TODAY

TODAY'S MANTRA

While I may not have been entirely myself in the past, I can shine bright with enthusiasm today.

TODAY'S RITUAL

Find an image of something sparkling—it could be a night sky, a painting, a fun graphic—and set it as your phone background for the day. Whenever you find your mind drifting to something negative, use this image to remind yourself of the endless possibilities that come from being you.

TODAY'S JOURNAL PROMPT

What limiting beliefs do I hold about being myself when it comes to relationships with others?

───────────────○───────────────

BORN ON THIS DAY

TONI BRAXTON, American singer-songwriter, pianist, actor, and television personality

MARGARETHE LENORE SELENKA, German anthropologist, feminist, and peace activist

"Differences are not intended to separate, to alienate. We are different precisely in order to realize our need of one another."—DESMOND TUTU, South African Anglican cleric and theologian and anti-apartheid and human rights activist

The Journey of Those Born on
OCTOBER 7

You were born of social conviction and an unyielding loyalty that can lead to self-denial. You will have to believe in yourself at all costs, as your journey is one of self-affirmation, psychological freedom, and impenetrable optimism.

Early on in your journey, you will meet your mysterious guide, *Power* (The Number Eight). Despite your diplomatic nature, *Power* calls you away from codependent comfort and toward a path of radical self-embodiment. *Power* invites you to shed all the layers of superficiality that block you from revealing yourself to the partners and friends you hold dear, so you can discover the true intimacy that comes from being real.

But if you choose this enriching path, you will have to contend with *Negativity* (Eight of Swords). *Negativity* highlights the voice of victimhood that tries to disempower you through subconscious restrictions. You will meet *Negativity* within internal blockages, when the world is yours for the taking but a part of you holds back because you feel you don't deserve it. If you can untangle yourself from these destructive voices, you will discover an entirely new sense of freedom.

By answering these self-revealing calls, you will uncover the promise of *Hope* (The Star). *Hope* reminds you that the past has no hold on your future and encourages you to wipe your internal slate clean as you run toward the pure excitement you have about your life's potential. You will meet *Hope* in the sparkling light of a new relationship or idea, when you wash away your fears and ride the wave of divine optimism.

―――――――――――――――○―――――――――――――――

LIBRA
RULERS: VENUS, URANUS

PURPOSE
To forgo the superficial and believe deeply in the divine potential of authenticity.

RELATIONSHIPS

You are naturally equipped for compromise within partnership, and your relationships should be a place of unapologetic authenticity and spacious compassion. By seeking out partners who hold endless space for your truth as well as your growth, you will discover that true love is limitless.

The Journey of
OCTOBER 8

Welcome to October 8, a healing adventure that restores your faith in your intuition.

Get up and out of your emotional comfort zone today. *Experience* (The Number Nine) invites you to embrace change, so ask someone out or try a new activity with your partner. By stepping out on the ledge of uncertainty, you may just find the romantic breakthrough you were looking for.

But be gentle if some *Anxiety* (Nine of Swords) comes up along the way. Vulnerability is as scary as it gets, so hold your fears with complete compassion while detaching from the stories they tell you. The worst-case scenarios are always more dire within the walls of the mind, so get curious rather than frozen by these fears.

Go deeper. *Memory* (The Moon) invites you to view your triggers as a reflection of the unhealed experiences of the past, so do the therapeutic work required to integrate your history into the present. More than likely, by acknowledging the hurts and grief of yesterday, you can make room for new emotional freedom for tomorrow.

JUST FOR TODAY

TODAY'S MANTRA

By trying to understand rather than deny my subconscious fears, they will become infinitely less powerful.

TODAY'S JOURNAL PROMPT

If fear wasn't an issue, what intimate relationships would I like to explore further?

TODAY'S RITUAL

Look up what sign the moon is in today and whether it's in a cardinal (Aries, Cancer, Libra, Capricorn), fixed (Taurus, Leo, Scorpio, Aquarius), or mutable (Gemini, Virgo, Sagittarius, Pisces) sign. If it is cardinal, try to take an active approach in your healing today. If it is fixed, try to work through discomfort. If it is mutable, try to just go with the flow.

BORN ON THIS DAY

URVASHI VAID, American LGBTQ+ rights activist, lawyer, and writer

BRUNO MARS, American singer-songwriter, record producer, musician, and dancer

"The power of love is stronger than the love of power."—DORIS TWITCHELL ALLEN, American psychologist

The Journey of Those Born on
OCTOBER 8

You were born of romantic honesty and an emotional depth that can feel intimidating to some. You will have to move toward the fear that chains you, as your journey is one of growth, psychological processing, and divine intuition.

Early on in your journey, you will meet your worldly guide, *Experience* (The Number Nine). Despite your introspective nature, *Experience* calls you away from morbid reflection and toward a path of higher knowledge. By saying "yes" to every personal adventure that comes your way, whether it be a new relationship or an exciting creative endeavor, you can expand your consciousness.

But if you choose this widening path, you will have to grapple with *Anxiety* (Nine of Swords). *Anxiety* introduces you to the fear factory that lives in your mind, the voices that churn out story after story of what could go wrong in your life. Rather than believing every headline that it comes up with, take *Anxiety* as an opportunity to practice mindfulness as you try to see yourself and your partners more clearly.

> ### YOUR GUIDES
>
> *Astrology: Your Energy*
> Libra (Venus, Uranus)
>
> *Numerology: Your Path*
> Experience (The Number Nine)
>
> *Minor Arcana: Your Lesson*
> Anxiety (The Nine of Swords)
>
> *Major Arcana: Your Highest Calling*
> Instinct (The Moon)

By answering these calls for growth, you will discover the importance of *Memory* (The Moon). *Memory* invites you back to the past, to the relationships and experiences that shaped how you approach intimacy and creativity today. You will meet *Memory* when you shed light on what was so that you can gain clarity around what is, releasing the outdated fears and illusions that cloud your judgment. By processing and clarifying the lessons of *Memory*, you can make room for the wildness of intuition.

LIBRA
RULERS: VENUS, URANUS

PURPOSE
To forgo the superficial and believe deeply in the divine potential of authenticity.

RELATIONSHIPS

You are naturally equipped for compromise within partnership, and your relationships should be a place of unapologetic authenticity and spacious compassion. By seeking out partners who hold endless space for your truth as well as your growth, you will discover that true love is limitless.

The Journey of
OCTOBER 9

Welcome to October 9, a self-empowering journey that can help you inspire others.

Libra season can leave you seeking affirmation from others, but *Autonomy* (The Number One) asks you to have faith in yourself instead. Listen to your intuitive direction and follow it with as much self-confidence as you can muster. How would you approach your day if you were to trust yourself?

And work on confident communication. *Clarity* (Ace of Swords) reminds you of how powerful your words can be if you don't cloud them with people-pleasing or self-doubt. If you feel like you have a strong idea at work or have a breakthrough on a personal level, trust in that potential. More than likely, by believing in your genius, you won't have to debate anyone about the validity of your thoughts.

So bask in the light of your authentic spirit. *Vitality* (The Sun) encourages you to be yourself in every aspect of your life today, embracing the beautiful rainbow of color that lives within and expressing it to the world around you. Whether you dress in a way that's true to you or hold your head higher than usual, know that it is not just okay but important to shine.

JUST FOR TODAY

TODAY'S MANTRA
I don't need permission from anyone to believe in my authentic power.

TODAY'S RITUAL
Give yourself the validation you need today. On a sticky note or a piece of paper with some tape and write down at least one compliment you wish you would receive from someone else. Stick this note on a mirror that you frequently look into and read the compliment aloud to yourself throughout the day.

TODAY'S JOURNAL PROMPT
When in life did I first learn to doubt or question my thoughts or ideas?

BORN ON THIS DAY

GUILLERMO DEL TORO, Mexican film director, producer, screenwriter, and author

JOHN LENNON, English rock singer-songwriter

"Self-reliance is the fine road to independence."—MARY ANN SHADD CARY, American Canadian civil rights activist, suffragist, and cofounder of Canada's first anti-slavery newspaper

The Journey of Those Born on
OCTOBER 9

You were born of peaceful wisdom and an introversion that keeps your innermost feelings at arm's length from others. You will have to shed light on the beauty that lies within, as your journey is one of independence, communication, and authentic vulnerability.

Early on in your journey, you will meet your aspiring guide, *Autonomy* (The Number One). Despite your gentle disposition, *Autonomy* calls you away from self-doubt and toward a path of intuitive action. By moving to the beat of your own drum, rather than giving away your power to the opinion of others, you can carve out a unique legacy that others will profoundly respect.

If you choose this self-reliant path, you will meet your incisive friend, *Clarity* (Ace of Swords). *Clarity* encourages you to trust your intrinsic genius and teaches you not to mince words as you translate your thoughts in meaningful ways to the world around you. You will meet *Clarity* in the purity of a mental breakthrough, when you have the internal momentum you need to express your truth with personal conviction.

By answering these calls for self-confidence, you will step into the light of *Vitality* (The Sun). *Vitality* teaches you the importance of vulnerability, encouraging you to integrate your deepest sense of self into your conscious identity. You will meet *Vitality* when you feel good in your own skin, embracing every inch of your imperfectly perfect humanity. If you can choose self-acceptance over self-protection, you will shine bright with the irrefutable power of authenticity.

YOUR GUIDES

Astrology: Your Energy
Libra (Venus, Uranus)

Numerology: Your Path
Autonomy (The Number One)

Minor Arcana: Your Lesson
Clarity (The Ace of Swords)

Major Arcana: Your Highest Calling
Vitality (The Sun)

LIBRA
RULERS: VENUS, URANUS

PURPOSE
To never apologize for daring to shine so bright.

RELATIONSHIPS

You are tenderhearted yet guarded, and your relationships should be a place of self-embodiment and radical support. By seeking out partners who empower you to be independent while boosting your confidence within yourself, you will discover that true love always wants you to shine.

The Journey of
OCTOBER 10

Welcome to October 10, a grounding journey that helps you embrace the truth.

Amidst the romantically volatile portion of Libra season, seek *Balance* (The Number Two) throughout the day. Rather than jumping to emotional or intellectual extremes, try to meet others halfway by finding internal peace. There's no need to waste time in fruitless debate as long as you feel comfortable with your perspective.

But watch out for *Doubt* (Two of Swords). If you find yourself questioning your point of view and getting lost in the opinions of others, try to center yourself in your intuitive intellect. Remember that your feelings and opinions matter most when it comes to your personal and professional decisions.

Don't gloss over any difficult truths. *Awakening* (Judgment) encourages you to be radically honest with yourself today, so if you have been denying the reality of a less-than-ideal relationship or an aspect of society at large, now is the time to accept what is rather than trying to change it. By looking at your life through a sober, discerning lens, you can make conscious choices that will benefit you and others in the long run.

JUST FOR TODAY

TODAY'S MANTRA
Accepting reality is rarely easy, but it is always freeing.

TODAY'S JOURNAL PROMPT
What big decision have I been second-guessing myself on for quite some time?

TODAY'S RITUAL
Rub some peppermint oil or leaves between your palms. Inhale deeply as you repeat the affirmation, "Through sober eyes I can make sober decisions."

BORN ON THIS DAY

CHRISTOPHER OFILI, English painter and winner of the Turner Prize

CLARE HOLLINGWORTH, English journalist, author, and first war correspondent to report the outbreak of World War II

"The difficult is what takes a little time; the impossible is what takes a little longer."—FRIDTJOF NANSEN, Norwegian Arctic explorer and refugee advocate

The Journey of Those Born on
OCTOBER 10

You were born of creative ingenuity and an ever-changing identity that can leave you feeling like you have no solid ground to stand on. You will have to find internal stability within radical honesty, as your journey is one of steadiness, resolution, and higher truths.

Early on in your journey, you will meet your earthly guide, *Balance* (The Number Two). Despite your ambitious nature, *Balance* calls you away from unpredictability and toward a path of interpersonal reliability. By taking life slowly and realistically rather than all at once, you can show up for the partners and projects that you are loyal to.

If you choose this sturdy path, you will have to contend with *Doubt* (Two of Swords). You will meet *Doubt* at the crossroads of an important decision, when the answer to which direction you should choose feels murky and uncertain. *Doubt* asks you to consider the ramifications of your actions, so you can make thoughtful decisions that benefit you and others in the long run.

By answering these calls to slow down, you will find your true footing within *Awakening* (Judgment). *Awakening* invites you to accept and embrace the unaltered version of the human experience, encouraging you to open your eyes to the complicated and imperfect nature of life itself. You will meet *Awakening* in the discomfort of reality, when by shifting your lens toward the truth, you break the bubble of fantasy and skyrocket into a more conscious, sober state of mind. If you can choose growth over denial, you can build a life based on radical honesty.

YOUR GUIDES

Astrology: Your Energy
Libra (Venus, Uranus)

Numerology: Your Path
Balance (The Number Two)

Minor Arcana: Your Lesson
Doubt (The Two of Swords)

Major Arcana: Your Highest Calling
Awakening (Judgment)

LIBRA
RULERS: VENUS, URANUS

PURPOSE
To find emotional grounding in the inconvenient yet irrefutable truth.

RELATIONSHIPS

You are independent and sporadically romantic, so your relationships should be a place of grounded tranquility and realism. By seeking out partners who aren't afraid to tell it like it is while working to grow into a deeper sense of shared understanding, you will discover that true love can withstand the weight of reality.

The Journey of
OCTOBER 11

W elcome to October 11, an enlightening journey of interpersonal growth.

Aim for *Flexibility* (The Number Three) rather than rigidity today by picking the brains and exploring the perspectives of those you are curious about. Whether you put together a task force at work or invite some friends out to dinner, be sure you are listening rather than trying to dominate the conversation.

But be gentle with yourself if you stumble upon a *Trigger* (Three of Swords). Amidst the social nature of Libra season, if you have a tough interaction with another person that pokes at an old wound, take a step back and evaluate what you have to learn from this deep hurt. By talking out your feelings with a trusted friend, therapist, or ancestor, you can begin to heal in ways you never expected.

And remember, imperfection is part of the human condition. *Perspective* (The World) invites you to have grace for yourself and others today. By taking a long walk in nature or sitting somewhere with a beautiful view, you can zoom out and see how the highs and lows of your growth journey connect you with the rest of humankind.

JUST FOR TODAY

TODAY'S MANTRA

I'll never know what someone else is going through, so I best extend them the grace I wish others would give me.

TODAY'S JOURNAL PROMPT

When my feelings are hurt, what are a few practical ways I can care for myself?

TODAY'S RITUAL

If you are in conversation with someone, when they are done sharing their perspective, repeat what you heard, saying, "So what I hear you saying is _____," and ask them if you understood them correctly. You might be amazed at what gets lost in translation.

BORN ON THIS DAY

AMITABH BACHCHAN, Indian actor, film producer, and politician

MARÍA ADELA GARD DE ANTOKOLETZ, Argentine human rights activist and cofounder of the Mothers of the Plaza de Mayo movement

"The future belongs to those who believe in the beauty of their dreams."—ELEANOR ROOSE-VELT, American diplomat, activist, and thirty-second first lady of the United States

The Journey of Those Born on
OCTOBER 11

You were born of diplomatic genius and a sense of fairness that can border on righteousness. You will have to zoom out to make peace with others, as your journey is one of learning, emotional release, and deep gratitude.

Early on in your journey, you will meet your free-thinking guide, *Flexibility* (The Number Three). Despite your strong code of ethics, *Flexibility* calls you away from dogmatism and toward a path of open-minded education. By putting yourself in other people's shoes, you can expand your perspective and grow through being in relationship with others.

But if you choose this people-oriented path, you will have to contend with *Trigger* (Three of Swords). You will meet *Trigger* when you are in the throes of emotional heartache, when a relationship or conversation did not go the way you had planned. Instead of getting lost in morbid reflection or hanging on to resentment, *Trigger* assures you that pain is a necessary part of growth, reminding you that this, too, shall pass.

By answering these enlightening calls, you will begin to find *Perspective* (The World). *Perspective* lies within the big picture, when you draw yourself out of the day-to-day pettiness of drama so that you can see the grand beauty of the human experience. *Perspective* invites you to see meaning in every peak and valley of your evolution so that you can support others in their quest for self-realization. If you can appreciate that we are all on a journey without a finite destination, you'll learn how to accept people where they are.

YOUR GUIDES

Astrology: Your Energy
Libra (Venus, Uranus)

Numerology: Your Path
Flexibility (The Number Three)

Minor Arcana: Your Lesson
Trigger (The Three of Swords)

Major Arcana: Your Highest Calling
Perspective (The World)

LIBRA
RULERS: VENUS, URANUS

PURPOSE
To take a step back and fall in love with the imperfections of the human condition.

RELATIONSHIPS

You are diplomatic and fair in partnership, and your relationships should be a place of strong communication and higher understanding. By seeking out partners who push you to grow and aren't afraid of tough conversations, you will discover that true love helps you see things from a different perspective.

The Journey of
OCTOBER 12

Welcome to October 12, a grounded journey that asks you to consider how you spend your creative energy.

Find your focus through *Discipline* (The Number Four) today. While Libra season can inspire artistic and romantic idealism, try to show the universe just how serious you are about your future by putting in the time and effort required to master your craft. Whether you check some mundane things off your to-do list or take a bite out of that huge project, be sure you execute your tasks with integrity.

But don't rush to start any new endeavors. *Restoration* (Four of Swords) reminds you how important it is to rest between efforts, so take some time today to consider how low you are on energy and what you might need to refuel for the future. What does self-care mean to you today?

Because at the heart of the matter, you are the CEO of your life. Zoom out and look at your creative and personal ambitions, asking where you might need to pull back and where it is important for you to invest more. Only you know what is best, and *Self-mastery* (The Emperor) empowers you to make objective decisions today that consider your long-term health and well-being.

———————————————◯———————————————

JUST FOR TODAY

TODAY'S MANTRA
Without a plan, my creative inspiration can never get off the ground.

TODAY'S JOURNAL PROMPT
How well have I been taking care of my holistic health as of late?

TODAY'S RITUAL
Organize your calendar into four-hour increments in which you'll execute your responsibilities. Between each of these work sessions, schedule ten minutes of pause. As you take these breaks, ask yourself what kind of energetic refueling (e.g., food, a supportive hug, an encouraging phone call) you need to carry out your next increment of work.

———————————————◯———————————————

BORN ON THIS DAY

HUGH JACKMAN, Australian actor and singer

DIANA ABGAR, Armenian writer, humanitarian, and first Armenian female diplomat

"People think I'm disciplined. It is not discipline. It is devotion. There is a great difference."
—LUCIANO PAVAROTTI, Italian operatic tenor

The Journey of Those Born on
OCTOBER 12

You were born of romantic abundance and a creative adaptability that can leave you feeling ungrounded most of the time. You will have to anchor yourself in integrity, as your journey is one of hard work, reevaluation, and self-respect.

Early on in your journey, you will meet your authoritative guide, *Discipline* (The Number Four). Despite your curious nature, *Discipline* calls you away from distractions and toward a path of hard-earned esteem. Back up your aspirations with thorough action, never resting on your laurels as you slowly but surely climb your way to indisputable mountaintops of success.

If you choose this consequential path, you will have to pay respect to *Restoration* (Four of Swords). *Restoration* asks you to pause between victories to replenish the emotional, physical, and spiritual fuel lost along the way. You will meet *Restoration* in moments of intentional time off, when you pull yourself out of the race and consider what it is you are ultimately looking to accomplish.

By answering these calls for intentionality, you will begin to embody the power of *Self-mastery* (The Emperor). *Self-mastery* inspires the rational, thoughtful authority that lives within, encouraging you to act from a place of reason rather than romantic idealism. By harnessing your creative and emotional power, keeping your soul deeply rooted in reality, you can channel your artistic genius into a higher purpose.

YOUR GUIDES

Astrology: Your Energy
Libra (Venus, Uranus)

Numerology: Your Path
Discipline (The Number Four)

Minor Arcana: Your Lesson
Restoration (The Four of Swords)

Major Arcana: Your Highest Calling
Self-mastery (The Emperor)

LIBRA
RULERS: VENUS, URANUS

PURPOSE
To root creativity in integrity and romance in reality.

RELATIONSHIPS

You are a romantic charmer and natural people person, but your relationships should be a place of deep respect and anchoring. By seeking out partners who root you in integrity and are never fooled by the whims of passion, you will discover that true love reminds you of what really matters.

The Journey of
OCTOBER 13

Welcome to October 13, a sage journey that helps you find your voice.

Speak up for what you believe in most today. *Courage* (The Number Five) invites you to tell the world what you're thinking, whether you do it through the written or spoken word or a creative project. It's time to share your truth and believe in the power of vulnerability.

But remember that honesty requires compassion. To channel the diplomatic nature of Libra season, *Maturity* (Five of Swords) asks you to choose your words wisely, making sure you convey your message without hurting others or damaging important relationships. If you feel yourself overcome with passion, take a second to breathe deeply and consider the impact of your words.

Because at the end of the day, everyone is entitled to their own experience. *Wisdom* (The Hierophant) reminds you that although your message is deeply important and valid, it doesn't cancel out other people's perspectives, and vice versa. Rather than getting lost in a war of opinions, tap into your sense of personal authority by listening to others while staying true to yourself. There is a balance between humility and confidence, so try to find the middle ground.

───────────────○───────────────

JUST FOR TODAY

TODAY'S MANTRA

I can be radically brave and deeply compassionate at the same time.

TODAY'S JOURNAL PROMPT

Do I tend to think before I speak? If not, how could I begin to practice more mindfulness with the words I say?

TODAY'S RITUAL

If passion or anger come up today, scream into a pillow for a minimum of five seconds to release some of that energy. If you find that your brain is still stewing on some old resentments, write down all the things you'd like to say to someone or something without holding anything back, and then rip up the paper and recycle it.

───────────────○───────────────

BORN ON THIS DAY

ARNA BONTEMPS, American poet, writer, librarian, and member of the Harlem Renaissance

SACHA BARON COHEN, English comedian and actor

"Give people the respect of your honest opinion, and always meet them where they're at."
—ALEXANDRIA OCASIO-CORTEZ, American politician and activist

The Journey of Those Born on
OCTOBER 13

Y ou were born of an emotional strength that often masks the difficulties you have endured. You will have to discover the power within vulnerability, as your journey is one of self-expression, thoughtfulness, and personal authority.

Early on in your journey, you will meet your inspired guide, *Courage* (The Number Five). Despite your humble nature, *Courage* calls you away from playing it small and toward a path of radical self-embodiment. By standing up and speaking out for what you believe, you can change the hearts and minds of many through your diplomatic genius.

But if you choose this public path, you will have to heed the warnings of *Maturity* (Five of Swords). *Maturity* asks you to be deeply careful with your words, reminding you that to get your point across, you must not get lost in the messy drama of battle. Instead, harness the strategy of communication, using your speech to incite great change rather than unnecessary conflict.

By answering these calls for bravery, you will begin to channel *Wisdom* (The Hierophant). The truth is highly subjective, so have grace and understanding for even your most adversarial opponents. You will meet *Wisdom* within humble self-confidence, when you are able to hold open space for the opinions of another without letting it rock you from your sense of certainty. If you can stand your ground while gracefully participating in the ethical debates of our time, you can be a voice of *Wisdom*.

YOUR GUIDES

Astrology: Your Energy
Libra (Venus, Mercury)

Numerology: Your Path
Courage (The Number Five)

Minor Arcana: Your Lesson
Maturity (The Five of Swords)

Major Arcana: Your Highest Calling
Wisdom (The Hierophant)

LIBRA
RULERS: VENUS, MERCURY

PURPOSE
To balance the courage of conviction with the courage of compassion.

RELATIONSHIPS

You are as emotionally grounded as they come, and your relationships should be a place of complete support and encouragement. By seeking out partners who inspire you to think and speak for yourself and champion your individuality, you will discover that true love never tries to quiet your voice.

The Journey of

OCTOBER 14

Welcome to October 14, a soul-led journey that asks you to consider who you want in your corner.

Rather than approaching your day with logic, soften to what your heart desires. *Devotion* (The Number Six) invites you to channel the romantic side of Libra season by prioritizing the relationships and creative endeavors that nourish your innermost needs.

But there may be some important emotional clearing you must do today. *Transition* (Six of Swords) asks you to do the harder, scarier thing of letting go of the mental and psychological patterns that aren't serving you any longer. Know that this shedding can free you for a more fulfilling existence.

Choice (The Lovers) reminds you that you have agency over who you let into your circle, so take thoughtful inventory of what partners, friends, and personal behaviors are in your highest and best interests. Take some time to connect with your internal world rather than dwelling on who isn't showing up. You are the lover and friend you've been searching for, so treat yourself accordingly.

JUST FOR TODAY

TODAY'S MANTRA

I'd rather build intimacy with myself than keep the company of those who don't have my back.

TODAY'S JOURNAL PROMPT

What are six traits that I tend to admire in others? Do these traits exist in myself? How can I nurture them?

TODAY'S RITUAL

Go near a body of water today, ideally the ocean. If you aren't near one, draw a bath or turn on the shower. As you mindfully stare at the water, repeat the spell, "Healing water, please help me free the internal patterns that are no longer serving me."

BORN ON THIS DAY

GEORGE FLOYD, American man murdered while restrained by Minneapolis police whose dying words, "I can't breathe," became a rallying cry at US protests against police brutality

NATALIE MAINES, American country musician

"Love, by its very nature, is unworldly, and it is for this reason rather than its rarity that it is not only apolitical but anti-political, perhaps the most powerful of all anti-political forces."—HANNAH ARENDT, German political philosopher and author

The Journey of Those Born on
OCTOBER 14

Y ou were born of the strength of compassion and a level of acceptance for others that can be mistaken for passivity. You will have to show the world the irrefutable force of love, as your journey is one of tenderness, transition, and radical empathy.

Early on in your journey, you will meet your gentle guide, *Devotion* (The Number Six). To channel your purpose-driven nature, *Devotion* calls you away from complacency and toward a path of deep meaning. Lead from the heart rather than the head and carve out a soul-led legacy that will leave a lasting imprint on the human experience.

But if you choose this path of sincerity, you will have to make friends with *Transition* (Six of Swords). *Transition* reminds you that an honest life requires change, inspiring you to let go of who you once were so you can grow freely toward the person you are meant to become. You will meet *Transition* in times of deep, internal uncertainty, when you walk the tightrope between grief and hope.

By answering these calls to meaningful action, you will uncover the healing nuance of *Choice* (The Lovers). *Choice* reflects who you are and what you stand for, inspiring you to make decisions that serve your emotional best interests. You will meet *Choice* in empathy, when you recognize the universal threads of humanity that connect us all, while maintaining the boundaries you need to protect your heart. If you can balance self-love with your love for others, *Choice* offers you a life of eternal meaning.

LIBRA
RULERS: VENUS, MERCURY

PURPOSE
*To find the purpose within love
and the love within purpose.*

RELATIONSHIPS

You are self-reliant yet diplomatic, and your relationships should be a place of unconditional support and gentle nurturing. By seeking out partners who generously give their heart without expectation of return, you will discover that true love mirrors your inherent value.

The Journey of
OCTOBER 15

W elcome to October 15, a fulfilling journey that empowers you to focus on what you do have, rather than what you don't.

Libra season can err on the side of idealism, but *Commitment* (The Number Seven) asks you what it is you truly want to invest in. Whether you tend to the health of a long-term relationship or work steadily toward a creative endeavor that you want to see come to fruition, now is the time to align your actions with your loyalties.

But beware of *Hypervigilance* (Seven of Swords). In the age of social media, it is all too easy to get lost in comparison and drown in the sorrows of what others have. Instead of falling for this trap, connect with yourself offline and consider what it is that makes you feel deeply content. More than likely, by detaching from all the noise, you can remember what nourishes your soul.

And when you let go of any fears of not-enoughness, you can work on your long-term *Evolution* (The Chariot). Spend the day devoting yourself to the person you are becoming, putting in the small yet meaningful efforts that will one day amount to your undisputable success. By laying the building blocks for your future, you can make meaningful progress.

———————————————— ○ ————————————————

JUST FOR TODAY

TODAY'S MANTRA
My definition of success is deeply personal and can't be compared to others'.

TODAY'S RITUAL
Put seven-minute time controls on your computer and phone to limit how long you spend on social media. Better yet, if you are able, don't log in to these platforms at all today. Rather than losing time comparing yourself to others, connect with yourself.

TODAY'S JOURNAL PROMPT
Who am I "jealous" of? What do they have that I fear I am lacking?

———————————————— ○ ————————————————

BORN ON THIS DAY

TERESA BILLINGTON-GREIG, English suffragist and cofounder of the Women's Freedom League

KIKO MIZUHARA, Korean American model, actor, singer, and designer

"That which does not kill us makes us stronger."—FRIEDRICH NIETZSCHE, German philosopher and writer

The Journey of Those Born on
OCTOBER 15

You were born of romantic compassion and a penchant for self-destruction that goes unnoticed by many. You will have to find healing within purpose, as your journey is one of discernment, radical trust, and hard-earned progress.

Early on in your journey, you will meet your serious guide, *Commitment* (The Number Seven). Despite your endless emotional capacity, *Commitment* calls you away from overextension and toward a path of clear direction. Examine what it is you truly care about, so you can avoid distraction and invest in your future.

But if you answer this call for maturity, you will have to contend with *Hypervigilance* (Seven of Swords). You will meet *Hypervigilance* when you are plotting and protecting your success, obsessively looking over your shoulder to see what your competitors are up to and what you might be missing. *Hypervigilance* asks you to turn your gaze inward, shutting off the hustle and scarcity that comes from comparison, so you can discover that true abundance comes from spiritual contentment.

By answering these calls for personal discretion, you will learn how to move with *Evolution* (The Chariot). *Evolution* asks you to devote yourself to the work at hand, never minding the results and finding purpose in the humility of discipline. By putting your most earnest foot forward and leaving your success up to fate, *Evolution* rewards you with unexpected success and sudden breakthroughs. If you can keep your efforts in the present, *Evolution* will take care of your brilliant future.

YOUR GUIDES

Astrology: Your Energy
Libra (Venus, Mercury)

Numerology: Your Path
Commitment (The Number Seven)

Minor Arcana: Your Lesson
Hypervigilance (The Seven of Swords)

Major Arcana: Your Highest Calling
Evolution (The Chariot)

LIBRA
RULERS: VENUS, MERCURY

PURPOSE
To find true fulfillment in the here and now.

RELATIONSHIPS

You are emotionally giving yet fearful of receiving, so your relationships should be a place of mutual trust and investment. By seeking out partners who are in it for the long haul and willing to put the work in required to grow together, you will discover that true love gets better with time.

The Journey of
OCTOBER 16

Welcome to October 16, a revealing journey that's about showing you who you really are when you aren't trying to be perfect.

Despite the socially pleasing nature of Libra season, *Power* (The Number Eight) invites you to discover your authentic nature. If you believe that certain parts of your truth are unlovable or unacceptable, begin to unveil these aspects of yourself to the people you trust. By being deeply vulnerable with yourself, you can inspire others to show up the same way.

But be aware of *Negativity* (Eight of Swords). If being honest or self-revealing hasn't worked out for you in the past, try not to let your mind convince you of all the reasons that might happen again. By witnessing while detaching from your fears, you can walk bravely into the unknown.

Because remember, through self-acceptance, you can handle anything. *Resilience* (Strength) invites you to dive in to the emotional depth of this day with openheartedness, allowing yourself to be tender and strong at the same time. If you are engaging in a vulnerable exchange with another person or with yourself, don't be afraid to admit your weaknesses and fears. You might just discover that this is where your true power lies.

JUST FOR TODAY

TODAY'S MANTRA

No one and nothing can diminish my power of authentic vulnerability.

TODAY'S JOURNAL PROMPT

When I have been vulnerable with my loved ones in the past, how have they reacted?

TODAY'S RITUAL

Try practicing vulnerability with yourself in the mirror. Speak aloud one truth about yourself that you fear others won't accept and try responding to yourself in a loving and encouraging manner. If you find you are not able to access this self-compassion, give yourself a warm hug instead.

BORN ON THIS DAY

BESSIE RISCHBIETH, Australian feminist and social activist

EUGENE O'NEILL, American playwright and Nobel Prize winner in literature

"You just gotta keep going and fighting for everything, and one day you'll get to where you want."—NAOMI OSAKA, Japanese tennis player

The Journey of Those Born on
OCTOBER 16

You were born of creative focus and an unpredictable emotional nature that can throw you off course. You will have to dig deep to find your grounding, as your journey is one of self-honesty, psychological opening, and emotional fortitude.

Early on in your journey, you will meet your mysterious guide, *Power* (The Number Eight). Despite your social charm, *Power* calls you away from niceties and toward a path of radical authenticity. You'll need to peel back the layers of people-pleasing that block you from the enigmatic force of nature that lives within. If you can choose to be real rather than liked, you'll tap into the gift of self-acknowledgment.

But if you choose this dynamic path, you will have to contend with *Negativity* (Eight of Swords). You will meet *Negativity* in the traps of the mind, when you subconsciously corner yourself into believing that there is no way out of your present circumstances. Instead of believing all the stories that your mind tells you, practice mindfulness as you detach from the destructive patterns of your brain and unlock the gates of personal freedom.

YOUR GUIDES

Astrology: Your Energy
Libra (Venus, Mercury)

Numerology: Your Path
Power (The Number Eight)

Minor Arcana: Your Lesson
Negativity (The Eight of Swords)

Major Arcana: Your Highest Calling
Resilience (Strength)

By answering these transformative calls, you will uncover your capacity for *Resilience* (Strength). *Resilience* introduces you to the limitless personal strength that lives within, inviting you to harness your passion toward self-realization rather than self-destruction. You will meet *Resilience* when you hit an emotional and spiritual bottom, only to discover that within the lowest of lows lies your infinite potential for growth.

LIBRA
RULERS: VENUS, MERCURY

PURPOSE
To view personal bottoms as a divine opportunity to begin again.

RELATIONSHIPS

You are prone to overcommitting in partnership, so your relationships should be a place of transcendent intimacy and divine trust. By seeking out partners who aim to grow together emotionally and psychologically, rather than getting hung up on societal expectations, you will discover that true love is a spiritual union.

The Journey of
OCTOBER 17

Welcome to October 17, an expansive journey that awakens you to your intuitive power. *Experience* (The Number Nine) invites you to look outward into the unknown today. Although Libra season can make you want to stick within your comfort zone, pursue someone or something that feels curious and foreign to you, or invest in a new creative endeavor that throws you into uncharted territory.

But give yourself some grace if *Anxiety* (Nine of Swords) comes up at any point. If you find yourself overwhelmed with the prospect of uncertainty, and your brain begins firing up its factory of worst-case scenarios, take a step back from the hustle and bustle and hold yourself with gentle understanding. Where is this fear coming from?

More than likely, through self-compassion, you can tap into a new level of bravery by getting in touch with your *Instinct* (The Hermit). Today's journey requires radical self-trust, making it a wonderful time to quiet the outside world and listen deeply to yourself. There are no hard-and-fast rules for how you should navigate the winding expansion this day, so look within, follow your intuitive compass, and be open to wherever it takes you.

———————————————○———————————————

JUST FOR TODAY

TODAY'S MANTRA

Adventure exists within the wildness of my soul.

TODAY'S RITUAL

Gain some unexpected knowledge by going to your local public library and walking through an aisle of subjects you would normally pass by. Close your eyes, grab a book at random, and if you are able, sit down and read it, or check it out. If you are not able, look it up online to get the general synopsis.

TODAY'S JOURNAL PROMPT

What is the biggest fear that comes up for me when I think about doing something new completely alone?

———————————————○———————————————

BORN ON THIS DAY

EMINEM, American rapper, songwriter, and record producer

NIRMALA DESHPANDE, Indian social activist

"Never be limited by other people's limited imaginations."—MAE C. JEMISON, American physician, engineer, and astronaut and first Black woman in space

The Journey of Those Born on
OCTOBER 17

You were born of limitless mercurial creativity and a desire for intimacy that, without caution, can leave you emotionally enmeshed with others. You will have to find the support you need from within, as your journey is one of expansion, psychological freedom, and internal intelligence.

Early on in your journey, you will meet your expansive guide, *Experience* (The Number Nine). Despite your introspective nature, *Experience* calls you away from the comforts of your mind and toward a path that teaches you to learn by doing. You will meet *Experience* when your consciousness shifts through embracing the wild unknown, when you choose growth over security.

But if you choose this ever-changing path, you will have to contend with *Anxiety* (Nine of Swords). You will meet *Anxiety* in the mental rabbit holes of fear, when your brain latches on to worst-case scenarios rather than searching for possibilities. By recognizing that this fearful thinking is a self-protective coping mechanism, you can find self-compassion.

By answering these spacious calls, you will come to rely on the power of *Instinct* (The Hermit). *Instinct* asks you to create a healthy sense of mental, emotional, or physical isolation so you can drown out the rest of the world and listen to the sound of your intuitive genius. *Instinct* gently guides you through the winding haze of your journey, step by step, leading you through the discomfort of uncertainty. If you can follow *Instinct* rather than fear, you can reach your highest destiny.

YOUR GUIDES

Astrology: Your Energy
Libra (Venus, Mercury)

Numerology: Your Path
Experience (The Number Nine)

Minor Arcana: Your Lesson
Anxiety (The Nine of Swords)

Major Arcana: Your Highest Calling
Instinct (The Hermit)

LIBRA
RULERS: VENUS, MERCURY

PURPOSE
To create a deeply intimate relationship with the intelligence of intuition.

RELATIONSHIPS

You are deep yet emotionally protective, but your relationships should be a place of radical compassion and higher understanding. By seeking out partners who expand your point of view while holding space for your fears of the unknown, you will discover that true love can open your eyes to new possibilities.

The Journey of
OCTOBER 18

Welcome to October 18, an unexpected journey that asks you to believe in fate as much as you believe in yourself.

As you navigate the interpersonal nature of Libra season, *Autonomy* (The Number One) invites you to create a deeper relationship with yourself instead. Take yourself on a date, listen to your favorite music, and by all means, do whatever it is you feel like doing. By acting on your intuition, you can strengthen that divine muscle.

And while you're at it, pay some respect for your innate genius as *Clarity* (Ace of Swords) encourages you to believe in your next greatest idea. Whether you have an ah-ha moment in your career or a breakthrough realization about your relationship, be sure to bring what is in your mind into the present moment.

But let the day unfold as it will. *Impermanence* (Wheel of Fortune) invites you to make friends with fate, trusting that even if the days seem like a loss on paper, the universe has a greater plan for you that will make complete sense in hindsight. Look for the good in each unexpected twist and turn that comes your way, making lemonade from life's juiciest lemons.

———————————○———————————

JUST FOR TODAY

TODAY'S MANTRA
By being completely true to myself, I can coconspire with my date, destiny.

TODAY'S JOURNAL PROMPT
What could taking a chance on my ideas look like today?

TODAY'S RITUAL
Get in touch with your internal genius by speaking out loud to yourself for one minute somewhere private. It may be uncomfortable at first but see what flows out of your mouth and try not to overthink what you say.

———————————○———————————

BORN ON THIS DAY

FREIDA PINTO, Indian actor

ZAC EFRON, American actor and singer

"We must work to preserve humanitarianism and to ensure that our planet is a safer and more suitable place in which to live. Essentially, we are all human beings who share a common fate."
—HAYA RASHED AL-KHALIFA, Bahrani lawyer, diplomat, Bahrain's first female ambassador, and the third female president of the United Nations General Assembly

The Journey of Those Born on
OCTOBER 18

You were born of sweet wisdom and a hidden depth that you do not trust to share with many. You will have to learn to bring your innate brilliance to the surface, as your journey is one of self-trust, free thinking, and karmic destiny.

Early on in your journey, you will meet your fearless guide, *Autonomy* (The Number One). Despite your observational nature, *Autonomy* calls you out from behind the scenes and toward a path of creative leadership. You will meet *Autonomy* when you strike out on your own, feeling the full spectrum of fear but doing it anyway.

If you choose this ambitious path, you will learn to work with *Clarity* (Ace of Swords). You will meet *Clarity* in the excitement of a good idea, when you forgo caution and manifest your internal breakthroughs into reality. *Clarity* asks you to steer clear of the mental traps of overanalysis and self-doubt, and instead, devote yourself deeply to the potential of your vision.

By answering these uninhibited calls to action, you will have to respect the laws of *Impermanence* (Wheel of Fortune). You will meet *Impermanence* when, by taking the road less traveled, you'll find yourself traversing the peaks and the valleys of the human experience, discovering value in even the toughest of circumstances. *Impermanence* invites you to be an active participant on the uncontrolled journey of fate, surrendering yourself spiritually to the fact that nothing lasts forever and yet nothing happens by chance.

YOUR GUIDES

Astrology: Your Energy
Libra (Venus, Mercury)

Numerology: Your Path
Autonomy (The Number One)

Minor Arcana: Your Lesson
Clarity (The Ace of Swords)

Major Arcana: Your Highest Calling
Impermanence (The Wheel of Fortune)

LIBRA
RULERS: VENUS, MERCURY

PURPOSE
To accept that true bravery looks like letting go.

RELATIONSHIPS

You are deeply compassionate yet unexpectedly private, and your relationships should be a place of individuality and mutual support. By seeking out partners who know how to fill their own emotional cup and inspire you to dance to the beat of your own dream, you will discover that true love just wants you to be yourself.

The Journey of
OCTOBER 19

Welcome to October 19, a diplomatic journey that centers you in the truth.

Reach for *Balance* (The Number Two) today. If you find yourself speaking out of turn or rushing through your work, take a deep, calming breath and slow down. Nothing needs to be rushed or forced, so pare back your responsibilities where you can and approach today with a sense of internal peace.

And while Libra season encourages you to see both sides of every decision, look out for *Doubt* (Two of Swords). If you are faced with a crossroads in your personal or professional life, don't get too hung up on making the perfect choice because there simply is no such thing today. More than likely, you don't have all the information you need, so rely on your intuition to decipher the best possible outcome.

All will end well, as long as you are prioritizing your moral *Truth* (Justice). Today encourages you to speak in accordance with your personal values, so consider the long-term consequences of your words. Whether you stay true to the people to whom you are loyal in conversation or speak up against a global issue, remember that what you do and what you say matters.

JUST FOR TODAY

TODAY'S MANTRA

What I don't say is as important as what I do say.

TODAY'S JOURNAL PROMPT

What personal, local, or global cause means a lot to me? How can I use my words to spread awareness?

TODAY'S RITUAL

Get your hands on some lavender (for peace) and sage (for wisdom). Rub them between your palms or place them in a bowl of water. As you inhale, repeat the affirmation, "My moral center keeps me balanced."

BORN ON THIS DAY

BINALAKSHMI NEPRAM, Indian humanitarian, author, and activist

REBECCA FERGUSON, Swedish actor

"Rise and demand; you are a burning flame. You are sure to conquer there where the final horizon Becomes a drop of blood, a drop of life, Where you will carry the universe on your shoulders, Where the universe will bear your hope."—MIGUEL ÁNGEL ASTURIAS, Guatemalan Nobel Prize–winning poet, diplomat, novelist, playwright, and journalist

The Journey of Those Born on
OCTOBER 19

Y ou were born of creative vitality and a zest for life that can burn you out when taken to extremes. You will have to simplify and focus on the issues that matter most, as your journey is one of equilibrium, intuitive action, and moral truth.

Early on in your journey, you will meet your tranquil guide, *Balance* (The Number Two). Despite your ambitious nature, *Balance* calls you away from overdoing it and toward a path of thoughtful prioritization. By considering where your energy is best utilized, rather than trying to take on everything at once, you can sustain your creative genius for the long haul.

But if you take this harmonious path, you will have to contend with *Doubt* (Two of Swords). You will meet *Doubt* when you are faced with a tough decision and don't have all the information you might need to make it. *Doubt* invites you to consider what you can, balancing your rational mind with intuition instead of losing sleep over making the perfect choice. By trusting yourself, you can't go wrong.

By answering these diplomatic calls, you will learn to honor your sense of *Truth* (Justice). *Truth* reveals the moral centeredness that lives within, helping you align your actions with your innate sense of right and wrong. *Truth* asks you to thoughtfully and consciously consider how you are impacting the people and places you belong to, inspiring you to live by your code of personal ethics. By seeking to be fair rather than right, you can make the world a more peaceful place.

LIBRA
RULERS: VENUS, MERCURY

PURPOSE
To slowly pare away unnecessary distractions to find a truthful moral purpose.

RELATIONSHIPS

You are bold and expressive in matters of the heart, and your relationships should be a place of balanced communication and easeful harmony. By seeking out partners who don't jump to conclusions in conflict and seek to live in peaceful coexistence with you, you will discover that true love is a soft place to land.

The Journey of
OCTOBER 20

Welcome to October 20, an enriching journey of pleasure and worthiness.

Despite the partnership-driven nature of Libra season, expand your perspective through friendship and community. *Flexibility* (The Number Three) reminds you how much there is to learn if you are willing to engage with new people, so take that new coworker out to lunch or enroll in a class with like-minded folks.

But watch out for *Trigger* (Three of Swords). If you find that the words or actions of another provoke hurt feelings or emotional tenderness, try to go inward rather than lashing out. More than likely, they poked at a sensitive part of you, presenting you with a crucial opportunity to heal a past heartache by holding yourself with gentle compassion.

And from there, open yourself to receiving the *Abundance* (The Empress) of the day. If an unexpected gift or compliment comes your way, try your best to accept it with open arms. But rather than waiting for others to fill your cup, seek out a nourishing and self-appreciative experience, like walking in a gorgeous park and indulging in your favorite meal. Let yourself enjoy some sweetness, knowing that you are worthy of such plenty.

JUST FOR TODAY

TODAY'S MANTRA
I can open myself, even just a little bit, to receiving some joy today.

TODAY'S JOURNAL PROMPT
What historical wounds do I have around friendship?

TODAY'S RITUAL
Close your eyes and imagine your perfect place, one that feels nourishing, safe, and downright happy. What would it look like, and what would it contain? This place can be completely made up, so don't limit yourself within the confines of reality. Whenever you find yourself feeling scarce today, close your eyes and transport yourself to this place.

BORN ON THIS DAY

JOHN DEWEY, American philosopher, educational theorist, and writer

PATRICIA VERDUGO, Chilean journalist, writer, and human rights activist

"That's why breaking those barriers is worth it. As much as anything else, it is also to create that path for those who will come after us."—KAMALA HARRIS, American politician, attorney, and first female, first Black, and first Asian American vice president of the United States

The Journey of Those Born on
OCTOBER 20

You were born of fierce diplomacy and an innate sense of responsibility that can lead to unnecessary burden. You will have to learn to let go and enjoy the sweetness in life, as your journey is one of curiosity, internal healing, and spiritual abundance.

Early on in your journey, you will meet your friendly guide, *Flexibility* (The Number Three). Although you may feel the most natural in a one-on-one partnership, *Flexibility* invites you to grow your support network by socially expanding. By opening yourself to the perspective-shifting and humor-inducing aspects of friendship, you can discover how to go with the flow and enjoy the company of many.

But if you take this sociable path, you will have to contend with *Trigger* (Three of Swords). You will meet *Trigger* within hurt feelings, when the words of a friend or foe pierce right at an unhealed wound. Rather than jumping to conclusions, *Trigger* invites you inward to address the hurts that were provoked. You must hold others accountable for their actions, but *Trigger* empowers you to be responsible for your reaction.

> ### YOUR GUIDES
>
> *Astrology: Your Energy*
> Libra (Venus, Mercury)
>
> *Numerology: Your Path*
> Flexibility (The Number Three)
>
> *Minor Arcana: Your Lesson*
> Trigger (The Three of Swords)
>
> *Major Arcana: Your Highest Calling*
> Abundance (The Empress)

By answering these calls for connection, you will open yourself to *Abundance* (The Empress). *Abundance* invites you to enjoy the fruits of your labor rather than getting bogged down in societal expectation. You will meet *Abundance* in the beauty of nature or the smile of a loved one, when you take the time to soak in the plentiful wonder of the present moment. If you can grow to accept the generosity and gifts that come your way, *Abundance* shows you how worthy you are of receiving.

───────────○───────────

LIBRA
RULERS: VENUS, MERCURY

PURPOSE
*To share burdens with loved ones
to create room for joy and pleasure.*

RELATIONSHIPS

You take partnership quite seriously, yet your relationships should be a place of community and effortless fun. By seeking out partners who help you lighten your emotional load through laughter and shared friendship, you will discover that true love feels like a breath of fresh air.

The Journey of

OCTOBER 21

Welcome to October 21, a humble journey that requires thoughtful action.

Despite the airy and romantic nature of Libra season, *Discipline* (The Number Four) asks you to keep your feet firmly planted in the work that today requires. Whether you show up for the personal or professional responsibilities you have today, be sure to bring your complete attention and integrity to everything you do.

But don't take on more than you can handle. Instead, make time for *Restoration* (Four of Swords), letting your mind cool off and restore itself before climbing the next mountain. Lie down for a few minutes, take off your shoes, and by all means, take a nap if you can afford it. By stopping the hustle for even a little while, you can discover that nothing meaningful comes from burnout.

And be a thoughtful leader toward yourself as you navigate today. *Self-mastery* (The Emperor) reminds you that through objective reason, you can make strategic yet compassionate decisions for yourself and the world around you. Instead of getting swept away by the ebbs and flows of emotion, get centered and tap into your sense of personal authority so you can create the boundaries you need to thrive.

JUST FOR TODAY

TODAY'S MANTRA

By creating structure in my day, I can show up for the responsibilities I have while taking care of myself.

TODAY'S RITUAL

Take advantage of calendar blocking and consider what obligations are not worth your energy today. If you find that your day is jam-packed and you cannot clear a single thing, try to schedule four minutes in your day to lie down and close your eyes.

TODAY'S JOURNAL PROMPT

How low on energy am I right now? How can I respect my limitations today?

BORN ON THIS DAY

KIM KARDASHIAN, American media personality, socialite, model, and businesswoman

CARRIE FISHER, American actor, writer, and activist for mental illness

"Peace is the effort of the human brain applied to the organization of human life and being of the peoples of the world on the basis of cooperation."—EMMELINE PETHICK-LAWRENCE, English women's rights activist and suffragist

The Journey of Those Born on
OCTOBER 21

You were born of divine wisdom and a sensual relationship with the material world that can be misperceived for superficiality. You will have to prove others wrong by living by your principles, as your journey is one of integrity, evaluation, and self-leadership.

Early on in your journey, you will meet your austere guide, *Discipline* (The Number Four). Despite your larger-than-life presence, *Discipline* calls you away from grandiosity and toward a path of painstaking diligence. You will meet *Discipline* in the hours of work and sweat that lie below the surface, when the rest of the world thinks it looks easy, but only you know what went into your worldly success.

But if you choose this gratifying path, you will have to take pause for *Restoration* (Four of Swords). Before you go climbing the next mountain, you must rest and reconsider where your mental and emotional energy would best be served moving forward. You will meet *Restoration* when you dig down to the root of your purpose and remember why it was that you started this work in the first place.

> ### YOUR GUIDES
>
> *Astrology: Your Energy*
> Libra (Venus, Mercury)
>
> *Numerology: Your Path*
> Discipline (The Number Four)
>
> *Minor Arcana: Your Lesson*
> Restoration (The Four of Swords)
>
> *Major Arcana: Your Highest Calling*
> Self-mastery (The Emperor)

By answering these calls for personal integrity, you will begin to channel *Self-mastery* (The Emperor). *Self-mastery* asks you to access the divine authority that lives within, empowering you to make objective yet compassionate decisions. *Self-mastery* encourages you to take up the right amount of space in the world, neither overshadowing others with self-centered ambition nor dimming your shine to make your naysayers comfortable. By making change through the power of your humble confidence, you will lead others by example.

―――――――――○―――――――――

LIBRA
RULERS: VENUS, MERCURY

PURPOSE
To let humble confidence and personal integrity speak for themselves.

RELATIONSHIPS

You are expansive and unstoppable, yet your relationships should be a place of emotional grounding. By seeking out partners who feel like home and inspire you to take the time you need to get clear on your purpose, you will discover that true love is a safe space to rest.

The Journey of
OCTOBER 22

Welcome to October 22, an inspired journey that honors, and respects, the freedom of speech.

Reach within to find the voice of *Courage* (The Number Five). Rather than holding back your innermost truths, seek out the opportunities that the day presents to share your honest perspective. Whether you take to social media or speak up at work, know that you are worthy of being heard.

But remember, everyone is entitled to their own opinion. To channel the diplomatic nature of Libra season, *Maturity* (Five of Swords) asks you to be thoughtful with your words, ensuring that they are being directed for positive change rather than cutting down the people around you. There is as much power in your thoughts as there is in your speech, so try to find respect for others from within.

Because at the end of the day, *Wisdom* (The Hierophant) is about understanding that the truth is highly subjective. Step into a place of higher consciousness today, respecting the varying and diverse perspectives of others while staying true to your internal genius. Just because someone may not agree with you doesn't mean you are wrong, nor does it mean either of you must be silenced.

JUST FOR TODAY

TODAY'S MANTRA

True diplomacy doesn't sound like silence; it sounds like thoughtful sharing and active listening.

TODAY'S JOURNAL PROMPT

What do I believe the limits are, if any, to free speech?

TODAY'S RITUAL

Spend five minutes looking up a quote by someone in history who you greatly admire. Write it down on a piece of paper, and carry it with you throughout this day, referencing it whenever you feel caught in a whim of passion or anger.

BORN ON THIS DAY

SHAGGY, Jamaican American reggae musician, singer, DJ, and actor

ROBERT CAPA, Hungarian American war photographer and photojournalist

"Whatever you're meant to do, do it now. The conditions are always impossible."—DORIS LESSING, English Zimbabwean Nobel Prize–winning novelist

The Journey of Those Born on
OCTOBER 22*

Y ou were born of intuitive charm and an emotional restraint that can block you from true personal freedom. You will have to find your authentic self within bravery, as your journey is one of self-expression, thoughtfulness, and higher knowledge.

Early on in your journey, you will meet your empowering guide, *Courage* (The Number Five). Despite your humble disposition, *Courage* calls you away from staying quiet and toward a path of radical honesty. You will meet *Courage* when you find your voice, carrying your truthful message in a confident yet diplomatic manner that gets the attention, and respect, of many.

But if you choose this visible path, you will have to pay respect to *Maturity* (Five of Swords). *Maturity* reminds you that straightforwardness without compassion is just cruel, encouraging you to choose your words wisely as you engage in healthy debate with others. Rather than trying to prove you are right at any cost, *Maturity* inspires you to listen to the opinions and feedback of others, without letting them get the best of you.

By answering these bold calls, you will learn to respect the subtleties of *Wisdom* (The Hierophant). *Wisdom* invites the intellectual leader that lives within to help you find self-confidence amidst the expansive sea of public and personal opinion. Hold your head high without the rigidity of ego, so you can grow from the perspectives and feedback that come your way, while staying deeply loyal to yourself. If you can strike the balance between authority and teachability, *Wisdom* offers you the power of authentic humility.

YOUR GUIDES

Astrology: Your Energy
Libra (Venus, Mercury)

Numerology: Your Path
Courage (The Number Five)

Minor Arcana: Your Lesson
Maturity (The Five of Swords)

Major Arcana: Your Highest Calling
Wisdom (The Hierophant)

LIBRA
RULERS: VENUS, MERCURY

PURPOSE
To learn to speak, and hear,
the nuances of truth.

RELATIONSHIPS

You are romantic yet deeply rational, and your relationships should be a place of uninhibited feeling. By seeking out partners who inspire you to speak your truth and offer you a safe space to be authentic, you will discover that true love accepts you as you are.

Are you a Scorpio born on this day? Head to page 760 to find your additional birthday guide!

WELCOME TO

SCORPIO
SEASON

The Journey of
OCTOBER 23

Welcome to October 23, a tenderhearted journey that asks you to commit to your inner healing.

Spend time on the things that matter today. To channel the depth and sincerity of Scorpio season, *Devotion* (The Number Six) invites you to disregard any superficial obligations so you can pour your emotional power into meaningful progress. What do you care about most?

Perhaps *Nostalgia* (Six of Cups) can help you decipher your priorities. Spend some time taking a trip down memory lane, rewatching old movies from your childhood or indulging in your favorite childhood treat. By getting in touch with your inner child, you will rediscover who you are on the deepest and most uninhibited level.

Through this self-discovery, you'll discover that how you treat your mental and emotional health involves *Choice* (The Lovers). Instead of getting caught up in emotional turmoil or spending time with spiritually needy people, hold yourself in high regard as you set the necessary boundaries required to thrive. Whether you begin a new form of therapy or make some much-needed changes to your personal life, it is a wonderful day to shed the destructive behaviors that block you from the love you deserve.

JUST FOR TODAY

TODAY'S MANTRA
I will get in touch with the pure-hearted version of me who knows what will make me emotionally fulfilled.

TODAY'S JOURNAL PROMPT
Is there a time in my life, or a specific memory from my childhood, in which I was being completely true to myself?

TODAY'S RITUAL
Start your morning in quiet meditation and visualize yourself at six years old. What did you look like, what were you excited about, and what did you love to do? Honor yourself at this age by doing something you loved as a kid today.

BORN ON THIS DAY

KATE HUDSON, English political activist and general secretary of the Campaign for Nuclear Disarmament

RYAN REYNOLDS, Canadian actor and film producer

"I think people are universal."—ANG LEE, Taiwanese filmmaker

The Journey of Those Born on
OCTOBER 23

Y ou were born of enigmatic emotional power and a self-reliance that can block you from getting the support you need. You will have to soften to the heart of the matter, as your journey is one of sincerity, healing, and unconditional love.

Early on in your journey, you will meet your earnest guide, *Devotion* (The Number Six). Despite your complicated disposition, *Devotion* calls you away from self-destruction and toward a path of meaningful work. You will meet *Devotion* within authentic generosity, when you release yourself from the traps of the ego and share the best of you.

If you choose this heartfelt path, you will stumble upon your gentle friend, *Nostalgia* (Six of Cups). *Nostalgia* invites you back to your past, to the young and uninhibited versions of you who carry the freedom of openheartedness. You will meet *Nostalgia* in the sweet smells and sounds that trigger meaningful memories, transporting you back to a simpler time. If you can find tender affection for your inner children, you'll appreciate how genius they really are.

By answering these calls for healing, you will come to understand the importance of *Choice* (The Lovers). You will meet *Choice* in the difficult yet crucial decisions you make to prioritize your holistic happiness over the needs of others. *Choice* asks you to pay respect to the ones you love while implementing the boundaries you require to live a life of emotional authenticity. By discovering a profound sense of self-loyalty, you will realize the most important relationship you have is the one you have with yourself.

SCORPIO
RULER: PLUTO

PURPOSE
To gently peel back the layers that block emotional freedom.

RELATIONSHIPS

You are strong and resilient by nature, yet your relationships should be a place of unconditional support and sweet tenderness. By seeking out partners who fill your cup with generous affection without expectation of return, you will discover that true love is even better than a fairy tale.

The Journey of
OCTOBER 24

Welcome to October 24, a solemn journey that asks you to take your future seriously. Show the universe where your *Commitment* (The Number Seven) lies. While Scorpio season can provoke some emotional upheaval, try to narrow your focus to the relationships and ambitions that you are deeply loyal to. There's no room for messing around, so show up for your obligations with complete sincerity.

But be wary of *Illusion* (Seven of Cups). If you find yourself fantasizing about an imagined romance or career that doesn't exist in the confines of reality, try to break the line of thinking that pulls you away from the present moment. Call a discerning friend or ground yourself in the facts so you can appreciate what you do have, rather than idealizing what you don't.

Because when you get clear on what you want and where you're going, you can blaze forward with complete confidence and faith. *Evolution* (The Chariot) reminds you that you can accomplish anything you set your mind to, so consider each action and decision you make today, ensuring that it gets you one step closer to your desired destiny.

JUST FOR TODAY

TODAY'S MANTRA

A little bit of hard work and emotional discernment can go a long way on the road to self-realization.

TODAY'S RITUAL

Come up with seven things you desire in life. Run them past a discerning friend or partner, or consider what a beloved ancestor or protective parent might say in response to the list. Do any seem like they're not in your best interests?

TODAY'S JOURNAL PROMPT

When I am deeply rooted in the reality of my circumstances, what goals and ambitions am I ready to pursue?

BORN ON THIS DAY

ANOHNI, English singer-songwriter and visual artist

BELVA ANN LOCKWOOD, American attorney, politician, educator, and author

"But until a person can say deeply and honestly, 'I am what I am today because of the choices I made yesterday,' that person cannot say, 'I choose otherwise.'"—STEPHEN COVEY, American educator, author, businessman, and speaker

The Journey of Those Born on
OCTOBER 24

You were born of powerful empathy and an attachment to love that can cloud your judgment. You will have to decide what is worth fighting for, as your journey is one of discernment, emotional sobriety, and personal conviction.

Early on in your journey, you will meet your formidable guide, *Commitment* (The Number Seven). Despite your limitless desires, *Commitment* calls you away from self-indulgence and toward a path of responsibility and focus. Set your sights on the goals and relationships that matter most, disregarding the superficial and letting go of useless distractions.

But if you choose this thoughtful path, you will have to watch out for *Illusion* (Seven of Cups). You will meet *Illusion* in the shiny objects that steal your focus, pulling you away from the parts of your life that are real and fulfilling. *Illusion* calls into question where your emotional priorities lie, forcing you to get honest about what you deem important in life. If you can recognize that when something seems too good to be true it probably is, you can break the spell of *Illusion*.

By answering these calls for maturity, you will earn the respect of *Evolution* (The Chariot). *Evolution* helps you find the divine momentum that carries you to new heights of self-realization, as long as you are willing to do the work required to get there. You will meet *Evolution* in moments of huge personal breakthroughs, when all the sweat and tears finally result in jaw-dropping success. If you can show the universe just how serious you are about your future, *Evolution* will ensure you get there.

SCORPIO
RULER: PLUTO

PURPOSE
To respect that meaningful progress leaves no room for games.

RELATIONSHIPS

You are romantic yet deeply complex, and your relationships should be a place of mutual commitment and shared responsibility. By seeking out partners who mean what they do and do what they say, you will discover that true love does not mess around.

The Journey of
OCTOBER 25

Welcome to October 25, an emotionally raw journey toward self-acceptance.
To harness the depth of Scorpio season, embrace your authentic *Power* (The Number Eight). Instead of worrying what others think, focus on accepting every part of yourself and integrating them into your conscious identity. You are inherently complicated, as are all humans, so find the majestic beauty that comes from being unapologetically you.

But know that self-honesty may come with its share of *Disappointment* (Eight of Cups). If a relationship, identity, or goal is not working out as you hoped, take today to come to terms with this loss as you begin to move away from this obligation. More than likely, by freeing yourself from a draining situation, you can fill your emotional cup in more fulfilling ways.

Because at the end of the day, you are capable of *Resilience* (Strength). Tap into your emotional strength throughout this healing journey, remembering how much you have endured in the past and believing in what you are capable of becoming. Know that discomfort is a natural part of the growth process, giving birth to spiritual muscles you never knew you had.

JUST FOR TODAY

TODAY'S MANTRA

As uncomfortable as it is to be honest, I choose to build a more authentic relationship with myself.

TODAY'S RITUAL

Pay special attention to hydration today. Whether you carry a reusable bottle with you or leave calendar reminders to grab a cup of water, make sure that you replenish yourself physically throughout this emotional day.

TODAY'S JOURNAL PROMPT

What aspect of myself do I have trouble accepting? Where does this self-denial come from?

BORN ON THIS DAY

CIARA, American singer-songwriter, dancer, model, and actor

MIDORI, Japanese-born American violinist

"Art is the lie that enables us to realize the truth."—PABLO PICASSO, Spanish painter, sculptor, printmaker, ceramicist, and theater designer

The Journey of Those Born on
OCTOBER 25

You were born of deep vigor and an insatiable ambition that can distract you from the truth. You will have to find the real strength that lies in authenticity, as your journey is one of integration, letting go, and rebirth.

Early on in your journey, you will meet your mysterious guide, *Power* (The Number Eight). To channel your hidden depth, *Power* calls you away from superficiality and toward a path of radical self-acceptance. Embrace every aspect of your enigmatic spirit, never denying a single inch of your imperfectly perfect humanity. If you can choose to be real rather than liked, you can uncover your authentic *Power*.

But if you choose this honest path, you will have to contend with *Disappointment* (Eight of Cups). You will meet *Disappointment* in the commitments that do not work out, when you poured your entire being into a relationship or obligation but it did not turn out how you planned. *Disappointment* invites you to feel the grief as well as the hope as you walk away, holding your head high and appreciating everything you took away from the past.

> ## YOUR GUIDES
>
> *Astrology: Your Energy*
> Scorpio (Pluto)
>
> *Numerology: Your Path*
> Power (The Number Eight)
>
> *Minor Arcana: Your Lesson*
> Disappointment (The Eight of Cups)
>
> *Major Arcana: Your Highest Calling*
> Resilience (Strength)

By answering these calls for internal healing, you will discover your capacity for *Resilience* (Strength). You will meet *Resilience* in the lowest of lows, when you can't imagine how to pick yourself up and yet a divine strength within slowly lifts you from the depths of despair. *Resilience* reminds you that you can handle anything, showing you the strength within vulnerability and the hope within change. If you can dig deep, *Resilience* teaches you how to be the light within the dark.

SCORPIO
RULER: PLUTO

PURPOSE
To realize that authentic strength is not visible to the naked eye.

RELATIONSHIPS

You are deeply committed to those you love, and your relationships should be a place of radical transformation and emotional learning. By seeking out partners who prefer things to be real rather than perfect, you will discover that true love can handle the truth.

The Journey of
OCTOBER 26

Welcome to October 26, a growth-inspiring journey through the unknown. Step out of the confines of your mind, and *Experience* (The Number Nine) something new today. Whether you explore a new part of town or dive into uncharted territory in your profession, make sure that you are doing something that inspires equal parts excitement and discomfort.

Although Scorpio season can lead to some morbid reflection, *Gratitude* (Nine of Cups) encourages you to focus on the gifts that the day offers. If you are completing some emotional or spiritual milestone, now would be a wonderful time to treat yourself to something sweet or celebrate with the people you love. Plus, by viewing today as a grand adventure rather than staying in your comfort zone, you may stumble upon a few unexpected blessings.

Above all else, celebrate the success that comes from trusting your *Instinct* (The Hermit). There is great power in following your intuition, so listen deeply to the direction you receive on a subconscious level throughout today. The map toward your true north lies within.

JUST FOR TODAY

TODAY'S MANTRA
Trusting myself is the most gratifying adventure of all.

TODAY'S RITUAL
Before you go to bed, consider or write down nine things that you are grateful for that you did today. They can be small or large, deep or seemingly mundane. If you find it difficult to come up with nine, write down some people you are grateful for to complete the list.

TODAY'S JOURNAL PROMPT
What internal and emotional growth is worth celebrating today?

BORN ON THIS DAY

MAHALIA JACKSON, American gospel singer

RAVEENA TANDON, Indian actor, model, and producer

"It is often when night looks darkest, it is often before the fever breaks that one senses the gathering momentum for change, when one feels that resurrection of hope in the midst of despair and apathy."—HILLARY CLINTON, American senator, secretary of state, Democratic presidential nominee, and forty-second first lady of the United States

The Journey of Those Born on
OCTOBER 26

You were born of intuitive power and mysteriousness that can leave you feeling profoundly misunderstood. You will have to search for the validation you desire from within, as your journey is one of growth, gratification, and internal trust.

Early on in your journey, you will meet your adventurous guide, *Experience* (The Number Nine). Despite your introspective nature, *Experience* calls you out of psychological probing and toward a path of higher knowledge. You will meet *Experience* in the great unknown, when you go toward the places that scare you in pursuit of consciousness-expanding truths.

And if you choose this widening path, you will have to pay respect to *Gratitude* (Nine of Cups). You will meet *Gratitude* in the spiritual and emotional wealth of your success, when you can't help but take a step back in awe at what you have accomplished. *Gratitude* encourages you to take a constant inventory of your blessings in life, rather than focusing on what is lacking, so you can experience the art of abundance.

By answering these expansive calls, you will have to follow the direction of *Instinct* (The Hermit) toward your ultimate purpose. *Instinct* illuminates the intuitive compass that lies within, subtly ushering you away from self-destruction and pointing you in the direction of true personal fulfillment. You will meet *Instinct* in moments of radical self-trust when you tune out the rest of the world to hear your deepest truth. If you can listen to *Instinct* rather than fear, you can create a life of profound consequence.

YOUR GUIDES

Astrology: Your Energy
Scorpio (Pluto)

Numerology: Your Path
Experience (The Number Nine)

Minor Arcana: Your Lesson
Gratitude (The Nine of Cups)

Major Arcana: Your Highest Calling
Instinct (The Hermit)

SCORPIO
RULER: PLUTO

PURPOSE
*To find divine purpose and meaning
in the wild unknown.*

RELATIONSHIPS

You are empathetic yet self-protective, so your relationships should be a place of emotional fulfillment and divine growth. By seeking out partners who expand your point of view and help you enjoy all the riches life has to offer, you will discover that true love is abundant.

The Journey of
OCTOBER 27

Welcome to October 27, a self-revealing journey that reminds you that there is no right way to be vulnerable.

Honor your intuition today. *Autonomy* (The Number One) invites you to act on your innermost feelings, so pursue the relationships, ideas, and ambitions that speak to your soul. There's no need to seek out permission or affirmation from others, but instead, turn inward to find the green light you are looking for.

And practice *Vulnerability* (Ace of Cups). Scorpio season can inspire much emotional upheaval, and today encourages you to hold your truths with gentle compassion, reminding yourself how brave it is to accept the emotions that are so difficult to digest. By uncovering what was buried in your psyche, you can discard what has been weighing you down.

By embracing your truest self, you can begin to let go of expectation. *Impermanence* (Wheel of Fortune) invites you to ride the waves of fate today, remembering that even the worst-case scenario may be a radical blessing in disguise. If you find that your hopes and plans aren't going according to plan, try to find faith that a power greater than yourself has a divine plan in mind.

JUST FOR TODAY

TODAY'S MANTRA
The most radical form of vulnerability is trusting that the universe will protect me emotionally.

TODAY'S RITUAL
Bring a token of self with you today. Whether you wear your favorite sneakers or keep your childhood blanket in your bag, use this physical object as a reminder that it is wonderful to be emotionally true to yourself.

TODAY'S JOURNAL PROMPT
What feeling or emotional epiphany am I ready to share with myself or another person today?

BORN ON THIS DAY

OLIVER TAMBO, South African lawyer, anti-apartheid politician, and cofounder of the African National Congress

ANNA LANGFORD, American politician, civil rights activist, and lawyer

"The worst enemy to creativity is self-doubt."—**SYLVIA PLATH**, American poet and novelist

The Journey of Those Born on
OCTOBER 27

You were born of deep introversion and an innate secrecy that makes you a mystery even to yourself. You will have to bring what is dark into the light, as your journey is one of self-belief, emotional openness, and divine trust.

Early on in your journey, you will meet your independent guide, *Autonomy* (The Number One). Despite your introspective nature, *Autonomy* calls you away from morbid reflection and toward a path of self-led breakthroughs. By following your instincts to their highest potential, you can create an authentic legacy that others will respect for decades to come.

But if you choose this brave path, you will have to open your heart to *Vulnerability* (Ace of Cups). Although you may prefer to keep your feelings to yourself, *Vulnerability* invites you to share your emotional depth. You will meet *Vulnerability* when you tell a loved one exactly how you feel or when you showcase a deeply personal piece of art, surrendering to the healing power of emotional honesty.

By answering these revealing calls, you will begin to understand the karmic laws of *Impermanence* (Wheel of Fortune). *Impermanence* reminds you that luck is ever-changing, encouraging you not to get too attached to any one outcome. Whether you are riding a high of good fortune or enduring a period of scarcity, *Impermanence* invites you to trust that the universe always has your best interests at heart. If you can flow with the highs as well as the lows, *Impermanence* offers you the gift of spiritual acceptance.

> ## YOUR GUIDES
>
> *Astrology: Your Energy*
> Scorpio (Pluto)
>
> *Numerology: Your Path*
> Autonomy (The Number One)
>
> *Minor Arcana: Your Lesson*
> Vulnerability (The Ace of Cups)
>
> *Major Arcana: Your Highest Calling*
> Impermanence
> (The Wheel of Fortune)

SCORPIO
RULER: PLUTO

PURPOSE
To be vulnerable for vulnerability's sake.

RELATIONSHIPS

You are highly emotionally intelligent but guarded, so your relationships should be a place of mutual self-revealing. By seeking out partners who know how to share their feelings without burdening you to take care of them, you will discover that true love is a safe space to be honest.

The Journey of
OCTOBER 28

Welcome to October 28, a gentle journey that requires moral conviction.

Despite the depth of Scorpio season, *Balance* (The Number Two) asks you to find a sense of tranquility amidst your greater responsibilities. Try to delegate where you can so that you can give yourself the time and space you need to accomplish things with ease.

And know that you deserve it. *Worthiness* (Two of Cups) invites you to honor your inherent value, never dismissing your need to please others. Instead, look within and consider what you need to feel supported and nourished throughout today.

Besides, equality is the only way forward. *Truth* (Justice) encourages you to stand up for yourself and others today, shedding light on the injustices and imbalances that exist in the world around you. It can be scary to call out others for their trespasses, but by doing so in a gentle and loving way, you can change the hearts and minds of many.

JUST FOR TODAY

TODAY'S MANTRA
My truth is valuable.

TODAY'S JOURNAL PROMPT
Which friends make me feel valued and cherished?

TODAY'S RITUAL
Spend eleven minutes outside, ideally sitting somewhere comfortable. Close your eyes and repeat the mantra, "Peace can only come from within."

BORN ON THIS DAY

JOAQUIN PHOENIX, American actor, producer, and animal rights activist

ANNA ELIZABETH DICKINSON, American orator, lecturer, and first woman to give a political address before the US Congress

"He who allows oppression shares the crime."—ERASMUS, Dutch philosopher and Catholic theologian; considered one of the greatest scholars of the Northern Renaissance

The Journey of Those Born on
OCTOBER 28

You were born of a stark paradox between independence and partnership. You will have to find your true needs in the middle ground, as your journey is one of peace, value, and interpersonal justice.

Early on in your journey, you will meet your tranquil guide, *Balance* (The Number Two). Despite your love of extremes, *Balance* calls you away from overdoing it and toward a path of easeful living. You will meet *Balance* when you slow down and calm your mind, investing in your sustainable happiness rather than instant gratification.

If you choose this peaceful path, you will have to contend with *Worthiness* (Two of Cups). *Worthiness* shines a light on your low self-esteem, inviting you to heal the wounds that taught you to expect less than you deserve. It pays to learn to be loyal to your needs.

By answering these calls for inner harmony, you will tap into the power of *Truth* (Justice). *Truth* invites you inward to a place of moral reason, a place from where you can make thoughtful and caring decisions for yourself and the people you care about most. You will meet *Truth* in moments of personal clarity, when you are able to separate your opinion from popular norms and navigate the world with a deep sense of personal accountability.

YOUR GUIDES

Astrology: Your Energy
Scorpio (Pluto)

Numerology: Your Path
Balance (The Number Two)

Minor Arcana: Your Lesson
Worthiness (The Two of Cups)

Major Arcana: Your Highest Calling
Truth (Justice)

SCORPIO
RULER: PLUTO

PURPOSE
To let equality and peace guide the way.

RELATIONSHIPS

You are intuitive and self-reliant, but your relationships should be a place of divine equality. By seeking out partners who honor your needs while respecting their own boundaries, you will discover that true love values your holistic well-being.

The Journey of
OCTOBER 29

Welcome to October 29, an emotion-shifting journey that asks you to let go. Scorpio season is not known for its *Flexibility* (The Number Three), but try to keep an open mind and heart as you move throughout this day. Rather than getting stuck on a thought pattern or dwelling on hurt feelings, get curious about what is coming up for you or another person by asking the right questions.

And seek out *Belonging* (Three of Cups). Whether you reach out to some joyful friends or develop a spiritual kinship with your ancestors or guides, create some sweet experiences with those who make you feel accepted. There's no need to waste time on fake friends or keep yourself in isolation, so call upon the loving support that is available to you.

But to truly make the most of this day, *Surrender* (The Hanged Man) your expectations and rigid ways of being. Try on something emotionally new for size, whether you embrace the contrary advice you get from a trusted person or you show up to an intimate conversation in a way you haven't tried before. By breaking out of what you typically do or how you innately react, you can enlarge your capacity for spiritual growth.

JUST FOR TODAY

TODAY'S MANTRA
I have the breadth of character to react to life in a different way than I did yesterday.

TODAY'S JOURNAL PROMPT
What are some tools or people I can lean on to begin to change my deeply programmed emotional responses?

TODAY'S RITUAL
Read about a spiritual, religious, or psychological practice that you are curious about. Notice if any discomfort or fear arises for you, and if it does, repeat the affirmation, "Knowledge can help me expand rather than contract."

BORN ON THIS DAY

SANAM NARAGHI ANDERLINI, English Iranian author and peace strategist

CARL DJERASSI, Austrian-born Bulgarian American chemist, novelist, and playwright, nicknamed the "father of the pill"

"When you finally accept that it's OK not to have answers and it's OK not to be perfect, you realize that feeling confused is a normal part of what it is to be a human being."—WINONA RYDER, American actor

The Journey of Those Born on
OCTOBER 29

You were born of deep empathy and an intensity that can keep you stuck in emotional extremes. You will have to let go to find new freedom, as your journey is one of learning, belonging, and spiritual breakthroughs.

Early on in your journey, you will meet your curious guide, *Flexibility* (The Number Three). Despite your powerful disposition, *Flexibility* calls you away from seeking control and toward a path of shared knowledge. By trying new things that extend beyond your emotional comfort zone and keeping an open mind as you get to know new people, you can grow in ways you never imagined possible.

If you choose this ever-changing path, you will meet your dear friend, *Belonging* (Three of Cups). *Belonging* invites you to share your innermost hopes and dreams with others, coconspiring with groups of like-minded individuals to make your life a work of art. You will meet *Belonging* in the connections that feed your soul, whether they be passing friendships or the sweet support of a beloved ancestor, reminding you that you are never alone.

By answering these heart-opening calls, you will come to understand the importance of *Surrender* (The Hanged Man). You will meet *Surrender* when you drop your preconceived notions and rigid fears and let life unfold as it should. Let go of how you thought you should be in favor of the radically new perspectives that come from living without expectation. If you can enjoy riding in fate's passenger's seat, *Surrender* offers you the gift of spiritual freedom.

SCORPIO
RULER: PLUTO

PURPOSE
To stop the struggle and embrace the generous arms of the universe itself.

RELATIONSHIPS

You are intense in all matters, including partnership, yet your relationships should be a place of lighthearted joy and supportive growth. By seeking out partners who help you see life as a miraculous adventure, you will discover that true love doesn't have to feel so serious.

The Journey of
OCTOBER 30

Welcome to October 30, a humbling journey that teaches you how to use your emotions productively.

Focus on *Discipline* (The Number Four) today. Scorpio season can feel emotionally destabilizing at times, but try to find some grounding within hard work and emotional perseverance. Whether you put in the effort to prioritize your mental health or show up to your responsibilities with personal integrity, now is the time to prove to the universe just how seriously you take your life.

And take some time for *Reflection* (Four of Cups). Assess the past few months or years, considering what you can learn in hindsight before jumping into your next endeavor. If you are grieving a relationship or a part of your identity, give yourself the space and grace you need to make room for new emotional freedom.

But if you find yourself getting carried away with morbid reflection, channel the power of *Self-mastery* (The Emperor). A certain level of detachment and objective reason can go a long way today, so make decisions that are logical and in your highest and best interests. Whether you set healthy boundaries with yourself or others, trust that you are the leader you need most.

JUST FOR TODAY

TODAY'S MANTRA
I can take leadership of my emotional and psychological well-being.

TODAY'S RITUAL
Do four things that bring you a healthy sense of confidence going into your day. Whether you meal-prep for the week or make your bed, remember that these small efforts can amount to a huge emotional shift.

TODAY'S JOURNAL PROMPT
What structures or boundaries could I add to my life to benefit my mental health?

BORN ON THIS DAY

GRACE SLICK, American artist, painter, and singer-songwriter

DIEGO MARADONA, Argentine footballer and manager

"Peace is not just the absence of war, it is about respect and tolerance."—GULALAI ISMAIL, Pakistani human rights activist

The Journey of Those Born on
OCTOBER 30

You were born of social prowess and an intensity that can feel too large to contain. You will have to harness your power through self-leadership, as your journey is one of hard work, integration, and personal authority.

Early on in your journey, you will meet your humble guide, *Discipline* (The Number Four). Despite your persuasive charm, *Discipline* calls you away from manipulation and toward a path of hard-earned respect. Rather than resting on your laurels or calling in favors, *Discipline* invites you to build an internal foundation from emotional grit and perseverance.

But if you choose this earnest path, you will have to make time for *Reflection* (Four of Cups). *Reflection* reminds you that without the time and space it takes to grieve, you can never internalize and grow from the experiences of the past. You will meet *Reflection* in times of profound reevaluation, when you take yourself off the hamster wheel of success and consider what you are doing and if it aligns with who you want to be.

By answering these calls for personal integrity, you will discover the importance of *Self-mastery* (The Emperor). *Self-mastery* teaches you how to be right-sized when in positions of power, encouraging you to admit when you are wrong while finding confidence in your intuitive intelligence. You will meet *Self-mastery* when you are a graceful authority who, instead of forcing the hands of others, holds yourself in high esteem by treating every perspective with profound respect. If you can believe that power is meant to be shared, you will become a leader among leaders.

SCORPIO
RULER: PLUTO

PURPOSE
To embody humble leadership by recognizing that no single person is an ultimate authority.

RELATIONSHIPS

You are socially powerful yet surprisingly distrusting of others, so your relationships should be a place of emotional grounding. By seeking out partners who feel like home, proving that they have your back over time, you will discover that true love is built on mutual respect.

The Journey of
OCTOBER 31

Welcome to October 31, an expressive journey that teaches you how to own your power. While Scorpio season can inspire great introversion, *Courage* (The Number Five) asks you to share your innermost feelings through creative art or interpersonal honesty. Take today to honor your truth, letting the rest of the world know who you are and what you stand for. A bit of vulnerability can go a long way.

But be gentle if you experience some *Grief* (Five of Cups) along the way. If someone does not respond to your honesty in the way you hoped, or if you find yourself overwhelmed with your own truth, accept these emotional reactions without judgment. Give yourself total permission to cry into your pillow or break down in fits of anger. By letting yourself feel exactly what you are feeling, you can move on with some level of closure.

And from there, remember that *Wisdom* (The Hierophant) looks like respecting the opinions of others without letting them overpower your sense of self. Step into a place of divine authority today, honoring your feelings and moving through the world with subtle confidence. No one has the power to take away or deny your truth, so guard your authenticity with fierce conviction.

JUST FOR TODAY

TODAY'S MANTRA
Vulnerability may be uncomfortable, but self-denial is much more painful.

TODAY'S RITUAL
To begin your day, spend five minutes in the shower or bath with your hand over your heart. Close your eyes and repeat the affirmation, "My sacred heart, you are allowed to feel what you are feeling."

TODAY'S JOURNAL PROMPT
When I am being vulnerable with myself or others, is there a harsh inner critic that tells me to stop? Where does this voice come from?

BORN ON THIS DAY

JULIETTE GORDON LOW, American activist and founder of the Girl Scouts of America

VALLABHBHAI PATEL, Indian freedom fighter and statesman

"Don't be afraid to be yourself and don't let anybody tell you that that's wrong. Because the best thing is you."—WILLOW SMITH, American singer, actor, and dancer

The Journey of Those Born on
OCTOBER 31

You were born of psychological depth and emotional restraint that can stop you from experiencing your most important feelings. You will have to find the healing within self-expression, as your journey is one of vulnerability, honesty, and personal power.

Early on in your journey, you will meet your inspired guide, *Courage* (The Number Five). Despite your humble disposition, *Courage* calls you away from self-denial and toward a path of radical self-revealing. You will meet *Courage* when you take your innermost truths and channel them into a creative masterpiece, making your emotions a profound work of art.

But if you choose this honest path, you will have to accept the inevitability of *Grief* (Five of Cups). You will meet *Grief* in moments of perceived failure or emotional loss, when something you poured your heart into didn't turn out as you once hoped. *Grief* invites you to feel the full breadth of these uncomfortable emotions, giving yourself full permission to grieve until the feelings run their natural course.

By answering these calls for vulnerability, you will

> ### YOUR GUIDES
>
> *Astrology: Your Energy*
> Scorpio (Pluto)
>
> *Numerology: Your Path*
> Courage (The Number Five)
>
> *Minor Arcana: Your Lesson*
> Grief (The Five of Cups)
>
> *Major Arcana: Your Highest Calling*
> Wisdom (The Hierophant)

step into the higher realms of *Wisdom* (The Hierophant). *Wisdom* encourages you to learn from the perspectives of others without giving away your power to the controlling authorities that aim to dull your shine. You will meet *Wisdom* when you differentiate your truth from popular opinion, learning to respect your own innate right to think and feel for yourself. If you can accept that not everyone will be able to handle your power, *Wisdom* will teach you the importance of self-approval.

SCORPIO
RULER: PLUTO

PURPOSE
To learn that no one can take away or diminish the power of authentic self-expression.

RELATIONSHIPS

You have learned how to contain your wild depth of emotion, but your relationships should be a place of unbridled self-expression and deep compassion. By seeking out partners who aren't afraid of honesty and encourage you to reveal your truth, you will discover that true love never asks you to hide your power.

The Journey of
NOVEMBER 1

W elcome to November 1, an emotionally freeing journey that inspires new forms of connection.

As you navigate the fixed, private nature of Scorpio season, reach for *Flexibility* (The Number Three). Rather than staying trapped in mental or psychological patterns, open yourself to unexpected conversations and new fields of study. More than likely, by stepping out of the confines of your mind, you can release yourself from the mental traps of fear and isolation.

And lean in to the relationships that feed your soul. *Belonging* (Three of Cups) invites you to form greater intimacy with others, whether they be good friends, ancestors, or spirit guides. Share as well as listen, so you can experience the transformative quality of authentic connection.

Because at the end of the day, radical breakthroughs often come from personal *Surrender* (The Hanged Man). Let yourself try new things, even if they make you uncomfortable, so you can begin to see your life from an entirely new perspective. Whether you try out a new spiritual practice or seek the guidance of a new mentor, look for the freedom that comes from not having all the answers.

JUST FOR TODAY

TODAY'S MANTRA
The quickest way to get out of a negative mental pattern is to seek the wisdom of others.

TODAY'S RITUAL
Throughout the day, keep an eye out for those around you whom you admire in some way. Ask them how they got there and listen for how you can learn from their experience.

TODAY'S JOURNAL PROMPT
When I am trudging through some emotional mud, which people or spiritual practices do I trust to lean on?

BORN ON THIS DAY

MIRIAM DECOSTA-WILLIS, American educator, writer, civil rights activist, and first Black faculty member at Memphis State University

AISHWARYA RAI BACHCHAN, Indian actor and 1994 winner of the Miss World pageant

"You want to touch the heavens, you want to feel glory and euphoria, but the trick is it takes work. You can't buy it, you can't get it on a street corner, you can't steal it or inject it or shove it up your ass, you have to earn it."—**ANTHONY KIEDIS**, American singer and member of the Red Hot Chili Peppers

The Journey of Those Born on
NOVEMBER 1

You were born of intuitive magic and an impulsiveness that can take you to the brink of uncertainty. You will have to discover a more meaningful kind of excitement, as your journey is one of learning, connection, and spiritual relief.

Early on in your journey, you will meet your curious guide, *Flexibility* (The Number Three). Despite your self-assured nature, *Flexibility* calls you away from stubbornness and toward a path of shared knowledge. You will meet *Flexibility* when you stay open-minded to the direction and absorb the expertise of others, rather than getting lost on the hamster wheel of self-seeking.

If you choose this changeable path, you will find yourself in the arms of *Belonging* (Three of Cups). You will meet *Belonging* in the warm embrace of the others, when you step out of isolation and let yourself become a part of something greater than yourself. Share your emotional abundance with others while receiving the support you need in return.

> ### YOUR GUIDES
>
> *Astrology: Your Energy*
> Scorpio (Pluto)
>
> *Numerology: Your Path*
> Flexibility (The Number Three)
>
> *Minor Arcana: Your Lesson*
> Belonging (The Three of Cups)
>
> *Major Arcana: Your Highest Calling*
> Surrender (The Hanged Man)

By answering these calls for connection, you will discover the freedom in *Surrender* (The Hanged Man). *Surrender* invites you to step out of emotional rigidity so that you can hang freely from the spiritual treetops of personal faith. You will meet *Surrender* in radical perspective shifts, when you take contrary action that goes against the natural grain of your psyche and discover the spiritual breakthrough you never knew you needed. If you can untangle yourself from the grips of ego, *Surrender* invites you through the door of personal enlightenment.

SCORPIO
RULER: PLUTO

PURPOSE
To let go, time and again, in order to find psychological freedom.

RELATIONSHIPS

You are as deep and intuitive as they come, but your relationships should be a place of light-hearted healing. By seeking out partners who draw you out of the rabbit holes of despair by reminding you not to take everything so seriously, you will discover that true love helps you unburden your mind.

The Journey of
NOVEMBER 2

Welcome to November 2, a transformative day that requires emotional accountability. As you move through the psychologically probing waters of Scorpio season, find your footing within *Discipline* (The Number Four). Whether you add some structure to your workday to ensure you fulfill all of your responsibilities or you show up with complete effort in your therapy session, know that personal integrity goes a long way today.

However, *Reflection* (Four of Cups) is an important thing to work on, too. Take a step back throughout today to consider where you are investing your emotional energy. If certain things are draining your cup recently, don't be shy to set the boundaries or say "no" to what is no longer serving you.

Because at the end of the day, you are always evolving. *Transformation* (Death) invites you to get honest about what in your life or identity has run its course. By grieving and honoring what was, you can open new space for hope and optimism for the magic that's to come. Remember, there is huge spiritual and psychological power in closing a chapter to begin a new one.

JUST FOR TODAY

TODAY'S MANTRA
I will pull out the old emotional weeds to free myself for new psychological growth.

TODAY'S JOURNAL PROMPT
What in my life, personally or professionally, has gone as far as it can and yet I am afraid to admit that it might be over?

TODAY'S RITUAL
Let go of items in your life that no longer serve you. You don't need to go through your whole apartment or home; simply take time to go through one drawer, creating space for what's to come.

BORN ON THIS DAY

AGA KHAN III, forty-eighth imam of the Nizari Ismaili sect of Islam, cofounder of the All-India Muslim League, and president of the League of Nations

MANDY CARTER, American LGBTQ+ activist

"Success and failure are both part of life. Both are not permanent."—**SHAH RUKH KHAN**, Indian actor, film producer, and television personality

The Journey of Those Born on
NOVEMBER 2

You were born of powerful empathy and a psychic ability to understand others that can take you out of your own experience. You will have to embrace the full depth of your authentic spirit, as your journey is one of grounding, self-awareness, and personal metamorphosis.

Early on in your journey, you will meet your forthright guide, *Discipline* (The Number Four). Despite your highly intuitive nature, *Discipline* calls you down from the treetops of the spiritual world and toward a hardworking path that is deeply grounded in reality. By accepting life on life's terms, you can be a force of integrity in the world around you.

But if you choose this honest path, you will have to make time for *Reflection* (Four of Cups). *Reflection* encourages you to take breaks along your road to growth to ensure that you are using your energy, and heart, wisely. You will meet *Reflection* when you hold out for complete internal alignment before taking any action.

By answering these calls for intentionality, you will meet your profound teacher, *Transformation* (Death). You will meet *Transformation* in the losses of identity that you experience along your journey, when you must say goodbye to a way of being or feeling that is no longer authentic to who you are. *Transformation* encourages you to walk through the doors of the unknown, leaving behind the parts of the past that don't need to accompany you in your future. If you can believe that there is new life within psychological death, you'll learn the divine art of metamorphosis.

YOUR GUIDES

Astrology: Your Energy
Scorpio (Pluto, Neptune)

Numerology: Your Path
Discipline (The Number Four)

Minor Arcana: Your Lesson
Reflection (The Four of Cups)

Major Arcana: Your Highest Calling
Transformation (Death)

SCORPIO
RULERS: PLUTO, NEPTUNE

PURPOSE
To build the emotional muscles that can withstand internal change.

RELATIONSHIPS

You are deeply attuned to your loved ones' psyches, and your relationships should be a place of earned respect and personal integrity. By seeking out partners who are willing to put in the time and effort required to make a relationship last a lifetime of change, you will discover that true love is forever evolving.

The Journey of
NOVEMBER 3

Welcome to November 3, an emotionally honest journey that teaches you how to keep yourself calm.

Find your sense of *Courage* (The Number Five) today. Whether you express yourself through a creative practice or by telling someone exactly how you feel, now is the time to hold nothing back as you honor your innermost truth. It is brave, and powerful, to step into the light of your authentic spirit.

But don't bypass *Grief* (Five of Cups). Although Scorpio season inspires emotional protection, let yourself feel the full breadth of whatever emotions come up today. Take the time to honor your internal experience through unapologetic tears or honest sharing with a trusted therapist or partner.

It is possible to balance emotional honesty with internal peace, as long as you are willing to do the work required to reach equilibrium. By releasing what is bottled up inside, you can tap into *Serenity* (Temperance). Whether you spend some time in silent meditation or engage with a meaningful spiritual practice, call upon the tools you need to calm your internal storms.

JUST FOR TODAY

TODAY'S MANTRA
I can express even the most uncomfortable feelings in a safe way.

TODAY'S RITUAL
Take fourteen minutes to sit quietly with yourself. Let your thoughts and feelings flow freely, not blocking their passage nor clamoring to hold on to them. Watch them pass by like a leaf floating along a stream and thank them for the gifts they bring.

TODAY'S JOURNAL PROMPT
What safe space or trusted person can I go to to express my emotions today?

BORN ON THIS DAY

ANNAPURNA MAHARANA, Indian activist for India's independence and social and women's rights

ANNA WINTOUR, English American journalist and editor in chief of *Vogue*

"Most people don't want to change. They're comfortable and set in their ways. But in order to change, you have to be able to agitate people at times."—COLIN KAEPERNICK, American civil rights activist and football player who knelt during NFL pregame national anthems in protest of police brutality and racial inequality in the United States

The Journey of Those Born on
NOVEMBER 3

Y ou were born of creative power and a social adaptability that can leave you feeling misunderstood. You will have to find yourself within your emotional truth, as your journey is one of self-expression, necessary hurt, and radical acceptance.

Early on in your journey, you will meet your bold guide, *Courage* (The Number Five). Despite your keen social awareness, *Courage* calls you away from being a chameleon and toward a path of emotional bravery. You will meet *Courage* when you reveal your innermost truths to the public, disregarding the opinions of others in favor of radical honesty.

But if you choose this magnificent path, you will have to contend with *Grief* (Five of Cups). *Grief* reminds you that it is not just okay, but it is necessary, to feel your feelings. You will meet *Grief* when you let yourself have a much-needed cry, allowing yourself the space and time it takes to heal. By acknowledging the entire spectrum of your emotions and seeing them through to completion, you can move forward with internal closure.

YOUR GUIDES

Astrology: Your Energy
Scorpio (Pluto, Neptune)

Numerology: Your Path
Courage (The Number Five)

Minor Arcana: Your Lesson
Grief (The Five of Cups)

Major Arcana: Your Highest Calling
Serenity (Temperance)

By answering these calls for self-acknowledgment, you will come to rely on the gift of *Serenity* (Temperance). You will meet *Serenity* in moments of spiritual grace, when you are able to withstand the highs and lows of a life of vulnerability without losing your sense of internal balance. *Serenity* invites you to practice emotional restraint through radical faith, never letting the world get the best of you. If you can seek balance over drama, you'll discover the gift of eternal peace.

○

SCORPIO
RULERS: PLUTO, NEPTUNE

PURPOSE
*To discover that emotional bravery
leads to internal peace.*

RELATIONSHIPS

You are compassionate yet deeply private, and your relationships should be a place of radical vulnerability and emotional grounding. By seeking out partners who encourage you to share your feelings and hold safe space for your truth, you will discover that true love is the most divine act of bravery.

The Journey of
NOVEMBER 4

Welcome to November 4, a healing journey that gets you in touch with the parts of you that need you most.

As you approach this day, show your *Devotion* (The Number Six) to the people and projects you cherish most. Rather than keeping up your guard or hustling for success, surrender to the meaningful connections you have and nourish them with the warmth of sincerity.

And connect with the joyous, loving child who lives within. *Nostalgia* (Six of Cups) invites you to release, even for just a moment, the burdens of adulting and embrace the lightheartedness of youth. What did you love to do as a kid? If you can, let yourself off the hook for some of your responsibilities so you can enjoy a full day of unapologetic freedom.

But don't be afraid if you meet your emotional *Shadow* (The Devil). To make the most of the introspective nature of Scorpio season, hold space for the internal fears and blockages that come up for you around happiness. More than likely, there were some formative experiences that forced you to put up walls or rely on destructive coping mechanisms as tools for survival. By doing some heavy psychological lifting, you can leave today feeling lighter than you ever have before.

JUST FOR TODAY

TODAY'S MANTRA

To integrate the full magic of my inner children, I must hold space for their joy as well as their sorrow.

TODAY'S RITUAL

Sit quietly for six minutes and immerse yourself in a cherished childhood memory, making the sights, sounds, and smells real again. Allow yourself to again experience the purity of feeling that goes hand in hand with youth, laughing when you feel joy and crying when you feel sad.

TODAY'S JOURNAL PROMPT

What is my relationship to therapy?

BORN ON THIS DAY

SHAKUNTALA DEVI, Indian mathematician, writer, and mental calculator known as the "Human Computer"

MATTHEW MCCONAUGHEY, American actor and producer

"Anybody who ever accomplished anything for his country was a fanatic."—SIMONNE MONET-CHARTRAND, Canadian labor activist, feminist writer, and pacifist

The Journey of Those Born on
NOVEMBER 4

You were born of irrefutable power and an emotional restraint that can block you from feeling your feelings. You will have to soften to the healing quality of self-acceptance, as your journey is one of sincerity, reminiscence, and psychological mending.

Early on in your journey, you will meet your tender guide, *Devotion* (The Number Six). Despite your natural sense of discipline, *Devotion* calls you away from overwork and toward a path of meaningful connection. By leading from the heart rather than the rigidity of the ego, you can be of authentic service to the world around you.

If you choose this earnest path, you will meet your sweet friend, *Nostalgia* (Six of Cups). *Nostalgia* asks you to hold on to the inner children who live within, never losing sight of their wonder as you navigate the rough terrain of adulthood. If you can seek out the experiences that ignite your childlike self, embracing the lightheartedness of naivete, *Nostalgia* will hand you the keys to eternal youth.

But if you answer these emotive calls, you will have to work with *Shadow* (The Devil). You will meet *Shadow* in moments of subconscious self-destruction, when you find yourself unable to cope with the vulnerability that true intimacy requires. *Shadow* invites you to shed light on what has been left in the darkness of your mind, freeing the unprocessed stories that block you from the connection you desire. If you can listen to the unhealed parts of you that need your support, *Shadow* shows you the transformative power of psychological reflection.

YOUR GUIDES

Astrology: Your Energy
Scorpio (Pluto, Neptune)

Numerology: Your Path
Devotion (The Number Six)

Minor Arcana: Your Lesson
Nostalgia (The Six of Cups)

Major Arcana: Your Highest Calling
Shadow (The Devil)

SCORPIO
RULERS: PLUTO, NEPTUNE

PURPOSE
To soften to the joy, as well as the heartbreak, of the past.

RELATIONSHIPS

You are hardworking and committed to those you are loyal to, and your relationships should be a place of unconditional support and internal healing. By seeking out partners who make you feel emotionally safe enough to be your most vulnerable self, you will discover that true love is a mirror to the healing you must give yourself.

The Journey of
NOVEMBER 5

Welcome to November 5, a transformative journey that asks you to accept change through emotional sobriety.

Focus on the relationships, goals, and obligations that matter today. To enhance the loyal nature of Scorpio season, *Commitment* (The Number Seven) encourages you to be steadfast in your responsibilities as you show the universe just how serious you are about the things you invest in.

But be wary of *Illusion* (Seven of Cups). If you find yourself getting lost in fantasy about a particular person, promotion, or object, try to cut through this daydream with sound reason. Whether you call a discerning friend or write down the facts of the situation, ground yourself in the reality and abundance of your present circumstances.

And if some unexpected change comes your way, assume it's for the best. *Upheaval* (The Tower) inspires incredible internal and external transitions, so lean in to whatever growth is being required of you today. Whether you break free from an old psychological pattern or get an unanticipated call to change within your relationships, trust that the universe has your highest and best interests in mind. Discomfort is a natural part of crucial evolution.

JUST FOR TODAY

TODAY'S MANTRA
Sometimes divine intervention is a much-needed call to take responsibility for my life.

TODAY'S RITUAL
Go for a walk today, ideally somewhere that has a breeze. As you move in your natural stride, repeat the affirmation, "There is no change that I can't handle."

TODAY'S JOURNAL PROMPT
In what ways have I recently been overly fixated on something I don't have?

BORN ON THIS DAY

VIRAT KOHLI, Indian cricketer and captain of India's national cricket team

ELIUD KIPCHOGE, Kenyan long-distance runner and Olympic marathon winner

"Effective movements are composed of two basic constituencies: those who are in the movement, and those who have the movement in them. The movement is in me, and I know it always will be."—VICTORIA GRAY ADAMS, American civil rights activist and cofounder of the Mississippi Freedom Democratic Party

The Journey of Those Born on
NOVEMBER 5

You were born of creative force and an unstoppable confidence that can make you forget at times that you are human. You will have to surrender to the powers greater than yourself, as your journey is one of thoroughness, emotional sobriety, and unexpected change.

Early on in your journey, you will meet your thoughtful guide, *Commitment* (The Number Seven). Despite your hunger for growth, *Commitment* calls you away from overindulgence and toward a path of interpersonal responsibility. By channeling your power into the relationships and ambitions you are most loyal to, you can create a life of profound consequence.

But if you choose this meaningful path, you will have to contend with *Illusion* (Seven of Cups). You will meet *Illusion* in the endlessness of desire, when you get so lost in the pursuit of what you think will make you happy that you forget that contentment only exists in the present moment. *Illusion* invites you to break the spell of not-enoughness, by realizing that when something seems too good to be true, it probably is.

By answering these calls for discernment, you will come to respect the humbling force of *Upheaval* (The Tower). You will meet *Upheaval* in times of ego-shattering change, the kind that you simply cannot plan for nor predict. *Upheaval* invites you to lean in, trusting that the walls of certainty are crumbling to the ground for a divine reason. Remember, only at ground zero can you master the art of beginning again.

YOUR GUIDES

Astrology: Your Energy
Scorpio (Pluto, Neptune)

Numerology: Your Path
Commitment (The Number Seven)

Minor Arcana: Your Lesson
Illusion (The Seven of Cups)

Major Arcana: Your Highest Calling
Upheaval (The Tower)

SCORPIO
RULERS: PLUTO, NEPTUNE

PURPOSE
To trust that the universe gives what matters and takes away what doesn't.

RELATIONSHIPS

You are deeply powerful and a tad dramatic, but your relationships should be a place of deep respect and emotional contentment. By seeking out partners who ground you in their loyalty and give you a sense of inner peace, you will discover that true love must be born from a solid emotional foundation.

The Journey of
NOVEMBER 6

Welcome to November 6, a self-empowered journey that asks you to have faith in your potential.

To make the most of the emotionally authentic nature of Scorpio season, *Power* (The Number Eight) invites you to own who you are in every way today. Whether you make peace with certain uncomfortable truths within yourself or create greater intimacy through honesty within your partnerships, now is the time to be real.

But prepare for some *Disappointment* (Eight of Cups). If through this radical self-honesty you end up realizing that a certain emotional obligation is no longer serving you, take this day to accept this inevitable loss. Grieve in whatever way feels necessary for closure, while remembering that by closing this door, you can open another.

And don't forget to reach out for *Hope* (The Star). Rely on the power of optimism, rather than getting stuck in morbid reflection of what hasn't worked out. If there is a secret dream that you have yet to realize, take some time to revel in the divine potential of what this wish could become. By washing away the debris of the past, you can make new room for the renewal that is to come.

JUST FOR TODAY

TODAY'S MANTRA
I can find light within the dark, hope within loss.

TODAY'S JOURNAL PROMPT
How honest have I been with myself and my partners? What hidden truth do I need to come to terms with today?

TODAY'S RITUAL
As you start your day, try to think of all the times that gifts have come to you disguised as woes. As you go about your day, do your best to be grateful for the seemingly terrible. Often they turn out to be the greatest gifts.

BORN ON THIS DAY

EMMA STONE, American actor

FANNY BIXBY, American philanthropist and anti-war writer

"People don't run out of dreams—people just run out of time."—GLENN FREY, American singer-songwriter, actor, and founding member of the Eagles

The Journey of Those Born on
NOVEMBER 6

Y ou were born of empathic power and a tenderheartedness that can make it difficult to implement emotional boundaries. You will have to learn to protect your shine, as your journey is
one of authenticity, emotion clearing, and divine renewal.

Early on in your journey, you will meet your emotionally intelligent guide, *Power* (The Number Eight).
While you put the needs of others first, *Power* calls you
away from playing it small and toward a path of radical
self-embodiment. Turn your compassion inward so
you can accept even the hardest-to-love corners of your
psyche and step into the full breadth of your authentic
spirit.

But if you follow this honest path, you will have to
contend with *Disappointment* (Eight of Cups). *Disappointment* reminds you that it is not just okay, but necessary, to untangle yourself from the emotional binds
that drain you. You will meet *Disappointment* when
you walk away from a relationship or identity that you
have invested deeply in so you can move toward a
greater sense of personal fulfillment.

By answering these calls to honor your truth, you will come to rely on *Hope* (The Star). *Hope*
asks you to tap in to the divine ray of light that exists within even the darkest of times, reminding
you that within each loss lies a profound opportunity to begin again. You will meet *Hope* in the
optimistic promise of tomorrow, when you wash your emotional slate clean to make room for a
brighter, and more fulfilling, dream for the future.

SCORPIO
RULERS: PLUTO, NEPTUNE

PURPOSE
*To invest in the potential, and promise,
of radical authenticity.*

RELATIONSHIPS

You are deeply attuned to the feelings of others, so your relationships should be a place of transcendent encouragement. By seeking out partners who give you the space to grow as an individual, while cheering you on through each personal breakthrough, you will discover that true love
is radically expansive.

The Journey of
NOVEMBER 7

W elcome to November 7, a psychological adventure that invites you to go deep within your subconscious.

Get out of your mental comfort zone and into the unknown today. Whether you begin a new therapeutic practice or explore new realms of your intimate relationships, *Experience* (The Number Nine) asks you to lean in to the discomfort of uncertainty.

And accept the gifts that come your way. Scorpio season can inspire emotional upheaval, but *Gratitude* (Nine of Cups) means taking some time today to revel in the emotional riches you have acquired. By recognizing what is filling your cup rather than wasting time on feelings of unworthiness, you can build a deeper sense of personal satisfaction.

But if the expansion of this day feels uncomfortable, search within to find the origin story of this emotional contraction. *Memory* (The Moon) invites you back to your past so you can find closure and perspective around the stories and experiences that shaped your emotional makeup. When did you first learn to close your heart to new experiences? By finding curiosity for the ebbs and flows of emotion that come up today, you can clear out the historical baggage that is weighing down your divine right to psychological freedom.

JUST FOR TODAY

TODAY'S MANTRA

Rather than judging or denying the fear that comes up for me today, I will view it as a portal into the experiences of my past that I need to heal.

TODAY'S JOURNAL PROMPT

What new psychological, spiritual, or emotional journey would I like to begin today?

TODAY'S RITUAL

Give yourself the time and space to fully feel what comes up for you today. Good or bad, right or wrong, lean in to whatever you are feeling and feel it intensely and without interruption for at least eighteen minutes.

BORN ON THIS DAY

LORDE, New Zealand singer-songwriter

ALBERT CAMUS, French philosopher, author, and journalist

"Nothing in life is to be feared, it is only to be understood. Now is the time to understand more, so that we may fear less."—MARIE CURIE, Polish French physicist and chemist

The Journey of Those Born on
NOVEMBER 7

Y ou were born of intuitive direction and a sense of conviction that can leave you inflexible to the ever-changing tides of life. You will have to learn to ebb and flow with the tides of life, as your journey is one of expansion, emotional satisfaction, and instinctual healing.

Early on in your journey, you will meet your high-minded guide, *Experience* (The Number Nine). Despite your desire for certainty, *Experience* calls you away from the illusion of control and toward a path of the spiritual unknown. You will meet *Experience* in times of wild uncertainty, when you forgo your comfort zone in favor of the uncharted wisdom of the road less traveled.

If you choose this wide path, you will get to know your dear friend, *Gratitude* (Nine of Cups). *Gratitude* reminds you of how important it is to take a step back from your hustle and appreciate the gifts that you have been given. It is easy to fixate on what you don't have, but try to appreciate the here and now, remembering that everything you need exists within gratitude.

By answering these perspective building calls, *Memory* (The Moon) will pull you to reconcile your past. You will meet *Memory* when you get to the root source of your emotions, drawing on your formative experiences to understand why it is you react to life the way you do. *Memory* empowers you to heal these deeply buried stories so that you can clear new space for your intuitive knowing. By seeking to understand your emotional tides, you can learn to be aligned with the divine rhythm of your soul.

YOUR GUIDES

Astrology: Your Energy
Scorpio (Pluto, Neptune)

Numerology: Your Path
Experience (The Number Nine)

Minor Arcana: Your Lesson
Gratitude (The Nine of Cups)

Major Arcana: Your Highest Calling
Memory (The Moon)

SCORPIO
RULERS: PLUTO, NEPTUNE

PURPOSE
To explore, rather than fear, the wild unknown of the subconscious.

RELATIONSHIPS

You are deeply loyal and attached to the people you love, but your relationships should be a place of psychological growth rather than comfort. By seeking out partners who unintentionally inspire you to confront the deep wounds of your past, you will discover that true love is a divine opportunity to heal.

The Journey of
NOVEMBER 8

Welcome to November 8, a spontaneous journey that teaches you how not to take everything so seriously.

Follow your instincts today. *Autonomy* (The Number One) invites you to act on your gut reactions as you pursue the ambitions and relationships that call to your soul. There's no need to wait for permission or get hung up on the opinions of others, but instead, give yourself radical permission to trust your intuition.

But don't forget to embrace your feelings. Although Scorpio season is not known for its *Vulnerability* (Ace of Cups), take a risk and reveal what it is that you truly care about. Perhaps, by putting your heart on the line and believing in the potential of your emotions, you may manifest the connection or breakthrough you were searching for.

Plus, there is something so freeing about allowing oneself to be authentic. *Vitality* (The Sun) reminds you that true self-embodiment is the greatest reward of all, so don't fret if others don't respond to you in the way you hoped. Instead, nurture the wildness that lives within by expressing yourself through creativity or dancing as if no one's watching. By owning who you are and what you love, you can inspire others to do the same.

———————————————○———————————————

JUST FOR TODAY

TODAY'S MANTRA
My heart always knows best, so I will let it shine in all its brilliance.

TODAY'S RITUAL
Have you laughed at yourself yet today? Dig through your closet, find a funny hat or sweater, and rock it all day long. It's hard to take life too seriously if you don't look too serious.

TODAY'S JOURNAL PROMPT
What hobby or activity gets me in touch with my creative inner child?

———————————————○———————————————

BORN ON THIS DAY

MARGARET MITCHELL, American novelist and journalist

ALAIN DELON, French actor, film director, producer, screenwriter, singer, and businessman

"The greatest challenge of the day is: how to bring about a revolution of the heart, a revolution which has to start with each one of us?"—DOROTHY DAY, American journalist, social activist, and anarchist

The Journey of Those Born on
NOVEMBER 8

Y ou were born of psychological strength and a highly introspective nature that can make it hard to let go and have a good time. You will have to grow younger as you grow older, as your journey is one of intuitive action, emotional risk-taking, and personal freedom.

Early on in your journey, you will meet your fiery guide, *Autonomy* (The Number One). Despite your emotional awareness, *Autonomy* calls you away from overthinking and toward a path of radical self-trust. By taking a chance on your potential, you can self-actualize your greatest ambitions as you follow the divine direction of your instinctual power.

But if you choose this daring path, you will have to take the biggest risk of all with *Vulnerability* (Ace of Cups). *Vulnerability* invites you to act on your innermost feelings, letting the people and projects you desire most know exactly where you stand. You will meet *Vulnerability* in the divine fragility of a new idea or relationship, when you aren't sure exactly how things will work out but you remain devoted to seeing them through.

> ### YOUR GUIDES
>
> *Astrology: Your Energy*
> Scorpio (Pluto, Neptune)
>
> *Numerology: Your Path*
> Autonomy (The Number One)
>
> *Minor Arcana: Your Lesson*
> Vulnerability (The Ace of Cups)
>
> *Major Arcana: Your Highest Calling*
> Vitality (The Sun)

By answering these calls to action, you will step into the light of *Vitality* (The Sun). *Vitality* encourages you to wear your heart on your sleeve, letting go of your inhibitions and expressing your innate brilliance to the world around you. You will meet *Vitality* when you feel so good in your own skin that protecting or shielding your deepest truths no longer seems necessary. If you can set yourself free from the confines of self-judgment, *Vitality* offers you the levity of self-acceptance.

───────────────○───────────────

SCORPIO
RULERS: PLUTO, NEPTUNE

PURPOSE
To care less about what others think in order to express yourself freely with the strength of heart.

RELATIONSHIPS

You are only interested in things that are real and emotionally weighty, but your relationships should be a place of divine fun and spontaneity. By seeking out partners who keep you on your toes and are always looking for a good time, you will discover that true love makes you feel lighter.

The Journey of
NOVEMBER 9

Welcome to November 9, a trust-building journey that inspires profound self-awareness. Despite the emotional weight of Scorpio season, seek out *Balance* (The Number Two) by leaning on others. Whether you confide in a trusted friend or partner or call upon the support of your spiritual practice, now is not the time to self-isolate and carry your burdens on your own. There is help out there if you are willing to look.

But be gentle if some fear comes up. *Worthiness* (Two of Cups) invites you to reflect on your emotional self-esteem, so consider where you first learned that a part of you was unlovable. If some formative experiences or learned behaviors still keep you at arm's length from others, try to bridge this gap with radical vulnerability and self-compassion.

And you may begin seeing things from an entirely new perspective. *Awakening* (Judgment) encourages you to rewrite some of the stories you tell yourself around intimacy, so you can break whatever psychological cycle you find yourself stuck in with partners and loved ones. By taking a discerning and critical lens to your personal life, you can make the crucial changes you need to experience true belonging.

———————————————○———————————————

JUST FOR TODAY

TODAY'S MANTRA
Even if I wasn't taught it, and even if I don't believe it yet, I trust that I am worthy of supportive love.

TODAY'S JOURNAL PROMPT
What partner, friend, loved one, ancestor, or guide makes me feel truly held and cherished? How do they do this for me?

TODAY'S RITUAL
On paper or in your mind, take an inventory of your past partnerships, platonic or romantic. What stories do you still carry from these experiences? While accepting what was, try to find the willingness to let them go.

———————————————○———————————————

BORN ON THIS DAY

BENJAMIN BANNEKER, American almanac author, surveyor, mathematician, and farmer

HARRIOT HUNT, American physician and women's rights activist

"People who have no hold over their process of thinking are likely to be ruined by liberty of thought."—MUHAMMAD IQBAL, British Indian writer, philosopher, and politician

The Journey of Those Born on
NOVEMBER 9

Y ou were born of intuitive power and an emotional privateness that keeps you at arm's length from the ones you love. You will have to transform your perspective through interpersonal trust, as your journey is one of harmony, intimacy, and spiritual truth.

Early on in your journey, you will meet your tranquil guide, *Balance* (The Number Two). Despite your instinctual independence, *Balance* calls you away from self-reliance and toward a path of shared responsibility. By leaning on others in times of personal strife and admitting that you need support, you will discover that life is much easier when you are not an emotional island.

If you answer these calls for interdependence, you will have to wrestle with *Worthiness* (Two of Cups). You will meet *Worthiness* in emotional scarcity, when you deem a part of yourself unlovable and block yourself from the connection you deserve. *Worthiness* invites you to take a closer look at where this self-rejection comes from so you can heal the wounds that block you from true belonging.

By answering these intimate calls, you will tap into the power of *Awakening* (Judgment). *Awakening* asks you to reconsider the stories you were told growing up around vulnerability and to see them through the sober eyes of adulthood. You will meet *Awakening* in the profound changes of heart, when you discover an emotional truth that, once digested, can never be denied again. By bringing consciousness to your emotional preprogramming, you can make radically honest decisions that reshape the course of your life.

YOUR GUIDES

Astrology: Your Energy
Scorpio (Pluto, Neptune)

Numerology: Your Path
Balance (The Number Two)

Minor Arcana: Your Lesson
Worthiness (The Two of Cups)

Major Arcana: Your Highest Calling
Awakening (Judgment)

SCORPIO
RULERS: PLUTO, NEPTUNE

PURPOSE
To awaken to the undeniable power of belonging.

RELATIONSHIPS

You are emotionally brave yet closed off from others, so your relationships should be a place of earned trust. By seeking out partners who are as loyal to you as they are to their word, you will discover that true love is a safe and reliable space to surrender.

The Journey of
NOVEMBER 10

Welcome to November 10, a heart-opening journey that helps you find a better point of view.

Try to channel *Flexibility* (The Number Three) today. Rather than getting stuck in the emotional stories you tell yourself, seek out the opinions and perspectives of other people. Whether you read a personal story or have an in-depth conversation with a coworker you admire, now is the time to expand your mind through active listening.

And despite the introverted nature of Scorpio season, search for a sense of *Belonging* (Three of Cups). Socializing is not second nature to everyone, so look for the communities of like-minded individuals of which you can belong. By dipping your toes in a new social circumstance that piques your curiosity, you just may find the sense of shared respect that you have been yearning for.

By getting out of your comfort zone, you may find a new *Perspective* (The World) on your day. Use a zoomed-out lens as you take inventory of your day, searching for the subtle details that inspire deep gratitude. Whether you notice the caring smile that a stranger gave you or the small act of kindness you witnessed on the street, look for the good within humanity.

―――――――○―――――――

JUST FOR TODAY

TODAY'S MANTRA
There is goodness in everyone if I am brave enough to search for it.

TODAY'S JOURNAL PROMPT
Are there any wounds around belonging that I need to unpack today?

TODAY'S RITUAL
Seek out opportunities to be generous today. Give a dollar to someone who needs it or make someone feel welcome. If you feel scarce at any point, repeat the affirmation, "When I open myself and put love and kindness into the world, I see love and kindness looking back at me."

―――――――○―――――――

BORN ON THIS DAY

ELLEN POMPEO, American actor and producer

MICHAEL JAI WHITE, American actor, director, and martial artist

"False friendship, like the ivy, decays and ruins the walls it embraces; but true friendship gives new life and animation to the object it supports."—RICHARD BURTON, Welsh actor

The Journey of Those Born on
NOVEMBER 10

Y ou were born of powerful independence and a stark realism that can make you focus on the worst of the human experience. You will have to learn to view life through a more generous lens, as your journey is one of seeking, community, and divine gratitude.

Early on in your journey, you will meet your curious guide, *Flexibility* (The Number Three). Despite your natural authority, *Flexibility* calls you away from pridefulness and toward a path of learning from others. By surrendering your fixed perspective for the experiences and genius of the people around you, you will discover that true wisdom comes from shared understanding.

If you choose this enlightening path, you will stumble upon your dear friend, *Belonging* (Three of Cups). *Belonging* invites you to share your heart with those you trust, building a sense of emotional community by leaning on and being there for others. You will meet *Belonging* when you extend the warmth of friendship to another person, putting your trust out there in the divine pursuit of authentic connection.

By answering these calls for openheartedness, you will come to find *Perspective* (The World). *Perspective* reminds you that your life has purpose and consequence for generations to come, encouraging you to pay your luck forward with selfless courage. You will meet *Perspective* when you find appreciation for the miracle of humanity, putting your best foot forward to leave the world a better place. By zooming out and seeing where you fit in the big picture, you will discover the divine threads that connect us all.

YOUR GUIDES

Astrology: Your Energy
Scorpio (Pluto, Neptune)

Numerology: Your Path
Flexibility (The Number Three)

Minor Arcana: Your Lesson
Belonging (The Three of Cups)

Major Arcana: Your Highest Calling
Perspective (The World)

SCORPIO
RULERS: PLUTO, NEPTUNE

PURPOSE
To search for commonality rather than dissonance with the world around you.

RELATIONSHIPS

You are highly emotionally intelligent yet wildly independent, and your relationships should be a place of enlightenment. By seeking out partners who expand your perspective, you will discover that true love is a source of wisdom.

The Journey of
NOVEMBER 11

W elcome to November 11, a grounding journey that requires you to act in your own best interest.

Channel your passion into *Discipline* (The Number Four) today. Whether you show up for therapeutic work or dig into a personal goal, use today to do the heavy lifting you would typically postpone until tomorrow. There is nothing more satisfying than a thorough effort, especially when it strengthens your sense of self-respect.

But don't disregard the emotional awareness that the day requires. To coincide with the psychologically aware nature of Scorpio season, *Reflection* (Four of Cups) invites you to reevaluate where you are investing your power. If you are giving it away to relationships or obligations that drain your cup, find the internal courage to walk away.

Because at the root of today, *Self-mastery* (The Emperor) wants you to remember that you are the CEO of your life. Make the tough but loving decisions you need to do to move your life forward using logic rather than fleeting emotion. Consider what will sustain your emotional contentment in the long run, and build out the emotional and psychological boundaries you need to thrive.

JUST FOR TODAY

TODAY'S MANTRA
I can be a trusted leader to my mental health by laying a strong foundation of self-respect.

TODAY'S JOURNAL PROMPT
Growing up, how was I taught to manage my emotions, if at all?

TODAY'S RITUAL
Take a moment to envision the type of person you would trust with your life, the type of leader you would follow. Now reflect on where you need to grow to become that person.

BORN ON THIS DAY

LEONARDO DICAPRIO, American actor, film producer, and environmental activist

SHIRLEY GRAHAM DU BOIS, American author, playwright, composer, and activist

"The mystery of human existence lies not in just staying alive, but in finding something to live for."—FYODOR DOSTOEVSKY, Russian novelist, short story writer, essayist, and journalist

The Journey of Those Born on
NOVEMBER 11

Y ou were born of empathic intelligence and a desire for intimacy that can take you away from your true power. You will have to become the partner you always needed, as your journey is one of personal integrity, reevaluation, and internal authority.

Early on in your journey, you will meet your stoic guide, *Discipline* (The Number Four). Despite your people-driven nature, *Discipline* calls you away from social distraction and toward a path of hard work. You will meet *Discipline* in the hours of unseen work that one day amounts to your impenetrable foundation of self-trust.

But if you choose this earnest path, you will have to make time for *Reflection* (Four of Cups). *Reflection* asks you to consider what it is you are investing in and whether it is filling or draining your emotional cup. You will meet *Reflection* in moments of retreat, when you shut out the rest of the world to find internal clarity. By bravely listening to yourself, you can build sustainable happiness through self-honesty.

By answering these calls for emotional maturity, you will begin to embody the strength of *Self-mastery* (The Emperor). *Self-mastery* reminds you that no one knows what is best for you better than you do. You will meet *Self-mastery* when you balance your emotions with objective reason, never minding the opinions of others as you step into your divine right to self-leadership. If you can set the boundaries you need to thrive, you will become the protective yet compassionate authority you always needed.

> ### YOUR GUIDES
>
> *Astrology: Your Energy*
> Scorpio (Pluto, Neptune)
>
> *Numerology: Your Path*
> Discipline (The Number Four)
>
> *Minor Arcana: Your Lesson*
> Reflection (The Four of Cups)
>
> *Major Arcana: Your Highest Calling*
> Self-mastery (The Emperor)

SCORPIO
RULERS: PLUTO, NEPTUNE

PURPOSE
To build emotional trust through deep self-awareness and personal integrity.

RELATIONSHIPS

You are highly attuned to the feelings of others, so your relationships should be a place of grounded respect and longevity. By seeking out partners who are willing to do the work required to build a foundation of trust, you will discover that true love grows stronger with time.

The Journey of
NOVEMBER 12

Welcome to November 12, a vulnerable journey that empowers you to be yourself.

As you swim through the deep psychological waters of Scorpio season, tap into *Courage* (The Number Five). Express yourself to the world around you in whatever way you feel called, whether it be on social media or via a treasured form of creativity. The more honest you are, the more impactful the day can feel.

Be gentle with *Grief* (Five of Cups). If you find yourself wading through some heavy regret or disappointment around a personal situation, don't rush through or limit your tough feelings. Instead, let yourself have the cry or stew in the resentment for as long as you need to let it go. But remember, the end goal is to move on.

Because at the end of the day, no one and nothing has power over your emotions. *Wisdom* (The Hierophant) encourages you to stand proudly in your authentic spirit, owning your feelings and never gaslighting yourself about your personal truths. If someone disagrees or tries to contradict your experience, take it as an opportunity to engage in a respectful exchange of emotional sharing, knowing that it will only strengthen your relationship with yourself.

―○―

JUST FOR TODAY

TODAY'S MANTRA
There is no feeling within me that I need to reject or that I will allow others to reject.

TODAY'S RITUAL
Keep an inventory of the emotions that come up today. About once every hour, write down the general feeling that you are experiencing (e.g., happy, sad, anxious). At the end of the day, read the list and take note of what emotions came up the most.

TODAY'S JOURNAL PROMPT
What creative, social, or personal platform is a safe outlet to express my innermost feelings?

―○―

BORN ON THIS DAY

AUGUSTE RODIN, French sculptor, generally considered the founder of modern sculpture

NEIL YOUNG, Canadian American singer-songwriter, musician, and activist

"Truth is the only safe ground to stand on."—ELIZABETH CADY STANTON, American writer, activist, and leader of the US women's rights movement

The Journey of Those Born on
NOVEMBER 12

Y ou were born of empathic power and an ability to transport into the emotional experiences of others that can take you far away from yourself. You will have to swim bravely back to who you truly are, as your journey is one of self-expression, vulnerability, and radical self-trust.

Early on in your journey, you will meet your bold guide, *Courage* (The Number Five). Despite your socially aware nature, *Courage* calls you away from niceties and toward a path of creative honesty. By revealing the full spectrum of your humanity on the center stage of life, you can build an inspired legacy of emotional authenticity.

But if you choose this brave path, you will have to hold space for *Grief* (Five of Cups). You will meet *Grief* in moments of profound heartache, when something you invested your soul into didn't turn out the way you had hoped. Rather than trying to bypass or numb these difficult feelings, *Grief* invites you to honor the pain you are in and see it through to fruition so that you can clear new space for hope.

By answering these emotive calls, you will come to understand the power of *Wisdom* (The Hierophant). *Wisdom* reminds you that no one knows you better than you know yourself, empowering you to listen deeply to your internal authority rather than falling prey to public opinion or societal pressure. By turning inward to decipher what an honest life looks like to you, you can experience the emotional freedom that comes from not caring what other people think.

SCORPIO
RULERS: PLUTO, THE MOON

PURPOSE
To realize that the only approval that matters is the approval of self.

RELATIONSHIPS

You quite easily take on the feelings of those you care about, but your relationships should be a place of emotional authenticity and self-accountability. By seeking out partners who honor your individuality and don't shy away from healthy conflict, you will discover that true love is more about being real than being nice.

The Journey of
NOVEMBER 13

Welcome to November 13, a healing journey that reminds you that vulnerability is born of emotional freedom.

Give your heart to what matters most today. *Devotion* (The Number Six) asks you what people and projects speak to your soul, pulling your focus away from the meaningless hustle and toward the aspects of life that bring deep meaning.

And perhaps the past will help you rediscover what you love most. Although Scorpio season is reflective in nature, *Nostalgia* (Six of Cups) invites you to reconnect with the joyful inner children who live within. Whether you practice your favorite creative hobby with no grand ambition in mind or double over with laughter with a childhood friend, know that there is profound wisdom within the joy.

You will need support, however, amidst this day of vulnerability. *Choice* (The Lovers) encourages you to honor your feelings throughout today, never pushing them away or denying their inherent value. By giving yourself endless grace, you can build the self-trust you need to practice emotional honesty moving forward. You are expanding in ways you may not recognize quite yet, so look for ways to nourish yourself amidst this growth.

JUST FOR TODAY

TODAY'S MANTRA

While vulnerability may not have been safe or possible in the past, I can give my inner child the permission it needs to be seen.

TODAY'S JOURNAL PROMPT

What did my formative experiences teach me about vulnerability?

TODAY'S RITUAL

When you are heading to sleep, make your bed in a way that you would have loved as a child. Whether you bring in some extra blankets, build a pillow fort, or leave a night-light on, try to nurture yourself to sleep tonight.

BORN ON THIS DAY

BARBARA BANGURA, Sierra Leonean women's rights activist

JIMMY KIMMEL, American television host and producer

"Normal is nothing more than a cycle on a washing machine."—WHOOPI GOLDBERG, American Emmy, Grammy, Oscar, and Tony Award–winning actor and comedian

The Journey of Those Born on
NOVEMBER 13

Y ou were born of the enigmatic power of transformation and an emotional restraint that makes it difficult for you to give your full self to others. You will have to surrender to the vulnerability of connection, as your journey is one of purpose, integration, and deep personal healing.

Early on in your journey, you will meet your tender guide, *Devotion* (The Number Six). Despite your guarded nature, *Devotion* calls you away from the rigidity of ego and toward a path of openheartedness. By leading from your heart, and generously giving your power to the people and causes that speak directly to your soul, you can build a life of profound meaning.

If you choose this personal path, you will stumble upon your reflective friend, *Nostalgia* (Six of Cups). *Nostalgia* reminds you of the childlike innocence that lives within, inspiring you to release the burdens of adulthood when you can. You will encounter *Nostalgia* in moments of joyful remembrance, when a deep belly laugh or an adored movie from your childhood reminds you that not everything in life has to be so serious.

YOUR GUIDES

Astrology: Your Energy
Scorpio (Pluto, The Moon)

Numerology: Your Path
Devotion (The Number Six)

Minor Arcana: Your Lesson
Nostalgia (The Six of Cups)

Major Arcana: Your Highest Calling
Choice (The Lovers)

By answering these softening calls, you will surrender to the healing of *Choice* (The Lovers). *Choice* knows that love is a decision, inspiring you to work through the hardened walls of self-protection that block you from the intimacy you deeply crave. You will meet *Choice* in moments of emotional free fall, when you take a risk on a person or project and find yourself held by the divine arms of compassion. If you can fight for love rather than survival, *Choice* shows you that you were born to thrive.

SCORPIO
RULERS: PLUTO, THE MOON

PURPOSE
To unburden and free the inner child who was taught to restrict their love and creativity.

RELATIONSHIPS

You are self-sustaining yet ever-changing, so your relationships should be a place of unconditional belonging. By seeking out partners who adore you for who you are becoming, rather than what you do or who you were, you will discover that true love comes from the soul.

The Journey of
NOVEMBER 14

W elcome to November 14, an emotionally discerning journey that offers you the rewards of integrity.

As you navigate the psychologically probing nature of Scorpio season, *Commitment* (The Number Seven) asks you to focus your energy on truthful and meaningful endeavors. Whether you invest some effort in a significant partnership or devote yourself to your internal healing, now is the time to show the universe just how serious you are about your future.

But be wary of *Illusion* (Seven of Cups). While pouring your heart into something important is favored today, watch out for the stories you have around such investments. If you find yourself believing that this treasured relationship or spiritual practice will be the answer to all your problems, try to cut through this noise with the sharp knife of honesty.

By handling yourself, and your dreams, with great emotional maturity, you can make radical progress. *Evolution* (The Chariot) invites you to push forward with earnest effort while trusting that a power greater than yourself will help you reach a higher destiny. By tending to your side of the street while working in harmony with the universe itself, you can progress in ways you never thought possible.

———————————————○———————————————

JUST FOR TODAY

TODAY'S MANTRA
There is no shortcut to emotional and spiritual progress; there is only good faith and hard work.

TODAY'S JOURNAL PROMPT
What is my relationship with psychological work? Do I tend to avoid any topics around my mental health?

TODAY'S RITUAL
Set down this book, put away your phone or other distractions, and get to work on writing a decisive *action* plan.

———————————————○———————————————

BORN ON THIS DAY

ANNA CATALDI, Italian humanitarian, journalist, film producer, and author

CLAUDE MONET, French painter and founder of impressionist painting

"Life is like a game of cards. The hand that is dealt you is determinism; the way you play it is free will."—JAWAHARLAL NEHRU, Indian anti-colonial nationalist and first prime minister of independent India

The Journey of Those Born on
NOVEMBER 14

Y ou were born of a creative force and an empathic diplomacy that can make you falter at times in your convictions. You will have to decide what is worth fighting for, as your journey is one of determination, clarity, and hard-earned progress.

Early on in your journey, you will meet your discerning guide, *Commitment* (The Number Seven). Despite your desire for growth, *Commitment* calls you away from taking on too much and toward a path of clear personal direction. By making the tough yet critical decisions that pull your focus away from the distractions of power and to the heart of what matters, you will build a reputation of humble loyalty.

But if you choose this sincere path, you will have to contend with *Illusion* (Seven of Cups). You will meet *Illusion* in the dreamlike ambitions that pull your attention away from reality, when you presume that someone or something will fill the spiritual hole within you. By cutting through this myth with incisive self-honesty, you can discover that personal integrity is the only sustainable solution to emotional contentment.

> ### YOUR GUIDES
>
> *Astrology: Your Energy*
> Scorpio (Pluto, The Moon)
>
> *Numerology: Your Path*
> Commitment (The Number Seven)
>
> *Minor Arcana: Your Lesson*
> Illusion (The Seven of Cups)
>
> *Major Arcana: Your Highest Calling*
> Evolution (The Chariot)

By answering these calls for maturity, you will come to understand the divine timing of *Evolution* (The Chariot). *Evolution* is the spiritual pace at which your potential is unfolding. It cannot be rushed by sheer force of will but rather humble work. You will meet *Evolution* in the unexpected yet well-deserved moments of success, when what feels like a lifetime of effort suddenly culminates in jaw-dropping progress. If you can keep your eyes on the daily growth rather than the goal, *Evolution* ensures you'll build a legacy worthy of respect.

SCORPIO
RULERS: PLUTO, THE MOON

PURPOSE
To build toward the divine satisfaction that comes from emotional grounding.

RELATIONSHIPS

You are emotionally intense yet undeniably fair in how you treat others, and your relationships should be a place of mutual and sustainable psychological effort. By seeking out partners who are willing to dig deep to make the partnership work, you will discover that true love can last a lifetime.

The Journey of
NOVEMBER 15

Welcome to November 15, an exercise in self-trust that shows you just how strong you really are.

Try to embrace all parts of yourself, rather than only the ones you think are socially acceptable. To make the most of the emotional authenticity of Scorpio season, *Power* (The Number Eight) invites you to reveal the hidden corners of your psyche to both yourself and the people you trust.

But don't shy away from any feelings of *Disappointment* (Eight of Cups). If a relationship, identity, or interpersonal obligation is no longer nourishing you on a personal level, now is the time to confront this reality and move forward. If a conversation of closure needs to happen, try to do so by balancing gentle compassion with self-respect.

And through this day of radical self-honesty, you might just discover how much you can handle. *Resilience* (Strength) calls you inward during times of strife, so tap into your power of emotional fortitude rather than letting your feelings get the better of you. Whether you let yourself have a good cry in the comfort of your home or release your toughest emotions into art, try to channel your truth in a self-respecting manner.

○

JUST FOR TODAY

TODAY'S MANTRA
While accepting certain aspects of my truth may be hard, it will inevitably set me free.

TODAY'S RITUAL
Today, give away one physical item that you associate with an identity or relationship you are grieving. Donate it, lend it to a friend, or, if it is biodegradable, bury it in the earth itself.

TODAY'S JOURNAL PROMPT
When I am navigating some tough emotions, what are some practical ways I can take care of myself?

○

BORN ON THIS DAY

WILLIAM HERSCHEL, German English astronomer who discovered Uranus

SARA JOSEPHINE BAKER, American physician who made contributions to public health, especially in New York City immigrant communities

"I've been absolutely terrified every moment of my life—and I've never let it keep me from doing a single thing I wanted to do."—**GEORGIA O'KEEFFE**, American modernist artist

The Journey of Those Born on
NOVEMBER 15

Y ou were born of unparalleled emotional intelligence and a devilish charm that can get you in trouble. You will have to turn your powers of the psyche inward, as your journey is one of self-acceptance, emotional honesty, and internal trust.

Early in your journey, you will meet your magnetic guide, *Power* (The Number Eight). Despite your desire for invulnerability, *Power* calls you away from self-denial and toward a winding road of self-intimacy. You will meet *Power* in moments of emotional free fall, when by living in emotional authenticity, you will find yourself in the warm embrace of universal empathy.

If you choose to walk this path of honesty, you will have to work through *Disappointment* (Eight of Cups). You will meet *Disappointment* in the emotional invest- ments that are long-expired and yet difficult to free yourself from. Your natural inclination may be to leave these responsibilities in the dark of night and hope to avoid any repercussions, but *Disappointment* asks you to give these entanglements the closure they deserve. It is never easy to say goodbye, but *Disappointment* teaches you the healing power of transparency.

YOUR GUIDES
Astrology: Your Energy Scorpio (Pluto, The Moon)
Numerology: Your Path Power (The Number Eight)
Minor Arcana: Your Lesson Disappointment (The Eight of Cups)
Major Arcana: Your Highest Calling Resilience (Strength)

By answering these brave calls, you will discover the power of *Resilience* (Strength). *Resilience* lies in your internal strength, the emotional backbone that holds you upright during the inevita- ble highs and lows in life. You will meet *Resilience* in moments of spiritual fortitude, when your animal instincts call you down to self-destruction but you choose to rise above to higher con- sciousness instead.

―――――――――――――――○―――――――――――――――

SCORPIO
RULERS: PLUTO, THE MOON

PURPOSE
To value internal strength over power over others.

RELATIONSHIPS

You are deeply empathic yet emotionally guarded, but your relationships should be a place of rad- ical intimacy and self-revealing. By seeking out partners who want to know all of you, even the darkest corners you try to hide, you will discover that true love is unconditionally accepting.

The Journey of
NOVEMBER 16

Welcome to November 16, an expansive journey that gets you in touch with your innate worthiness.

Seek to learn something new today. Scorpio season can keep you stuck in your head, but *Experience* (The Number Nine) asks you to look outward in search of higher knowledge and deep meaning. By throwing yourself into a new emotional or psychological perspective, you can unlock the internal breakthrough you were looking for.

And try to find *Gratitude* (Nine of Cups) in the blessings that come your way. More than likely, something or someone will fill your emotional cup today, so work to accept these magical gifts and know that you have the right to enjoy them. Whether you splurge on a treat for yourself or revel in the embrace of a loved one, try to disregard the feelings of unworthiness that may come up.

But know that this self-love may require some time alone. *Instinct* (The Hermit) encourages you to build a relationship with your intuition today, so quiet the distractions of the outside world and listen for the divine direction that lies within. By drawing yourself away from the hustle and bustle of society, you can get clear on what you need to thrive moving forward.

———————————————O———————————————

JUST FOR TODAY

TODAY'S MANTRA
The most divine antidote to morbid reflection is getting out of my comfort zone, following my intuition, and embracing the abundant unknown.

TODAY'S JOURNAL PROMPT
What does self-love look like to me? How can I practice that today?

TODAY'S RITUAL
At the end of your day, make a mental list of nine things you were grateful for. When you are finished with your list, say the prayer, "Thank you, universe, for everything you've given me and everything you've taken away."

———————————————O———————————————

BORN ON THIS DAY

LILIAN STEVENSON, Irish Christian peace activist and historian

PETE DAVIDSON, American comedian, actor, writer, and producer

"You'll never miss the water 'til the well runs dry."—W. C. HANDY, American composer

The Journey of Those Born on
NOVEMBER 16

Y ou were born of otherworldly conviction and a self-destructive unpredictability that leaves you uncertain if you can trust yourself. You will have to grow to respect your divine intelligence, as your journey is one of seeking, perspective, and internal trust.

Early on in your journey, you will meet your sage guide, *Experience* (The Number Nine). Despite your desire for certainty, *Experience* calls you out of the driver's seat and into the wild unknown. By breaking free of the confines of comfort, you can explore the vast wisdom that the universe has to offer and expand your emotional perspective.

If you choose this far-reaching path, you will meet your dear friend, *Gratitude* (Nine of Cups). *Gratitude* invites you to love yourself by enjoying the blessings that come your way, rather than getting stuck in the self-deprecating feelings of unworthiness. You will meet *Gratitude* when your emotional cup runs over and you can't help but find gratitude for the miracles that have been sent your way.

By answering these calls for abundance, you will come to trust in the direction of *Instinct* (The Hermit). *Instinct* reminds you of how important it is to spend time alone, encouraging you to tune out the noise of the outside world so you can get centered in the divine truth that lies within. You will meet *Instinct* in moments of intentional isolation, when, by nourishing the relationship you have with yourself, you gain the clarity you need to move forward. If you can follow your internal compass, rather than denying your power, *Instinct* will teach you how to trust yourself.

YOUR GUIDES

Astrology: Your Energy
Scorpio (Pluto, The Moon)

Numerology: Your Path
Experience (The Number Nine)

Minor Arcana: Your Lesson
Gratitude (The Nine of Cups)

Major Arcana: Your Highest Calling
Instinct (The Hermit)

SCORPIO
RULERS: PLUTO, THE MOON

PURPOSE
To build faith, and trust, in the innate intelligence that lives within.

RELATIONSHIPS

You are quite attached and loyal to the ones you love, and your relationships should be a place of emotional expansion and deep learning. By seeking out partners whose perspective and experience are quite different from your own, you will discover that true love is a portal for internal growth.

~ 499 ~

The Journey of
NOVEMBER 17

Welcome to November 17, an emotionally daring journey that asks you to trust your instincts and the universe itself.

Listen to the intuitive voice that lies within today. *Autonomy* (The Number One) asks you not to follow the feelings or opinions of others today, but instead, to stand proudly on your own. Act on the desires or ideas that feel deeply true, trusting they will guide you to a higher sense of personal fulfillment.

So take a chance on your feelings. As you navigate the emotionally immersive nature of Scorpio season within your partnerships, *Vulnerability* (Ace of Cups) invites you to share your emotions freely. Whether you take a risk and tell someone how you feel or channel your internal world into a creative piece of art, know that a bit of self-revealing will go a long way.

But don't get too hung up on expectations. *Impermanence* (Wheel of Fortune) reminds you that even the worst of circumstances might be a blessing in disguise, encouraging you to look for the silver lining in whatever transpires today. Even if you come up against some temporary disappointment, perhaps tomorrow you will see that this day was a miracle after all.

JUST FOR TODAY

TODAY'S MANTRA
True vulnerability requires me to trust in the divine unknown outcome of living with an open heart.

TODAY'S JOURNAL PROMPT
When I share my innermost feelings with another person, how do I attempt to control their reaction?

TODAY'S RITUAL
Begin your day by standing up, firmly rooted, and saying to yourself out loud, "I will stand up for what I believe and for what is true."

BORN ON THIS DAY

PADMAJA NAIDU, Indian freedom fighter and politician

RUTH BLEIER, American neurophysiologist and one of the first feminist scholars to explore how gender biases have shaped biology

"Fulfillment isn't found over the rainbow—it's found in the here and now. Today I define success by the fluidity with which I transcend emotional land mines and choose joy and gratitude instead."
—RUPAUL, American drag queen, actor, singer, and television personality

The Journey of Those Born on
NOVEMBER 17

Y ou were born of personal resilience and a depth of power that can convince you that you can control anything. You will have to surrender to a higher level of vulnerability, as your journey is one of intuition, hope, and divine fate.

Early on in your journey, you will meet your independent guide, *Autonomy* (The Number One). Despite your introspective nature, *Autonomy* calls you away from overanalysis and toward a path of radical self-belief. You will meet *Autonomy* when you trust your instinct and proceed with the authentic confidence that comes from internal alignment.

If you choose this path of self-realization, *Vulnerability* (Ace of Cups) will ask you to lead from the heart. Rather than protecting your pride, *Vulnerability* invites you to trust in the potential of putting yourself out there and believing that the right people and opportunities will reciprocate your affection. You will meet *Vulnerability* when you put everything on the table and discover that emotional bravery is the greatest gift of all.

> ## YOUR GUIDES
>
> *Astrology: Your Energy*
> Scorpio (Pluto, The Moon)
>
> *Numerology: Your Path*
> Autonomy (The Number One)
>
> *Minor Arcana: Your Lesson*
> Vulnerability (The Ace of Cups)
>
> *Major Arcana: Your Highest Calling*
> Impermanence
> (The Wheel of Fortune)

By answering these daring calls, you will begin to move in stride with the karmic laws of *Impermanence* (Wheel of Fortune). You will meet *Impermanence* in the natural ebbs and flows of life, when you have no choice but to move with the rhythm of divine timing. *Impermanence* asks you not to struggle or force your way out of fate, but instead, to detach from expectation and surrender to a power greater than yourself. By witnessing the larger divine intelligence at play, you will discover that everything happens for a reason.

SCORPIO
RULERS: PLUTO, THE MOON

PURPOSE
To uncover the irrefutable power of emotional surrender.

RELATIONSHIPS

You are deeply empathic toward the ones you love, and your relationships should be a place of loving trust and independence. By seeking out partners who feel complete on their own and inspire you to do the same, you will discover that true love is the merging of two whole hearts rather than two halves.

The Journey of
NOVEMBER 18

Welcome to November 18, an emotionally balancing journey that connects you to others. As you navigate the emotionally private waters of Scorpio season, try to find *Balance* (The Number Two) within your relationships. Share your innermost feelings when you can while relying on the healing power of silent support when you simply cannot find the words to explain your experience. Look for the people who make you feel inherently understood and unconditionally accepted.

And know that it is okay to ask for what you need. *Worthiness* (Two of Cups) invites you to state your emotional and mental needs to yourself and others, even if you fear that they are too much. Dip your toes in this level of vulnerability, slowly revealing who you are and what you stand for.

Because at the end of the day, compassionate honesty is what will connect you with others. Be a beacon of *Truth* (Justice) today, calling out the injustices you see without slandering anyone's character. By bringing a fair yet empathetic lens to how you communicate and express yourself today, you can inspire a new sense of equality and intimacy with the people you trust.

JUST FOR TODAY

TODAY'S MANTRA

Honesty with kindness, rather than judgment, bridges the gap between me and others.

TODAY'S RITUAL

On a piece of paper, write down a situation or relationship that has been bothering you recently. Beneath that, write a version of this truth that is lacking in compassion for others or yourself. And beneath that, write a version of this truth that gives everyone involved the absolute benefit of the doubt. Which one feels more true to you?

TODAY'S JOURNAL PROMPT

How do I typically communicate tough or uncomfortable feelings with people I trust?

BORN ON THIS DAY

BRENÉ BROWN, American professor, lecturer, author, and podcast host

MARGARET ATWOOD, Canadian poet, novelist, literary critic, and environmental activist

"Truth is powerful and will prevail."—SOJOURNER TRUTH, American abolitionist and feminist

The Journey of Those Born on
NOVEMBER 18

You were born of otherworldly wisdom and an emotional sensitivity that can move you toward the extremes of isolation. You will have to find connection in the middle ground between yourself and others, as your journey is one of partnership, boundaries, and shared truths.

Early on in your journey, you will meet your harmonizing guide, *Balance* (The Number Two). Despite your hermitlike nature, *Balance* calls you away from self-protective solitude and toward a path of mutual vulnerability. By accepting the gifts as well as the excruciating fears that come from vulnerability, you will discover that life is much richer when shared.

If you choose this compassionate path, you will have to learn the lessons of *Worthiness* (Two of Cups). Although you may believe you will never get the support and affection you desire, *Worthiness* reminds you that you are inherently valuable and deserve the universal call for connection. You will meet *Worthiness* when you crawl out of your comfort zone and admit to a person, and most importantly to yourself, that you have emotional needs.

By answering these trust-building calls, you will awaken to the *Truth* (Justice). Underneath the social constructs and self-centeredness that divide, common threads unite the human experience. *Truth* shows you the power of diplomacy, encouraging you to look for commonalities that can bridge the huge distance that the wars of the ego cause. If you can understand rather than be understood, you'll transform your compassion into interpersonal breakthroughs.

SCORPIO
RULERS: PLUTO, THE MOON

PURPOSE
To search fearlessly for the threads of emotion that connect us all.

RELATIONSHIPS

You are highly attuned to the feelings of others, and your relationships should be a place of deep belonging. By seeking out partners who make you feel accepted for who you are, rather than what you do, you will discover that true love heals wounds you never knew existed.

The Journey of
NOVEMBER 19

Welcome to November 19, an emotionally nourishing journey that reconnects you with the joys of connection.

Despite the psychologically fixed nature of Scorpio season, *Flexibility* (The Number Three) invites you out of the rabbit holes of the mind and into the present moment. By staying open-hearted to every person and idea that crosses your path, you can learn to flow in harmony with the beauty that surrounds you.

And you just may find yourself surrendering to the warmth of *Belonging* (Three of Cups). Whether you embrace the comradery of trusted friends or deepen your relationships with your spirit guides, push yourself out of isolation and remember that you are never truly alone. If you need to call upon some emotional support, know that the universe has your back.

By opening yourself to the emotional and spiritual *Abundance* (The Empress) of this day, you can fill your energetic cup in a meaningful and sustainable way. Let in the good things that come your way, whether it be the gorgeous scent of a flower on your walk to work or the affectionate words of a loved one. You are worthy of such generosity, so let yourself absorb the joyful gifts that are yours to keep.

○

JUST FOR TODAY

TODAY'S MANTRA
There is profound surrender and beauty in letting in the love, support, and joy that I need.

TODAY'S RITUAL
As you go about your day, try to take note of someone who seems quite positive. Study their behavior, and if you find the courage and it feels appropriate, ask them about how they stay so optimistic.

TODAY'S JOURNAL PROMPT
What person, community, spiritual practice, or ancestor makes me feel truly accepted and nourished?

○

BORN ON THIS DAY

JOSÉ RAÚL CAPABLANCA, Cuban world champion chess player

ANNA SEGHERS, German writer

"Acting is really about having the courage to fail in front of people."—ADAM DRIVER, American actor and Marine Corps veteran

The Journey of Those Born on
NOVEMBER 19

Y ou were born of fierce bravery and a strength of spirit that can convince others that you are completely okay on your own. You will have to learn to receive the gifts of connection, as your journey is one of sharing, community, and unapologetic happiness.

Early on in your journey, you will meet your curious guide, *Flexibility* (The Number Three). Despite your self-assured nature, *Flexibility* calls you away from pridefulness and toward a path of interpersonal understanding. By opening your mind as well as your heart to the perspectives of others, you can grow and change in ways you never could have on your own.

If you choose this social path, you will meet your great teacher, *Belonging* (Three of Cups). *Belonging* asks you to question why you prefer to do things on your own, encouraging you to reveal your innermost feelings to people you hope to build an authentic community with. While it is far easier and safer to put up walls and tell yourself that no one will understand you, instead, try to find the strength in vulnerability.

By answering these intimate calls, you will open yourself to *Abundance* (The Empress). *Abundance* reminds you how good it feels to receive love and affection from others, even if at times, it seems easier to try to fill your cup on your own. It is more than okay to acknowledge your independence and the fears that come up around interdependency, but *Abundance* pushes you to honor the universal need for connection instead.

YOUR GUIDES

Astrology: Your Energy
Scorpio (Pluto, The Moon)

Numerology: Your Path
Flexibility (The Number Three)

Minor Arcana: Your Lesson
Belonging (The Three of Cups)

Major Arcana: Your Highest Calling
Abundance (The Empress)

SCORPIO
RULERS: PLUTO, THE MOON

PURPOSE
To find a new lightness and levity through divine connection.

RELATIONSHIPS

You are generous with others without expecting much in return, but your relationships should be a place of deep emotional reciprocation and nourishment. By seeking out partners who go out of their way to fill your cup with joy and laughter, you will discover that true love is never draining.

The Journey of
NOVEMBER 20

Welcome to November 20, a psychologically grounding journey that builds real self-esteem.

To close out the psychologically probing Scorpio season, *Discipline* (The Number Four) invites you to focus on what you can control today. Whether you show up to your work responsibilities with complete integrity or create some structure around how you care for your mental health, discover how empowering it can be to get in the driver's seat of your day.

And make some time for *Reflection* (Four of Cups). Reconsider where it is you have been devoting your emotional energy, and if any of these relationships or goals have been draining you for quite some time, try to make peace with this inevitable ending. While it undoubtedly is upsetting and may require some grieving, know that this level of honesty will guide you toward a deeper sense of fulfillment.

Because at the end of the day, you are the leader of your destiny. *Self-mastery* (The Emperor) invites you into a position of personal authority today, encouraging you to take charge of your present happiness as well as your future success. Make the tough but crucial decisions to honor your power so you can move out of survival mode and into a thriving life.

JUST FOR TODAY

TODAY'S MANTRA
I can be a strong emotional authority toward myself.

TODAY'S RITUAL
Spend four minutes lying on your back on the floor to ground yourself. Try not to think of anything in particular; just feel the weight of the ground beneath you.

TODAY'S JOURNAL PROMPT
What obligation in my life has been draining me from a mental health perspective?

BORN ON THIS DAY

JOE BIDEN, American politician and forty-sixth president of the United States

NADINE GORDIMER, South African writer and political activist

"What is often called exceptional ability is nothing more than persistent endeavor."—PAULI MURRAY, American civil and women's rights activist, lawyer, Episcopal priest, and author

The Journey of Those Born on
NOVEMBER 20

Y ou were born of deep psychological awareness that, on your worst day, can make you judgmental to the emotional shortcomings of others. You will have to discover the strength
within personal integrity, as your journey is one of hard work, careful consideration, and humble
authority.

Early on in your journey, you will meet your grounding guide, *Discipline* (The Number Four). Despite your
compassionate nature, *Discipline* calls you away from
codependency and toward a path of rigorous effort.
You will meet *Discipline* in the long, arduous hours of
work that go unnoticed by the public but can one day
amount to a reputation worthy of profound respect.

But if you choose this enduring path, you will have to
pause from time to time for *Reflection* (Four of Cups).
Reflection wants you to use your emotional reserves
wisely, asking you to take thorough and constant inventory of where your devotions lie. You will meet *Reflection* when you say "no" to what has been draining you,
sticking through the discomfort of disappointing others as you stay true to your internal knowledge.

YOUR GUIDES

Astrology: Your Energy
Scorpio (Pluto, The Moon)

Numerology: Your Path
Discipline (The Number Four)

Minor Arcana: Your Lesson
Reflection (The Four of Cups)

Major Arcana: Your Highest Calling
Self-mastery (The Emperor)

By answering these calls for integrity, you will begin to embody *Self-mastery* (The Emperor).
Self-mastery invites you into a position of personal leadership, asking you to temper the unpredictability of feeling into a higher state of objective reason. You will meet *Self-mastery* when you
do what is right, rather than what is popular, helping you discover the everlasting satisfaction of
humility. If you can aim to be good, rather than liked, *Self-mastery* will propel you into a position
of divine authority.

SCORPIO
RULERS: PLUTO, THE MOON

PURPOSE
*To care more about moral responsibility
than the opinions of others.*

RELATIONSHIPS

You are deeply partnership-driven, and your relationships should be a place of emotional grounding and pragmatism. By seeking out partners who work to build a solid foundation of respect and
trust, you will discover that true love requires personal integrity.

The Journey of
NOVEMBER 21

Welcome to November 21, an enlightening journey that connects you to the rest of humanity.

Tap into your *Courage* (The Number Five) today. To make the most of the last day of Scorpio season, take what you have learned about your emotional and psychological truth over the past month and share it with the world around you. Whether you channel it via social media or into a piece of art, you never know who will identify with your story.

But be gentle if you experience some *Grief* (Five of Cups). If you find that something you have poured your soul into isn't quite working out, let yourself experience the entire range of emotions that come with this loss. Even better, call a trusted friend or therapist—you don't have to go through this personal release on your own.

Through the process of such vulnerability, you may tap into a new sense of *Wisdom* (The Hierophant). What have you discovered about yourself that brings you a new perspective on the human experience? More than likely, through the process of becoming more emotionally honest and open with yourself, you can look for the commonalities you have with others rather than focusing on the divide.

JUST FOR TODAY

TODAY'S MANTRA
If I am human, then you are human, and we all deserve some grace.

TODAY'S RITUAL
If you have some tough emotions coming up today, spend five minutes alone with your inner children. Close your eyes as you let the feelings come up and ask yourself what part of you is getting triggered. If you can imagine this part, ask it when it was born and what it needs you to hear.

TODAY'S JOURNAL PROMPT
What emotions make me feel connected to others when I see them?

BORN ON THIS DAY

RENÉ MAGRITTE, Belgian surrealist artist

LOUISE YIM, South Korean educator, politician, and the country's first female minister

"Judge a man by his questions rather than his answers."—VOLTAIRE, French Enlightenment writer, historian, and philosopher

The Journey of Those Born on
NOVEMBER 21*

Y ou were born of intuitive wisdom and a transcendent intelligence that can make you feel far removed from your peers. You will have to learn to share your thoughts as well as your feelings with the rest of humankind, as your journey is one of expression, emotional honesty, and higher knowledge.

Early on in your journey, you will meet your inspired guide, *Courage* (The Number Five). Despite your philosophic disposition, *Courage* calls you away from reclusive thinking and toward a path of psychological bravery. By sharing your innermost truths with the world around you and daring to stand on your own, you can build an unfounded legacy of radical honesty.

But if you choose this bold path, you will have to contend with *Grief* (Five of Cups). *Grief* reminds you that sadness is a natural part of life, encouraging you to surrender to your emotions without letting the depths of despair overshadow the silver lining. If you can embrace the vulnerability required to call upon the support you need, *Grief* teaches you how to feel your feelings without letting them get the best of you.

> ### YOUR GUIDES
>
> *Astrology: Your Energy*
> Scorpio (Pluto, The Moon)
>
> *Numerology: Your Path*
> Courage (The Number Five)
>
> *Minor Arcana: Your Lesson*
> Grief (The Five of Cups)
>
> *Major Arcana: Your Highest Calling*
> Wisdom (The Hierophant)

By answering these calls for vulnerability, you will come to respect the subtle power of *Wisdom* (The Hierophant). *Wisdom* reminds you that everyone is powerful in their own way, so remain open to the knowledge of others without backing down from your unique perspective. You will meet *Wisdom* when you gracefully oscillate between an authority and a student, realizing that true personal authority comes from asking the right questions rather than demanding clear answers.

SCORPIO
RULERS: PLUTO, THE MOON

PURPOSE
To discover that vulnerability is the thread that binds the human experience.

RELATIONSHIPS

You are psychically attuned to everyone you encounter, and your relationships should be a place of emotional bravery. By seeking out partners who aren't afraid to share their scariest feelings, and encourage you to do the same, you will discover that true love is born from vulnerability.

Are you a Sagittarius born on this day? Head to page 761 to find your additional birthday guide!

WELCOME TO

The Journey of
NOVEMBER 22

Welcome to November 22, a fulfilling journey that inspires self-acknowledgment.

As you set about the generous-hearted nature of Sagittarius season, *Devotion* (The Number Six) asks you to direct your abundant energy toward the matters of the heart. Whether you give an empowering pep talk to a friend in need or share your wealth of wisdom with a new client, now is the time to give what you have with no expectation of return.

But you will get a return anyway because *Confidence* (Six of Wands) rewards you with the applause you deserve today. It could be the acknowledgment you have been waiting for from a trusted adviser or a joyous tarot card that affirms for you the progress you have made. Either way, the universe will be giving you a grand thumbs-up for the work you have been doing.

So let yourself enjoy it. *Choice* (The Lovers) reminds you that you can receive only the love you think you deserve, so try to widen your emotional capacity for good things. If you find yourself coming up against any feelings of unworthiness, hold yourself gently with compassion. By acknowledging the past experiences that may have taught you to contract in fear, you can leave today with some profound emotional expansion.

JUST FOR TODAY

TODAY'S MANTRA

As I give generously, I also will try to open myself to receiving.

TODAY'S RITUAL

Put on your favorite outfit, stand in front of a mirror, and repeat the affirmation, "I am worthy of feeling good about myself."

TODAY'S JOURNAL PROMPT

In my personal relationships, do I tend to feel safer when I am giving or receiving?

BORN ON THIS DAY

MUM SHIRL, Wiradjuri woman, social worker, and humanitarian activist

JAMIE LEE CURTIS, American actor and writer

"It is never too late to be what you might have been."—GEORGE ELIOT, English novelist, poet, journalist, and translator

The Journey of Those Born on
NOVEMBER 22

You were born of grounded optimism and a sense of responsibility that can overburden you at times. You will have to learn to fill your own cup first, as your journey is one of purpose, self-acknowledgment, and profound self-love.

Early on in your journey, you will meet your unassuming guide, *Devotion* (The Number Six). *Devotion* asks you what you're working for and what you're working toward, moving your gaze away from popular opinion and toward a path of divine usefulness. If you can keep your eyes on your own path and not compare yourself to others, *Devotion* will help you build a life of high esteem through estimable action.

If you choose this path of meaning, you will be greeted by your joyous friend, *Confidence* (Six of Wands). *Confidence* brings you the recognition you deserve, helping you embrace your hard-earned success while not letting it go to your head. If you can enjoy the rewards while keeping your focus on the places you'd like to grow, *Confidence* will keep the applause going.

> ### YOUR GUIDES
>
> *Astrology: Your Energy*
> Sagittarius (Jupiter)
>
> *Numerology: Your Path*
> Devotion (The Number Six)
>
> *Minor Arcana: Your Lesson*
> Confidence (The Six of Wands)
>
> *Major Arcana: Your Highest Calling*
> Choice (The Lovers)

If you answer these calls for meaning, you will meet your greatest teacher, *Choice* (The Lovers). *Choice* adores your generous spirit but knows that you cannot absorb the love you seek without giving yourself the love you deserve. You will meet *Choice* in moments of self-recognition, when you redirect your path toward the goals and relationships that seek to nourish you in return for your sincerest effort. If you can choose yourself, rather than giving away your power, you'll discover you are more than enough.

———————————————○———————————————

SAGITTARIUS
RULER: JUPITER

PURPOSE
To grow self-confidence by turning unconditional generosity and divine loyalty inward.

RELATIONSHIPS

You are deeply wise yet emotionally restrained, so your relationships should be a place of unconditional compassion and support. By seeking out partners who genuinely wish the best for you and encourage you to thrive, you will discover that true love is a window into the love you must give to yourself.

The Journey of
NOVEMBER 23

Welcome to November 23, an insightful journey that reminds you that growth takes time. As you navigate the expansive wanderlust of Sagittarius season, *Commitment* (The Number Seven) asks you to rein in your focus to the obligations that matter most. What are you working toward? By narrowing your efforts and energy to the people and projects you are invested in, you can make meaningful progress.

But don't give up if you face any opposition today. *Perseverance* (Seven of Wands) wants to see you sweat, so kick your motivation into high gear rather than giving up at the first hint of adversity. Whether you stand up to an authority who disagrees with your plans or jump through some hoops to make your ideas come to life at work, now is the time to believe in yourself.

Because at the end of the day, your meaningful *Evolution* (The Chariot) happens during life's marathon rather than at the finish line. Look for the small wins within the work you are doing today, noticing how you are growing stronger with each hurdle you overcome. By showing the universe just how earnest you are about your dreams, you can move one meaningful step closer to making them a reality.

JUST FOR TODAY

TODAY'S MANTRA
Passion without clear direction and effort won't bring me the results I desire.

TODAY'S RITUAL
As you begin your day, close your eyes and visualize what responsibilities you have coming up. Imagine yourself carrying out each task with confidence and strength. As you open your eyes, say aloud the word, "Onward."

TODAY'S JOURNAL PROMPT
What kind of personal growth am I most interested in investing in right now?

BORN ON THIS DAY

MILEY CYRUS, American actor and singer

MAUDE ROYDEN, English preacher, suffragist, and campaigner for the ordination of women

"Dream big, but focus on the small."—ROBIN ROBERTS, American television broadcaster and the first woman of color and first openly LGBTQ+ woman to host *Jeopardy!*

The Journey of Those Born on
NOVEMBER 23

You were born of wild exuberance and an impatient passion for growth that can make you feel like nothing is ever quite enough. You will have to discover the personal development that truly fulfills you, as your journey is one of intention, persistence, and spiritual development.

Early on in your journey, you will meet your sage guide, *Commitment* (The Number Seven). Despite your free-loving nature, *Commitment* calls you away from unreliability and toward a path of divine dedication. By sticking to your word and remaining loyal to the people, projects, and ambitions you believe help make you a better person, you will discover the undeniable payoff of good faith.

But if you walk this discerning path, you will have to make friends with *Perseverance* (Seven of Wands). You might prefer to pack up and start over when the going gets tough, but *Perseverance* asks you to dig in your heels as you see your obligations through to completion. You will meet *Perseverance* in the face of opposition or the lull of dissatisfaction, when your enthusiasm for the fight has waned and yet you find yourself tapping into a deeper strength of personal conviction.

By answering these calls for loyalty, you will come to respect the subtle brilliance of *Evolution* (The Chariot). You will meet *Evolution* in the slow, arduous effort that, over time, can lead to profound and unexpected personal breakthroughs. While these revelations don't possess the shock value you would typically seek, the hard work and resolve they require ensure that their effects last a lifetime.

YOUR GUIDES

Astrology: Your Energy
Sagittarius (Jupiter)

Numerology: Your Path
Commitment (The Number Seven)

Minor Arcana: Your Lesson
Perseverance (The Seven of Wands)

Major Arcana: Your Highest Calling
Evolution (The Chariot)

SAGITTARIUS
RULER: JUPITER

PURPOSE
To accept that the most important spiritual breakthroughs happen over time.

RELATIONSHIPS

You are as adventurous, creative, and dramatic as they come, yet your relationships should be a place of mutual commitment and good faith. By seeking out partners who are willing to work with you through even the toughest of challenges, you will discover that true love is a worthwhile investment.

The Journey of
NOVEMBER 24

W elcome to November 24, an overwhelmingly expansive journey that asks you to use your vital energy wisely.

Take up more space in the world today because *Power* (The Number Eight) invites you to embrace every inch of your wild humanity. Rather than dimming your enthusiasm to make others comfortable, forge ahead with the unbridled confidence of self-trust. You are the courageous authority you always needed.

And why not make some moves? *Momentum* (Eight of Wands) asks you to take swift action in your desire and dreams today. If you get an internal green light, move ahead with complete focus, and don't back down just because someone tells you to. It's time to strike while the iron's hot, with nothing to lose and everything to gain.

But as you navigate this intense energy, tap into *Resilience* (Strength). It is easy to give up or lose steam as the day progresses, so reach within to rediscover the spiritual muscles that have carried you through great victories in your life. When did you persevere through a seemingly insurmountable obstacle in the past? By recognizing and utilizing just how strong you are, you can make monumental growth internally as well as externally.

JUST FOR TODAY

TODAY'S MANTRA

I don't need permission and I don't need to wait to act in alignment with my personal power.

TODAY'S JOURNAL PROMPT

If I weren't afraid of others' opinions of me, what personal or spiritual goal would I like to grow toward?

TODAY'S RITUAL

Wear a piece of clothing or jewelry that makes you feel powerful. Whether it is your favorite combat boots or a statement necklace, be sure it enhances your innate strength.

BORN ON THIS DAY

YARA SALLAM, Egyptian feminist and human rights advocate

SARAH HYLAND, American actor

"When I'm dead twenty-five years, people are going to begin to recognize me."—SCOTT JOPLIN, American composer and pianist known as the "King of Ragtime"

The Journey of Those Born on
NOVEMBER 24

Y ou were born of boundless compassion and an unbridled generosity that makes it unclear when your body, mind, and soul have had enough. You will have to learn to invest deeply in yourself, as your journey is one of authenticity, alignment, and spiritual fortitude.

Early on in your journey, you will meet your emotionally intelligent guide, *Power* (The Number Eight). Despite your desire to be adored, *Power* calls you away from people-pleasing and toward a path of radical self-embodiment. By honoring the full rainbow of your humanity rather than denying the parts you deem unlovable, you will discover the profound influence you can have on others when you are being unapologetically real.

If you choose this self-honest path, you will have to keep pace with *Momentum* (Eight of Wands). *Momentum* asks you to act quickly whenever you feel a profound "yes" from your intuition. You will meet *Momentum* in times of personal velocity, when your life is moving at an intense speed and yet your passion keeps burning with the fire of self-belief.

> ### YOUR GUIDES
>
> *Astrology: Your Energy*
> Sagittarius (Jupiter)
>
> *Numerology: Your Path*
> Power (The Number Eight)
>
> *Minor Arcana: Your Lesson*
> Momentum (The Eight of Wands)
>
> *Major Arcana: Your Highest Calling*
> Resilience (Strength)

By answering these stimulating calls to action, you will come to rely on the magic of *Resilience* (Strength). You will meet *Resilience* when the hustle becomes too much and exhaustion pervades every ounce of passion you once had. Rather than continuing to run on empty, cease fighting and tap into the deeper spiritual source of power that lies within. If you can unburden yourself from the notion that you must handle everything, you'll discover the radical strength that lies within surrender.

SAGITTARIUS
RULER: JUPITER

PURPOSE
To discover that true personal power means knowing when to push and when to surrender.

RELATIONSHIPS

You have so much love and excitement to offer, yet your relationships should be a place of emotional unburdening and deep trust. By seeking out partners who embrace even the hardest-to-love corners of your psyche and help carry the weight of your hardest truths, you will discover that true love is as real as it gets.

The Journey of
NOVEMBER 25

Welcome to November 25, a soul-opening adventure that needs your energy to last.
Look for opportunities to expand your perspective today. *Experience* (The Number Nine) invites you to step outside your norm as you explore the ideas, projects, and spiritual practices that are foreign and exciting to you. It's the perfect time to be a beginner, so throw your expertise out the window as you try something new.

But don't give up if you get overwhelmed. *Persistence* (Nine of Wands) asks you to take note of your energy levels throughout the day, giving yourself the emotional, physical, and spiritual nourishment you need to sustain yourself. Whether you give yourself a thirty-minute power nap or proactively drink water, consider what you need to thrive.

If you find yourself lost in the wildness of this plentiful day, reach within to discover your *Instinct* (The Hermit). While there is much uncertainty in risk-taking, only you have the answers of where to go next, so tap into your intuition whenever you are deciding what the next right move could be. By trusting in your gut and never second-guessing your wisdom, you can grow in step with the universe itself.

―――――――――――――――○―――――――――――――――

JUST FOR TODAY

TODAY'S MANTRA

The unknown is only scary if I don't trust myself and only exhausting if I don't nourish myself.

TODAY'S JOURNAL PROMPT

What new spiritual practice am I interested in researching or trying?

TODAY'S RITUAL

On a piece of paper, draw three circles. Above the first circle, write "Emotional energy," over the second, write "Physical energy," and over the third, write "Mental energy." Then fill in a portion of the circle to represent how full or drained this aspect of your energy is.

―――――――――――――――○―――――――――――――――

BORN ON THIS DAY

LINA MORGENSTERN, German writer, educator, feminist, and pacifist

RINGO SHEENA, Japanese singer-songwriter and musician

"In trying to make something new, half the undertaking lies in discovering whether it can be done."—HELEN GAHAGAN DOUGLAS, American actor, politician, and the first Democratic woman from California elected to Congress

The Journey of Those Born on
NOVEMBER 25

Y ou were born of sage wisdom and a sense of personal duty that can distract you from the wild adventure of the human experience. You will have to find purpose within the unknown, as your journey is one of growth, resilience, and spiritual direction.

Early on in your journey, you will meet your expansive guide, *Experience* (The Number Nine). Despite your responsible nature, *Experience* calls you away from the mundanity of work and toward a path of divine uncertainty. You will meet *Experience* as you explore uncharted heights of understanding, breaking free of your comfort zone and making the world your greatest teacher.

If you choose this far-reaching path, you will have to pay respect to *Persistence* (Nine of Wands). *Persistence* asks you not to burn out too quickly as you traverse the long road of your soul's evolution. You will meet *Persistence* in the small but consequential moments of restoration along the way, when you recharge your energetic batteries long enough to move ahead.

By answering these sweeping calls for growth, you

will have to rely on the power of *Instinct* (The Hermit). *Instinct* calls you inward when you are in need of direction, inviting you to trust the intuitive compass within. You will meet *Instinct* when you are lost in the wilderness of the unknown and have no choice but to place one foot in front of another, trusting that your divine intelligence can guide you through. If you can listen deeply to yourself, *Instinct* teaches you that the soul always knows the right way forward.

SAGITTARIUS
RULER: JUPITER

PURPOSE
To nurture the power of intuition amidst the wild unknown.

RELATIONSHIPS

You are deeply devoted to your people, but your relationships should be a place of spiritual expansion and personal growth. By seeking out partners who push you outside of your comfort zone and remind you of how much there is to learn, you will discover that true love is an adventure of its own.

The Journey of
NOVEMBER 26

Welcome to November 26, a risk-taking journey that requires you to have some faith.
Create your own adventure today. As you navigate the wanderlust of Sagittarius season, *Autonomy* (The Number One) invites you to strike out into the unknown guided by nothing but the magic of your intuition. Where is your gut asking you to go?

Believe deeply in your *Potential* (Ace of Wands). This is not a day that requires planning or logic, but rather, a time to take a chance on the limitless ideas that you have within. Whether you pursue a new creative, spiritual, or personal endeavor, know that the simple excitement behind the idea ensures that it will blossom into something quite profound.

But try not to sit around waiting for things to turn out how you hoped. *Impermanence* (Wheel of Fortune) asks you to take your fate in stride today, neither fighting upstream against it nor giving up completely on your hopes. Instead, see how you can coconspire with these spiritual forces, turning each hand that you are dealt into something greater with good faith and a bit of optimism.

JUST FOR TODAY

TODAY'S MANTRA
I will act on my instincts as if I have nothing to lose by trying.

TODAY'S JOURNAL PROMPT
What do I want to explore that lies far outside my comfort zone? What steps can I take today to begin?

TODAY'S RITUAL
Go buy a lottery ticket or scratcher from your local gas station, just to roll the dice and see what happens.

BORN ON THIS DAY

RITA ORA, English singer-songwriter and actor

CHARLES M. SCHULZ, American cartoonist and creator of the comic strip *Peanuts*

"The real power behind whatever success I have now was something I found within myself—something that's in all of us."—TINA TURNER, American-born Swiss singer-songwriter and actor

The Journey of Those Born on
NOVEMBER 26

You were born of limitless power and an abundance of strength that can make you believe at times that you can control fate. You will have to learn to fly with the winds of uncertainty, as your journey is one of independence, risk-taking, and karmic destiny.

Early on in your journey, you will meet your brave guide, *Autonomy* (The Number One). To channel your sage confidence, *Autonomy* calls you away from dependence and toward a path of radical self-trust. By listening to your gut and pursuing your instincts with the boldness of personal faith, you can carve out a one-of-a-kind legacy that others will look to with amazement.

If you choose this bold path, you will have to make friends with *Potential* (Ace of Wands). *Potential* invites you to take a chance on your next best idea rather than getting lost in the what-ifs of doubt. You will meet *Potential* at the very beginning of an adventure, when your enthusiasm for expansion keeps your eyes wide with hope.

By answering these risk-taking calls to action, you will have to surrender to the laws of *Impermanence* (Wheel of Fortune). *Impermanence* reminds you that life itself is an adventure, encouraging you to embrace the ups and downs, ebbs and flows. You will meet *Impermanence* when you are forced to accept and respect the divine twists and turns along your journey, when you have no choice but to make the most out of every aspect of the human experience. If you can remember that nothing lasts forever, *Impermanence* teaches you how to trust in the present moment.

YOUR GUIDES

Astrology: Your Energy
Sagittarius (Jupiter)

Numerology: Your Path
Autonomy (The Number One)

Minor Arcana: Your Lesson
Potential (The Ace of Wands)

Major Arcana: Your Highest Calling
Impermanence
(The Wheel of Fortune)

SAGITTARIUS
RULER: JUPITER

PURPOSE
To take great risks while trusting that fate is unfolding as it should.

RELATIONSHIPS

You are generously wise yet secretly guarded, so your relationships should be a place of transcendent trust and independence. By seeking out partners who let you do your thing and are content with who they are, you will discover that true love is a merging of two whole individuals.

The Journey of
NOVEMBER 27

Welcome to November 27, a slow and careful journey that asks you to live with integrity.
Aim for *Balance* (The Number Two) today. Although Sagittarius season makes you want to take on the world all at once, begin your day in quiet meditation as you consider what matters and what you can handle. Aim for quality rather than quantity when it comes to your ambitions, ensuring that you can get everything done without breaking a major sweat.

Besides, today is mostly for *Preparation* (Two of Wands). If there is a large venture you plan to take on professionally or personally, take this day to decide upon what this endeavor will require of you. By taking a step back to consider every obstacle as well as the larger ramifications of your vision, you can proceed with peaceful confidence as soon as tomorrow.

But for now, focus on your why. *Truth* (Justice) asks you to look at how your plans are working in harmony with, or in contrast to, your moral values. Are you living by your own code of ethics? Your actions have great consequences, so take a fair yet honest look at your motives and don't be afraid to pivot course if necessary.

JUST FOR TODAY

TODAY'S MANTRA
I will carefully consider where I am heading today, rather than acting impulsively and regretting it later.

TODAY'S JOURNAL PROMPT
What is an important moral value that I want to live by?

TODAY'S RITUAL
Light two candles, one for peace and one for honesty. As you stare into their flames, repeat the spell, "Magic fire, help me be truthfully patient and patiently truthful."

BORN ON THIS DAY

JIMI HENDRIX, American musician and singer-songwriter

LOUISE NØRLUND, Danish feminist and pacifist

"All fixed set patterns are incapable of adaptability or pliability. The truth is outside of all fixed patterns."—BRUCE LEE, Hong Kong American actor, director, martial artist, and philosopher

The Journey of Those Born on
NOVEMBER 27

You were born of worldly wisdom and an insatiable wanderlust that can make you feel like you have to be in a hundred places at once. You will have to slow down to find the truth you seek, as your journey is one of tranquility, patience, and higher truths.

Early on in your journey, you will meet your easeful guide, *Balance* (The Number Two). Despite your excitable nature, *Balance* calls you away from overdoing it and toward a path of energetic harmony. By never biting off more than you can chew, and taking time to rest when you need to, you can savor each experience along life's grand adventure.

If you choose this peaceful path, you will have to pay respect to *Preparation* (Two of Wands). Your ideas are inspired, but take a step back and consider which ones are worth exploring. You will meet *Preparation* in the lead-up to your most profound personal mission, when you have taken the time you need to align your mind with your heart and your body with your soul.

By answering these calls for patience, you will begin to notice the subtlety of *Truth* (Justice). *Truth* invites you to take spiritual accountability for your actions, considering on an objective and soul level how your life has impacted the world around you. You will meet *Truth* when you zoom out and see how you fit into the bigger picture, inspiring you to live with deep moral integrity. If you can gauge your success from the lens of quality rather than quantity, *Truth* offers you the gift of self-respect.

YOUR GUIDES

Astrology: Your Energy
Sagittarius (Jupiter)

Numerology: Your Path
Balance (The Number Two)

Minor Arcana: Your Lesson
Preparation (The Two of Wands)

Major Arcana: Your Highest Calling
Truth (Justice)

SAGITTARIUS
RULER: JUPITER

PURPOSE
To do less and consider more in order to live a life of profound consequence.

RELATIONSHIPS

You are high-minded and easily bored with partnership, but your relationships should be a place of lasting harmony. By seeking out partners who complement your wild nature with a peaceful calm, you will discover that true love balances you.

~ 523 ~

The Journey of
NOVEMBER 28

Welcome to November 28, a perspective-shifting journey that asks you to switch up the norm.

As you navigate the wanderlust of Sagittarius season, let *Flexibility* (The Number Three) be your guide. Rather than seeking to control or navigate your destiny, try to remain open to whatever the day throws at you. Whether you have an unplanned lunch with a new coworker or check out a new neighborhood on the other side of town, seek to break free from your everyday routine.

And why not enlarge your expertise along the way? *Expansion* (Three of Wands) invites you to try out a new field of study or skill, so put your ego to the side and practice the willingness that comes with beginning new things.

Besides, the most enriching of days come from not being in the driver's seat. *Surrender* (The Hanged Man) invites you to see life from an entirely new vantage point by not trying to force your will. If a friend or event beckons you in a new direction, follow it with innocent curiosity, and you may just uncover the spiritual breakthrough you have been waiting for.

JUST FOR TODAY

TODAY'S MANTRA

By unburdening myself from the illusion of control, I can explore the clear skies of the unknown.

TODAY'S JOURNAL PROMPT

What foreign subject, land, or spiritual practice am I super curious to study?

TODAY'S RITUAL

Go outside and find three twigs or sticks. These each represent a skill or field of study you'd like to explore. Plant the twigs upright in soft soil and repeat the mantra, "I can take one step toward learning something new." If you are not able to perform this in real life, close your eyes and carry out the entire ritual in your imagination.

BORN ON THIS DAY

YAMI GAUTAM, Indian actor

HELEN MAGILL WHITE, American educator and the first US woman to earn a PhD

"I didn't want to be a big record mogul . . . I just wanted to write songs and make people laugh."
—BERRY GORDY, American songwriter and record, film, and television producer

The Journey of Those Born on
NOVEMBER 28

Y ou were born of expansive self-confidence and an independent spirit that can leave you in a permanent position of authority. You will have to discover the transformative power of being a student, as your journey is one of learning, personal progress, and spiritual breakthroughs.

Early on in your journey, you will meet your light-hearted guide, *Flexibility* (The Number Three). Despite your innate wisdom, *Flexibility* calls you away from being an expert and toward a path of childlike curiosity. By staying eternally open to the experiences and knowledge of others, you can grow your perspective in an entirely new and fulfilling direction.

If you choose this exciting path, you will make good friends with *Expansion* (Three of Wands). *Expansion* reminds you that you can always benefit from learning new skills, so consider stepping outside your field of knowledge and pursuing something foreign. You will meet *Expansion* when you approach a subject or field as a humble student, with your eyes wide open and your brain ready to absorb.

By answering these spacious calls, you will come to respect the power of *Surrender* (The Hanged Man). *Surrender* asks you to release the rigid walls of the ego so that you can remain forever open to receiving the wisdom of the universe. You will meet *Surrender* in comfort-shattering experiences that alter your point of view in an unexpected but profound way. If you seek the growth that comes from not having all the answers, *Surrender* opens the door to enlightenment.

YOUR GUIDES

Astrology: Your Energy
Sagittarius (Jupiter)

Numerology: Your Path
Flexibility (The Number Three)

Minor Arcana: Your Lesson
Expansion (The Three of Wands)

Major Arcana: Your Highest Calling
Surrender (The Hanged Man)

SAGITTARIUS
RULER: JUPITER

PURPOSE
*To discover humble wisdom
that comes from not knowing.*

RELATIONSHIPS

You are radically independent with a wealth of knowledge to share, yet your relationships should be a place of deep learning. By seeking out partners who shed light on points of view that you can't quite see on your own, you will discover that true love expands your perspective.

The Journey of
NOVEMBER 29

Welcome to November 29, a self-respecting journey that teaches you when enough is enough.

Approach today with a sense of *Discipline* (The Number Four). Whether you create a rigorous plan of action or stick to your spiritual practices with complete integrity, try to show the universe and yourself just how reliable you can be. Keep your feet firmly planted in reality as you make great progress.

But make sure your to-do list includes some time for *Celebration* (Four of Wands). Too much unfulfilling work can lead to serious burnout, so create some space in your day to indulge in something that is plain fun. Call the friends you consider family and have a night on the town or sit back and enjoy the movie that always makes you laugh. A little bit of joy goes a long way.

And don't feel any guilt over it. *Self-mastery* (The Emperor) empowers you to own each decision you make today, as long as it is serving your long-term best interests. If you need to add boundaries as you navigate this day, see them as an opportunity to re-parent yourself and to practice profound self-respect.

JUST FOR TODAY

TODAY'S MANTRA

By creating some self-proposed structure in my day, I can make time for work and play.

TODAY'S JOURNAL PROMPT

What is my favorite nourishing way to blow off steam?

TODAY'S RITUAL

Close your eyes and manifest a dream party you would like to throw for yourself. Consider your guest list, the location, your menu, and what activities you would include. If you feel inspired, spend some time today planning how to implement this in real life. You deserve it!

BORN ON THIS DAY

CHADWICK BOSEMAN, American actor and playwright

LOUISA MAY ALCOTT, American author

"Failures, repeated failures, are finger posts on the road to achievement. One fails forward toward success."—C. S. LEWIS, English writer and lay theologian

The Journey of Those Born on
NOVEMBER 29

Y ou were born of compassionate diplomacy and a pervasive generosity that can leave your cup empty. You will have to protect yourself with the strength of personal authority, as your journey is one of hard work, energetic restoration, and necessary boundaries.

Early on in your journey, you will meet your no-nonsense guide, *Discipline* (The Number Four). Despite your happy-go-lucky disposition, *Discipline* calls you away from capitulation and toward a path of rigorous perseverance. By devoting hours of mental, physical, and spiritual energy to the ambitions you hold dear, you can create an unshakable foundation upon which to build sustainable success.

If you choose this diligent path, you will have to make time for *Celebration* (Four of Wands). *Celebration* asks you to stop the hustle, even for a second, to reconnect with uninhibited joy and good fun. You will meet *Celebration* when you are indulging in the present moment, surrounded by the people and activities that refill your energy tank so you can keep fighting another day.

By answering these calls for endurance, you will come to understand the importance of *Self-mastery* (The Emperor). *Self-mastery* reminds you that you are the highest authority when it comes to your overall well-being, encouraging you to set the necessary structures, systems, and boundaries you need to sustain a lifetime of meaningful action. You will meet *Self-mastery* when you practice self-respect, letting yourself and the rest of the world know where you begin and the work ends. If you can seek to be respected rather than well liked, you'll learn the art of self-preservation.

SAGITTARIUS
RULER: JUPITER

PURPOSE
To work hard, but never at the expense of joy and longevity.

RELATIONSHIPS

You are giving to the ones you love, even to a fault, yet your relationships should be a place of mutual responsibility and joyful support. By seeking out partners who seek to share your burdens and help you find time to have some fun, you will discover that true love is a wonderful place to come home to.

The Journey of
NOVEMBER 30

Welcome to November 30, a self-empowering journey that opens you to higher truths. Sagittarius season can expand your perspective, but *Courage* (The Number Five) invites you to share what you have been learning. Tell the world about the radical revelations or global issues you have been studying without holding back in the hopes of making others comfortable. A bit of bravery can go a long way.

In fact, lean in to any healthy *Conflict* (Five of Wands) that comes your way. If you find yourself in stark disagreement with a person, place, or institution, don't back down in the name of compromise. Instead, participate in a detached form of debate, standing firm in the facts that back up your point of view.

Because at the end of the day, no one has a monopoly on the truth. *Wisdom* (The Hierophant) advises you to balance personal authority with humility, so try to walk the line between being a good listener and an empowered individual. By finding spiritual confidence in your perspective and believing deeply in your innate intelligence, you can engage in radically transformative conversations that reshape the nature of disagreement.

JUST FOR TODAY

TODAY'S MANTRA
Authentic confidence allows me to accept and grow from the fact that others may disagree with my point of view.

TODAY'S JOURNAL PROMPT
What issue do I feel called to speak up about? Is there more research I can do to strengthen my authority on this subject?

TODAY'S RITUAL
Take five minutes to sit in silent meditation. As you close your eyes, place your hand over your right shoulder and repeat the affirmation, "I won't let others get the best of me."

BORN ON THIS DAY

MARINA ABRAMOVIĆ, Serbian conceptual and performance artist, philanthropist, writer, and filmmaker

MARK TWAIN, American writer, humorist, entrepreneur, publisher, and lecturer

"If they don't give you a seat at the table, bring a folding chair."—SHIRLEY CHISHOLM, American politician, educator, author, and the first Black woman elected to the US Congress

The Journey of Those Born on
NOVEMBER 30

Y ou were born of expansive curiosity and an abundance of potential that you might not know what to do with. You will have to find your purpose through wild bravery, as your journey is one of honesty, necessary conflict, and higher knowledge.

Early on in your journey, you will meet your daring guide, *Courage* (The Number Five). Despite your flexible disposition, *Courage* calls you away from passivity and toward a path of radical candor. By speaking out from a place of divine conviction, you can change the hearts and minds of many.

But if you choose this audacious path, you will have to contend with *Conflict* (Five of Wands). *Conflict* reminds you that adversity is a natural obstacle amidst a journey of fierce bravery. You will meet *Conflict* in the face of adversaries and naysayers who try to dim your shine and question your point of view. If you can learn not to take criticism too seriously, you'll learn how not to let others get the best of you.

By answering these valiant calls to action, you will begin to channel the humble confidence of *Wisdom* (The Hierophant). The truth is all too easy to dispute, so stay true to your beliefs amidst the rocking tides of public opinion. You will meet *Wisdom* in moments of sage confidence, when you respectfully allow others to share their point of view while holding your head high with graceful self-trust. If you can seek internal over external approval, *Wisdom* will offer you the gift of spiritual authority.

YOUR GUIDES

Astrology: Your Energy
Sagittarius (Jupiter)

Numerology: Your Path
Courage (The Number Five)

Minor Arcana: Your Lesson
Conflict (The Five of Wands)

Major Arcana: Your Highest Calling
Wisdom (The Hierophant)

SAGITTARIUS
RULER: JUPITER

PURPOSE
*To dare to be honest among
a sea of followers.*

RELATIONSHIPS

You have much joy and wisdom to share with others, and your relationships should be a place of radical vulnerability. By seeking out partners who say it like it is and inspire you to disrupt the status quo, you will discover that true love is the highest act of bravery.

The Journey of
DECEMBER 1

Welcome to December 1, a journey of metamorphosis that reminds you of the importance of joy amidst transition.

As you navigate the fiery passion of Sagittarius season, *Discipline* (The Number Four) asks you to direct your energy toward meaningful work. Whether you create a thoughtful to-do list or organize your calendar, be sure to add some helpful structure to this expansive day.

And while you're at it, pencil in some time for *Celebration* (Four of Wands). Acknowledge how hard you have been working by spending some quality time with friends or having an uninhibited dance party with yourself. While it may feel as if you don't have enough time to play on a day like this, remember that sometimes the most productive thing to do is nothing productive at all.

You will need some joyful energy to spare as you embrace *Transformation* (Death). You may be mourning an outdated version of yourself, so give yourself some grace as you shed old layers of personal protection. As you navigate whatever internal or external transition you are going through, remind yourself that it is brave, and radical, to move toward a more authentic version of yourself.

JUST FOR TODAY

TODAY'S MANTRA

I will pay respect to my internal and external needs amidst this season of growth.

TODAY'S JOURNAL PROMPT

What is a quick but effective activity that helps me get out of my head and into the present moment?

TODAY'S RITUAL

Throw a celebration for a version of yourself that you are ready to let go. Whether you execute this in your imagination on the way to work or carry it out in real life, give this version of yourself the appreciation and acknowledgment it deserves so you can release it with joy rather than sadness.

BORN ON THIS DAY

ZOË KRAVITZ, American actor, singer, and model

KOTHAINAYAKI AMMAL, Tamil activist, feminist, and writer hailed as the "Queen of Fictions"

"If only I'd known my differentness would be an asset, then my earlier life would have been much easier."—BETTE MIDLER, American singer, actor, and comedian

The Journey of Those Born on
DECEMBER 1

You were born of expansive independence and an impulsiveness that can waste your potential on fruitless effort. You will have to direct your energy toward the most essential of growth, as your journey is one of hard work, restoration, and spiritual renewal.

Early on in your journey, you will meet your serious guide, *Discipline* (The Number Four). Despite your spirited disposition, *Discipline* calls you away from blind passion and toward a path of humble progress. By showing up with integrity for all your work, both the gratifying and the seemingly mundane, you can build an infallible foundation of authentic self-esteem.

If you choose this diligent path, you will have to make time for *Celebration* (Four of Wands). *Celebration* reminds you to acknowledge your hard-earned success, inviting you to take time between ambitions for nourishing rest and uninhibited joy. You will meet *Celebration* within metaphorical and literal homecomings, when you pause from your hustle long enough to refill your energetic cup.

By answering these calls for self-respect, you will find your ultimate potential within *Transformation* (Death). *Transformation* reminds you that it is not just okay, but imperative, for you to grow out of old versions of yourself. You will meet *Transformation* within the discomfort of transition, when you are simultaneously grieving what once was and beginning to open your soul's doors to the potential of who you could become. If you can trust that there is new, beautiful life within the natural deaths of identity, you'll tap into the divine art of metamorphosis.

> ## YOUR GUIDES
>
> *Astrology: Your Energy*
> Sagittarius (Jupiter)
>
> *Numerology: Your Path*
> Discipline (The Number Four)
>
> *Minor Arcana: Your Lesson*
> Celebration (The Four of Wands)
>
> *Major Arcana: Your Highest Calling*
> Transformation (Death)

SAGITTARIUS
RULER: JUPITER

PURPOSE
To realize that to be truly alive,
you must constantly transform.

RELATIONSHIPS

You have enough optimism to power the world, and your relationships should be a place of restorative joy. By seeking out partners who help you relax through fun, laughter, and play, you will discover that true love is where you go to recharge.

The Journey of
DECEMBER 2

Welcome to December 2, an empowering journey that teaches you to keep your cool amidst drama.

Find your sense of *Courage* (The Number Five) today. Channel the sage confidence of Sagittarius season by sharing your truth and passion with the rest of the world. Whether you dare greatly in your creative, personal, or spiritual life, try to find the willingness to risk it all.

And rise to the occasion if you run into any *Conflict* (Five of Wands). If you find that someone or something is standing in the way of you fulfilling your dreams, hold true in your convictions no matter what. By embracing the inevitability of pushback, you can strengthen your resilience muscles and learn to sustain a lifetime of vulnerability.

But don't get burnt out with passion. *Serenity* (Temperance) asks you to find peace throughout this brave day, taking a few minutes here and there to quiet your mind and calm your nervous system. There is no battle, or desire, that is worth losing your sense of internal contentment over, so call upon your spiritual resources and support systems to center yourself amidst the wild excitement of vulnerability.

———————○———————

JUST FOR TODAY

TODAY'S MANTRA
Internal peace helps me win the fight for my creative ambitions.

TODAY'S JOURNAL PROMPT
When I am in an argument with someone, what spiritual tools can I rely on to keep myself calm?

TODAY'S RITUAL
To begin your day, sit in silent meditation for fourteen minutes. As you close your eyes, visualize yourself going into battle with fierce bravery and with no inhibitions or self-doubt. Carry this image with you throughout your day and draw upon its power when you need it most.

———————○———————

BORN ON THIS DAY

BRITNEY SPEARS, American singer-songwriter and dancer

NELLY FURTADO, Canadian singer-songwriter

"Deeds, not words."—HÉLÈNE MONASTIER, Swiss peace activist and teacher

The Journey of Those Born on
DECEMBER 2

Y ou were born of divine optimism and a limitless generosity that can leave you vulnerable to the self-seeking nature of others. You will have to learn to fight for your right to personal peace, as your journey is one of bravery, imperative conflict, and spiritual tranquility.

Early on in your journey, you will meet your brave guide, *Courage* (The Number Five). Despite your accommodating personality, *Courage* calls you away from playing it small and toward a path of unapologetic self-expression. You will meet *Courage* in moments of excruciating vulnerability, when the world shines its spotlight directly on your creative brilliance. If you live freely from the depths of your soul, *Courage* brings you a lifetime of jaw-dropping applause.

If you take this road of self-expression, you will have to contend with *Conflict* (Five of Wands). You will meet *Conflict* in the jealous haters and naysayers who seek to set fire to your brilliance. *Conflict* invites you to combat this adversity with self-belief, learning in the process that authentic power is untouchable.

By answering these lionhearted calls, you will discover the value of *Serenity* (Temperance). *Serenity* reminds you that internal harmony is always available to you, even in the rockiest of external circumstances. You will meet *Serenity* when you tune out the rest of the chaos and tap into the divine quiet that guards your wild soul. If you can reach for this spiritual support amidst the inevitable drama of an honest life, you'll discover the gift of eternal contentment.

YOUR GUIDES
Astrology: Your Energy
Sagittarius (Jupiter, Mars)
Numerology: Your Path
Courage (The Number Five)
Minor Arcana: Your Lesson
Conflict (The Five of Wands)
Major Arcana: Your Highest Calling
Serenity (Temperance)

SAGITTARIUS
RULERS: JUPITER, MARS

PURPOSE
To protect creative brilliance with internal peace.

RELATIONSHIPS

You are endlessly giving to the people you are committed to, but your relationships should be a place of protection and peace. By seeking out partners who help keep your creative flame alive while bringing you a sense of personal contentment, you will discover that true love is your best advocate.

The Journey of
DECEMBER 3

Welcome to December 3, a self-healing journey that invites you to feel good about yourself. Proceed from the heart today. *Devotion* (The Number Six) invites you to bring the optimistic energy of Sagittarius season into the relationships and goals you cherish most. There's no room for superficial interactions or draining obligations; instead, prioritize the aspects of your life that nourish your soul.

And you may just stumble upon some unexpected applause. *Confidence* (Six of Wands) encourages you to own how much good work you have done, patting yourself on the back and accepting any praise that comes your way. Many of us have been taught to feel shame around accepting compliments, but now is the time to experience some well-deserved acknowledgment.

But be gentle and curious if some emotions get triggered throughout this fulfilling day. *Shadow* (The Devil) invites you inward to heal the emotional blockages you have around letting in good things. When did you first learn to fear, or reject, intimacy and joy? By using a reflective lens to explore the wounds that lie deep within your subconscious, you can discover a profound sense of emotional freedom.

JUST FOR TODAY

TODAY'S MANTRA
I won't beat myself up over the unconscious fears I have around happiness.

TODAY'S JOURNAL PROMPT
How do I typically react to compliments?

TODAY'S RITUAL
To start your day, light a candle and recite the spell, "Devil magic, please help me release the character defects that burden the peace within me."

BORN ON THIS DAY

DARYL HANNAH, American actor and environmental activist

RAMA DEVI, Indian freedom fighter and social reformer

"Maybe it's not too late to learn how to love and forget how to hate."—OZZY OSBOURNE, English singer-songwriter and television personality

The Journey of Those Born on
DECEMBER 3

You were born of abundant genius and a wildness that can make it hard to sustain real intimacy, even with yourself. You will have to soften to the healing quality of connection, as your journey is one of sincerity, self-acknowledgment, and true vulnerability.

Early on in your journey, you will meet your open-hearted guide, *Devotion* (The Number Six). Despite your expansive personality, *Devotion* calls you away from overindulgence and toward a path of meaningful service. By sharing your magnificent power with the people and projects that speak directly to your soul, you can build a life of deep consequence.

If you take this purposeful path, you will meet your inspired friend, *Confidence* (Six of Wands). *Confidence* invites you to celebrate your accomplishments, never confusing humility for self-denial. You will meet *Confidence* when you take a step back from all your work and appreciate how much progress you have made. While you may be your toughest critic, *Confidence* asks you to focus on the good you have done.

By answering these emotionally significant calls, you can go deeper with *Shadow* (The Devil). *Shadow* asks you to take a closer look at your emotional defenses and unconscious self-destructive tendencies, shedding a compassionate light on what lies beneath the surface. You will meet *Shadow* in profound psychological healing, when you uncover, discover, and discard the internal wounds that block your emotional freedom. If you can gently go toward the places within that scare you, you'll remember who you are underneath it all.

YOUR GUIDES

Astrology: Your Energy
Sagittarius (Jupiter, Mars)

Numerology: Your Path
Devotion (The Number Six)

Minor Arcana: Your Lesson
Confidence (The Six of Wands)

Major Arcana: Your Highest Calling
Shadow (The Devil)

SAGITTARIUS
RULERS: JUPITER, MARS

PURPOSE
To soften to and embrace your inherent goodness.

RELATIONSHIPS

You are brave in most areas of your life, but your relationships should be a place of deep vulnerability. By seeking out partners whom you don't feel you always have to be strong around and with whom you can reveal your truth, you will discover that true love is a profound portal for healing.

The Journey of
DECEMBER 4

Welcome to December 4, a surprising journey that reminds you that you can handle anything.

Show up with great *Commitment* (The Number Seven) to the responsibilities and relationships that help you grow. Whether you put in some extra work within your partnership to better understand each other or devote yourself to a new project in your professional life, now is the time to use your energy in a meaningful way.

But don't take it as a bad sign if you run into any obstacles along the way. *Perseverance* (Seven of Wands) asks you to fight even harder for what you want in the face of opposition, defending and protecting the dreams of the soul. Although Sagittarius season can inspire some flightiness, channel this energy into persistence instead.

By building some of these muscles, you will be able to make the most out of any change that comes your way. *Upheaval* (The Tower) may bring an internal or external shift to you today, so lean in to whatever the universe throws at you. More than likely, it is a shift you have been needing to make for quite some time, presenting you with a radical opportunity to grow.

———————————————○———————————————

JUST FOR TODAY

TODAY'S MANTRA
With the power of personal persistence, I can embrace any fateful change that comes my way.

TODAY'S RITUAL
Set an alarm for 7 p.m. this evening and spend sixteen minutes making a list of what you accomplished today. Ask yourself whether you used your time wisely, and if there is anything you did that doesn't feel worth your while.

TODAY'S JOURNAL PROMPT
What big internal or external change am I need of in my life?

———————————————○———————————————

BORN ON THIS DAY

SELINA COOPER, English suffragist and the first woman to represent the Independent Labour Party

STELLA CORNELIUS, Australian businesswoman and peace and conflict resolution activist

"Everyone needs a chance to evolve."—JAY-Z, American rapper, songwriter, record executive, and businessman

The Journey of Those Born on
DECEMBER 4

Y ou were born of expansive authority and limitless ambition that can keep you reaching for power rather than purpose. You will have to discover your ultimate potential through fateful change, as your journey is one of intention, commitment, and unexpected revelations.

Early on in your journey, you will meet your steadfast guide, *Commitment* (The Number Seven). Despite your wide-ranging interests, *Commitment* calls you away from unreliability and toward a path of deep loyalty and dedication. You will meet *Commitment* in the crucial decisions that move your life forward in a specific, and focused, direction.

But if you choose this deliberate path, you will have to pay respect to *Perseverance* (Seven of Wands). *Perseverance* reminds you that when the going gets tough, you have the power to persist by drawing on your internal resources. You will meet *Perseverance* in the face of your competitors and obstacles, when you dig deep within your conviction and rise to the occasion.

By answering these devotional calls to action, you will meet your greatest teacher, *Upheaval* (The Tower).

You will encounter *Upheaval* in the change that you neither caused nor asked for, when your reality as it stands begins to shift in a radical and unexpected way. By looking for the purpose and the opportunity within these divine acts of intervention, you can recognize your limitless resilience. If you can trust that the universe is doing for you what you cannot do for yourself, you'll discover the art of starting over.

───────○───────

SAGITTARIUS
RULERS: JUPITER, MARS

PURPOSE
To remain fiercely loyal to the soul's commitments amidst the wild winds of change.

RELATIONSHIPS

You are a natural authority figure in most areas of your life, yet your relationships should be a place of deep respect and mutual hard work. By seeking out partners who are willing to grow together rather than apart when things get hard, you will discover that true love is a faithful bond.

The Journey of
DECEMBER 5

W elcome to December 5, an inspired journey that asks you to believe in your resilience. Step into your *Power* (The Number Eight) today. To make the most of the fierce bravery of Sagittarius season, try to accept and embrace every inch of your authentic spirit. If there is something you have been holding back due to fear of rejection, test out how it feels to honor this aspect of your truth.

And follow through on this self-affirmation with some action. *Momentum* (Eight of Wands) invites you to take action on your desires today. Whether you sign up for that trip abroad or purchase the URL for your new business, now is the time to move forward with your internal plans.

By putting faith in your true self, you may just discover a new sense of *Hope* (The Star). If you are grieving an aspect of your life that is ending or reeling from a personal mistake, try to actively search for the silver lining as you move your gaze toward the future. The more you know, the better you can do, so get excited about what you hope to create with this deeper sense of perspective.

JUST FOR TODAY

TODAY'S MANTRA
Now that I know myself better, I am ready to move forward.

TODAY'S JOURNAL PROMPT
What significant thing have I learned about myself by making a mistake recently?

TODAY'S RITUAL
Take a cold shower, as cold as you can stand, to start your morning. As you let this refreshing water wash over your body, repeat the affirmation, "Hope will outlast any of my deep fears of rejection."

BORN ON THIS DAY

MARGARET CHO, American stand-up comedian, actor, musician, fashion designer, and author

MILDRED SCOTT OLMSTED, American Quaker peace activist

"Character—the willingness to accept responsibility for one's own life—is the source from which self-respect springs."—JOAN DIDION, American writer

The Journey of Those Born on
DECEMBER 5

Y ou were born of intuitive authority and a deep-seated fear of being wrong that can cause internal paralysis. You will have to take a leap of faith to discover your innate brilliance, as your journey is one of authenticity, self-trust, and personal renewal.

Early on in your journey, you will meet your enigmatic guide, *Power* (The Number Eight). To make the most of your intrinsic fire, *Power* calls you away from approval-seeking and toward a path of self-derived confidence. You will meet *Power* when you embrace the full breadth of your authentic spirit, never making yourself small to make others comfortable.

If you choose this self-affirming path, you will have to make moves with *Momentum* (Eight of Wands). *Momentum* asks you to strike while the iron's hot, putting complete faith in your instincts rather than falling prey to the overanalysis of self-doubt. You will meet *Momentum* when you leave behind what is no longer serving you and your head, heart, and soul converge in a resounding "yes" to move onward.

By answering these calls for self-belief, you will come to rely on *Hope* (The Star). *Hope* reminds you that within every disappointment lies a chance for radical renewal, encouraging you to wash away the past with the divine waters of optimism. You will meet *Hope* in the aftermath of grief, when you begin to see the ray of sunlight peeking through the debris and rubble of loss. Just as the stars can't shine without darkness, *Hope* shows you that within the seemingly worst of circumstances, you can unlock your true brilliance.

> ### YOUR GUIDES
>
> *Astrology: Your Energy*
> Sagittarius (Jupiter, Mars)
>
> *Numerology: Your Path*
> Power (The Number Eight)
>
> *Minor Arcana: Your Lesson*
> Momentum (The Eight of Wands)
>
> *Major Arcana: Your Highest Calling*
> Hope (The Star)

SAGITTARIUS
RULERS: JUPITER, MARS

PURPOSE
To find your power in the uncertainty of self-trust.

RELATIONSHIPS

You are fiercely powerful yet self-protective, so your relationships should be a place of deep honesty and self-revealing. By seeking out partners who aren't afraid to know even the darkest corners of your truth, you will discover that true love asks you to be real.

The Journey of
DECEMBER 6

Welcome to December 6, a fearless journey into your internal world.

To make the most of the wanderlust of Sagittarius season, try to have a new *Experience* (The Number Nine) today. Instead of trying to control or conquer your ambitions, put adventure at the top of your to-do list. Whether you explore a new subject in your chosen field or go on an unexpected date on a different side of town, embrace the foreign and unknown.

And make sure you have enough energy to sustain this growth. *Persistence* (Nine of Wands) asks that you keep a careful eye on your emotional, physical, and spiritual needs today, never draining yourself of your most valuable resources. If you need to take a power nap or add fifteen minutes to your lunch break, give yourself what you need to carry forward.

You will need this nourishment as you do the heavy reflective work with your *Memory* (The Moon). Get curious about the emotional reactions you have today, looking inward to decipher what experiences within you are getting triggered. By bringing what is underneath the surface of your psyche to your conscious mind, you can begin tomorrow with a clean mental slate.

JUST FOR TODAY

TODAY'S MANTRA
I will bravely get to know the parts of myself that I normally keep buried.

TODAY'S JOURNAL PROMPT
What are small but impactful ways I can take care of myself amidst an emotionally heavy day?

TODAY'S RITUAL
On a piece of paper, draw an approximately three-inch circle. Draw a line down the middle of the circle and on the left side, write down three things that you are afraid of at this very moment. On the right side, write down six things that you are curious to explore.

BORN ON THIS DAY

ICHIKAWA EBIZŌ XI, Japanese Kabuki actor and stage producer

LUCIA RIJKER, Dutch boxer, kickboxer, and actor

"It is easy enough to vote right and be consistently with the majority. But it is more often more important to be ahead of the majority and this means being willing to cut the first furrow in the ground and stand alone for a while if necessary."—PATSY MINK, American attorney and politician

The Journey of Those Born on
DECEMBER 6

You were born of expansive compassion and an optimism that can border on naivete. You will have to grow wiser through the process of getting to know yourself, as your journey is one of exploration, perseverance, and intuitive healing.

Early on in your journey, you will meet your worldly guide, *Experience* (The Number Nine). Despite your tenderhearted nature, *Experience* calls you away from emotional safety and toward a path of the expansive unknown. You will meet *Experience* when you set bravely out into the wilderness of new opportunities, relying on nothing but the excitement of what's to come.

If you choose this widening path, you will have to show your grit to *Persistence* (Nine of Wands). *Persistence* reminds you that just because you are close to the finish line, doesn't mean you can call it in due to exhaustion. Instead, *Persistence* encourages you to fill your energetic cup along the way, making sure you have enough resources to last the lifetime of your journey.

YOUR GUIDES

Astrology: Your Energy
Sagittarius (Jupiter, Mars)

Numerology: Your Path
Experience (The Number Nine)

Minor Arcana: Your Lesson
Persistence (The Nine of Wands)

Major Arcana: Your Highest Calling
Memory (The Moon)

By answering these growth-inspiring calls, you will discover the healing power of *Memory* (The Moon). *Memory* knows that no matter how far you go, you can never escape your past. *Memory* calls you back inward to heal the unaddressed parts of your story so that you can begin to live out your true purpose with the gift of self-awareness. You will meet *Memory* in the repressed experiences that carry a profound truth that you must reclaim. If you can clear out the rubble of the subconscious, *Memory* offers you the gift of a clear conscience.

SAGITTARIUS
RULERS: JUPITER, MARS

PURPOSE
To grow into the wild unknown in order to reclaim what was lost within.

RELATIONSHIPS

You are unconditionally generous with the people you love, and your relationships should be a place of emotional maturity. By seeking out partners who push you to question your spiritual and psychological status quo, you will discover that true love inspires you to grow.

The Journey of
DECEMBER 7

Welcome to December 7, a courageous journey that reminds you how magical you truly are.

Trust in your instincts today. To make the most of the bravery of Sagittarius season, *Autonomy* (The Number One) asks you to do what feels right to you rather than relying on the opinions of others. Take a chance on your next greatest idea, diving headfirst into the grand adventure of self-trust.

All you need to do is believe in its *Potential* (Ace of Wands). This is not a day for rigid planning or conservative thinking, but instead, a wonderful time to take a chance on your inspiration. What grand vision have you been sitting on for quite some time? Be bold and be brave.

By investing in yourself, you can begin to experience the full power of your authenticity. *Vitality* (The Sun) invites you to feel good about who you are and where you are going, so shine a conscious light on the things that are going well in your life right now. Whether you wear that outfit that makes you feel gorgeous or give yourself a giant smile in the mirror, do something that reminds you how lucky you are to be uniquely you.

―――――――――○―――――――――

JUST FOR TODAY

TODAY'S MANTRA
Perhaps I am brilliant, after all!

TODAY'S JOURNAL PROMPT
In what situations do I feel the most myself?

TODAY'S RITUAL
Give yourself a pep talk in the mirror to start your day. It can be uncomfortable at first, but put on a smile (real or fake!) and tell yourself all the empowering words you wish you could hear from a person you admire.

―――――――――○―――――――――

BORN ON THIS DAY

HARRIET NAHANEE, Pacheedaht Indigenous rights and environmental activist

YUZURU HANYU, Japanese figure skater and first Asian men's singles skater to win the Olympic gold

"Optimism is a strategy for making a better future. Because unless you believe that the future can be better, you are unlikely to step up and take responsibility for making it so."—NOAM CHOMSKY, American linguist, philosopher, cognitive scientist, historian, social critic, and political activist

The Journey of Those Born on
DECEMBER 7

You were born of bold ambition and a certainty of purpose that makes you forget at times that life is meant to be enjoyed. You will have to find the freedom that comes from growing into your true self, as your journey is one of leadership, intuitive action, and boundless authenticity.

Early on in your journey, you will meet your audacious guide, *Autonomy* (The Number One). Despite your desire for security, *Autonomy* calls you away from careful planning and toward a path of radical self-belief. You will meet *Autonomy* in the roads that you carve out for yourself, never minding the rules and plans that others have drawn out for you.

If you choose this bold path, you will meet your inspired friend, *Potential* (Ace of Wands). *Potential* encourages you to act without a set plan, reminding you that it is possible to fake it until you make it. You will meet *Potential* in the very beginning stages of your next venture, when you have no idea what is to come. If you can trust your instincts, you will be a trailblazer and tastemaker.

By answering these calls for confidence, you will open yourself to the light of *Vitality* (The Sun). *Vitality* invites you to be completely and unapologetically true to your innate brilliance, never dimming your shine to make others comfortable. You will meet *Vitality* when you step into the sunlight of your authentic spirit, letting the warm glow of self-acceptance keep your embers of passion glowing for the rest of your life.

───────────○───────────

SAGITTARIUS
RULERS: JUPITER, MARS

PURPOSE
To take leaps of faith in yourself to uncover authentic self-confidence.

RELATIONSHIPS

You are generously committed to the people you are loyal to, and your relationships should be a place of unconditional encouragement. By seeking out partners who are confident enough in themselves to celebrate your boundless brilliance, you will discover that true love wants you to shine.

The Journey of
DECEMBER 8

Welcome to December 8, an eye-opening journey that teaches you that you can notice when you are slowing down.

As you navigate the fiery passion of Sagittarius season, temper this energy by seeking *Balance* (The Number Two). There's no need to overindulge or overcommit yourself today, but instead, practice self-restraint as you decipher what projects and relationships are truly worth your while.

And why not spend some thoughtful time in *Preparation* (Two of Wands). Some days are made for wild action, but use this day to plan for your next grand adventure. Take careful note of everything you might need or could stumble into along the way so that you can set out tomorrow with a thorough and decisive strategy for success.

But if you run up against an inconvenient truth today, don't run away. *Awakening* (Judgment) encourages you to come to terms with reality as it stands rather than getting lost in fantastical thinking or idealization. By meeting yourself and the world exactly where it is, you can make thoughtful decisions that will sustain your long-term well-being and satisfaction. If you find that you need to pivot from your plans, take it as a welcome sign that you are moving closer to your true purpose.

JUST FOR TODAY

TODAY'S MANTRA
I will take a step back from my plans to be sure I'm seeing everything clearly.

TODAY'S JOURNAL PROMPT
What plans can I afford to cancel to simplify my day?

TODAY'S RITUAL
Watch a documentary about a current social or political issue that is tough for you to swallow. If you find it quite difficult to digest, hold your hand over your chest and repeat the affirmation, "I am capable of handling the truth."

BORN ON THIS DAY

SAMMY DAVIS JR., American singer, dancer, actor, vaudevillian, and comedian

BERNICE FISHER, American civil rights activist and union organizer, called the "godmother of the restaurant 'sit-in' technique"

"To be an artist, one must . . . never shirk from the truth as he understands it, never withdraw from life."—DIEGO RIVERA, Mexican painter who established the mural movement in Mexican and international art

The Journey of Those Born on
DECEMBER 8

Y ou were born of boundless authenticity and a depth of passion that can overwhelm even you at times. You will have to find your truth within the middle ground, as your journey is one of peace, thoughtfulness, and higher understanding.

Early on in your journey, you will meet your tranquil guide, *Balance* (The Number Two). Despite your limitless power, *Balance* calls you away from extremes and toward a path of easeful living. Rather than taking everything all at once, *Balance* teaches you how much more effective you can be when you pare back your ambitions and focus on sustainable action.

If you choose this path of reason, you will have to make time for *Preparation* (Two of Wands). *Preparation* reminds you that a bit of planning can go a long way, encouraging you to set yourself up for success in advance rather than making things up as you go. You will meet *Preparation* on the eve of your next adventure, when you have considered and reconsidered what you will need to see your plan through to completion.

By answering these calls for patience, you will begin to live in harmony with *Awakening* (Judgment). *Awakening* asks you to make peace with reality as it stands, never denying the harsh truths of life but instead integrating them into your personal evolution. You will meet *Awakening* in the toughest of ah-ha moments, when you see things as they really are rather than how you would like them to be. If you can choose truth over comfort, *Awakening* will hand you the keys to higher consciousness.

—————————————————○—————————————————

SAGITTARIUS
RULERS: JUPITER, MARS

PURPOSE
To make life simpler in order to awaken to what really matters.

RELATIONSHIPS

You are prone to instantaneous passion and intimacy, but your relationships should be a place of earned trust and peaceful coexistence. By seeking out partners who don't tolerate drama of any kind but instead demand compassionate truth, you will discover that true love is a source of wisdom.

The Journey of
DECEMBER 9

Welcome to December 9, a playful adventure that offers you sage wisdom.

Keep your mind and heart open to others as you navigate the adventurous winds of Sagittarius season. *Flexibility* (The Number Three) invites you to engage in conversation with the world that surrounds you today, so don't get stuck in fixed opinions or rigid thinking. Instead, approach others with curiosity and find the courageous willingness to be proven wrong.

And with this humility, you might just learn a new skill. *Expansion* (Three of Wands) encourages you to try something foreign to increase your database of knowledge and enhance the expertise you already have. Whether you try out a new technology at work or let a friend show you a new spiritual practice, move toward the opportunities that excite you.

As you explore these bountiful possibilities, try to keep things in *Perspective* (The World). No adventure has ever gone seamlessly, so whenever you have a moment, take a step back and thank the universe for everything it has given you and everything it has taken away. By practicing active gratitude for each peak and valley you travel today, you can find purpose in even the most uncomfortable of circumstances.

JUST FOR TODAY

TODAY'S MANTRA
I am grateful for all the things I have yet to know.

TODAY'S RITUAL
Look up one of the three famous people born on this day and research the times in which they pivoted from their perspective to draw inspiration for how you can approach the rest of your day.

TODAY'S JOURNAL PROMPT
What spiritual subjects or practices help me see the big picture of my life?

BORN ON THIS DAY

WHINA COOPER, Māori leader who led a nonviolent march against the loss of Māori lands

GRACE HOPPER, American US Navy rear admiral and computer scientist

"Most things don't work out as expected, but what happens instead often turns out to be the good stuff."—JUDI DENCH, English actor

The Journey of Those Born on
DECEMBER 9

You were born of expansive wisdom and a spirited introversion that can keep you stuck in the confines of your comfort zone. You will have to become grateful for the unexpected, as your journey is one of connection, learning, and deep appreciation.

Early on in your journey, you will meet your excitable guide, *Flexibility* (The Number Three). Despite your sage intelligence, *Flexibility* calls you away from being an expert and toward a path of thorough listening and humble sharing. By engaging in an open-minded dialogue with everyone, including the universe itself, you will grow in ways you never imagined possible.

If you choose this fruitful path, you will meet your coconspirator, *Expansion* (Three of Wands). *Expansion* reminds you that no matter how much of an expert you become at your chosen crafts, there is always more to explore. You will meet *Expansion* in the new skills, hobbies, subjects, and relationships you take on for the sake of childlike curiosity.

By answering these inspired calls for growth, you will find a new lens for life with *Perspective* (The World). You will meet *Perspective* at each peak along your ever-winding journey, when you are able to take a step back and witness the inexplicable brilliance of the human experience. *Perspective* invites you to find meaning in every twist and turn, practicing gratitude for even the most trying of personal setbacks. If you can zoom out and see the big picture, you'll discover the gift of spiritual intelligence.

YOUR GUIDES

Astrology: Your Energy
Sagittarius (Jupiter, Mars)

Numerology: Your Path
Flexibility (The Number Three)

Minor Arcana: Your Lesson
Expansion (The Three of Wands)

Major Arcana: Your Highest Calling
Perspective (The World)

―――――○―――――

SAGITTARIUS
RULERS: JUPITER, MARS

PURPOSE
To bear witness to the unexpected brilliance of life.

RELATIONSHIPS

You are as wise as they come, yet your relationships should be a place of newness. By seeking out partners who direct your gaze to the aspects of life that would have gone unnoticed in your usual view, you will discover that true love is an eye-opening experience.

The Journey of
DECEMBER 10

Welcome to December 10, a gratifying journey that teaches you to take responsibility for yourself.

Despite the impulsivity of Sagittarius season, *Discipline* (The Number Four) asks you to be reliable and accountable to the responsibilities you have in your day. Make a thorough to-do list, trying your best to carry it through to completion and communicating clearly with others as you go.

And be sure to schedule some time for *Celebration* (Four of Wands). Whether you go out for the night with some cherished friends or stay inside watching your favorite movies, try to do one thing today to acknowledge all the hard work you have been putting in. By doing so, you can restore some of the energy and enthusiasm you may have lost along the way.

Because at the end of the day, you are the leader of your journey. *Self-mastery* (The Emperor) empowers you to take a position of authority in your life today, executing the boundaries and tough decisions required to make sustainable progress toward your ultimate potential. Don't be afraid to say "no" when necessary, remaining objective as you decipher what it is you need to make the most of the time that you have today.

JUST FOR TODAY

TODAY'S MANTRA
I will do all that I can today to ensure my success for tomorrow.

TODAY'S RITUAL
Dress up. Whether you put on your fanciest pair of shoes or style your hair a new way, let yourself celebrate how good it feels to be you.

TODAY'S JOURNAL PROMPT
When do I have a hard time saying "no" to taking on new responsibilities?

BORN ON THIS DAY

ADA LOVELACE, English mathematician, considered the first computer programmer

NELLY SACHS, German Swedish Nobel Prize–winning poet and playwright

"To live is so startling it leaves little time for anything else."—EMILY DICKINSON, American poet

The Journey of Those Born on
DECEMBER 10

You were born of unbridled independence and a wanderlust that can cause you to be unreliable when it comes to the things that matter most. You will have to find the growth within restraint, as your journey is one of duty, restoration, and objective self-leadership.

Early on in your journey, you will meet your stern guide, *Discipline* (The Number Four). Despite your boundless interests, *Discipline* calls you away from overextension and toward a path of earnest effort. You will meet *Discipline* when you devote yourself completely to the improvement of your brilliance, wasting no time on fruitless distraction and building a solid foundation of personal integrity.

If you choose this deliberate path, you will get to spend time with your joyous friend, *Celebration* (Four of Wands). *Celebration* applauds you for your hard work, encouraging you to take some well-deserved time off between ventures to recharge your emotional, physical, and spiritual batteries. You will meet *Celebration* in moments of self-care, when you replenish what has been lost in the exhaustion of endurance.

YOUR GUIDES

Astrology: Your Energy
Sagittarius (Jupiter, Mars)

Numerology: Your Path
Discipline (The Number Four)

Minor Arcana: Your Lesson
Celebration (The Four of Wands)

Major Arcana: Your Highest Calling
Self-mastery (The Emperor)

By answering these calls for accountability, you will begin to embody the grace of *Self-mastery* (The Emperor). You will meet *Self-mastery* in moments of personal discernment, when you are able to make thoughtful and self-preserving choices for your future. *Self-mastery* empowers you to enforce these internal boundaries so that you can actualize your ultimate potential and inspire others to do the same. If you can choose objective reason over the impulses of passion, you'll discover the gift of self-respect.

SAGITTARIUS
RULERS: JUPITER, MARS

PURPOSE
To protect, preserve, and nurture the profound potential that lives within.

RELATIONSHIPS

You are independent and self-sufficient by nature, but your relationships should be a place of reliable and restorative comfort. By seeking out partners who make you feel held and supported no matter what life hurls your way, you will discover that true love feels like home.

The Journey of
DECEMBER 11

W elcome to December 11, an enlightening journey that asks you to be bold but never prideful.

As you navigate the passionate nature of Sagittarius season, generously share your truth with the world around you. *Courage* (The Number Five) empowers you to practice transparency in your personal and professional life, letting others know where you stand without actively hurting anyone's feelings.

You'll need this social nuance as you navigate some necessary *Conflict* (Five of Wands). If you find yourself in a standoff with someone or something today, embrace the discomfort as you strengthen your debate skills. If your stance gets questioned, take it as an opportunity to further develop your point of view.

Because at the end of the day, no human is the ultimate authority on any one subject, except themselves. *Wisdom* (The Hierophant) invites you to practice radical humility today, so actively listen to the perspectives and opinions of others without losing your internal sense of right and wrong. There's no need to dig in your heels in disagreement, but instead, open yourself to the possibility that you may be wrong in one way and deeply right in another.

JUST FOR TODAY

TODAY'S MANTRA

The bravest act of all is to admit that I could be wrong.

TODAY'S RITUAL

Every five or so hours today, splash your face with cold water. Today can feel quite impulsive and fiery, so use this element to refresh and clear your state of mind.

TODAY'S JOURNAL PROMPT

When it comes to my spirituality, do I feel open-minded or quite rigid in my beliefs?

BORN ON THIS DAY

ANNIE JUMP CANNON, American astronomer, suffragist, and feminist whose cataloging work was instrumental in the development of contemporary stellar classification

JOHN KERRY, American politician, diplomat, and climate activist

"In life, you have ups and downs, but you should never give up. You should always try to get ahead."—YALITZA APARICIO, Mexican actor and preschool teacher

The Journey of Those Born on
DECEMBER 11

Y ou were born of fierce compassion and a sense of diplomacy that can hold you back from speaking your entire truth. You will have to be bravely open-minded, as your journey is one of self-expression, necessary strife, and higher understanding.

Early on in your journey, you will meet your bold guide, *Courage* (The Number Five). Despite your tactful social skills, *Courage* calls you away from people-pleasing and toward a path of radical vulnerability. To empower others to embrace the full breadth of their authentic spirit, you must first give yourself full permission to express your truth.

If you choose this daring path, you will have to contend with *Conflict* (Five of Wands). *Conflict* reminds you that being agreeable is not the same as being accepted, so view criticism and discord as a sign that you are living a life of bravery. You will meet *Conflict* when you agree to disagree, allowing others to speak their piece while holding your head high.

By answering these valiant calls, you will open yourself to the subtle genius of *Wisdom* (The Hierophant). There are never clear answers to life's toughest questions, so feel free to surrender your fixed thinking while questioning the powers that be. You will meet *Wisdom* when you are curious rather than prideful, listening deeply to the genius of the universe instead of deferring to the limits of the human mind.

YOUR GUIDES

Astrology: Your Energy
Sagittarius (Jupiter, Mars)

Numerology: Your Path
Courage (The Number Five)

Minor Arcana: Your Lesson
Conflict (The Five of Wands)

Major Arcana: Your Highest Calling
Wisdom (The Hierophant)

SAGITTARIUS
RULERS: JUPITER, MARS

PURPOSE
To realize that true courage is the willingness to change your mind.

RELATIONSHIPS

You are prone to giving others the benefit of the doubt, but your relationships should be a place of complete honesty. By seeking out partners who aren't afraid to tell it like it is and encourage radical transparency, you will discover that true love is an act of courage.

The Journey of
DECEMBER 12

Welcome to December 12, a self-validating journey that requires you to soften to your inherent worthiness.

Show your *Devotion* (The Number Six) to the person you hope to become today. Focus on the meaningful work that feeds your soul rather than pleasing others with trivial and unfulfilling obligations. By acting with sincerity, you can produce exceptional results for your efforts.

To make the most of the optimism of Sagittarius season, *Confidence* (Six of Wands) asks you to take note of the positive momentum you have in your life. Let yourself feel good in your own skin, and if you happen to receive any external praise or validation, embrace this well-deserved recognition with open arms.

But at the end of the day, the love that you truly need must come from within. *Choice* (The Lovers) invites you to take an active role in your mental and spiritual health, giving yourself the sweet words of encouragement that you need to continue forward in your growth. What are you proud of yourself for? By speaking to yourself as you would a loved one, you can come out of today with a profound sense of self-confidence that will send you soaring into the potential of tomorrow.

―――――――――○―――――――――

JUST FOR TODAY

TODAY'S MANTRA
I will acknowledge the exceptional person I am becoming, rather than waiting for others to validate my growth.

TODAY'S JOURNAL PROMPT
How does shame come up for me when I try to give myself a compliment?

TODAY'S RITUAL
Try to come up with six things you have done in the past year that you are proud of. They can be small or substantial. If you find it hard to come up with all six, call a dear friend and see if they can help you see your progress.

―――――――――○―――――――――

BORN ON THIS DAY

ELIZABETH MARTÍNEZ, American feminist, community organizer, activist, author, and educator

FRANK SINATRA, American singer and actor

"If you crush the ego, you'll understand who you are."—**RAJINIKANTH**, Indian actor, producer, and screenwriter

The Journey of Those Born on
DECEMBER 12

You were born of expansive knowledge and a chameleon-like flexibility that can make you unsure of who you are on the deepest level. You will have to discover yourself through vulnerability, as your journey is one of sincerity, recognition, and self-acceptance.

Early on in your journey, you will meet your earnest guide, *Devotion* (The Number Six). Despite your limitless intelligence, *Devotion* calls you away from superficial ambition and toward a path of meaningful service. By giving yourself completely to the work that feeds your soul, rather than your ego, you will build a life of deep consequence.

If you choose this heartfelt path, you will meet your dear friend, *Confidence* (Six of Wands). *Confidence* encourages you to take humble pride in a job well done, sending the applause you deserve your way. You will meet *Confidence* when you hit your stride, recognizing how your gifts and talents fit into the bigger picture.

By answering these calls for sincerity, you will come to understand the importance of *Choice* (The Lovers). *Choice* asks you to take a look in the mirror of your soul to find your inherent value, rather than looking to others to validate your worth. You will meet *Choice* in moments of internal recognition, when you come to realize that the only person who can love you the way you seek is yourself. If you can look inward for the love you need most, *Choice* offers you the gift of authentic self-esteem.

SAGITTARIUS
RULERS: JUPITER, THE SUN

PURPOSE
To choose to love yourself over the applause of many.

RELATIONSHIPS

You are as socially intelligent as they come, and your relationships should be a place of unconditional support. By seeking out partners who cherish you for who you are underneath the facade, you will discover that true love is as real as it gets.

The Journey of
DECEMBER 13

Welcome to December 13, a consequential journey that asks you to serve the soul, rather than the ego.

Live with high integrity today. To make use of the abundant optimism of Sagittarius season, *Commitment* (The Number Seven) asks you to show your loyalty to the dreams you believe in most. Whether you pour your energy into a professional endeavor or invest in the progress of a relationship, make your intentions known.

And don't give up so easily. *Perseverance* (Seven of Wands) wants to see you sweat, so dig in your heels if you find yourself in the face of an obstacle or an opponent. By fighting for what you believe in, and bravely protecting what is rightfully yours, you can prove to the universe that you mean business.

This conviction will be the key to meaningful progress today. *Evolution* (The Chariot) reminds you that it is the small but crucial efforts that eventually amount to radical success, so keep your eyes on the road ahead and your feet moving forward toward your ultimate goals. By never straying from your intended purpose, you can accomplish more in a day than you thought was possible in a lifetime.

JUST FOR TODAY

TODAY'S MANTRA
There is no momentum quite like personal focus.

TODAY'S JOURNAL PROMPT
What dream have I been sitting on for quite some time now?

TODAY'S RITUAL
Make a vision board of where you'd like your life to be in seven years. Whether you do it online, with images torn out of magazines, or in your imagination, consider the city you'd like to be in, where you'd like to be professionally and personally, and how you'd like to feel.

BORN ON THIS DAY

TAYLOR SWIFT, American singer-songwriter

JAMIE FOXX, American actor, comedian, and musician

"I didn't break the rules, but I challenged the rules."—ELLA BAKER, American civil and human rights activist and director of the Student Nonviolent Coordinating Committee

The Journey of Those Born on
DECEMBER 13

You were born of boundless integrity and a penchant for transformation that can at times steer you away from who you are truly meant to become. You will have to aim your focus directly at the source of your power, as your journey is one of investment, perseverance, and inspired progress.

Early on in your journey, you will meet your earnest guide, *Commitment* (The Number Seven). Despite your limitless potential, *Commitment* calls you away from overindulgence and toward a path of complete intentionality. *Commitment* doesn't care for half-hearted promises or fair-weather entanglements, but instead wants you to devote yourself deeply to the spiritual contracts made between you and the universe itself.

If you choose this forthright path, you will have to pay respect to *Perseverance* (Seven of Wands). With all your abundant optimism, it won't be easy to face the inevitable backlash from the naysayers and skeptics. Instead of backing down, or worse, sinking to their level, *Perseverance* invites you to face your most ruthless opponents, drawing on the only weapon you truly have—the light of self-belief.

> ### YOUR GUIDES
>
> *Astrology: Your Energy*
> Sagittarius (Jupiter, The Sun)
>
> *Numerology: Your Path*
> Commitment (The Number Seven)
>
> *Minor Arcana: Your Lesson*
> Perseverance (The Seven of Wands)
>
> *Major Arcana: Your Highest Calling*
> Evolution (The Chariot)

By answering these serious calls to action, *Evolution* (The Chariot) will ensure you grow far beyond your highest expectations. You will meet *Evolution* in moments of self-affirming breakthroughs, when what feels like a lifetime of hard work suddenly amounts to a level of success that feeds the soul, rather than the ego. If you can continue to lay these bricks of integrity, you will build the lasting achievements that come from personal investment.

———————————————○———————————————

SAGITTARIUS
RULERS: JUPITER, THE SUN

PURPOSE
To invest fearlessly in the spiritual contracts of the soul.

RELATIONSHIPS

You are self-reliant and forever evolving, yet your relationships should be a place of mutual investment and earned trust. By seeking out partners who put in the emotional effort required to withstand the rocking tides of life, you will discover that true love is always worth fighting for.

The Journey of
DECEMBER 14

Welcome to December 14, a self-revealing journey that requires you to dig down into the recesses of your soul.

Step into the full breadth of your authentic *Power* (The Number Eight). As you approach anyone and anything today, don't be afraid to show up exactly as you are without compromising to make others feel comfortable. Instead, by accepting every aspect of your humanity, you can inspire others to do the same.

To make the most of this confidence and the general enthusiasm of Sagittarius season, *Momentum* (Eight of Wands) encourages you to act on your instincts rather than hanging around for self-doubt to kick in. What would you do if you weren't afraid? Strike while the iron's hot—you won't regret listening to your gut.

And no matter how the day unfolds, know that you can rely on yourself. *Resilience* (Strength) invites you to the place of spiritual fortitude that lives deep inside you that you have built up over a lifetime of hard work. If you find your animal instinct of fight or flight kicking in, temper this natural fear with profound emotional courage. By remembering how much you have endured, you can reconnect with the infallible fire that burns within.

JUST FOR TODAY

TODAY'S MANTRA
I will run toward my innate power with radical self-acceptance.

TODAY'S JOURNAL PROMPT
When in my adult life have I witnessed my own capacity for resilience?

TODAY'S RITUAL
At both 8 a.m. and 8 p.m., light a candle and repeat the spell, "Fire magic, help me run toward the direction my instinct wants me to go."

BORN ON THIS DAY

NOSTRADAMUS, French astrologer, physician, and reputed seer

SHIRLEY JACKSON, American writer, notable for her horror and mystery works

"To Want and To Dare! Never hesitate to act when the feeling of injustice revolts us. To give one's measure with all good faith, the rest will follow as a logical consequence."—DORIA SHAFIK, Egyptian feminist, poet, and leader of Egypt's women's liberation movement

The Journey of Those Born on
DECEMBER 14

You were born of limitless wisdom and a penchant for overthinking that at times can make it hard to act on your instincts. You will have to trust your instincts, as your journey is one of authenticity, movement, and personal strength.

Early on in your journey, you will meet your mysterious guide, *Power* (The Number Eight). To make the most of your natural authority, *Power* calls you away from being accommodating and toward a path of radical self-acceptance. You will meet *Power* when you embrace every inch of your enigmatic force, never denying the full breadth of your influence.

If you choose this authentic path, you will have to keep pace with *Momentum* (Eight of Wands). *Momentum* invites you to act on your instincts, pursuing and fulfilling the internal callings of the soul. You will meet *Momentum* when you choose self-trust over self-doubt, blazing toward your future and realizing your potential in the process.

> ### YOUR GUIDES
>
> *Astrology: Your Energy*
> Sagittarius (Jupiter, The Sun)
>
> *Numerology: Your Path*
> Power (The Number Eight)
>
> *Minor Arcana: Your Lesson*
> Momentum (The Eight of Wands)
>
> *Major Arcana: Your Highest Calling*
> Resilience (Strength)

By answering these daring calls to action, you will build a deep relationship with *Resilience* (Strength). *Resilience* reminds you that fear is not a barrier to your success, encouraging you to push past this natural emotion and build the spiritual muscles required to thrive. You will meet *Resilience* in the circumstances that you once thought could kill you, but instead, now introduce you to the divine strength that lives within. If you can move bravely toward the places that scare you, you'll discover that there is no end to your magnificence.

SAGITTARIUS
RULERS: JUPITER, THE SUN

PURPOSE
To dig deep enough to realize there is no limit to what the soul can handle.

RELATIONSHIPS

You are outgoing on the surface yet surprisingly guarded, so your relationships should be a place of deep connection and self-revealing. By seeking out partners who aren't fooled by your facade of confidence and push you to let down your walls, you will discover that true love isn't afraid to go deeper.

The Journey of
DECEMBER 15

W elcome to December 15, an inspired adventure that forces you to lean on your intuition. To make the most of the wanderlust of Sagittarius season, *Experience* (The Number Nine) invites you to take a chance on the unknowns that the day presents you. Whether you tackle a foreign project in your work or dive into a completely new spiritual practice, it's okay to wander far from your comfort zone.

And stick through the discomfort. *Persistence* (Nine of Wands) asks you not to give up when the going gets tough, encouraging you to nurture your needs to see your ambitions through to completion. Drink enough water, don't skip meals, and take small breaks to ensure you have enough energy to make the most of the wonder of this day.

But above all else, listen to your *Instinct* (The Hermit). There is no clear set of directions for how today should unfold, so look within for guidance whenever you feel the anxiety of uncertainty creeping in. Where are your instincts beckoning you? By silencing the noise of other people's opinions as well as the imposter syndrome you may feel, you can realize how spot-on your intuition really is.

JUST FOR TODAY

TODAY'S MANTRA

As scary as the unknown is, it presents me with a unique opportunity to trust myself.

TODAY'S RITUAL

Spend nine minutes in silent visualization to begin your day. Sit comfortably, close your eyes, and envision a sphere of fire that burns within your lower stomach, representing your gut instinct. As you go about your day, keep this image with you whenever you feel unsure of yourself.

TODAY'S JOURNAL PROMPT

When I am exploring something new, how can I nurture myself through this understandable fear?

BORN ON THIS DAY

MAURICE WILKINS, New Zealand–born English biophysicist and Nobel Prize winner

MICHELLE DOCKERY, English actor

"My dream is to see all people smiling. Not because they have to, but because it comes from within."—MARTINE BONNY DIKONGUE, Cameroonian economist and trainer for nonviolent conflict resolution

The Journey of Those Born on
DECEMBER 15

You were born of expansive generosity and a compassion for others that you don't extend toward yourself as easily. You will have to create a deeper relationship with your intrinsic power, as your journey is one of expansion, self-care, and internal trust.

Early on in your journey, you will meet your worldly guide, *Experience* (The Number Nine). To make the most of your confident spirit, *Experience* calls you away from your comfort zone and toward a path of the wild unknown. You will meet *Experience* when you run toward, rather than away from, the boundless possibilities that lie in the depths of uncertainty.

If you choose this winding path, you will have to pay respect to *Persistence* (Nine of Wands). *Persistence* reminds you that you cannot withstand a lifetime of adventure without taking care of your fundamental needs. You will meet *Persistence* in the small but meaningful breaks you must take along your journey, when you pull off and recharge to regain your enthusiasm for the work that lies ahead.

By answering these far-reaching calls, you will come to rely on the genius of *Instinct* (The Hermit). *Instinct* encourages you to listen to your gut, rather than gaslighting yourself into thinking that your intuition is just a figment of your imagination. You will meet *Instinct* in the wilderness of uncharted territory, when you have no one and nothing to consult for direction except your internal compass. If you can respect this intrinsic gift, you'll discover that *bravery* is just another word for self-trust.

> ### YOUR GUIDES
>
> *Astrology: Your Energy*
> Sagittarius (Jupiter, The Sun)
>
> *Numerology: Your Path*
> Experience (The Number Nine)
>
> *Minor Arcana: Your Lesson*
> Persistence (The Nine of Wands)
>
> *Major Arcana: Your Highest Calling*
> Instinct (The Hermit)

SAGITTARIUS
RULERS: JUPITER, THE SUN

PURPOSE
To learn to respect the power of instinct within the wilderness of the unknown.

RELATIONSHIPS

You crave emotional intimacy, and your relationships should be a place of perspective-shifting experiences. By seeking out partners whom you trust enough to travel far outside your comfort zone, you will discover that true love inspires you to fly.

The Journey of
DECEMBER 16

Welcome to December 16, an inspired journey that teaches you how to fall forward.

Go your own way today. *Autonomy* (The Number One) invites you to move to the beat of your intuition, never minding social norms and disregarding the opinions of others. Where is your inspiration leading you? By listening to your internal genius, you can fulfill your deepest curiosity.

All you have to do is believe in your *Potential* (Ace of Wands). To make the most of the optimism of Sagittarius season, have complete faith in your next best idea. Although some days are meant for careful planning and rigorous follow-through, now is the time to just begin with radical enthusiasm and leave the details for tomorrow.

So take things as they come. *Impermanence* (Wheel of Fortune) reminds you that fate has a mind of its own, encouraging you to remain dynamic as the day unfolds as it will. Instead of getting stuck on how you think things should go, embrace each unexpected circumstance by drawing on your innate creativity and resilience. By building a relationship with the greater forces at play, you can show the universe just how innovative you truly are.

JUST FOR TODAY

TODAY'S MANTRA
Just like life itself, I will stay dynamic.

TODAY'S JOURNAL PROMPT
In what ways do I consider myself a risk-taker?

TODAY'S RITUAL
Consider someone you admire for their innovation, whether it's a personal friend or a historical figure. Write down ten qualities you see in them that allow them to be so daring and carry this list with you throughout your day to try to embody these characteristics.

BORN ON THIS DAY

JANE AUSTEN, English novelist

FANNY GARRISON VILLARD, American suffragist, pacifist, and cofounder of the NAACP

"If the future is to remain open and free, we need people who can tolerate the unknown, who will not need the support of completely worked out systems or traditional blueprints from the past."—MARGARET MEAD, American cultural anthropologist

The Journey of Those Born on
DECEMBER 16

You were born of fierce confidence and a sense of certainty that can make it difficult to withstand the unpredictable nature of life. You will have to be willing to risk it all, as your journey is one of independence, intuitive action, and radical detachment.

Early on in your journey, you will meet your fearless guide, *Autonomy* (The Number One). To make the most of your ambitious spirit, *Autonomy* calls you away from following the rules and toward a path of self-leadership. You will meet *Autonomy* when you disregard the norms and traditions that came before you, carving out a one-of-a-kind adventure that others will follow in wonder.

If you choose this audacious path, you will make good friends with *Potential* (Ace of Wands). *Potential* reminds you that you don't need a set plan to pursue your wildest dreams, but instead, encourages you to propel yourself forward with nothing but the flame of enthusiasm. You will meet *Potential* within the uncertainty of new beginnings, when all you can do is hope for the best.

But in answering these wild calls, you will have to surrender to the laws of *Impermanence* (Wheel of Fortune). You will meet *Impermanence* in the unexpected twists and turns that fate hurls your way, when you are forced to draw on the resilience of inspiration as you adapt to the reality of your present circumstance. If you can learn to dance in harmony with the ever-changing winds of fate, making up new moves as you go, *Impermanence* offers you the gift of adaptability.

SAGITTARIUS
RULERS: JUPITER, THE SUN

PURPOSE
To make friends with risk by remaining eternally responsive to change.

RELATIONSHIPS

You are quite loyal to the people you care about, so your relationships should be a place of mutual independence and encouragement. By seeking out partners who propel your dreams forward with their enthusiasm, you will discover that true love wants you to soar.

The Journey of
DECEMBER 17

Welcome to December 17, an enlightening journey that asks you not to assume anything. Seek out spiritual *Balance* (The Number Two) today. Rather than jumping to extremes, try to remain open as you peacefully navigate the lessons and perspectives that the day offers. If you find yourself in deep conversation with another person, aim to meet them halfway rather than engaging in any form of hostile debate.

And although Sagittarius season can ignite some spiritual consciousness, don't assume that your conclusions are correct. *Preparation* (Two of Wands) encourages humble consideration, so do your research and thoughtfully contemplate every angle before taking a strong stance. By viewing the day as a journey rather than a destination, you can enjoy the adventure of not knowing anything for sure.

Because at the end of the day, the *Truth* (Justice) always hangs in the balance. Try to practice ambivalence as you explore the social, spiritual, or political topics that come up, ensuring that you aren't dogmatic in your point of view. More than likely, by opening yourself to the possibility that you might be wrong, you can step into a higher state of consciousness and experience the breakthrough you were searching for all along.

JUST FOR TODAY

TODAY'S MANTRA
True wisdom looks like admitting when I don't know the answer.

TODAY'S RITUAL
Practice saying, "I'm not sure" throughout today. Whether someone asks you a question you aren't entirely certain about at work or your partner invites you to plan for next year, find the freedom that comes from taking your time.

TODAY'S JOURNAL PROMPT
Do I tend to jump to conclusions or take my time when developing an opinion?

BORN ON THIS DAY

EUGENE LEVY, Canadian actor, comedian, producer, director, and writer

LOUISE SAUMONEAU, French socialist, union leader, and feminist

"To me, most of life kind of lives in the grey and I don't just mean morally. I just mean kind of everything. If things were black and white it would be a lot clearer as to what to do all the time."—SARAH PAULSON, American actor

The Journey of Those Born on
DECEMBER 17

You were born of powerful optimism and an intensity that at times can make it difficult to handle the nuances of life. You will have to find the beauty within ambivalence, as your journey is one of simplicity, consideration, and spiritual breakthroughs.

Early on in your journey, you will meet your tranquil guide, *Balance* (The Number Two). Despite your limitless hunger for understanding, *Balance* calls you away from dogmatism and toward a path of patient open-mindedness. By taking in knowledge bit by bit, rather than jumping to conclusions, you can discover the wisdom that comes from personal moderation.

If you choose this thoughtful path, you will have to pay respect to *Preparation* (Two of Wands). *Preparation* reminds you that to have a meaningful perspective to share, you must take time to do your research. You will meet *Preparation* in the weeks leading up to your next breakthrough, when you practice the patience required to consider and question your point of view.

By answering these calls for patience, you will become a messenger for *Truth* (Justice). *Truth* teaches you that there is no room for extremes when it comes to justice, encouraging you to temper your passion with the coolness of fair reason. You will meet *Truth* in the excruciatingly and magnificently gray areas in life, when you slowly melt into the vastness of spiritual openness. If you can embrace the discomfort of not knowing, *Truth* shows you that the change you seek must start from within.

YOUR GUIDES

Astrology: Your Energy
Sagittarius (Jupiter, The Sun)

Numerology: Your Path
Balance (The Number Two)

Minor Arcana: Your Lesson
Preparation (The Two of Wands)

Major Arcana: Your Highest Calling
Truth (Justice)

SAGITTARIUS
RULERS: JUPITER, THE SUN

PURPOSE
*To develop a patience
for uncertainty.*

RELATIONSHIPS

You may like to throw yourself into intimacy, but your relationships should be a place of emotional boundaries and patience. By seeking out partners who like to build trust over time rather than diving into things right away, you will discover that true love is a slow burn.

The Journey of
DECEMBER 18

Welcome to December 18, a nourishing journey that broadens your capacity for receiving. Approach today with sincere *Flexibility* (The Number Three). Rather than coming up with a firm plan, let the day take you in an unexpected direction. Whether you get invited on a social outing with new friends or are encouraged to take on a foreign project at work, say a daring "yes" to the things that are outside of your norm.

To make the most of the adventurous spirit of Sagittarius season, *Expansion* (Three of Wands) asks for your willingness to be a beginner at a new skill or interest. By picking up an intriguing book or spiritual subject, you can increase your mental, emotional, and psychological capacity. There is nothing to fear, so jump headfirst into something that piques your interest.

And don't forget to enjoy yourself. *Abundance* (The Empress) reminds you that happiness is one of the most vital human emotions, so let yourself crack up in laughter or internalize the generous love you receive from others. By accepting and embracing every gift of goodness that this day has to offer, you can enter tomorrow with energy to spare and pay forward.

JUST FOR TODAY

TODAY'S MANTRA
I will open myself to the unexpected gifts and wild beauty that the day sends my way.

TODAY'S JOURNAL PROMPT
How can I discover new books or podcasts that are outside my wheelhouse of knowledge?

TODAY'S RITUAL
Spend your morning somewhere outside, whether it be your backyard or a local park. As you sit and enjoy the fresh air, consider three new skills you hope to learn in the next year. If you feel inspired, try taking steps to start learning one of them today.

BORN ON THIS DAY

BILLIE EILISH, American singer-songwriter

ZAINAB BANGURA, Sierra Leonean politician and social activist

"The sky is the limit. I'm just following where life takes me. It's been an incredible journey."
—**CHRISTINA AGUILERA**, American singer

The Journey of Those Born on
DECEMBER 18

Y ou were born of intuitive brilliance and a deep-seated anxiety that can keep you from embracing new experiences. You will have to open yourself to the lightness of life because your journey is one of humility, growth, and spiritual fulfillment.

Early on in your journey, you will meet your curious guide, *Flexibility* (The Number Three). Despite your wise and self-reliant disposition, *Flexibility* calls you away from introversion and toward a path of shared knowledge. By remaining open to the fruitful adventures of collaboration, you can shift your perspective and learn how rewarding it can feel to just go with the flow.

If you choose this open-minded path, you will meet your inspired friend, *Expansion* (Three of Wands). *Expansion* reminds you that there is always more to learn, encouraging you to explore the fields, topics, and relationships that interest you the most. You will meet *Expansion* when you are a complete beginner, drawing only briefly on your foundational expertise as you dive headfirst into the unknown.

By answering these prolific calls, you will come to appreciate the healing quality of *Abundance* (The Empress). *Abundance* reminds you that you are worthy of receiving, pushing you to accept the loving support and nourishment that come your way. You will meet *Abundance* when you let yourself feel unapologetically good, never denying your hunger for happiness and embracing the wild beauty of the human experience. If you can learn to welcome the gifts that your journey brings, you will find true purpose in paying it forward.

SAGITTARIUS
RULERS: JUPITER, THE SUN

PURPOSE
To push through the discomfort of expansion into the beauty of abundance.

RELATIONSHIPS

You are highly sensitive to the feelings of others, yet your relationships should be a place of light-hearted adventure and pure joy. By seeking out partners who teach you how not to take life so seriously, you will discover that true love keeps you feeling young.

The Journey of
DECEMBER 19

W elcome to December 19, a self-gratifying journey that asks you to take your potential seriously.

Add some *Discipline* (The Number Four) to your day. Although Sagittarius season can inspire waves of enthusiasm, temper this unpredictability with thorough to-do lists and high integrity. By showing up for the responsibilities that matter, you can experience the highs of a job well done.

But that doesn't mean you won't have time for *Celebration* (Four of Wands). Set aside a few minutes or a few hours to relish all the effort you have put into your future recently, and recharge your energetic battery for the work that lies ahead. Whether you throw yourself a literal party or get in bed at a ridiculously early hour, know that you deserve it.

And remember that you have the authority to make good decisions for your future. *Self-mastery* (The Emperor) empowers you to think objectively about your long-term health and well-being today, so set the boundaries or make the tough choices required to thrive. By being a decisive and objective leader toward yourself rather than falling prey to distractions or procrastination, you can build a deep sense of self-respect.

JUST FOR TODAY

TODAY'S MANTRA

I have authority over how I show up today, so I will do my very best to set myself up for a better tomorrow.

TODAY'S JOURNAL PROMPT

What are the things that distract me the most from my goals (e.g., social media, television, socializing)?

TODAY'S RITUAL

Try to think of someone, a friend or historical figure, you consider to have good discipline. As you visualize this person, repeat the affirmation, "I am capable of the very same level of discipline."

BORN ON THIS DAY

ANNIE MURPHY, Canadian actor

ÉDITH PIAF, French singer and France's "national chanteuse"

"The special gift of that suffering, I have learned, is how to be strong while we are weak, how to be brave when we are afraid, how to be wise in the midst of confusion, and how to let go of that which we can no longer hold."—LE LY HAYSLIP, Vietnamese American writer, memoirist, and humanitarian

The Journey of Those Born on
DECEMBER 19

You were born of wild exuberance and a blind optimism that can leave you ill-equipped in times of personal strife. You will have to discover the beauty in grit, as your journey is one of hard work, restoration, and objective leadership.

Early on in your journey, you will meet your stern guide, *Discipline* (The Number Four). Despite your happy-go-lucky disposition, *Discipline* calls you away from resting on your laurels and toward a path of earning your keep. You will meet *Discipline* when you choose diligence over instant gratification, helping you build an indestructible foundation of personal integrity.

If you choose this intrepid path, you will meet your joyful friend, *Celebration* (Four of Wands). *Celebration* invites you to take some well-deserved time off between ambitions to replenish the energy you lost in the painstaking labor of a job well done. You will meet *Celebration* in the laughter of your loved ones as well as the crystal-clear silence of rest, when you absorb the nourishment you need to move forward.

By answering these weighty calls, you will step into the large shoes of *Self-mastery* (The Emperor). *Self-mastery* teaches you that nothing worth keeping comes easy, empowering you to rise to the occasion whenever the burdens of life try to squash your convictions. You will meet *Self-mastery* when you act as the CEO of your future, making the clear and kind decisions for yourself that will carry you toward a better tomorrow. By investing deeply in your potential, you will earn something that no one can take away from you: self-respect.

SAGITTARIUS
RULERS: JUPITER, THE SUN

PURPOSE
To realize that the most satisfying wins in life are the hardest to achieve.

RELATIONSHIPS

You were born with energy to spare, but your relationships should be a place of emotional grounding and restoration. By seeking out partners who offer a safe place to rest your head at the end of a long day, you will discover that true love is the home you always needed.

The Journey of
DECEMBER 20

Welcome to December 20, a sage journey that reminds you how powerful it can be to take risks.

To make the most of the more extroverted end of Sagittarius season, *Courage* (The Number Five) invites you to share who you are and what you stand for. Whether you post your perspective on social media or ensure your voice is heard at work, don't be afraid to take up some well-deserved space.

But don't fret if you run into some *Conflict* (Five of Wands). Today encourages healthy discourse, so empower yourself to clap back at any of the naysayers or contrarians that come your way. More than likely, by defending your point of view and staying true to your convictions, you can inspire others to do the same.

This vulnerability will be worth your while because *Wisdom* (The Hierophant) comes from experience. It is intimidating to engage in honest conversation and risk rejection, but you can learn a lot more about yourself through this process than by staying in your comfort zone. Try to move your ego out of the way by not taking your pride so seriously, and you can discover that honesty is the birthplace of personal freedom.

———————————○———————————

JUST FOR TODAY

TODAY'S MANTRA
I will not back down from my truth just because someone may reject, dispute, or disregard its value.

TODAY'S JOURNAL PROMPT
What is the worst that could happen if I share my perspective with others today?

TODAY'S RITUAL
Wear something red today, whether it be a bright red top or red lipstick. Try to bring the fire of this powerful color with you as you act with great courage.

———————————○———————————

BORN ON THIS DAY

JONAH HILL, American actor, filmmaker, and comedian

DYLAN WANG, Chinese actor and model

"Man, I fear neither your weapons nor your threats; they are powerless."—LAURA SMITH HAVILAND, American abolitionist, suffragist, and social reformer who documented the history of the Underground Railroad

The Journey of Those Born on
DECEMBER 20

Y ou were born of expansive diplomacy and a self-awareness that can stop you from being fearlessly yourself. You will have to become willing to fail bravely, as your journey is one of vulnerability, healthy conflict, and sage intelligence.

Early on in your journey, you will meet your bold guide, *Courage* (The Number Five). Despite your easygoing disposition, *Courage* calls you away from complacency and toward a path of radical self-expression. You will meet *Courage* when you dare to stand out among your peers, speaking your truth far and wide for all the world to hear.

If you choose this public path, you will have to contend with *Conflict* (Five of Wands). *Conflict* reminds you that a friend to all is a friend to none, encouraging you to drop your old ways of people-pleasing so that you can engage in the enriching experience of healthy debate. You will meet *Conflict* when you are brave enough to disagree with others, firmly stating your point of view while absorbing their unique and differing perspectives.

By answering these brave calls, you will come to understand the nuance of *Wisdom* (The Hierophant). *Wisdom* teaches you that even the most admired of leaders has no idea what they are doing most of the time, empowering you to think for yourself, take some risks, and learn from your mistakes. You will meet *Wisdom* in the profound intelligence that comes with age and experience, when by knowing better, you are able to do better. If you can learn not to take your failures so seriously, *Wisdom* will hand you the keys to higher consciousness.

─────────────────○─────────────────

SAGITTARIUS
RULERS: JUPITER, THE SUN

PURPOSE
To be brave enough to fail, smart enough to learn, and wise enough to try again.

RELATIONSHIPS

You are quite accommodating to the people you love, yet your relationships should be a place of radical honesty and healthy conflict. By seeking out partners who aren't afraid to tell you how they feel and demand that you do the same, you will discover that true love doesn't waste time on niceties.

The Journey of
DECEMBER 21

Welcome to December 21, an emotionally enriching journey that invites you to fall in love with yourself.

Lead from the heart rather than your head today. There's simply no time for superficial obligations and ambitions because *Devotion* (The Number Six) asks you to set your sights on the relationships and projects that feed your soul. How can you move toward a higher purpose today?

To make the most of the enthusiasm of Sagittarius season, *Confidence* (Six of Wands) encourages you to give yourself the affirmation you need. Whether you pat yourself on the back for a job well done or accept a sincere compliment from another person, let yourself bask in the sunlight of your authentic spirit.

Because at the end of the day, you are the love you need most. *Choice* (The Lovers) invites you to notice the spark of your individuality, offering yourself the acknowledgment and praise you would a dear friend. Although it can be uncomfortable at first to turn your generosity inward, you can discover a new sense of emotional contentment by giving yourself the tender affection you normally seek from others. Hold up a compassionate mirror to yourself today so you can see just how beautiful you truly are.

○

JUST FOR TODAY

TODAY'S MANTRA
I can show myself that I am worthy of love.

TODAY'S RITUAL
To start your day, hold up a mirror to yourself, and look deep within your eyes for six minutes. If you find your critical gaze wandering to other parts of your face and body, actively try to redirect your focus to the beauty and wonder of your eyes.

TODAY'S JOURNAL PROMPT
Growing up, how was self-love encouraged or discouraged in my household?

○

BORN ON THIS DAY

SAMUEL L. JACKSON, American actor and producer

EMMA TENAYUCA, American labor organizer and civil rights activist

"It's never too late—never too late to start over, never too late to be happy."—JANE FONDA, American actor, political activist, and environmentalist

The Journey of Those Born on
DECEMBER 21*

Y ou were born of expansive curiosity and a social drive that can cause you to care more about public acceptance than the acceptance of yourself. You will have to learn to embrace every bit of complexity within you, as your journey is one of devotion, acknowledgment, and self-love.

Early on in your journey, you will meet your earnest guide, *Devotion* (The Number Six). Despite your plethora of interests, *Devotion* calls you away from superficial work and toward a path of meaningful service. You will meet *Devotion* when you move into alignment with your purpose, silencing the allure of instant gratification and listening deeply to the motivations of the soul.

If you choose this sincere path, you will meet your inspired friend, *Confidence* (Six of Wands). *Confidence* reminds you that it is not just okay but wonderful to like who you are becoming. You will find *Confidence* in cheers and applause for a job well done, when you allow yourself to accept the gift of acknowledgment.

By answering these fulfilling calls, you will come to understand the importance of *Choice* (The Lovers). *Choice* knows how much easier it is to seek the love of others than it is to love oneself but encourages you to push past this emotional blockage with the power of personal agency. You will meet *Choice* when you realize happiness is a decision you must make inside yourself rather than a fleeting object you must chase. By taking ownership of your emotional well-being, you can discover that you are the person you have been waiting for.

> ### YOUR GUIDES
>
> *Astrology: Your Energy*
> Sagittarius (Jupiter, The Sun)
>
> *Numerology: Your Path*
> Devotion (The Number Six)
>
> *Minor Arcana: Your Lesson*
> Confidence (The Six of Wands)
>
> *Major Arcana: Your Highest Calling*
> Choice (The Lovers)

SAGITTARIUS
RULERS: JUPITER, THE SUN

PURPOSE
To discover that external applause will never make up for the fundamental need for self-love.

RELATIONSHIPS

You have enough enthusiasm to fuel the sun, and your relationships should be a place of unconditional support. By seeking out partners who mirror how special you are, you will discover that true love is a direct reflection of self-acceptance.

Are you a Capricorn born on this day? Head to page 761 to find your additional birthday guide!

WELCOME TO

The Journey of
DECEMBER 22

Welcome to December 22, a momentous journey that asks you to focus on the work at hand.

To mark the first day of the hardworking Capricorn season, *Commitment* (The Number Seven) asks you to direct your focus toward the people and projects that you plan to keep in your future. If you find yourself juggling a fair number of responsibilities, consider which ones are more important to prioritize because you only have so much time in a day.

And contemplate what you will need to do to nurture these investments beyond today. *Sustainability* (Seven of Pentacles) encourages you to take the long view, implementing the structures and systems you need to bring these goals to fruition in spite of the unpredictable tides of life.

Amidst all this sincere effort, try to notice the small and meaningful progress you are making toward these long-term ambitions. *Evolution* (The Chariot) reminds you that fulfillment lies in the journey rather than the destination, so try to appreciate where you are right now in your life. What success have you made so far that is worth acknowledging? More than likely, you are further ahead than you give yourself credit for.

JUST FOR TODAY

TODAY'S MANTRA

I will invest in my long-term future while acknowledging how far I have come.

TODAY'S RITUAL

Divide a sheet of paper into two columns. In the left column, write down seven things you have been doing this year that you would like to stop doing next year. In the right column, write down seven things you haven't done this year that you would like to begin doing next year.

TODAY'S JOURNAL PROMPT

How do I tend to compare my progress to that of peers my age?

BORN ON THIS DAY

MARION WALLACE DUNLOP, Scottish artist, author, and suffragist, and one of the first suffragists in Britain to hunger strike

MITSUO TSUKAHARA, Japanese artistic gymnast and five-time Olympic gold medalist

"I think the one lesson I have learned is that there is no substitute for paying attention."—**DIANE SAWYER**, American television journalist

The Journey of Those Born on
DECEMBER 22

You were born of profound integrity and a desire for control that can make it difficult to embrace change. You will have to devote yourself to your growth, as your journey is one of focus, persistence, and radical progress.

Early on in your journey, you will meet your no-nonsense guide, *Commitment* (The Number Seven). To channel your serious disposition, *Commitment* calls you away from over-responsibility and toward a path of intentional action. By pouring your discipline into only the relationships and ideas that speak directly to your soul, you will build a life of profound consequence.

If you choose this focused path, you will have to pay respect to *Sustainability* (Seven of Pentacles). *Sustainability* asks you to consider what you will need to bring your ambitions to fruition while finding deep satisfaction in the daily work. You will meet *Sustainability* when you tend to the health of your long-term goals, nourishing them with the humble hand of perseverance.

> ### YOUR GUIDES
>
> *Astrology: Your Energy*
> Capricorn (Saturn)
>
> *Numerology: Your Path*
> Commitment (The Number Seven)
>
> *Minor Arcana: Your Lesson*
> Sustainability
> (The Seven of Pentacles)
>
> *Major Arcana: Your Highest Calling*
> Evolution (The Chariot)

By answering these grounding calls, you will find yourself working in harmony with *Evolution* (The Chariot). *Evolution* asks for nothing but your sincerest efforts in exchange for life-altering progress. You will meet *Evolution* in radical personal breakthroughs, when all the behind-the-scenes work you have put in finally culminates in profound success. If you can put one foot in front of the other, never minding the outcome of your efforts, *Evolution* will soar you to new heights of self-realization.

CAPRICORN
RULER: SATURN

PURPOSE
To find purpose within progress rather than success.

RELATIONSHIPS

You are serious about most everything in life, and your relationships should be a place of long-term investment. By seeking out partners with whom you want to build trust and respect over a lifetime of hard work, you will discover that true love grows stronger with each passing day.

The Journey of
DECEMBER 23

Welcome to December 23, a dynamic journey that asks you to dig deep.
Step into your *Power* (The Number Eight) by being an authentic authority when it comes to yourself. Instead of seeking the approval of others, reach within to decipher how and where your energy would best be utilized. There's no need to waste time on superficial endeavors; just expand into the areas that speak to your soul.

To make the most of the hardworking nature of Capricorn season, *Repetition* (Eight of Pentacles) reminds you that mastery takes time, so put in the hours you must to hone your chosen craft. Whether you spend some time studying for a test you have coming up at school or practicing a skill at work, know that this invisible effort will pay off in the long run.

And if you feel drained at any point, tap into your *Resilience* (Strength). Rather than letting your feelings get the best of you, reach within to find the strength to move forward with grace. By remembering why you are working so hard in the first place, you can reignite your enthusiasm for the ambitions and goals you have laid out for your future.

JUST FOR TODAY

TODAY'S MANTRA

I have limitless energy to pursue the goals that are deeply authentic to me.

TODAY'S JOURNAL PROMPT

What obligations do I have that are draining some of my most vital energy?

TODAY'S RITUAL

If you find yourself overwhelmed at any point today, set aside eight minutes to do some wrist tapping. Using your index and middle fingers on your dominant hand, tap on the inside of your nondominant wrist while repeating the affirmation, "I am worthy of embracing my full authentic power."

BORN ON THIS DAY

EDDIE VEDDER, American singer-songwriter and musician

GEORGE WASSOUF, Syrian singer

"What success I have obtained is the result of many sleepless nights and real hard work." —MADAM C. J. WALKER, American entrepreneur, philanthropist, political and social activist, and the first female self-made millionaire in America

The Journey of Those Born on
DECEMBER 23

You were born of emotional maturity and a respect for authority that can keep you from realizing how influential you innately are. You will have to grow into the force of nature you were always meant to be, as your journey is one of authenticity, mastery, and internal strength.

Early on in your journey, you will meet your enigmatic guide, *Power* (The Number Eight). Despite your desire to follow the rules, *Power* calls you away from the rigidity of tradition and toward a radical path of self-realization. You will meet *Power* when you expand into your full potential, never making yourself small or denying your truth to make others comfortable.

But if you choose this path of self-embodiment, you will have to pay respect to *Repetition* (Eight of Pentacles). *Repetition* reminds you that to master your chosen craft, you must put in the mundane and tedious time that will one day amount to your irrefutable success. You will meet *Repetition* in the hours of unseen work that help you build a lasting relationship with integrity.

If you answer these calls for expansion, you will come to rely on the power of *Resilience* (Strength). Whenever life tests your limits, *Resilience* asks you to dig deep rather than give up in the face of opposition. You will meet *Resilience* when you strengthen your emotional muscles by taking each personal setback as a profound opportunity to rise strong. If you can hold your ground through even the rockiest of times, you'll learn that you can handle anything.

YOUR GUIDES

Astrology: Your Energy
Capricorn (Saturn)

Numerology: Your Path
Power (The Number Eight)

Minor Arcana: Your Lesson
Repetition (The Eight of Pentacles)

Major Arcana: Your Highest Calling
Resilience (Strength)

CAPRICORN
RULER: SATURN

PURPOSE
To look for power within rather than outside yourself.

RELATIONSHIPS

You are as strong as they come, yet your relationships should be a place of deep sharing and vulnerability. By seeking out partners who recognize your innate brilliance while holding space for the darkest corners of your emotional truth, you will discover that true love takes you as you are.

The Journey of
DECEMBER 24

W elcome to December 24, an expansive journey that asks you to rewild your intuition. Despite the risk-averse nature of Capricorn season, *Experience* (The Number Nine) invites you to explore the unknown that the day offers you. Enroll in a new course, take on a foreign project at work, or plan your next adventure abroad—the more out of your comfort zone, the better.

And know that you can rely on yourself. *Self-sufficiency* (Nine of Pentacles) asks you to look within whenever you feel scarce or fearful today, drawing on your innate resourcefulness to get your needs met. Whether you treat yourself to a nourishing meal or spend some time relishing your favorite public garden, know that you can unlock the abundance you seek.

As you travel this uncharted territory, rely on your *Instinct* (The Hermit). There may be no clear plan of action for you to follow, so take things one step at a time as you consult your intuitive intelligence. Where is your gut telling you to go next? If you can let go of certainty and embrace the grand adventure of self-trust, you can discover how good it feels to listen to yourself.

JUST FOR TODAY

TODAY'S MANTRA

For today, bravery might mean feeling fear but trusting my intuition anyway.

TODAY'S RITUAL

Try to recall a time in your life when you felt deeply uncertain of where to go next. How did you move through this discomfort? Bring this memory with you as you move through the unknowns of this day.

TODAY'S JOURNAL PROMPT

What is a small indulgence that brings me emotional comfort?

BORN ON THIS DAY

TARJA HALONEN, Finnish politician and first female president of Finland

ANTHONY FAUCI, American physician, scientist, immunologist, and public health adviser to every US president since Ronald Reagan

"Now I hold the full conviction that my true happiness lies in living my life freely, without any fears or false pretexts."—RICKY MARTIN, Puerto Rican singer-songwriter and actor

The Journey of Those Born on
DECEMBER 24

You were born of deep devotion to the ones you love and a need for connection that can keep you from living out true personal freedom. You will have to rewild yourself to reclaim your power, as your journey is one of fearlessness, abundance, and radical self-trust.

Early on in your journey, you will meet your worldly guide, *Experience* (The Number Nine). Despite your desire for emotional safety, *Experience* calls you away from codependency and toward a path of the unknown. You will meet *Experience* in the opportunities that take you far away from where you began so you can expand your perspective and soar through new heights of knowledge.

If you choose this expansive path, you will meet your elegant friend, *Self-sufficiency* (Nine of Pentacles). *Self-sufficiency* teaches you that you have everything you need within, encouraging you to rely on your own powers of abundance rather than entangling yourself with others. You will meet *Self-sufficiency* in moments of personal wealth, when you take a step back and witness all the good you have acquired.

YOUR GUIDES

Astrology: Your Energy
Capricorn (Saturn)

Numerology: Your Path
Experience (The Number Nine)

Minor Arcana: Your Lesson
Self-sufficiency
(The Nine of Pentacles)

Major Arcana: Your Highest Calling
Instinct (The Hermit)

By answering these bountiful calls, you will come to rely on the power of *Instinct* (The Hermit). You will meet *Instinct* in the wilderness of uncertainty, when you make an active choice to follow the intuitive calls of your soul. *Instinct* encourages you to move forward through the divine mystery of your journey guided by nothing but the light of your internal compass. If you can run toward your truth rather than away from it, *Instinct* will introduce you to yourself.

─────────────────────○─────────────────────

CAPRICORN
RULER: SATURN

PURPOSE
*To reclaim the wildness of power
that lives within.*

RELATIONSHIPS

You are deeply attached to the people you trust, yet your relationships should be a place of radical growth and freedom. By seeking out partners who expand your perspective and encourage you to push the boundaries of your comfort zone, you will discover that true love is the greatest adventure of all.

The Journey of
DECEMBER 25

Welcome to December 25, a fruitful journey that asks you to take fate as it comes.

Do your own thing today. Despite the conservative nature of Capricorn season, *Autonomy* (The Number One) invites you to choose your own adventure by following your instinct rather than the opinions of others. What do your mind, body, and soul feel like pursuing today?

By trusting in this divine intelligence, you can tap into your powers of *Manifestation* (Ace of Pentacles). Today is a wonderful day to plant some seeds for your future, so purchase that URL for your new business or begin laying the groundwork for your next promotion at work. Anything is possible, as long as you are willing to nurture its potential with personal integrity and grounded optimism.

But don't fret if things don't go quite as you envisioned. *Impermanence* (Wheel of Fortune) asks you to trust that your day is unfolding as it should, so aim to make the most out of every card that you are dealt. Whether you feel like you are riding a high of good luck or trudging through mud, take each circumstance as a divine opportunity to showcase your resilience.

———————————————○———————————————

JUST FOR TODAY

TODAY'S MANTRA

I will throw myself toward my next goal without overthinking the outcome.

TODAY'S JOURNAL PROMPT

Do I consider myself an optimist, a pessimist, or a realist, and why?

TODAY'S RITUAL

Tuck one dollar in your pocket this morning and wait for an instinctual opportunity either to give it away or to spend it on something. Don't overthink it; just see what your intuition guides you toward.

———————————————○———————————————

BORN ON THIS DAY

FLEMMIE PANSY KITTRELL, American nutrition expert who helped establish the US's Head Start program and the first Black woman to earn a PhD in nutrition

ANNIE LENNOX, Scottish singer-songwriter, political activist, and philanthropist

"For me, life is a series of little moments, insane happiness or a split-second decision."—DIDO, English singer-songwriter

The Journey of Those Born on
DECEMBER 25

You were born of personal conviction and a need for security that can stop you from moving on to bigger and better things. You will have to risk big to win big, as your journey is one of intuitive action, abundance, and divine trust.

Early on in your journey, you will meet your courageous guide, *Autonomy* (The Number One). Despite your desire for certainty, *Autonomy* calls you away from playing it safe and toward a path of self-led breakthroughs. You will meet *Autonomy* when you trust in your instincts, carving out a unique legacy that balances bravery with personal integrity.

If you choose this inspired path, you will make friends with *Manifestation* (Ace of Pentacles). *Manifestation* encourages you to bring your best ideas into the folds of reality, rather than letting them wilt within the walls of your imagination. You will meet *Manifestation* when your dreams come to fruition, leaving you in awe at the wealth that comes from taking chances.

By answering these brave calls, you will come to trust the laws of *Impermanence* (Wheel of Fortune). You will meet *Impermanence* in the ebbs and flows of success, when fate waves its magic wand and you have no choice but to roll with the present. *Impermanence* reminds you that nothing lasts forever, encouraging you to take it easy rather than struggle as you await your next stroke of good fortune. If you can learn not to hold on to things so tightly, you'll discover the universe always gives you what you need.

CAPRICORN
RULER: SATURN

PURPOSE
To take a chance on fate to develop a relationship with the universe itself.

RELATIONSHIPS

You are committed and loyal to the people you care about, yet your relationships should be a place of abundance that stems from independence. By seeking out partners who know how to meet their own needs and encourage you to do the same, you will discover that true love is the meeting of two whole individuals.

The Journey of
DECEMBER 26

Welcome to December 26, an enlightening journey that requires your complete attention. Seek to find *Balance* (The Number Two) within your goals today. Rather than taking on everything at once, seek out the support and relief you need to put forth the most high-quality work possible. It is not a day for cutting corners, so if you find yourself short on time, aim to do less.

And how exactly? The key will be *Prioritization* (Two of Pentacles). Although Capricorn season inspires great ambition, try to delegate the responsibilities that simply aren't serving your long-term goals. Whether you give up on an old ambition that has run its course or go to your boss and let them know that you have outgrown an old task, remember that these tough decisions can make you more effective in the long run.

Besides, you'll need more space in your day to open to the *Truth* (Justice). Zoom out and look at the big picture of your life to see where things are being pulled to extremes. By refocusing your efforts, you can come back to center and remember what it is you are building toward.

JUST FOR TODAY

TODAY'S MANTRA

By slowing down and paring back my day, I can reconsider if my goals still ring true.

TODAY'S RITUAL

Schedule at least one eleven-minute break between the other obligations you have today. In these eleven minutes, try to quiet your mind and not fret about any of the things you have to do. Just sit in silence and give yourself some mental space.

TODAY'S JOURNAL PROMPT

What aspect of my life feels out of balance recently?

BORN ON THIS DAY

SUSHILA NAYYAR, Indian physician and politician

KIT HARINGTON, English actor

"The aim of life is to live, and to live means to be aware, joyously, drunkenly, serenely, divinely aware."—HENRY MILLER, American writer and artist

The Journey of Those Born on
DECEMBER 26

You were born of personal strength and a depth of understanding that can keep you stuck in morbid reflection. You will find the answers you seek by taking a step back, as your journey is one of stability, assessment, and higher knowledge.

Early on in your journey, you will meet your earthly guide, *Balance* (The Number Two). Despite your limitless power, *Balance* calls you away from taking on too much and toward a path of peaceful living. You will meet *Balance* when you rethink your responsibilities and ambitions so you can sustain a lifetime of hard work and personal integrity.

If you take this intentional path, you will have to pay respect to *Prioritization* (Two of Pentacles). *Prioritization* reminds you that quality is better than quantity, encouraging you to say "no" to the ambitions that feed your ego rather than your soul. You will meet *Prioritization* when you decide what people and projects are truly worth your while, simplifying your life and narrowing your focus.

By answering these calls to slow down and remain present, you will awaken to the nuance of *Truth* (Justice). You will meet *Truth* within balance, when you are able to surrender the black-and-white thinking of the ego and embrace the mystical gray areas in life. *Truth* invites you to persevere through the discomfort of ambivalence until you come out the other side with a radically new perspective. If you trust that nothing is certain and yet everything has meaning, you'll tap into the gift of spiritual consciousness.

―――――――――――――――――○―――――――――――――――――

CAPRICORN
RULER: SATURN

PURPOSE
To work to decode the nuanced simplicity of the truth.

RELATIONSHIPS

You are deep and introspective, and your relationships should be a place of ease and tranquility. By seeking out partners who are not interested in drama and keep their feet firmly planted in peaceful reality, you will discover that true love is simpler than you think.

The Journey of
DECEMBER 27

Welcome to December 27, a connected journey that invites you out of your comfort zone. Get out of your head and into conversation with the rest of the world today. While Capricorn season inspires some rigidity, *Flexibility* (The Number Three) asks you to remain open to the diverse opinions and perspectives of others, whether you read your news from a different outlet or engage in discussion with an unexpected individual.

From there, look for the merit in *Collaboration* (Three of Pentacles). If you find yourself stuck on an issue at work or home, enlist the expertise and support of the people around you. Even if no one is available to you, seek out help from your spirit guides or ancestors. There is always some form of help available to you if you are willing to look.

To make the most of this social day, you will have to *Surrender* (The Hanged Man) your ego. There's no use for being proud, so admit what you don't know and try something new. By breaking free from your instinctual responses to life, you may just crack open an entirely new perspective that transforms your consciousness for the better.

JUST FOR TODAY

TODAY'S MANTRA
Not doing things my way can be the biggest blessing in disguise.

TODAY'S JOURNAL PROMPT
When working within a group, what position do I tend to take on (e.g., leader, helper)?

TODAY'S RITUAL
To begin your day, lie down on your back in bed, with your head dangling off the edge. Repeat the affirmation, "I will remain flexible to whatever new information comes my way today."

BORN ON THIS DAY

TIMOTHÉE CHALAMET, American actor

SAHAR GHOREISHI, Iranian actor

"If anyone wants to ask a question or to suggest something, I'm always open."—SHELLY-ANN FRASER-PRYCE, Jamaican track and field sprinter

The Journey of Those Born on
DECEMBER 27

You were born of profound self-reliance and a capacity for aloneness that can keep you at arm's length from others. You will need to surrender to belonging, as your journey is one of curiosity, skill-sharing, and meaningful sacrifice.

Early on in your journey, you will meet your energetic guide, *Flexibility* (The Number Three). Despite your worldly wisdom, *Flexibility* calls you away from having the answers and toward a path of humble understanding. You will meet *Flexibility* in the unexpected conversations you share with others, when an unlikely teacher says just the right thing to help you move forward into new freedom.

If you say "yes" to this connected path, you will meet your divine friend, *Collaboration* (Three of Pentacles). *Collaboration* knows that the best work comes from the hands and hearts of many, inspiring you to find your role in a team that shares your vision. You will meet *Collaboration* in moments of skill sharing, when you lay your talents at the feet of the group and trust that they will flourish with the brilliance of others.

> ## YOUR GUIDES
>
> *Astrology: Your Energy*
> Capricorn (Saturn)
>
> *Numerology: Your Path*
> Flexibility (The Number Three)
>
> *Minor Arcana: Your Lesson*
> Collaboration (The Three of Pentacles)
>
> *Major Arcana: Your Highest Calling*
> Surrender (The Hanged Man)

By answering these calls for social growth, you will come to appreciate the power of *Surrender* (The Hanged Man). *Surrender* knows how easy it would be for you to spend this lifetime on a solo adventure but instead asks you to surrender to the intimacy of long-term connection. If you can release yourself from the grip of ego's ambitions and run toward the warmth of community, *Surrender* teaches you that some of the hardest choices to make are ultimately the most gratifying.

CAPRICORN
RULER: SATURN

PURPOSE
*To choose joyful connection
over isolated control.*

RELATIONSHIPS

You are private when it comes to your feelings, yet your relationships should be a place of radical communication. By seeking out partners who are first and foremost a dear and trusted friend who you can tell anything to, you will discover that true love sends your walls tumbling to the ground.

The Journey of
DECEMBER 28

W elcome to December 28, a gratifying journey that seeks to reground you in humility.
Do what you say you are going to do today. *Discipline* (The Number Four) invites you to be ambitious and thorough in your goals, so pour everything that you have into the people and projects that you are obligated to. By showing up with self-accountability, you can reap the benefits of hard work.

But despite the rigor of Capricorn season, be careful not to burn out through self-neglect. *Conservation* (Four of Pentacles) reminds you that your fundamental needs must be attended to in order for you to show up with such intensity. Whether you prepare meals to sustain a long day of work or go to bed early to replenish your energy, take care of your mind, body, and soul.

Because at the end of the day, you are the leader of your future. *Self-mastery* (The Emperor) empowers you to act with great maturity today as you set the expectations and boundaries you need to thrive. By putting the unpredictability of emotions to the side, you can make thorough and objective decisions that will benefit you well beyond the scope of this day.

———————————————◯———————————————

JUST FOR TODAY

TODAY'S MANTRA
To be a true authority toward myself, I must be accountable for my actions not just today, but every day.

TODAY'S JOURNAL PROMPT
How do I treat my body on a daily basis?

TODAY'S RITUAL
Cook something at home made from whole foods. Whether it is your favorite childhood dish or a quick stew, be sure it is nourishing to your soul.

———————————————◯———————————————

BORN ON THIS DAY

RATAN TATA, Indian industrialist and philanthropist

STAN LEE, American comic book writer, editor, and publisher and film producer

"You pray for rain, you gotta deal with the mud too. That's a part of it."—DENZEL WASHINGTON, American actor, director, and producer

The Journey of Those Born on
DECEMBER 28

You were born of intuitive confidence and an impulsivity that can distract you from your true purpose. You will have to choose long-term gratification over whims of passion, as your journey is one of integrity, grounding, and self-leadership.

Early on in your journey, you will meet your humble guide, *Discipline* (The Number Four). Despite your ever-evolving interests, *Discipline* calls you away from spreading yourself too thin and toward a path of earnest effort. By putting in the time, sweat, and energy required to master your chosen craft, you can build a lasting legacy of respect.

If you choose this hardworking path, you will have to contend with *Conservation* (Four of Pentacles). *Conservation* asks you to take inventory of what you need to sustain a lifetime of service, rather than draining all your energy in fits of inspiration. You will meet *Conservation* when you take care of your physical and material needs, ensuring that you never lose steam due to burnout.

By answering these calls for restraint, you will begin to embody the wisdom of *Self-mastery* (The Emperor). *Self-mastery* reminds you that you have agency over your choices, empowering you to take an objective and discerning look at how you are utilizing your potential. You will meet *Self-mastery* when you act in your long-term best interests, setting the boundaries and making the calls that build an internal sense of trust. If you can work to honor your highest self, you can become the authority you always hoped to be.

YOUR GUIDES

Astrology: Your Energy
Capricorn (Saturn)

Numerology: Your Path
Discipline (The Number Four)

Minor Arcana: Your Lesson
Conservation (The Four of Pentacles)

Major Arcana: Your Highest Calling
Self-mastery (The Emperor)

CAPRICORN
RULER: SATURN

PURPOSE
To make personal integrity the highest marker of success.

RELATIONSHIPS

You are independent and self-sufficient, but your relationships should be a place of spiritual and physical grounding. By seeking out partners who help you create a stable sense of home in which you can decompress, you will discover that true love is a foundation you can always fall back on.

The Journey of
DECEMBER 29

Welcome to December 29, an intrinsically motivated journey that requires you to trust in yourself.

Although Capricorn season can cause you to act conservatively in your professional life, *Courage* (The Number Five) asks you to take the risk to share your truth when appropriate. Whether you are in a position of leadership or are early on in your career, now is the time to step up and into your power.

But be gentle with yourself if feelings of *Scarcity* (Five of Pentacles) come up. It is quite scary and intimidating to approach your work with honesty in a society that encourages you to stay small and quiet. If you find yourself navigating some heavy uncertainty or anxiety, enlist the support of the people or spiritual practices that have your best interests at heart.

Above all else, remember that you are the decision-maker of your life. *Wisdom* (The Hierophant) invites you to discern the true from the false from within throughout today, never minding the opinions of others and trusting deeply in your intuitive intelligence. By staying true to your convictions while engaging in healthy discussions with others, you can come out tomorrow with a new sense of self-confidence.

JUST FOR TODAY

TODAY'S MANTRA
When it comes to my professional purpose, I am the ultimate authority.

TODAY'S RITUAL
Put on a cozy, soft outfit that brings you a sense of emotional comfort. It could be an old pair of jeans or your partner's well-worn sweatshirt; just make sure that you feel held and comfortable in it.

TODAY'S JOURNAL PROMPT
Growing up, what was I taught about how to engage with authority?

BORN ON THIS DAY

MARY TYLER MOORE, American Emmy and Tony Award–winning actor and producer

RADHA PAUDEL, Nepalese nurse, activist, and writer

"A child is a quicksilver fountain spilling over with tomorrows and tomorrows and that is why she is richer than you and I."—TOM BRADLEY, American politician, police officer, and first Black mayor of Los Angeles

The Journey of Those Born on
DECEMBER 29

You were born of interpersonal integrity and a sense of diplomacy that can keep you from speaking your entire truth. You will have to learn to stand up and out for what you believe in most, as your journey is one of self-expression, bravery, and higher knowledge.

Early on in your journey, you will meet your bold guide, *Courage* (The Number Five). Despite your harmonious disposition, *Courage* calls you away from codependency and toward a sunlit path of creative vulnerability. You will meet *Courage* in moments of heart-racing visibility, when you choose to abandon the mask of niceties and take center stage in a life of honesty.

If you choose this spirited path, you will have to contend with *Scarcity* (Five of Pentacles). *Scarcity* shines an unflattering light on your belief of not-enoughness, helping you realize that your fears of loss are the only thing blocking you from true creative fulfillment. You will meet *Scarcity* in moments of perceived lack, when you feel there is no cushion to fall back on so you must sacrifice the full breadth of your ambitions in exchange for safety.

> ## YOUR GUIDES
>
> *Astrology: Your Energy*
> Capricorn (Saturn)
>
> *Numerology: Your Path*
> Courage (The Number Five)
>
> *Minor Arcana: Your Lesson*
> Scarcity (The Five of Pentacles)
>
> *Major Arcana: Your Highest Calling*
> Wisdom (The Hierophant)

By answering these calls for bravery, you will discover the power of *Wisdom* (The Hierophant). *Wisdom* emboldens you to be the spiritual leader in your life, prioritizing no one's expertise higher than your own intuition. You will meet *Wisdom* within self-trust, when your innate genius pierces through the fog of false promises and into the sunlight of personal authority. If you can remember that no one else has the keys to your truth, *Wisdom* gladly unlocks your intrinsic spiritual wisdom.

───────────────○───────────────

CAPRICORN
RULER: SATURN

PURPOSE
To be brave enough to place self-respect above the opinions of others.

RELATIONSHIPS

You are committed and serious by nature, yet your relationships should be a place of play and passion. By seeking out partners who make you feel loved and accepted when you let go of your inhibitions, you will discover that true love is a place of freedom.

The Journey of
DECEMBER 30

Welcome to December 30, a healing journey that overflows with emotional possibility. Show your *Devotion* (The Number Six) through meaningful action today. To make the most of the hard work that Capricorn season inspires, give your very best to the ambitions and relationships that speak to your soul. There's no need to spend time on the superficial today, so curate your to-do list to include only the most fulfilling of obligations.

And consider where you need to give and where you need to receive. *Reciprocity* (Six of Pentacles) reminds you that good deeds go both ways, so try not to deny the help and affection that come your way today so that you can extend this same abundance to someone else.

But if some fears or psychological blocks come up around all the good that today offers, get curious rather than frustrated with yourself. *Shadow* (The Devil) encourages you to take an empathetic look at your emotional triggers, considering where and when you first learned to reject the excruciating vulnerability of joy. By doing some reflective work with these hidden parts of yourself, you can clear new space to invite all the wonder that awaits you tomorrow.

JUST FOR TODAY

TODAY'S MANTRA

While I may consciously know I am worthy of happiness, I will be compassionate with the buried parts of myself that don't.

TODAY'S RITUAL

Turn off the lights in a room in your home, light a candle, and repeat the affirmation, "There is no darkness within me that doesn't contain a ray of light."

TODAY'S JOURNAL PROMPT

What is an emotional need of mine that I typically try to deny? What steps could I take to start receiving this nourishment?

BORN ON THIS DAY

FATIMA JIBRELL, Somali American environmental activist

V, South Korean singer-songwriter

"Maybe my pain was motivation."—LEBRON JAMES, American basketball player, philanthropist, and activist

The Journey of Those Born on
DECEMBER 30

Y ou were born of abundant strength and a compassion for others that you don't as easily extend toward yourself. You will have to learn to receive the healing you need, as your journey is one of sincerity, reciprocation, and psychological opening.

Early on in your journey, you will meet your tender-hearted guide, *Devotion* (The Number Six). Despite your responsible nature, *Devotion* calls you away from stark objectivity and toward a path of fulfillment through vulnerability. *Devotion* asks you to pursue not what you feel you have to do, but rather the ambitions that speak to the deepest recesses of your soul.

If you choose this path of meaning, you will meet your dear friend, *Reciprocity* (Six of Pentacles). *Reciprocity* teaches you the art of paying it forward, encouraging you to accept the help and gifts that come your way when you are down on your luck so that one day you can extend this same benevolence to another.

By answering these calls for compassion, you will meet your greatest teacher, *Shadow* (The Devil). You will meet *Shadow* in the subconscious defensive mechanisms that keep you at arm's length from the intimacy you truly seek. *Shadow* invites you inward to a place of radical nonjudgment to understand the formative experiences that taught you to fear good things so that you can heal these dark corners of your internal world. If you can shine a light on the parts of you that you find hardest to love, *Shadow* will offer you the gift of self-belonging.

YOUR GUIDES

Astrology: Your Energy
Capricorn (Saturn)

Numerology: Your Path
Devotion (The Number Six)

Minor Arcana: Your Lesson
Reciprocity (The Six of Pentacles)

Major Arcana: Your Highest Calling
Shadow (The Devil)

CAPRICORN
RULER: SATURN

PURPOSE
To let down the deepest psychological barriers and let good things in.

RELATIONSHIPS

You are quite comfortable being in the position of giving love, but your relationships should be a place of unconditional support. By seeking out partners whose cup is overflowing with self-contentment and pouring over into yours, you will discover that true love is abundant rather than draining.

The Journey of
DECEMBER 31

Welcome to December 31, a personally significant journey that asks you to invest in the long term.

To channel the high level of integrity that Capricorn season inspires, *Commitment* (The Number Seven) invites you to invest in your most important personal and professional goals. Show up to these obligations with as much accountability and loyalty as you can muster, demonstrating to others and to yourself just how reliable you are.

And make decisions that are going to allow you to keep up this intentionality in the long run. *Sustainability* (Seven of Pentacles) asks you to take a step back and consider how you can consistently and effectively nurture these goals moving forward. Whether you make a one-month or one-year plan, contemplate how to tend to your most valuable ambitions.

As you navigate this day of meaningful work, try to notice the small breakthroughs that you are experiencing on a personal level. *Evolution* (The Chariot) encourages you to move forward with a momentum of purpose while appreciating how far you have come. You are not the same person you were even a day ago, so give yourself the recognition you deserve for the internal and external advancements you have made.

JUST FOR TODAY

TODAY'S MANTRA

Every day is an opportunity to move closer to the person I am meant to become.

TODAY'S RITUAL

Compose an email to your future self seven years from now, letting them know where you hope to grow toward. If you feel compelled, look up an email service that automates this email to be sent to yourself in seven years.

TODAY'S JOURNAL PROMPT

How have I changed in the past year?

BORN ON THIS DAY

GABBY DOUGLAS, American artistic gymnast

ANTHONY HOPKINS, Welsh actor, director, and producer

"Don't wait for inspiration. It comes while one is working."—HENRI MATISSE, French painter, draftsman, printmaker, and sculptor

The Journey of Those Born on
DECEMBER 31

Y ou were born of unparalleled integrity and a work ethic that can keep you stuck on the hamster wheel of goals that are no longer serving your best interests. You will have to channel your force into the person you are becoming, as your journey is one of intention, consistency, and radical progress.

Early on in your journey, you will meet your forthright guide, *Commitment* (The Number Seven). To make the most of your serious temperament, *Commitment* calls you away from over-responsibility and toward a path of personal discernment. By saying "no" to what is draining your bountiful resources, you can invest in the higher callings of the soul.

If you choose this earnest path, you will have to pay respect to *Sustainability* (Seven of Pentacles). *Sustainability* asks you to consider the long term, making sure that you are putting in the forethought and boundaries required to maintain a lifetime of meaningful work. You will meet *Sustainability* when you take a step back and confirm that you never waste time on fruitless work.

By answering these calls for maturity, you will find true fulfillment within *Evolution* (The Chariot). *Evolution* invites you to see success as a journey rather than a destination, encouraging you to seek gratification in the lessons you've learned rather than dwelling on the experiences you believe to be mistakes. You will meet *Evolution* in deeply personal breakthroughs, when you feel the universe nodding at you in recognition that you are on the right path. If you can keep your mind, heart, and soul moving forward toward the future, *Evolution* will teach you how not to regret the past.

CAPRICORN
RULER: SATURN

PURPOSE
To invest in invisible progress that amounts to radical breakthroughs.

RELATIONSHIPS

You are serious about most everything in life, and your relationships should be a place of long-term, mutual commitment. By seeking out partners who understand that trust must be proven over time, you will discover that true love is an investment for a lifetime.

The Journey of
JANUARY 1

Welcome to January 1, an intuitive journey that requires you to trust your gut, and your partners, as you pursue your deepest goals.

Marking the beginning of the Western calendar year, today drips with Capricorn season's promise of self-improvement. Despite this yearning, however, *Balance* (The Number Two) asks you not to tackle your hopes and dreams alone or with haste. Instead, approach this day with ease, take your time, make a sustainable plan, and invite feedback and participation from the people you trust most.

Besides, you might have too much on your plate to begin with. *Prioritization* (Two of Pentacles) asks you to take on only as much as you can handle, checking in throughout the day to make sure you haven't drained your cup through people-pleasing or blind ambition. Ask for help when you can, and don't be afraid to share your burdens. You never know who would love to help.

All this patience will help you hear today's greatest teacher, *Intuition* (The High Priestess). *Intuition* asks you what you're working so hard for and if your goals truly align with your deepest needs. By sensing rather than planning today, you will come out the other side with a profound peace with who you are and a clarity about who you hope to become.

JUST FOR TODAY

TODAY'S MANTRA

My gut will tell me what I can and cannot take on.

TODAY'S JOURNAL PROMPT

How can I gently, intuitively, and sustainably approach my long-term goals?

TODAY'S RITUAL

Turn the lights off and lie down on your back with your legs open or crossed to open your pelvis. Place your hands on your lower stomach, and as you breathe in and out, imagine the intuitive knowing that lives inside your womb or stomach. Carry this image with you throughout your day, knowing that your inner wisdom will tell you what you need to know today.

BORN ON THIS DAY

BETSY ROSS, American seamstress credited with creating the first American flag

QI BAISHI, Chinese painter known for modernizing classical Chinese painting

"Don't ever tell anybody anything. If you do, you start missing everybody."—J. D. SALINGER, American novelist

The Journey of Those Born on
JANUARY 1

Y ou were born of earthly ambition and fierce self-will that can err on the side of stubbornness. You will have to learn to go with the flow, as your journey is one of partnership, harmony, and trusting your intuition.

Early on in life, you will meet your gentle guide, *Balance* (The Number Two). *Balance* invites you down a path of companionship, showing you the many blessings that come from sharing your life with others. Rather than proving that you are right or in charge, as you oftentimes are, *Balance* encourages you to reach for compassion and harmony in your partnerships.

If you choose to take this peaceful road, you will inevitably cross paths with your adversary, *Prioritization* (Two of Pentacles). *Prioritization* reminds you that to have it all, you must learn to delegate and strategize. Just because you can juggle two dozen tasks at once does not mean that you will be able to do them well. If you can release your need for control and credit, *Prioritization* will teach you how much easier it is to travel with a lighter pack.

By answering these calls for patience, *Intuition* (The High Priestess) will reveal your true power. Rather than caring for worldly success or outside influence, *Intuition* asks you to believe deeply in the power of the unseen realm as you trust your intuition over institutional power. You will meet *Intuition* in moments of spiritual clarity, when the material world asks you to move one way but your gut, heart, and soul pull you in the right direction instead. If you can quiet the noise of capitalism, *Intuition* will offer you the gift of divine purpose.

―――――――――――――――○―――――――――――――――

CAPRICORN
RULERS: SATURN, VENUS

PURPOSE
To trust that the unfolding of fate is never rushed, never greedy, and never frantic.

RELATIONSHIPS

You are independent at heart, yet your relationships should be a place of complete reciprocity. By seeking out partners and friends who are skilled at the art of connection, you will discover that true love asks you to lean on others and participate in the equal exchange of true intimacy.

The Journey of
JANUARY 2

Welcome to January 2, a fruitful journey of unexpected joy and shared adventure.
The pressure of Capricorn season may have you feeling bogged down in responsibility, but *Flexibility* (The Number Three) asks you to find freedom in your day anyway. Go wherever the moment takes you, especially saying "yes" to unexpected invitations from others, even if they seem to get in the way of your original to-do list.

As you say "yes" to the unknown of today, pay special attention to the people who want to create with you. *Collaboration* (Three of Pentacles) encourages teamwork of any kind, so remain humble as you welcome and absorb the expertise and feedback of others, and as you share your gifts. There's no need to compare or compete today, as long as you are aiming toward a common goal.

The undercurrent of this sociable day is nourishment through joy, teammates, and ideas. It is a day to appreciate the small and large blessings, soaking in every inch of spiritual sunlight that crosses your path. So enjoy. Create. Share. Smile. Feel free to relish the happy moments and mini breakthroughs, as *Abundance* (The Empress) aims to fill your cup.

JUST FOR TODAY

TODAY'S MANTRA

There is no greater joy than creating with others.

TODAY'S JOURNAL PROMPT

What are my greatest blocks when it comes to trusting and enjoying collaboration?

TODAY'S RITUAL

Sit in front of a mirror and maintain deep eye contact with yourself as you repeat the chant, "I am lovable. I am loving. I am loved."

BORN ON THIS DAY

ALICE MARY ROBERTSON, American educator, social worker, and second woman elected to the US Congress

DAX SHEPARD, American actor and comedian

"A person, who no matter how desperate the situation, gives others hope, is a true leader." —**DAISAKU IKEDA**, Japanese Buddhist philosopher, educator, author, and nuclear disarmament advocate

The Journey of Those Born on
JANUARY 2

Y ou were born of internal balance and a fierce loyalty that can keep you from meeting new people. You will have to open yourself to the joy of unexpected connection, however, as your path is one of curiosity, collaboration, and divine creative power.

Early on in your journey, you will meet your sociable guide, *Flexibility* (The Number Three). *Flexibility* shows you the genius of having none of the answers and all of the questions, encouraging you to humbly enter each day with no particular plan in mind. You will meet *Flexibility* in moments of chanced fate, when your day starts out looking one way and the universe leads you through a winding, fantastical, exciting path of blind curiosity.

If you choose this widening path, you will meet your earthly teacher, *Collaboration* (Three of Pentacles). *Collaboration* shows you the power of teamwork, encouraging you to share your skills and learn from others rather than staying in isolation. You will meet *Collaboration* in moments of shared inspiration, when your skills perfectly complement others' and you allow yourself and others a space to shine.

> ### YOUR GUIDES
>
> *Astrology: Your Energy*
> Capricorn (Saturn, Venus)
>
> *Numerology: Your Path*
> Flexibility (The Number Three)
>
> *Minor Arcana: Your Lesson*
> Collaboration (The Three of Pentacles)
>
> *Major Arcana: Your Highest Calling*
> Abundance (The Empress)

By answering these calls for connection, *Abundance* (The Empress) will invite you to receive and embrace the grace and beauty that live within and around you. While you are realistic and hardworking, *Abundance* reminds you that life is best when enjoyed and nourished, encouraging you to remain present in moments of profound bliss. If you can release yourself from the burden of the hustle and tap into your innate flow, *Abundance* teaches you that happiness is a birthright.

―――――――――――○―――――――――――

CAPRICORN
RULERS: SATURN, VENUS

PURPOSE
To bloom in the unknown.

RELATIONSHIPS

You are a balanced and committed partner to those you love, and your relationships should be a place of expansion and connection. By seeking out partners who are willing to change and evolve, you will discover that true love teaches you how good it feels to question the norm.

The Journey of
JANUARY 3

Welcome to January 3, a grounded journey of humility, restoration, and the harnessing of the will.

You may be bouncing off the walls with ideas and anticipation, but *Discipline* (The Number Four) asks you to direct your attention solely toward the tasks that matter. A slow and steady approach is most favorable today, so don't skip over any seemingly mundane tasks for easy gratification. The small actions will amount to a meaningful day's work.

To complement the serious nature of Capricorn season, *Conservation* (Four of Pentacles) asks you to treat your body, mind, and resources in a sustainable manner. Pause for regular mealtimes and mental breaks so you can refuel your energetic tank. There is no accomplishment that can be rushed today, so know that the most productive thing you can do is to be patient with yourself and your goals.

All of today's work aims to help you understand the importance of *Self-mastery* (The Emperor). Rather than falling prey to whims of emotion, today encourages you to take responsibility for your feelings and find self-esteem through estimable actions. By showing up as an objective and fair parent to yourself today, you can balance the responsibilities you have in the world while taking care of and satisfying your most fundamental needs.

JUST FOR TODAY

TODAY'S MANTRA
It is the small actions that make long-lasting change.

TODAY'S RITUAL
Make a thorough list of what and whom you are responsible for today and carry it with you. Whenever you get lost in the activity of the day, refer to this list.

TODAY'S JOURNAL PROMPT
What type of structure and discipline could I add to my day today?

BORN ON THIS DAY

CICERO, Roman philosopher

J. R. R. TOLKIEN, English author of *The Hobbit* and The Lord of the Rings series

"Since our leaders are behaving like children, we will have to take the responsibility they should have taken long ago."—GRETA THUNBERG, Swedish climate change activist

The Journey of Those Born on
JANUARY 3

You were born of grounded curiosity and a relentless desire for new opportunities. You have to temper your need for change, however, as your journey is one of hard work, reflection, and leadership.

Early on in your journey, you will meet your judicious guide, *Discipline* (The Number Four). *Discipline* requires you to put short-term gratification at the bottom of your to-do list in favor of long-term stability. Rather than acting from a place of unbridled passion, *Discipline* asks you to walk a more spiritual path of personal integrity and self-restraint. You will meet *Discipline* in the drips of sweat that pour down your face and the gratifying exhaustion of a job well done.

If you choose this discerning path, you will meet your grounded friend, *Conservation* (Four of Pentacles). *Conservation* asks if all this hard work is sustainable, ensuring that your hustle doesn't get the better of you. You will meet *Conservation* when you are forced to take a break from the pursuit of material growth and realize that all the stability you need exists within.

YOUR GUIDES

Astrology: Your Energy
Capricorn (Saturn, Venus)

Numerology: Your Path
Discipline (The Number Four)

Minor Arcana: Your Lesson
Conservation (The Four of Pentacles)

Major Arcana: Your Highest Calling
Self-mastery (The Emperor)

If you answer these pragmatic calls, you will come upon your ultimate teacher, *Self-mastery* (The Emperor). *Self-mastery* calls you inward, to a place of divine self-awareness, where discipline and control find their true spiritual purpose. You will meet *Self-mastery* in moments of crucial decision-making when you choose to be honest rather than to look good. By recognizing the importance of thoughtful action and emotional regulation, *Self-mastery* allows you to develop a reputation worthy of respect.

CAPRICORN
RULERS: SATURN, VENUS

PURPOSE
To achieve satisfaction in personal integrity.

RELATIONSHIPS

You are full of energy and ideas, but your relationships should be a place of divine rest. By seeking out partners who aim to calm you down rather than rile you up, you will discover that true love is the rock you can always fall back on.

The Journey of
JANUARY 4

Despite the disciplined, grounded energy of Capricorn season, January 4 invites you on a journey of self-expression and spiritual knowledge.

Early on in the day, look for ways to show the world who you are in all your splendid uniqueness. *Courage* (The Number Five) beckons you down a path of creative wonder and total vulnerability, helping you show your true colors in each professional or personal endeavor you take on today.

True vulnerability is no easy task, so take note of when *Scarcity* (Five of Pentacles) rears its fearful head. If you find yourself stuck in overthinking or self-criticism, actively seek out positive friends and family members who can remind you of your worth. Don't let insecurity get the best of you, because today, optimism and self-confidence are achieved through a simple shift in perspective.

At the heart of things, today's journey is leading you toward greater self-trust and *Wisdom* (The Hierophant). It is an important day to trust your gut and follow your desires, drowning out the authority figures who try to tell you you're wrong. You are the maker of your own destiny, and if you can listen deeply to your inner callings, you will realize that all the answers lie within.

———————————◯———————————

JUST FOR TODAY

TODAY'S MANTRA
I will trust my gut over the critical voices inside my head.

TODAY'S RITUAL
In front of a mirror or with a trusted friend, speak out loud all the criticism you direct toward yourself on a regular basis. Then hold your hand over your heart and ask your higher self to release these false, limiting beliefs.

TODAY'S JOURNAL PROMPT
What would I reveal about myself to others if I weren't afraid of rejection?

———————————◯———————————

BORN ON THIS DAY

LOUIS BRAILLE, French educator and inventor of a system of reading and writing for the blind

ISAAC NEWTON, English mathematician, physicist, and astronomer

"Sometimes you have to put a wrench in the gears to get people to listen."—ALICIA GARZA, American civil rights activist, writer, and cofounder of the international Black Lives Matter movement

The Journey of Those Born on
JANUARY 4

Y ou were born of unmatched discipline and a level of self-control that can block your inner-most feelings. You will have to embrace the power of imperfection, however, as your journey is one of fearlessness, manifestation, and teachability.

Early on in your journey, you will meet your magnanimous guide, *Courage* (The Number Five). *Courage* asks you to follow your heart instead of your head, inspiring you toward a life of deep meaning rather than material success. You will meet *Courage* in moments of wild vulnerability, when you discard the safer path and walk heroically to center stage, showing the rest of us exactly who you are.

If you choose this brave path, you will meet your toughest adversary, *Scarcity* (Five of Pentacles). *Scarcity* highlights your financial fears, forcing you to separate the true from the false. You will meet *Scarcity* in moments of radical self-investment when you choose to save in one area to take a chance on the life of your dreams.

> ### YOUR GUIDES
>
> *Astrology: Your Energy*
> Capricorn (Saturn, Venus)
>
> *Numerology: Your Path*
> Courage (The Number Five)
>
> *Minor Arcana: Your Lesson*
> Scarcity (The Five of Pentacles)
>
> *Major Arcana: Your Highest Calling*
> Wisdom (The Hierophant)

By answering these soulful calls to action, *Wisdom* (The Hierophant) asks you to discard your preconceived notions about how the world works and who is worth listening to. You will meet *Wisdom* in moments of disillusionment with so-called authorities and prophets, when you begin to realize that there are no clear-cut answers to life's greatest questions. As you realize that no one has a monopoly on the truth, you will discover that all you need to do is have faith in yourself.

○

CAPRICORN
RULERS: SATURN, VENUS

PURPOSE
To realize that internal freedom is a choice.

RELATIONSHIPS

You are as sturdy and reliable as they come, but your relationships should be a place of passion. By seeking out partners who follow their heart rather than their head in life's greatest decisions, you will discover that true love is the most worthwhile risk of all.

The Journey of
JANUARY 5

Welcome to January 5, a heartfelt journey of sincere generosity and connection. Rather than wasting the hardworking nature of Capricorn season on self-centered ambition, *Devotion* (The Number Six) asks you to give your energy to a meaningful cause instead. Whether it be personal or professional, find ways that you can be useful to the world around you, paying special attention to the humble work that can make the lives of others easier.

And give with no expectation of return. *Reciprocity* (Six of Pentacles) asks you to share the gift of service with others so you can discover how fulfilling it is to live in spiritual abundance. What inside you do you possess in plenty and how can you give it away to the people who need it most? Whether it be material, emotional, or spiritual, share your luck and watch it grow.

If you can answer the calls of usefulness today, *Choice* (The Lovers) fills you with connection and self-love. Take a look around you and witness the relationships that you have nourished, paying special attention to the intimacy you have nurtured within yourself. If you can appreciate the love that you have cultivated inside as well as outside yourself, today helps you find a profound sense of emotional wholeness.

JUST FOR TODAY

TODAY'S MANTRA
The most meaningful thing I can do is to give.

TODAY'S JOURNAL PROMPT
How can I uniquely and lovingly be of service to others today?

TODAY'S RITUAL
Write a short list of the qualities you desire and look for in other people (e.g., compassion, integrity, emotional intelligence), and make an active effort to personify these qualities throughout the day.

BORN ON THIS DAY

MAIKKI FRIBERG, Finnish educator, suffragist, and peace activist

HAYAO MIYAZAKI, Japanese animator and filmmaker

"The creative process is not controlled by a switch you can simply turn on or off; it's with you all the time."—ALVIN AILEY, American dancer, director, choreographer, and activist

The Journey of Those Born on
JANUARY 5

You were born of great intensity and a sense of pridefulness that can make it hard to surrender to your innate tenderness. You will have to find the power within emotional surrender, as your journey is one of service, reciprocity, and choice.

Early on in your journey, you will meet your humble guide, *Devotion* (The Number Six). *Devotion* asks you to walk the path of deep meaning, showing you the fulfillment that comes from acting from the heart rather than the ego. You will meet *Devotion* in moments of heartfelt work, when every inch of your being is being thrust toward a sincere cause.

If you choose this path of dedication, you will meet your bounteous teacher, *Reciprocity* (Six of Pentacles). *Reciprocity* invites you to share your gifts with others, reminding you that giving is the eternal spring from which abundance grows. You will meet *Reciprocity* in moments of financial or material gain, when you choose to let go and share rather than grip tightly to the wealth that comes your way.

By answering these calls for emotional openness, you will discover the power of *Choice* (The Lovers). You will meet *Choice* in profound moments of visibility, when by revealing your true vulnerability, you allow love from others to smooth out your rougher edges. No longer must you hide in the recesses of self-reliance. No longer must you give without receiving anything in return. Instead, *Choice* mirrors all the love that you deserve.

───────────────○───────────────

CAPRICORN
RULERS: SATURN, VENUS

PURPOSE
To show love for yourself and others through action.

RELATIONSHIPS

You are passionate with an undeniable desire for intensity in relationships, yet your relationships should be a place of tenderness. By seeking out emotionally vulnerable partners who show their love through thoughtful action, you will discover that true love never has to play it cool.

The Journey of
JANUARY 6

Welcome to January 6, a meaningful journey of internal commitment and external growth.

Complementing the disciplined air of Capricorn season, *Commitment* (The Number Seven) asks you to sink your teeth into the projects and relationships that matter the most to you today. Rather than scattering your attention, start your day by meditating to gain internal clarity on what simply and undeniably needs to get done. Don't falter, no matter who or what stands in your way.

And be sure that you're working toward your long-term future because *Sustainability* (Seven of Pentacles) is not interested in quick fixes or instant gratification. Don't be afraid to pause and reassess your strategy throughout the day, constantly taking inventory of where your energy would be utilized best. If you feel that you're getting lost in petty drama, know that you have a choice to walk away.

This big-picture work that you are called to do today lies within your personal *Evolution* (The Chariot). Zoom out and see where you would like life to take you and who you would like to become. Today may feel like you're biting off more than you can chew, but if you take it minute by minute and hour by hour, you will be amazed by where your efforts can land you at the end of the day.

JUST FOR TODAY

TODAY'S MANTRA
I will be infallible when it comes to my personal growth today.

TODAY'S RITUAL
Start your day by going for a quick sprint, go outside and walk in the direction of the wind, or close your eyes and visualize yourself flying. Do something that makes you feel like you are moving onward and upward.

TODAY'S JOURNAL PROMPT
Who do I want to become, and what will it take to get there?

BORN ON THIS DAY

SYD BARRETT, English guitarist, singer-songwriter, and cofounder of Pink Floyd

MARIAN CRIPPS, English anti-war activist

"You are an aperture through which the universe is looking at and exploring itself."—ALAN WATTS, English writer and speaker known for interpreting and popularizing Buddhism, Taoism, and Hinduism for a Western audience

The Journey of Those Born on
JANUARY 6

Y ou were born of great practical kindness and a generosity that can make you put the dreams of others before your own. You will have to learn to invest in yourself, however, as your journey is one of promise, perseverance, and personal growth.

Early on in your journey, you will meet your steadfast guide, *Commitment* (The Number Seven). *Commitment* asks you to sink your teeth into the ambitions, relationships, and ideas that matter most to you, and to stand up for them no matter what. You will meet *Commitment* in moments of uncertainty and insecurity, when life tests your devotion and forces you to dive deeper into the promises you've made to yourself and others.

If you choose this path of sincerity, you will meet your sage teacher, *Sustainability* (Seven of Pentacles). *Sustainability* asks you to take a step back from your work and reassess where your energy and money could best be utilized. You will meet *Sustainability* when you are looking through a wider lens at your life and planning for a more fruitful future.

By answering these calls for maturity, you will meet

your ultimate potential in *Evolution* (The Chariot). *Evolution* wishes you only the realization of your own power, pushing you to stop at nothing on your way to achieving your long-term goals. You will meet *Evolution* in moments of personal breakthroughs, when you push past your fear of failure and enter a new realm of power and responsibility. If you remain fiercely dedicated to your vision, *Evolution* ensures that you will get to where you've always wanted to grow.

CAPRICORN
RULERS: SATURN, VENUS

PURPOSE
To commit to your personal evolution.

RELATIONSHIPS

You have love for all humankind, and your relationships should be a place of profound commitment and loyalty. By seeking out partners who are willing to work side by side toward a greater future, you will discover that true love is the most important investment of all.

The Journey of
JANUARY 7

Welcome to January 7, an internal journey to discover the power that lies within.
Despite the pragmatism of Capricorn season, *Power* (The Number Eight) asks you to take the deeper, more expansive path today. Look for opportunities to practice honesty with yourself and with others, fearlessly pursuing the shared truth that lies in every moment. It is not a time for restriction, but instead a time for intimacy, so share your imperfect humanness.

And as your day opens, don't be afraid to put in the work that comes along with expansion. *Repetition* (Eight of Pentacles) asks you to show up for the humble work that others may pass off as trivial. See these small responsibilities as a large opportunity for growth, helping you end the day with a sense of pride and mastery over your personal progress.

This honest work will introduce you to today's highest calling, *Resilience* (Strength). Rather than letting your perceived failures cloud your day, *Resilience* wants you to appreciate that the courage it takes to show up to life's arena is proof enough of your strength. Each emotional obstacle will give birth to new spiritual muscles, leaving you with an even deeper reserve to tap into tomorrow.

JUST FOR TODAY

TODAY'S MANTRA
There is no truth I can't handle today.

TODAY'S JOURNAL PROMPT
When, growing up, did I learn to fear my own truth and my own power?

TODAY'S RITUAL
Write down a buried personal truth that you are ready to heal and bring it into the sun or under a light. Repeat the chant, "Dark truths, I seek from thee sun-soaked healing to bring lightness to me."

BORN ON THIS DAY

SADAKO SASAKI, Japanese victim of the Hiroshima bombing, known for her attempt to fold one thousand paper origami cranes before her death from cancer

CHARLES ADDAMS, American artist and cartoonist and *Addams Family* creator

"There are years that ask questions and years that answer."—ZORA NEALE HURSTON, American author, anthropologist, and filmmaker

The Journey of Those Born on
JANUARY 7

Y ou were born of creative intelligence and a fierce ambition that can cause you to overinvest in areas that don't feed your highest purpose. You will be asked to pursue only what you truly desire, as your journey is one of honesty, intentionality, and fortitude.

Early on in your journey, you will meet your transcendental guide, *Power* (The Number Eight). *Power* beckons you away from the confines of society, inviting you along a winding and elusive path of self-uncovering. Through the process of deep emotional honesty, *Power* will help you shed the superficial layers that mask your authentic wholeness, introducing you to a life of radical expansion and self-acceptance.

If you choose this road less traveled, you will shake hands with your humble teacher, *Repetition* (Eight of Pentacles). *Repetition* knows the value of quiet tasks and will teach you to pay respect to the generosity that life has shown you. If you can never let your pride make you believe that you have outgrown modest work, *Repetition* makes you a masterful apprentice of the spiritual world.

> ## YOUR GUIDES
>
> *Astrology: Your Energy*
> Capricorn (Saturn, Venus)
>
> *Numerology: Your Path*
> Power (The Number Eight)
>
> *Minor Arcana: Your Lesson*
> Repetition (The Eight of Pentacles)
>
> *Major Arcana: Your Highest Calling*
> Resilience (Strength)

By answering these calls for personal integrity, you will uncover your capacity for *Resilience* (Strength). *Resilience* shows you what you are made of, helping you draw on the endless emotional reserves that lie within you. You will meet *Resilience* in moments of self-realization, when you thought life got the best of you but instead, the setback catapulted you further into your power. If you can recognize the depth of your strength, you will see that the universe only gives you what you can handle.

CAPRICORN
RULERS: SATURN, VENUS

PURPOSE
To uncover the endless internal strength within.

RELATIONSHIPS

You are driven by forward momentum, yet your relationships should be a place of deep understanding and vulnerability. By seeking out partners who don't shy away from the truth, you will discover that true love doesn't need you to be perfect, it just needs you to be honest.

The Journey of
JANUARY 8

Welcome to January 8, an expansive journey that encourages freedom over control.
As you approach today, look for any and every opportunity to seek *Experience* (The Number Nine). Explore a new part of town, teach yourself a new skill in your work, or reach out to that expert you've been hoping would mentor you. If you can remain humbly curious throughout this day, you can open your mind to new understanding.

To honor the disciplined nature of Capricorn season, take some time to appreciate how far you've come. *Self-sufficiency* (Nine of Pentacles) asks you to acknowledge your hard-earned success, whether it be material, emotional, or spiritual. Look around you, witness the abundance you have built, and rest satisfied in this personal power.

Throughout each minute of this fruitful day, listen to your *Instinct* (The Hermit). It is not the time to seek outside authority and advice, but rather a perfect opportunity to quiet the opinions of others so you can hear the intuitive truth-teller that exists within. If your gut has been urging you toward a spiritual path, make a concerted effort to say "yes" to this invitation today. There's no mistake to be made, as long as you are listening deeply to yourself.

JUST FOR TODAY

TODAY'S MANTRA
I will rely on internal trust as I pursue external freedom.

TODAY'S RITUAL
Place a blindfold over your eyes as you carry out a mundane task, like brushing your teeth or making your bed. While it's destabilizing at first, let this sensory deprivation help you tap into your intuition and physical intelligence.

TODAY'S JOURNAL PROMPT
What do I instinctively want to learn more about?

BORN ON THIS DAY

STEPHEN HAWKING, English theoretical physicist

EMILY GREENE BALCH, American economist, sociologist, and pacifist

"Always go a little further into the water than you feel you're capable of being in. Go a little bit out of your depth. And when you don't feel that your feet are quite touching the bottom, you're just about in the right place to do something exciting."—**DAVID BOWIE**, English singer-songwriter

The Journey of Those Born on
JANUARY 8

Y ou were born of grounded power and an intensity that can make it difficult to let go of control. You will have to surrender to the abundance of the unknown, however, as your journey is one of seeking, satisfaction, and internal trust.

Early on in your journey, you will meet your wild guide, *Experience* (The Number Nine). *Experience* steers you away from your comfort zone and encourages you to seek out the answers to life's biggest questions. By humbly searching your way through life, rather than attempting to control the outcome, you allow *Experience* to take you to uncharted heights of consciousness.

If you choose this winding path, you will be greeted with open arms by your earthly friend, *Self-sufficiency* (Nine of Pentacles). *Self-sufficiency* holds up a gold-plated mirror to your intrinsic abundance, revealing to you the riches that you have accumulated of your own accord. You will meet *Self-sufficiency* in moments of well-earned material success, when you have no one to thank for your wealth but your own work ethic and personal integrity.

By answering these calls for growth, you will come to rely on the wisdom of *Instinct* (The Hermit). *Instinct* asks you time and again to trust yourself, above all else, as you carve out a life of meaning. You will meet *Instinct* in moments of intentional isolation, when you drown out the external pressures so you can listen deeply to what your gut is trying to tell you. If you can rely on *Instinct* in the darkest of moments, putting one intuitive foot in front of the other, you will align yourself with authentic spiritual direction.

CAPRICORN
RULERS: SATURN, VENUS

PURPOSE
To search fearlessly for spiritual direction.

RELATIONSHIPS

You are probing and introspective, but your relationships should be a place of wanderlust and expansion. By seeking out partners who help you get out of your head and into the present moment, you will discover that true love reveals the endless possibilities that life has to offer.

The Journey of
JANUARY 9

Welcome to January 9, a gratifying journey of independence and self-actualization.

As you navigate the seriousness of Capricorn season today, try your best to stay on the path of *Autonomy* (The Number One). Rather than waiting for others to show up as you wish, seize every opportunity you can to accomplish your goals and responsibilities on your own. It is a day to say, "I can do this."

And don't be surprised if you find yourself in a position of leadership. *Manifestation* (Ace of Pentacles) wants you to share your wealth of optimism with others, filling up their cup with your confidence. Encourage the people on your team at work, hype up a friend who is low on self-esteem, or simply give a stranger on the street a compliment.

And take each of your personal ups and downs in stride today. *Impermanence* (Wheel of Fortune) wants you to remember that life's circumstances are fleeting and unreliable, and so it is best to find happiness in acceptance. If today is on the upswing, stay present with this joy. If today has you feeling down on your luck, find peace in the knowledge that it won't last forever. Trust that the tides of today are guiding you to where you are supposed to be.

JUST FOR TODAY

TODAY'S MANTRA
I will hold on to my personal power while I ride today's roller coaster.

TODAY'S RITUAL
To get right-sized, sit underneath the sky at any point today, ideally when the sun or the moon is most visible to you. Notice yourself in relation to the vastness of the sky and extend gratitude to the powers that be.

TODAY'S JOURNAL PROMPT
In what part of my life am I not practicing acceptance?

BORN ON THIS DAY

CARRIE CHAPMAN CATT, American suffragist

KENNY "KLOOK" CLARKE, American jazz drummer and major innovator of the bebop style

"I am incapable of conceiving infinity, and yet I do not accept finity. I want this adventure that is the context of my life to go on without end."—**SIMONE DE BEAUVOIR**, French writer, intellectual, existentialist philosopher, political activist, feminist, socialist, and social theorist

The Journey of Those Born on
JANUARY 9

You were born of earthly wisdom and a wanderlust that can keep you away from the ambitions you seek. You will have to decide what you stand for, however, as your journey is one of autonomy, legacy, and unpredictability.

Early on in your journey, you will meet your fearless guide, *Autonomy* (The Number One). *Autonomy* asks you to carve out your own unique path, disregarding the preconceived notions of what others expect you to become. You will meet *Autonomy* in moments of divine ambition when you find yourself hurling yourself toward the seemingly impossible, guided by nothing but your intuition.

It can be frightening to travel uncharted territory, but know that your steps will leave behind a crucial road map for others to follow in the future. *Manifestation* (Ace of Pentacles) asks you to believe in your raw talent and helps you discover the "why" and "how" of your success. You will meet *Manifestation* in the very beginning of a new personal or professional opportunity, when you know you are about to do what no one has done before.

> ### YOUR GUIDES
>
> *Astrology: Your Energy*
> Capricorn (Saturn, Venus)
>
> *Numerology: Your Path*
> Autonomy (The Number One)
>
> *Minor Arcana: Your Lesson*
> Manifestation (The Ace of Pentacles)
>
> *Major Arcana: Your Highest Calling*
> Impermanence
> (The Wheel of Fortune)

Just know that anything you receive must be shared because *Impermanence* (Wheel of Fortune) knows that nothing good can last forever. Your highest calling is not only to accept, but to embrace the cyclical ups and downs of life. You will meet *Impermanence* in moments of surrendered freedom, when you detach completely from the notion that life owes you security and instead can laugh joyfully at the creative genius of it all. If you can hang on to your hat throughout life's wild ride, *Impermanence* will teach you how to get out of destiny's way.

CAPRICORN
RULERS: SATURN, VENUS

PURPOSE
To surrender your legacy to divine destiny.

RELATIONSHIPS

You are both wise and curious, and your partnerships should be your place of trusting independence. By seeking out partners who admire and respect your need for space, you will deepen your personal life while forever expanding your consciousness.

The Journey of
JANUARY 10

W elcome to January 10, a relational journey guided by your moral compass.
　　Amidst the discipline of Capricorn season, it can be easy to get bogged down in personal to-do lists. But as you set out today, look for opportunities to work with others. *Balance* (The Number Two) knows the value of shared responsibility and invites you to team up with someone who complements your skill set.

Besides, there's a lot you will be juggling today. *Prioritization* (Two of Pentacles) asks you to pour your energy solely into the projects and relationships that mean the most to you right now. It is not a day to spread yourself thin, but instead a day to offload or discard the extraneous burdens that are not yours to carry any longer.

If you find yourself lost in the choices that today requires, slow down and get in touch with *Truth* (Justice). Your moral compass will be the true guiding force for the day, breathing new clarity into even the murkiest of situations. Because today asks you to engage with others, it's all the more important for you to seek some alone time to get in touch with your personal values and sense of right and wrong. Look inward so you can point your compass toward the true north.

○

JUST FOR TODAY

TODAY'S MANTRA
To work with others, I must first know myself.

TODAY'S JOURNAL PROMPT
Whom can I intuitively trust to share my responsibilities with today?

TODAY'S RITUAL
Sit with your back against a wall with your legs crossed, and place one object that is meaningful to you on each inner knee. Close your eyes and feel the weight of your body ground you into the floor beneath you. Recognize your effortless ability to hold these two objects in balance.

○

BORN ON THIS DAY

GEORGE FOREMAN, American boxer, entrepreneur, minister, and author

MAX ROACH, American jazz drummer and composer

"How far you go in life depends on your being tender with the young, compassionate with the aged, sympathetic with the striving and tolerant of the weak and strong. Because someday in your life you will have been all of these."—GEORGE WASHINGTON CARVER, American agricultural scientist

The Journey of Those Born on
JANUARY 10

You were born of disciplined ambition and a self-reliance that can stop you from asking for help when you need it most. You will have to share your dreams as well as your burdens with those you can trust, as your journey is one of harmony, delegation, and sacred justice.

Early on in your journey, you will meet your tranquil guide, *Balance* (The Number Two). *Balance* asks you to drop your guard and walk toward the meaningful intimate relationships that make your life more easeful. Just because you can do everything on your own, doesn't mean you should. By learning to work in harmony with others, *Balance* shows you how to achieve your goals in a more sustainable way.

If you choose this path of intimacy, you will meet your wise teacher, *Prioritization* (Two of Pentacles). *Prioritization* asks you what all this work is for and if it's really worth the effort and time it requires. You will meet *Prioritization* in moments of overwhelm, when you learn to ask for help—and most importantly learn when to say "no"—helping you take on only what you can handle.

> ## YOUR GUIDES
>
> *Astrology: Your Energy*
> Capricorn (Saturn, Venus)
>
> *Numerology: Your Path*
> Balance (The Number Two)
>
> *Minor Arcana: Your Lesson*
> Prioritization (The Two of Pentacles)
>
> *Major Arcana: Your Highest Calling*
> Truth (Justice)

By answering these calls for peace, you will slow down enough to hear the voice of *Truth* (Justice). *Truth* invites you inward to a place of sound judgment, helping you intuitively decipher between right and wrong. You will meet *Truth* in moments of moral clarity, when your gut tells you what impenetrable laws you stand by and what you are willing to fight for. If you can remain calm, *Truth* will show you the clarity of moral reason.

CAPRICORN
RULERS: SATURN, VENUS

PURPOSE
To trust your moral compass as you lean on those who align with your values.

RELATIONSHIPS

You are independent and ever-changing, yet your relationships should be a place of complete trust. By seeking out emotionally sincere partners who naturally harmonize with your energy, you will discover that true love is the art of letting go of your need for control.

The Journey of
JANUARY 11

W elcome to January 11, a spiritual journey of community and understanding.
As you navigate the grounded nature of Capricorn season, be sure to leave behind your expectations so you can make room for *Flexibility* (The Number Three). This is not a time to overthink, but instead to remain malleable and open to the day's plans for you. If you receive unexpected invitations from friends or colleagues, welcome them with open arms and view each pivot in your day as an opportunity to learn.

If you choose to flow through this day, you will find yourself enveloped in the arms of *Collaboration* (Three of Pentacles). Today doesn't need you to work or plan in isolation, but instead favors community-building and group brainstorming. Seek out people you admire, pick their brain on the tasks you have to do, and see where *Collaboration* can take you.

But don't try to control the outcome. *Surrender* (The Hanged Man) encourages you to seize new opportunities to surrender your will and trust that the universe has your back. By letting go of expectation and ego, you'll discover an entirely new perspective on your circumstances. Perhaps life is going well, after all, if you can only get out of your own way.

JUST FOR TODAY

TODAY'S MANTRA
My goals can be better achieved if I surrender to new ideas and perspectives.

TODAY'S JOURNAL PROMPT
How can I incorporate pleasure and gratitude into my collaborations today?

TODAY'S RITUAL
Start your morning with a refreshing herbal tea, like hibiscus or ginseng, that invigorates you while flowing through your system.

BORN ON THIS DAY

ALICE PAUL, American suffragist and leader of the National Woman's Party

EZRA CORNELL, American businessman, politician, philanthropist, founder of Western Union, founder of Ithaca's first library, and cofounder of Cornell University

"The greatest discovery of any generation is that a human can alter his life by altering his attitude."—WILLIAM JAMES, American psychologist, philosopher, and author of *Varieties of Religious Experience*

The Journey of Those Born on
JANUARY 11

You were born of deep personal integrity and a humble caution that make it difficult to make important decisions. You will have to learn to let go, however, as your journey is one of joyful collaboration, teamwork, and leaps of faith.

Early on in your journey, you will meet your charming guide, *Flexibility* (The Number Three). *Flexibility* asks you to bend your rigid ways of thinking so that you can traverse a path of intellectual freedom. You will meet *Flexibility* in moments of collaborative compromise, when you choose to sacrifice your singular goals in favor of new ideas and perspective-shifting relationships.

If you choose this wide-open path, you will have to contend with *Collaboration* (Three of Pentacles). *Collaboration* asks you to no longer work in isolation, inviting you to release and to trust that the work and responsibility is best put in the capable hands of others. If you can pay deep respect to the skills of the people around you while believing deeply in your own, *Collaboration* teaches you the art of teamwork.

> **YOUR GUIDES**
>
> *Astrology: Your Energy*
> Capricorn (Saturn, Mercury)
>
> *Numerology: Your Path*
> Flexibility (The Number Three)
>
> *Minor Arcana: Your Lesson*
> Collaboration (The Three of Pentacles)
>
> *Major Arcana: Your Highest Calling*
> Surrender (The Hanged Man)

By answering these eye-opening calls, you will come to understand the power of *Surrender* (The Hanged Man). *Surrender* reminds you that you cannot force your way to a spiritual experience, but instead, by releasing your need for control you can free-fall into a state of enlightenment. By believing that the universe may have a better plan in store for you, *Surrender* encourages you to sacrifice your preconceived notions and embrace an entirely new and exciting perspective.

─────────────────○─────────────────

CAPRICORN
RULERS: SATURN, MERCURY

PURPOSE
To make room for community, spontaneity, and new perspectives.

RELATIONSHIPS

You are naturally attracted to deep intimacy, but your relationships should be a place of social expansion. By seeking out partners who add spontaneity and community to your life, you will discover that true love never has a dull moment.

The Journey of
JANUARY 12

W elcome to January 12, an intentional journey of self-actualization.
To make the most of the hardworking nature of Capricorn season, actively work toward *Discipline* (The Number Four). It is not a day for short-sighted goals or instant gratification, but instead, a day for accomplishing the small and mundane tasks that normally fall through the cracks. Write a thorough list of what must be done and make no excuses as you go about completing them.

But be sure you take them slowly and steadily. *Conservation* (Four of Pentacles) warns of burnout, encouraging you to view today as a marathon rather than a sprint. There is nothing important that can be accomplished in haste. Instead, if you can place one foot in front of the other deliberately and methodically, you will end up where you need to go.

All this work will help you reach today's true inner calling, *Transformation* (Death). This day encourages you to let go and grieve what no longer serves you, whether it be a relationship, an aspiration, or an identity. You are building toward something far truer and more authentic today, so it is time to clear out the past so you can make room for a deeper sense of self.

―――――――――○―――――――――

JUST FOR TODAY

TODAY'S MANTRA
Slowly but surely, I will work toward being truer to myself.

TODAY'S RITUAL
Go outside and find either a tree or a small piece of bark. Sit up with your back against the tree or with the bark in your lap and bring your awareness to your chest. Slowly but surely breathe in and out as you expand into your power.

TODAY'S JOURNAL PROMPT
What habits distract me from my productivity and sense of self?

―――――――――○―――――――――

BORN ON THIS DAY

JACK LONDON, American short-story writer and adventure novelist

BANG, Swedish journalist, writer, pacifist, and feminist

"If you only read the books that everyone else is reading, you can only think what everyone else is thinking."—HARUKI MURAKAMI, Japanese writer

The Journey of Those Born on
JANUARY 12

You were born of emotional maturity and a social awareness that can cause you to care more about the opinions of others than your own. You will have to find true self-esteem through action, however, as your journey is one of personal integrity, fiscal freedom, and self-leadership.

Early on in your journey, you will meet your intentional guide, *Discipline* (The Number Four). Discipline asks you to walk away from the intoxicating draw of social capital in favor of a more discerning, thoughtful path of self-work. You will meet *Discipline* in moments of personal restraint, when you could stay at the party until dawn but you choose to invest in your future instead.

If you follow this sturdy path, you will have to contend with your wise adversary, *Conservation* (Four of Pentacles). *Conservation* asks you why you're holding on so tightly to control and scarcity, hoping that one day you will trust that you don't have to work yourself into the ground. You will meet *Conservation* when you choose to relax and enjoy the fruits of your labor.

If you can answer these high callings, you will meet

YOUR GUIDES
Astrology: Your Energy
Capricorn (Saturn, Mercury)
Numerology: Your Path
Discipline (The Number Four)
Minor Arcana: Your Lesson
Conservation (The Four of Pentacles)
Major Arcana: Your Highest Calling
Transformation (Death)

your greatest teacher, *Transformation* (Death). *Transformation* asks you time and again to let go of what once was so that you can fully embrace who you are becoming. You will meet *Transformation* in moments of metamorphosis, when you have grieved one version of yourself and are consciously walking toward a newer, and truer, manifestation of your being. If you can accept that nothing, and no one, is meant to stay the same, *Transformation* teaches you the art of renewal.

———————————————○———————————————

CAPRICORN
RULERS: SATURN, MERCURY

PURPOSE
To build toward a more honest, authentic truth of the self.

RELATIONSHIPS

You are social and flexible, but your relationships should be a place of solid emotional ground. By seeking out partners who share your sense of pragmatism and purpose, you will discover that true love can stand the test of time.

The Journey of
JANUARY 13

Welcome to January 13, a fearless journey of personal fulfillment.

Despite the pragmatic nature of Capricorn season, prepare for the possibility of vulnerability. *Courage* (The Number Five) not only encourages you to share your heart, but may push you unexpectedly into sharing it without your choosing. Whether it be posting something authentic on social media or quite literally communicating your deepest feelings with another, make an effort to be seen.

But don't be surprised if fear pops up along the way. *Scarcity* (Five of Pentacles) highlights your critical beliefs and the limiting stories you tell yourself around authenticity. So reach out to supportive friends and family members, and rely on their optimism and belief in you until you can access your own. There is so much good that can come from asking for help today.

Amidst all this vulnerability, however, be sure to find the middle ground. *Serenity* (Temperance) knows that extremes only lead to drama, so act with peaceful reason no matter what the circumstances. Meditate, sip a calming cup of tea, or call a soothing friend who knows how to talk you off any emotional ledge. And no matter what, seek to find the balance between authenticity and inner harmony.

JUST FOR TODAY

TODAY'S MANTRA
As long as I am aligned within, no one can knock me off balance.

TODAY'S RITUAL
Channel the color red. By either dressing in something red or making it the lock screen on your phone, keep the energy and vibrance of red in your mind as you fearlessly travel through this creative day.

TODAY'S JOURNAL PROMPT
Whose opinions or criticisms block me from pursuing my deepest desires?

BORN ON THIS DAY

ERNESTINE LOUISE ROSE, Swedish suffragist, abolitionist, and freethinker

GEORGE IVANOVICH GURDJIEFF, Russian philosopher, mystic, spiritual teacher, and composer

"I am smart, I am talented, I take advantage of the opportunities that come my way and I work really, really hard. Don't call me lucky. Call me a badass."—SHONDA RHIMES, American television producer, screenwriter, and author

The Journey of Those Born on
JANUARY 13

You were born of fierce integrity and an emotional control that can keep you from processing your most vital feelings. You will have to learn to lean in to the messiness of emotion, however, as your journey is one of personal risk-taking, spiritual abundance, and inner peace.

Early on in your journey, you will run into your unbounded guide, *Courage* (The Number Five). *Courage* asks you to dance toward the path of creative freedom, believing deeply in the special powers that only you can offer to the world around you. You will meet *Courage* in moments of personal faith, when you choose to believe in your innate magic and follow your heart rather than your head.

If you choose this vulnerable path, you will have to contend with your greatest hurdle, *Scarcity* (Five of Pentacles). *Scarcity* asks you to look at your limiting beliefs, forcing you to question why you believe others are more worthy of support than you are. You will meet *Scarcity* in moments of self-investment, when you accept the help that comes your way as you pour your own resources into matters of the heart.

> ### YOUR GUIDES
>
> *Astrology: Your Energy*
> Capricorn (Saturn, Mercury)
>
> *Numerology: Your Path*
> Courage (The Number Five)
>
> *Minor Arcana: Your Lesson*
> Scarcity (The Five of Pentacles)
>
> *Major Arcana: Your Highest Calling*
> Serenity (Temperance)

By answering these calls for authenticity, you will come to understand the importance of *Serenity* (Temperance). Amidst your wild journey, *Serenity* asks you to find the middle road within yourself, the peaceful voice that tells you exactly where you need to go next. *Serenity* knows that nothing needs to be done in the extreme, showing you that you can have your creativity without all the drama. If you can always choose tranquility over fear, you can build a sustainable life from the heart.

CAPRICORN
RULERS: SATURN, MERCURY

PURPOSE
To strike the balance between external creativity and inner peace.

RELATIONSHIPS

You are steady and reliable, but your relationships should be a place for unbridled passion and fire. By seeking out partners who make you feel alive and provoke a healthy sense of vulnerability, you will discover that true love is the most fulfilling risk of all.

The Journey of
JANUARY 14

Welcome to January 14, an emotive journey of generosity and self-awareness. Amidst the hardworking nature of Capricorn season, look for how your actions can benefit others, with no expectation of return. *Devotion* (The Number Six) inspires you to pursue the small, seemingly insignificant acts of service that make the world that much sweeter for those around you. So pick up that piece of trash on the street, smile at that stranger on the subway, or look your barista in the eye and thank them for that perfect cup of coffee.

Perhaps the most direct way you can care for the world today is through physical service. *Reciprocity* (Six of Pentacles) encourages an abundance mentality, allowing you to share what you have in plenty without fear of personal loss. Whether it be lending a few dollars to a person in need or treating a friend to lunch, today asks you to give in order to receive the joy you desire.

But don't be surprised if some fear comes up as your heart expands. *Shadow* (The Devil) invites you inward to reflect upon the blockages you have around receiving love, affection, and joy. Try to notice your emotions without judgment, remembering that vulnerability is not as easy as it seems.

JUST FOR TODAY

TODAY'S MANTRA
I will be as tender with my feelings as I am with others'.

TODAY'S JOURNAL PROMPT
What do I have in plenty that I can share with others?

TODAY'S RITUAL
Revel in something sweet today, whether it be a piece of fruit or candy or a bubble bath scented with your favorite aroma. As you set about your day giving to others, see how good it feels to receive.

BORN ON THIS DAY

IMMACULÉE ILIBAGIZA, Rwandan American author and survivor of the Rwandan genocide

JULIAN BOND, American civil rights activist, politician, professor, and writer

"True beauty is something that attacks, overpowers, robs, and finally destroys."—YUKIO MISHIMA, Japanese novelist, poet, playwright, and actor

The Journey of Those Born on
JANUARY 14

You were born of tempered power and an emotional discipline that can block you from receiving the healing you need most. You will have to learn to soften to the wounds of the heart, however, as your journey is one of service, benevolence, and self-acceptance.

Early on in your journey, *Devotion* (The Number Six) will call you away from your desire for power and prestige and direct you toward a path of humble purpose. Rather than encouraging a lifetime of self-serving goals, *Devotion* inspires you to act from a place of divine duty. You will meet *Devotion* in moments of personal integrity, when you choose to do the right thing even though no one is watching.

If you choose this path of purpose, you will fall into the arms of your spiritual teacher, *Reciprocity* (Six of Pentacles). *Reciprocity* knows that the gifts of the universe exponentially grow in value when shared with others, inspiring you to give when you receive. You will meet *Reciprocity* in moments of personal plenty, when your cup is so full that you cannot help but share it with those who need it most.

YOUR GUIDES

Astrology: Your Energy
Capricorn (Saturn, Mercury)

Numerology: Your Path
Devotion (The Number Six)

Minor Arcana: Your Lesson
Reciprocity (The Six of Pentacles)

Major Arcana: Your Highest Calling
Shadow (The Devil)

By answering these calls for expansion, you will meet your healing teacher, *Shadow* (The Devil). *Shadow* knows how much old fear, shame, and anxiety come up when life begins to get big and full of happiness. *Shadow* invites you to witness your conscious and unconscious coping mechanisms for these feelings, encouraging you to address the deep emotional holes that can only be filled by self-love. If you can believe that you are worthy of healing, *Shadow* gladly steps out of your way to reveal the light.

CAPRICORN
RULERS: SATURN, MERCURY

PURPOSE
To love yourself and others through generous compassion.

RELATIONSHIPS

You are controlled and self-reliant by nature, yet your relationships should be a place of emotional devotion. By seeking out partners who give their affection with no expectation of return, you will discover that true love is the most healing act of all.

The Journey of
JANUARY 15

Welcome to January 15, an intensive journey of self-actualization.

As you navigate the grounded nature of Capricorn season, pursue the goals that you want to sink your teeth into so you can walk the path of *Commitment* (The Number Seven). Show the universe how serious you are about today by favoring earnest efforts over pompous displays of showmanship and focusing on the most important tasks and people at hand.

As you travel this sincere path, don't forget about the sentiment of *Sustainability* (Seven of Pentacles). Not all the projects you start will come to fruition immediately, but tend to these investments thoughtfully anyhow. Put in the slow and steady work required to accomplish your goals and find the intrinsic joy that comes from honest effort.

And expect the unexpected. *Upheaval* (The Tower) will throw some curveballs your way, pushing you into unexpected changes that serve a greater purpose. Let go of "the plan" today, and trust-fall into whatever circumstances you are thrown into. If you can integrate integrity with blind faith, you will awaken to divine direction.

JUST FOR TODAY

TODAY'S MANTRA
I will commit deeply to the universe's plans for me.

TODAY'S RITUAL
Find some peppermint oil or extract, drop it into the palm of your hand, and rub it around. Close your eyes, inhale deeply from your palm, and chant, "Peppermint, clear my mind so I can see where I need to go."

TODAY'S JOURNAL PROMPT
Do I trust that the universe has my back?

BORN ON THIS DAY

NÂZIM HIKMET, Polish Turkish poet, playwright, and novelist

MOLIÈRE, French playwright, actor, and poet

"Darkness cannot drive out darkness: only light can do that. Hate cannot drive out hate: only love can do that."—MARTIN LUTHER KING JR., minister, civil rights movement leader, and Nobel Peace Prize winner

The Journey of Those Born on
JANUARY 15

Y ou were born of emotional sincerity and a subconscious penchant for self-destruction that can throw you off course. You will have to learn how to build trust with yourself, however, as your journey is one of perseverance, investment, and radical change.

Early on in your journey, you will meet your formidable guide, *Commitment* (The Number Seven). *Commitment* asks you to walk a path of sincere purpose, investing in the change you can make in the world around you rather than getting lost in personal melodrama. You will meet *Commitment* in moments of maturity, when you choose to not let the ghosts of the past get the best of you and instead keep your focus on the work that lies ahead.

If you follow this intentional path, you will have to pay respect to your wise teacher, *Sustainability* (Seven of Pentacles). *Sustainability* asks you time and again if you're working toward the long haul or simply shooting for short-term gratification. You will meet *Sustainability* when you execute the seemingly mundane tasks that will one day amount to irrefutable success.

By answering these calls for maturity, you will build the emotional muscles required to withstand the power of *Upheaval* (The Tower). You will meet *Upheaval* in moments of divine intervention, when the universe makes the necessary change that you were not able to make for yourself. If you can believe that every unexpected change serves a higher purpose, you will discover that personal integrity always catches you when you fall.

YOUR GUIDES
Astrology: Your Energy
Capricorn (Saturn, Mercury)
Numerology: Your Path
Commitment (The Number Seven)
Minor Arcana: Your Lesson
Sustainability
(The Seven of Pentacles)
Major Arcana: Your Highest Calling
Upheaval (The Tower)

CAPRICORN
RULERS: SATURN, MERCURY

PURPOSE
To build the emotional maturity required to embrace change.

RELATIONSHIPS

You are generous and devoted, and your relationships should be a place of divine teamwork and loyalty. By seeking out partners with whom you are able to share the responsibilities that keep you up at night, you will discover that true love always has your back.

The Journey of
JANUARY 16

Welcome to January 16, a hardworking journey fueled by internal optimism.

Today is not a day to get lost in appearances, but rather a time to embrace your *Power* (The Number Eight). By taking a deeper look underneath all the layers of superficiality, show who you really are so that others feel safe enough to do the same. The best way to combat shame is honesty, so reveal your true colors, and own your authenticity.

As you lean in to the person you truly are, don't be afraid to roll up your sleeves and improve your craft. *Repetition* (Eight of Pentacles) asks you to humble yourself at the feet of your goals, never bypassing the work required to achieve greatness. Tackle today's tasks bit by bit, slowly but surely, and recognize yourself as both the apprentice and the master.

But at the heart of things today, reach for *Hope* (The Star). No matter where you are or what you have gone through, lean in to the inspiration and dreams that fill your imagination with wonder and make your eyes twinkle with pure potential. By using optimism to wash away the debris of the past, you can respark your enthusiasm for the future.

JUST FOR TODAY

TODAY'S MANTRA

With self-honesty and hard work, the past will never hold me back from my potential.

TODAY'S RITUAL

Make a two-column list. On the left, list the values you would like to embody (e.g., honesty). On the right, list the actions you could take to become this higher self (e.g., sharing the imperfect but true sides of yourself on social media).

TODAY'S JOURNAL PROMPT

What small, concrete steps can I take toward self-belief today?

BORN ON THIS DAY

SUSAN SONTAG, American author and film director

DIAN FOSSEY, American primatologist and conservationist

"I stay true to myself and my style, and I am always pushing myself to be aware of that and be original."—AALIYAH, American singer, actor, dancer, and model

The Journey of Those Born on
JANUARY 16

You were born of deep loyalty and a subconscious need for chaos that can overcomplicate your life. You will have to learn to focus only on what's real and positive, however, as your journey is one of authenticity, intentionality, and divine optimism.

Early on in your journey, you will meet your enigmatic guide, *Power* (The Number Eight). *Power* asks you to unmask your self-protective layers as you walk bravely along a winding path of self-honesty. By getting to know yourself and all your perfect imperfections, *Power* teaches you that your life's potential only increases through radical self-acceptance.

If you choose this path of authenticity, you will have to shake hands with your formidable teacher, *Repetition* (Eight of Pentacles). *Repetition* reminds you that there is no shortcut to mastery, inspiring you to put in the long and arduous hours required to harness your talents. You will meet *Repetition* in moments of profound humility, when your ego tells you that you have outgrown the mundanity of your work but you choose to pay respect to your craft anyway.

YOUR GUIDES

Astrology: Your Energy
Capricorn (Saturn, Mercury)

Numerology: Your Path
Power (The Number Eight)

Minor Arcana: Your Lesson
Repetition (The Eight of Pentacles)

Major Arcana: Your Highest Calling
Hope (The Star)

By answering these calls for personal integrity, you will discover the divine purpose of *Hope* (The Star). You will meet *Hope* in the darkest of moments, when a spark of enthusiasm lights up deep within your subconscious mind. Like an encouraging parent, *Hope* reminds you that the past has no hold on your future, as long as you are willing to believe. If you can get to know the magic that lives within, *Hope* shows you how to turn dreams into reality.

CAPRICORN
RULERS: SATURN, MERCURY

PURPOSE
To turn radical authenticity into divine possibility.

RELATIONSHIPS

You are intense yet controlled, but your relationships should be a place of total erotic freedom and honesty. By seeking out partners who make you feel understood and adored for your complexity, you will discover that true love is a path to self-acceptance.

The Journey of
JANUARY 17

Welcome to January 17, an introspective journey that leads to higher consciousness.

As you navigate the intellectual side of Capricorn season, be sure to incorporate *Experience* (The Number Nine) into your plans. Question every accepted truth today, embrace your power of intellectual autonomy, and search for greater personal truths. Humble yourself at the feet of the unknown.

Amidst the wisdom of this day, *Self-sufficiency* (Nine of Pentacles) invites you to practice abundance in your relationship with the material world. Whether it be preparing a delicious lunch for yourself or splurging on that new mattress you've been desiring, favor the necessary indulgences that make life that much richer.

You will need to nourish your internal resources because *Memory* (The Moon) asks you to self-reflect today. Carve out extra time to check in with how the past is still affecting your present and embrace this opportunity for historical healing. If you are at a crossroads in any aspect of your life, now is the time for deep soul-searching rather than outside counseling. By staying true to your innermost voice, you can reach the personal breakthroughs you've been needing.

JUST FOR TODAY

TODAY'S MANTRA
I will embrace the unknowns within and around me.

TODAY'S JOURNAL PROMPT
What am I deeply questioning in my life right now?

TODAY'S RITUAL
Go into a safe room of your choosing, light a small candle, and turn off the lights or shut the blinds. Meditate on this small fire of light, knowing that it represents the power of your intuition today.

BORN ON THIS DAY

MUHAMMAD ALI, American world heavyweight boxing champion and Olympic gold medalist

ALVA BELMONT, American socialite and suffragist

"For me, becoming isn't about arriving somewhere or achieving a certain aim. I see it instead as forward motion, a means of evolving, a way to reach continuously toward a better self. The journey doesn't end."—MICHELLE OBAMA, American attorney, author, and the forty-fourth first lady of the United States

The Journey of Those Born on
JANUARY 17

You were born of intellectual power and impenetrable focus on the future that can keep you from acknowledging the heartbreaks of the past. You will have to look back to look forward, however, as your journey is one of seeking, personal abundance, and deep introspection.

Early on in your journey, you will meet your wise guide, *Experience* (The Number Nine). Rather than getting lost in the rat race of achievement or blindly trusting the authority of others, *Experience* asks you to define your own set of truths through a search for greater self-understanding. You will meet *Experience* in moments of personal revelation, when your humble curiosity has led you to a new levels of consciousness.

If you choose this fearless path, you will be greeted by your glamorous friend, *Self-sufficiency* (Nine of Pentacles). *Self-sufficiency* teaches you the art of personal plenty, encouraging you to ask for what you deserve on an emotional and material level. You will meet *Self-sufficiency* in moments of abundance, when you can't help but pat yourself on the back for all the riches you have acquired in your search for meaning.

> ## YOUR GUIDES
>
> *Astrology: Your Energy*
> Capricorn (Saturn, Mercury)
>
> *Numerology: Your Path*
> Experience (The Number Nine)
>
> *Minor Arcana: Your Lesson*
> Self-sufficiency (The Nine of Pentacles)
>
> *Major Arcana: Your Highest Calling*
> Memory (The Moon)

By answering these calls for expansion, you will come to understand the importance of *Memory* (The Moon). *Memory* knows where you have been and what you have gone through, gently encouraging you to sift through the past so that you can understand how it has shaped your present. It is brave to remember and accept the reality of what you have experienced. But if you are willing, *Memory* helps you clear out the emotional baggage that is no longer serving you and reveal your emotional wholeness.

CAPRICORN
RULERS: SATURN, MERCURY

PURPOSE
*To uncover the true essence
that lies within.*

RELATIONSHIPS

You are emotionally powerful and intense, and your relationships should be a place of radical growth and expansion. By seeking out partners who enlarge your perspective and push you outside your comfort zone, you will discover that true love helps you evolve.

The Journey of
JANUARY 18

Welcome to January 18, a fearless journey of learning when to give and when to take.
Look for ways to embrace *Autonomy* (The Number One) today. Whether it be starting a solo project or conquering a new task without outside help, rely on your personal gifts rather than waiting for others to give you the green light. See what you can accomplish by believing deeply in your power to succeed.

To make the most of the hardworking nature of Capricorn season, lean in to your powers of *Manifestation* (Ace of Pentacles). Quiet the voices of imposter syndrome and pursue your next goal with blind enthusiasm. Take on a position of leadership today, encouraging others to step into their own personal power and leading with complete vulnerability. You have much enthusiasm to share, so spread it widely.

Besides, *Vitality* (The Sun) wants you to give yourself permission to shine. Access your authentic confidence by drawing on your innermost strength as you share your optimism and hope with the world around you. There is a natural radiance that comes from self-belief, so take a chance on yourself and channel the fearlessly vulnerable child who lives within.

JUST FOR TODAY

TODAY'S MANTRA
I will shine bright for myself and others today.

TODAY'S RITUAL
Sit out in the sun, even if it is covered by clouds, for nineteen minutes. Repeat the mantra, "Sun magic, please help me sing the beautiful song that lives within me."

TODAY'S JOURNAL PROMPT
How can I take on a position of generous leadership in my life today?

BORN ON THIS DAY

DANIEL HALE WILLIAMS, American heart surgeon who performed the first open-heart surgery

A. A. MILNE, English playwright, poet, and author of the Winnie-the-Pooh books

"To become truly great, one has to stand with people, not above them."—**MONTESQUIEU**, French judge and political philosopher

The Journey of Those Born on
JANUARY 18

Y ou were born of humble wisdom and an introversion that can stop you from pursuing your biggest dreams. You will have to dare greatly, however, as your journey is one of independence, self-belief, and authenticity.

Early on in your journey, you will meet your fearless guide, *Autonomy* (The Number One). *Autonomy* asks you to stop overthinking and act on your intuition, zipping you along a path of fearless self-reliance. You will meet *Autonomy* in moments of powerful self-trust, when you throw caution to the wind and act on your deepest ambitions.

If you choose this trailblazing path, you will meet your inspired teacher, *Manifestation* (Ace of Pentacles). *Manifestation* asks you to believe in the sheer potential of your goals, never losing sleep over the possibility of failure. You will meet *Manifestation* in moments of personal investment, when you take the first step toward realizing your dreams.

By answering these calls for confidence, you will come to rely on the strength of *Vitality* (The Sun). *Vitality* knows the importance of authenticity, encouraging you to shed light on all your inner children so that you can integrate them into your conscious identity. You will meet *Vitality* in moments of self-actualization, when you are able to channel your internal enthusiasm into your physical reality. If you can give yourself permission to shine, you will allow others to do the same.

YOUR GUIDES

Astrology: Your Energy
Capricorn (Saturn, Mercury)

Numerology: Your Path
Autonomy (The Number One)

Minor Arcana: Your Lesson
Manifestation (The Ace of Pentacles)

Major Arcana: Your Highest Calling
Vitality (The Sun)

CAPRICORN
RULERS: SATURN, MERCURY

PURPOSE
*To manifest a joyous life
of authentic power.*

RELATIONSHIPS

You are quite thoughtful and introspective, and your relationships should be a place of optimism and growth. By seeking out partners whose confidence and enthusiasm remind you of the limitless possibilities in life, you will discover that true love is an endless source of inspiration.

The Journey of
JANUARY 19

W elcome to January 19, an enlightening journey of personal balance and self-awareness. Despite the rigor of Capricorn season, approach your day gently. *Balance* (The Number Two) is not impressed by fits of passion, nor is it fooled by unsustainable efforts. Look for ways in which you can do things more harmoniously today, whether it be taking something off your to-do list or enlisting help from a trusted companion.

You will need this steady approach because *Prioritization* (Two of Pentacles) asks you to trim the unnecessary burdens of the day. Take an honest look at where you are spreading yourself too thin, and don't be shy to delegate or walk away from the projects or relationships that are simply not worth your time.

Besides, *Awakening* (Judgment) will need your full and undivided attention. Approach each relationship and goal with complete honesty and awareness, reflecting on the fears that have kept you closed-minded to the greater truths that are awaiting you. It is a day to brave the temporary discomfort of clarity, all in the name of higher consciousness.

JUST FOR TODAY

TODAY'S MANTRA
Internal balance allows me to handle the weight of truth.

TODAY'S RITUAL
Get outside and sit under a tree or somewhere that feels sturdy to you. Drop into the weight of your body until you reach a place of unshakable centeredness.

TODAY'S JOURNAL PROMPT
What outside distractions or burdens keep me away from the truth?

BORN ON THIS DAY

EDGAR ALLAN POE, American writer, poet, and critic

PAUL CÉZANNE, French artist and Postimpressionist painter

"Don't compromise yourself, you're all you got."—JANIS JOPLIN, American rock and blues singer-songwriter

The Journey of Those Born on
JANUARY 19*

You were born of self-confidence and an enthusiasm that can make it hard to accept uncomfortable realities. You will have to learn how to slowly awaken to the truth, however, as your journey is one of sustainability, delegation, and radical awareness.

Early on in your journey, you will be called away from your fierce ambition so you can walk the path of *Balance* (The Number Two). *Balance* asks you what the hurry is all about and why you have to sacrifice your needs for your desires. You will meet *Balance* in moments of intentional slowness, when you choose to steady your heart and tend to your internal sense of harmony.

If you choose this patient path, you will come upon your sage friend, *Prioritization* (Two of Pentacles). *Prioritization* highlights your propensity to overwork, forever asking you to let go of some responsibility and share the burden with others. You will meet *Prioritization* in moments of choice, when you have to say "no" to one area of your life so that you can run wholeheartedly toward the things that really matter.

And what matters exactly? *Awakening* (Judgment) will inspire you to new heights of understanding through fearless self-inventory. By recognizing where and how you have lost your sense of clarity along the way, *Awakening* calls you to get honest about where you have faltered. If you can forgo the traps of shame and regret, *Awakening* shows you that it's never too late to wake up to the truth.

> ### YOUR GUIDES
>
> *Astrology: Your Energy*
> Capricorn (Saturn, Mercury)
>
> *Numerology: Your Path*
> Balance (The Number Two)
>
> *Minor Arcana: Your Lesson*
> Prioritization (The Two of Pentacles)
>
> *Major Arcana: Your Highest Calling*
> Awakening (Judgment)

CAPRICORN
RULERS: SATURN, MERCURY

PURPOSE
To slowly but surely awaken to the truth.

RELATIONSHIPS

You are bold and brave, but your relationships should be a place of peace and harmony. By seeking out partners who bring balance into your life rather than drama, you will discover that true love is the most easeful experience of all.

Are you an Aquarius born on this day? Head to page 761 to find your additional birthday guide!

WELCOME TO

The Journey of
JANUARY 20

Welcome to January 20, an inspired journey of emotional expansion.

Marking the first day of Aquarius season, *Flexibility* (The Number Three) invites you to expand your consciousness by engaging with the people around you. Seek out others' opinions and perspectives, and don't be afraid to dive into something new intellectually.

But try not to take everything too personally. *Trigger* (Three of Swords) may bring old resentments and fears to the surface today, making you extra sensitive to the words and actions of others. It can be easy to get lost in the stories we tell ourselves, but try to remain objective and give others the benefit of the doubt while tending to your wounds in private.

To help you keep the peace, find the grace within *Perspective* (The World). There is an emotional wholeness to this day, so take a step back and witness just how far you have come in life. If you have reached a personal or professional milestone, or if you simply can appreciate the progress you have made, take some time to sit in deep gratitude for the people and experiences that have impacted you for the better along the way.

JUST FOR TODAY

TODAY'S MANTRA
I will look for the spiritual perfection of the present moment.

TODAY'S RITUAL
End your day in silent gratitude. Set a timer for twenty-one minutes and close your eyes. Visualize where you were one year ago and bring forward images of the people and places that have helped you grow since then.

TODAY'S JOURNAL PROMPT
What old stories keep me stuck in a state of emotional victimhood?

BORN ON THIS DAY

JOY ADAMSON, Austrian naturalist and author

RAINN WILSON, American actor and comedian

"Remember, your mind is like a parachute: If it isn't open, it doesn't work. So keep an open mind!"—BUZZ ALDRIN, American astronaut and fighter pilot

The Journey of Those Born on
JANUARY 20

Y ou were born of deep loyalty and an existential dread that can make it all too easy to focus on negativity. You will have to learn to get out of your mind's way, however, as your journey is one of openness, emotional accountability, and spiritual wealth.

Early on in your journey, you will meet your sociable guide, *Flexibility* (The Number Three). *Flexibility* asks you to keep an open mind rather than getting stuck in the comfort of self-reliance. *Flexibility* introduces you to folks from many walks of life, allowing you to expand your understanding well beyond your lived experience.

If you choose this collaborative path, you will have to contend with your lower companion, *Trigger* (Three of Swords). *Trigger* holds up a mirror to your sensitivity, highlighting the unhealed wounds of the past that cause you to take well-meaning comments personally and offensively. You will meet *Trigger* when you want to react with anger, but instead you turn inward and address the true reason why that spot was so sore to begin with.

By answering these calls for self-awareness, you will learn to enjoy the view with *Perspective* (The World). *Perspective* invites you to take a step back when you reach huge milestones and witness the wholeness of your experience. You will meet *Perspective* when you can see how all the trials and tribulations you went through have made you the person you were meant to become. Through undeniable hard work, community-building, and a bit of gratitude, *Perspective* will teach you that emotional contentment is the greatest achievement of all.

YOUR GUIDES

Astrology: Your Energy
Aquarius (Uranus)

Numerology: Your Path
Flexibility (The Number Three)

Minor Arcana: Your Lesson
Trigger (The Three of Swords)

Major Arcana: Your Highest Calling
Perspective (The World)

AQUARIUS
RULER: URANUS

PURPOSE
To learn to appreciate the twists and turns on the journey of life.

RELATIONSHIPS

You are as solid and loyal as they come, and your relationships should be a place of social and mental expansion. By seeking out partners who help grow your level of understanding and nourish your sense of community, you will discover that true love is something to be eternally grateful for.

The Journey of
JANUARY 21

W elcome to January 21, a grounded journey of self-improvement.
At the height of the erratic Aquarius season, temper your rebellious spirit and follow the path of *Discipline* (The Number Four). It is a wonderful time to set a firm to-do list and slowly but surely work your way through it. Via consistent action and humble integrity, you can build a solid foundation of self-trust.

Be sure to leave time for *Restoration* (Four of Swords). Although you may have grand ambitions, make sure to pause and contemplate before taking on your next goal. Focus on seemingly mundane and achievable tasks, like washing the dishes or folding the laundry. This will leave you extra mental space to process the past as you make room for the vision of your future.

All this grounded progress will awaken you to the spiritual strength of *Self-mastery* (The Emperor). Despite the natural ebbs and flows of emotion, remember that there is one thing in life you always can control—your actions. If you can remain detached and objective as you go about your day, you can build a profound sense of self-respect.

JUST FOR TODAY

TODAY'S MANTRA
It is the daily, diligent work that will one day amount to the person I hope to become.

TODAY'S JOURNAL PROMPT
What small but important tasks can I manage to accomplish today?

TODAY'S RITUAL
Make a thorough to-do list and set an alarm for the top of every hour of the working day. When the alarm rings, turn your attention back to the list and see where you need to go next.

BORN ON THIS DAY

CHRISTIAN DIOR, French fashion designer

HELEN CHAVEZ, American labor activist

"You keep your eyes on the prize, you try to do what's right, and eventually, you'll reach your goal."—ERIC HOLDER JR., American lawyer, judge, and first Black US attorney general

The Journey of Those Born on
JANUARY 21

Y ou were born of progressive ideals and a genius that can leave you far from grounded. You will have to bring your powers back down to Earth, however, as your journey is one of hard work, patience, and integrity.

Early on in your journey, you will meet your demanding guide, *Discipline* (The Number Four). *Discipline* asks you to channel your fierce intellect into tangible productivity, pushing you toward a path of humble work. You will meet *Discipline* in moments of grit, when your hard efforts have yet to pay off, but you persevere anyhow. If you can walk the walk, *Discipline* ensures that your voice is heard.

If you choose this grounded path, you will have to pay respect to *Restoration* (Four of Swords). *Restoration* knows that there is a time to act and a time to regroup, inspiring you to take necessary breaks between each mountain you aim to climb. You will meet *Restoration* in moments of solitary contemplation, when you pause long enough to heal as you wait for the next intuitive voice of direction.

By answering these calls for personal integrity, you will discover the strength of *Self-mastery* (The Emperor). *Self-mastery* knows your potential for leadership, encouraging you to harness your passion, and temper, so that you can be a voice of reason. You will meet *Self-mastery* in moments of spiritual maturity, when your estimable actions speak even louder than your words. If you can worship humility rather than grandiosity, you will leave a lasting influence on the minds and hearts of others.

AQUARIUS
RULER: URANUS

PURPOSE
*To find your higher purpose within
each drop of humble sweat.*

RELATIONSHIPS

You are larger than life, with energy to spare, yet your relationships should be a place of emotional grounding. By seeking out partners who quite literally bring you down to earth, you will discover that true love is as real and reliable as it gets.

The Journey of
JANUARY 22

W elcome to January 22, a creative journey toward spiritual consciousness.

The beginning of Aquarius season often encourages behind-the-scenes work, but *Courage* (The Number Five) asks you to dance through your day with self-expression. Look for outlets to channel your creativity in any capacity. Instead of dimming your brilliance to make others comfortable, shine a light on the things that make you uniquely you.

But be careful of what you say and how you say it. *Maturity* (Five of Swords) encourages you to think before you speak, watching out for hotheadedness born from emotional defensiveness. If you receive any criticism or negative feedback today, let it roll off you. If you can't manage to let it go, call a trusted friend or scream into a pillow. The goal is simply to not harm anyone in the process.

If you can grow in these ways, you will find yourself in the divine consciousness of *Wisdom* (The Hierophant). It is a day to worship at the altar of truth rather than pride, neither acting as an all-knowing authority nor believing in the false prophets who claim to be. Practice humility as you question everything and discover the spiritual freedom that comes from knowing nothing.

JUST FOR TODAY

TODAY'S MANTRA
No one is perfect, so I will shine in all my brilliant imperfection.

TODAY'S JOURNAL PROMPT
What do I hope to self-express, and how can I practice humility in this self-expression?

TODAY'S RITUAL
Get out a piece of paper and draw or write without judgment or much thought. Simply put on the paper what is immediately coming to you, and don't question the process. Instead, discover the freedom that comes from not having to be perfect.

BORN ON THIS DAY

GEORGE BALANCHINE, Russian-born American ballet composer and choreographer who founded the New York City Ballet

LORD BYRON, English poet and politician

"Well that's very kind of you, but voices ought not be measured by how pretty they are. Instead they matter only if they convince you that they are telling the truth."—SAM COOKE, American singer-songwriter and entrepreneur

The Journey of Those Born on
JANUARY 22

Y ou were born of subtle genius and a reserved humility that can stop you from getting the recognition you deserve. You will have to learn to express yourself when needed, however, as your journey is one of self-expression, awareness, and spiritual trust.

Early on in your journey, you will run into your passionate guide, *Courage* (The Number Five). *Courage* asks you why you're holding back your true magic, inspiring you toward a path of total vulnerability. You will meet *Courage* in moments of creative rebirth, when you choose to unearth the gifts and truths that lie within and share them with the world around you.

If you choose this lively path, you will have to contend with your lower companion, *Maturity* (Five of Swords). You will meet *Maturity* in the ruthless critics who question your work, forcing you to use your words as weapons or as tools for understanding. If you can remember to always take the high road, *Maturity* makes you untouchable to the cowardly naysayers who simply envy your genius.

> ### YOUR GUIDES
>
> *Astrology: Your Energy*
> Aquarius (Uranus)
>
> *Numerology: Your Path*
> Courage (The Number Five)
>
> *Minor Arcana: Your Lesson*
> Maturity (The Five of Swords)
>
> *Major Arcana: Your Highest Calling*
> Wisdom (The Hierophant)

By answering these calls for personal growth, you will open the gates of *Wisdom* (The Hierophant). *Wisdom* knows that there is no such thing as an authority in the spiritual world, encouraging you to think for yourself and not get bogged down by those who aim to steal your power. If you can humbly listen to the deepest truths that live within, *Wisdom* teaches you the divine art of believing in yourself.

AQUARIUS
RULER: URANUS

PURPOSE
To vulnerably self-express through spiritual trust.

RELATIONSHIPS

You are steady, logical, and detached, but your relationships should be a place of total vulnerability and honesty. By seeking out partners who are courageously honest and true, you will discover that true love holds nothing back in the pursuit of connection.

The Journey of
JANUARY 23

W elcome to January 23, a heartfelt journey of emotional release and regrowth. Although Aquarius season can block vulnerability, *Devotion* (The Number Six) asks you to show where your heart lies through meaningful action. Look out for where, and to whom, your time is best put, and don't be afraid to abandon any superficial obligations in favor of purposeful work.

But don't get too attached to any outcome because *Transition* (Six of Swords) needs you to leave behind old ways of thinking in favor of greater mental clarity. For this reason, it is a good time to journal, talk to a close friend, or engage with a therapeutic practice to help you free yourself from old emotional blockages and embrace radical growth.

As today opens your mind and heart to healing, *Choice* (The Lovers) sweetly calls you home to yourself. This is a day of simple yet difficult decision-making, where each action moves you closer to either self-love or self-abandonment. Show your loyalty to yourself by actively choosing to spend your time with the work, people, and community that remind you how worthy you are of love.

JUST FOR TODAY

TODAY'S MANTRA
To love myself, in all my complexity, is an active choice I can make today.

TODAY'S JOURNAL PROMPT
What would I love about myself today if I weren't afraid of what other people think?

TODAY'S RITUAL
Because this season lacks the element of water, draw a bath, drink some tea, or swim in a nearby body of water. Being in touch with the vastness and fluidity of water will give your tense emotions room to flow with greater ease.

BORN ON THIS DAY

ÉDOUARD MANET, French Impressionist painter

GERTRUDE B. ELION, American biochemist and drug researcher who developed leukemia and herpes drug treatments

"Every day we wake up, we have an opportunity to do some good, but there's so much bad that you have to navigate to get to the good."—CHESLEY "SULLY" SULLENBERGER III, American pilot who successfully executed an emergency landing in the Hudson River

The Journey of Those Born on
JANUARY 23

You were born of thunderous ingenuity and a pridefulness that can make it difficult to surrender to your true emotional tenderness. You will have to learn to soften to the healing you need most, as your journey is one of humble service, personal transition, and emotional growth.

Early on in your journey, you will meet your gentle guide, *Devotion* (The Number Six). *Devotion* asks you to walk the path of spiritual humility, forever favoring small acts of integrity over grand gestures of showmanship. You will meet *Devotion* in moments of quiet resolve, when you know your good deeds may go unnoticed, but you do them for the greater good anyhow.

If you choose this path of service, you will meet your psychological mentor, *Transition* (Six of Swords). You will meet *Transition* in monumental rites of passage, when you are called to abandon old ways of thinking to embrace a newer and truer phase of growth. If you can embrace the grief of change and transition, *Transition* helps you make room for healing.

By answering these heartfelt calls, you will discover the importance of *Choice* (The Lovers). *Choice* holds up a mirror to your relationships with others, helping you see whether you are acting from a place of self-hatred or self-loyalty. You will meet *Choice* in moments of disillusionment, when you realize that a lover, an identity, or an opportunity will not fill the emotional hole that lies within. If you can seek to accept yourself entirely, *Choice* teaches you that love is an inside job.

YOUR GUIDES

Astrology: Your Energy
Aquarius (Uranus)

Numerology: Your Path
Devotion (The Number Six)

Minor Arcana: Your Lesson
Transition (The Six of Swords)

Major Arcana: Your Highest Calling
Choice (The Lovers)

AQUARIUS
RULER: URANUS

PURPOSE
To surrender to the fact that self-love is the way forward.

RELATIONSHIPS

You are forever inspired and at times dramatic, so your relationships should be a place of gentle compassion and healing. By seeking out partners who give you the support and understanding you need most, you will discover that true love is a mirror to the relationship you must build with yourself.

The Journey of
JANUARY 24

W elcome to January 24, an introspective journey that inspires personal progress.
As you navigate the erratic nature of Aquarius season, orient your plans around the ideals of *Commitment* (The Number Seven). Instead of taking on everything at once, devote your energy to the people and objectives that ring the truest to you. Even if you only get one thing done today, it is a success if you do it with your full attention.

But don't get lost in the anxieties of the mind. *Hypervigilance* (Seven of Swords) can create unease today, making you feel like you must look behind your back to ensure that no one and nothing is getting the best of you. Instead of giving in to this feeling, aim for spiritual trust rather than manipulative strategy, surrendering your fears to the universe itself.

Just keep your eyes on your personal *Evolution* (The Chariot). The small bits of work will one day amount to your irrefutable success, so pay respect to the tasks at hand throughout today. By staying earnest in your efforts and believing deeply that they are leading you to something greater, you can make great strides in your self-development.

JUST FOR TODAY

TODAY'S MANTRA
I will commit to my growth, rather than my success.

TODAY'S JOURNAL PROMPT
What am I afraid will happen if I surrender my goals and ambitions to a higher spiritual power?

TODAY'S RITUAL
Lie facedown in a comfortable and safe space. Spread your arms and legs into a starfish position, one of the most surrendered positions the body can take. Repeat the mantra, "The universe has my back," until it begins to feel true. If you happen to fall asleep, enjoy it, because you have truly surrendered to this exercise.

BORN ON THIS DAY

MARIA TALLCHIEF, Osage ballerina and first Native American prima ballerina

CATHERINE HAMLIN, Australian obstetrician and gynecologist

"I'm lucky. Hard work is the key but luck plays a part."—NEIL DIAMOND, American singer-songwriter

The Journey of Those Born on
JANUARY 24

Y ou were born of open-mindedness and a wealth of compassion that can make you more committed to the growth of others than to your own success. You will have to devote yourself to your deepest ambitions instead, as your journey is one of intentionality, trust, and personal development.

Early on in your journey, you will meet your serious guide, *Commitment* (The Number Seven). *Commitment* asks you to sharpen your soft focus, leading you through a path of meaning and responsibility. Rather than pleasing everyone, *Commitment* encourages you to get serious about what you care about most and to do away with the rest.

If you choose this formidable path, you will have to contend with your lower companion, *Hypervigilance* (Seven of Swords). *Hypervigilance* highlights your distrust of others, forcing you to surrender your strategies of self-protection, such as manipulation or deception. By recognizing that no one can hurt you as long as you are aligned with your sense of personal integrity, *Hypervigilance* teaches you to trust by becoming trustworthy.

YOUR GUIDES

Astrology: Your Energy
Aquarius (Uranus)

Numerology: Your Path
Commitment (The Number Seven)

Minor Arcana: Your Lesson
Hypervigilance (The Seven of Swords)

Major Arcana: Your Highest Calling
Evolution (The Chariot)

By answering these calls for discernment, you will find yourself being carried by the divine winds of *Evolution* (The Chariot). *Evolution* knows where you must grow, directing you toward a higher purpose and asking nothing of you but total perseverance. You will meet *Evolution* in moments of radical progress, when you must pinch yourself for how far you've come. If you can commit to the work you are doing without focusing on results, *Evolution* offers you the rewards of sincerity.

AQUARIUS
RULER: URANUS

PURPOSE
To carry out your purpose with complete integrity and focus.

RELATIONSHIPS

You are gentle yet hard to pin down, but your relationships should be a place of total commitment. By seeking out partners who are as serious about you as they are about the rest of their responsibilities, you will discover that true love is a gratifying act of interpersonal responsibility.

The Journey of
JANUARY 25

W elcome to January 25, a mystical journey of personal strength.

Despite the highly logical nature of Aquarius season, *Power* (The Number Eight) invites you to go on an emotional deep dive today. Peel back any protective layers of superficiality and share your true nature with everyone and everything you encounter today, including yourself. Make sure to be caring when others show vulnerability as well because this will be repaid to you tenfold.

This empathy must be turned inward, as *Negativity* (Eight of Swords) asks you to take note of the mean and limiting voices in your head that come up today, neither ignoring them nor believing them to be true. Simply bring awareness to the self-restricting cages of your mind and speak to yourself in the kind voice that you would use with a friend.

And if you can show up for this emotional growth, you will uncover your capacity for *Resilience* (Strength). Rely on your inner resources throughout today, drawing on the unshakable spiritual muscles that exist within. By maintaining your composure and sense of integrity amidst the ebbs and flows of emotion, you can discover your impenetrable emotional strength.

———————————————○———————————————

JUST FOR TODAY

TODAY'S MANTRA
If life were always easy, I wouldn't discover how strong I truly am.

TODAY'S RITUAL
Acknowledge the infinite sky above you so you can gain perspective. Go out tonight, with a blanket and a friend if needed, and sit underneath the night sky, witnessing your connection to the larger forces at play.

TODAY'S JOURNAL PROMPT
What are the persistent mean thoughts that enter my mind about myself, and where did they come from?

———————————————○———————————————

BORN ON THIS DAY

CORAZON AQUINO, Filipina politician and eleventh president and first female president of the Philippines

ALICIA KEYS, American singer-songwriter

"Lock up your libraries if you like; but there is no gate, no lock, no bolt that you can set upon the freedom of my mind."—VIRGINIA WOOLF, English author

The Journey of Those Born on
JANUARY 25

Y ou were born of high ideals and a fierce ambition that can distract you from looking inward. You will have to uncover your true personal depth, as your journey is one of emotional honesty, clearing, and internal strength.

Early on in your journey, you will meet your probing guide, *Power* (The Number Eight). Power asks you to part ways with any superficial identities and directs you toward a path of radical self-honesty. You will meet *Power* in moments of emotional visibility, when you begin to understand yourself on a deeper level and find the willingness to be honest with those you trust. If you can value sincerity over perfection, *Power* shows you the abundance that comes from self-acceptance.

If you choose this deeper path, you will have to cross swords with *Negativity* (Eight of Swords). *Negativity* highlights your cruel self-talk, revealing the voices in your head that keep you from enjoying the full breadth of your power. If you can witness these seemingly destructive parts of yourself, and aim to understand where they are coming from, *Negativity* releases you from these mental cages through total empathy.

YOUR GUIDES

Astrology: Your Energy
Aquarius (Uranus)

Numerology: Your Path
Power (The Number Eight)

Minor Arcana: Your Lesson
Negativity (The Eight of Swords)

Major Arcana: Your Highest Calling
Resilience (Strength)

By answering these calls for self-reflection, you will tap into *Resilience* (Strength). *Resilience* shows you just how sturdy your emotional foundation is, empowering you to harness this intrinsic strength in times of personal turmoil. By believing deeply in your capacity to handle even the toughest of emotional hurdles, *Resilience* teaches you that the hardest truths only make you stronger.

―――――――――――○―――――――――――

AQUARIUS
RULER: URANUS

PURPOSE
To rely on your inner strength as you grow toward radical self-honesty.

RELATIONSHIPS

You are fierce and authoritative, but your relationships should be a place of emotional unveiling. By seeking out partners who want to peel back the layers of your emotional complexity, you will discover that true love is born from excruciating vulnerability.

The Journey of
JANUARY 26

Welcome to January 26, a solitary journey of higher consciousness.

To coincide with the intellectual side of Aquarius season, *Experience* (The Number Nine) asks you to grow in your understanding and effectiveness today. Don't be afraid to ask questions and seek out new perspectives that speak to your curious nature. By humbling yourself at the feet of the unknown, you can explore new realms of possibility.

But watch out for those mental fears that block you today. *Anxiety* (Nine of Swords) warns against future-tripping and overanalyzing, forcing you to unearth the historical wounds that cause you to consider the worst-case scenario. If you can witness yet detach from these hypervigilant thoughts, today brings you an opportunity to clear out some heavy mental baggage.

And if you walk through these spiritual doors, you will gain access to the power of *Instinct* (The Hermit). It is time to build internal trust, so make decisions from a place of divine intuition rather than scarcity. If your gut, not your fear, is pulling you in any one direction today, follow it with complete cooperation. If you can believe in your powers of perception, your genius will light the way forward.

JUST FOR TODAY

TODAY'S MANTRA
My intuition is the higher knowledge of which I seek.

TODAY'S RITUAL
Close your eyes and visualize your mind with a cage surrounding it, knowing that the cage is a visual representation of your fears. Now, visualize a key that was in your hand all along, and feel the power and release that comes from unlocking this cage and freeing your mind.

TODAY'S JOURNAL PROMPT
What fears or traumas block me from listening to my gut?

BORN ON THIS DAY

SEÁN MACBRIDE, Irish politician and Nobel Peace Prize recipient

ELLEN DEGENERES, American comedian and television personality

"Radical simply means 'grasping things at the root.'"—ANGELA DAVIS, American political activist, philosopher, academic, and author

The Journey of Those Born on
JANUARY 26

Y ou were born of wild passion and a hunger for more that can make it difficult to appreciate what you have in the present moment. You will have to learn that less is more, as your journey is one of spiritual seeking, perspective-shifting, and necessary isolation.

Early on in your journey, you will meet your sage guide, *Experience* (The Number Nine). *Experience* calls you away from your worldly desires and toward a path of deep spiritual understanding. You will meet *Experience* in moments of fearless reevaluation, when you burn the script that was given to you at birth in favor of a map of the abundant unknown.

If you choose this path of enlightenment, you will have to reckon with your lower companion, *Anxiety* (Nine of Swords). You will meet *Anxiety* in your obsessive fear-based thinking, the part of you that tries to wrap its head around worst-case scenarios that may never happen. *Anxiety* wants you to know that intellectualizing your emotions is not the same as feeling your

feelings, inviting you to acknowledge your fears rather than letting them get the best of you.

By answering these calls for personal growth, you will come upon your highest teacher, *Instinct* (The Hermit). *Instinct* believes deeply in the power of your intuition and at times invites you to pause from your earthly obligations in favor of the unseen work that can only be done when alone. If you can trust that in the process of withdrawal comes renewed understanding, *Instinct* shows you the spiritual productivity of isolation.

─────────────────○─────────────────

AQUARIUS
RULER: URANUS

PURPOSE
*To turn inward
before you grow outward.*

RELATIONSHIPS

You are the life of the party, and your relationships should be a place of free spaciousness and understanding. By seeking out partners who offer you generous freedom and unconditional compassion, you will discover that true love will never hold you back.

The Journey of
JANUARY 27

W elcome to January 27, a fearless journey of spiritual surrender.
As you engage with the progressive energy of Aquarius season, lean in to the power of *Autonomy* (The Number One). Walk a path of self-reliance, trusting deeply in your intuitive powers and never minding the people who try to get in your way. Seize this opportunity to realize your strength by tackling the projects and objectives you usually would pass on out of fear.

You will need this personal optimism because *Clarity* (Ace of Swords) asks you to pursue your next best idea with complete personal faith. You have the gift of a beginner's mind today, so don't fret about not being an expert. Instead, throw yourself headfirst into a new project or subject.

Within these leaps of faith, *Impermanence* (Wheel of Fortune) invites you to accept the cyclical nature of life so that you can enjoy the ride. Life is ever-changing, with luck being as fleeting as a butterfly in the wind. So enjoy each high and low that comes up, believing in the inevitable upswing that will soon grace your presence.

JUST FOR TODAY

TODAY'S MANTRA
I will thank the universe for everything it's given me, and everything it's taken away.

TODAY'S RITUAL
Go to a nearby body of water, whether it be a pool or the ocean, and completely fall backward into it, letting the water catch you on your way down. Float on your back and stare up at the sky, practicing gratitude for the things in your life that hold you through even the toughest of times.

TODAY'S JOURNAL PROMPT
What in my life do I need to let go of so I can make room for something new?

BORN ON THIS DAY

ASMA JAHANGIR, Pakistani human rights lawyer and social activist

LEWIS CARROLL, English author

"I pay no attention whatever to anybody's praise or blame. I simply follow my own feelings."
—WOLFGANG AMADEUS MOZART, Austrian musical prodigy and composer

The Journey of Those Born on
JANUARY 27

You were born of radical wisdom and a desire for solitude that can keep you from actualizing your true potential. You will have to learn to take a leap of faith in yourself, as your journey is one of innovation, enthusiasm, and letting go.

Early on in your journey, you will meet your fearless guide, *Autonomy* (The Number One). *Autonomy* asks you to do what has not been done before, beckoning you toward the road never traveled. You will meet *Autonomy* in moments of intuitive movement, when you realize that you are building the blueprint of a life beyond your wildest dreams. If you can accept that others may not understand your actions, *Autonomy* teaches you the art of self-reliance.

If you choose this courageous path, you will have to make friends with *Clarity* (Ace of Swords). *Clarity* asks you time and again to believe in the potential of an idea, rather than losing sleep over what could go wrong or caving to your internal imposter syndrome. If you can move toward the projects and concepts that light your brain with pure enthusiasm, *Clarity* will offer you the gift of self-belief.

> ### YOUR GUIDES
>
> *Astrology: Your Energy*
> Aquarius (Uranus)
>
> *Numerology: Your Path*
> Autonomy (The Number One)
>
> *Minor Arcana: Your Lesson*
> Clarity (The Ace of Swords)
>
> *Major Arcana: Your Highest Calling*
> Impermanence (The Wheel of Fortune)

By internalizing these empowering lessons, you will come to understand and accept the rhythm of *Impermanence* (Wheel of Fortune). *Impermanence* knows that nothing was made to stay the same, inviting you to surrender to the idea that the only constant in life is change. If you can acknowledge that your circumstances are neither bad nor good, but perfectly fated, *Impermanence* teaches you that everything happens for a reason.

AQUARIUS
RULER: URANUS

PURPOSE
To trust that fate is unfolding as it should.

RELATIONSHIPS

You are high-minded and quirky, and your relationships should be a place of complete freedom to be exactly who you are. By seeking out partners who don't just tolerate but embrace your uniqueness, you will discover that true love comes from radical acceptance.

The Journey of
JANUARY 28

W elcome to January 28, a balanced journey toward justice.

Although Aquarius season can feel a bit extreme, try to aim for *Balance* (The Number Two). Whether it be sharing a friendly ride to work with a colleague or taking a much-needed break in the middle of your workday, find ways to manage your stress and make life easier. There's no need to tackle a million projects at once; instead, seek to create harmony with the world around you.

But don't expect decisions to come easily. *Doubt* (Two of Swords) enhances feelings of uncertainty, forcing you to question each action you take today. It is okay not to have all the answers, so where possible, don't make any concrete or finite changes to your life on this day. Instead, gather the information you can and let yourself off the hook.

Besides, *Truth* (Justice) encourages you to focus your attention on the issues that really matter. Whether it be social, political, or interpersonal, stand up for what you believe in, and live in deep integrity. If you can get clear on what your heart cares to devote itself to today, you will be the change you wish to see.

JUST FOR TODAY

TODAY'S MANTRA
Balance comes from only spending time on the things that matter.

TODAY'S RITUAL
Whenever you get aggravated or stuck today, take a restful moment to meditate. Shut off from the outside world so you can quiet the thoughts and drama of the day and drop into the innate truth that lives within you.

TODAY'S JOURNAL PROMPT
What change would I like to see in the world, and what is a sustainable way I can devote myself to this cause?

BORN ON THIS DAY

JACKSON POLLOCK, American Expressionist painter

SARAH MCLACHLAN, Canadian singer-songwriter and philanthropist

"Hope costs nothing."—COLETTE, French novelist and performer

The Journey of Those Born on
JANUARY 28

You were born of rebellious ingenuity and an impulsiveness that can lead you to both good and bad extremes. You will have to learn how to take the middle road, as your journey is one of harmony, uncertainty, and justice.

Early on in your journey, you will meet your graceful guide, *Balance* (The Number Two). *Balance* wants to know what you're chasing and why you're moving so fast, calling you toward a path of less resistance. If you can calm your restless spirit enough to get in touch with your needs, *Balance* helps you build a life of sustainable tranquility.

If you choose this path of reason, you will have to reckon with your lower companion, *Doubt* (Two of Swords). *Doubt* stirs up your feelings of uncertainty, forcing you to confront your fears around decision-making. You will meet *Doubt* in moments of overwhelm, when you know that you must act but you are terrified of making a wrong move. It is wise to consider all your options, but *Doubt* asks you to learn the difference between patience and avoidance.

By answering these calls for self-awareness, you will open yourself to the power of *Truth* (Justice). *Truth* knows how to sit on the fine line between right and wrong, good and evil, and encourages you to tap into your own moral compass and decipher your unique code of ethics. By doing your research and sifting through all the different perspectives at play, *Truth* teaches you how to find personal clarity amidst the gray areas in life.

―――――――――――――――○―――――――――――――――

AQUARIUS
RULER: URANUS

PURPOSE
To find the truth that hangs in the balance.

RELATIONSHIPS

You are brave, detached, and innovative, yet your relationships should be a place of restful ease. By seeking out partners who harmonize with your personality and make your heart beat peacefully, you will discover that true love can sustain a lifetime.

The Journey of
JANUARY 29

Welcome to January 29, a curious adventure that aims to shift your perspective.
As you traverse the social air of Aquarius season, stay receptive to all perspectives as you walk the path of *Flexibility* (The Number Three). Reach for open-mindedness and curiosity, making a special effort to embrace whatever life throws at you, whether it be an unexpected invitation from a friend or a new opportunity for learning.

But watch out for *Trigger* (Three of Swords). You may feel extra sensitive today, but dig deep to understand your reactions rather than blaming your feelings on others. If you can take inventory of your past and discover why you are so sore about certain subjects, you'll encounter a new sense of emotional progress.

And as you aim to keep the peace, look for the grace of *Abundance* (The Empress). There is a fruitfulness to this day, so take extra time to savor the sweetest encounters and experiences that come your way. Whether it be taking in a warm compliment from a friend or enjoying a gorgeous sunset, embrace the divine generosity that exists within each moment.

JUST FOR TODAY

TODAY'S MANTRA
Perhaps everything I need is in the present moment.

TODAY'S RITUAL
Release tension in your body. Lie down on your back and close your eyes. Scan your body from head to toe, releasing the muscles that are tense and holding on to your deeper sense of stress.

TODAY'S JOURNAL PROMPT
What am I grateful for today?

BORN ON THIS DAY

GREG LOUGANIS, American Olympic diver, LGBTQ+ activist, and author

GERMAINE GREER, Australian writer and public intellectual

"I trust that everything happens for a reason, even if we are not wise enough to see it."—OPRAH WINFREY, American television talk show host, actor, and philanthropist

The Journey of Those Born on
JANUARY 29

You were born of radical justice and a sense of right and wrong that can make it difficult for you to accept the differing opinions of others. You will have to stay open to grow, as your journey is one of curiosity, inner healing, and spiritual sacrifice.

Early on in your journey, you will stumble upon your social guide, *Flexibility* (The Number Three). *Flexibility* calls you toward a path of understanding, encouraging you to ask questions rather than demanding to have your singular voice heard. If you can harness the interpersonal power of genuine curiosity, *Flexibility* introduces you to colleagues, friends, and mentors who serve to expand your consciousness.

If you choose to walk this ever-changing path, you will cross swords with your toughest teacher, *Trigger* (Three of Swords). *Trigger* asks you why you're taking things so personally and if there may be a deeper story underneath the hurt you are feeling toward others. If you can tend to these unhealed wounds, *Trigger* teaches you how to take emotional responsibility for yourself.

By answering these calls for self-awareness, you will discover the healing power of *Abundance* (The Empress). *Abundance* shows you how important it is to fill your emotional cup, inspiring you to receive the goodness that life has to offer without guilt or shame. If you can make a consistent effort to savor the sweetness of each day, and practice gratitude for these gifts, *Abundance* teaches you the art of personal contentment.

YOUR GUIDES

Astrology: Your Energy
Aquarius (Uranus)

Numerology: Your Path
Flexibility (The Number Three)

Minor Arcana: Your Lesson
Trigger (The Three of Swords)

Major Arcana: Your Highest Calling
Abundance (The Empress)

AQUARIUS
RULER: URANUS

PURPOSE
To learn to receive the goodness that comes from staying open-minded.

RELATIONSHIPS

You are relationship-driven and emotionally loyal, so your relationships should be a place of personal growth and radical freedom. By seeking out partners who make your life and perspective larger rather than smaller, you will discover that true love is eternally expansive.

The Journey of
JANUARY 30

W elcome to January 30, a pragmatic day of self-leadership.

As you navigate the chaotic winds of Aquarius season, ground yourself in the path of *Discipline* (The Number Four). Channel your mental inspiration into tangible results, rather than getting lost in philosophical thought. Make a thorough and realistic to-do list inspired by the people you can help today, putting service and honor at the forefront of your mind.

As you walk this arduous path, leave room to pause. *Restoration* (Four of Swords) asks you to rest before you act and carve out intentional time to regroup as you go about today's list of responsibilities. There is no point in tackling this on an empty battery, so when necessary, take a break until you get your next intuitive direction.

If you can embrace these lessons, you will understand the power of *Self-mastery* (The Emperor). Work to harness the power of emotional regulation rather than getting swept away in the impermanence of feeling. If you can step into a role of authority in your own life as well as with others today, *Self-mastery* introduces you to the humble leader who exists within.

—○—

JUST FOR TODAY

TODAY'S MANTRA

I will act as my own objective leader so that I can empower others to do the same.

TODAY'S JOURNAL PROMPT

How can I be of service to the world around me today?

TODAY'S RITUAL

Make a two-column list, the left column being today's goals and the right column being the steps required to achieve them. Carry this with you throughout the day and refer to it when you are feeling overwhelmed.

—○—

BORN ON THIS DAY

FRANKLIN ROOSEVELT, thirty-second president of the United States

MARÍA JULIA HERNÁNDEZ, Salvadoran human rights advocate

"The people I admire most are those who struggle for everyone."—VANESSA REDGRAVE, English actor and activist

The Journey of Those Born on
JANUARY 30

Y ou were born of progressive ideals and insatiable curiosity that can make it difficult for you to remain loyal to just one thing. You will have to find great meaning in reliability, as your journey is one of integrity, patience, and spiritual maturity.

Early on in your journey, you will meet your no-nonsense guide, *Discipline* (The Number Four). *Discipline* reminds you that your unique skills are meant for something greater, inspiring you toward a path of grounded hard work. You will meet *Discipline* in moments of seemingly thankless labor, when you persevere through the toughest hurdles in search of deeper purpose. If you can put one foot in front of the other, *Discipline* introduces you to your integrity.

If you choose this meaningful path, you will have to contend with your wise teacher, *Restoration* (Four of Swords). *Restoration* asks you time and again to pause between battles, making sure that your intentions are clear as you set about your next goal. You will meet *Restoration* in moments of patience, when you choose to wait to act until your mind is aligned with your intuition.

By answering these calls for responsibility, you will tap into the resource of *Self-mastery* (The Emperor). *Self-mastery* knows what you are capable of, inspiring you to harness your powers of objectivity and leadership amidst the ever-changing tides of human emotion. If you can remain humble in your well-earned power, *Self-mastery* helps you build a profound legacy of respect.

───────────────○───────────────

AQUARIUS
RULERS: URANUS, MERCURY

PURPOSE
To work steadily and patiently toward self-leadership.

RELATIONSHIPS

You are sociable and adventurous, yet your relationships should be a place of emotional grounding. By seeking out partners who make you feel safe and secure in your loyalty to one another, you will discover that true love anchors you in the toughest of times.

The Journey of
JANUARY 31

W elcome to January 31, a humble journey of radical self-expression.
　　　To make the most of the authenticity that Aquarius season inspires, *Courage* (The Number Five) invites you to come out of your comfort zone and shine brightly in your truest colors. Look for opportunities to express yourself, whether it be in your intimate relationships, in your work, or on social media. If there is a piece of truth you're ready to share, now would be the time.

There's no such thing as oversharing today, as long as you don't aim your words at the expense of others. *Maturity* (Five of Swords) requires you to harness the power of choice in your communication, favoring the restraint of pen and tongue. Watch out for buried resentments and do the necessary processing it takes to heal these ill feelings toward others.

The root of today calls for *Wisdom* (The Hierophant), asking you to remain right-sized in your relationship with the world around you. By recognizing the essential truth that you are neither superior nor inferior to others, you can find the balance between expertise and teachability. Share your knowledge and embrace your power while remaining receptive to the knowledge that surrounds you.

JUST FOR TODAY

TODAY'S MANTRA
I can learn the humble balance between sharing and listening.

TODAY'S RITUAL
Channel the magic of the owl, with its ever-searching eyes and internal strength. While visualizing an owl of your choosing, repeat this chant, "Owl wisdom, show me my knowledge and let me hear others'."

TODAY'S JOURNAL PROMPT
Where do I question my own authority and give away my power to others?

BORN ON THIS DAY

HENRI DESGRANGE, French cyclist, journalist, and founder of the Tour de France

CONCEPCIÓN ARENAL, Spanish author, journalist, poet, law school graduate, the first woman to attend university in Spain, and a pioneer in Spanish feminism

"The most luxurious possession, the richest treasure anybody has, is his personal dignity."—JACKIE ROBINSON, American baseball player and the first Black major league player

The Journey of Those Born on
JANUARY 31

Y ou were born of humble genius and an emotional control that can block you from expressing your true creative brilliance. You will have to take a leap of faith eventually, as your journey is one of vulnerability, unbridled passion, and self-empowerment.

Early on in your journey, you will meet your bold
guide, *Courage* (The Number Five). No matter how
much you drag your feet, *Courage* jumps at any opportunity to thrust you into moments of unexpected visibility
and vulnerability. You will meet *Courage* when you drop
your defenses and show the world your true colors, revealing the many layers that lie beneath the surface.

If you choose this brave path, you will inevitably
cross swords with your sage teacher, *Maturity* (Five of
Swords). *Maturity* asks you to speak up and speak out,
not to hurt others, not to win, not to be proven right,
but for the sake of profound understanding. You will
meet *Maturity* in moments of self-expression, when
you use words for connection rather than self-
protection, allowing you to hear and be heard.

By answering these calls for vulnerability, *Wisdom*
(The Hierophant) reminds you that humility is the birthplace of understanding. You will meet
Wisdom in moments of emotional and mental openness, when you are willing to do away with
preconceived notions in favor of greater consciousness. If you can surrender to the fact that there
are no black-and-white answers to life's biggest questions, you will show the rest of us how to ask
the right questions.

———————————————————○———————————————————

AQUARIUS
RULERS: URANUS, MERCURY

PURPOSE
*To be brave enough not to
have all the answers.*

RELATIONSHIPS

You are quite serious and emotionally withholding, yet your relationships should be a place of
openheartedness and childlike joy. By seeking out partners who help you drop your defenses and
stay in the present moment, you will discover that true love is the birthplace of emotional
freedom.

The Journey of
FEBRUARY 1

Welcome to February 1, a communicative journey of personal abundance.
During the mercurial part of Aquarius season, make sure to channel *Flexibility* (The Number Three). Work on your communication from all angles, remembering to be an equally good listener as you are a talker. It is a crucial time to consider different perspectives and not get too bogged down in stubbornness, so stay open to changing your mind.

But as you open yourself to the thoughts of others, be wary of *Trigger* (Three of Swords). *Trigger* shows itself in your social sensitivity, when the words of another person can strike at the center of an unhealed wound. If someone or something offends you to the core, take inventory of the history behind why this pain still exists, rather than blaming your feelings on another.

The interpersonal legwork of today offers the promise of *Abundance* (The Empress). Pay attention to the sweetness of your social interactions and find gratitude for the interpersonal miracles that fill your emotional cup. Whether it be exchanging smiles with a stranger or accepting a sincere compliment from a dear friend, remember that you are worthy of joyous connection.

JUST FOR TODAY

TODAY'S MANTRA
I can soak in the miracles of others today.

TODAY'S RITUAL
Express gratitude for the ones you love. Think of three people in your intimate life you would like to acknowledge and send them a heartfelt and nuanced thank you for the unique role that they play in your life.

TODAY'S JOURNAL PROMPT
What old wounds around friendship and communication block me from trusting others?

BORN ON THIS DAY

LEYMAH ROBERTA GBOWEE, Liberian peace activist and winner of the Nobel Peace Prize

HARRY STYLES, English singer-songwriter and actor

"Perhaps the mission of an artist is to interpret beauty to people—the beauty within themselves."—LANGSTON HUGHES, American poet and playwright

The Journey of Those Born on
FEBRUARY 1

Y ou were born of personal freedom and a deep self-reliance that make it hard to lean on others. You will have to open yourself to the power of authentic connection, as your journey is one of curiosity, interpersonal healing, and spiritual harvest.

Early on in your journey, you will meet your mentally engaging guide, *Flexibility* (The Number Three). *Flexibility* asks you to walk a path of community-building, leaving your penchant for self-reliance behind as you embrace the power of shared understanding. You will meet *Flexibility* in moments of compromise, when you choose to accommodate the needs of the group rather than demanding your singular point of view.

If you choose this open-minded path, you will have to contend with your toughest teacher, *Trigger* (Three of Swords). You will meet *Trigger* in moments of interpersonal conflict that feel like emotional betrayal, when someone close to you pokes at an ancient wound that needs to be healed. If you can look beyond the superficial circumstances of these conflicts, *Trigger* brings endless opportunities to address the hidden fears that lie deep within.

> ## YOUR GUIDES
>
> *Astrology: Your Energy*
> Aquarius (Uranus, Mercury)
>
> *Numerology: Your Path*
> Flexibility (The Number Three)
>
> *Minor Arcana: Your Lesson*
> Trigger (The Three of Swords)
>
> *Major Arcana: Your Highest Calling*
> Abundance (The Empress)

By answering these calls for interpersonal growth, you will find yourself in the endless grace of *Abundance* (The Empress). *Abundance* knows the value of happiness in a world that is so distracted by the pursuit of power, inspiring you to cultivate an internal sense of beauty, creativity, and joy. By planting many diverse seeds of personal satisfaction, rather than placing your dependence on outside forces, *Abundance* shows you how to harvest the life of your dreams.

AQUARIUS
RULERS: URANUS, MERCURY

PURPOSE
To invest in the connections that will one day grow into personal fulfillment.

RELATIONSHIPS

You are autonomous and rebellious, so your relationships should be a place of social growth and understanding. By seeking out partners who have an expansive network of friends from diverse walks of life, you will discover that true love makes the world grow in front of your eyes.

The Journey of
FEBRUARY 2

Welcome to February 2, an earthly journey of self-leadership.

The untethered quality of Aquarius season will make your impulses hard to contain, but do your best to channel *Discipline* (The Number Four). Rather than dreaming up a million improbable ideas, keep your feet firmly planted on the ground as you aim for tangible results. If you can balance innovation with humility, you'll get things done.

But as you do, make sure to incorporate *Restoration* (Four of Swords). Feverish work can yield less-than-ideal results, so pause between projects and tap into your intuition. Some of your best plans simply can't come to fruition yet, but by pouring your attention into the undeniable callings of the day, you can leave the rest on tomorrow's doorstep.

If you answer these humble calls, you will become the CEO of your day. *Self-mastery* (The Emperor) invites you to embrace this position of leadership, encouraging you to trust your gut while maintaining an objective eye on the tasks at hand. If you can follow through on your promises to yourself and others, you can discover the power of personal authority.

―――――――――――――○―――――――――――――

JUST FOR TODAY

TODAY'S MANTRA

I will harness my innovative ideas through hard work and discipline, yielding radical results.

TODAY'S JOURNAL PROMPT

What structure and boundaries do I need to make the most out of today?

TODAY'S RITUAL

Make a thorough action plan from the vantage point of a loving leader, giving yourself tasks that both nurture your needs and contribute to the world around you.

―――――――――――――○―――――――――――――

BORN ON THIS DAY

INA GARTEN, American author and television cooking show host

JAMES JOYCE, Irish novelist and poet

"You can't achieve anything in life without a small amount of sacrifice."—**SHAKIRA**, Colombian singer-songwriter

The Journey of Those Born on
FEBRUARY 2

Y ou were born of balanced genius and a desire for external acceptance that can lead you away from your true purpose. You will have to find unshakable confidence through estimable action, as your journey is one of hard work, quiet patience, and personal authority.

Early on in your journey, you will meet your unrelenting guide, *Discipline* (The Number Four). *Discipline* calls you away from the traps of flightiness and unreliability and asks you to walk a path of sincere meaning. By putting one foot in front of the other as you aim for each tangible goal, *Discipline* grounds you in the truth that anything is possible as long as you work at it.

If you choose this honorable path, you will be asked to slow down by your wise teacher, *Restoration* (Four of Swords). *Restoration* knows that nothing can be accomplished on an empty battery, encouraging you to pause between efforts and to find clarity in these moments of rest. You will meet *Restoration* in moments of reevaluation, when you have completed one huge milestone and are waiting on spiritual direction for where to go next.

> ### YOUR GUIDES
>
> *Astrology: Your Energy*
> Aquarius (Uranus, Mercury)
>
> *Numerology: Your Path*
> Discipline (The Number Four)
>
> *Minor Arcana: Your Lesson*
> Restoration (The Four of Swords)
>
> *Major Arcana: Your Highest Calling*
> Self-mastery (The Emperor)

By answering these calls for personal evaluation, you will step into the power of *Self-mastery* (The Emperor). *Self-mastery* shows you how to bridge humility and authority, throwing you into positions of leadership through divine intervention. You will meet *Self-mastery* in moments of emotional and intellectual discernment, when you are able to make an executive decision for the good of many. If you are willing to trust that you are worthy and capable of great responsibility, *Self-mastery* introduces you to the leader who lives within.

AQUARIUS
RULERS: URANUS, MERCURY

PURPOSE
To let your hard work and integrity speak for themselves.

RELATIONSHIPS

You are effortlessly social and a great communicator, yet your relationships should be a place of unspoken trust. By seeking out partners who reveal their loyalty through action rather than words, you will discover that true love is built upon the foundation of interpersonal integrity.

The Journey of
FEBRUARY 3

W elcome to February 3, a courageous adventure of intellectual self-trust.

As you navigate the progressive air of Aquarius season, reach for *Courage* (The Number Five). Pursue a high level of vulnerability, looking for every opportunity to share your perspective with the world around you. Get on social media, speak up in a meeting, or tell that friend what you've really been thinking.

But make sure not to cram your opinions down anyone's throat. *Maturity* (Five of Swords) asks you to use your words not as weapons but rather as a birthing place for understanding. Listen as well as you speak today, encouraging those around you to express themselves as honestly as you are. There's no need to fight for your voice to be heard, so simply speak your piece and surrender to the outcome.

Besides, *Wisdom* (The Hierophant) encourages different points of view. Be willing to be wrong as well as to question the authority figures who try to tell you what is right. The truth hangs in the balance, so stay humble and open to receiving new information. If you can be both the student and the teacher, you will reach new levels of consciousness.

JUST FOR TODAY

TODAY'S MANTRA
I will share and listen, teach and learn.

TODAY'S RITUAL
Send loving-kindness to your perceived enemies, as difficult as this may sound. You don't have to change how you feel about them, but simply taking the action will make all the difference. Close your eyes, visualize a ray of love, and send it their way.

TODAY'S JOURNAL PROMPT
Am I willing to be wrong about the subjects I think I know best?

BORN ON THIS DAY

ELIZABETH BLACKWELL, English American physician and the first woman to receive a medical degree in the United States

NORMAN ROCKWELL, American painter and illustrator

"We are always the same age inside."—GERTRUDE STEIN, American novelist, poet, playwright, and art collector

The Journey of Those Born on
FEBRUARY 3

You were born of expansive intellect and a mental flexibility that makes it difficult to know where you stand on any given issue. You will have to run directly toward the truth, as your journey is one of honesty, perspective-shifting, and humility.

Early on in your journey, you will meet your magnificent guide, *Courage* (The Number Five). *Courage* asks you to surrender your flighty nature and get serious about a path of vulnerability. You will meet *Courage* in moments of daring greatly, when you tell the world what you stand for as you shout it from the spiritual rooftops.

If you choose this path of visibility, you will have to contend with your toughest teacher, *Maturity* (Five of Swords). *Maturity* tests your sensitivity, asking you to grow a thick skin of self-confidence no matter what criticism is thrown your way. You will meet *Maturity* in moments of perceived threat, when the words of another aim to provoke but you choose to surrender your pride in favor of being the bigger person.

By answering these calls for humility, you will step into the divine realm of *Wisdom* (The Hierophant). *Wisdom* reminds you that everyone has a right to their own opinion, as long as they share their perspective rather than claim it as fact. You will meet *Wisdom* in moments of humble exchange when you are able to hold peaceful space for the truth of another. If you can find the personal growth within open-mindedness, *Wisdom* hands you the keys of spiritual knowledge.

> ## YOUR GUIDES
>
> *Astrology: Your Energy*
> Aquarius (Uranus, Mercury)
>
> *Numerology: Your Path*
> Courage (The Number Five)
>
> *Minor Arcana: Your Lesson*
> Maturity (The Five of Swords)
>
> *Major Arcana: Your Highest Calling*
> Wisdom (The Hierophant)

AQUARIUS
RULERS: URANUS, MERCURY

PURPOSE
To courageously share and listen for the sake of understanding.

RELATIONSHIPS

You are social and flexible, and your relationships should be a place of profound truth. By seeking out partners who tell it like it is and encourage you to share honestly, you will discover that true love comes from being radically seen for your perfect imperfections.

The Journey of
FEBRUARY 4

Welcome to February 4, a heartfelt journey of progress and connection.

As you look for where to aim your focus today, shoot for *Devotion* (The Number Six). Although Aquarius season can scatter your focus, prioritize meaningful work over trivial pursuits to ensure that your actions serve a greater purpose. Whether it be volunteering for something outside your job description at work or helping out a neighbor in need, be thoughtful.

And as you look for meaning, don't be afraid to leave behind old ways of thinking. *Transition* (Six of Swords) asks you to mentally move forward today, no longer letting your subconscious's limiting beliefs hold you back from progressing toward your deepest desires and highest potential.

As you tackle this humble work, *Choice* (The Lovers) asks you to do it for yourself. There's no need to depend on outside praise or acceptance; simply look inward for the confidence and love that you crave most. Give yourself a sincere compliment in the mirror or pat yourself on the back. If you can find love for yourself, you'll find the sense of purpose you've been seeking all along.

JUST FOR TODAY

TODAY'S MANTRA
I will learn to value myself through estimable actions.

TODAY'S JOURNAL PROMPT
What old patterns of thinking or behavior are holding me back from self-love?

TODAY'S RITUAL
Do some mental clearing. Draw a bath and fill it with eucalyptus leaves or Epsom salt. As you soak in this healing energy, breathe in and out six times and visualize releasing the mental baggage you have been carrying around.

BORN ON THIS DAY

CHARLES LINDBERGH, American aviator and the first person to fly solo across the Atlantic Ocean

BETTY FRIEDAN, American feminist and writer

"You must never be fearful about what you are doing when it is right."—**ROSA PARKS**, American civil rights activist who refused to give up her bus seat to a white passenger

The Journey of Those Born on
FEBRUARY 4

You were born of rational innovation and an emotional restraint that can hold you back from true vulnerability. You will have to soften to matters of the heart, as your journey is one of sincerity, emotional progress, and true love.

Early on in your journey, you will meet your unassuming guide, *Devotion* (The Number Six). *Devotion* gently pulls you away from your rigid ways of being and toward a path of meaningful service. You will meet *Devotion* in moments of sincere purpose, when your actions are aligned with your deepest priorities.

If you choose this path of sincerity, you will have to contend with your probing teacher, *Transition* (Six of Swords). *Transition* asks you to let go of the mental patterns that keep you from moving forward in your personal development. You will meet *Transition* in moments of emotional clearing, when you shed the memories, fears, and beliefs that unconsciously weigh you down. If you choose mental clarity over chaos, *Transition* helps you move forward in the right direction.

YOUR GUIDES

Astrology: Your Energy
Aquarius (Uranus, Mercury)

Numerology: Your Path
Devotion (The Number Six)

Minor Arcana: Your Lesson
Transition (The Six of Swords)

Major Arcana: Your Highest Calling
Choice (The Lovers)

By answering these calls for meaningful work, you will find yourself in the healing light of *Choice* (The Lovers). *Choice* knows that love is simply a decision away, inspiring you to fight for your happiness in every aspect of your life. You will meet *Choice* in moments of emotional reciprocity, when you pursue the people and things that want the best for you. By letting go of the relationships, dynamics, and mental patterns that keep you stuck in sadness or discomfort, *Choice* teaches you the vulnerable art of self-advocacy.

AQUARIUS
RULERS: URANUS, MERCURY

PURPOSE
To humbly work to love and be loved in return.

RELATIONSHIPS

You are serious and formidable, yet your relationships should be a place of vulnerability and service. By choosing partners who give from the heart and don't expect anything in return, you will discover that true love is the intuitive art of emotional intimacy.

The Journey of
FEBRUARY 5

Welcome to February 5, a self-guided journey toward radical evolution.

Commitment (The Number Seven) asks you to narrow your focus to the projects and relationships you are invested in most. Rather than saying "yes" to anything and everything that comes your way, show up for who and what you plan to grow with in the future. Quality wins over quantity.

Amidst the socially expansive nature of Aquarius season, look out for *Hypervigilance* (Seven of Swords). Be leery of paranoia and deceitful self-protection, staying present to the fear-based stories your anxiety tells you today. There is no point in trying to get away with subtle trickery, so act in earnest and trust that others are doing the same.

And if you can proceed with complete sincerity, you will find yourself in a state of personal *Evolution* (The Chariot). You have momentous potential for growth, so accept every invitation to step out of your comfort zone and into a new level of self-realization. Whether it be a promotion at work or the next serious step in your personal relationship, pledge your heart and soul toward a greater future.

JUST FOR TODAY

TODAY'S MANTRA
I will sincerely invest myself in the life I want.

TODAY'S RITUAL
Draw on the power of black tourmaline, a crystal known for its strong protective powers. Keep it in your right pocket, or even better, tuck it into your bra or shirt pocket.

TODAY'S JOURNAL PROMPT
What fears, conscious or subconscious, do I have around betrayal?

BORN ON THIS DAY

CRISTIANO RONALDO, Portuguese footballer

FRANTIŠKA PLAMÍNKOVÁ, Czech feminist and suffragist

"All progress has resulted from people who took unpopular positions."—ADLAI STEVENSON II, American lawyer, politician, and diplomat

The Journey of Those Born on
FEBRUARY 5

Y ou were born of heartfelt courage and a hunger for more that can make it difficult to remain loyal to just one thing. You have to get serious about what you care about most, as your journey is one of investment, sincerity, and self-actualization.

Early on in your journey, you will meet your formidable guide, *Commitment* (The Number Seven). *Commitment* asks you to drop the act of uncertainty and set your sights on a path of complete devotion. By working toward the things you want to invest in most, *Commitment* ensures that you slowly but surely build upon a faithful foundation of trust.

If you choose this intentional path, you will have to contend with your lower companion, *Hypervigilance* (Seven of Swords). *Hypervigilance* knows how scary it is to trust in others, shedding light on your subconscious need to protect yourself against outside betrayal. If you can work through these fears and come to understand that these self-protective and at times deceitful measures block you from true intimacy, *Hypervigilance* shows you the strength of emotional surrender.

YOUR GUIDES

Astrology: Your Energy
Aquarius (Uranus, Mercury)

Numerology: Your Path
Commitment (The Number Seven)

Minor Arcana: Your Lesson
Hypervigilance (The Seven of Swords)

Major Arcana: Your Highest Calling
Evolution (The Chariot)

By answering these calls for personal accountability, you will uncover the power of *Evolution* (The Chariot). You will meet *Evolution* in the pinch-me moments of success, when you can't believe how far your commitment to yourself and the ones you love has taken you. Through powerful self-determination and complete faith in a power greater than yourself, *Evolution* takes your sincerity and catapults you into unbounded realms of personal progress.

AQUARIUS
RULERS: URANUS, MERCURY

PURPOSE
*To commit your heart, mind, and body
to your personal evolution.*

RELATIONSHIPS

You are romantic and at times dramatic, yet your relationships should be a place of total sincerity and commitment. By seeking out partners who are as straightforward as they are devoted, you will discover that true love always points you in the right direction.

The Journey of
FEBRUARY 6

W elcome to February 6, a winding journey of emotional strength.
Despite the mercurial nature of Aquarius season, *Power* (The Number Eight) asks you to get out of your head and into your inner truth. Reach for opportunities to share your wild vulnerability internally and externally today, never making yourself small or keeping secrets to make others comfortable.

But watch out for *Negativity* (Eight of Swords), the voice inside you that likes to point out everything you have ever done wrong. If you find yourself stuck in a mental rabbit hole full of shame and self-hatred, call a close friend or trusted partner and ask them to ground you in the truth of your lovability.

Besides, *Resilience* (Strength) knows how much you are capable of healing. Tap into your intrinsic emotional strength to remember how much you have survived and how much you are learning to thrive. If the weight of your emotions feels insurmountable today, slow down, drop into your place of internal safety, and know that it is yours to keep.

JUST FOR TODAY

TODAY'S MANTRA
I will trust my feelings with myself and the ones I love today.

TODAY'S RITUAL
Cast off the chains of negative self-talk by getting your inner critic out onto paper. Write a letter to yourself from the perspective of your inner critic using your nondominant hand. Write back to this part of yourself, using your dominant hand, from the perspective of a compassionate and loving friend.

TODAY'S JOURNAL PROMPT
Where do the mean voices inside my head come from?

BORN ON THIS DAY

MARY LEAKEY, English paleoanthropologist who discovered the earliest human footprints

BABE RUTH, American baseball player

"You never know how strong you are, until being strong is your only choice."—BOB MARLEY, Jamaican singer-songwriter and musician

The Journey of Those Born on
FEBRUARY 6

You were born of innovative humanitarianism and a compassion for others that you do not extend toward yourself as easily. You will have to fall in love with the beautiful complexity of your humanity, as your journey is one of authenticity, inner healing, and emotional strength.

Early on in your journey, you will meet your enigmatic guide, *Power* (The Number Eight). *Power* calls you away from the mundane and superficial aspects of life and toward a path of complete self-honesty and intimacy. You will meet *Power* in moments of inexplicable and divine connection, when the most shameful experiences of your past end up being the birthplace of everlasting trust with another human being.

If you choose this expansive path, you will have to cross swords with your deepest blockage, *Negativity* (Eight of Swords). If you can both recognize and seek to understand the voice of self-sabotage that lives within, *Negativity* helps you untangle from these mental burdens through radical compassion.

By answering these calls for emotional accountability, you will tap into the undeniable miracles of *Resilience* (Strength). *Resilience* invites you to reconnect with the higher emotional intelligence that lives within, allowing you to heal yourself from the inside out. You will meet *Resilience* in moments of internal strength, when you are able to act and react to difficulties from a place of divine fortitude. If you can believe in your intuitive capacity to heal, *Resilience* shows you how far it can go.

YOUR GUIDES

Astrology: Your Energy
Aquarius (Uranus, Mercury)

Numerology: Your Path
Power (The Number Eight)

Minor Arcana: Your Lesson
Negativity (The Eight of Swords)

Major Arcana: Your Highest Calling
Resilience (Strength)

AQUARIUS
RULERS: URANUS, MERCURY

PURPOSE
To be fiercely vulnerable to the healing powers within and around you.

RELATIONSHIPS

You are a giver in matters of the heart, and your relationships should be a place of complete emotional surrender. By seeking out partners who can hold space for your deepest shame, you will discover that true love is a portal for radical healing.

The Journey of
FEBRUARY 7

Welcome to February 7, a self-revealing journey of intuitive knowledge.

As you channel the mental power of Aquarius season, seek out *Experience* (The Number Nine) rather than staying in your comfort zone. Walk a path of understanding, questioning everything while staying curious about the lessons that are available to you. Whether you begin a long-term study or book your next great adventure, look outward for more information.

But beware of *Anxiety* (Nine of Swords). Instead of engaging in obsessive angst-based thinking, address the deeper fears that lie underneath. Call a close friend or seek outside help if the voices get too loud today, and know that they are only protecting you against a worst-case scenario that likely will never come.

And if speaking to someone doesn't help, go inward and access *Instinct* (The Hermit). Celebrate your intuitive powers of direction, trust your gut, and act on this sacred knowledge. If you receive any internal messages today, loud or quiet, listen to them with complete faith so you can realize your innate powers of perception.

JUST FOR TODAY

TODAY'S MANTRA
I will look outward for practical knowledge and inward for sacred truths.

TODAY'S RITUAL
Move your body to free yourself of mental angst. Whether it be a dance while doing the dishes or a quick sprint around the block, take the time to get out of your fear-based thinking, for even five minutes, and into the presence of your physical body.

TODAY'S JOURNAL PROMPT
When was the last time that I listened to my gut and I turned out to be right?

BORN ON THIS DAY

LAURA INGALLS WILDER, American writer

AN WANG, Chinese American computer engineer and inventor

"Suffering has been stronger than all other teaching, and has taught me to understand what your heart used to be. I have been bent and broken, but—I hope—into a better shape."—CHARLES DICKENS, English novelist

The Journey of Those Born on
FEBRUARY 7

You were born of innovative ambition and a fierce focus that can make it hard to notice the lessons that life throws at you along the way. You will have to seek to learn more about yourself and the world around you, as your journey is one of understanding, letting go, and internal knowing.

Early on in your journey, you will meet your wise guide, *Experience* (The Number Nine). *Experience* calls you away from narrow-mindedness and toward a path of endless searching. You will meet *Experience* in moments when you are a student of life, absorbing all the information around you so that you can discern your unique point of view.

If you choose this forever-expanding path, you will meet your great teacher, *Anxiety* (The Nine of Swords). While it is scary to let go of your attempts to control the outcomes in life, *Anxiety* encourages you to find empathy for your fear so that you can integrate it and move forward. It is not by self-denial that you will find new strength, but rather by acknowledging your weakness and embracing the healing power of vulnerability.

YOUR GUIDES

Astrology: Your Energy
Aquarius (Uranus, Mercury)

Numerology: Your Path
Experience (The Number Nine)

Minor Arcana: Your Lesson
Anxiety (The Nine of Swords)

Major Arcana: Your Highest Calling
Instinct (The Hermit)

By answering these calls for growth, you will learn to rely on *Instinct* (The Hermit). *Instinct* asks you to listen to the humble voice of intuition that lives deep within, lighting your way through even the murkiest of passages. You will meet *Instinct* in moments of intuitive journeying, when you find your feet following an invisible path of divine purpose. If you can quiet the outside noise enough to hear your intrinsic genius, *Instinct* teaches you how to trust yourself completely in the dark.

AQUARIUS
RULERS: URANUS, MERCURY

PURPOSE
To be spiritually available to the knowledge that lives within.

RELATIONSHIPS

You are a serious go-getter, and your relationships should be a place of unbounded exploration. By seeking out partners who never let fear stop them from experiencing the adventure of life, you will discover that true love pushes you to new heights of understanding.

The Journey of
FEBRUARY 8

W elcome to February 8, an independent journey of karmic fate.
Despite the social nature of Aquarius season, *Autonomy* (The Number One) asks you to rely on yourself. Look for ways to create your own destiny today, whether it be starting a new project or putting in motion your next plan for self-improvement. No one can get in your way today, as long as you believe in yourself.

You'll need this enthusiasm for the future, as *Clarity* (Ace of Swords) asks you to pursue your next greatest idea. Whether you act on a long-standing dream today or speak up in your role at work, now is the time to find an outlet for the genius that lives within you.

But to bring you some perspective during this ambitious day, *Impermanence* (Wheel of Fortune) encourages you to see the best in every hiccup and unexpected change that comes your way. You certainly can't control fate, but a positive mindset and a belief in your own luck can go a long way as you ride the divine roller coaster of today.

──────────○──────────

JUST FOR TODAY

TODAY'S MANTRA
I believe in my ability to move forward no matter what the circumstances.

TODAY'S RITUAL
Find a private spot to sit and speak aloud for ten minutes. Allow yourself to express any stream of consciousness that appears in your mind. Don't hold back or judge what comes through; just remain curious about what is on your mind.

TODAY'S JOURNAL PROMPT
What mental strengths do I possess?

──────────○──────────

BORN ON THIS DAY

DMITRI MENDELEEV, Russian chemist and inventor who devised the periodic table of elements

PEGGY DUFF, English political activist

"Anything one man can imagine, other men can make real."—JULES VERNE, French writer known as the "father of science fiction"

The Journey of Those Born on
FEBRUARY 8

You were born of expansive genius and an introspection that can keep you stuck in morbid reflection. You will have to throw yourself into the potential of the moment instead, as your journey is one of self-belief, possibility, and ever-changing luck.

Early on in your journey, you will encounter your precocious guide, *Autonomy* (The Number One). *Autonomy* calls you away from the distractions of intimacy and toward a path of fierce self-reliance. You will meet *Autonomy* in moments of blind faith in yourself, when you have no idea how to move forward but you find your feet moving toward your future anyway.

If you accept this unyielding path, you will meet your intelligent coconspirator, *Clarity* (Ace of Swords). *Clarity* invites you to listen closely to the instincts of the mind, encouraging you to follow through on the exciting ideas that keep you up at night. Rather than getting stuck on the details, *Clarity* asks you to chase the enthusiasm and figure it out as you go.

By answering these calls for self-belief, you will come to respect the laws of *Impermanence* (Wheel of Fortune). *Impermanence* asks you to embrace the cyclic nature of success, never holding on too tight to any one circumstance because you know it will inevitably transform. You will meet *Impermanence* in moments of optimism born from complete faith, when you are willing to trust that the changes that are occurring in your life are fated for the better.

YOUR GUIDES

Astrology: Your Energy
Aquarius (Uranus, Mercury)

Numerology: Your Path
Autonomy (The Number One)

Minor Arcana: Your Lesson
Clarity (The Ace of Swords)

Major Arcana: Your Highest Calling
Impermanence
(The Wheel of Fortune)

AQUARIUS
RULERS: URANUS, MERCURY

PURPOSE
*To control what you can and faithfully
let go of the rest.*

RELATIONSHIPS

You are deeply introspective and intuitive, and your relationships should be a place of personal freedom and change. By seeking out partners who give you the space and trust to grow within and outside the relationship, you will discover that true love can withstand the unpredictable tides of life.

The Journey of
FEBRUARY 9

Welcome to February 9, a harmonious journey toward radical justice.

As you navigate the more romantic side of Aquarius season, be sure to keep *Balance* (The Number Two) in mind. *Balance* encourages peace over drama and intimacy over isolation, so look for ways that you can compromise with others. By seeking to understand rather than to be understood, you can find new harmony within your personal relationships.

But don't get too in your head, as *Doubt* (Two of Swords) warns against the overthinking that leads to indecision. If you come to a difficult crossroads in your day, take inventory of the factors at play and seek outside counsel to help you see the big-picture solution to your problems. Try your best to face any issue head-on and know that the only bad decision is to make no decision at all.

Besides, *Truth* (Justice) encourages you to anchor your fretful mind through spiritual alignment. When you are feeling most confused today, take a moment to meditate on your circumstances, dropping into a place of internal peace. Tap into your moral compass, the divine arrow that always points you toward your true north.

JUST FOR TODAY

TODAY'S MANTRA
The truth lies in my internal balance.

TODAY'S RITUAL
Calm your racing mind. Find a piece of lavender or sandalwood, and as you inhale its aroma, chant, "Inner scales, help me see the beautiful balance that exists within me."

TODAY'S JOURNAL PROMPT
What decision am I most afraid to make right now?

BORN ON THIS DAY

BETSY MIX COWLES, American feminist, educator, and early leader of the abolition movement

BRENDAN BEHAN, Irish author and poet

"No person is your friend who demands your silence, or denies your right to grow."—ALICE WALKER, American novelist

The Journey of Those Born on
FEBRUARY 9

Y ou were born of artistic genius and a need for solitude that can push away the companionship you desire most. You will have to learn to be true to yourself in relationship with others, as your journey is one of partnership, crucial decision-making, and radical justice.

Early on in life, *Balance* (The Number Two) calls
you away from your hermetic desires and toward a path
of interpersonal peace. Rather than overcomplicating
your existence, *Balance* asks you to slow down and
smell the roses, finding complete relief in the present
moment and in the company of trustworthy partners.

If you choose this gentle path, you will stumble
upon your sage teacher, *Doubt* (Two of Swords). You
will meet *Doubt* in the decisions that feel too uncertain to face, growing like weeds around you the longer
they are left unattended. *Doubt* urges you to make
tough decisions rather than procrastinating in fear,
teaching you there's no such thing as a mistake if you
try with the best of intentions.

By answering these calls for trust, you will come to
understand the importance of *Truth* (Justice). You will

YOUR GUIDES

Astrology: Your Energy
Aquarius (Uranus, Venus)

Numerology: Your Path
Balance (The Number Two)

Minor Arcana: Your Lesson
Doubt (The Two of Swords)

Major Arcana: Your Highest Calling
Truth (Justice)

meet *Truth* when you drop into the spiritual anchor of your soul, the untouchable and undeniable source that defines the difference between right and wrong, good and evil. Truth knows that
no action goes without consequence, inspiring you to act with complete intention. If you can stay
honest with yourself no matter what the voices around you may say, *Truth* teaches you to live in
harmony with the laws of the universe, doing unto others as you would like them to do unto you.

———————————————○———————————————

AQUARIUS
RULERS: URANUS, VENUS

PURPOSE
*To find the internal balance that carries
your moral compass.*

RELATIONSHIPS

You are prone to isolation, yet your relationships should be a place of healing equality. By seeking
partners who want to meet you halfway, never taking more than they are willing to give, you will
discover that true love is both trusting and fair.

The Journey of
FEBRUARY 10

Welcome to February 10, a freeing journey of personal surrender.
To complement the airy creativity of this part of Aquarius season, *Flexibility* (The Number Three) encourages you to keep an open mind and heart regarding the people you meet as you float through this day. There's no need to come up with a thorough to-do list or plan, but instead, put yourself out there and take a chance on the social engagements that come your way.

As you engage with the world around you, look out for *Trigger* (Three of Swords). The words of others can often bring up moments of insecurity and fear, but try your best not to take anything too personally. *Trigger* encourages emotional maturity and self-awareness, so if needed, take a break to compose yourself and get back to center.

The best way to thrive today is to let go. *Surrender* (The Hanged Man) asks you to take on a new perspective, sacrificing your natural way of approaching things for the sake of personal growth and potential spiritual awakenings. Release your grip on control today and find new freedom as you hang gracefully from the treetops of the unknown.

―――――――――――――――――――○―――――――――――――――――――

JUST FOR TODAY

TODAY'S MANTRA
I will take a chance on the unknowns that today offers.

TODAY'S RITUAL
To see things from a different perspective, hang upside down—literally. Lie on your back at the edge of your bed, and if you are able, bend so that your head is fully dangling off the edge. Hold this pose as long as it feels comfortable so you can see things differently.

TODAY'S JOURNAL PROMPT
Where does life seem to be asking me to release control?

―――――――――――――――――――○―――――――――――――――――――

BORN ON THIS DAY

HIRATSUKA RAICHŌ, Japanese writer, journalist, political activist, anarchist, and feminist

BORIS PASTERNAK, Russian poet, novelist, and literary translator

"We like our archetypes and heroes to be what they are at face value. And life doesn't work out like that."—LAURA DERN, American actor

The Journey of Those Born on
FEBRUARY 10

Y ou were born of radical confidence and an intellectual independence that make it difficult to hear the differing opinions of others. You will have to grow with an open mind, as your journey is one of malleability, self-awareness, and ego sacrifice.

Early on in your journey, you will meet your community-oriented guide, *Flexibility* (The Number Three). *Flexibility* calls you away from self-reliance and toward a path of social discovery. By embracing the friends, colleagues, and teammates who help sharpen your innate intelligence, you will grow your understanding and effectiveness with the world around you.

If you choose this convivial path, you will have to contend with your emotional teacher, *Trigger* (Three of Swords). *Trigger* knows how much words can hurt wounds of the past, encouraging you to self-reflect whenever someone hits you in a psychological sore spot. Rather than taking it personally or blaming your feelings on others, *Trigger* encourages you toward emotional accountability.

YOUR GUIDES

Astrology: Your Energy
Aquarius (Uranus, Venus)

Numerology: Your Path
Flexibility (The Number Three)

Minor Arcana: Your Lesson
Trigger (The Three of Swords)

Major Arcana: Your Highest Calling
Surrender (The Hanged Man)

By answering these calls for consciousness, you will discover the power of *Surrender* (The Hanged Man). *Surrender* knows that spiritual breakthroughs are merely a shift in perspective, encouraging you to abandon your rigid ways of thinking in favor of the universe's grander vision. You will meet *Surrender* in moments of unexpected epiphany, when life ceases to go according to plan and you find yourself on new mental ground. If you can remember to release expectation, *Surrender* teaches you that through sacrificing your pride, you gain eternal wisdom.

AQUARIUS
RULERS: URANUS, VENUS

PURPOSE
To discover a spiritual experience in the act of letting go.

RELATIONSHIPS

You are powerfully autonomous and high-minded, yet your relationships should be a place of total open-mindedness and fluidity. By seeking out partners who are as free-spirited as they are curious, you will discover that true love is the most enlightening adventure of all.

The Journey of
FEBRUARY 11

Welcome to February 11, a rigorous journey of personal metamorphosis.
To make the most of today, *Discipline* (The Number Four) asks you to keep your head down and commit to your work. Bit by bit, tackle the mundane tasks you have been putting off. Whether it be personal or professional, do the necessary legwork to prove to the universe that you mean business.

But be sure to pursue humble progress over unsustainable ambition. *Restoration* (Four of Swords) asks you to pause when you're overwhelmed, giving yourself time to reassess your plans for the day and hopefully leading you to more meaningful action. Despite the dreamy nature of Aquarius season, slow and steady wins the race, so remain open to the intuitive callings of the soul.

Besides, *Transformation* (Death) knows who you are becoming. Let go of outdated versions of yourself by giving up an old way of thinking or embracing a new style of self-expression. No matter what you are shedding, embrace the radical emotional shifts that reveal new layers of authenticity. Don't be afraid of the changes you see in yourself today; you are growing closer to the truth of who you are.

JUST FOR TODAY

TODAY'S MANTRA
I will slowly work to reveal the person I truly am.

TODAY'S JOURNAL PROMPT
What outdated parts of myself am I ready to shed?

TODAY'S RITUAL
Today you might feel a bit like the phoenix rising from the ashes, so elderberry tea is in order. It can be found at most local health food stores. As you sip it by a black candle of your choosing, visualize this tea helping you detox from whatever old versions of yourself that you are shedding.

BORN ON THIS DAY

FLORYNCE KENNEDY, American lawyer, radical feminist, and civil rights advocate

SHERYL CROW, American singer-songwriter

"I have not failed. I've just found 10,000 ways that won't work."—THOMAS EDISON, American inventor

The Journey of Those Born on
FEBRUARY 11

You were born of interpersonal compassion and an idealism that can keep you far from reality. You will have to ground yourself in your spiritual development, as your journey is one of hard work, necessary rest, and personal growth.

Early on in your journey, you will meet your humble guide, *Discipline* (The Number Four). *Discipline* calls you away from the distractions of romance and toward a path of grounded work. Through a complete commitment to the goals you lay out for your life, *Discipline* helps you build a stable foundation of integrity within yourself.

If you choose this deliberate path, you will be asked to slow down by your sage teacher, *Restoration* (Four of Swords). *Restoration* knows that the body and mind can only handle so much for so long, encouraging you to take the necessary time off to recharge. You will meet *Restoration* in moments of personal burnout when you finally let yourself collapse into the arms of comfort, home, and nourishment.

> ### YOUR GUIDES
>
> *Astrology: Your Energy*
> Aquarius (Uranus, Venus)
>
> *Numerology: Your Path*
> Discipline (The Number Four)
>
> *Minor Arcana: Your Lesson*
> Restoration (The Four of Swords)
>
> *Major Arcana: Your Highest Calling*
> Transformation (Death)

By answering these calls for maturity, you will build the emotional muscles required to embrace *Transformation* (Death). You are not the same person you were even a year ago, and *Transformation* inspires you time and again to shed the layers of the past that you simply cannot carry into your authentic future. Whether it be relationships, jobs, or identity, *Transformation* reminds you of the importance of closing one door so that you can open a truer one.

AQUARIUS
RULERS: URANUS, VENUS

PURPOSE
To humbly work to shed old layers and reveal new levels of self-honesty.

RELATIONSHIPS

You are relationship-driven and romantic, and your relationships should be a place of radical transparency. By seeking out partners who work as diligently on their spiritual and emotional growth as you do, you will discover that true love only requires complete authenticity.

The Journey of
FEBRUARY 12

Welcome to February 12, a heroic journey toward inner balance.

To channel the authenticity of Aquarius season, be bold and brave as you channel the power of *Courage* (The Number Five), revealing your most authentic self for the sake of shared understanding. It is impossible to predict the outcome of these efforts, so try your best to enjoy each moment of self-revealing.

But if you pursue this daring path, work to practice *Maturity* (Five of Swords). Be restrained when it comes to what you say in the heat of emotion, particularly around triggering topics that could potentially harm others. If you happen to receive any negative feedback or criticism today, talk it out with a close friend or supporter, and try your best to let it roll off your back.

Besides, *Serenity* (Temperance) knows that internal peace comes from spiritual alignment. Meditate on how best to carry out the universe's wishes rather than succumbing to the drama of the ego. Aim for the middle road of patience and moderation in everything you create and share today. There's no need to be the best or to be "right" on this day; instead, aspire toward a profound sense of inner harmony.

JUST FOR TODAY

TODAY'S MANTRA
To courageously share from a place of internal balance.

TODAY'S RITUAL
Meditate to get in touch with the serenity that the day requires. If you find meditation difficult, sit with your back against a wall, set a timer for five minutes, and repeat, "Serenity" over and over until the timer goes off.

TODAY'S JOURNAL PROMPT
How can I bring patience and moderation to my creativity today?

BORN ON THIS DAY

JOHN L. LEWIS, American organized labor leader

RANDI BLEHR, Norwegian feminist, liberal politician, and suffragist

"Ignorance more frequently begets confidence than does knowledge: it is those who know little, not those who know much, who so positively assert that this or that problem will never be solved by science."—**CHARLES DARWIN**, English naturalist

The Journey of Those Born on
FEBRUARY 12

Y ou are a fierce humanitarian with an ability to sacrifice for what you believe in most, which at times can drain most of your vital resources. You will have to learn the art of moderation, as your journey is one of bravery, personal growth, and inner balance.

Early on in your journey, you will meet your brave guide, *Courage* (The Number Five). *Courage* applauds you for your curiosity and encourages you toward a path of vulnerable leadership, inviting you to take big risks as you make your voice heard. You will meet *Courage* in moments of visibility, when you take a leap of faith outside your comfort zone and suddenly find yourself at the center stage of your life.

If you embrace this wild path, you will have to contend with your toughest teacher, *Maturity* (Five of Swords). *Maturity* asks you to harness the power of authentic speech, forcing you to get clear on your values so that you can deliver an incisive message that can withstand any negative feedback. If you can stand by what you believe in most, *Maturity* teaches you how to grow beyond the fear of opposition.

> ### YOUR GUIDES
>
> *Astrology: Your Energy*
> Aquarius (Uranus, Venus)
>
> *Numerology: Your Path*
> Courage (The Number Five)
>
> *Minor Arcana: Your Lesson*
> Maturity (The Five of Swords)
>
> *Major Arcana: Your Highest Calling*
> Serenity (Temperance)

By answering these calls for strength, you will come to rely on the gifts of *Serenity* (Temperance). *Serenity* shows you the middle road to truth, revealing the power of gray areas and the purpose of patience. You will meet *Serenity* in moments of personal moderation, when you choose to fight for the peaceful big picture rather than get lost in the daily imbalance of opinion. If you can seek to align with the greater forces of good, *Serenity* helps you change the hearts and minds of many.

─────────────────○─────────────────

AQUARIUS
RULERS: URANUS, VENUS

PURPOSE
To courageously pursue a path of peaceful internal alignment.

RELATIONSHIPS

You are lovingly detached in most aspects of your life, yet your relationships should be a place of passionate compromise. By seeking out partners who use honesty as a tool for shared understanding, you will discover that true love is born from unapologetic authenticity and radical kindness.

The Journey of
FEBRUARY 13

Welcome to February 13, an expressive journey of self-acceptance.

Amidst the emotionally detached air of Aquarius season, *Devotion* (The Number Six) asks you to approach today from the heart instead. Rather than playing it safe and protecting your pride, spend unapologetic time with the people and projects you adore most. Look for how you can be most useful to whatever your soul belongs to.

But as you do, *Transition* (Six of Swords) asks you to part ways with the old and outdated mental patterns that keep you from true emotional freedom. Whether it be fear of abandonment or betrayal, unburden yourself of this historical baggage. Take a look at where your mind gets the best of you in your relationships and turn this fear over to someone you trust.

There's more introspective work to be done, however, as *Shadow* (The Devil) asks you to acknowledge your subconscious penchant for self-sabotage. By recognizing that your destructive habits are really masking a deeper belief that you are unworthy of happiness, you can find new freedom in self-acceptance. If you can reach for empathy for the parts of you that learned to fear expansion, you'll thrive.

JUST FOR TODAY

TODAY'S MANTRA
I will work through the fears and destructive behaviors that block me from openheartedness.

TODAY'S JOURNAL PROMPT
When and where did I learn to fear my own happiness?

TODAY'S RITUAL
Spend some time in the dark. Find an enclosed room in your home or place of work that feels safe, shut the lights off, and if possible, draw the blinds. Place your hand over your heart's center, and repeat the words, "Without darkness, there would be no light."

BORN ON THIS DAY

FEODOR CHALIAPIN, Russian opera singer

GEORGES SIMENON, Belgian French writer

"We want deeper sincerity of motive, a greater courage in speech and earnestness in action." —**SAROJINI NAIDU**, Indian political activist and poet known as the "Nightingale of India"

The Journey of Those Born on
FEBRUARY 13

Y ou are an objective humanitarian with an emotional mysteriousness that can keep you at arm's length from the people you love most. You will have to soften to the healing of connection, as your journey is one of vulnerability, progress, and deep expansion.

Early on in your journey, you will meet your graceful guide, *Devotion* (The Number Six). *Devotion* calls you away from your rigid ways of being and toward a path of emotional purpose. *Devotion* asks you to make your biggest decisions in life from the heart, inspiring you to act from a place of love rather than scarcity.

If you choose this meaningful path, you will cross swords with your greatest teacher, *Transition* (Six of Swords). *Transition* knows that unprocessed emotional baggage slows down the process of becoming, pushing you to address and heal the subconscious stories you have outgrown. You will meet *Transition* in moments of internal transition, when you accept what parts of yourself you must leave behind as you journey toward new personal freedom.

By accepting these calls to emotionally soften, you will find yourself in the healing realm of *Shadow* (The Devil). *Shadow* understands how excruciatingly vulnerable it is to be free, helping you find empathy for the unconscious destructive behaviors and addictions that hold you back from true personal expansion. You will meet *Shadow* in moments of spiritual acceptance, when the simple act of admitting your fears releases all the shame attached to them. If you can aim for complete self-honesty, *Shadow* teaches you how to integrate darkness into the light.

YOUR GUIDES

Astrology: Your Energy
Aquarius (Uranus, Venus)

Numerology: Your Path
Devotion (The Number Six)

Minor Arcana: Your Lesson
Transition (The Six of Swords)

Major Arcana: Your Highest Calling
Shadow (The Devil)

AQUARIUS
RULERS: URANUS, VENUS

PURPOSE
*To let love heal the shame that blocks
true personal freedom.*

RELATIONSHIPS

You are private in most areas of your life, yet your relationships should be a place of divine vulnerability and empathy. By seeking out partners who love you because of, not in spite of, your emotional complexity, you will discover that true love is an act of interpersonal healing.

The Journey of
FEBRUARY 14

W elcome to February 14, a focused journey of unexpected change.
 Commitment (The Number Seven) asks you to remain faithful to the people and
projects you care about most. Be cognizant of your time today, spending the better part of your
energy on meaningful work and sincere interpersonal connection. Choose sincerity over popu-
larity by taking serious actions toward what truly matters.

But amidst the most social time of Aquarius season, look out for *Hypervigilance* (Seven of
Swords). Instead of indulging social paranoia and engaging in defensive strategies, drop your
weapons and believe in those who are trustworthy. If you find yourself feeling self-protective and
skeptical of the behavior of another, however, check in with your gut and get clear on what is fear
versus intuition.

You'll need to keep a strong emotional footing, as *Upheaval* (The Tower) requires change. If
you find the foundation beneath you shaking today, whether it be an unexpected change in your
job or an unanticipated confrontation in your personal life, try your best to understand the
method to the madness. Even if it's just on an emotional level, there may be a much-needed ad-
justment occurring in your life today, so surrender to the possibility of what could become.

○

JUST FOR TODAY

TODAY'S MANTRA
I will commit to the inevitability of change.

TODAY'S JOURNAL PROMPT
Where is life forcing me to change and grow, and what about that is making me uncomfortable?

TODAY'S RITUAL
Invite the unexpected into your life. Bring a two-sided coin with you as you go
for a walk. At each intersection, flip the coin—heads for left and tails for right.
Do this for at least seven minutes and embrace wherever fate takes you.

○

BORN ON THIS DAY

MARION MAHONY GRIFFIN, American architect and one of the first licensed female architects
in the US

DANAI GURIRA, American actor and playwright

"If there is no struggle, there is no progress."—**FREDERICK DOUGLASS**, American abolitionist,
lecturer, and editor who escaped enslavement

The Journey of Those Born on
FEBRUARY 14

You were born of courageous ingenuity and a need for internal peace that can make it difficult to accept the crucial invitations for change that come your way. You will have to get serious about your radical growth, as your journey is one of sincerity, trust, and unstoppable change.

Early on in your journey, you will encounter your formidable guide, *Commitment* (The Number Seven). *Commitment* steers you away from the whims of passion and toward a path of interpersonal responsibility. By devoting yourself completely to the people, projects, and ideas that you believe in most, *Commitment* shows you how meaningful life can be when you don't stray from your intended purpose.

If you choose this path of personal integrity, you will have to reckon with your lower companion, *Hypervigilance* (Seven of Swords). You will meet *Hypervigilance* in the faces of those who once betrayed you, when you poured your heart and soul into something yet the person could not honor their end of the relationship. *Hypervigilance* asks you to forgive others for their trespasses rather than arming yourself with weapons of deception.

YOUR GUIDES

Astrology: Your Energy
Aquarius (Uranus, Venus)

Numerology: Your Path
Commitment (The Number Seven)

Minor Arcana: Your Lesson
Hypervigilance (The Seven of Swords)

Major Arcana: Your Highest Calling
Upheaval (The Tower)

By answering these calls for personal responsibility, you will be prepared to embrace the genius of *Upheaval* (The Tower). *Upheaval* invites you to surrender to the power of change, forcing you to let go of what once was so that you can fall freely into the arms of a better tomorrow. You will meet *Upheaval* in moments of divine intervention, when the universe does for you what you knew must be done for your personal growth and future happiness.

AQUARIUS
RULERS: URANUS, VENUS

PURPOSE
To live in integrity and leave the rest up to fate.

RELATIONSHIPS

You are wildly loving, yet your relationships should be a place of complete focus and commitment. By seeking out partners who honor their word and act from a place of personal integrity, you will discover that true love is an unbreakable bond of trust.

The Journey of
FEBRUARY 15

W elcome to February 15, a reflective day that is brimming with possibility.
To make the most of today, *Power* (The Number Eight) asks you to see beyond the superficial. Whether it be processing old wounds or deeply listening to a close partner as they share their truth, work with the unseen aspects of life. No matter what you're working on or who you're working with, make the effort to go a bit deeper.

But amidst the dreamier end of Aquarius season, don't get lost in any mental spirals. *Negativity* (Eight of Swords) warns against incessant fear-based thinking today, the kind that stops you from approaching new ideas and keeps you awake at night. As negative thoughts come up, as they always do, acknowledge them without giving them any more power. Simply let them pass, and keep it moving.

Besides, *Hope* (The Star) has far greater plans for you. Bring your hidden dreams into the light of day, putting personal faith in even the craziest of ideas. As you do the reflective work that this day requires, reach down into the divine optimism that lives beneath all the emotional baggage. Whether it be learning to play an instrument or telling someone you love them, remember that anything is possible if you are willing to believe.

JUST FOR TODAY

TODAY'S MANTRA
I will dig deep to uncover my truest dreams.

TODAY'S JOURNAL PROMPT
What secret dream, talent, or idea do I hope to bring into my real life?

TODAY'S RITUAL
Wish upon a star. Whether it's dark enough to see the stars or they are out of sight, go outside tonight and tell the sky exactly what dreams you hope will come true.

BORN ON THIS DAY

ERNEST SHACKLETON, English Irish polar explorer

SUSAN B. ANTHONY, American social reformer and women's suffrage movement leader

"You cannot teach a man anything, you can only help him find it within himself."—GALILEO GALILEI, Italian astronomer, physicist, and engineer who has been called the "father of science"

The Journey of Those Born on
FEBRUARY 15

Y ou were born of radical love and an inner turmoil that can make it hard for you to find compassion for yourself. You will have to dig deep to find your true magic, as your journey is one of authenticity, self-awareness, and divine optimism.

Early on in your journey, you will meet your authentic guide, *Power* (The Number Eight). *Power* calls you away from the mundane and toward a path of total self-honesty through deep reflection. You will meet *Power* in moments of truth, when you are able to see past the physical facade of yourself or another person and witness the profound complexity of the human experience.

If you choose this self-aware path, you will have to contend with your toughest teacher, *Negativity* (Eight of Swords). You will meet *Negativity* in your compulsive fear-based thinking, when your mind runs away with a scary possibility that may never happen. If you can bring awareness and detachment to these mental patterns, *Negativity* shows you how important it is to be present of mind.

> ### YOUR GUIDES
>
> *Astrology: Your Energy*
> Aquarius (Uranus, Venus)
>
> *Numerology: Your Path*
> Power (The Number Eight)
>
> *Minor Arcana: Your Lesson*
> Negativity (The Eight of Swords)
>
> *Major Arcana: Your Highest Calling*
> Hope (The Star)

By answering these calls for self-reflection, you will uncover the mystical optimism of *Hope* (The Star). *Hope* knows underneath all your fear and shame lies complete self-belief, encouraging you to find faith in your dreams so you can turn them into reality. You will meet *Hope* in moments of divine confidence, when you somehow muster the courage and strength to actualize your deepest potential. If you can look within for the enthusiasm you need, *Hope* will introduce you to your limitless potential.

AQUARIUS
RULERS: URANUS, VENUS

PURPOSE
*To uncover the fear and shame
that block optimism.*

RELATIONSHIPS

You are emotionally devoted yet private, so your relationships should be a place of radical self-revealing. By seeking out partners who don't scare easily and who believe deeply in your divine potential, you will discover that true love is born from perfect imperfection.

The Journey of
FEBRUARY 16

Welcome to February 16, a psychic journey toward higher consciousness.

As you navigate the intuitive end of Aquarius season, set your sights on *Experience* (The Number Nine). Humbly search, opening yourself to new possibilities and perspectives. Whether it be finding a new mentor or searching for a new spiritual practice, discover the consciousness-expanding power of not knowing.

As you travel this path of understanding, look out for *Anxiety* (Nine of Swords). Be careful of the fretful hamster wheels that can block you from mental expansion. If you are feeling overwhelmed or stuck, take a moment to call a friend or adviser and get a grounded perspective on reality. Nothing is as bad or unmanageable as it seems.

And if you get the mental relief you are needing, get to know the intuitive waters of *Memory* (The Moon). Reach within to see how deep your intuitive powers can run if you can release the unhealed and unprocessed memories that cloud this inner clarity. Block out the incessant noise of your brain so you can get in touch with the true flow of your emotions, letting them guide you to the answers you need most.

JUST FOR TODAY

TODAY'S MANTRA
I will release the historical fears that block my intuitive powers.

TODAY'S RITUAL
Get outside at night and notice what phase the moon is in—is it waxing or waning? If you are not sure what these phases mean, do some research before you head out this evening.

TODAY'S JOURNAL PROMPT
What old stories or mental patterns block me from trusting my gut?

BORN ON THIS DAY

LEONORA O'REILLY, American feminist, suffragist, and trade union organizer

THE WEEKND, Canadian singer-songwriter and record producer

"At the end of the day, we're all spirits having a physical experience."—MAHERSHALA ALI, American actor and rapper

The Journey of Those Born on
FEBRUARY 16

You were born of fearless genius and a penchant for chaos that can leave you feeling destabilized. You will have to pursue internal healing rather than self-destruction, as your journey is one of understanding, mental healing, and intuitive awareness.

Early on in your journey, you will stumble upon your unbounded guide, *Experience* (The Number Nine). *Experience* knows that there is always more to be learned, inviting you to question authority and seek out the answers to the questions you desire most. If you can remain as curious as you are adventurous, *Experience* leads you on an enlightening path of self-understanding.

If you choose this unpredictable path, you will have to contend with your lower companion, *Anxiety* (Nine of Swords). *Anxiety* sheds light on your deepest fears, forcing you to confront the darkest corners of your subconscious. You will meet *Anxiety* in moments of internal awareness, when your mind tries to take you down a rabbit hole of worst-case scenarios but you choose to stay in the present moment instead.

By answering these calls for bravery, *Memory* (The Moon) will ask you to reconnect with your past so that you can access the intuitive voice that got blocked over time. You will meet *Memory* in moments of unconscious reaction, when your body and gut are telling you something that your mind has yet to understand. By processing and releasing the ancient stories that stop you from trusting this innate instinct, *Memory* reveals to you the divine power of the subconscious.

AQUARIUS
RULERS: URANUS, VENUS

PURPOSE
To search for the intuitive knowledge that exists within.

RELATIONSHIPS

You are wild and unyielding in your passions, yet your relationships should be a place of wisdom and healing. By seeking out partners who are working their way through their own demons while supporting your inner journey, you will discover that true love illuminates parts of you that you never knew existed.

The Journey of
FEBRUARY 17

W elcome to February 17, a sovereign journey of self-confidence.
As you wrap up the highly social Aquarius season, *Autonomy* (The Number One)
asks you to lean on yourself completely today. When making an action plan for the day, think
only of your set of skills and your capacity to accomplish without the burdens or limitations of
others. The more you can get done on your own, the better.

And don't be afraid to walk away from what can't serve your future. *Clarity* (Ace of Swords)
encourages you to invest in the potential of new ideas today, so make peace with letting go of
whatever way of thinking or believing no longer fits. By washing away the debris of mental clut-
ter, you can move toward a new sense of purpose with complete freedom.

The good news is, *Vitality* (The Sun) knows how much you have grown and encourages you to
share your personal progress. Step into a place of leadership in your life today, never backing
down from an invitation to be more visible in the world around you. Whether it be sharing a
piece of art or speaking on a topic you know in great detail, be ready to step into the spotlight at
any moment.

JUST FOR TODAY

TODAY'S MANTRA
I will find self-confidence through self-reliance.

TODAY'S RITUAL
Get out in the sun! Even if it's hidden behind a cloud, spend ten full minutes
lying beneath the giver of life, and chant in your head or aloud, "Sun power,
I seek from thee the vital confidence to be freely me."

TODAY'S JOURNAL PROMPT
What have you grown out of or grown away from that you need to let go?

BORN ON THIS DAY

MICHAEL JORDAN, American basketball player, NBA champion, Basketball Hall of Fame in-
ductee, and entrepreneur

FUKI KUSHIDA, Japanese peace and women's rights activist

"Finally, she mused that human existence is as brief as the life of autumn grass, so what was there
to fear from taking chances with your life?"—MO YAN, Chinese Nobel Prize–winning novelist

The Journey of Those Born on
FEBRUARY 17

You were born of social power and an emotional expansiveness that can make it difficult to know where to focus your energy. You will have to invest in your long-term happiness, as your journey is one of self-reliance, inspiration, and authentic confidence.

Early on in your journey, you will meet your fearless guide, *Autonomy* (The Number One). *Autonomy* calls you away from morbid self-reflection and toward a path of courageous innovation, pushing you time and again to make things up as you go. This is not a time to follow someone else's blueprint, but rather, a wild invitation to follow your own set of rules. If you can throw out the script and trust your intuition, *Autonomy* helps you carve out a life beyond your wildest dreams.

And know that a bit of naivete goes a long way. *Clarity* (Ace of Swords) asks you to believe in the pure potential of your ideas, rather than getting stuck on what could go wrong or how you might fail. You will meet Clarity in the excitement of your next greatest ambition, when you are brimming with enthusiasm for the work that is to come.

> ## YOUR GUIDES
>
> *Astrology: Your Energy*
> Aquarius (Uranus, Venus)
>
> *Numerology: Your Path*
> Autonomy (The Number One)
>
> *Minor Arcana: Your Lesson*
> Clarity (The Ace of Swords)
>
> *Major Arcana: Your Highest Calling*
> Vitality (The Sun)

By answering these calls for confidence, you will find yourself basking in the glow of *Vitality* (The Sun). *Vitality* knows how good it feels to be yourself, encouraging you to let down your facades and giving you permission to shine. You will meet *Vitality* in moments of total authentic self-expression, when your creativity is aligned with your true identity and you discover what it means to feel truly alive.

AQUARIUS
RULERS: URANUS, VENUS

PURPOSE
To be fiercely driven in your pursuit of authenticity.

RELATIONSHIPS

You are emotionally reflective and creatively deep, and your relationships should be a place of pure happiness. By seeking out partners who make you laugh and help you not take everything so seriously, you will discover that true love blooms in the light of the present moment.

The Journey of
FEBRUARY 18

W elcome to February 18, a harmonious journey that leads to internal clarity.

On the last day of the sociable Aquarius season, *Balance* (The Number Two) asks you to seek peace with yourself and others. There's no need to rush or create any drama, but instead, practice patience as you work through your day's interpersonal obligations. Whether it be asking help from a partner or taking something off your to-do list, favor sustainability over showmanship.

But beware of *Doubt* (Two of Swords). Be mindful of overthinking your decisions today and seek outside counsel if you are unclear on what to do next. Sometimes there is no perfect solution, so make use of the partnerships you trust as you untangle the fears and limiting beliefs that block you from moving forward with your day.

Besides, if you slow down enough, you can hear the truth. *Awakening* (Judgment) invites you to see some aspect of your life today with new clarity, helping you let go of any old crutches of denial. Whether it be understanding a relationship or a part of yourself with more perspective, favor radical awareness over emotional safety. If you can reach for honesty, you'll find your next spiritual awakening.

JUST FOR TODAY

TODAY'S MANTRA
Sometimes spiritual awakenings can be slow, peaceful, and gradual.

TODAY'S RITUAL
Today can feel overwhelmingly honest at times, so burn some sage to ground yourself in reality. If a particular room in your house needs clearing, burn the sage in the corners of the ceiling and any hidden nooks and crannies.

TODAY'S JOURNAL PROMPT
What honest and forthright partner can I lean on for support today?

BORN ON THIS DAY

ANDRÉ BRETON, French writer, poet, and founder of Surrealism

YOKO ONO, Japanese singer and artist

"The peace I am thinking of is the dance of an open mind when it engages another equally open one."—TONI MORRISON, American writer and first Black woman to win the Nobel Prize for Literature

The Journey of Those Born on
FEBRUARY 18*

Y ou were born of higher consciousness and an attachment to the past that can make it difficult to accept the reality of the present. You will have to slowly awaken to the truth, as your journey is one of harmony, trust, and radical awareness.

Early on in your journey, you will encounter your slow and steady guide, *Balance* (The Number Two). *Balance* calls you away from your grandiose plans and toward a peaceful path of longevity. *Balance* will always favor your long-term health and happiness over the short-lived promises of passion. If you can take life bit by bit, rather than all at once, *Balance* teaches the art of the slow burn.

If you choose this gentle path, you will have to contend with your lower companion, *Doubt* (Two of Swords). *Doubt* sheds light on your lack of self-trust, forcing you to address your predisposition toward overanalyzing your every move. If you can talk out your fears with trusted friends and counselors, *Doubt* will show you that there's no such thing as a wrong decision.

By answering these calls for patience, *Awakening* (Judgment) will tell you what you need to know. You will meet *Awakening* in moments of divine clarity, when you finally have the perspective you need to make self-aware choices about who you are and how you want to operate moving forward. If you can lead a life of deep consciousness, *Awakening* helps integrate the truth into your life, no matter how uncomfortable it may seem at first.

○

AQUARIUS
RULERS: URANUS, VENUS

PURPOSE
To slowly but surely awaken to the truth.

RELATIONSHIPS

You are intuitive and idealistic, and your relationships should be a place of stability, patience, and honesty. By seeking out partners who are as grounded as they are self-aware, you will discover that true love builds a foundation of long-term emotional satisfaction.

Are you a Pisces born on this day? Head to page 761 to find your additional birthday guide!

WELCOME TO

PISCES
SEASON

The Journey of
FEBRUARY 19

Welcome to February 19, a social journey of spiritual contentment.

Marking the first day of the empathic Pisces season, *Flexibility* (The Number Three) asks you to let go of your rigid plans and embrace every unexpected invitation that comes your way. Whether you meet someone new or study a new subject, forget what you think you know and open your mind to the perspectives of others.

Plus, *Belonging* (Three of Cups) invites you to make the most of your relationships with the people around you. Seek out opportunities to get to know your colleagues, call a childhood friend on your lunch break, or attend that happy hour you would otherwise pass up. Revel in the joys of community and remember that life can be that much sweeter when shared with the love of others.

As you embrace this social day, *Perspective* (The World) asks you to take a step back and appreciate it all. Rather than getting lost in the minutiae of conversation, listen openly to the words of others and find peace in the diversity of the human experience. Remember, you don't have to agree with everyone today, but there's always more to discover if you're open to seeing the big picture.

JUST FOR TODAY

TODAY'S MANTRA
I will take a step back and appreciate the diversity of others.

TODAY'S RITUAL
Text three close friends, from varying walks of life, and ask them a question you've always been too shy to ask. That's it! See where the conversation takes you.

TODAY'S JOURNAL PROMPT
What friend, colleague, or companion truly enriches my life experience?

BORN ON THIS DAY

NICOLAUS COPERNICUS, Polish mathematician and astronomer who theorized that planets revolve around the sun

MILLIE BOBBY BROWN, English actor

"Then you must teach my daughter this same lesson. How to lose your innocence but not your hope. How to laugh forever."—**AMY TAN**, American author

The Journey of Those Born on
FEBRUARY 19

You were born of intuitive brilliance and personal magnificence that can unintentionally steal the spotlight from others. You will have to find emotional fulfillment in shining your light on others, as your journey is one of connection, community, and personal contentment.

Early on in your journey, you will meet your fun-loving guide, *Flexibility* (The Number Three). *Flexibility* calls you away from your penchant for independence and isolation and toward a path of open-minded connectedness. You will meet *Flexibility* in times of rethinking, when the words and wisdom of others strike a chord with you and your perspective begins to shift. If you can remain humble enough to learn from the world around you, *Flexibility* teaches your mind how to run free.

If you choose this curious path, you will meet your loving teacher, *Belonging* (Three of Cups). *Belonging* knows that life is most enriching when filled with the laughter and joy of loving companions, encouraging you to be a lifelong team player. You will meet *Belonging* in moments of true belonging, when your power is deeply valued and seen by others.

By answering these calls for connection, you will discover the importance of *Perspective* (The World). *Perspective* knows how wild yet short life is, inspiring you time and again to take a step back and witness all the magic and wonder you have experienced. You will meet *Perspective* at great personal milestones, when you can't help but pause and soak in appreciation for it all. If you can remember to always come back to gratitude, *Perspective* will make a wise soul out of you.

PISCES
RULER: NEPTUNE

PURPOSE
To appreciate the grand emotional adventure of life, love, and belonging.

RELATIONSHIPS

You are independent and highly intuitive, and your relationships should be a place of freedom and social expansion. By seeking out partners who are as much of a friend to you as they are a lover, you will discover that true love helps you build a sense of community.

The Journey of
FEBRUARY 20

W elcome to February 20, an emotionally grounded journey of self-respect.
Discipline (The Number Four) asks you to approach this day with your feet firmly planted in reality. Drink your morning cup of coffee or tea and plan out a thorough to-do list that you can strategically execute throughout today. Amidst the dreamiest time of Pisces season, get grounded in the reliability of hard work and integrity.

You'll need this sense of safety, as *Reflection* (Four of Cups) requires you to reevaluate the projects, relationships, and ideas you have been pouring your heart into. Preference emotional discernment over burnout, and don't be afraid to say "no" to the things in your life that are weighing you down. If it's time to walk away, your gut will let you know.

All this personal restraint offers you the greater lessons of *Self-mastery* (The Emperor). Your sense of integrity runs deep, which means you should act from a place of leadership as you practice maturity with the world around you. Rather than getting caught up in the whims of passion, harness the power of emotional regulation today, and lead by example.

———————————◯———————————

JUST FOR TODAY

TODAY'S MANTRA
I will be the objective and humble leader I always needed.

TODAY'S RITUAL
Get clear on exactly what you're feeling. Look up a list of different emotions, and if you are able, print it out or save it to your phone. Circle or write down the feelings that resonate with you the most today, and practice mindfulness throughout the day.

TODAY'S JOURNAL PROMPT
Who in my life or in history is a living example of emotional maturity?

———————————◯———————————

BORN ON THIS DAY

KURT COBAIN, American singer-songwriter and member of Nirvana

ANSEL ADAMS, American landscape photographer

"You can't master your future if you're still a slave to your past."—**RIHANNA**, Barbadian singer-songwriter

The Journey of Those Born on
FEBRUARY 20

You were born of immersive empathy and a transcendent creativity that can take you far away from reality. You will have to keep your feet firmly planted in integrity, as your journey is one of hard work, contemplation, and self-leadership.

Early on in your journey, you will encounter your discerning guide, *Discipline* (The Number Four). *Discipline* calls you away from the ease of comfort and toward a meaningful path of personal growth. Rather than resting on your creative laurels, *Discipline* asks you time and again to back up your divine gifts with personal integrity and honor. As you put in the hours required to master your craft, *Discipline* teaches you how to walk the walk.

If you choose this grounded path, you will have to contend with your emotional teacher, *Reflection* (Four of Cups). *Reflection* knows the importance of saying "no," inspiring you to check in with your gut before saying "yes" to any big invitations. But don't let the hurt from your past cloud your decision-making process because *Reflection* encourages you to wipe the slate clean as you welcome new opportunities for growth.

> ## YOUR GUIDES
>
> *Astrology: Your Energy*
> Pisces (Neptune)
>
> *Numerology: Your Path*
> Discipline (The Number Four)
>
> *Minor Arcana: Your Lesson*
> Reflection (The Four of Cups)
>
> *Major Arcana: Your Highest Calling*
> Self-mastery (The Emperor)

And if you integrate these lessons, you will learn to embody the power of *Self-mastery* (The Emperor). *Self-mastery* understands how intense yet unpredictable emotions can be, inspiring you to self-regulate through awareness and discernment. By never getting carried too far away from your moral values by the spells of passion, *Self-mastery* teaches you how to lead a life worthy of respect.

PISCES
RULER: NEPTUNE

PURPOSE
To harness the power of emotion through self-leadership.

RELATIONSHIPS

You are harmonious and romantic, and your relationships should be a place of grounded respect and healthy boundaries. By seeking out partners whose words match their actions, you will discover that true love is born of earned trust.

The Journey of
FEBRUARY 21

Welcome to February 21, a heartfelt journey toward self-knowledge.

As you look for where to channel the emotive qualities of Pisces season, *Courage* (The Number Five) asks you to take the risk of vulnerability. Whether it be telling a close friend how you feel or sharing a piece of art with the internet, opt for acts of personal bravery over playing it cool. Show the world who you are and what you believe.

But don't get lost in *Grief* (Five of Cups). Just because people may not respond to your vulnerability in the way you hoped or anticipated does not mean your moment of vulnerability was a failure. Avoid wallowing in regret or morbid reflection and keep your head up as you find satisfaction in the radical work of honesty. As long as you are true to yourself, you will be a success.

If you can maintain this emotional maturity, you'll embrace the power of *Wisdom* (The Hierophant). By courageously sharing your perspective while respecting others' right to disagree, you'll practice deep humility. You can be both the teacher and the student, the performer and the critic, and in the process, discover the depth of knowledge available to you.

JUST FOR TODAY

TODAY'S MANTRA
I will share my heart while listening to the hearts of others.

TODAY'S RITUAL
Draw on the calming powers of chamomile tea. And if you have access to it, add some rose water to the tea to add even more healing properties. Sip the tea and mindfully repeat, "I am worthy of love and understanding."

TODAY'S JOURNAL PROMPT
What historical fears do I have around emotional rejection?

BORN ON THIS DAY

NINA SIMONE, American singer and civil rights activist

ELLIOT PAGE, Canadian actor

"Freedom is not a state; it is an act. It is not some enchanted garden perched high on a distant plateau where we can finally sit down and rest. Freedom is the continuous action we all must take, and each generation must do its part to create an even more fair, more just society."—JOHN LEWIS, American politician and prominent civil rights leader

The Journey of Those Born on
FEBRUARY 21

You were born of creative ingenuity and an emotional wisdom that can put you in a perpetual position of authority. You will have to find the freedom in not having all the answers, as your journey is one of vulnerability, self-accountability, and higher consciousness.

Early on in your journey, you will run into your unbounded guide, *Courage* (The Number Five). *Courage* calls you away from a life of aimless dreaming and toward a path of personal authenticity. You will meet *Courage* in moments of profound visibility, when you choose to reveal your emotions to the world around you and are met with grand applause from the universe itself.

But if you choose this daring path, you will have to contend with *Grief* (Five of Cups). It's difficult when others do not react to vulnerability in the way you hoped, forcing you to heal the parts of you that are left in pain by the harshness of your critics. But if you can accept that a life of truth will always come with its own bag of trolls, *Grief* teaches you how to grow a thick skin of self-love.

By answering these calls for bravery, *Wisdom* (The Hierophant) will ask you to find your divine place as both the teacher and the student. *Wisdom* asks you to discover what true humility looks like by finding your voice while remaining open enough to absorb the knowledge of others. You will meet *Wisdom* in the ah-ha moments of enlightenment, when you come to realize there is no one-size-fits-all answer to life's greatest questions. If you can find the freedom in not knowing, *Wisdom* helps you uncover your own personal truth.

YOUR GUIDES

Astrology: Your Energy
Pisces (Neptune)

Numerology: Your Path
Courage (The Number Five)

Minor Arcana: Your Lesson
Grief (The Five of Cups)

Major Arcana: Your Highest Calling
Wisdom (The Hierophant)

PISCES
RULER: NEPTUNE

PURPOSE
To realize that there is no singular truth, but limitless personal truths.

RELATIONSHIPS

You are dreamy and at times flighty, yet your relationships should be a place of radical self-revealing. By seeking out partners who are as honest with themselves as they are with you, you will discover that true love inspires you to be completely true to yourself.

The Journey of
FEBRUARY 22

W elcome to February 22, a sincere journey of love and connection.

To complement the compassionate nature of Pisces season, *Devotion* (The Number Six) asks you to lead generously with your heart today. Send a love note to your partner, lend a financial hand to someone on the street, or buy the coffee of the person behind you in line. Prioritize empathetic acts of service over self-serving motives.

To add to the sweetness of today, *Nostalgia* (Six of Cups) invites you to take a trip down memory lane. What do you still adore from your past? Whether it is watching an old childhood movie or reminiscing about fun times with your family, remember the best from the past so you can manifest it in the present.

Besides, *Choice* (The Lovers) knows that happiness is something to seek. Make conscious decisions to nurture your psychological health, rather than getting stuck in self-destructive patterns and feelings. In each moment today, choose to fill your cup with supportive relationships and creatively fulfilling projects, and walk away from those that are no longer serving your best interests.

JUST FOR TODAY

TODAY'S MANTRA
I will fill up my cup so I can share it with others.

TODAY'S JOURNAL PROMPT
What were the parts of my childhood, small or large, that I would like to integrate into my present life?

TODAY'S RITUAL
Gather a piece of rose quartz or simply start with an open heart. Place your hand over your heart and conjure your favorite childhood memory. Meditate on this memory throughout the day, and channel its energy into everything you do.

BORN ON THIS DAY

THILLAIYADI VALLIAMMAI, South African Tamilian who worked with Mahatma Gandhi to implement nonviolent methods to fight the apartheid regime

STEVE IRWIN, Australian naturalist and television personality

"I am glad that I paid so little attention to good advice; had I abided by it I might have been saved from some of my most valuable mistakes."—EDNA ST. VINCENT MILLAY, American lyrical poet and playwright

The Journey of Those Born on
FEBRUARY 22

Y ou were born of empathic leadership and an emotional restraint that can block others from knowing what you need most. You will have to shed old protective coping mechanisms to reveal your heart, as your journey is one of divine service, joy, and emotional fulfillment.

Early on in your journey, you will discover your tender guide, *Devotion* (The Number Six). *Devotion* calls you away from the mundanity of labor and toward a path of heartfelt service. By aiming to make the world a better place through any means possible, *Devotion* teaches you that a life of meaning is spent in a deep state of generosity.

If you choose this purposeful path, *Nostalgia* (Six of Cups) asks you to fill your cup in the present by reconnecting with the joy of the past. You will experience *Nostalgia* in moments of remembering, when you smile in recognition of the happiness attached to the past. If you can integrate the sweetness of the past into every moment, *Nostalgia* helps you create everlasting emotional contentment.

By answering these calls for emotional meaning, you will uncover the sacred knowledge of *Choice* (The Lovers). The most important relationship you have is the one you have with yourself, so work on creating a deep and respectful sense of internal loyalty. You will meet *Choice* in moments of self-love, when you either embrace or walk away from something to serve your best emotional interest. If you can believe that you are inherently enough, *Choice* teaches you how to love yourself unconditionally.

YOUR GUIDES

Astrology: Your Energy
Pisces (Neptune)

Numerology: Your Path
Devotion (The Number Six)

Minor Arcana: Your Lesson
Nostalgia (The Six of Cups)

Major Arcana: Your Highest Calling
Choice (The Lovers)

PISCES
RULER: NEPTUNE

PURPOSE
To love yourself in order to truly love others.

RELATIONSHIPS

You are emotionally contained, yet your relationships should be a place of boundless love. By seeking out partners who give their heart as generously as you give yours, you will discover true love never holds back due to pride or fear.

The Journey of
FEBRUARY 23

Welcome to February 23, an earnest journey toward self-progress.

Despite the changing tides of Pisces season, *Commitment* (The Number Seven) asks you to devote yourself completely to the causes that mean the most to you today. It is not a call for flighty promises or fair-weather friendship, but instead a crucial time to align with the people and projects that speak to your soul. Show the world your conviction.

But be careful what you wish for. *Illusion* (Seven of Cups) warns against fantasy-based thinking, so get clear on what the healthiest choice is for you in the long run. If the spells of romance or the allure of prestige is clouding your vision today, take a break from dreaming and call your most straightforward friend to get their two cents on the matter. A bit of reality is needed.

And if you answer these stern calls, *Evolution* (The Chariot) invites you to climb new heights of personal progress. Level up in your life by saying "yes" to the invitations that propel your life forward. Whether it be taking the next step in your partnership or asking for a promotion at work, you are ready to move onward and upward.

JUST FOR TODAY

TODAY'S MANTRA
I will take myself, my relationships, and my future seriously today.

TODAY'S JOURNAL PROMPT
What am I ready to get serious about in my life?

TODAY'S RITUAL
Draw on the potent and sobering power of mint. Whether you brew fresh mint tea or slowly inhale peppermint oil, repeat the chant, "I will clear the illusion for the sake of my self-evolution."

BORN ON THIS DAY

LUCY GODIVA WOODCOCK, Australian pacifist, teacher, trade union official, and women's activist

AMSCHEL ROTHSCHILD, German banker and the founder of the Rothschild banking dynasty

"Now is the accepted time, not tomorrow, not some more convenient season. It is today that our best work can be done and not some future day or future year. It is today that we fit ourselves for the greater usefulness of tomorrow."—W. E. B. DU BOIS, American civil rights activist, writer, and founder of the NAACP

The Journey of Those Born on
FEBRUARY 23

Y ou were born of creative freedom and an intuitive wisdom that can make it hard to admit when you are wrong. You will have to discover your capacity for humility, as your journey is one of responsibility, fantasy-breaking, and deep progress.

Early on in your journey, you will meet your deliberate guide, *Commitment* (The Number Seven). *Commitment* steers you away from the distractions of emotional drama and toward a purposeful path of self-investment. You will meet *Commitment* in moments of active decision-making, when you choose to point your arrow straight at the heart of what matters to you most. If you can keep your eye on the prize, *Commitment* ensures you hit a bull's-eye.

But if you choose this honest path, look out for *Illusion* (Seven of Cups). You will meet *Illusion* in moments of wishful thinking, when you think you have found the quick solution to your problems, but it is simply a figment of your imagination. Not everything you wish for in life is in your best interest, and *Illusion* forces you to separate self-destructive fantasy from true possibility.

By answering these calls for emotional sobriety, you will discover true fulfillment within *Evolution* (The Chariot). *Evolution* knows how far you can grow, encouraging you to do the legwork required while aligning your vision with the winds of fate. You will meet *Evolution* in the pinch-me moments of personal progress, when you can't quite believe how far you've come. If you can hurl your will and your life in the direction of purpose, you'll soar to new heights of self-actualization.

PISCES
RULER: NEPTUNE

PURPOSE
To channel your will toward a realistic and meaningful purpose.

RELATIONSHIPS

You are emotionally dramatic yet deeply sincere, and your relationships should be a place of grounded commitment. By seeking out partners who are as true to their word as you are to the relationship, you will discover true love is the slow building of trust.

The Journey of
FEBRUARY 24

W elcome to February 24, an introspective journey of personal strength.

To coincide with the emotionality of Pisces season, *Power* (The Number Eight) calls you inward to self-reflect and get honest about who you are. Quiet the noise and opinions of others today as you search through the dark and unseen corners of your emotional makeup. Discover the complexity of your soul, and if you feel called, share it with someone you trust.

As you do this digging, *Disappointment* (Eight of Cups) encourages you to walk away from the emotional binds that are keeping you stuck and unfulfilled. It can be difficult to cut ties with the people, projects, or ideas that you once devoted your heart to, but know that there is something bigger and better waiting for you on the other side of grief.

If you can hold yourself through this temporary withdrawal, *Resilience* (Strength) reminds you of your innate power. Rather than getting carried away with troublesome emotions or fits of rage, tap into the endless divine resources that live within you. If you can harness these feelings and channel them into personal progress, you'll build a sense of spiritual fortitude.

―――○―――

JUST FOR TODAY

TODAY'S MANTRA
I can handle the necessary emotional changes that come up today.

TODAY'S JOURNAL PROMPT
What emotional bonds (to people, places, or beliefs) are no longer making me happy?

TODAY'S RITUAL
Run a very hot shower, letting the steam fog up your bathroom mirror. Turn off the water, and, using your finger, write your deepest truth in the fog on the mirror. As you wipe it away, look yourself in the eye in self-recognition.

―――○―――

BORN ON THIS DAY

WILHELM GRIMM, German lexicographer and author, and one of the Brothers Grimm

GIOVANNI PICO DELLA MIRANDOLA, Italian Renaissance nobleman and philosopher

"Your time is limited, so don't waste it living someone else's life. Don't be trapped by dogma—which is living with the results of other people's thinking. Don't let the noise of others' opinions drown out your own inner voice."—STEVE JOBS, American computer entrepreneur and co-founder of Apple

The Journey of Those Born on
FEBRUARY 24

You were born of spiritual generosity and an empathy that you extend toward others far more easily than you do to yourself. You will have to heal from the inside out, as your journey is one of self-acceptance, emotional boundaries, and internal strength.

Early on in your journey, you will meet your enigmatic guide, *Power* (The Number Eight). *Power* draws you away from the mundanity of work and toward a path of radical self-compassion. Nothing that is true is superficial, so drop the masks and facades that keep you from your true, authentic nature. *Power* asks you time and again to go to the places that scare you, helping you release the shame that holds you back from loving yourself.

If you choose this revealing path, *Disappointment* (Eight of Cups) will ask you to walk away from the emotional bonds that are no longer fulfilling their promises. You will meet *Disappointment* in moments of withdrawal, when you have surrendered the relationship, idea, or identity that no longer fills your cup. If you can confront these endings with clarity and intention, *Disappointment* offers you greater emotional contentment.

By embracing these tough emotional calls, you will uncover the power of *Resilience* (Strength). What doesn't kill you makes you stronger, so you'll need to practice believing in yourself no matter what. You will meet *Resilience* in moments of emotional fortitude, when the worst has happened and yet you find yourself standing on stronger spiritual ground because of it. If you can actively reinforce these emotional muscles, you'll learn what you are made of.

PISCES
RULER: NEPTUNE

PURPOSE
To find strength in the endless power that lives within.

RELATIONSHIPS

You are dreamy and idealistic in matters of the heart, yet your relationships should be a place of radical truth. By seeking out partners who are as authentic with themselves as they are with the world around them, you will discover that true love comes from dropping your mask.

The Journey of
FEBRUARY 25

Welcome to February 25, a fulfilling journey of self-trust.

Experience (The Number Nine) invites you to grow in your understanding and effectiveness. Open a book that feels out of your league or seek the knowledge of someone well beyond your years. It's a day to take on the subjects and beliefs that are most foreign to you, so embrace your role as life's greatest student.

But rather than getting lost in the dreaminess of Pisces season, make sure to savor the present moment. *Gratitude* (Nine of Cups) asks you to look at the world around you and appreciate even the smallest of gifts. Whether it be enjoying the breeze on your face or indulging in a scrumptious feast, actively try to see the most of it.

But above all else today, trust yourself. *Instinct* (The Hermit) calls you inward to the place of divine reason, so make the big decisions from your gut today. If at any point you are lost in the noise of society, find a place of deep solitude so that you can hear the voice of wisdom that is forever available and waiting for you to listen.

JUST FOR TODAY

TODAY'S MANTRA
I will learn and grow with the world around me, while deeply trusting myself.

TODAY'S JOURNAL PROMPT
What am I most emotionally grateful for today?

TODAY'S RITUAL
Seek out isolation. No matter how much you have on your plate, find nine minutes in your day to sit down and spend time alone, in whatever way your intuition guides you.

BORN ON THIS DAY

JAMEELA JAMIL, English television actor and activist

PIERRE-AUGUSTE RENOIR, French artist and leader in the development of Impressionism

"Happiest is he who expects no happiness from others. Love delights and glorifies in giving, not receiving. So learn to love and give, and not to expect anything from others."—MEHER BABA, Indian spiritual master

The Journey of Those Born on
FEBRUARY 25

You were born of creative ambition and a fierce loyalty that can keep you from embracing new people and places. You will have to search for more than meets the eye, as your journey is one of seeking, perspective, and intuitive work.

Early on in your journey, you will be called away from consistent, linear growth and toward a winding path of *Experience* (The Number Nine). *Experience* asks you to be an eternal student of life, forever questioning and considering the things beyond your scope of understanding. By being courageous enough to pursue the unknowns around you, *Experience* soars to new heights of consciousness.

And when you're up there, be sure to reach for *Gratitude* (Nine of Cups). *Gratitude* asks you to keep your perspective on the good, pushing you to acknowledge the many gifts that life has bestowed upon you. You will meet *Gratitude* in moments of awe, when you take a step back and see just how miraculous this world of wonder can be.

> ## YOUR GUIDES
>
> *Astrology: Your Energy*
> Pisces (Neptune)
>
> *Numerology: Your Path*
> Experience (The Number Nine)
>
> *Minor Arcana: Your Lesson*
> Gratitude (The Nine of Cups)
>
> *Major Arcana: Your Highest Calling*
> Instinct (The Hermit)

By answering these calls for growth, you will come to rely on the power of *Instinct* (The Hermit). *Instinct* asks you to consult the voice of intuition that lives within you, humbly guiding you toward a life of authentic purpose. You will meet *Instinct* in moments when, on paper, you are lost, and yet something profound within you still ushers you to where you are meant to go. If you can listen to this divine intelligence with trust, *Instinct* lights your way through the darkest of times.

PISCES
RULER: NEPTUNE

PURPOSE
To grow inward to a place of divine self-trust.

RELATIONSHIPS

You are seriously romantic and romantically serious, yet your relationships should be a place of expansive wonder. By seeking out partners who never cease to amaze you with their depth of character, you will discover that true love brings you endlessly new perspectives on life.

The Journey of
FEBRUARY 26

Welcome to February 26, a fearlessly emotional journey of karmic destiny. Despite the passive nature of Pisces season, *Autonomy* (The Number One) asks you to approach this day with complete self-confidence and passion. Trust your gut as you lead yourself through your responsibilities, relying completely on your internal power rather than waiting for permission from others.

But when you can, *Vulnerability* (Ace of Cups) asks you to take a step back and find gratitude for the life that you have nurtured. Whether it be the family you have created or the dreams you have built, look for the emotional good that exists in every moment. Perhaps, for today, personal fulfillment is just a small shift in perspective.

You'll need this positive view, as *Impermanence* (Wheel of Fortune) pushes you to find meaning in both the highs and the lows of the day. If your stock is up, share it generously with the world around you, holding nothing back due to scarcity. And if your day isn't going according to plan, thank the universe for the unseen gifts that are right around the corner. Luck is fleeting, but happiness is a choice.

JUST FOR TODAY

TODAY'S MANTRA
Gratitude lies in perspective.

TODAY'S JOURNAL PROMPT
What times in my life did I hit an emotional bottom that ended up leading me somewhere better?

TODAY'S RITUAL
Go to the ocean (or find a video on the internet) and watch the tides go in and out. Meditate on this image, and repeat the phrase in your mind, "Thank you for everything you've given me and everything you've taken away."

BORN ON THIS DAY

JOHNNY CASH, American singer-songwriter

ERYKAH BADU, American singer-songwriter, record producer, and actor

"To put everything in balance is good, to put everything in harmony is better."—VICTOR HUGO, French poet, novelist, and dramatist of the Romantic movement

The Journey of Those Born on
FEBRUARY 26

You were born of deep intuition and a limitless power that can make it hard to accept what you cannot control. You will have to learn to roll with the tides of life, as your journey is one of independence, emotional fulfillment, and karmic fate.

Early on in your journey, you will encounter your fearless guide, *Autonomy* (The Number One). *Autonomy* beckons you away from the spells of emotional reflection and toward a path of action and innovation. By only following the beat of your own intuition, you'll learn how to carve out a life that is custom-made for your creative talents.

If you choose this road less traveled, you will meet your emotional teacher, *Vulnerability* (Ace of Cups). It is easy to never be completely satisfied with life as it is, but *Vulnerability* asks you time and again to take a step back and witness the emotional wholeness that exists within the love around you. If you can practice deep gratitude for life on life's terms, you'll realize how much you have been given.

By answering these calls for courage, *Impermanence* (Wheel of Fortune) reminds you that luck is fleeting and finite, but love is endless. *Impermanence* teaches you how to appreciate the highs and lows that come with each season, opening your eyes to a greater perspective on what this journey is all about. You will meet *Impermanence* in moments of karmic trust, when on paper you may be down on your luck, but you know in your gut that the next best thing is waiting for you just around the bend.

PISCES
RULER: NEPTUNE

PURPOSE
*To fearlessly believe in
the perfection of fate.*

RELATIONSHIPS

You are deep and introspective, and your relationships should be a place of joy, peace, and emotional wholeness. By seeking out partners who fill your heart's cup so full that you cannot ask for anything more, you will discover that with true love, any outside success is just a cherry on top of a beautiful life.

The Journey of
FEBRUARY 27

Welcome to February 27, a harmonious journey toward emotional justice.

To go with the flow of Pisces season, *Balance* (The Number Two) asks you to take a slow and steady approach to this day. There's no need to overwork or overextend yourself; instead, try to practice a certain level of calm as you accomplish your responsibilities. And if you're ever overwhelmed, seek out a romantic or platonic partner to help you share the load.

Besides, *Worthiness* (Two of Cups) asks you to remember your value in relationship with others. Come to the table as equals with the ones you love, advocating for your needs while also staying open and available to their perspective. Seek out equality in your exchanges with others, prioritizing the people who aim to meet you halfway.

You'll need this self-confidence, as *Truth* (Justice) asks you to get clear on your moral compass and stand up for what you believe in today. Whether it be sticking up for someone you love or volunteering for a cause that is meaningful to you, practice bravery over keeping the peace. There are no black-and-white answers to life's toughest questions, so fight for what is true to you.

JUST FOR TODAY

TODAY'S MANTRA
I will peacefully share the harmonious truth that lives within me.

TODAY'S RITUAL
Fill a cup with the drink of your choice, ideally one that evokes positive memories. Drink, and when the cup is empty, refill it, reminding yourself that there is always more to receive.

TODAY'S JOURNAL PROMPT
With whom in my life do I share similar moral values?

BORN ON THIS DAY

ELIZABETH TAYLOR, English American actor, businesswoman, and humanitarian

ALICE HAMILTON, American physician, research scientist, and author

"And now that you don't have to be perfect, you can be good."—JOHN STEINBECK, American author and Nobel Prize winner

The Journey of Those Born on
FEBRUARY 27

You were born of creative intuition and an otherworldly mind that can lead you to extreme thinking. You will have to discover the truth that hangs in the balance, as your journey is one of tranquility, reciprocity, and divine justice.

Early on in your journey, you will meet your easy-going guide, *Balance* (The Number Two). *Balance* calls you away from emotional illusion and toward a grounded path of partnership and peace. Rather than burning out on the hamster wheel of desire, *Balance* invites you time and again to find happiness in the present moment with the people you love. Remember, life is only as complicated as you make it.

If you choose this intimate path, *Worthiness* (Two of Cups) will ask you if you are getting what you need from your closest partnerships. *Worthiness* reminds you how important it is to show up entirely as yourself in relationship with others so you can show them how much you value yourself. You will meet *Worthiness* in the partners who reciprocate your generosity and who appreciate the wonder of your authentic being.

> ### YOUR GUIDES
>
> *Astrology: Your Energy*
> Pisces (Neptune)
>
> *Numerology: Your Path*
> Balance (The Number Two)
>
> *Minor Arcana: Your Lesson*
> Worthiness (The Two of Cups)
>
> *Major Arcana: Your Highest Calling*
> Truth (Justice)

By answering these calls for emotional healing, you will awaken to the power of *Truth* (Justice). *Truth* highlights the unreliability of opinion, encouraging you time and again to come up with your own set of values and ethics so that you can navigate the messiness of this human experience. You will meet *Truth* in moments of personal justice-seeking, when you find the clarity of consciousness to call out the imbalances in the world that you would like to see change.

PISCES
RULER: NEPTUNE

PURPOSE
To calmly and fairly stand up for the truth.

RELATIONSHIPS

You are a lonely dreamer at heart, yet your relationships should be your place of complete companionship. By seeking out partners who are your true equal and who always aim to meet you halfway, you will discover the long-term success of balanced love.

The Journey of
FEBRUARY 28

Welcome to February 28, a sociable journey that teaches you how to receive.

To complement the mutable waters of Pisces season, *Flexibility* (The Number Three) asks you to go with the flow today. By staying open to the invitations that come your way, even if they're outside your comfort zone, you'll learn by doing. So say "yes" to that happy hour, say "yes" to that first date, or say "yes" to that new project.

And make sure to incorporate *Belonging* (Three of Cups). Favor comradery of any kind, whether it be teaming up with your colleagues or reconnecting with your childhood friends. Look for ways that you can create new communities around you today, and don't be afraid to merge some of your social circles and see how they mix.

Abundance (The Empress) asks you to do your best to receive every blessing that comes your way today, remembering how deeply worthy you are of true happiness. If these positive emotions feel overwhelming at any point, take a moment to sit alone with yourself and practice gratitude for the people around you. When you're ready, step back out in the wonder of this day and celebrate the joy that surrounds you.

JUST FOR TODAY

TODAY'S MANTRA
I will get out of my comfort zone of loneliness and say "yes" to happiness.

TODAY'S JOURNAL PROMPT
Which of my friends would I like to get to know each other?

TODAY'S RITUAL
Today works best in threes. Find three of something you adore—three roses, three crystals, three pieces of chocolate. Whatever they are, keep them with you throughout the day, and when you are feeling low on energy, use them to come back to the present moment.

BORN ON THIS DAY

FRANK GEHRY, Canadian-born American architect

JULIA SEBUTINDE, Ugandan judge and first African woman to sit on the International Court of Justice

"Do not let either the medical authorities or the politicians mislead you. Find out what the facts are, and make your own decisions about how to live a happy life and how to work for a better world."—LINUS PAULING, American chemist and peace activist

The Journey of Those Born on
FEBRUARY 28

Y ou were born of loner like creativity and an emotional self-reliance that can keep you stuck in isolation. You will have to break out of your shell to find the connection you need most, as your journey is one of open-mindedness, community, and true joy.

Early on in your journey, you will encounter your airy friend, *Flexibility* (The Number Three). *Flexibility* calls you away from the comforts of isolation and toward a path full of connection and understanding. You will meet *Flexibility* when you thought things would go one way but fate and friendship brought you to a new destination beyond your wildest dreams.

If you choose this connected path, *Belonging* (Three of Cups) will encourage you to reveal your true colors to those you love most. You will meet *Belonging* in the warmth of community, when the adoration from your dearest friends holds you through even the toughest of times. If you can place deep value in your connections with others, *Belonging* ensures they will always have your back.

By embracing these calls for expansion, you will

YOUR GUIDES

Astrology: Your Energy
Pisces (Neptune)

Numerology: Your Path
Flexibility (The Number Three)

Minor Arcana: Your Lesson
Belonging (The Three of Cups)

Major Arcana: Your Highest Calling
Abundance (The Empress)

open yourself to *Abundance* (The Empress). *Abundance* encourages you to enjoy life, soaking in every blessing that comes your way. You will meet *Abundance* in moments of overwhelming happiness, when you must steady your heart so that you can truly appreciate and witness the beauty that surrounds you. If you can stay present and know that you are worthy of this grace, *Abundance* teaches you how to pay it forward.

———————————————◯———————————————

PISCES
RULER: NEPTUNE

PURPOSE
To let friendly curiosity blossom into true emotional happiness.

RELATIONSHIPS

You are a passionate and independent dreamer, but your relationships should be a place of community and curiosity. By seeking out partners with whom you can share both your greatest friends and your greatest ideas, you will discover true love expands your perspective as well as your sense of happiness.

The Journey of
FEBRUARY 29

W elcome to February 29, an emotionally mature journey of self-respect.
As you contend with the varying emotions of Pisces season, *Discipline* (The Number Four) asks you to narrow your focus to the tangible tasks at hand. Approach your day from a place of structure and restraint, grounding yourself in the humble work that can't wait until tomorrow. If your feelings get the best of you, attend to a mundane task like folding the laundry as you process these emotions.

Besides, *Reflection* (Four of Cups) asks you to reevaluate what you have been giving your heart to. Whether it's a relationship or a project, say "no" to what is no longer filling your cup so that you can say a resounding "yes" to something better.

If you are willing to answer these grounded calls, you'll step into a new level of *Self-mastery* (The Emperor). To harness the power of emotion is a rare and coveted skill, so bring awareness to your feelings without letting them get the best of you today. If you are feeling overwhelmed at any point, take a deep, calming breath and listen to the leader who lives within.

JUST FOR TODAY

TODAY'S MANTRA

I will feel my feelings without letting them overpower me.

TODAY'S RITUAL

Pick a mundane task, like vacuuming, and put your entire focus and effort into this simple work. As you do, repeat the chant, "I am responsible for my actions, and I choose to do things to the utmost of my ability."

TODAY'S JOURNAL PROMPT

What are ways I can ground myself in my body when my emotions are getting the best of me?

BORN ON THIS DAY

ANN LEE, founding leader of the United Society of Believers in Christ's Second Appearing, or the Shakers

KOREDE BELLO, Nigerian singer-songwriter

"I did not consciously go after dance. It found me."—RUKMINI DEVI ARUNDALE, Indian dancer, choreographer, theosophist, and animal activist

The Journey of Those Born on
FEBRUARY 29

Y ou were born of intuitive knowledge and an empathy that can make you a sponge to the erratic feelings of others. You will have to learn to harness your feelings, as your journey is one of integrity, reevaluation, and divine leadership.

Early on in your journey, you will meet your formidable guide, *Discipline* (The Number Four). *Discipline* calls you away from the spells of emotion and toward a path of intention and purpose. By putting one foot in front of the other as you climb your way to the top of each personal mountain, *Discipline* teaches you how to transform your wildest dreams into reality.

But don't be afraid to say "no" to the things that drain you. *Reflection* (Four of Cups) encourages you to pause and reconsider where you are investing the best of you, helping you get clear on who and what is draining your emotional energy. You will meet *Reflection* in moments of necessary withdrawal, when you have closed the door on all toxic engagements and made room for better things to come.

YOUR GUIDES

Astrology: Your Energy
Pisces (Neptune)

Numerology: Your Path
Discipline (The Number Four)

Minor Arcana: Your Lesson
Reflection (The Four of Cups)

Major Arcana: Your Highest Calling
Self-mastery (The Emperor)

By answering these calls for emotional maturity, you will step into the power of *Self-mastery* (The Emperor). *Self-mastery* asks you to channel your immense empathy into personal authority, pushing you to uncharted heights of internal leadership. You will meet *Self-mastery* in moments of development, when you are able to move forward from a place of integrity despite any drama or emotional upheaval around you.

PISCES
RULER: NEPTUNE

PURPOSE
*To take a humble, spiritual approach
to self-development.*

RELATIONSHIPS

You are gentle and compassionate, and your relationships should be a place of respectful boundaries. By seeking out partners who honor your needs and have strong personal integrity, you will discover that true love comes from loving structure.

The Journey of
MARCH 1

W elcome to March 1, a humble journey toward emotional regulation.
Today, *Discipline* (The Number Four) asks you to focus on what is manageable. Whether it be drying the dishes or answering your emails, prioritize work that produces tangible results. To temper the dreaminess of Pisces season, act with integrity and intention, and make the most out of each responsibility.

You may have things you need to process while you work. *Reflection* (Four of Cups) encourages you to say "no" when possible, giving yourself the time and space to reevaluate the emotional engagements in your life. If a relationship or responsibility has been draining your cup, now is the time to decide to part ways. If you can use today to heal, tomorrow you will be ready to move forward.

Besides, *Self-mastery* (The Emperor) empowers you to be a strong leader for yourself today. By making pragmatic and mature decisions rather than emotionally reacting, this day offers you a new kind of self-confidence that is born from estimable action. Act as the protector toward yourself you always needed and begin moving toward a life that is worthy of respect.

——————————◯——————————

JUST FOR TODAY

TODAY'S MANTRA
I can make the tough objective calls that will lead me to greater emotional health.

TODAY'S JOURNAL PROMPT
How can I implement healthy boundaries with myself and others today?

TODAY'S RITUAL
Tap into the leader within. Stand in front of a mirror with your shoulders pulled slightly back, your head held high, and your feet hip width apart. Chant four times, "I know what is best for my heart."

——————————◯——————————

BORN ON THIS DAY

FRÉDÉRIC CHOPIN, Polish French pianist and composer

JUSTIN BIEBER, Canadian singer and musician

"You can't eat beauty, it doesn't sustain you. What is fundamentally beautiful is compassion, for yourself and those around you. That kind of beauty inflame[s] the heart and merchants the soul."—LUPITA NYONG'O, Kenyan Mexican actor

The Journey of Those Born on
MARCH 1

You were born of creative independence and a limitless imagination that makes reality difficult to grasp. You will have to look for the beauty within structure, as your journey is one of hard work, personal inventory, and divine order.

Early on in life, you will meet your no-nonsense guide, *Discipline* (The Number Four). *Discipline* asks you to devote yourself seriously to this lifetime, earnestly following the path of personal integrity rather than personal satisfaction. You will meet *Discipline* in the things that don't come naturally to you, when you are forced to rely on humble daily practice to achieve your next goal.

If you choose this grounding path, you will have to heal your historical wounds with *Reflection* (Four of Cups). You will meet *Reflection* in the events of the past that hold you back from fully embracing the new opportunities coming your way. Rather than holding on to old stories that keep you trapped in fear and resentment, uncover, discover, and discard them so that you can make room for hope.

YOUR GUIDES

Astrology: Your Energy
Pisces (Neptune, The Moon)

Numerology: Your Path
Discipline (The Number Four)

Minor Arcana: Your Lesson
Reflection (The Four of Cups)

Major Arcana: Your Highest Calling
Self-mastery (The Emperor)

By answering these calls for personal accountability, you will meet your most important teacher, *Self-mastery* (The Emperor). *Self-mastery* empowers you to harness the unreliability of emotion, neither denying nor giving in to its force, so that you can act from a place of humble strength. If you can consistently and persistently take inventory and responsibility for your feelings, *Self-mastery* brings you a life of profound honor.

———————————————————○———————————————————

PISCES
RULERS: NEPTUNE, THE MOON

PURPOSE
*To build self-trust through
estimable action.*

RELATIONSHIPS

You are inspired and independent, and your relationships should be a place of emotional grounding and healthy boundaries. By seeking out partners who are as humble as they are reliable, you will discover that true love can turn your wildest hopes into a sustainable reality.

The Journey of
MARCH 2

Welcome to March 2, a daring journey toward higher consciousness.

To channel the creative waters of Pisces season, *Courage* (The Number Five) invites you to move out of the shadows and into the sunlight of your authentic spirit. Look for ways to express yourself and try your best not to hold anything back. You'll never know where these wild acts of bravery may take you, but more than likely, they'll end with a huge round of applause.

But be careful not to take others' reactions too personally. *Grief* (Five of Cups) warns against hypersensitivity today, encouraging you to find the infallible confidence to withstand any positive or negative public perception. If you can stay true to yourself, there will be no need to fixate on the opinions of others.

Besides, *Wisdom* (The Hierophant) knows that opinions are not facts. Trust your gut as you question outside authority and the systems that keep you from expanding into the fullest version of yourself. Use today to rebel against these limited and fear-based societal norms. If you can aim to think and feel for yourself, you can end today with a deep appreciation for the divine power that lives within.

JUST FOR TODAY

TODAY'S MANTRA
I will be courageously and unapologetically myself.

TODAY'S JOURNAL PROMPT
When did I first learn to fear my individuality?

TODAY'S RITUAL
Put pen to paper and unpack the wounds you have around vulnerability. On one page, write the times when you received negative criticism for being yourself. On the next page, write a response to that criticism from a place of self-confidence and love.

BORN ON THIS DAY

SHIDZUE KATŌ, Japanese feminist and birth control movement pioneer

LOU REED, American musician, singer-songwriter, and poet

"Today you are you! That is truer than true! There is no one alive who is you-er than you!"—DR. SEUSS, American children's author

The Journey of Those Born on
MARCH 2

You were born of empathic diplomacy and a harmonious heart that can make it uncomfortable for you to stand out. You will have to be daring enough to be yourself, as your journey is one of bravery, guts, and internal truth.

Early on in your journey, you will meet your untamed guide, *Courage* (The Number Five). *Courage* calls you away from a life of people-pleasing and toward a path of radical vulnerability. You will meet *Courage* in moments of emotional unveiling, when you take off the masks that protect you from rejection to reveal the true nature that exists underneath. If you can love yourself more than people's idea of you, you'll pursue a life of authenticity.

But if you choose this daring path, you will have to contend with *Grief* (Five of Cups). You will meet *Grief* in moments when your confidence feels low and you aren't certain that your bravery was worth all the trouble. Although it's easy to view vulnerability as a failure when people don't react as you hoped, if you can forget about the outcome, you'll find the emotional satisfaction that comes from being real.

YOUR GUIDES

Astrology: Your Energy
Pisces (Neptune, The Moon)

Numerology: Your Path
Courage (The Number Five)

Minor Arcana: Your Lesson
Grief (The Five of Cups)

Major Arcana: Your Highest Calling
Wisdom (The Hierophant)

By answering these wild calls, you will tap into the divine realm of *Wisdom* (The Hierophant). *Wisdom* knows that truth is subjective, encouraging you time and again to believe in your gut over the fair-weather preachers and false prophets. You will meet *Wisdom* in moments of personal resolve, when you are so aligned with your intuition that no one, and nothing, can sway you from your truth.

PISCES
RULERS: NEPTUNE, THE MOON

PURPOSE
*To courageously fight for the truth
that lives within.*

RELATIONSHIPS

You are gentle and accommodating, but your relationships should be a place of radical authenticity and individuality. By seeking out partners who are completely themselves and who encourage you to be the same, you will discover that true love is never judgmental.

The Journey of
MARCH 3

Welcome to March 3, a service-oriented journey toward unconditional love.

Devotion (The Number Six) asks you to use your energy to help others today. Look for ways, big and small, to generously give your gifts to an individual or a greater cause. There's no need to expect any return on your efforts because the universe will repay you plenty with deep emotional satisfaction.

But try to center your efforts around topics of the past. To coincide with the emotive nature of Pisces season, *Nostalgia* (Six of Cups) invites you to take a trip down memory lane today so that you can tap into a deeper sense of meaning in the work that you do. Whether it be checking in with a childhood friend who is down on their luck or stopping by your elementary school and seeing if they need any help, find your purpose from the past.

In general today, make a *Choice* (The Lovers) to put your heart first. Love is always an option, but unfortunately, love is rarely something that our society champions. So aim to be a spiritual example for others, living from the soul and acting in accordance with your deepest sense of emotional integrity.

JUST FOR TODAY

TODAY'S MANTRA
Love is the only guiding force I need today.

TODAY'S RITUAL
Grab a rose quartz or some object that symbolizes love to you and lie on your back in a starfish position. Put the rose quartz or other object directly over your heart as you send loving-kindness to those you care about most.

TODAY'S JOURNAL PROMPT
Who or what helped fill my emotional cup as a kid, and how can I pay that forward?

BORN ON THIS DAY

BEATRICE WOOD, American artist and studio potter known as the "Mama of Dada"

CAMILA CABELLO, Cuban-born American singer-songwriter

"I promise I will get up every day, determined to make a difference. . . . I am ready to serve."
—TEDROS ADHANOM GHEBREYESUS, Ethiopian biologist, public health researcher, and director-general of the World Health Organization

The Journey of Those Born on
MARCH 3

You were born of intuitive intelligence and an ability to chameleon yourself to fit in that blocks you from being seen for who you truly are. You will have to show the world your heart, as your journey is one of purpose, reflection, and unconditional love.

Early on in your journey, you will meet your sincere guide, *Devotion* (The Number Six). *Devotion* calls you away from the distractions of instant gratification and toward a path of deep emotional service, nurturing your heart over your ego. By giving your time, effort, and energy generously to the people and causes that speak to your soul, you'll discover how to build a life of deep meaning.

And if you choose this generous path, *Nostalgia* (Six of Cups) will ensure you never forget where you came from. You will meet *Nostalgia* in moments of heart-warming reflection, when something in the present sparks a vivid memory of a deep and joyful experience from your past. If you can take these positive memories wherever you go, you'll integrate the sweetness of what was into the reality of what is.

> ## YOUR GUIDES
>
> *Astrology: Your Energy*
> Pisces (Neptune, The Moon)
>
> *Numerology: Your Path*
> Devotion (The Number Six)
>
> *Minor Arcana: Your Lesson*
> Nostalgia (The Six of Cups)
>
> *Major Arcana: Your Highest Calling*
> Choice (The Lovers)

By answering these calls for sincerity, you will discover the importance of *Choice* (The Lovers). Love is born from conscious action but can die out like a fire if left unattended. *Choice* encourages you to devote yourself to the deep connections in your life, especially the one that you have with yourself. If you can prioritize these matters of the heart above all else, you will never have to yearn for more.

PISCES
RULERS: NEPTUNE, THE MOON

PURPOSE
To work humbly and generously
toward a life full of love.

RELATIONSHIPS

You are a forever-evolving social butterfly, yet your relationships should be a place of unconditional support and love. By seeking out partners who love you for who you are rather than what you do, you will discover that true love is born from the heart rather than the ego.

The Journey of
MARCH 4

Welcome to March 4, a purposeful journey toward self-progress.

Commitment (The Number Seven) asks you to narrow your focus to the things that your heart belongs to today. There's no room to be flaky or a fair-weather friend, so stick to your word and show up for your responsibilities. If you find yourself overcommitted and overwhelmed, practice straightforward communication to show your respect for other people's time.

But be careful what you set your sights on. Pisces season has a way of blurring the truth, and *Illusion* (Seven of Cups) warns against fantasy-based thinking and believing. If something seems too good to be true today, it probably is. If you get lost in dreams of what could be, ground yourself by calling a no-nonsense friend who can set you back on the straight and narrow.

Besides, *Evolution* (The Chariot) has more important things for you to move toward. In the spirit of emotional progress, take a leap of faith and reveal your heart to the world around you. Whether it be taking that next step in your intimate partnership or asking for that promotion you've been coveting at work, find the strength to move forward.

JUST FOR TODAY

TODAY'S MANTRA
My grounded intuition tells me where I need to grow.

TODAY'S RITUAL
Break the spell of illusion by grabbing fresh peppermint or peppermint oil and rubbing it in your hands. As you inhale its aroma, repeat the mantra, "Dreams are divine, but fantasy is not. Please help me see the difference."

TODAY'S JOURNAL PROMPT
What fantasies are blocking me from reality right now?

BORN ON THIS DAY

ANTONIO VIVALDI, Italian Baroque violin virtuoso and composer

MARGARET OSBORNE DUPONT, American tennis player

"Be careful, think about the effect of what you say. Your words should be constructive, bring people together, not pull them apart."—MIRIAM MAKEBA, South African singer-songwriter, actor, United Nations Goodwill Ambassador, and civil rights activist

The Journey of Those Born on
MARCH 4

You were born of grounded intuition and an unconscious desire for control that can distract you from your highest purpose. You will have to learn to set your sights on the aspects of life that matter most, as your journey is one of intention, spell-breaking, and meaningful progress.

Early on in your journey, you will meet your faithful guide, *Commitment* (The Number Seven). *Commitment* calls you away from the hamster wheel of work and along a path of emotional purpose. You will meet *Commitment* in moments of intentional choice, when you walk away from the distractions in life so you can run toward the responsibilities that mean the most to you. If you can choose substance over facade, you'll discover the gifts of sincerity.

But if you take this meaningful path, you will have to contend with your lower companion, *Illusion* (Seven of Cups). You will meet *Illusion* in the shiny objects that steal your focus by igniting your imagination, beckoning you away from your higher purpose. If you can surrender to the idea that some things are simply too good to be true, *Illusion* helps you differentiate between the true and the false.

By answering these sobering callings, you will discover the divine momentum of *Evolution* (The Chariot). *Evolution* knows how far you can go, pushing you toward your ultimate potential and asking nothing of you except your sincerest of efforts. You will meet *Evolution* in moments of astounding personal progress, when you can't quite believe how miraculously your dreams are unfolding. If you can act with courage of heart, *Evolution* invites you to new heights of self-realization.

PISCES
RULERS: NEPTUNE, THE MOON

PURPOSE
To act with intention and focus as life unfolds with divine purpose.

RELATIONSHIPS

You are intuitive yet realistic, and your relationships should be a place of sincere commitment and respect. By seeking out partners who acknowledge your needs and boundaries without question, you will discover that true love is nurtured with personal integrity.

The Journey of
MARCH 5

Welcome to March 5, an introspective journey toward internal strength.

Power (The Number Eight) invites you inward to a place of radical self-honesty and vulnerability. By surrendering to the truth that lies underneath your external facades, you'll shed light on even the darkest corners of your soul. If fear comes up, welcome it and know that you are moving closer to the truth.

Pisces season can gloss over tougher realities, so prepare for some necessary *Disappointment* (Eight of Cups). With internal clarity comes unexpected revelations, so if you find yourself disillusioned with some aspect of your life today, now is the time to emotionally prepare yourself to walk away. Whether it be a long-overdue breakup or an important loss of identity, prioritize progress over stagnation.

Besides, *Resilience* (Strength) knows that you can handle anything. Tap into your deep emotional resources today as you awaken to the truth that has been calling you for some time now. By witnessing your feelings rather than giving in to their dramatic ebbs and flows, you'll strengthen your emotional muscles and recognize that the universe only gives you as much as you can handle.

JUST FOR TODAY

TODAY'S MANTRA
I can integrate any difficult truth as long as it serves my growth.

TODAY'S RITUAL
Tackle a mundane and tangible fear. Whether it be trapping a spider in your house and taking it outside or sitting alone in complete darkness, do something small but actionable around fear to tap into your internal strength.

TODAY'S JOURNAL PROMPT
What times in my life have I shown great emotional resilience?

BORN ON THIS DAY

MOMOFUKU ANDO, Taiwanese Japanese inventor of instant ramen noodles and cup noodles

CHARLES H. FULLER JR., American playwright and Pulitzer Prize winner

"Those who do not move, do not notice their chains."—ROSA LUXEMBURG, Polish Marxist philosopher, economist, anti-war activist, and revolutionary socialist

The Journey of Those Born on
MARCH 5

Y ou were born of creative strength and a subconscious desire for drama that can keep you
stuck in cycles of self-destruction. You will have to harness your emotions to something
true, as your journey is one of introspection, disillusionment, and emotional fortitude.

Early on in your journey, you will meet your enigmatic guide, *Power* (The Number Eight). *Power* calls
you away from subconscious chaos and toward a path
of emotional self-awareness. You will meet *Power* when
you confront the internalized shame that was never
yours to carry in the first place. If you can do the courageous digging required to know yourself, *Power* helps
you reveal your true magnificence.

But if you choose this thoughtful path, you will
have to contend with *Disappointment* (Eight of Cups).
The more honest you become, the more disillusioned
you may be with the interpersonal connections and responsibilities you have made. You will meet *Disappointment* in moments of personal withdrawal, when
you break free from the connections that drain you,
knowing that your heart belongs somewhere better.

> ### YOUR GUIDES
>
> *Astrology: Your Energy*
> Pisces (Neptune, The Moon)
>
> *Numerology: Your Path*
> Power (The Number Eight)
>
> *Minor Arcana: Your Lesson*
> Disappointment (The Eight of Cups)
>
> *Major Arcana: Your Highest Calling*
> Resilience (Strength)

By answering these calls for self-honesty, you will discover the importance of *Resilience*
(Strength). *Resilience* knows how strong you are, reminding you that you can handle even the
toughest of personal lessons. You will meet *Resilience* in moments of emotional tenacity, when
the worst has happened and yet you find yourself moving forward with complete faith. If you can
strengthen your spiritual muscles, *Resilience* teaches you how good it feels to lean on yourself.

PISCES
RULERS: NEPTUNE, THE MOON

PURPOSE
*To go inward to access limitless
emotional resources.*

RELATIONSHIPS

You are emotionally attuned and at times dramatic, yet your relationships should be a place of
healing intimacy. By seeking out partners who embrace the truth of who you are with complete
nonjudgment, you will discover that true love gives you limitless room to be yourself.

The Journey of
MARCH 6

Welcome to March 6, an adventurous journey toward self-trust.

Today, seek out new *Experience* (The Number Nine). Whether you pick the brain of an esteemed mentor or start an exciting new course, step outside your lived experience and absorb the wisdom around you. To expand on the mutable qualities of Pisces season, seize every opportunity to increase your understanding and perspective.

And make sure to practice *Gratitude* (Nine of Cups). Rather than getting hung up on what you are lacking, take inventory of the many gifts in your life today. Even if it's something as small as the breeze blowing through the grass, you can find happiness in every moment.

But if you're feeling overwhelmed or lost at any point in the day, make sure to lean on yourself. *Instinct* (The Hermit) encourages you to rely on the intuitive genius that lives within. It is the small voice that beckons you toward a life of personal meaning, so quiet the noise of the outside world as you tap into this internal compass. Spend time alone, or even better in nature, and trust that your gut will tell you everything you need to know today.

───────○───────

JUST FOR TODAY

TODAY'S MANTRA

While I am open to the wisdom of others, the most important information I need lies within.

TODAY'S JOURNAL PROMPT

When in the past has my gut moved me in the right direction?

TODAY'S RITUAL

Spend time alone but searching. Get out a tarot deck or a two-sided coin and ask yourself anything. Pull a card or flip the coin and see how your gut responds to the knowledge within that draw.

───────○───────

BORN ON THIS DAY

ELIZABETH BARRETT BROWNING, English poet

VALENTINA TERESHKOVA, Soviet cosmonaut and first woman in space

"I saw the angel in the marble and carved until I set him free."—**MICHELANGELO**, Italian sculptor, painter, architect, and poet of the High Renaissance

The Journey of Those Born on
MARCH 6

You were born of endless compassion and an empathy that can make you lose your sense of self. You will have to tap into the truth that can only come from within, as your journey is one of searching, appreciation, and self-trust.

Early on in your journey, you will stumble upon your wise guide, *Experience* (The Number Nine). *Experience* calls you away from a life of self-sacrifice and toward a path of higher understanding. You will meet *Experience* in moments of deep questioning, when you disregard the facts and explore the world to decipher your own set of truths. If you can remain forever teachable, you'll reach new heights of consciousness.

And if you choose this fulfilling path, be sure to pause for *Gratitude* (Nine of Cups). *Gratitude* asks you to always count your blessings, even when you feel like you are down on your luck. You will meet *Gratitude* in the small and seemingly insignificant moments of bliss, when you can't help but smile at the miraculous experience of being alive.

> ### YOUR GUIDES
>
> *Astrology: Your Energy*
> Pisces (Neptune, The Moon)
>
> *Numerology: Your Path*
> Experience (The Number Nine)
>
> *Minor Arcana: Your Lesson*
> Gratitude (The Nine of Cups)
>
> *Major Arcana: Your Highest Calling*
> Instinct (The Hermit)

By answering these calls for expansion, you will come to rely on *Instinct* (The Hermit). *Instinct* asks you to listen to the intuitive voice within that directs you toward an unknown but fateful purpose. You will meet *Instinct* in moments when you feel lost, yet your faith in your powers of perception allows you to move forward with complete self-confidence. If you can quiet the distracting noise of society and authority, you'll be able to listen deeply to yourself.

───────────────○───────────────

PISCES
RULERS: NEPTUNE, THE MOON

PURPOSE
To travel fearlessly through the unknown, guided by nothing but the sound of intuition.

RELATIONSHIPS

You are sweet and endlessly compassionate, and your relationships should be a place of growth and freedom. By seeking out partners who lovingly give you the space you need to reach new heights of instinctual consciousness, you will discover that true love doesn't need limits.

The Journey of
MARCH 7

Welcome to March 7, an emotionally fulfilling journey of trust.

Despite the passive nature of Pisces season, *Autonomy* (The Number One) begs you to be fearless and courageous today. Trust your intuition, and don't depend on others as you tackle each moment head-on. It is a wonderful day to start the project or relationship that scares you most, favoring bravery over safety.

But make sure not to forget about *Vulnerability* (Ace of Wands). Surrender to your humanity and bring your tenderheartedness to every new situation you encounter. It's okay to be afraid and excited at the same time, so wear your heart on your sleeve as you show the world how compassionate you are.

Besides, *Impermanence* (Wheel of Fortune) knows that the only constant in life you can control is your intention. Today can feel like an emotional roller coaster at times, so try to find the best in every twist and turn that comes your way. If your luck is up, make sure to pay that forward. But if you feel the cards are stacked against you, know that the universe has something better for you on the other side.

JUST FOR TODAY

TODAY'S MANTRA
The only thing I can control is my surrender.

TODAY'S RITUAL
Put your hand over your heart and press into your heart's center as you hold the wide range of emotion that today contains. Repeat the affirmation, "Vulnerability won't kill me. In fact, everything good is born from it."

TODAY'S JOURNAL PROMPT
When was a low point in my life that ended up being a miracle in disguise?

BORN ON THIS DAY

GERTRUD LUTZ-FANKHAUSER, Swiss humanitarian activist who helped rescue thousands of Jews in Hungary from Nazi Germany

KŌBŌ ABE, Japanese writer, playwright, musician, photographer, and inventor

"I learned long ago to focus on things you can control and don't even pay attention to things you don't."—BRYAN CRANSTON, American actor

The Journey of Those Born on

MARCH 7

You were born of fierce empathy and a single mindedness that can make it hard to adjust course amidst unexpected change. You will have to learn to roll with the punches, as your journey is one of ambition, perspective, and karmic fate.

Early on in your journey, you will run into your powerful guide, *Autonomy* (The Number One). *Autonomy* calls you away from the depths of emotional enmeshment and toward a path of radical self-reliance. You will meet *Autonomy* in moments of personal momentum, when your actions are in complete alignment with your intuition. If you can trust your own direction, you'll reach new heights of self-confidence.

But if you choose this brave path, *Vulnerability* (Ace of Cups) will ask you to let down your guard. There's no need to be too cool for school; instead, open your heart and reveal your cards to people and projects you love. You have so much compassion to give, so share it unapologetically.

By answering these calls to action, you will come to respect the laws of *Impermanence* (Wheel of Fortune). The only constant in life is change, so let go of expectation and ride the roller coaster of fate. You will meet *Impermanence* in moments of divine trust, when your cards are down but you know that the upswing is only a celestial heartbeat away. If you can hang on to the belief that the universe has your back, you'll learn to enjoy the ride of your life.

YOUR GUIDES

Astrology: Your Energy
Pisces (Neptune, The Moon)

Numerology: Your Path
Autonomy (The Number One)

Minor Arcana: Your Lesson
Vulnerability (The Ace of Cups)

Major Arcana: Your Highest Calling
Impermanence
(The Wheel of Fortune)

PISCES
RULERS: NEPTUNE, THE MOON

PURPOSE
To throw yourself into love and leave the rest up to fate.

RELATIONSHIPS

You are deeply committed and sincere, so your relationships should be a place of independence and radical trust. By seeking out partners who know how to fill their own cup and encourage you to do the same, you will discover that true love does not require self-sacrifice.

The Journey of
MARCH 8

W elcome to March 8, a harmonious journey toward intuitive justice.

Balance (The Number Two) asks you to find your footing somewhere solid. Look for the people, projects, and ideas that feel easy and natural, rather than seeking out any turmoil. Partnership can also serve a divine purpose in your life today, so ask for help from those who are trustworthy.

And don't forget how valuable you are. As you wade through the empathic waters of Pisces season, *Worthiness* (Two of Cups) asks you to prioritize the relationships that reciprocate your generosity. If you are beginning a partnership with someone, take things slowly today as you observe their intentions. And if you are fully committed, don't be afraid to ask for what you need and see how others respond.

Besides, *Truth* (Justice) calls you to stand up for what you believe in most. In the spirit of radical honesty, consult your internal compass as you express your thoughts and opinions to the world around you. Get emotionally and mentally clear on your beliefs so that they can withstand any opposition while remaining open to the productive feedback of others.

JUST FOR TODAY

TODAY'S MANTRA
I will practice balance as I stand up for my intuitive sense of justice.

TODAY'S JOURNAL PROMPT
Which partners, friends, or colleagues do I intuitively trust?

TODAY'S RITUAL
Find two objects of sentimental meaning for you small enough to fit in a pocket or backpack. Place each object in either pocket of your pants or either side of your bag, and visualize them balancing you out.

BORN ON THIS DAY

ADDIE L. WYATT, American labor movement leader, civil rights activist, and first Black woman elected as the international vice president of a major US labor union

MILANA VAYNTRUB, Soviet-born American actor, comedian, and activist

"Strength doesn't necessarily come from resisting fear, weakness, or any other feeling and overcoming it. Strength comes from looking at those things straight on—and accepting them as they really are."—KAT VON D, American tattoo artist, entrepreneur, and television personality

The Journey of Those Born on
MARCH 8

You were born of otherworldly strength and an emotional depth that can leave you lost in morbid reflection. You will have to learn to swim peacefully through the gray areas in life, as your journey is one of harmony, partnership, and intuitive justice.

Early on in life, you will meet your easeful guide, *Balance* (The Number Two). *Balance* calls you away from the murky waters of self-reflection and toward a path of peaceful and grounded living. Time and again, you'll be reminded that life doesn't have to be such a struggle, inspiring you to lean on trustworthy partners and seek out the goals that are in harmony with your values.

If you choose this tranquil path, you will meet your emotionally intelligent friend, *Worthiness* (Two of Cups). *Worthiness* asks you to dip your toes before you dive into partnership, teaching you to trust your own timing rather than rushing intimacy. By taking things slowly and listening deeply to your sense of safety, you will ensure that you never have to sacrifice your emotional safety for the sake of another.

By answering these calls for emotional peace, you will tap into the higher realm of *Truth* (Justice). Life is deeply complicated, so you'll need to consult your moral compass as you navigate the ever-moving targets of right and wrong. You will meet *Truth* in moments of personal conviction, when you have reached a place of internal alignment that allows you to stand firmly for what you believe in. If you can trust yourself to separate the true from the false, you'll deeply influence the minds and hearts of others for the better.

PISCES
RULERS: NEPTUNE, THE MOON

PURPOSE
To slowly but surely grow to trust yourself completely.

RELATIONSHIPS

You are deeply intuitive and sensitive to the feelings of others, but your relationships should be a place of grounded equality and reciprocity. By seeking out partners whose actions align with their words, you will discover that true love is always capable and willing to honor your needs and boundaries.

The Journey of
MARCH 9

Welcome to March 9, an inquisitive journey that builds new perspective.

Flexibility (The Number Three) invites you not to take your plans so seriously today. Embrace the unexpected in every form, whether it is saying "yes" to a last-minute party or welcoming a new member of your company. Pursue a wide variety of emotional experiences so that your heart can stay open and fresh.

This openheartedness will come in handy, as *Belonging* (Three of Cups) encourages you to have fun with others. Seek out the loving support of your community today in the form of old companions or new. Better yet, combine some of your social circles, and expand your sense of community.

And if you embrace these social callings, you may find yourself relating to life in an entirely new way. *Surrender* (The Hanged Man) requires you to let go of your rigid ways of being so that you can experience new spiritual breakthroughs. If someone invites you out of your comfort zone to a place that threatens your sense of understanding, take the risk and see what you can discover. As with much of Pisces season, today invites you on an emotional adventure, so put your heart on the line.

JUST FOR TODAY

TODAY'S MANTRA
I will let my heart explore new perspectives today.

TODAY'S JOURNAL PROMPT
What friends, groups, or communities help expand my perspective?

TODAY'S RITUAL
Channel the freedom of the butterfly. Close your eyes and visualize the most gorgeous butterfly your imagination can conjure, taking note of its delicate wings and ever-changing pattern of flight. Take this lightness with you today, and if you happen to see a butterfly in real life, make sure to say hi.

BORN ON THIS DAY

BOBBY FISCHER, American chess player

EMMA BONINO, Italian politician and philanthropist

"It was when I found out I could make mistakes that I knew I was on to something."—**ORNETTE COLEMAN**, American jazz saxophonist and composer

The Journey of Those Born on
MARCH 9

Y ou were born of otherworldly consciousness and a deep introversion that can keep you from experiencing new things. You will have to take the risk of connection, as your journey is one of curiosity, community, and perspective shifting.

Early on in your journey, you will bump into your enthusiastic guide, *Flexibility* (The Number Three). *Flexibility* calls you away from a life of wanderlust and toward a sociable path of emotional connection. You will meet *Flexibility* in moments of interpersonal understanding, when you step out of your lived experience and realize that when it comes to emotion, there's no such thing as right or wrong.

And if you choose this path of connection, *Belonging* (Three of Cups) shows you the gifts of understanding through close, intimate relationships with people from different walks of life. You will meet *Belonging* when you and others take off your masks and accept each other for exactly who you are.

By answering these calls for community, you will find yourself with an entirely new perspective. *Surrender* (The Hanged Man) asks you to never get stuck in deep-rooted emotional patterns, encouraging you time and again to open your heart to new experiences. You will meet *Surrender* in the unexpected spiritual breakthroughs in life, when, by walking in someone else's shoes, you end up traveling on entirely new emotional soil. If you can relinquish the safety that comes from having all the answers, you'll find the keys to enlightenment.

YOUR GUIDES

Astrology: Your Energy
Pisces (Neptune, The Moon)

Numerology: Your Path
Flexibility (The Number Three)

Minor Arcana: Your Lesson
Belonging (The Three of Cups)

Major Arcana: Your Highest Calling
Surrender (The Hanged Man)

PISCES
RULERS: NEPTUNE, THE MOON

PURPOSE
*To search for the emotional adventure
that lies in connection.*

RELATIONSHIPS

You are deeply introverted and emotionally self-reliant by nature, yet your relationships should be a place of community-building and belonging. By seeking out partners who are as socially adept as they are compassionate, you will discover that true love expands your world in ways you never thought possible.

The Journey of
MARCH 10

W elcome to March 10, a grounded journey toward emotional transformation.
　　To contain the unpredictable emotions of Pisces season, *Discipline* (The Number Four) asks you to get real about what you can manage today. Focus on the humble and seemingly mundane tasks ahead of you so you don't get too carried away with the unpredictability of feeling. Whether it be methodically folding the laundry or cleaning out your garage, stay close to reality.

As you work to stay grounded, *Reflection* (Four of Cups) asks you to reevaluate the things that have been draining your emotional cup recently. Take a much-needed inventory of your personal obligations and get honest about the ones that are not reciprocal. If it is time to walk away from something, take today to prepare for the next step.

Besides, *Transformation* (Death) means you are growing toward something truer anyhow. Shed old versions of your emotional self or relationships so that you can begin to embody the true authenticity of your soul. There may be some grief that comes with this transition, but remember that you are blossoming into the person you were always meant to become.

JUST FOR TODAY

TODAY'S MANTRA
I will shed the emotional layers that I have outgrown today.

TODAY'S JOURNAL PROMPT
What emotional obligations or patterns are holding me back from true authenticity?

TODAY'S RITUAL
Say a grieving prayer for the person you once were. Light a candle and dim the lights as you repeat, "I release who I was. Thank you for everything you have done for me, and for making space for something new."

BORN ON THIS DAY

LILLIAN WALD, American nurse and social activist who started American community nursing

TAMARA KARSAVINA, Russian prima ballerina and cofounder of the Royal Academy of Dance

"Do not think your single vote doesn't matter much. The rain that refreshes the parched ground is made up of single drops."—KATE SHEPPARD, New Zealand suffragist

The Journey of Those Born on
MARCH 10

Y ou were born of intuitive confidence and restlessness that can distract you from meaningful growth. You will have to work hard for true authenticity, as your journey is one of integrity, reevaluation, and metamorphosis.

Early on in your journey, you will meet your stern guide, *Discipline* (The Number Four). *Discipline* calls you away from a life of unbridled passion and toward a grounded path of hard work. You will meet *Discipline* in moments of self-leadership, when you harness your powerful emotions and channel them into productivity. If you can put one foot in front of the other, *Discipline* offers you the gifts of self-respect.

If you choose this humble path, *Reflection* (Four of Cups) will ask you to pause from time to time to reconsider where you are devoting your energy. If someone or something is draining you of your emotional resources, walk away and make peace with what was. You will meet *Reflection* in moments of deep contemplation, when you know what you must say "no" to but are not quite sure where to go next.

By answering these calls for personal accountability, *Transformation* (Death) will ask you to let go of old and outdated emotional coping mechanisms in favor of radical authenticity. You will meet *Transformation* in moments of personal metamorphosis, when you are unveiling yet another emotional mask and revealing the true heart that lies underneath. If you can find the courage to break old norms, you'll also discover the freedom of being yourself.

———————————————————○———————————————————

PISCES
RULERS: NEPTUNE, THE MOON

PURPOSE
To build the emotional muscles required
for powerful authenticity.

RELATIONSHIPS

You are emotionally independent and optimistic, yet your relationships should be a place of deep rooting. By seeking out partners who are the salt of the earth and true to their word, you will discover that the loyalty and dependability of true love makes your heart feel safe.

The Journey of
MARCH 11

Welcome to March 11, a brave journey toward emotional moderation.

Courage (The Number Five) invites you to share what you have inside today. While it is scary to reveal things from the heart, now is the time for vulnerability, so seize the moment and put yourself out there. Stand by the deeply held personal beliefs that make you uniquely you.

But don't get too hung up on the outcome. *Grief* (Five of Cups) warns against morbid reflection today, so steer away from the emotions that lead you down an unproductive shame spiral. Even if things don't go perfectly your way, know you are growing toward a more authentic version of yourself. Reach for self-love over emotional victimhood.

Besides, nothing is as bad as it seems. To channel the peacefulness of Pisces season, *Serenity* (Temperance) asks you to take the middle road with your emotions today, never letting them bring you too high or too low. Meditate to calm your racing mind and tap into that grounded sacred space of peace that lives within. If you can reach for spiritual alignment over unnecessary drama, you'll find the eternal gift of tranquility.

JUST FOR TODAY

TODAY'S MANTRA
With internal peace, I will not get emotionally rocked by vulnerability.

TODAY'S RITUAL
Seek out the color light blue. Whether it be in how you dress, the background color on your phone, or the color of the ocean, light blue is known for its calming and relaxing qualities, helping you access the serenity of this day.

TODAY'S JOURNAL PROMPT
What spiritual practices or rituals keep me the most emotionally peaceful?

BORN ON THIS DAY

RALPH ABERNATHY, American civil rights leader and head of the NAACP

MARIUS PETIPA, French ballet dancer, choreographer, and teacher

"If you really want to understand something, the best way is to try and explain it to someone else."—DOUGLAS ADAMS, English author, screenwriter, essayist, and humorist

The Journey of Those Born on
MARCH 11

Y ou were born of harmonic creativity and a moral conviction that can err on the side of judgment when taken to extremes. You will have to find the power within moderation, as your journey is one of self-expression, consciousness, and emotional peace.

Early on in your journey, you will encounter your magnificent guide, *Courage* (The Number Five). *Courage* calls you to step out of the shadows of others and into the light of your creative spirit. You will meet *Courage* in moments of radical vulnerability when you find yourself taking center stage in your life.

But if you choose to dance to the beat of your own drum, *Grief* (Five of Cups) will ask you not to take things so personally. It is easy to get hung up on the opinions and reactions of others when leading with authenticity, but *Grief* invites you to detach from expectation and accept that everything is as it should be. By trusting that the universe has your back, you'll begin to see your glass as half full.

By answering these brave calls, you will come to respect the importance of *Serenity* (Temperance). *Serenity* invites you to take the middle road in life, worshipping the calm waters of tranquility rather than the rattling cages of turmoil. You will meet *Serenity* in moments of meditation, when you take a step back from your frantic thoughts and realize that everything you need is in the present moment. Sure, the truth isn't always as sexy as the highs and lows of drama, but remember that internal peace is a gift that keeps on giving.

> ### YOUR GUIDES
>
> *Astrology: Your Energy*
> Pisces (Neptune, Pluto)
>
> *Numerology: Your Path*
> Courage (The Number Five)
>
> *Minor Arcana: Your Lesson*
> Grief (The Five of Cups)
>
> *Major Arcana: Your Highest Calling*
> Serenity (Temperance)

PISCES
RULERS: NEPTUNE, PLUTO

PURPOSE
To discover that radical vulnerability does not have to sacrifice emotional serenity.

RELATIONSHIPS

You are partnership-driven and compassionate, and your relationships should be a place of endless support and encouragement. By seeking out partners who champion your vulnerability and cheer you on throughout your journey, you will discover that true love is the only applause you need.

The Journey of
MARCH 12

W elcome to March 12, a sweet journey toward self-healing.

Pisces season always champions kindness, but *Devotion* (The Number Six) calls you to act entirely from a place of generous love today. Look for ways to be of service to the people and projects to which your heart belongs, lending a helping hand without having to be asked or requiring anything in return.

Besides, *Nostalgia* (Six of Cups) offers you plenty. Reconnect with the happiest of times by taking a romantic trip down memory lane. Call an old friend and have a belly laugh about shared experiences, or rewatch your favorite childhood movie as many times as you can stomach. Use the past as a wonderful portal into the joy of the present today.

You'll need this levity, as *Shadow* (The Devil) asks you to heal the subconscious behaviors that are holding you back from true freedom. Witness the ways in which you reject or deny happiness today and try to understand these parts of you with complete nonjudgment. When and where did you learn that it wasn't okay to enjoy your life? Do what you can to release this old shame, shedding light on the wounds that need it most.

―――――○―――――

JUST FOR TODAY

TODAY'S MANTRA
I will open my heart to the present and past while having compassion for the fears that may come up.

TODAY'S JOURNAL PROMPT
What memories from my childhood or early life experiences are sweet and soothing to me?

TODAY'S RITUAL
Use scent to transport you to the past. Pick up a favorite childhood food, flower, perfume, or something with a vivid smell. Hold it under your nose and ask the universe to bring the happy memories to the surface.

―――――○―――――

BORN ON THIS DAY

VASLAV NIJINSKY, Polish ballet dancer and choreographer

CHARMAINE WHITE FACE, Oglala Lakota leader, defender of Native American rights, biologist, and journalist

"Practice kindness all day to everybody and you will realize you're already in heaven now."—JACK KEROUAC, American Beat writer

The Journey of Those Born on
MARCH 12

You were born of intuitive intellect and an empathic flexibility that can make you a sponge to the feelings of others. You will have to protect your heart and surrender to your deepest emotions, as your journey is one of sincerity, sentimentality, and self-forgiveness.

Early on in your journey, you will stumble upon your gentle guide, *Devotion* (The Number Six). *Devotion* calls you away from a life of endless searching and toward a path of meaningful connection. By giving generously to every person, project, and idea that your heart belongs to, *Devotion* teaches you the endless grace that comes from being of service. If you can put ego to the side and give without caution, you'll discover love without conditions.

If you choose this heartfelt path, *Nostalgia* (Six of Cups) will encourage you to reflect kindly on the past. No one's early life experiences were perfect, yet *Nostalgia* reminds you of the small wonders that helped you through even the toughest of times. You will meet *Nostalgia* in moments of sweet reminiscence, when the simple taste of a childhood treat transports you back to a brief moment of happiness.

> ## YOUR GUIDES
>
> *Astrology: Your Energy*
> Pisces (Neptune, Pluto)
>
> *Numerology: Your Path*
> Devotion (The Number Six)
>
> *Minor Arcana: Your Lesson*
> Nostalgia (The Six of Cups)
>
> *Major Arcana: Your Highest Calling*
> Shadow (The Devil)

By answering these calls for openheartedness, *Shadow* (The Devil) will help you heal the blockages you have around vulnerability. You will meet *Shadow* in moments of self-sabotage, when the sweetness of life is far too overwhelming to bear and you find yourself seeking immediate escape. If you can practice deep understanding for the parts of you that learned to fear good things, *Shadow* offers you self-compassion as a tool for emotional freedom.

PISCES
RULERS: NEPTUNE, PLUTO

PURPOSE
To be emotionally generous with others and especially with yourself.

RELATIONSHIPS

You are dreamy and curious, and your relationships should be a place of complete support and devotion. By seeking emotionally tender and heartfelt partners who aim to fill your emotional cup, you will discover the limitless healing that comes from true love.

The Journey of
MARCH 13

Welcome to March 13, a valiant journey toward unexpected revelations.

Commitment (The Number Seven) asks you to narrow your focus to the relationships and responsibilities that matter the most to you today. If you have given someone your word, follow through on every promise you have made. Despite the emotionally passive nature of Pisces season, show your loyalty through meaningful action.

But don't get too wistful about any outcomes today. *Illusion* (Seven of Cups) warns against fantasy-based decision-making, so check in with yourself or a grounded friend to make sure you are not wishing for something that isn't in your long-term best interest.

Besides, *Upheaval* (The Tower) has enough change in store for you. Expect the unexpected today, welcoming every twist and turn in your day's plan with humble gratitude. You never know what seeming mistake may end up being a miracle, so trust that the universe is doing for you what you cannot do for yourself. The deeper meaning of today may not reveal itself immediately but have faith that you are moving closer to the truth.

―――――――――◯―――――――――

JUST FOR TODAY

TODAY'S MANTRA
I will do my part to live in integrity and leave the rest up to the universe.

TODAY'S RITUAL
Cleanse your mind of expectation by going somewhere where you can feel the breeze on your face and surrendering your day's plans to the powers that be as you repeat, "Thank you, universe, for everything you've given me and everything you've taken away."

TODAY'S JOURNAL PROMPT
What fantasies do I have that may not be healthy for me?

―――――――――◯―――――――――

BORN ON THIS DAY

MAHAWA BANGOURA CAMARA, Guinean diplomat, politician, and the first woman to serve as the foreign minister of Guinea

LUAN SANTANA, Brazilian singer-songwriter

"Imagination is as vital to any advance in science as learning and precision are essential for starting points."—PERCIVAL LOWELL, American astronomer, mathematician, and author

The Journey of Those Born on
MARCH 13

You were born of grounded creativity and an emotional depth that can keep you stuck in the darkness of the human experience. You will have to throw yourself into the unknown, as your journey is one of intention, choice, and unexpected revelation.

Early on in your journey, you will meet your focused guide, *Commitment* (The Number Seven). *Commitment* calls you away from a life of tireless work and toward a path of intentional effort. By aiming your time, energy, and heart only toward the things you care about most, you'll learn how to build deep loyalty to the world around you.

But if you choose this narrow path, be careful where you aim. *Illusion* (Seven of Cups) reminds you that just because you want something, doesn't mean it is in your long-term best interest. You will meet *Illusion* in moments of dreamlike desire, when the intoxicating draws of what could be take you away from what is. If you can accept that if a dream seems too good to be true, it probably is, you'll learn to separate fantasy from reality.

By answering these calls for self-awareness, you will come to respect the power of *Upheaval* (The Tower). You will meet *Upheaval* in entirely unpredicted events, when the universe steps in and does for you what you were unwilling or unready to do for yourself. *Upheaval* forces you out of stagnation time and again so that you can reach your highest potential. If you can find faith in these acts of spiritual force, you'll learn to embrace the divinity in chaos.

> ### YOUR GUIDES
>
> *Astrology: Your Energy*
> Pisces (Neptune, Pluto)
>
> *Numerology: Your Path*
> Commitment (The Number Seven)
>
> *Minor Arcana: Your Lesson*
> Illusion (The Seven of Cups)
>
> *Major Arcana: Your Highest Calling*
> Upheaval (The Tower)

───────────○───────────

PISCES
RULERS: NEPTUNE, PLUTO

PURPOSE
To make decisions with integrity and leave the outcome up to the universe.

RELATIONSHIPS

You are self-reliant and emotionally private, yet your relationships should be a place of grounded trust and mutual respect. By seeking out partners who always keep their word and tell it like it is, you will discover that true love is a spiritual commitment that can sustain a lifetime.

The Journey of
MARCH 14

W elcome to March 14, a brilliantly honest journey toward personal faith.
Power (The Number Eight) calls you inward to heal the places that scare you. To help you master the empathy of Pisces season, pursue deep self-intimacy today, giving yourself the space and compassion to reveal the truths that lie underneath the truth. Seek out someone safe and empathetic to share these revelations with.

There may be something important you need to reveal today. *Disappointment* (Eight of Cups) encourages you to walk away from the relationships and emotional ties that are draining your cup, and to do so directly. Rather than fleeing the scene without a proper goodbye, find the courage to confront these letdowns head-on and give them the closure they deserve, so all parties involved can move forward.

And if you brave this high calling, *Hope* (The Star) reminds you that honest change always leads you somewhere better. Reach down into the depths of your soul and discover what it is you truly believe in because therein lies your eternal optimism. Whether you want to pursue a new dream job or a meaningful relationship, have faith that your intuition will tell you where you need to flourish next.

JUST FOR TODAY

TODAY'S MANTRA
Even the hardest truths shall set me free.

TODAY'S RITUAL
Channel the star with candlelight. Light one of your most cherished candles and turn out the lights. Set a timer for seventeen minutes and meditate on the mantra, "Starlight. Candlelight. Light up my soul."

TODAY'S JOURNAL PROMPT
What deep, private dreams am I ready to bring into the light today?

BORN ON THIS DAY

ALBERT EINSTEIN, German-born American theoretical physicist and Nobel laureate

STEPHEN CURRY, American basketball player

"I was built this way for a reason, so I'm going to use it."—**SIMONE BILES**, American gymnast and Olympic gold medalist

The Journey of Those Born on
MARCH 14

Y ou were born of great emotional depth and self-restraint that can hold you back from realizing your true potential. You will find the proper channels for all your creative wonder, as your journey is one of interpersonal trust, emotional emancipation, and divine optimism.

Early on in life, you will meet your enigmatic guide, *Power* (The Number Eight). *Power* invites you to leave behind emotional denial in favor of a spiraling path of personal truth-seeking. You will meet *Power* in moments of radical self-acceptance, when you realize that the very parts of you that you desperately tried to bury are the very things that make you universally human.

If you choose this introspective path, you will have to contend with your great teacher, *Disappointment* (Eight of Cups). You will meet *Disappointment* in moments of temporary grief when you know must walk away from a relationship, job, or dream that is no longer fulfilling your soul. If you can walk away from the bags that are weighing down your true potential, you can move forward with a divine sense of freedom.

By answering these calls for emotional growth, you will come to believe in the power of *Hope* (The Star). *Hope* is that tingling of excitement in your belly reminding you that you are destined for something special, something magic. You will meet *Hope* in moments when you wash away the imposter syndrome of the past and pursue your dreams with complete faith. By moving beyond the fear of failure, you can find the eternal flame of optimism that lies within.

> ### YOUR GUIDES
>
> *Astrology: Your Energy*
> Pisces (Neptune, Pluto)
>
> *Numerology: Your Path*
> Power (The Number Eight)
>
> *Minor Arcana: Your Lesson*
> Disappointment (The Eight of Cups)
>
> *Major Arcana: Your Highest Calling*
> Hope (The Star)

PISCES
RULERS: NEPTUNE, PLUTO

PURPOSE
To dig deep to a place of divine optimism.

RELATIONSHIPS

You are an intuitive diplomat, and your relationships should be a place of radical acceptance and unconditional support. By seeking out partners who value mental health and mutual honesty, you will discover that true love accepts you for exactly who you are.

The Journey of
MARCH 15

W elcome to March 15, an adventurous journey toward subconscious healing.
    Experience (The Number Nine) invites you to expand your mind and embrace the unknowns of the day. Enroll in that course you've been curious about, seek out that mentor you've been too shy to reach out to, or dive into that book that felt a bit out of your league. Favor a fearless approach to understanding and explore widely.

And don't forget to appreciate all the wonder that comes your way. Amidst the intense compassion of Pisces season, *Gratitude* (Nine of Cups) asks you to find a deep appreciation for the emotionally fulfilling aspects of your life today. If things are feeling scarce or you are having a hard time finding perspective, make a list of nine things, big or small, that you are grateful for.

Besides, *Memory* (The Moon) needs you to integrate your past into the present. If you are feeling triggered in any way today, do the emotional digging to find the origin story behind your unconscious reaction. You are responsible for your feelings in the present, so make an effort to clear out the ancient internal cobwebs that are blocking your deep and intuitive powers.

JUST FOR TODAY

TODAY'S MANTRA
While there is much to learn in this world, all the information I need to heal exists within me.

TODAY'S JOURNAL PROMPT
What was I going through and what was I like when I was age nine?

TODAY'S RITUAL
Align yourself with the moon. Go outside somewhere safe and sit in the moonlight. Is it waxing or waning? New or full? Stare up at the moon as you repeat the chant, "Moon magic, sing to me the tales of my past that can bring healing to me."

BORN ON THIS DAY

SAMUEL "LIGHTNIN'" HOPKINS, American blues musician

WILL.I.AM, American rapper, songwriter, record producer, entrepreneur, television personality, and actor

"Fight for the things that you care about, but do it in a way that will lead others to join you."
—RUTH BADER GINSBURG, American Supreme Court Justice

The Journey of Those Born on
MARCH 15

You were born of emotional generosity and a subconscious penchant for self destruction. You will have to heal before you can bloom, as your journey is one of searching, perspective, and deep emotional clearing.

Early on in your journey, you will meet your sage guide, *Experience* (The Number Nine). *Experience* calls you away from a life of selfless service and toward a path of divine understanding. By questioning the large authorities and institutions in your life, you can break through limited and outdated ways of thinking in search of higher truths.

If you choose this far-reaching path, *Gratitude* (Nine of Cups) will ask you time and again to count your blessings. By taking a step back to find perspective in your life, you'll find appreciation for the unimaginable peaks and valleys that you have traveled. If you can remain humble enough to never take things for granted, you'll learn the art of emotional contentment.

By answering these calls for emotional expansion, you will be asked to do the inner healing required to truly soar. *Memory* (The Moon) values the importance of the subconscious, inviting you to address historical wounds to make emotional space for new and better experiences. You will meet *Memory* in moments when the past projects itself onto the present and you are forced look inward to understand what is being triggered. If you can create emotional safety for the inner child who carries these deep fears, you'll become the intuitive caretaker you always needed.

YOUR GUIDES

Astrology: Your Energy
Pisces (Neptune, Pluto)

Numerology: Your Path
Experience (The Number Nine)

Minor Arcana: Your Lesson
Gratitude (The Nine of Cups)

Major Arcana: Your Highest Calling
Memory (The Moon)

PISCES
RULERS: NEPTUNE, PLUTO

PURPOSE
To remember that internal healing is as important as external growth.

RELATIONSHIPS

You are more prone to giving than receiving, yet your relationships should be a place of wild encouragement and intuitive trust. By seeking out partners who champion your outward ambitions as much as they appreciate your inward growth, you will discover that true love is the only acknowledgment you'll ever need.

The Journey of
MARCH 16

Welcome to March 16, a personally fulfilling journey toward positivity.

Autonomy (The Number One) invites you to trailblaze through this day guided by nothing but your own ambition. The world is yours for the taking, so approach everything head-on and don't wait for permission to do the things your soul is calling for. Everything that you need to thrive lies within.

So why not practice *Vulnerability* (Ace of Cups)? Get excited about the emotional possibilities of today by making a limitless list of the things you hope to give yourself to. Big or small, concrete or abstract, harness the gifts of an open heart. To make the most of the spiritual waters of Pisces season, you don't need to know what you're doing or how to do it; just throw your generous spirit into the unknown.

And then share this perspective with the rest of us. *Vitality* (The Sun) empowers you to self-express today, lighting the world around you with your authenticity. Post that piece of art you've been working on to your social media or make someone smile with your unique sense of humor. Get out there and be you, giving yourself total permission to shine while inspiring others to do the same.

———————————————○———————————————

JUST FOR TODAY

TODAY'S MANTRA
I am lovable. I am loving. I am loved.

TODAY'S JOURNAL PROMPT
Where and when do I shine the brightest?

TODAY'S RITUAL
Get some spice. Add some cinnamon, ginger, garlic, or any other spice to your meals throughout today to keep you feeling alive. It doesn't matter what kind, so choose your own adventure.

———————————————○———————————————

BORN ON THIS DAY

ANNA ATKINS, English botanist, photographer, and the first person to publish a book illustrated with photographic images

JHENÉ AIKO, American singer-songwriter

"You have to show reality as it is, not as you wish it to be."—JORGE RAMOS, Mexican American journalist and author

The Journey of Those Born on
MARCH 16

You were born of deep loyalty and an unconscious need for chaos that can keep you stuck in a cycle of self-destruction. You will have to take the vulnerable risk of true happiness, as your journey is one of intuition, fulfillment, and optimism.

Early on in your journey, you will meet your precocious guide, *Autonomy* (The Number One). *Autonomy* calls you away from a life of interdependence and toward a radical path of self-determination. You will meet *Autonomy* in moments of resourcefulness when you have nothing to rely on but the strength of your intuition. If you can trust yourself above all else, *Autonomy* offers you the gift of tenacity.

But if you choose this ambitious path, you will have to swim through the emotional waters of *Vulnerability* (Ace of Cups). *Vulnerability* is about the power of love, inspiring you to share openheartedly with people and projects that align with your personal values. You will meet *Vulnerability* in moments of deeply fulfilling connection, when you put yourself out there and discover the rewards of authenticity.

By answering these brave calls, you will tap into the lightness of *Vitality* (The Sun). *Vitality* asks you to tap into the beam of sunshine you emit when you are living freely in your authentic nature. You will meet *Vitality* in moments of joyous self-expression, when your emotional cup is so full that you don't have to hold back any part of your wild spirit. If you can find the courage to dance to the beat of your own drum, *Vitality* will have the rest of us dancing along with you.

───────────────────────○───────────────────────

PISCES
RULERS: NEPTUNE, PLUTO

PURPOSE
To live, love, and act from a place of total authenticity.

RELATIONSHIPS

You are seriously committed to love, and your relationships should be a place of independence and trusting space. By seeking out partners who know how to fill their own cup and encourage you to do the same, you will discover that true love is born from unconditional freedom.

The Journey of
MARCH 17

Welcome to March 17, a relationship-driven journey toward self-awakening.

Balance (The Number Two) encourages you to partner up today. Seek out the people who can make your life a bit smoother, and lean in to the wonders that come from sharing your hopes and dreams with the people you love. To make the most of the empathic waters of Pisces season, remember that you are not alone.

But don't accept any less than you deserve. *Worthiness* (Two of Cups) encourages you to prioritize relationships with those who know your value. Take note of the way that others treat you and do the internal digging to clarify exactly what you need from partnerships. By recognizing your own needs and placing them first, you can set healthy boundaries.

And don't be afraid to make any tough decisions, as *Awakening* (Judgment) asks you to champion honesty, no matter how harsh it may be. Surrender to reality so that you can ensure that your actions align with the greater good. Whether it be integrating new and profound truths about the world you live in or the people you are in relationships with, know that the truth shall set you free.

JUST FOR TODAY

TODAY'S MANTRA
I can handle the truth about my relationships.

TODAY'S JOURNAL PROMPT
What do I need from partnership, and do I feel that those needs are currently being met?

TODAY'S RITUAL
Write down the truth about your current partnerships, platonic or romantic. Write down the good, the bad, and the ugly. Don't hold back anything as you write the truth that you have always known.

BORN ON THIS DAY

KATIE LEDECKY, American swimmer and Olympic gold medalist

ANNA WESSELS WILLIAM, American pathologist and the first woman to be elected chair of the laboratory section of the American Public Health Association

"We are all one—and if we don't know it, we will learn it the hard way."—BAYARD RUSTIN, American civil rights leader

The Journey of Those Born on
MARCH 17

Y ou were born of deep empathy and an eternal optimism that can make it difficult to swallow the harshness of reality. You will have to make peace with the truth through partnership, as your journey is one of harmony, reciprocity, and emotional revelation.

Early on in your journey, you will encounter your grounding guide, *Balance* (The Number Two). *Balance* calls you away from a life of emotional isolation and toward a path of harmonious connection. You will meet *Balance* when you take the middle road in your relationships, offering the benefit of the doubt to everyone you encounter and especially yourself. There's no need for unnecessary drama or black-and-white thinking as you pursue a life of peaceful coexistence.

If you choose this path of connection, *Worthiness* (Two of Cups) asks you to remember your value as you enter into partnership with others. You will meet *Worthiness* in relationships built upon mutual respect, when you are able to be fully and unapologetically yourself, discovering the long-term benefits of emotional reciprocity.

By answering these calls for interpersonal growth, *Awakening* (Judgment) will replace your rose-tinted glasses with the beauty of truth. You will meet *Awakening* in moments of self-revelation, when you are able to see your emotional circumstances as they truly are rather than how you want them to be. Reality may never be easy to digest, but if you are willing to experience the raw and unfiltered aspects of the human experience, you'll learn that honesty is the key to emotional contentment.

PISCES
RULERS: NEPTUNE, PLUTO

PURPOSE
To be fully awake to complexity of emotion.

RELATIONSHIPS

You prefer to charge your emotional batteries in isolation, yet your relationships should be a place of faithful connection and mutual dependency. By seeking out partners who are deeply devoted to you by nature, you will discover that true love is even better than the movies.

The Journey of
MARCH 18

Welcome to March 18, a lively journey that builds perspective.

Pisces season always encourages free thinking, and *Flexibility* (The Number Three) invites you to view today as an open-ended adventure. Say "yes" to every social or professional invitation that comes your way without attaching any unnecessary expectation to what may come of it. Invite new perspectives and ideas into your life and remember that there is always more to learn.

And this knowledge may very well come in the form of *Belonging* (Three of Cups). Invest in your community, calling old friends or new ones as you include them in your day of wonder. Even better, blend your social worlds, introducing your wide range of loved ones to each other.

And from there, take a step back and enjoy. *Perspective* (The World) encourages you to zoom out and see the big picture, appreciating the many little triumphs that have gotten you to this day. You may have completed some type of season in your life and be preparing for a new phase of development, so use today to celebrate how far you've come.

○

JUST FOR TODAY

TODAY'S MANTRA

Before I make my next move, I will celebrate my progress with the people I love.

TODAY'S RITUAL

Reach out to three friends. Even if you haven't spoken to them in years, call them or ring their doorbell, and ask them what the greatest lesson is they've learned in life thus far. Listen closely to broaden your perspective.

TODAY'S JOURNAL PROMPT

What cycle of my life am I completing?

○

BORN ON THIS DAY

FRED SHUTTLESWORTH, American minister and civil rights activist

F. W. DE KLERK, South African president and Nobel Peace Prize winner

"To define is to kill. To suggest is to create."—STÉPHANE MALLARMÉ, French symbolist poet whose work inspired Cubism, Futurism, Dadaism, and Surrealism

The Journey of Those Born on
MARCH 18

You were born of intuitive intelligence and a gift for introspection that can keep you stuck in reflection. You will have to learn to enjoy the present moment, as your journey is one of unpredictability, community, and perspective.

Early on in your journey, you will meet your excitable guide, *Flexibility* (The Number Three). *Flexibility* calls you away from relentless self-analysis and toward a path of curious connection. You will meet *Flexibility* in times of perspective-building, when the experiences and knowledge of others bring you the ah-ha moment you were seeking.

If you choose this sociable path, *Belonging* (Three of Cups) will welcome you with open arms. You will meet *Belonging* when you find yourself held by the loving support of others. By sharing your deepest feelings and dreams with those who have proven their trust, you'll discover the profound emotional breakthroughs that come from moving out of isolation.

By embracing these calls for openheartedness, you will begin to see things through new eyes. *Perspective* (The World) reminds you that life is a grand adventure, inviting you to take a step back and witness the many mountains you have climbed along the way. You will meet *Perspective* in the jaw-dropping silence of a completed milestone, when you are filled with the deepest sense of gratitude for the experiences you have had. If you can zoom out and look at the big picture, the beauty of your journey will leave you speechless.

YOUR GUIDES

Astrology: Your Energy
Pisces (Neptune, Pluto)

Numerology: Your Path
Flexibility (The Number Three)

Minor Arcana: Your Lesson
Belonging (The Three of Cups)

Major Arcana: Your Highest Calling
Perspective (The World)

PISCES
RULERS: NEPTUNE, PLUTO

PURPOSE
To accept the grand invitation for life's big adventure.

RELATIONSHIPS

You are deeply reflective and even brooding, but your relationships should be a place of fun-filled adventure and community. By seeking out partners who always keep things interesting as they push you out of your comfort zone, you will discover that true love doesn't have to be so serious after all.

The Journey of
MARCH 19

Welcome to March 19, an objective journey toward self-trust.

Discipline (The Number Four) asks you to channel your feelings into tangible work. What can you concretely accomplish today? Whether it be organizing your office or tending to the more mundane aspect of your job, choose humble service over acts of grandiosity.

But to harness the intuitive power of Pisces season, *Reflection* (Four of Cups) calls you to re-evaluate the emotional obligations you have in your life. If a relationship or contract has been depleting you of your internal resources for some time, use today to consider how you could better use your energy without this baggage.

You'll need to make clear decisions, as *Self-mastery* (The Emperor) inspires you to step into a position of self-leadership. Make the tough but loving calls that will move your life forward, executing them with humble compassion and clarity of mind. Say what you need to say without letting your emotions get in the way, stating your boundaries while respecting the needs of others. Know that you are the CEO of your day, and don't be afraid to act accordingly.

JUST FOR TODAY

TODAY'S MANTRA

Being straightforward is a loving act of kindness to myself and others.

TODAY'S RITUAL

Get clear on your responsibilities. Make a list of the current obligations you have on your plate. Go through each one with an objective eye and ask yourself whether the effort to handle each drains or fills your emotional cup.

TODAY'S JOURNAL PROMPT

If I were a true leader to myself, what changes would I like to make?

BORN ON THIS DAY

ALBERT PINKHAM RYDER, American painter

GLENN CLOSE, American actor and producer

"To get what you want, *stop* doing what isn't working."—**EARL WARREN**, governor of California and fourteenth chief justice of the US Supreme Court

The Journey of Those Born on
MARCH 19

You were born of intuitive resilience and a dramatic creativity that can be difficult to contain. You will have to ground yourself in emotional maturity, as your path is one of integrity, reevaluation, and powerful objectivity.

Early on in your journey, you will meet your formidable guide, *Discipline* (The Number Four). *Discipline* calls you away from fantasy and toward a path that favors usefulness over laziness and integrity over desire. You will meet *Discipline* in moments of satisfying exhaustion, when you take a step back and witness the unshakable, self-made ground upon which you stand.

If you choose this hardworking path, don't worry, as *Reflection* (Four of Cups) will force you to take a break. Before making the next big move, *Reflection* invites you to evaluate the past to gain clarity around the future. If you can stay honest with yourself about the failures and successes of your circumstances, you'll learn to use your energy wisely.

By answering these calls for accountability, you will tap into the power of *Self-mastery* (The Emperor). *Self-mastery* reveals the wise authority that lives within, helping you make clear and effective decisions in even the most complicated of situations. You will meet *Self-mastery* in moments of emotional fortitude, when you are able to channel your immense feelings into concrete and sustainable long-term solutions. If you can always reach for integrity over drama, you'll earn the eternal gift of self-respect.

YOUR GUIDES

Astrology: Your Energy
Pisces (Neptune, Pluto)

Numerology: Your Path
Discipline (The Number Four)

Minor Arcana: Your Lesson
Reflection (The Four of Cups)

Major Arcana: Your Highest Calling
Self-mastery (The Emperor)

PISCES
RULERS: NEPTUNE, PLUTO

PURPOSE
To channel hard work and optimism into personal integrity.

RELATIONSHIPS

You are an intuitive and autonomous ray of light, so your relationships should be a place of grounded mutual respect. By seeking out partners who keep their word as well as maintain their personal integrity, you will discover that true love comes from earned trust.

The Journey of
MARCH 20

Welcome to March 20, an openhearted journey toward self-confidence.
Courage (The Number Five) invites you to throw caution to the wind and express yourself to the world around you. Seize every opportunity to show us who you are, and don't apologize for shining so brightly. It's a day to be the main character in your life and step into the light of your authentic spirit.

But don't get too stuck in the morbid reflection that Pisces season can bring up. *Grief* (Five of Cups) warns against endless and unproductive self-pity today. If something doesn't go your way, notice the grief that comes up and find compassion for yourself without spending too long in this state. Pick yourself up and dust yourself off, knowing that with each perceived failure, you are growing closer to your ultimate potential.

And what is that potential exactly? *Wisdom* (The Hierophant) empowers you to think for yourself rather than getting lost in the opinions of others. Don't give away your power to any real-life or internet trolls today. Get centered in the intuitive knowledge that lives within you and know that just because your truth is different from others doesn't make it wrong.

○

JUST FOR TODAY

TODAY'S MANTRA
I will trust in my truth as I express it to the world around me.

TODAY'S RITUAL
Draw a heart—no really, draw a heart. Draw it once, or over and over in your journal. As you draw, celebrate your emotional wholeness, release self-pity, and embrace the courage today requires.

TODAY'S JOURNAL PROMPT
When did I learn to give away my power to others' opinion of me?

○

BORN ON THIS DAY

SPIKE LEE, American film director

ANDRÉE CHEDID, Egyptian French poet and novelist

"As human beings, our job in life is to help people realize how rare and valuable each one of us really is, that each of us has something that no one else has—or ever will have—something inside that is unique to all time."—FRED ROGERS, American children's television host

The Journey of Those Born on
MARCH 20*

Y ou were born of deep empathy and a self-critical nature that can stop you from expressing your greatest truths. You will have to be brave enough to be yourself, as your journey is one of self-revealing, temporary grief, and higher consciousness.

Early on in your journey, you will meet your open-hearted guide, *Courage* (The Number Five). *Courage* calls you away from a life of passivity and toward a path of radical authenticity. You will meet *Courage* in moments of self-expression, when the dreamlike creativity that lives within finally reaches the surface for the rest of us to witness in awe. If you can outwardly channel your inner genius, you'll discover the strength of heart.

If you choose this bold path, you will have to contend with your emotional teacher, *Grief* (Five of Cups). It's easy to get lost in the what-ifs and what-could-have-beens in life, but *Grief* asks you not to get stuck in this trap of self-pity for eternity. Instead, acknowledge this temporary disappointment and grief for only a moment, as you raise your eyes toward the possibilities that lie ahead.

> ### YOUR GUIDES
>
> *Astrology: Your Energy*
> Pisces (Neptune, Pluto)
>
> *Numerology: Your Path*
> Courage (The Number Five)
>
> *Minor Arcana: Your Lesson*
> Grief (The Five of Cups)
>
> *Major Arcana: Your Highest Calling*
> Wisdom (The Hierophant)

By answering these calls for bravery, you will unlock the gates of *Wisdom* (The Hierophant). *Wisdom* knows that there are no monopolies on truth, inspiring you to question all false prophets and systems that try to oppress and repress your intuitive voice of reason. If you can remember that there is no right way, there is only your way, you'll move inward to a place of radical self-trust.

———————————————○———————————————

PISCES
RULERS: NEPTUNE, PLUTO

PURPOSE
To be completely yourself and empower others to do the same.

RELATIONSHIPS

You are gentle yet self-aware, and your relationships should be a place of passion and courageous vulnerability. By seeking out partners who give their heart as freely and openly as you give yours, you will discover that true love never asks you to hold back your true feelings.

*Are you an Aries born on this day? Head to page 761 to find your additional birthday guide!

APPENDIX
Cusp Birthdays

If you were born on the last day of a zodiac season—April 19, May 20, June 20, July 22, August 22, September 22, October 22, November 21, December 21, January 19, February 18, or March 20—there is a chance you were born in the next sign, depending on the exact time of your birth. For example, if you were born on April 19, the last day of Aries season, there is a possibility that you are, in fact, a Taurus. In this instance, your birthday spread is still just as relevant, but you get an extra Minor Arcana guide to help you along your journey (yay!).

To find out if this applies to you, you will need to determine your exact time of birth and the location. Then, using an online astrology birth chart tool (e.g., astro-charts.com), calculate what sign your sun is in. If you were, in fact, born with a different sun sign, look for your additional Minor Arcana guide in the following sections.

APRIL 19 *(Sun in Taurus)*

The additional guide of your journey is *Scarcity* (Five of Pentacles). You will meet *Scarcity* in moments of perceived lack, when you focus on what you don't have rather than finding gratitude for what you do. *Scarcity* invites you to shift your mindset through generosity and vulnerability, sharing what you have and asking for the help you need.

MAY 20 *(Sun in Gemini)*

The additional guide of your journey is *Hypervigilance* (Seven of Swords). You will meet *Hypervigilance* when your distrust of others stems from a lack of trust in yourself. *Hypervigilance* invites you to act in accordance with your ethics, believing in the fundamental goodness of humanity, rather than losing sleep over the actions of others.

JUNE 20 *(Sun in Cancer)*

The additional guide of your journey is *Disappointment* (Eight of Cups). You will meet *Disappointment* when you know you must walk away from something that is no longer serving you. *Disappointment* invites you to pause and mourn what was, rather than bypassing the necessary reflection required to move forward with clarity.

JULY 22 *(Sun in Leo)*

The additional guide of your journey is *Preparation* (Two of Wands). You will meet *Preparation* in the necessary planning that must be done before you set out to accomplish a goal. *Preparation* invites you to survey all the potential hurdles and difficulties you may experience along the way to ensure that you are as ready as you can be to succeed.

AUGUST 22 *(Sun in Virgo)*

The additional guide of your journey is *Collaboration* (Three of Pentacles). You will meet *Collaboration* when you entrust your goals to like-minded folks with varying skills and backgrounds. *Collaboration* invites you to see how three heads are far better, and faster, than one, encouraging you to recognize the inherent value in teamwork.

SEPTEMBER 22 *(Sun in Libra)*

The additional guide of your journey is *Restoration* (Four of Swords). You will meet *Restoration* in moments of burnout, when you have no choice but to pause to regain what was lost in your ambition. *Restoration* invites you to see the importance of such recovery, encouraging you to quiet your mind and rest your body until the light of enthusiasm returns.

OCTOBER 22 *(Sun in Scorpio)*

The additional guide of your journey is *Grief* (Five of Cups). You will meet *Grief* in sadness and loss, when a situation or relationship hasn't turned out how you hoped. *Grief* invites you to feel the full weight of these feelings so that you can internalize and learn from these necessary losses without getting stuck in regret.

NOVEMBER 21 *(Sun in Sagittarius)*

The additional guide of your journey is *Conflict* (Five of Wands). You will meet *Conflict* within adversity, when a person, place, or institution questions or threatens your stance or authority. *Conflict* invites you to stand tall in your sense of self without letting your ego stop you from hearing constructive, and necessary, criticism from others.

DECEMBER 21 *(Sun in Capricorn)*

The additional guide of your journey is *Reciprocity* (Six of Pentacles). You will meet *Reciprocity* in the harmonious give and take of resources, both emotional and material. *Reciprocity* invites you to share what you have with love, while also remaining humble and vulnerable enough to receive the gifts that others offer you.

JANUARY 19 *(Sun in Aquarius)*

The additional guide of your journey is *Doubt* (Two of Swords). You will meet *Doubt* within indecision, when your mind can't seem to decipher the "right" course of action. *Doubt* reminds you that nothing in life is certain or clear and that you have nothing to lose from trying with the best intentions.

FEBRUARY 18 *(Sun in Pisces)*

The additional guide of your journey is *Worthiness* (Two of Cups). You will meet *Worthiness* within intimacy, when you are called to share who you are and what you need with another person. *Worthiness* reminds you not to make yourself small because true connections require you to be the whole of who you are.

MARCH 20 *(Sun in Aries)*

The additional guide of your journey is *Conflict* (Five of Wands). You will meet *Conflict* in external roadblocks and critics who try to thwart you from achieving your highest potential. *Conflict* reminds you that there is always something to learn from adversity, encouraging you to surrender your pride in favor of growth.

NADINE JANE is an expert astrologer with a background as a digital designer who makes astrology accessible, relatable and beautiful. She has long sought out the mysteries and magic tucked into every corner of our lives and uses her work to share the tools of self-discovery and self-knowledge that her astrology practice has given her. As one of the internet's leading astrologers, she has collaborated with popular brands such as Mejuri and Glossier and she has been featured in *Elle* and on *MTV*.